Mastering™
Active Directory for
Windows® Server 2003 R2

D1404763

Mastering™
Active Directory for Windows® Server 2003 R2

Brad Price

John Price

Scott Fenstermacher

Wiley Publishing, Inc.

Acquisitions Editor: Tom Cirtin

Development Editor: David Clark

Technical Editor: Jim Kelly

Production Editor: Angela Smith

Copy Editor: Liz Welch

Production Manager: Tim Tate

Vice President and Executive Group Publisher: Richard Swadley

Vice President and Executive Publisher: Joseph B. Wikert

Vice President and Publisher: Neil Edde

Book Designer: Maureen Forys, Happenstance Type-O-Rama

Illustrator: Jeffrey Wilson, Happenstance Type-O-Rama

Compositor: Chris Gillespie, Happenstance Type-O-Rama

Proofreader: Nancy Riddiough

Indexer: Nancy Guenther

Cover Designer: Margaret Rowlands

Cover Image: Wiley Publishing, Inc.

Wiley Publishing, Inc. End-User License Agreement

For Mom—your strength is an inspiration to everyone!

To Chris—you have laughed in the face of adversity and proven you can do anything you put your mind to. You are a far better man than I ever will be.

To DeAnn, Jami, and Becca—thank you for believing in me.

—*Brad Price*

For Hallie and Kathy—your strength and courage are my greatest inspiration.

—*John Price*

Acknowledgments

As I sit here during the high school football playoff season and think back on all that has happened while I have been working on this book, I realize that there are so many people I need to include in this short area I have for acknowledgments. Although I know it is inevitable that I will forget someone, I hope that I don't!

I need to express my gratitude and love to my wife and daughters.

DeAnn—again I sit here at the close of writing a book and think about everything you had to do while I was sitting at my desk testing, researching, writing, and editing. I have so much to catch up on and you have been great at allowing me to indulge in this writing game once more. You are the foundation of our family. Without you, my world would crumble.

Jami—as you are going through this final year of your primary education, I marvel at how you could have grown up so fast. You are a very caring, intelligent, beautiful young woman and I am very proud to be known as your father. I know you will be successful in anything that you set your mind to, and I look forward to watching you grow as an adult.

Becca—I sit and wonder as to how my baby could be sweet sixteen and driving! Your charm, intelligence, and thoughtfulness are the cornerstones to a personality that makes everyone around you consider you a friend. As you enter the final years of high school, I watch with fascination as you maneuver through all the potholes with grace. I am so very lucky to have you as a daughter.

To the rest of my family—again I thank you for putting up with my excuses for not making some of the get-togethers, although, who knows, it may come as a relief. But most of all, Mom and Dad, you two are great. Thanks for everything you do for everyone. Mom, you have had a rough year and all of us are so proud of your strength. Even when you thought you were a burden to others, you didn't realize that we still owe you more than we will ever be able to give. And Dad, you have always been there for everyone, no matter what was asked of you. You proved once again that you are a truly great and selfless man. I am proud to call you my father.

During the course of writing this book I still had other commitments, and without some good friends I would not have been able to perform all of my duties. During the summer, softball runs through my veins. Without Dennis Mefford and April Miller I would not have been able to keep our softball team running smoothly. They took on most of the management chores and I was able to show up to the games and help out. You two made this season one of the most enjoyable. We didn't win the tournament, but we had a great time all summer long! To the team—Amanda, Cassie, Savannah, Dana, Jami, Lisa, April, Becca, Felicia, Haley, Maeghan, Megan, and Tiffany—you are the best. I find each summer is made better by having hard-working, friendly, humorous, and pleasant young ladies on the team. Each of you has a special place in my heart.

And for all of the characters that make my life interesting—Dennis and Amy, Mike and Gretchen, Dan and Terri, Jim and Elaine, Chris and Connie, and Mark and Eros, my Bestest Friend and all of the kids at the ROWVA school; and my crazy cohorts at work—Dan, Michelle, Penny, Ron, Marcellus, Krista, Margaret, Courtney, Gina, Dawn, Karen, Diane, and Susan—thank you for your friendship, confidence, trust, and knowledge.

—Brad Price

Putting a book like this together takes many hours of research, testing, writing, re-writing, etc. If I did not have a solid network of people behind me, both in my professional life and my personal life, there is no way I would be able to pull it off.

I would like to start off by thanking my wife and daughter. Thank you for understanding the long nights and weekends of writing. Without you, I would not be where I am today. You are my inspiration and motivation for doing the work that I do. I love you both more than anything in the world. I can't wait to resume full-time Dad status again soon, and spend my evening reading children's books, working on puzzles, and chasing "the maniac" around the house.

My mom and dad have not only helped shape me into the person that I am in my professional life, but have helped mold me into the man that I am today. Thank you for always believing in me and teaching me that I can succeed in whatever I set my mind to as long as I work hard and give it my best effort.

Making the transition from family acknowledgments to professional acknowledgments, I have to thank someone who falls into both categories. From the time we were young, my brother Brad has inspired me to not only dream big, but work hard to make those dreams a reality. Thank you; you are my best friend.

Professionally, there are many people who have helped me along the way, and many who continue to inspire me. Of those people, I would like to personally thank Roy Bowen, whose Group Policy expertise is reflected in Chapter 9 of this book. You are a wise man, and I hope that we work together for many years to come.

This is the portion of the acknowledgments that will get me the most grief from my coworkers. This is where I thank each of my three bosses, right up the line. I would like to thank Eric Mickels, Michael Giannou, and Jim Simpson. The vision that you outlined and presented to me had me excited from day one, and I love being part of it and watching it come to fruition each and every day. That vision, and its subsequent reality, is the reason I am happy that my name is on the MSI roster. Now, about that raise…

—*John Price*

I would like to thank Brad and John for the chance to write a few a words with them and the team of editors at Wiley for translating them into English. Not said often enough, thanks to my wife Lori for all the innumerable things you do. To the kids, Jaina and Shelby, here's the reason I spent so much time downstairs. Finally, big thanks go to Craig and Carol, the parents, for encouraging me to pursue a career with those new-fangled computers.

—*Scott Fenstermacher*

There were several people involved with this book. Without them you wouldn't be holding this tome. John and Scott worked diligently and provided some great material. Randy Muller wrote chapters 8 and 14. He carried part of this load when things came down to the wire and did a great job. Tom Cirtin is not only a great Acquisitions Editor, I also consider him to be a friend and confidant. Rachel Gunn started out as the Production Editor and did a great job through her tenure. She saw this book through some interesting times and never seemed to doubt it. Angela Smith, who took over for Rachel, jumped on board and made it seem as if she was there all along. Jim Kelly — you did an amazing job as the Technical Editor and helped keep the content of the book accurate and complete, which is a feat considering the vast number of topics that are included. David Clark and Liz Welch—you two helped keep us in line as we strayed from the appropriate styles, but even more impressive is your ability to make our words sound good!

—*Brad Price, John Price, and Scott Fenstermacher*

Contents at a Glance

Contents

Introduction

As I sit here and contemplate what I am going to say in the pages of this introduction, I find myself thinking, "Why would I want to buy this book?" And the first thing that comes to mind is the realization that if I'd had a book in front of me as I was learning the new tools and utilities that Microsoft has included in this new release, I wouldn't have had to spend so much time trudging through the menus and help dialog boxes, and surfing the Net. And then I thought, "Wow, I should have let someone do this for me and I could have spent my time doing something a little more fun!"

This book is a labor of love. I really do enjoy going through the new material and learning what I can do with an operating system. And I didn't have to go through all of it myself. Truth be told, I am not qualified for some of this, especially the scripting section. The code I write is nearly illegible! If you notice on the front of this book, there are three authors listed: Brad Price, John Price, and Scott Fenstermacher. We divided up the chores, with John and I writing the core of the book, which includes the designing, planning, managing, and troubleshooting sections, while Scott was busy working on the final section on scripting.

Who Should Read This Book

Everyone. Well, okay, maybe not Aunt Myrtle who works as a part-time karaoke bar bouncer. But anyone responsible for Active Directory, or at least part of an Active Directory installation, needs to learn the lessons that are available in this book. If the title alone intrigued you, maybe this is the book for you. Included on the pages herein is detailed coverage of Active Directory as it is used in Windows Server 2003 R2. The topics covered range from the design options you need to consider before deploying Active Directory to management and troubleshooting. If you are responsible for the day-to-day operations of Active Directory, this book is for you. If you are responsible for designing a new Active Directory rollout for a company, this book is for you. If you need to learn some troubleshooting tips and want to see how some of the utilities work, this book is for you.

But most important, the final part of this book delves into scripting. Smart administrators know that any shortcut you can take in order to perform an action will be helpful, especially since we usually don't have all the time we would like to perform all of the duties we are responsible for, let alone the emergencies that arise. These administrative shortcuts can be as simple as creating a Microsoft Management Console (MMC) that includes all of the administrative tools that you use on a daily basis so that you don't have to open each administrative tool in its own window, to writing scripts and batch files that will perform those repetitive tasks.

If you have been hesitant to jump into the scripting side of administration, you will want to check out the final part of this book. Scott has started with the basics and will lead you through the steps to create your very own scripts. He has included several examples that you can use in your environment. What you learn from this section alone will save you more in administrative costs than this book will set you back.

The Contents at a Glance

The first part of this book deals with designing and planning your Active Directory rollout. The information that you find in this part is not geared solely toward Windows Server 2003 R2. As a matter of fact, you could use these chapters to help you design and plan an Active Directory implementation based on either Windows Server 2003 or Windows Server 2003 R2. If you are already familiar with the Active Directory and are ready to introduce it into your organization, you should check out the chapters dedicated to design and planning. The information that you take from these chapters will help you build a rock-solid design. You will learn the best method of naming your forest, trees, and domains; how to organize objects using containers and organizational units; and how to plan your group policy implementation. The chapters that make up this section include:

◆ Chapter 1: Active Directory Fundamentals

◆ Chapter 2: Domain Name System Design

◆ Chapter 3: Active Directory Forest and Domain Design

◆ Chapter 4: Organizing the Physical and Logical Aspects of Active Directory

◆ Chapter 5: Flexible Single Master Operations Design

The second part of the book deals with managing your Active Directory implementation once it has been put into place. The day-to-day operations of Active Directory will rely on you knowing how to manage the infrastructure. This includes some of the new features that are part of Windows Server 2003 R2, such as Active Directory Federation Services and Identity Management for Unix. The more you know, the easier it is for you to effectively manage your environment. But even more important, the more you know about the inner workings and interoperability of the features, the easier it will be for you to effectively troubleshoot issues. The chapters in this part include:

◆ Chapter 6: Managing Accounts: User, Group, and Computer

◆ Chapter 7: Managing Access with Active Directory Services

◆ Chapter 8: Maintaining Organizational Units

◆ Chapter 9: Managing Group Policy

◆ Chapter 10: Managing Site Boundaries

◆ Chapter 11: Managing the Flexible Single Master Operations Roles

◆ Chapter 12: Maintaining the Active Directory Database

Troubleshooting is the core of the Part 3. As we all know, there is no perfect operating system. And the more complex the operating systems become, the more likely the chance of something breaking. Your best friend during a crisis is knowledge. If you possess the necessary troubleshooting skills and tools when something goes wrong, you will be able to fix the problem faster than if you were stumbling around in the dark. The chapters in this part will help you learn the troubleshooting tools that are at your disposal, as well as provide some tips you'll find useful when faced with problems. The chapters in this part include:

◆ Chapter 13: Microsoft's Troubleshooting Methodology for Active Directory

◆ Chapter 14: Troubleshooting Problems Related to Network Infrastructure

◆ Chapter 15: Troubleshooting Problems Related to the Active Directory Database

◆ Chapter 16: Troubleshooting Active Directory with Microsoft Operations Manager

As we have already mentioned, the final part of this book, which includes three long chapters, is dedicated to administrative scripting. Building and understanding how scripts work and affect Active Directory can make you stand out in the crowd, as well as make your life easier. Here's a small sampling of what you can do when using administrative scripts: run a script to create several users; have a script inform users who never log off that their password is about to expire; or manipulate the group membership of a group so that only authorized users are members of the group. And the nice thing is that, once you are comfortable with the scripting basics and administrative options available, the knowledge you gain will allow you to move on and use scripts to affect other services, not just Active Directory. The final chapters of the book include:

◆ Chapter 17: ADSI Scripting Primer

◆ Chapter 18: Active Directory Scripts

◆ Chapter 19: Monitoring Active Directory

Final Comments

As this book is going to print, the zygort.com website is going live. Zygort is the fictional company that John and I have used in all of the books that we have written. We decided to capitalize on the name and use it as a central repository for our Active Directory and Windows Server knowledge. While the website will not duplicate the information we have included in this book, we will be posting additional information from time to time as well as using the site as a portal to some of the best Active Directory information that we find. Other topics that might make your life a little easier will also become part of the content, so you may find tips for anything from server virtualization to application virtualization to product integration. We will also post at the Zygort site any updates to the Active Directory information we have included in this book. We understand how fast the computing world changes, and we would like to keep you as up-to-date as possible.

So sit back and enjoy this ride into the wondrous adventure known as Active Directory. We hope that the information in this book helps you in all of your Active Directory endeavors. And we hope that we can cut down on the amount of time it takes you to perform an administrative task. We understand how much time administrators need to put in just to stay on top of things, and if we can make your life a little easier and give you a little more free time, then we have done our jobs.

Part 1

Active Directory Design

In this part:

Chapter 1

Active Directory Fundamentals

Ever since the inception of network operating systems, the men and women who have the responsibility of administering and managing them have desired an easy way to work with them. Networks have gone through the natural evolution from peer-to-peer networks to directory-based networks. Directory-based networks have become the preferred type of network due to the fact that they can ease an administrator's workload.

To address the needs of organizations, the IEEE organization developed a set of recommendations that defined how a directory service should address the needs of administrators and efficiently allow management of network resources. These recommendations, known as the X.500 recommendations, were originally envisioned to include a large centralized directory that would encompass the entire world, divided by geopolitical boundaries. Even though X.500 was written to handle a very large amount of data, designers reviewing the drafts of these recommendations saw merit in the directory and soon the recommendations were adopted by several companies the two best known, Novell and Microsoft.

Active Directory is Microsoft's version of the X.500 recommendations. Battles rage between directory services camps, each one touting theirs as the most efficient directory service. Since some of the directory services, like Novell's NDS, have been around longer than Active Directory, those that are familiar with NDS will attack Active Directory. Their attacks are usually centered on the fact that Active Directory does not perform functions the same way as NDS.

When it is all said and done, companies that develop X.500-based directory services can interpret the recommendations and implement them to fit their design needs. Microsoft interpreted and utilized the X.500 recommendations to effectively manage a Windows-based network. Novell did the same for a Novell-based network and the two have been at odds over which one is more efficient for years. With all that notwithstanding, Microsoft has enjoyed great success with Active Directory. It has been adopted by thousand of organizations and will more than likely continue to be used for many years to come.

Do I Need Active Directory?

So just how do you know if you need Active Directory? There are factors that you should address in order to determine whether you should defer installation of a domain controller. Some of the questions you should ask are:

Do I want to centrally manage my resources?

Do I want to control user accounts from one location?

Do I have applications that rely on Active Directory?

If you answered "yes" to any of these questions, you will want to take advantage of the features that Active Directory provides. Taking each one of the questions into account, you will find that your life as an administrator will be much easier if you use Active Directory over using no directory service whatsoever. The tools that become available to you when you implement Active Directory will ease your administrative load, although there is the inherent learning curve that is associated with any new technology that you need to learn.

If you answered "yes" to the last of the three questions posed above, then you have no choice but to implement Active Directory. Most of the Active Directory-enabled applications on the market rely on a full version of Active Directory to be installed within your network. There are some Active Directory-enabled applications that can take advantage of using Active Directory Application Mode (ADAM) based systems. ADAM is discussed later in this chapter.

The first two questions relate to something administrators have striven for over the years. Having one central location to manage users and resources makes an administrator's life easier. If you have to continually move from server to server to administer the resources contained on them you would spend more time tracking down the resources than you would performing your job. If you have to maintain user accounts on several systems, you will need to make sure you have an efficient method of cataloging the accounts so that you know where they reside.

With Windows 2000 Server, Windows Server 2003 or Windows Server 2003 R2, you can use Active Directory as the central repository for user, group and computer accounts as well as shared folders and printers. Having the ability to manage these resources from any domain controller within your domain allows you to greatly reduce your administrative overhead.

The Basics

When you break it down, Active Directory is a type of database, but one built as a "directory". The difference between a relational database and a directory is that the former is optimized for updating, while the latter is optimized for reading. In this manner, Active Directory was developed with the understanding that the objects contained within the directory would not be changing often, but would be used in order for users, computers and administrators to control, manage and discover the organization's resources.

One of the most basic functions that Active Directory provides is a centralized repository for user account information. When an administrator creates a user account, the account information is held on a domain controller within the domain where the user resides. All of the domain controllers within the domain will receive an identical copy of the user account so that the user is able to authenticate using any domain controller in the domain.

Any changes to the user account are made on one of the domain controllers and then sent to every other domain controller within the domain. This transfer of data is called replication. Replication of information can be a burden on the network, especially in environments with several thousand users, group, computers, and other objects. To alleviate the replication burden on the network, Active Directory only replicates the attributes that have been changed and not the entire object.

In order to get a good understanding of how active Directory works, you must first understand what the schema is and the role it plays in the directory service. The following section will outline the major roles of the schema.

Schema

The schema is the building blocks of Active Directory, much like DNA molecules are the building blocks for our bodies. Just as our DNA holds all of the information necessary to build our leg, ears, hair, etc., the schema holds all of the information to create users, groups, computers, etc. within Active Directory. The schema defines how each attribute can be used and the properties associated with the attribute. Take for instance a child's toy that we have grown up with; Legos. When you first take a look at Legos, you see hundreds of tiny pieces that really don't seem to represent anything. Some are short, some long, and some are special shapes. These are the individual pieces, or building blocks, that will go into creating the cars, airplanes and dioramas.

Active Directory schema is pretty much the same thing. If you look within the Active Directory Schema snap-in, shown in Figure 1.1, you will see hundreds of entries that are used when creating objects within Active Directory. These entries are known as attributes and they allow you to create new objects or modify existing objects within your directory.

NOTE   To add the Active Directory Schema snap-in, you will first need to register the dynamic link library. To do so, open the Run line or use a command prompt and type in `regsvr32 schmmgmt.dll`.

ATTRIBUTES

In order to standardize Active Directory, the schema defines the attributes that can be used when creating objects. Unlike our Legos though, these attributes are only defined once and can be used for any object. Defining the attribute once and using it in multiple objects allows for a standardized approach of defining objects, especially when searching for the attribute. Take the `Name` attribute for example. Whenever an object uses the `Name` attribute you know that the name has to be at least 1 character in length and cannot exceed 255 characters. You would know this due to the syntax and rules that are applied to the attribute.

FIGURE 1.1
Active Directory
Schema snap-in

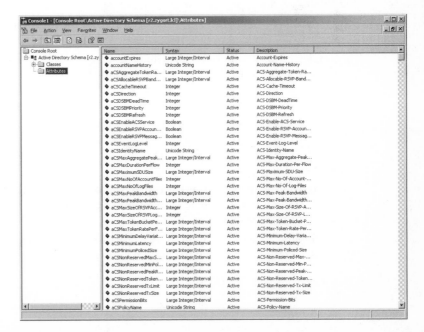

Take a look at Figure 1.2. Shown in that figure is the properties page of the name attribute. There is a lot of information within this property page, but right now we are only interested in the Syntax and Range area. Notice that the attribute is a Unicode String that has to be at least 1 character in length and cannot exceed 255 characters. Each attribute within the schema is defined in such a way, although the syntax for each of the attributes could be different.

In Figure 1.3, the properties for Bad-Pwd-Count are shown. This is another attribute that makes up a user object. Notice that the X.500 Object ID (OID) is different from that of the Name attribute. Each attribute within the schema has to have a unique OID. OIDs are registered and maintained by the Internet Assigned Numbers Authority (IANA). Once assigned, the OID should not be used by any other attribute. Within Active Directory, the default attributes are already assigned OIDs, and those OIDs are protected in a way that will not allow another application to overwrite them.

New attributes will need to be assigned an OID. If you are adding an attribute for use in an object, to safeguard your attribute and make sure that you do not step on any other attributes, you should register is with the IANA. Registration is free, and as long as your OID is unique, you should be issued an OID for your attribute. The attributes that Microsoft uses will all be within their own OID range, which starts with 1.2.840.113556. For a complete list of the registered OIDs, you can go to http://asn1.elibel.tm.fr/oid/index.htm and perform a search on the OID. If you have registered an OID, it will appear in this database once the entry is added.

Within an attribute's properties you will find several check boxes that you can select. Each of them is described in the following list:

Allow This Attribute To Be Shown In Advanced View If selected, whenever you choose View ➢ Advanced within an MMC, the attribute can be shown within a property page or within the details pane.

Attribute Is Active You can deactivate attributes that you no longer need within Active Directory. Note that the default attributes cannot be deselected. Nor can attributes that are still in use within an object.

Index This Attribute In The Active Directory If this is an attribute that you are going to allow searches on, you may want to index the attribute to increase the search responsiveness.

Replicate This Attribute To The Global Catalog Not every attribute needs to reside within the Global Catalog. The rule of thumb is: if you need to locate an object based upon an attribute, or the object's attribute is needed within another domain, you should add it. Otherwise, to reduce the total size of the domain partition, you should not add in any superfluous attributes.

Attribute Is Copied When Duplicating A User When you copy a user account, several attributes are copied from the original account to the new account. If you want the attribute to copy, select the box. Do note that many attributes are unique to a user, so select this option with care.

Index This Attribute For Containerized Searches In The Active Directory If you select this option, the attribute can be indexed for searches within containers in Active Directory, such as Organizational Units.

Ambiguous Name Resolution (ANR) Selecting this option allows for an LDAP-based client to resolve a request when only partial data is available.

FIGURE 1.2
Name attribute
property page

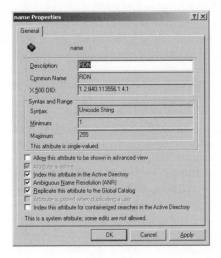

FIGURE 1.3
Bad-Pwd-Count
attribute property page

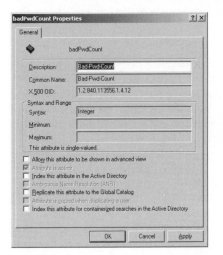

OBJECT CLASSES

An object class is a defined grouping of attributes that make up a unique resource type. One of the most common object classes is the user class. You use the user object class as the template for a user account. When you create a user account, the attributes that are defined for the user object class are used to define the new account. Information that you populate within the add user wizard, or enter within the `dsadd` command line become the properties within the attributes.

If we go back for a minute to the Legos we were playing with, you can use some of the brown blocks to create a roof on a house, some red bricks to make the walls, and tan bricks to make a door. The clear pieces can be used as windows and the white piece form the porch. All of these are considered attributes. Putting these attributes together form the object class house. When you build your first house you have built your first object. Subsequent houses will have the same attributes, but you may build the porch with tan pieces instead of the white ones.

So, when I create a user account for Mary, that user account will have unique values stored within the attributes for her user account. Bob's user account will be created using identical attributes, but will not have the same values within each attribute. Mary's phone number may be 555.1234, and Bob's 555.9876.

Not all of the attributes that make up an object class are shown within the administrative tools. Many of them hide behind the scenes and will rarely, if ever, need to be changed. One such attribute is the user's Security ID or SID. The user's SID will change when a user is moved from one domain to another, but will not change while the user remains within a domain. Active Directory Users and Computers does not have the ability to change this attribute. A default set of attributes fields appear within the utilities, and if you decide to make an attribute available for updating, you may need to programmatically add the fields to the utilities.

Attributes are defined as mandatory or optional. Mandatory attributes have to be populated or the object will not be created. One such attribute is a computer's name. Optional attributes do not necessarily need to have values. Attributes such as the Manager attribute within a user object does not need to be populated, but it is always nice to include that information. The more complete the information, the more complete Active Directory becomes.

The Two Sides of AD

Active Directory has both a logical side and a physical side. Each of the two parts has a very important role to play. The physical side of Active Directory is made up of the domain controllers and physical locations where the domain controllers reside. When you promote a system to domain controller status, you will usually place that domain controller close to the user population that will use it for authentication and access. Domain controllers need to communicate with one another in order to share the information they have.

The logical side is a little more nebulous; it is made up of objects within Active Directory that define how the domain controllers will communicate with one another as well as the objects that define how the resources are organized and accessed. Active directory sites and site links define which domain controllers will replicate directly with each other, and which ones will have to communicate indirectly through other domain controllers.

Domains dictate the replication scope. When you create a domain, the domain partition is only replicated to domain controllers from the same domain. The domain partition is not copied to domain controllers outside of the domain. This allows you to partition your directory service and reduce the size of the database file that holds all of the forest's objects.

Organizational Units (OUs) are used to organize objects for easy administration and to manage those objects easily using group policies. In order to have efficient administration of resources, it is recommended that you design your Active Directory with administration in mind.

The design of the logical and physical sides of Active Directory are discussed in great detail in Chapter 3. If you are in the process of rolling out Active Directory, make sure that you develop a detailed plan for the roll-out. Without a good design, Active Directory may not work efficiently for your environment. If your design does not meet the needs of your organization, you may be faced with either suffering through working with an inadequate design or rebuilding your Active Directory infrastructure from the ground up. Neither of these options will sit well with your user base or the management of the company.

What's New in R2?

Windows Server 2003 shipped in the spring of 2003. When it was released it was the most advanced network operating system Microsoft had ever developed. The advances that it made over Windows 2000 Server were obvious almost immediately, even though most of the new functionality was seen only by administrators. The new features were appreciated by administrators. Microsoft went to great lengths, not only to enhance the security and functionality of Windows Server 2003, they added in additional administrative tools to make an administrator's life easier. And if you know anything about administrators, anything you can do to make their life easier, the better they like it.

Over the course of the two and a half years from the time Windows Server 2003 shipped and Windows Server 2003 R2 became available, there were several new technologies that had been developed that Microsoft wanted to take advantage of, as well as new attack vectors that posed security risks to an organization's resources. With the next major release of the Windows Server operating system, known as Longhorn Server, not shipping until the 2007 timeframe, Microsoft decided an interim release would be the best

Windows Server 2003 R2 is based on the Service Pack 1 (SP1) codebase and will not install on a Release To Manufacturing (RTM) version of Windows Server 2003. Whereas SP1 added some new features to the operating system, mainly in an attempt to improve security, Windows Server 2003 R2 is a means of adding additional functionality and features to the already robust operating system.

There are several enhancements to the original version of Windows Server 2003 that have been incorporated into the R2 release, although we will only be concerned about the enhancements to Active Directory in this book. Those enhancements include Active Directory Application Mode (ADAM), Active Directory Federation Services (ADFS) and UNIX Identity Management. If you are really interested in the other features, such as Windows Sharepoint Services, Common Log File System, DFS Replication enhancements, Windows Subsystem for UNIX Applications, Auto-add Network Printers, Print Management Console, and SAN Storage Manager, you should consult our sister publication, Mastering Windows Server 2003 R2.

Active Directory Application Mode (ADAM)

Active Directory Application Mode (ADAM) allows administrators to create small versions of Active Directory that run as non-operating system services. Because ADAM does not run as an operating system service, it does not require deployment on a domain controller. Any workstation or server can host an instance of ADAM, or multiple instances. Instead of building a domain controller so that developers have an Active Directory database to work with, you could create an instance of ADAM on their workstations for them to test against. You could also use it as a repository for data used by a Customer Relations Management program or an address book directory. If you have a need for a directory to hold data instead of a database, you may want to consider using ADAM.

One of the biggest benefits of using ADAM is the administrative benefits you receive from it. Since ADAM is a user version of Active Directory, anyone familiar with how to manage objects within Active Directory should be at ease when working with object in ADAM. And like Active Directory, you can control your replication scope, or the systems that you replicate objects. If you have three systems that need to host the directory, you can specify that the ADAM partitions are hosted on those systems.

While you may find developers more interested in ADAM than most administrators, the possibilities that ADAM provides are only limited by your imagination. If an application's primary use of data is mainly reading that data and performing queries against that data, not making mass changes, then ADAM should fit the bill. For more information on ADAM and how to manage ADAM within your infrastructure, go to Chapter 12: Managing the Active Directory Database.

Active Directory Federation Services (ADFS)

Many organizations are partnering with businesses in order to efficiently deliver products and services. As businesses form these alliances, there needs to be a secure method of authenticating users from the partners' organizations. Part of the challenge to allowing authentication into your network is the security needed to maintain the connection between partners, while keeping hostile entities at bay. In the past this was possible with several tools and utilities, none of which appeared to work well with each other.

ADFS extends Active Directory to the Internet while guaranteeing the authenticity of the accounts attempting to authenticate. Using this technology will enable organizations to not only work with partner organizations more efficiently, it will also allow interoperability with a with range of applications and platforms, such as Netegrity, Oblix, and RSA, as well as leverage client systems that can utilize Simple Object Access Protocol (SOAP)-based command sets.

When using ADFS, an organization can allow divisions that exist within separate forests, as well as partner organizations, to have access to the organization's web applications and utilize a single sign on. ADFS is based on the Web Services (WS-*) architecture that is being developed with the cooperation of several companies, including IBM and Microsoft. Chapter 8, "Managing Access to Active Directory Objects" will cover managing and maintaining ADFS integration between organizations and within an organization.

UNIX Identity Management

UNIX has been around for nearly as long as computers have needed operating systems. Several different versions of UNIX exist, and an offshoot of UNIX, LINUX has taken a strong foothold in the open source community. In order for organizations that utilize both a Windows-based and UNIX-based infrastructure, Microsoft has included its next version of UNIX integration products into the Windows Server 2003 R2 product.

Both pieces of the Unix Identity Management tool, Password Synchronization administrator and Server for Network Information Service (NIS) were part of Microsoft's Services for UNIX 3.5 product. The utilities have been enhanced for inclusion with R2. You will find UNIX Identity Management covered in more detail in Chapter 8.

Pre-Design Criteria

When working with any design, you should make sure that you have a good framework to work off of. Throughout the years, Microsoft has identified what they term the "Microsoft Solutions Framework" (MSF), which is based on four principles:

Work toward a shared vision.

Stay agile, expect things to change.

Focus on delivering business value.

Foster open communication.

This set of guidelines can be used to control nearly any design and, if used correctly, can help stabilize the operations rollout.

Microsoft Solutions Framework

When you adopt MSF, you are taking on a set of principles and models that can aid you in a successful design. When you look at the high-level view of the MSF model, you will see five distinct phases: Envisioning, Planning, Developing, Stabilizing, and Deploying. Each phase within the cycle moves one step closer to the final product, with the Envisioning phase containing the design tasks.

The Envisioning phase can then be broken down into discrete functions, the first of which should be the creation of the design team. This team will be responsible for putting together the initial design specifications and determining if the project should move forward. The roles that will be included within the design team should include individuals within six categories: Program Management, Development, Test, Release Management, User Experience, and Product Management.

The Program Management role is responsible for making sure that the project is delivered on time and within budget. The team members that hold this role will need to make sure that they are on top of the overall project and are monitoring the progress. This role becomes the de facto project owner.

The Product Management role is responsible for making sure that the project meets the organization's business needs. The individuals who are holding this role are responsible for making sure that the needs of the organization are met, and that trade-offs in the plan are handled correctly. They will need to have a good sense of the business and understand what the customers ultimately need.

The Development role needs to have a good technical understanding of the project's design criteria and are responsible for making sure that the technical constraints of the project are met.

The Test role is responsible for making sure that the success criterion of the design is met. They need to have a good understanding of the business processes and need to create the milestones that the design will have to pass in order to be approved.

Release Management is a role that is often ignored during the design phase, but is vital to any technical rollout. They are responsible for making sure that the piloting phase of the project moves forward without a problem, and if there are problems, can communicate those issues with the rest of the team so that an efficient solution can be devised.

The final role is that of User Experience. If the users are not happy, your life will not be pleasant. The individuals that make up this role are responsible for making sure that the users' needs are met and that the design will addresses the need for ease of use.

While each project that goes through the design phase will have these six roles assigned to it, smaller projects may include individuals who are members of more than one team. On larger projects you may have several members within a role. No matter how many members for each role you have, make sure that the team members can perform the functions for which they are responsible, as well as make sure that they know what function they are to perform. Set guidelines and train each member so that they have the appropriate skill if necessary.

Risk Assessment

Every project is going to have some risks involved. Risk is the possibility that you will incur some type of loss. Don't confuse the possibility of loss with the certainty of loss. Just because you have identified that a loss could occur, doesn't mean that it will occur. Many projects have been stopped due to nervous program managers and corporate sponsors fearing that the project will cause a problem. Instead of pulling the plug on a project, the risk assessment should be used so that you have a basis for risk mitigation and management.

If you look at risk assessment as a positive instead of a negative, you can plan out the requirements to alleviate problems within the project and stop catastrophes from completely wiping out the budget. However, you should remember that risk assessment does not stop after you first identify the risks that you could be facing. You should continually assess the risks during the entire project lifecycle, because you could introduce new risk vectors as you progress.

There are six steps for you to follow during risk assessment and management:

Risk identification   Identify the conditions that could lead to a loss and the ramifications of that loss.

Risk analysis and prioritization   Analyze each risk and determine which risks will be considered the most dangerous, or highest priority for the design team

Risk management planning and scheduling   Develop plans that will address how risks will be controlled.

Risk status tracking and reporting   Continually monitor the process in order to identify when a risk condition has been triggered.

Risk control   Carry out the contingency plans if a risk has been triggered.

Risk education   Develop a database of information that will aid in the control of risks in the future.

NOTE   For more information concerning the Microsoft Solutions Framework, visit http://www
.microsoft.com/technet/itsolutions/msf/default.mspx

Once the risk assessment is out of the way, you are ready to take on the responsibility of designing the Active Directory infrastructure. This can be a daunting task to undertake considering there are so many variables to take into account. Over the course of the next few chapters we are going to introduce the criteria you will need to take into account in order to build an effective design.

Coming Up Next...

The next few chapters are all going to deal with making sure that you know the criteria for designing a rock solid Active Directory infrastructure. Without a good design, you will probably not have a stable infrastructure. Of course everything within an Active Directory environment relies on a solid DNS infrastructure. If your DNS infrastructure is not stable, the Active Directory will not be stable and your users will not be happy with the design.

The next chapter outlines the requirements for a viable DNS design that Active Directory can use. Since there are several options at your disposal when it comes to designing the DNS infrastructure, you should understand the options so that you can make informed decisions. The more you understand the design options, the more reliable your infrastructure will be.

Chapter 2

Domain Name System Design

You cannot have Active Directory without having the Domain Name System (DNS) in place. I know that is a blunt way to open the chapter, but it is the fundamental truth with this chapter. DNS is required when you implement Active Directory. Although you do not have to run Microsoft's version of DNS, there are many reasons why you would want to do so.

As with all services that are used within a network, you have many options as to how you will implement DNS. However, you should follow some general guidelines if you want to make sure you are taking advantage of the best way to use DNS. Failure to do so could cause severe problems with name resolution and Active Directory functionality. Throughout this chapter, we are going to look at why DNS is required and how you can implement an efficient and secure DNS infrastructure. Later, in Chapter 14, "Maintaining DNS," I will cover troubleshooting DNS.

Tied Together

When implementing Active Directory within your environment, DNS is required. Active Directory cannot exist without it. The two entities are like trains and railroad tracks. The train's engines are mighty powerful machines that can pull thousands of tons of equipment, but without the tracks, they cannot move. If the tracks are not aligned correctly, the train may derail. If the tracks are not switched in the right direction, the train will not arrive at the correct destination.

If you haven't immersed yourself in the finer details of DNS, now is the time. If you think you understand how DNS works, you should still go back and review all of the new options that have been added to the DNS service in Windows Server 2003 and Windows Server 2003 R2. Where Windows 2000 added some fancy new features into the Microsoft DNS world, such as support for dynamic updates and Service locator (SRV) records, Windows Server 2003 upped the ante even more with support for stub zones and the ability to use directory application partitions for Active Directory–integrated zones.

As I mentioned in the introduction to this chapter, you are not required to use Microsoft's implementation of DNS; UNIX BIND DNS will work just fine as long as it meets certain criteria. As a matter of fact, there are several companies that already invested deeply in a BIND DNS solution and are not about to completely restructure with a new DNS implementation. As the old saying goes, don't fix what is not broken. We will look at using BIND within your infrastructure later in the chapter.

Looking at the correlation between your Active Directory and DNS, you will find the two will share the same zone naming conventions. If your Active Directory domain name is going to be zygort.lcl, the DNS namespace will also be zygort.lcl. Notice that the top level domain (TLD) name for DNS, in this case lcl, does not have an equivalent domain within Active Directory. The reason for this is that for most companies, the top level domain is not unique, and not owned by the company. Take for instance a company that is using widgets.com as its Active Directory namespace. The

TLD used in this case, com, is owned by the Internet Consortium for Assigned Names and Numbers (ICANN) and is shared by hundreds of thousands of Internet based websites. When designing Active Directory, the designers decided to make sure that the root of the Active Directory forest could be unique, so they required the domain names to take on two domain components, the company's DNS domain and the TLD that it resides under.

As a domain controller comes online, part of its startup routine is to attempt registration of the SRV records that identify the services that are running on the domain controller. The only requirement for a DNS server to work with Active Directory is that the DNS server support SRV records. It does not matter to Active Directory clients if the records are entered manually by an administrator or automatically by the domain controller itself, all that matters is that the records are correct. If the SRV records are not listed within the zone, or entered incorrectly, the client will not be able to locate the domain controller. If the SRV records are correctly listed within the DNS zone, the host name of the server that is providing the service is returned to the client. The client will then query the DNS server for the A record of the domain controller in order to resolve the IP address.

How to Resolve

The most basic of all DNS services provide the ability for a client system to send a query to the DNS server asking for the DNS server to return the IP address of a host system. This type of resolution is referred to as forward name resolution. DNS provides this functionality by hosting resource records that specify the IP address for each of the host systems within the DNS namespace. The namespace is referred to within the DNS server as the zone. For instance, if your DNS namespace is zygort.lcl, and you have a server named APFS01 with an IP address of 192.168.29.75, your zone name would be zygort.lcl and the server would have a resource record that tied the name APFS01 to IP address 192.168.29.75. When a client sent a query to the DNS server looking for APFS01.zygort.lcl, the DNS server would reply to the query with a response containing the IP address.

This is the most fundamental purpose of DNS, and probably the most utilized function, finding an IP address when a client sends a query. There is another resolution type known as reverse name resolution. Reverse name resolution allows a client to query for a host name when it knows the IP address of the system in question. This works in much the same way as the caller ID system on your telephone. If you have entered information into your caller ID system, when a phone number comes in to your home, the caller's name shows up on the display. If you have not entered the identifying information, the phone number will display. There are several programs and utilities that use reverse name resolution and you may find it beneficial to make sure you have the correct information included within the zone.

DNS servers will resolve queries within the zones that are configured on them. You can have more than one zone on a server and the server will accept and respond to queries for records in those zones. When a client sends a query for a zone that is not hosted on the DNS server, the DNS server has to perform additional tasks in order to respond correctly to the client. The DNS server will look to the top of the DNS hierarchy, known as the root, for help. These root DNS servers are listed within the Root Hints tab of the DNS server properties. The DNS server will send a query of its own to one of these root servers asking for resolution. The root servers will refer the DNS server to the appropriate TLD DNS server. The DNS server will then query the TLD DNS server for assistance. The TLD server will refer the DNS server to the appropriate Second Level Domain DNS server. This process will continue until a DNS server with the resource record resolves the request.

There are problems that can be encountered with the typical DNS resolution methods. First off, not every namespace is accessible from the Internet. Our example zygort.lcl is a prime example of that. If you were to perform a lookup on a server name within that namespace using conventional DNS methods, the lookup would fail. There needs to be another method of resolving the DNS queries for these zones. The other problem lies with companies that do not want their DNS servers to query outside of their organization. Since DNS servers look to the root of the Internet as the de facto starting point for name resolution, you need a way to keep them from attempting to do so. New options have been introduced to address these issues.

Windows 2000 DNS servers introduced *forwarders* to the Microsoft DNS world. Using forwarders, you can specify another DNS server that will attempt to resolve queries when the local DNS server cannot. By default, a DNS server will use the DNS servers that are configured within the Root Hints tab of the DNS server properties. If your DNS server cannot reach the root servers, or you want to control the servers that perform the iterative queries from your organization, you can enter the server's IP address within the forwarders tab on the properties sheet for the DNS server. Once configured, the queries that cannot be resolved by the DNS server will be sent to the first DNS server listed in the forwarders tab.

One problem that occurs when you define a forwarder is that the DNS server identified as the forwarder will have to take on the task of resolving all the queries outside of the DNS server's zones. This can be a considerable amount of traffic. Another problem occurs when the forwarder does not have the ability to query for certain zones. Windows Server 2003 introduced another method of forwarding, *conditional forwarding*. Using conditional forwarding, you can specify a DNS server that will be used to resolve queries based on the domain name in question. For example, if a user needs to resolve an address for `zygort.com` and if a conditional forwarder is created for the `zygort.com domain`, the DNS server will send a recursive query to the server specified within the forwarder setting. Figure 2.1 shows conditional forwarders configured for the zones `zygort.com` and `bloomco.org`. Notice the All Other DNS Domains entry. Configuring DNS addresses within that setting specifies which servers will be used as standard forwarders if no conditional forwarders meet the query needs.

NOTE   For more information on conditional forwarding, see the TechNet article 304991 at `http://support.microsoft.com/default.aspx?kbid=304491&product=winsvr2003`.

FIGURE 2.1
Conditional forwarders

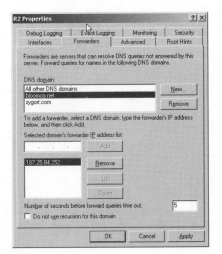

Another item to note, if a DNS server is configured as the root server for the organization, you cannot configure it to forward requests to another DNS server. If by accident this has happened to you, you can simply delete the root zone from the DNS server, which is specified by the dot (.), as seen in Figure 2.2. In the case of a Windows 2003 Server, the root zone is designated by .(root), as seen in Figure 2.3. Once the root zone is deleted, you can enter external root servers into the root hints, as well as configure forwarders.

FIGURE 2.2

Root zone in Windows 2000

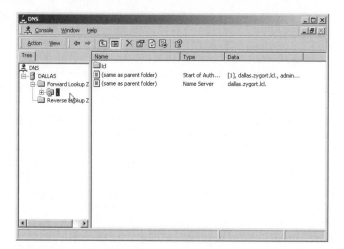

FIGURE 2.3

Root zone in Windows Server 2003

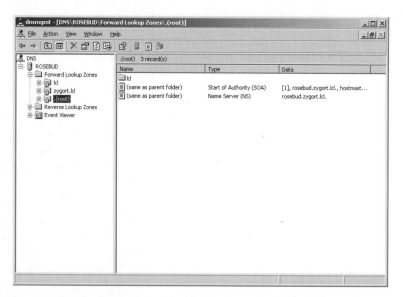

This behavior does not occur within a Windows Server 2003 DNS server when you promote the first domain controller. This doesn't mean that you need let Dcpromo install the DNS service; you could configure the DNS zone first, and then promote the domain controller. Doing so will allow you to configure the zone the way you want and then allow the domain controller to register. There are other considerations to take into account if you create the zone first when promoting the first domain controller for your forest, and we will discuss those options later in the chapter. First and foremost, if you create the zone manually, make sure that you configure the zone for dynamic updates, otherwise, you will receive an error message stating the domain is not configured.

So Many Zone Types

For every zone that you use, you will need to determine how you will configure the DNS servers to use them. There are basically three zone types within Windows Server 2003 and Windows Server 2003 R2: primary, secondary, and stub. The data for the zone can be contained within a file on the system drive of the DNS server and read into memory at startup, or it can be held in Active Directory. The former option is known as a standard zone type, which uses zone transfers as a means of sending the data to other DNS servers that host the zone. The latter is known as Active Directory–integrated and uses Active Directory replication to send the data. Of the three zone types, you have the choice of making primary and stub zones Active Directory–integrated, but secondary zones cannot be Active Directory–integrated. Each of them has their place within your infrastructure, but knowing when to choose one over the other can be confusing.

PRIMARY ZONES

Primary zones have traditionally been held on a single system and are known in the Microsoft world as *standard primary zones*. Primary zones are the update point within DNS. The limitation to these zones is their inherent single point of failure. Although the zone data can be transferred to another server that acts as the secondary zone, if the server holding the primary zone fails, you no longer have an update point. In order to make updates to the zone while the server holding the original primary zone is unavailable, you have to change a secondary zone to a primary.

Another limitation to standard primary zones also stems from the single update point. When using clients that support dynamic DNS updates, the only server in the zone that can receive the updates is the server holding the primary zone. Whenever a dynamic DNS client comes online, it queries its preferred DNS server for the Start of Authority (SOA) record for the zone in which it is preparing to register. The SOA record informs the client of the server that is authoritative for the zone. The client then sends the dynamic DNS registration information to the server holding the primary zone. This is not a problem unless the server with which the client is registering is across a slow or over-consumed WAN link. The additional DNS registration traffic may become too cumbersome. In addition, the same data then has to travel back across the WAN link if a server holding the secondary zone requires a zone transfer.

This has led administrators to create subdomains within the DNS hierarchy to support the remote locations. In this manner, the remote locations have their own DNS servers to hold their primary zones, with the parent domain holding delegation records to the subdomain. Clients within the zone register locally, and the only data that needs to be sent across the WAN link are the queries for zone information and zone transfers if a secondary zone is configured on another server.

However, this scenario has two problems: you may not have an administrative staff in place at the remote locations, and query traffic could consume more bandwidth on the WAN link than the registration traffic would. So what is an administrator to do?

Besides evaluating the traffic that would be generated from either of the two scenarios to determine which will be the lesser of two evils, you could break away from the archaic DNS methodologies and start using the new and improved Microsoft DNS technologies. Using Active Directory–integrated zones greatly enhances your DNS infrastructure. Gone are the days of having one update point and tedious zone transfers. (Do I sound like a salesman yet?)

Active Directory–integrated primary zones store the zone records within Active Directory. These records can then be used by any Active Directory–integrated DNS server. The domain controllers that hold the data will replicate changes amongst one another. This allows for any of the Active Directory–integrated DNS servers to be updated, and the updates are replicated to every other Active Directory–integrated DNS server. Later in this chapter we will discuss the replication options that are available once you configure a zone as Active Directory–integrated.

SECONDARY ZONES

Secondary zones have been around as long as primary zones. When an administrator wanted another DNS server to host the same zone information as the primary zone, a secondary zone would be created, which would then host identical information as the primary. The zone data within a secondary zone is a read-only copy of the primary zone database. Secondary zones still have their place within an organization. If you have a remote location where you do not want to support a domain controller but want to provide local resolution to the clients, you can create a secondary zone on a server within that location. This will reduce the amount of query traffic that has to pass across the WAN link, but you will be required to send zone transfers from a master server across the WAN link to the secondary. Typically, there will be more queries sent by clients than there will be dynamic updates from clients. Even so, you should monitor the traffic that is passing across the WAN link to determine if you are using the link appropriately.

STUB ZONES

New to Windows Server 2003 is the stub zone. Although the name may sound a little strange, it does perfectly describe this zone type. Stub zones do not contain all of the resource records from the zone, as the primary and secondary zones types do. Instead, only a subset of records populates the zone, just enough to provide the client with the information necessary to locate a DNS server that can respond to a query for records from the zone.

When you create the stub zone, it is populated with the SOA record along with the NS records and the A records that correspond to the DNS servers identified on the SOA record. All this is done automatically. The administrator of the zone is not required to create the SOA, NS, or A records. Instead, as the zone is created, the DNS server will contact a server that is authoritative for the zone and request a transfer of those records. Once populated, the DNS server holding the stub zone will contact the authoritative server periodically to determine if there are any changes to the SOA, NS, and A records. You can control how often the DNS server requests updates by configuring the Refresh Interval on the SOA record for the zone.

As a client queries the DNS server to resolve the IP address for host, the DNS server is going to attempt to locate the A record for the host name. If the DNS server is configured with a stub zone for the domain name contained within the query, the DNS server will send an iterative query directly to an authoritative DNS server for the zone. In Figure 2.4, you will find the common query path that is taken when a client is trying to resolve an address. In this case, the client is trying to locate `server1.dallas.bloomco.com`. When the client in `chicago.zygort.com` sends the recursive query to its DNS server, the DNS server will "walk the tree" by sending iterative queries to DNS servers along the path to eventually get to a DNS server that is authoritative for `dallas.bloomco.com`.

In Figure 2.5, we have configured the same server with a stub zone for `dallas.bloomco.com`. When the client sends the recursive query to its DNS server, the DNS server has a zone listed within its database that lets it know which servers to contact when trying to locate `dallas.bloomco.com`. The DNS server can then send a single iterative query to the authoritative server and then send the result back to the client, thereby making the resolution process far more efficient.

FIGURE 2.4
Standard name
resolution

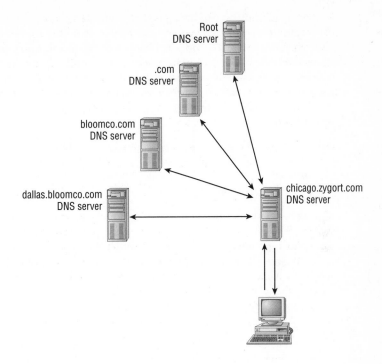

FIGURE 2.5
Name resolution
using a stub zone

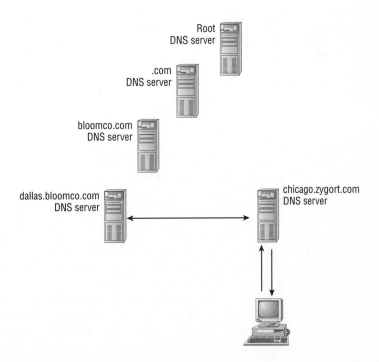

So the question on your mind is "Why not use a conditional forwarder instead of the stub zone?" There are two reasons why you would want to use a stub zone over a conditional forwarder. First, the stub zone has automatic updating features. When the refresh interval on the SOA record is reached, the server holding the stub zone will contact an authoritative server for the zone and update the list of name servers and their associated addresses. Conditional forwarders rely on administrative staff to keep them updated. Secondly, conditional forwarders will require more processing power to perform the logic of evaluating the conditions to determine which one matches. Stub zone information is held within the DNS database and can be parsed far more quickly.

NOTE For more information on conditional forwarding and stub zones, see the Microsoft webcast at http://support.microsoft.com/default.aspx?kbid=811118&product=winsvr2003.

How to Name a Zone

Trying to determine what you are going to name your zone can be one of the more difficult things you will do. The name should be descriptive enough so that it can be easily remembered while at the same time short enough so that it is not too difficult to type. Even though it may sound fun, you will not want to have supercalifragilisticexpialidocious.com as a domain name. Or if you do, your users will probably want to torture you for torturing them. If you are using any other DNS servers within your environment besides Windows DNS server, you should follow the DNS naming guidelines, as set forth in RFC 952. This document spells out the characters that can be used within a DNS implementation. Any character within the ANSI character set is legal to use. Essentially you have the option of using any of the following:

- Uppercase letters A-Z
- Lowercase letters a-z
- Numerals 0-9
- Hyphen -

Other Rules:

- Every name should start with a letter, not a number.
- Names cannot contain spaces.
- The period (.) is used as a delimiter between subdomains.
- Names should not end with a dash.
- Single character names are not allowed.

However, if your network uses only Windows-based DNS servers, or other DNS implementations that support extended character sets, you can use extended characters from the UTF-8 character set. This includes the underscore (_) character that is so popular amongst Windows NT administrators. During migration from Windows NT to Windows 2000 or Windows Server 2003, you will not have to rename computers that use an underscore in their name in order for them to be added to the DNS zone. This keeps you from having a domain named chi-corp.zygort.lcl as the DNS name, and CHI_CORP as the domain's NetBIOS name. Be wary, however. If you have any DNS servers that cannot handle the extended character set, you will receive errors during zone transfers when using UTF-8 characters.

TIP　You must register your Internet presence with an Internet registration authority so that you are ensured of owning your domain name. If you do not register your domain name, another company could register it and use it. Even if you do not plan to use the name on the Internet, register it so that it is reserved in case you ever do need an Internet presence.

Internal and External Name Options

Basically, you have two options when you are choosing internal and external namespaces for your organization: using different namespaces or using the same namespace. Each of the options presents its own trials and tribulations for administrators, so you should take the time to plan which method you will implement. Making changes to an existing namespace is a nightmare that you probably do not want to go through. You should make sure that you design your DNS/Active Directory namespace to support your organization's business needs as well as security requirements.

Keeping Them Separate

If you have determined that your organization will need an Internet presence, you need to determine the name with which you will be identified. Your name should identify your company. Users who are accessing your external resources should find your name easy to understand. One guideline is to make your name short, yet understandable. The easier it is to remember and type, the easier it will be for users to return to your site. The name `zygort.com` is much easier to remember and type than `zygort-manufacturing-inc.com`. Plus, if you are using a subdomain as your internal name, the longer the external DNS name is, the longer the internal namespace will be as you append the subdomain. Users will not appreciate having to enter **`accountspayable.accounting.corp.zygort.lcl`**.

To keep your internal resources hidden from external users, you should keep the internal namespace different than the Internet namespace. If you want to keep the two namespaces separate, you have the option of making the internal domain name a child domain from the Internet namespace or having two completely different namespaces.

COMPLETELY SEPARATE NAMESPACES

Using a completely separate namespace can help protect your internal infrastructure by having records for external resources stored within the external DNS servers, while internal resources can only be resolved by internal DNS servers. By hiding your DNS namespace in such a manner, you do not have as much to worry about when it comes to attackers trying to find out how your Active Directory infrastructure is configured. There are two methods that administrators will use when creating a separate namespace; public namespaces and private namespaces.

Public Namespace　When a company uses a public namespace, they will use one namespace that is generally known by the public, and another that they do not make readily available to external users. A case may be a company that has registered `zygort.com` and `zygort.org`. Using the `zygort.com` namespace for the external namespace and `zygort.org` as the internal namespace keeps the two separate. As long as the internal resources are not registered within the DNS servers that are publicly accessible, the Active Directory infrastructure should be relatively secure.

Private Namespace　Take for instance the company that is using `zygort.com` as their external namespace. By using an internal namespace of `zygort.lcl`, none of the resources within the `zygort.lcl` namespace are accessible from the Internet by default. An administrator would have to configure additional mechanisms for the Active Directory infrastructure and internal resources to be made externally available.

DELEGATING A SUBDOMAIN

Another naming scheme is to create a subdomain beneath the company's Internet presence. While this method does not protect the internal resources as efficiently as a private namespace, you can effectively use the 'security by obscurity' method. In other words, if a company uses an external namespace of zygort.com and an internal namespace of internal.zygort.com, the internal namespace should not be available within the external DNS servers. Even if you never add any delegation records to the Internet domain so that the internal domain name is available from the Internet , you will still be using a domain name structure that will make sense to your users. If you decide to make the internal domain accessible, you can add a delegation record to the DNS servers that are used for your Internet presence or create a subdomain to allow specific servers to be accessed.

Identical Confusion

Using the same name for your internal infrastructure that you are using to identify your organization on the Internet can be very time consuming and confusing. While users will not have any problem remembering just a single namespace, the administrative staff will have the burden of allowing users the ability to access both internal and external resources.

One of the basic rules for protecting your resources is not allowing external entities to discover your internal resources. If you want to use the same namespace internally as well as externally, you will have to use two completely different zones with the same namespace, in order to guarantee that they will not share any zone information. Otherwise, zone transfers or Active Directory replication will populate the DNS servers that the external clients use with information about your internal network. Letting anyone outside of your organization access this information is not a good thing.

Therein lies the problem. How do you allow your internal clients the ability to access resources outside of your internal infrastructure? For each of the web servers, SMTP servers, and any other server that is part of your Internet presence, you will have to manually enter the records into your internal DNS zones. If anything changes, you must make sure that you update the records accordingly. Missing any updates or forgetting to enter records for resources that the users need to access will cause plenty of phone calls to come your way!

Understanding the Current DNS Infrastructure

DNS has been around for many years, and chances are you will already have DNS within your infrastructure. Whether or not your current DNS implementation will support your needs will have to be determined. After all, what works for the Unix or Novell side of your network may not work the best for Active Directory. Case in point, DNS is normally a single master database. This means that updates and entries into the database can only be made on one server—the server holding the primary zone. Every other DNS server that holds a copy of the zone will use secondary zone types that contain read-only copies of the zone database. In order for clients that support dynamic update to enter their resource records within the database, they have to be able to contact the DNS server that hosts the primary zone. As mentioned earlier in the chapter, this is an inefficient method of utilizing DNS.

Unix and Novell DNS solutions that are already in place may not support the Active Directory requirements. At the very least, your DNS has to support SRV records as recorded in RFCs 2052 and 2782. If it doesn't, Active Directory domain controllers will not be found by Active Directory–aware clients. The best environment would be to have a DNS server that not only supports SRV records, but also support dynamic updates as recorded in RFC2136. If the DNS server does not support dynamic updates, you will have to manually enter the correct information for the domain controllers, which will include all of the SRV records that are found within the NETLOGON.DNS file that is created when the domain controller is promoted. Doing so could be a time-consuming, boring task.

After determining if the current DNS servers will support Active Directory, take a look at where the DNS servers are located and the client population that they serve. You probably retain DNS functionality at those locations. You should also determine whether or not you want to place DNS servers in locations that are not supported by local DNS servers. Ask yourself if the clients would be better served to have a local DNS server. The answer will be based on the difference between the queries made by the clients and the zone replication between DNS servers. In a large zone, you may have a large amount of zone transfer data, so you need to weigh that against the number of queries the clients are making. Use a network monitoring tool, such as Microsoft's Network Monitor or McAfee's Sniffer, to analyze the data that is traveling through your network links to determine where the majority of the data is coming from.

That Other DNS Server

What are you supposed to do if another division is responsible for the DNS infrastructure? Some companies have a complete division of responsibilities, and the DNS servers may not be under your control. People are very possessive of the things they manage, and you may find yourself fighting a battle to get the support you need in order to implement Active Directory.

The Windows-based DNS service was designed to interoperate with the latest DNS standards. It was also designed to support additional features that are available only to a Microsoft DNS implementation. These additional features are beneficial to administrators who want to have easier administration and additional security options.

Due to Windows Server 2003's compliance with DNS standards, it will interoperate with Berkeley Internet Name Domain (BIND) DNS servers running versions 9.1.0, 8.2, 8.1.2, and 4.9.7. Windows Server 2003 DNS is also fully compliant with Microsoft Windows NT 4's DNS service.

As you will note in Table 3.1, Windows Server 2003's DNS service and BIND 9.1.0 support some important DNS features. Other versions of DNS do not support all of the options.

TABLE 2.1:   DNS Features Supported on Multiple Platforms

	SRV RECORDS	DYNAMIC UPDATES	INCREMENTAL ZONE TRANSFER	STUB ZONES	CONDITIONAL FORWARDING
Windows Server 2003	x	x	x	x	x
Windows 2000	x	x	x		
Windows NT 4			x		
BIND 9.1.0	x	x	x	x	x
BIND 8.2	x	x	x		
BIND 8.1.2	x	x			
BIND 4.9.7	x				

Additional features are present in a Windows Server 2003 DNS environment that are not supported by other DNS servers. A list of additional features is presented in Table 3.2.

When attempting to integrate Windows Server 2003 DNS into an existing environment, take the previously mentioned interoperability into account. If the existing infrastructure does not support some of the features, you may be forced to upgrade the current infrastructure to Windows Server 2003 DNS so that all of the features that you need for your design are met.

In many companies, a DNS infrastructure is already controlled by a DNS group. If this group is unwilling to relinquish control of DNS or will not allow you to implement your own Windows Server 2003 DNS server, you may be forced to use the existing DNS services. Some organizations do have separate divisions that are responsible for specific portions of the network infrastructure. If your organization is one of them and you are not allowed to implement DNS due to departmental standards and regulations, you will be forced to use what the DNS administrative staff dictates. Be aware of the requirements for Active Directory, however. You may need to force them to upgrade their existing servers to handle the service locator (SRV) records and dynamic updates that Active Directory uses.

TABLE 2.2:   DNS Features Not Supported on Non-Windows Platforms

	SECURE DYNAMIC UPDATES	WINS INTEGRATION	UTF-8 CHARACTER ENCODING	ACTIVE DIRECTORY INTEGRATED ZONES	APPLICATION DIRECTORY-SUPPORT	OBSOLETE-RECORD SCAVENGING
Windows Server 2003	x	x	x	x	x	x
Windows 2000	x	x	x	x		x
Windows NT 4		x				
BIND 9.1.0						
BIND 8.2						
BIND 8.1.2						
BIND 4.9.7						

Propagating the Changes

In order to have an effective DNS solution, you will want to make sure that the clients have access to a local DNS server. In order to have DNS servers close to the clients, you will probably need to propagate the zone data to DNS servers in several locations.

Zone transfers come in two flavors: *authoritative zone transfers (AXFRs)* and *incremental zone transfers (IXFRs)*. An AXFR, sometimes referred to as a complete zone transfer, transfers the entire zone database when the zone transfer is initiated. An IXFR, as defined in RFC1995, only transfers the changes in the zone since the last zone transfer. As you can probably guess, the amount of data that is transferred during an IXFR transfer could be substantially less than that of an AXFR.

The choice to use zone transfers is usually made because the DNS servers in your environment are not Windows 2000– or Windows Server 2003–based. Third-party DNS servers do not participate in Active Directory replication, nor can they read the Active Directory database to determine the resource records that are used. To keep the network usage as low as possible, you should make sure the DNS servers all support IXFR. Otherwise, every time a zone transfer is initiated, the entire zone records will be passed to all of the appropriate DNS servers.

Active Directory–integrated zones can take advantage of Active Directory replication to propagate the changes made to resource records. When you use Active Directory replication, not only do you have the additional benefit of only having one replication topology, but a smaller amount of data is usually passed across the network. For instance, take a record that changes a couple of times before the replication or zone transfer occurs. In the case of a zone transfer, if the record changes twice before the transfer is initiated, both changes have to be sent, even if some of the data is no longer valid. In the case of Active Directory replication, only the effective changes are replicated. All of the intermediate changes are discarded.

You also gain the advantage of the built-in functionality of replication. In an environment where you have multiple sites, many of which could be connected through WAN links, if there are considerable amounts of zone information to be transferred, the replication traffic that is sent between domain controllers in different sites is compressed to reduce network overhead.

Active Directory–integrated zones boast the benefit of being able to share the responsibility of updating the zone, whether it is from dynamic DNS clients or manually entered records. The single point of administration and single point of failure disappear. There are limitations to using Active Directory–integrated zones, however.

First, you can create an Active Directory–integrated zone only on a DNS server that is also a domain controller. If you have a location where you do not want to place a domain controller, you will not be able to take advantage of Active Directory–integrated zones on a DNS server at that location. Of course, if you do not have enough clients to warrant placing a domain controller at that location, you probably will not have dynamic update client issues either.

The second limitation is only a limitation of Windows 2000 domain controllers and not typically a problem with Windows Server 2003 domain controllers. The zone data is replicated to every domain controller within the domain. As you will see in the section "Propagating the Changes," Active Directory replication is far more efficient than zone transfers, but there are still some problems with replicating changes. Windows 2000 domain controllers will only replicate changes to other domain controllers within the same domain, and that replication goes out to all domain controllers, not just those that are DNS servers.

Windows Server 2003 made Active Directory–integrated zones more efficient, but at the same time, using the zones gave the administrators a little more to think about. Active Directory–integrated zones within a Windows Server 2003 environment do not hold the zone data within the domain partition; instead, a separate partition, a directory application partition, is used. An application directory partition does not rely on any specific domain within Active Directory, it can be replicated to any domain controller in the forest. If you look at the partitions within a Windows Server 2003 domain controller, you will find the typical partitions (Schema, Configuration, and Domain), and you will also find directory application partitions for the forest and domain.

When you create an Active Directory–integrated zone on a Windows Server 2003 domain controller, you have the option of determining the scope of replication for the zone. Four options are available, as seen in Figure 2.6:

◆ Replicating to all DNS servers in the forest

◆ Replicating to all DNS servers within a domain

◆ Replicating to all domain controllers within the domain

◆ Replicating to all domain controllers defined in the replication scope of a DNS application directory partition

If you choose the first option—replicating to all DNS servers within the forest—every DNS server within the forest will receive the DNS zone information. The zone information will be held within an application partition. This will cause the most replication because every DNS server within the forest will hold the records for the zone, but the only domain controllers that will receive the data will be those that host the DNS service. You cannot have any Windows 2000–based domain controllers in this scenario.

The second option—replicating to all DNS servers within the domain—will reduce the amount of replication traffic because only the domain controllers that are DNS servers for the domain in question will hold a copy of the domain records. As with the previous option, the zone is stored in an application partition. Again, as with the previous option, you cannot have any Windows 2000–based domain controllers within the domain.

The third option—replicating to all domain controllers within the domain—essentially makes all domain controllers within the domain behave as if they are Windows 2000 domain controllers. Every domain controller, whether or not it is a DNS server, will hold the data for the zone. If you still have some Windows 2000–based domain controllers that are DNS servers, this is the option you will choose.

FIGURE 2.6
Replication scope
options

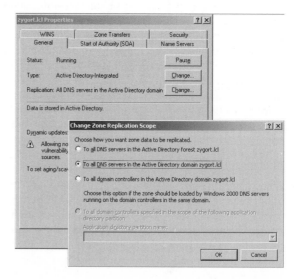

The final option—replicating to all domain controllers defined in the replication scope of a DNS application directory partition—is also an option that is only available to Windows Server 2003 domain controllers. Using an application directory partition, you can choose which of the domain controllers will host a copy of the partition. In this manner, you can control exactly which domain controllers, that are also DNS servers, will host the zone data. If you do not want to replicate the zone to a server that is across a WAN, you will not have to replicate it.

Protecting DNS

DNS has been a popular service to attack because so many clients rely on it in order to locate the host systems that they are attempting to contact. Without DNS, you would not be able to locate `http://www.microsoft.com`. You could call the web server by its IP address, but how many of us have the IP address of the server memorized?

Two methods of attack are usually attempted against DNS servers: denial of service (DoS) attacks and abusing the name resolution. Earlier in this chapter I used an analogy that compared DNS to train tracks. When someone attacks DNS, they are essentially attempting to derail or misguide our trains by adversely affecting the tracks. With denial of service attacks, the attacker attempts to block the DNS server from answering client queries, thereby derailing the clients. When abusing the name resolution that a DNS server provides, either the attacker will cause the DNS server to return incorrect results to the client, or the attacker will gather information about a company from the data that the DNS server returns. This method does not stop the DNS service from responding to the clients, it simply misdirects them, sending them to the wrong destination.

Understanding just how important DNS is to a company's infrastructure, the designers of DNS built the service to be redundant and able to withstand attacks that attempt to take down the DNS servers that support a company. Nevertheless, some attackers will try to knock down your DNS so that they can reduce the effectiveness of your implementation, annoy your clients as they attempt to perform their jobs, and just plain dampen your spirits. Denial of service attacks can be devastating, but you can take steps to put yourself at ease. The following sections cover practices you should take into account when you are designing your DNS infrastructure. You may not need to implement each of the methods identified here, but you should identify the systems that are at risk and use every precaution to make sure that your systems are protected from attack.

Limit the Dynamic Updates

I am going to assume that you are working in an Active Directory environment because that is the main thrust of this book. An Active Directory–integrated DNS server can be configured so that it accepts dynamic update requests only from authorized systems. Once you configure a zone as Active Directory–integrated, you should change the dynamic updates so that only secure updates are allowed. At that point, only members of Active Directory can update the zone records. Once secure updates are turned on, an attacker will not be able to easily add false records to your database that could cause the domain controller to become overloaded as it tries to replicate the changes. Figure 2.7 shows the zone properties for zygort.lcl. Notice that the Dynamic Updates option is set to Secure Only.

FIGURE 2.7

Properties of the zygort. com zone showing secure updates enabled

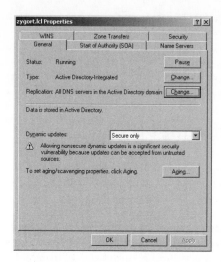

In a Windows Server 2003–based domain, you can take this one step further by making sure that the DNS data is replicated only to domain controllers that are DNS servers or by specifying that the records are replicated only to the DNS servers that are included within the scope of an application partition. Later in this chapter we will discuss the replication options that are available when using Windows Server 2003 DNS.

Monitor for Traffic

If the DNS server appears to be overloaded and you believe the resource overhead is due to an attack, you can use a monitoring tool, such as Microsoft's Network Monitor, or a product, such as Sniffer, to detect where the traffic is originating. If the traffic is from outside of your company, you can assume that you are being attacked. If this is the case, you can attempt to quell the traffic by putting firewall rules into place that will reject packets that originate from the addresses that you identify from the network trace. Most firewalls can be configured to drop spoofed packets. Check with your firewall administrator to determine what you can do with the firewalls in your infrastructure.

If you do put rules into place, that does not mean you will stop the attack. The attacker was probably spoofing their address in the first place, so you may end up being attacked again from the same entity but through another address. Some firewalls have intrusion-detection capabilities, and you may be able to have the firewall dynamically drop packets if they are deemed an attack. You should develop a plan for monitoring the traffic that enters your network, whether it is bound for DNS or not. This plan should take into account the necessity of watching for attack types as well as determine how much monitoring you should perform so that it does not adversely affect the network performance.

The DNS monitoring policy should include references to who will be responsible for designing the monitoring solution, who will implement the policy, where the settings will be applied and who will be responsible for reviewing the data that is collected. In traditional organizations you may have several individuals who are responsible for each part of the monitoring of DNS. There are new monitoring tools available such as Microsoft Operations Manager that will consolidate the monitoring of several systems into one cohesive solution.

Set Quotas

In Windows Server 2003–based Active Directory domains, you have the ability to set quotas on the number of objects that a user is allowed to create within the Active Directory partitions. You can set quotas differently on each Active Directory partition because each partition is evaluated separately. By using quotas, you are able to effectively control the number of objects that can be created by an account, thereby quelling any attempt to flood an Active Directory–integrated zone with too many false objects.

You can set a quota limit on either user accounts or group accounts. An account that has been explicitly added to the quota list that is also a member of a group that has quotas applied to it will be able to create as many objects as the *least* restrictive of the quota policies will allow. When a user attempts to create an object within the container where a quota limit has been set, the existing objects are compared against the quota limit. If the user has not met the quota, the object can be created, but the user will be denied the ability to create the object if the quota has been met.

The command dsadd is used in order to create a quota limit for an Active Directory partition. You can set quotas on any of the partitions, schema, configuration, domain, or any application partitions. However, the quota can only be created or modified on a Windows Server 2003 domain controller because Windows 2000 domain controllers are unfamiliar with the command-line utilities that are used to work with the Active Directory partitions.

Figure 2.8 shows the switches that are available when you are using the dsadd quota command. In its most basic form, you can use it to simply set a quota on a partition. For example, the command dsadd quota -part zygort.lcl -acct zygort\jprice -qlimit 10 would restrict the account jprice so that it is able to create only 10 objects within the zygort.lcl domain partition.

FIGURE 2.8

Syntax of the dsadd quota command

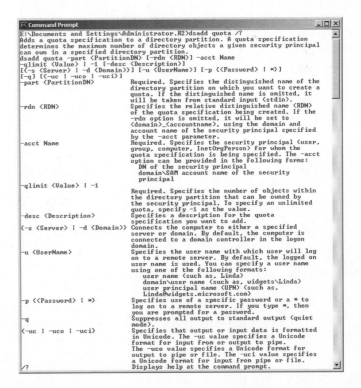

You should take note that the quota limit that you set on an account will include tombstoned objects in the quota count. Tombstones objects are objects that are marked for deletion, but have not yet been purged from the database because a deleted object needs to replicate the deletion action to all domain controllers before purging the object. Once the tombstoned object has met the tombstone lifetime, then all of the domain controllers will purge the object during the next database cleanup cycle. If an object were simply deleted from one domain controller and not marked as tombstoned, the object would simply replicate from another domain controller and reappear in the database.

If you want to ignore tombstoned objects, you can use the `dsmod partition` command with the -qtmbstnwt switch. If you specify a value of 0, then all tombstoned objects will be ignored when objects are evaluated against a user's quota. If you want to reduce the percentage that a tombstone object goes against a user's quota, you can use a weight value between 0 and 100. This value is a percentage, and is used to calculate an active object's full value to a tombstoned object's value. For instance, if you set the -qtmbstnwt switch to 50, each tombstoned object will only count as half of an active object. A value of 10 will count each tombstoned object as 1/10 of each active object.

If at a later time you want to modify the number of objects that `jprice` could create, you could use the `dsmod quota` command. The syntax for `dsmod quota` is shown in Figure 2.9. Notice that you will have to know the fully distinguished name for the quota entry before you can change the quota limit. You can use the `dsquery quota` command to list the quotas that are set. As you can see in Figure 2.10, nearly all of the same options that are available from `dsadd` are also available from `dsquery`.

FIGURE 2.9

Syntax of the `dsmod` `quota` command

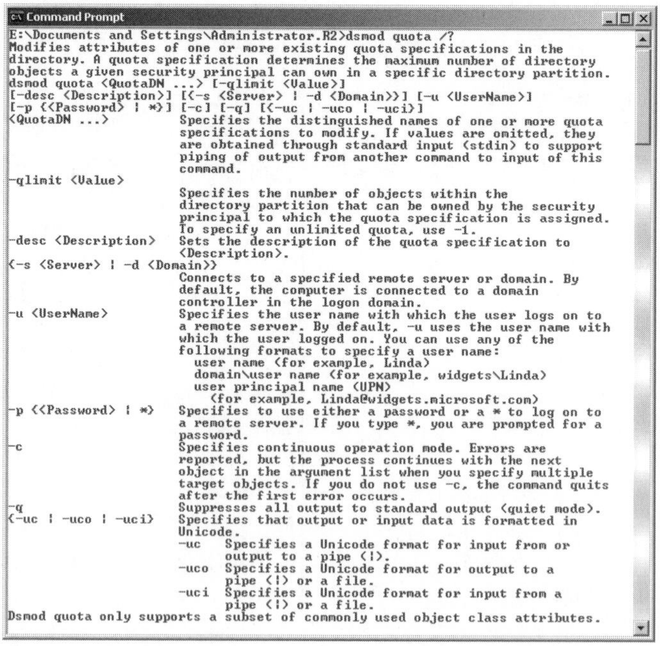

To find the quota entry for the `jprice` account, you would enter `dsquery quota -acct zygort\` `jprice` at the command prompt. If you want to start your search at a specific partition, you can enter the partition's fully distinguished name in the command by using the `startnode` option. Of course your best bet for maintaining your DNS server is to make sure you have good documentation, and we know we all document everything. If you end up having to support an Active Directory implementation that another administrator had set up, you will be able to find out what has been set by querying for the information.

Once you know the quota entry, you can issue the `dsmod quota "CN=zygort_jprice,CN=NTDS Quotas,dc=zygort,dc=lcl" -qlimit 15` command, which will set a new quota of 15 objects for the `jprice` account. Note that when you have a space within the fully qualified name of an object, you need to enclose the entire name in quotes.

NOTE If you are familiar with ADSI scripting, you can also manage quota limits on Active Directory partitions. For more information on ADSI scripting, check out the Scripting section at the end of this book.

FIGURE 2.10

Syntax of the `dsquery quota` command

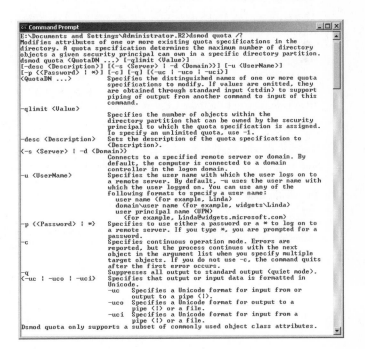

Disable Recursion

The typical behavior for a DNS server is to take over the name resolution process whenever a client is attempting to resolve a host name. Clients typically send an iterative query to their DNS server, and the DNS server starts the recursion process to locate a DNS server that can identify the IP address for the host name in question. An attacker can take advantage of this scenario and start attacking the DNS server with several queries in an attempt to limit its ability to respond to valid queries.

When you disable recursion on a DNS server, you are essentially telling the DNS server that it will no longer be a slave to the client, and it should only return a referral to the client. In this scenario, the DNS server takes on far less of a load, but the client will incur more of the work. As the clients send queries to their DNS servers, the DNS servers will check their zone data for a match. If the DNS server is not authoritative for the zone and has not cached the entry, the DNS server will refer the client to another DNS server to contact.

In order to disable recursion, you can open the properties of the DNS server and select the option Disable Recursion (Also Disables Forwarders), as seen in Figure 2.11.

This takes most of the resolution responsibility off of the DNS server; however, you should note that DNS servers that have been stripped of their recursive abilities cannot be configured to forward, by using either a standard or conditional forwarder. This is due to the recursive nature of forwarding. The DNS server would normally send a recursive query to the server listed within the Forwarders tab of the DNS server properties.

Use Appropriate Routing

There are several ways to resolve a query when it is sent to a DNS server. If the DNS server that receives the query cannot resolve the query from a zone in which the DNS server is authoritative, the server will attempt to locate the host name within the query by asking other servers. As long as you have not disabled recursion, you can still configure a server to act as a forwarder. You can also configure any Windows Server 2003 DNS server with a stub zone.

Which routing method should you choose when you are attempting to maintain a secure system? If you are worried about a denial of service attack, you should use the method that is the least resource intensive. Conditional forwarding is the most resource intensive of the routing methods, because it has to process the conditions before it decides where to forward the query. However, if you have implemented a firewall to block traffic, you may need to use another method besides a stub zone, because stub zones require access to remote systems by using TCP and UDP port 53. Make sure you work in conjunction with the network infrastructure team to determine where you have firewall rules that will block traffic on TCP port 53.

FIGURE 2.11
Disabling recursion

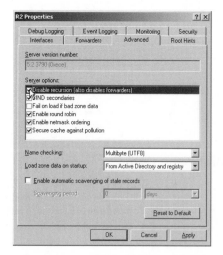

Keeping the System Accurate

Attacks are not always attempts to stop the system from responding. Sometimes attacks are meant to discover information about a company or to redirect clients to incorrect hosts. Two of the most common attacks on a DNS implementation are *database manipulation* and *cache poisoning*. In either of these scenarios, data in entered into the DNS server that does not correspond to the correct host with which the client is attempting to communicate.

To alleviate attacks on your system, you should take steps to help guarantee that the DNS database can be modified only by authorized entities and to ensure that the DNS resolver cache does not contain invalid records. The options discussed in the following sections will help you protect your systems and alleviate problems for your users.

Use IPSec

If you want to make sure that you have control over the systems that are able to connect to your DNS server and ensure that those systems are authorized to do so, you could implement IPSec and use a policy that requires the clients to have IPSec in order to communicate with the DNS servers. You could even go so far as to configure policies that are specific to certain clients in order to allow only a subset of clients to connect to a DNS server. Clients from remote sites, or outside of a specific department, may not have the appropriate settings to allow them to connect to a DNS server, while authorized clients are allowed to update records within the zone and communicate with the DNS server in order to query for other hosts.

You can create your own IPSec policies that have rules in place that will allow only the appropriate clients to access the DNS server. At the same time, you can include a rule that will allow all of the DNS servers that need to communicate with one another to do so. If you are using Active Directory–integrated DNS servers, make sure the IPSec rules that govern the domain controllers are configured to allow any replication partner the ability to connect and communicate.

IPSec is covered in a later chapter, but you should determine at this point what type of IPSec policies you will need to implement. Not all client types support IPSec, so you should determine if it is supported within your organization. If it is, you will need to make sure that the appropriate level of security. The three basic policies that are preconfigured allow for connection types, Client, Server and Secure Server, as seen in Figure 2.12.

Client   The client IPSec policy will not initiate IPSec communication with any other system. Instead, it will enable the system to communicate using IPSec, but only if another system initiates an IPSec enable connection. If not asked to talk IPSec, it will continue to communicate clear text.

Server   The server IPSec policy will attempt to initiate IPSec communication with all of the systems it is communicating with, but if a system is not configured to use IPSec, or the IPSec policies do not match, the two systems will still communicate using clear text.

Secure Server   The secure server IPSec policy becomes the network equivalent of the snob. Assigning this policy will configure the system to only communicate with other IPSec-enabled systems. If a system is not able to talk IPSec, or the IPSec policies between the two systems do not match, they will not be able to connect to one another.

FIGURE 2.12
Built-in IPSec
Security Policies

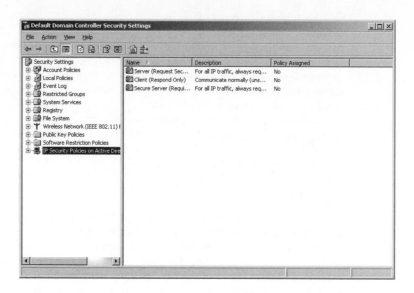

Use Secure DDNS

As mentioned before, if you want to make sure the records that are entered within your DNS zones are valid records, you can implement the Secure Only option from the General tab of the zone properties, as seen in Figure 2.13. Once enabled, the only clients that can enter records within the zone are clients that are members of your Active Directory.

The greatest benefit of using only secure updates is that you can be guaranteed that the records that are entered are valid. An attacker would not be able to register records that would redirect the client to an invalid host or bad records that would cause the failure of the client's access attempt.

FIGURE 2.13
Enabling secure
dynamic updates

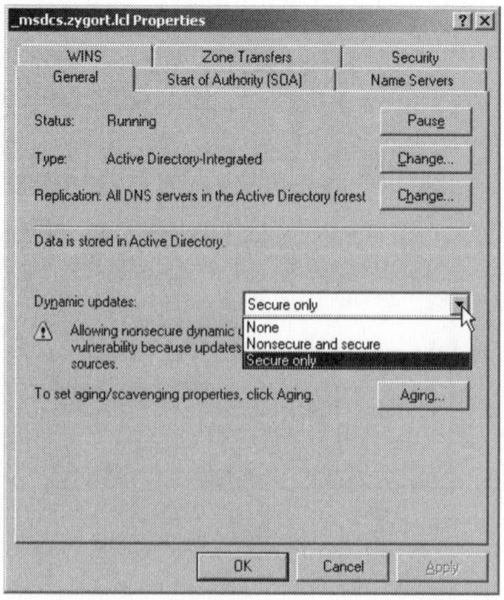

The only way you would be able to make the zone more secure would be to completely disable the ability to use dynamic updates. Usually, this is not an option because the administrative staff would have to manually enter every record within the zone. This could be a very time-consuming task, and it would be prone to human error, which could cause the same problems you are trying to alleviate.

If you implement secure updates, make sure that the clients that need to register within your zone are still able to do so. You might need to allow DHCP to register on behalf of some of the clients within your network, and you might have to manually create the records for others.

Avoid Cache Poisoning

An attacker could attempt to populate the cache on your DNS server with incorrect information in an attempt to either stop name resolution or to redirect clients to incorrect systems. If an attacker were able to populate the cache with an entry that would redirect a client to the wrong DNS server, the client could receive a response to their query that redirected them to a compromised host.

To make sure that the entries within the DNS cache are complete and accurate entries that are part of the name resolution path that the DNS server has obtained during resolution, you can enable the Secure Cache Against Pollution option, as seen in Figure 2.14. You can reach this option by opening the properties of your DNS server and selecting the Advanced tab.

During normal query operations, DNS servers will query other DNS servers to resolve the query. If a DNS server holds the correct information within cache, it can respond with a complete answer to the query, but it is not the authoritative server. If someone wants to cause a misdirection, they could enter information into the DNS server's cache, which would in turn give wrong data back to all other DNS servers that are using it to resolve. Once enabled, your DNS server will ignore records that were not obtained from the DNS server that is authoritative for the zone in question. This will place additional resource requirements on your DNS server because it will need to perform more queries due to the dropping of records that are not obtained from authoritative DNS servers. However, it will allow you to guarantee the authenticity and accuracy of the records.

FIGURE 2.14
Securing against
cache pollution

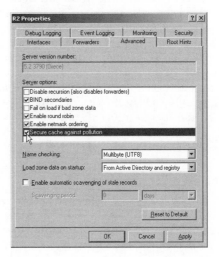

Allow Appropriate Access

Keeping attackers away from the data contained in your database should be of high concern. If an attacker is able to access the records, or able to damage the database so that it no longer responds correctly to queries, either your clients will become victims of redirection attacks or they will not have the ability to access the hosts with which they were intending to communicate. The following sections cover options that you should consider when you are attempting to secure both Active Directory–integrated and non–Active Directory–integrated zones.

ACTIVE DIRECTORY–INTEGRATED ZONES

By default, members of the domain's Administrators group, Domain Admins, Enterprise Admins, and DNS Admins groups have the ability to manage DNS zones. If you want to control the administrative staff who can manage a zone, you can configure the permissions on the zone within the DNS console. If special groups are responsible for specific zones, make sure you remove the other administrative groups from the zones' access control lists. If you don't, a rogue administrator could make unauthorized changes to the zones.

NON–ACTIVE DIRECTORY–INTEGRATED ZONES

Stub zones, secondary zones, and primary zones that are not Active Directory–integrated do not have access control lists associated with them. This is not necessarily a bad thing for stub and secondary zones because the records contained within them cannot be modified directly. The primary zone is the only one that can be modified directly. Non–Active Directory–integrated primary zones are at risk, however. You should make sure that you monitor the accounts within the groups that have the ability to work on the DNS server, and you should consider turning off the dynamic update option.

Zone data is stored within a file on the DNS server when the zone is not Active Directory–integrated. These zone files are protected using file system access control lists. The default members of the access control list include the Users and Power Users groups. Typically, neither of these groups needs access to the zone files; therefore, you should modify the access control list so that only the Administrators group, any special DNS administrative groups, and the System account have access. Remember that any dynamic updates are performed within the DNS service, and it is up to the System account to update the zone's associated file; therefore, users do not need to have access to the these files.

You should also consider moving the zone files to another partition away from the system files. Such a move would effectively reduce the chance of a zone file being compromised by a buffer overflow and allowing an attacker to browse the files stored on the system partition. Once you move the files to another partition, make sure that you adjust the access control list so that only the appropriate DNS administrators and system have access to the files.

Lock Down Transfers

An Active Directory–integrated zone can send zone transfers to a secondary zone if the DNS server is configured to do so. You may want to review your settings to make sure that you only allow zone transfers to DNS servers that are authorized to receive the transfer. This is especially important if your zones are not Active Directory–integrated. All of the zone information will need to pass between the DNS servers as zone transfers. You should make sure that all of the DNS servers that need to receive the transfer are listed, and that no other servers are allowed to receive a transfer.

If you can be certain that all of the DNS servers that are listed within the Name Servers tab of the zone properties are valid servers, you can use the setting shown in Figure 2.15. By using the option Only To Servers Listed In The Name Servers tab, you can allow all servers that have a secondary zone configured for the namespace to receive zone transfers when a change occurs.

However, if you think you might have a rogue administrator, or someone has built a DNS server to capture records for your namespace, you may want to kick up your level of security a notch by using the Only To The Following Name Servers option. When using this setting you will need to manually enter the IP address of every valid DNS server that needs to receive a zone transfer. Of course, this will not keep a rogue administrator who has permissions to view the zone data away from your DNS records. If you have granted them the privileges, there is not much you can do besides revoke their power.

If your zones are Active Directory–integrated, you can probably use the default setting of not allowing zone transfers. This guarantees that only domain controllers hold the zone records, but limits you if there are any non–Active Directory–integrated DNS servers within your environment.

FIGURE 2.15

Allowing zone transfer to servers listed as name servers

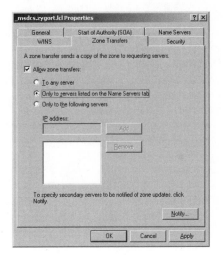

Coming Up Next

Just like the chicken and the egg, the debate rages on as to whether you should design the Active Directory domains or the DNS infrastructure first. We decided that since the AD relies on DNS, we should discuss it first. In the next chapter we are going to go in depth on the criteria you should take into account when designing your Active Directory domains.

Chapter 3

Active Directory Forest and Domain Design

How do you optimally design a database that replicates only parts of itself to as many as thousands of domain controllers at differing intervals? Therein lies the need for the first section of this chapter. Active Directory may very well become one of the largest database implementations within your organization. If you talk to very many database administrators, you will see them cringe when you mention that you would like to replicate a database to multiple servers. But that is exactly what you are going to do with Active Directory and your domain controllers. In all fairness, the Active Directory database is not nearly as complex as you will find with a relational database used for data warehousing, but it is still not a trivial task.

Active Directory is a technology that is unlike most directory services in that it is an integral part of the operating system (OS). The many other directory services out there "sit on top" of the OS. For example, Novell's NetWare Directory Services (NDS), now termed eDirectory, can be easily upgraded independently of an OS upgrade. But that's not the case for Active Directory. To update the directory service on the Microsoft platform, you currently need to upgrade to the latest server OS or service pack. Each service pack brings a host of bug and security fixes for Active Directory as well as additional functionality; therefore, you should apply the latest service pack on all of your domain controllers within a month of its release—although that is easier said than done.

Don't get me wrong; you can extend Active Directory to support new attributes and object classes at any time. When you deploy Active Directory–enabled applications, you will usually need to add the additional attributes and object classes to Active Directory in order to support those applications. That is different from making structural changes to Active Directory, which requires that you make changes to the OS to support the updates.

Take note that Active Directory enhancements, features, and functionality are greatly upgraded by Windows Server 2003. The move from Windows 2000 to 2003 requires very little planning. The two databases are built on the same underlying technologies, but Microsoft learned a lot after the initial rollout with Active Directory under Windows 2000. Consider Active Directory in Windows Server 2003 as version 2.0 to the 1.0 Active Directory version in Windows 2000—this is an unofficial versioning that's included just for illustrative purposes. Windows Server 2003 R2 is not such a large update to Active Directory. It came as more of an enhancement to some of the features of the OS.

New administrative tools have been added and additional functionality has been included with both Windows Server 2003 and the new R2 version. However, for most of the added functionality, you will need to retire all of your Windows 2000 domain controllers. I'll discuss more on that later in this chapter as we review the functional levels for domains and forests.

You should consider moving to Windows Server 2003 for a myriad of reasons, not the least of which is the support timeline expiration of Windows 2000. Mainstream product support expires five years after a product release. Many in the IT industry will take the conspiracy theorist's stance and accuse Microsoft of retiring products in order to keep companies on the purchasing side of the table. However, in our industry, you must admit that the technologies that develop over the course of five years tend to make operating systems and applications obsolete. For those of you who have left Windows NT 4 for the greener pastures of Windows 2000/2003 and Active Directory, could you even imagine trying to perform some of the administrative tasks on Windows NT 4 that you can perform with the newer technologies?

TIP For more information on the life cycle of operating systems and applications, peruse the article on Microsoft's website at http://support.microsoft.com/default.aspx?pr=lifecycle.

In the following sections, we're going to look at the criteria you should consider when developing your Active Directory design. Most of the information included comes from working with Active Directory over the past few years and the methodology that has proven to work the best. Although some of the information may seem like simple common sense, there are times when common sense seems to take a backseat to the desire to implement technology. Also, this chapter is not going to delve deeply into the technology; we're saving that for the upcoming administration, maintenance, management, and troubleshooting chapters. Instead, in this chapter we concentrate on the requirements and options for a solid forest and domain design.

Active Directory Forest Design Criteria

Active Directory design requires both technical expertise and organizational acceptance. It requires compromise among diverse groups that may be used to doing tasks their own way—Domain Name System (DNS) administrators can use Unix for DNS, Novell NetWare administrators have a different architecture of directory services that they want to implement, enterprise resource planning (ERP) packages use their own directory service, proxy/firewall/Internet access might use its own directory service, email uses its own directory service—you get the idea. How do you please everyone in your design? You probably can't. Start by developing the ideal design by yourself, if possible, and then let each group have its turn telling you what modifications they would like to see or, in a worst-case scenario, why your design won't work. If you let each group try to design Active Directory, you will never complete the project.

Get executive sponsorship in the design phase. I cannot stress this point enough. In other words, find an executive to approve the design phase of Active Directory. If you make an executive ally within the organization and that executive trusts and likes your plan, you will find that getting the design approved and moving on to the planning stages will be much easier. Of course, you need to make sure that the executive with whom you ally yourself has a basic understanding of the whole picture when it comes to Active Directory.

Active Directory design is about putting structure around a confused mass of unorganized objects. It's about administrative control and separating the service owners accountable for maintaining Active Directory and the services that support it from data owners who are responsible for maintaining the objects within the directory. It is about architecting a solution that takes into account the limitations of the technology you are working with (Windows Server and Active Directory) and designing around the organizational day-to-day business. Your design needs to take into consideration speed/latency, name resolution, availability, security, disaster recovery, hardware, and so on.

Forest design should be your first architectural element when designing Active Directory. A forest is a single instance of Active Directory. The forest is the topmost container in Active Directory. It is scalable beyond 5,000 domain controllers, 5,000 sites, and millions of users, according to Microsoft's Branch Office Deployment Guide. Even the largest organizations should be able to contain all of the necessary objects within a single forest. You will find that other considerations will come into play when developing your design. Legislative, political, or organizational reasons may force you to move to a multiple-forest design, but make sure there is a valid reason to do so. Later in this chapter, we discuss the pros and cons of single- and multiple-forest implementations.

Although a forest is almost insanely easy to build, it is far, far more complex to design. Several options are available, and you need to know what roles forests and domains play within your organization. As you will see in the next section, the domain is no longer the security boundary, as it was under Windows NT 4. I will discuss the differences and the new technologies that make up the security boundary, replication boundary, administration boundary, schema, and global catalog.

Schema

A forest shares a single *schema,* which can be defined as the rules of what can go into a directory service. Active Directory is made up of *objects,* which are instances of an object class that have been defined by combining attributes to form what can be allowed within the directory. These rules also define where objects can be created and used within the directory service. Because all of the objects within the forest have to follow the same rules, there can be only one schema per forest.

Because of the important nature of the schema, you should not take its existence lightly. Although you may not have to think about it on a daily basis, you will need to make sure that you do not allow anyone to have access to the schema. If changes are enacted within the schema, the results could be disastrous. Your organization may be one of the lucky ones that never have to modify their schema, but very few organizations are so lucky.

Many organizations will modify their default schema so that it will support directory-enabled applications. One such example, and probably the most prevalent, is the need to implement Microsoft Exchange. Both Exchange 2000 Server and Exchange Server 2003 add many attributes and object classes to the schema. Prior to implementing an Active Directory–enabled application within your production environment, make sure you understand the ramifications of altering your schema. Test the application first in a test environment.

NOTE If you would like to see the schema extensions that are installed with Exchange 2000/2003, check out the information at `http://msdn.microsoft.com/library/default.asp?url=` `/library/en-us/e2k3/e2k3/e2k3_ldf_diff_ad_schema_intro.asp`.

When designing your Active Directory infrastructure, determine which Active Directory–enabled applications you will be implementing and determine which of them will extend the schema. You should then determine when you want to extend the schema for each one. Extending the schema is not something that should be taken lightly. You will be adding attributes that will possibly change existing objects, and adding new object classes that will be used to create new objects. As all of these changes occur, take into consideration how much additional replication will occur, to which domain controllers these changes will take effect, and the additional global catalog replication that will start consuming network traffic throughout every domain within your forest.

Schema Considerations

If you are extending the schema for an in-house application, consider contacting an object ID (OID) issuing authority for the proper classification. Failure to do so could cause problems with other applications when they are installed within your environment. If an application needs to use an OID that is already in use, the application will fail the install. Windows Server 2003 will allow you to reclassify an attribute; however, Windows 2000 will not. As a best practice, you should contact one of the following organizations to verify that the OID is not in use:

◆ Internet Assigned Numbers Authority (IANA) hands out OIDs for free under the "Private Enterprises" branch.

◆ American National Standards Institute (ANSI) hands out OIDs under the "US Organizations" branch for $1,000.

◆ British Standards Institute (BSI) hands out OIDs under the "UK Organizations" branch.

◆ Visit www.iso.ch for information on your country's National Registration Authority.

While you are at it, register the OID so that no one else can use it for their commercial applications. Microsoft will validate all applications that you want to be certified for use within Active Directory. If you register your OID and someone else tries to use it, Microsoft will fail the application and the software vendor will have to change its application accordingly.

For information on registering OIDs for the ISO or if you are registering an OID under Microsoft's branch, see the following websites:

◆ http://msdn.microsoft.com/library/en-us/ad/ad/obtaining_a_root_oid_from_an_iso_name_registration_authority.asp

◆ http://msdn.microsoft.com/library/en-us/ad/ad/obtaining_an_object_identifier_from_microsoft.asp

NOTE   For more information on registering OIDs for your Active Directory environment, see Chapter 12, "Maintaining the Active Directory Database."

Security Boundary

The rules have changed since Windows NT 4. Under NT, the domain was the security boundary. If you were a member of the Domain Admins group, you had full control of your domain and were isolated from Domain Admins from other domains. Now with Active Directory, the forest is the security boundary in Active Directory, not the domain. I get a kick out of clients who want to argue this point with me. Any Domain Admin on any domain controller throughout the forest can bring down the entire AD forest—either on purpose or by mistake. There are some simple ways to do this:

◆ Impersonate any user in the forest (in any domain).

◆ Read, change, or delete any Windows-secured resource or configuration setting on any machine (especially domain controllers) in the forest.

◆ Modify service accounts that run in the *system context*—that means OS privileges.

◆ Run code in the system context.

◆   Hide (bury) domain administrator–equivalent accounts for later use.

◆   Cause changes to replicate to other DCs. This is not a problem with database corruption, but it is for a denial-of-service (DoS) attack, which would be easy with a simple script that added users endlessly.

◆   Take ownership of files, folders, objects, attributes, and, thereby, breach privacy.

These are just a few of the many ways to bring down the AD forest. Granted, being a member of the Domain Admins group from the forest root makes it easier to carry out some of these attacks, but having Domain Admin membership anywhere within the forest could be a potential risk if the user who is granted that level of control is not trustworthy.

When you are creating your AD design, you must account for who will become the forest owner. The forest owner is any account that has full control access to every domain within the forest. Any domain administrator in the root domain of the forest (the first domain created in the forest) is automatically made a member of the Enterprise Admins and Schema Admins groups. You should be thinking like the rest of us and take users and administrators out of this group immediately. You can then create a set of standards and procedures detailing when an account can be added to these groups in order to perform the administrative duty.

Replication Boundary

Active Directory forests provide for a complete replication boundary. Every domain controller within the forest will participate in the replication topology, sharing information between them so that each domain controller can respond correctly when a client requests it. Two AD partitions, the configuration and schema partitions (or naming contexts), replicate on a forest-wide basis. Every domain controller within the forest will share identical data for these two partitions. The schema partition holds all of the rules pertaining to how objects can be created within the forest. If any of the domain controllers within your forest had a different set of attributes or object class rules, the objects that were created by that domain controller would not work with the other domain controllers.

The configuration partition specifies how the domain controllers communicate and the domain is designed. Other systems, such as Exchange 2000/2003, use the configuration partition to hold data about the systems that provide the email service. Having this information replicated to all domain controllers within the forest gives you the ability to hold the configuration data in one location, Active Directory, and allows other systems to look to the domain controllers to find out how they are supposed to run. This also means that you only have to configure one replication topology when synchronizing changes instead of having Active Directory–specific data replicating through domain controllers and Exchange data replicating through Exchange servers.

Note that data does not replicate between domain controllers in different forests. Even if you have domain controllers from two forests within the same physical location, they will not share configuration and schema partition data; only those from the same forest will.

Another partition type, the application partition, can be configured to replicate to all domain controllers within the forest, but it is not mandatory that it do so. With an application partition, you have the ability to choose which domain controllers the partition will replicate to, thereby giving you a means of controlling some of the replication traffic within your organization. This technology is not available with Windows 2000 systems, but is available when you're using Windows Server 2003. Having the ability to replicate the data within the partition to all Active Directory–integrated DNS servers within the forest, restrict it to all Active Directory–integrated DNS servers within the domain, host the data within the domain partition, or choose which domain controllers will hold the partition can help you control the replication traffic in your environment. Later in this chapter we look at how the application partition works and the benefits of using this new partition type.

You can see the naming contexts upon opening Active Directory Services Interface (ADSI) Edit, which is provided in the Support Tools on the Windows 2000 or Windows 2003 CD under \SUPPORT\ TOOLS. Figure 3.1 shows ADSI Edit with the naming contexts opened. You can also view the naming contexts that are held on a domain controller using the NTDSUTIL command-line utility.

NOTE For more information on NTDSUTIL, see Chapter 12.

As you'll see in the following chapter, the last partition, the domain partition, or domain-naming context as it is sometimes referred, is replicated only to other domain controllers within the same domain. Although this does improve performance by restricting the amount of replication throughout the organization, it causes issues when users are trying to locate objects within other domains. To alleviate some of the problems associated with partitioning the forest into separate domains, Microsoft introduced the concept of a global catalog.

FIGURE 3.1
ADSI Edit and the
naming contexts

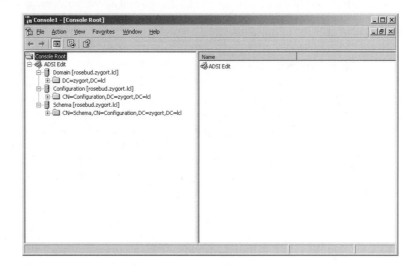

A Common Global Catalog

A forest also provides for a common global catalog (GC) within the forest. A global catalog is a domain controller that hosts objects from every domain naming context within the forest. At first you might think that could be a lot of data for a domain controller to host. If the GC server were to hold all of the attributes from every domain within the forest, you'd be correct. However, to keep network traffic at a minimum, only about 200 of the 1,700+ available attributes for each object are copied into the GC. The GC is like a giant cache of directory objects and attributes that keep you from needing to query beyond a single domain controller. For example, you could easily take a laptop from domain to domain, country to country inside the same forest and authenticate immediately because your user object (and every user object in the forest) is cached in the GC, which replicates forest-wide.

You can control which attributes populate the GC with the Schema Management Microsoft Management Console (MMC) snap-in. Attributes that are selected to replicate to the GC are referred to as the Partial Attribute Set (PAS). When you load the Active Directory Schema snap-in, you can open the properties of any attribute and view whether or not the attribute will be part of the GC. Figure 3.2 shows the properties of the Bad Password Count attribute. Notice that the check box for Replicate This Attribute To The Global Catalog is not checked. Once selected, the attribute would then need to replicate to all GCs within the forest.

Be warned though; in Windows 2000, when you make a change to the PAS, you cause a full GC replication throughout the forest. Windows 2000 domain controllers do not know how to efficiently handle the PAS. This is not a big deal in an office of 200 people, but it is very much a concern when you have a 9GB GC such as Microsoft. This does not happen in Windows Server 2003; instead, only the changed or added attributes are replicated throughout the forest. If you want to maintain efficient control of the GCs in your infrastructure, you should think about only allowing Windows Server 2003 systems to have the GC role.

NOTE   Later, as we determine the placement of domain controllers, we come back to the GC server. There will be specific locations where you should place GC servers so that users and applications have access to the GC. For instance, the GC holds the Exchange 2000/2003's global address list (GAL), so you need to provide constant access to the GC for all of your Exchange servers.

Always start your design with the most basic design options. If finding a resource easily across domain boundaries is important, without additional software services, consider a single forest. A single forest will allow all of the objects from every domain to be seen through the GC. If you must use multiple forests, there are applications, such as Microsoft Identity Integration Server 2003 (MIIS), formerly Microsoft Metadirectory Services (MMS), that can replicate objects and attributes between forests and differing directory services such as Novell's NDS to Active Directory. These applications have a definite learning curve to them and will usually require additional design and planning. Make sure you exhaust every other option before deciding to create more than one forest.

TIP   For more information concerning Microsoft Identity Integration Server 2003, visit Microsoft's website at www.microsoft.com/miis.

FIGURE 3.2
Properties of the
Bad Password Count
attribute

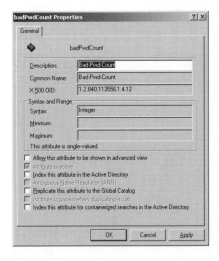

When you have multiple domains within your forest, you need to have a method to gain access to the resources in each domain. The GC servers must have the ability to pull data from domain controllers in each of the other domains. To do so, trust relationships are used to determine which domains can contact each other.

Kerberos and Trusts

Under the Windows NT 4 model, every domain was its own security boundary. To allow users to access resources within another NT domain, you had to create a trust relationship between the two domains. When you created a trust relationship, only one domain was allowed to trust users from the other domain. If you wanted to allow both sets of users to access each other's resources, you had to create two trust relationships. To make matters worse, there was no sharing of trust. In other words, the trust relationships were not transitive. If DomainA had a trust relationship with DomainB, and DomainB had a trust relationship with DomainC, DomainA was still restricted from accessing DomainC until an explicit trust was set up between DomainA and DomainC. To make matters worse, these trust relationships were only one-way trusts so you needed to create two trusts just so that two domains could trust one another. Needless to say, planning and maintaining the correct trust relationships in a large NT infrastructure caused many administrators to lose sleep.

Windows 2000 and Windows Server 2003 have changed the trust relationship game. Within a forest, all of the domains are interconnected through two-way transitive trusts. This allows every user within the forest to access resources within any domain within the forest so long as they have been granted permissions to access the resource. All of this is accomplished using the fewest trust relationships possible. Take a look at Figure 3.3. This is a typical forest that has two trees and several domains within each tree. In a Windows 2000/2003 forest, you will need only the trust relationships shown in the graphic. If you were to implement the same number of domains within a Windows NT 4 environment, you would need 20 trusts.

In order for the trust relationships to work within our forest, the Kerberos authentication service is used. With Kerberos, each of the domains and all of the security principles within each domain are identified and given access to the resources through a process known as *delegation*. Later in this chapter, as we look at domain design, we take a closer look at Kerberos and how it works across domain boundaries.

FIGURE 3.3
Active Directory trusts
within a forest

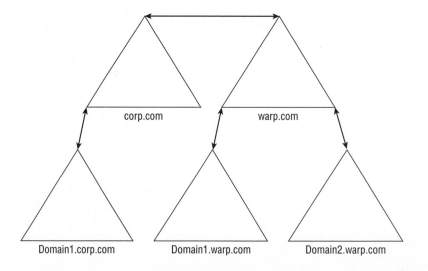

Political and Administration Boundary

These two topics, political and administration boundaries, are tied together due to the fact that there is usually an underlying political reason for creating separate forests. As I mentioned earlier, the forest is the security boundary. Administrative accounts from the root domain of the forest have the ability to become the forest owners and, as such, can control all of the objects within the forest. Although there are other reasons why you may want to create separate forests, doing so to appease a faction within your organization might end up being the deciding factor. You may not like it, but some divisions simply do not like allowing other administrators to be able to access their data, and they may have a corporate sponsor who has enough power to override your design. The only way that you can isolate their data is to create a separate forest and assign them as the forest owners.

The drawbacks to giving them their own forest are that you will have additional administrative overhead and you will need to make sure that they are properly trained to use Active Directory. When you have two forests, you have two completely separate administrative structures. If you can get by with a single forest, do so. You will reduce the total administrative costs. Later in this chapter, we review the advantages and disadvantages associated with single and multiple forests.

The key to deciding where the administrative boundaries should be drawn will be dictated by whether you have to isolate services or data from other portions of the organization. Creating a separate forest is the only way you can isolate the directory services and data from groups of users. Before you make the decision to create a separate forest, review the arguments from all sides. You may be able to create a separate domain in order to give autonomy over services and data. Autonomy allows the administrators of certain resources to control them, while at the same time limiting the access to those resources from the other domains. Weigh the cost of a separate forest where isolation can be granted against the ease of administration with a single forest where you can apply autonomy. Of course, the political battles will ensue, as each division wants to have complete control over all of its resources. Don't forget what I mentioned earlier about executive sponsorship. If the battles rage on and you need to settle the disputes, there is nothing like having someone with lots of clout in your corner.

Multiple Forests: Pros and Cons

Seeing multiple forests within a medium-sized client is not uncommon. One of my Active Directory clients had about 2,000 people and six forests. They used one for production, one for development, two for extranet applications, and two for development that mimicked the extranet production forests. This was a good, secure design for them. Although not every organization will need to go to this extreme, I often recommend that you have a separate forest in which to test changes to Active Directory and software interaction. Creating a miniature version of your production environment will allow you to test changes before they are implemented within your production environment. Most companies that have a test environment have far fewer problems within their infrastructure than those that "shoot from the hip." I can't tell you how many times a service pack or hotfix has caused instability within a network.

I also like to recommend using a development forest if an organization has developers who need to test their software prior to implementing it within the production forest. Developers need their own forest if they require excess privileges or if they touch Active Directory. Often developers feel like they need Domain Admin access and a domain controller under their desk. I would never give developers this much power over my forest. As I mentioned in the "Schema" section earlier, changes to the schema are not easily undone. Although Windows Server 2003 is a great deal friendlier when it comes to modifying the schema, you should never make any changes without first testing the implementation to determine what the ramifications will be. I always recommend that developers do their work in a separate forest or, if possible, on virtual machine technology. Running a virtual system on an existing system is an easy way to mimic the production environment. The drawback is that the computer on which you are running the virtual system should have enough horsepower to run multiple operating systems at the same time. Two premier virtual system software applications are available. Microsoft sells its version, Microsoft VirtualPC (`www.microsoft.com/virtualpc`), which was originally marketed by Connectix, and EMC markets its own version called VMWare (`www.vmware.com`).

I also briefly mentioned a forest used for extranet applications. This is one area where you will need to determine the level of security you need for users who access your infrastructure across the Internet. Some organizations will implement a completely different forest for their perimeter network than they use within their internal network. This adds an additional layer of security to your design. If you were to use the same forest in both locations, you could run the risk of exposing information about your internal network if someone were able to hack into your perimeter network.

Figure 3.4 is a flowchart that will assist you in making decisions for your forest design. Within this flowchart, I take into account isolation and autonomy needs and choose the best forest design based on the needs of the organization. Table 3.1 shows the advantages and disadvantages of using a single forest. Table 3.2 compares the multiple-forest pros and cons.

FIGURE 3.4

Flowchart to determine isolated or autonomous control

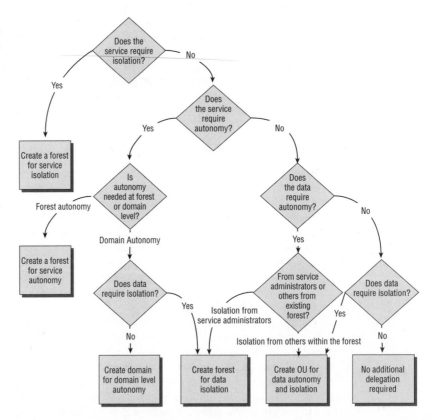

TABLE 3.1:   Single-Forest Pros and Cons

SINGLE-FOREST PROS	SINGLE-FOREST CONS
Easier to administer	Less secure for multiple business units with unknown/untrusted administrators.
Easier to troubleshoot	Forests cannot be merged or split.
A single security boundary	Domains cannot join other forests.
Single schema	Schema differences are sometimes needed between business units.
Easier to support	Cannot agree on change control within a domain.
	Users cannot search GCs of other forest without additional software.

TABLE 3.2:   Multiple-Forest Pros and Cons

MULTIPLE-FOREST PROS	MULTIPLE-FOREST CONS
More secure.	More administration.
May have different schema in each forest (e.g., one business unit uses Exchange and another doesn't want its schema extended with the Exchange attributes).	Difficult to remember what schema extensions have been added and from which application they were added.
More control over outside trusts.	Don't have complete transitive trusts.
Trusts between forests in W2K3 are transitive Kerberos secured.	Trusts between two forests are one-way, nontransitive NTLMv2 in W2K.
	Certain Exchange 2000 mailbox features are not available when users exist in a different forest than their user object.

Most small and medium-sized companies will correctly opt for a single forest. Possible exceptions could be when:

◆ Extranet application(s) use Active Directory.

◆ Acquisitions and/or businesses break off into their own entities.

◆ Pilot deployments are needed to roll out application or new systems.

◆ Network administration is separated into autonomous groups that do not trust one another.

◆ Business units are politically separated.

◆ Business units must be separately maintained for legal reasons.

◆ There is a need to isolate the schema or configuration containers.

◆ There is a need to limit the scope of trusts between domains.

NOTE If part of your organization needs to have additional schema attributes and objects, and those attributes and objects are specific to an application, you could be able to use an Active Directory Application Mode (ADAM) partition, sometimes referred to as an application partition, instead of creating a separate forest. Note that if the objects are used for security purposes, they will have to be stored within Active Directory and not as an ADAM partition.

If you are considering a multiforest implementation, realize that you will need to do special planning for the following:

DNS name resolution Your solution is easy in W2K3 because you can use *conditional forwarding*, forwarding to preferred DNS servers depending on the domain name.

Resource sharing This includes things like printers, global catalog, certificate synchronization, trust relationships, and access control. The solution here is simply MIIS Server, a free download for W2K3 Enterprise Server users.

Network infrastructure It doesn't permit communication in a single forest (sites, subnets).

WARNING If you plan to use Active Directory in an outward-facing mode (extranet application), use a separate forest. If you need to synchronize accounts, download the free version of MIIS (formerly MMS) from www.microsoft.com/miis. You must be using W2K3 Enterprise Server to run it.

To get the most functionality from your AD implementation, you will want to move to one of the higher *functional levels*. A functional level is a mode in which you can run AD that allows it to utilize new tools that are not available if you have domain controllers from other operating systems within your infrastructure. Depending on what operating systems are running on your domain controllers, you will have the ability to change AD's functional level to suit your needs.

Designing with Change Control Policies in Mind

This is an often-overlooked planning step. Realize that extending the schema later (to implement or upgrade to Exchange, for instance) affects the entire forest, every object, and the domain controller. Have a change control policy in place that emphasizes proper operational processes. I know this is boring and a pain to implement, but it is sorely needed. Everything you do should be verified in a lab first, monitored, rolled out to a pilot group, verified, and then deployed in a systematic approach. Anticipate change, reorganizations, politics, and so forth.

Before deciding to make any type of change, make sure you verify that the change that will be implemented is required. If you are simply adding an attribute to an object class, make sure none of the existing attributes will support your needs. There are 15 custom attributes that can be used for any purpose. Using these attributes will only cause replication traffic to the domain controllers in the domain where the object exists. If the change needs to be added to the global catalog, the change will replicate throughout the forest. Be aware of the additional replication you will be introducing.

If you do add an additional attribute or attributes to an object class, the new object class will need to replicate to all domain controllers within the forest. If you have wide area network (WAN) links where replication is controlled through a schedule, you could introduce inconsistencies between your domain controllers until the replication has completed. You will also cause additional replication across those WAN links, which could pose other problems for the users who are trying to use them. Make sure you know how you are going to roll out the changes and the schedule you will enforce.

A well-defined change control policy will reduce the problems associated with making changes to your infrastructure. Debates will rage among the administrators of the domains within the forest. The battles that need to be fought to prove the change needs to be put into place are hard enough without having to decide on all of the criteria to include within your policy. The criteria should include the following:

Planning and testing   The planning documents that must be completed and the types of tests that the change will need to pass

Who is able to make the change   The appropriate parties that will be able to enact the change within the schema

The rollout schedule   Project guidelines for how the change will be made

Where the change can be made   The systems that will be used to change the schema

Prior to implementing Active Directory, decide who will make up the approval committee. Meet with the administrators of all of the domains within the forest to gain approval of the policy. Everyone who will be affected needs to buy in. Getting them to do so may not be a simple task, especially in an environment where you have service or data autonomy. Some administrators may not have a great deal of trust in other administrators. As mentioned before, make sure you have the appropriate allies so that you can get approval from the highest-level stakeholder.

Building a Design Based on the Standard Forest Scenarios

There are three basic forest design scenarios: the organization-based forest, the resource forest, and the restricted-access forest. Each of them is used for specific design goals.

Organization-based forest   Organization-based forests are the most common type of forest. Under this design, an organization's resources are placed within the forest and organized so that the appropriate groups have control over the resources they need. Although companies will choose the decentralized model for several reasons, one of the primary reasons is autonomy of control. If autonomy is required, a department or division could have a domain created for them, or organizational units (OUs) could be built within a domain.

Resource forest   If certain resources need to be isolated from the rest of the organization, then a resource forest can be created. A resource forest is one in which the resources (such as shared folders, printers, member servers, etc.) are located within their own forest so that the owners of the resource can control them. Usually, the resource forest will not have any user accounts within the forest (with the exception of the service administrator accounts that are required to maintain the forest). Using this type of forest, an organization can make sure that the resources contained within the resource forest are not affected by the loss of services in any other forest.

Restricted-access forest   A restricted-access forest creates complete separation of service administrators. Although trust relationships can be built to allow users to access the resources within the remote forest, the service administrators from the two forests will not be allowed to administer the other forest services. If there is any need for isolation of services, this is the type of forest structure that will need to be built.

Separating Extranet Applications into Their Own Forest

I can't stress enough that security is too important to take administrative shortcuts. Don't allow an extranet application in your demilitarized zone (DMZ) to use the same forest as your production users. Simple hacks (such as enumeration, DoS, and elevated privileges attacks) against your extranet could cause catastrophic damage to your internal network AD structure if the two are linked with a single forest.

If you are running Windows Server 2003 as the OS upon which AD is operating, you will have options, such as conditional forwarding, that will make implementing separate forests easier. Even if you are still running Windows 2000, you should take the time to design a secure foundation for your AD infrastructure, even if it will take additional administration and time.

New features within Windows Server 2003 R2 make using multiple forests a little less intimidating. Active Directory Federation Services takes advantage of using a single sign-on for users who are in separate forests. You can extend that functionality to the DMZ by using ADFS to authenticate accounts to your internal AD infrastructure. For more information on working with ADFS, see Chapter 7, "Managing Access to Active Directory Resources."

Forest Functionality Mode Features in Windows 2003

Windows 2000 introduced mixed and native mode functionality. When Window NT 4 backup domain controllers were used in conjunction with Windows 2000 domain controllers in the same domain, the domain had to use mixed-mode functionality. This limited what functions were available to Active Directory because every domain controller had to work under the Windows NT 4 domain rules. Windows Server 2003 adds additional functionality to Active Directory, and in doing so has expanded into *forest functionality* and *domain functionality*. Choosing to move your domain or forest to a higher functional level will give you the added benefit of additional AD functionality. Your goal in any migration, upgrade, or clean installation is to get to Windows Server 2003 Forest Functional mode as soon as possible.

Your goal in any upgrade, migration, or installation is to get to Windows 2000 native mode or Windows Server 2003 Forest Functional mode as soon as you can. When you switch your domains from Windows Server 2000 mixed mode to native mode, you lose the ability to support Windows NT 4 backup domain controllers. From that point on, the backup domain controllers will not be allowed to participate in replication. When switching from native mode to Windows Server 2003 Functional level, you excommunicate the Windows 2000 domain controllers from the domain. In return, because all of the domain controllers are at their highest level, you can take advantage of all of the advanced feature sets of Windows Server 2003.

To switch your forest from Windows 2000 to Windows Server 2003 Forest Functional level, you must be a member of the Enterprise Admin group. All of the domains within the forest must be at least at the Windows 2000 native mode. As long as all of the domains within the forest are at that level, when you choose to switch the forest to Windows Server 2003 Forest Functional level, all of the domains will switch at the same time. If any of the domains are still at the Windows 2000 mixed mode, you will not be able to raise the Forest Functional level. As you can see in Figure 3.5, you will find the Raise Forest Functional Level choice in Active Directory Domains and Trusts. You can, however, also manually edit the functionality levels in ADSI Edit, and/or LDP.EXE, although I don't recommend doing so unless Microsoft support tells you to manually edit them.

FIGURE 3.5
Forest Functionality
level

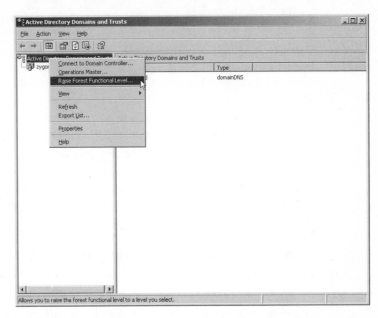

When going to Windows Server 2003 Forest Functionality level, you gain the following features:

Domain rename   This ability is accessed through the `netdom` command-line utility or the `random` resource kit utility.

Link value replication   This is the ability, for example, for a group to replicate a single member when a change is made instead of the entire group being replicated each time (which is what Windows 2000 does). This also removes the 5,000-member limit on groups.

The ability to convert a user in AD to INetOrgPerson on the fly   You also gain the ability to put a user password on the InetOrgPerson Lightweight Directory Access Protocol (LDAP) object.

Schema redefine   This is not deletion, though it is the next best thing.

Dynamic auxiliary classes   Use this when you need to have a departmental schema extension that doesn't affect the rest of the forest. For example, use it when a department needs to put employee IDs put into Active Directory and you, as the forest owner, don't want to extend the schema for this small department's needs.

Basic and query group types   Basic group types, Security and Distribution, are available with all versions of Active Directory. Query groups types become available when the forest level is raised to Windows Server 2003 Functional level. Query based groups allow you to create an email distribution list that dynamically updates its members based on an LDAP query.

Improved Knowledge Consistency Checker (KCC) algorithms and scalability   This feature is a big deal. In Windows 2000, you were told to turn off the KCC for implementations where you had about 100 DCs in a domain. Now, the KCC can scale to more than 4,000 DCs in a domain, although you'd probably never want to have a domain that big.

Additional attributes automatically added to the global catalog   Since forest level trusts are now available, the global catalog has a few additional attributes that it keeps track of so that the trusts can be efficiently utilized by clients.

Inter-site Topology Generator (ISTG) enhancements   You can allow for complex site designs that have more than 100 sites and the ability to stop replicating with an "offline" domain controller automatically.

Constrained delegation   This allows you to control the service principle names of the service accounts that another service account can be delegated.

Application groups   This is a method of controlling the accounts that have access to an application.

Cross-forest trusts   These are perfect for Exchange clients that exist in one forest, but have their Exchange mailbox in another forest. They eliminate the need to login again. Windows 2000 has NTLMv2 cross-forest trusts. Windows Server 2003 uses Kerberos trusts. (Can you say single sign-on?)

The ability to update logon time stamp as a fast-synching replicated attribute   When a user logs on, the logon time stamp is updated within the domain controller to which they authenticate, and that attribute is replicated as an urgent update to all of the other domain controllers

Universal groups   This is the same as in native mode for Windows 2000.

Group nesting   This is the same as in native mode for Windows 2000.

The ability to switch distribution groups to security groups, and vice versa   This is the same as in native mode for Windows 2000.

SID history as an attribute of a user object   This is the same as in native mode for Windows 2000. It is a very important part of migrations that happen over time. An NT 4 or Windows 2000 SID can be brought over during migration so that authentication against resources and objects in the NT 4 or Windows 2000 domain/forest that have not been migrated will still work.

ADDITIONAL RESOURCES

The following are white papers and websites that will help you familiarize yourself with some of the important Active Directory topics:

Multiple Forest Considerations Whitepaper   www.microsoft.com/downloads/details .aspx?displaylang=en&familyid=B717BFCD-6C1C-4AF6-8B2C-B604E60067BA

Design Considerations for Delegation of Administration in Active Directory   http://www .microsoft.com/technet/prodtechnol/windows2000serv/technologies/activedirec- tory/plan/addeladm.mspx

Best Practice Active Directory Design for Managing Windows Networks   www.microsoft .com/technet/prodtechnol/windows2000serv/technologies/activedirectory/plan/ bpaddsgn.mspx

Active Directory Information   www.microsoft.com/ad and www.microsoft.com/technet/ad

How to Create a Cross-Reference to an External Domain in Active Directory in W2K   support .microsoft.com/?id=241737

Active Directory Domain Design

So far we have looked at what goes into a forest design. The criteria that I introduced for forests will flow over into domain design. You are still going to base your design decisions on one major design criterion: administrative control. Keep this in mind as you work through the rest of this chapter. All of your decisions will have administrative control as the primary priority, and then group policies and security policies will help you refine your design.

As many administrators will tell you, designing the domain structure can be troubling. If you have separate administrative teams within your organization, you will probably find that they do not trust outside influences and will demand that they have their own forest so that they can have complete control over their resources. Although there may be cases where you will give in and allow them to have their own forest, you should try to avoid creating an additional forest under most conditions.

To create a forest, you must first promote a stand-alone server to a domain controller. During that promotion, you will specify the details that will control the very destiny of the forest. Think about that for a moment, because that statement does imply the gravity of the design decisions you are making. Creating an AD infrastructure takes planning and understanding of the options you have available to you. We are going to look at the design decisions for domains, which ultimately will affect the forest structure as well.

We start with the design criteria that you should take into consideration and then move into a discussion of the administrative and replication issues that pertain to domains. From there we go through a quick rundown of the benefits and drawbacks when you have a single domain design as compared to a multiple-domain and multiple-tree design. We examine trust relationships and look at the different trusts that can be built, as well as alternatives to creating additional trust relationships. Because some domains will need to support previous versions of Windows domain controllers, we study the functional modes of Windows 2000 and Windows Server 2003 domains.

Active Directory Domain Design Criteria

I'm going to say it again, and you are probably going to tire of hearing this, but administrative control will become the primary domain design criterion. As you remember from earlier in this chapter, the forest is the security boundary. Because you cannot guarantee that a domain cannot be affected by an account from outside the domain, the forest becomes the security boundary within Active Directory. So then, the domain becomes the autonomous administrative boundary. This means that administrators for a domain have control over the resources within their domain, but no other domain. The reason I state that they have autonomy over their domain is that they are responsible for resources within their domain, but those same resources can be controlled by members of the forest root high-level group Enterprise Admins.

However, before planning multiple domains, you should think about the ramifications of having multiple domains within your environment. Later in this chapter, I spell out the advantages and disadvantages of having multiple domains and trees. Always start simple—single forest, single domain—and work from there. You will encounter plenty of political battles as you design your domain structure, so plan your battles well. Create a design that you think will work, and just as with the forest structure, let others review it so that you can refine it to fit their needs.

Defining Domain Requirements

Effectively, a domain can host millions of objects. Theoretically, you are restricted only by the hardware limitations of your domain controllers. With that said, you will find that other factors will force you to limit the size of your domain in order to make your AD infrastructure efficient. If all the accounts that you have created within your domain are within a large well-connected network where you have plenty of available bandwidth for all your network traffic to flow upon, you could probably get by with a single domain. Problems begin cropping up when you start working with locations that are separated by WAN links that may not have enough available bandwidth to support the replication traffic.

Domain Boundaries

As we mentioned earlier, the forest is the administrative boundary for Active Directory. Because the Enterprise Admins group has the ability to affect any domain within the forest, administrators will not have complete isolated control of their domain. However, account policies that consist of password, lockout, and Kerberos policies are defined for an individual domain. The same can be said about the replication boundary. The schema and configuration naming contexts are replicated throughout the forest. Application mode partitions can also be replicated throughout the forest. The domain naming context, on the other hand, only replicates between domain controllers within a single domain. In this section, we look at how this can affect your domain design.

ACCOUNT POLICY BOUNDARY

An account policy is enforced at the domain level and will not affect other domains within the forest. Account policies are not inherited from domain to domain, so a parent domain's policy will not affect any child domain. At the same time, you cannot override the account policy within the domain by using another policy that is linked elsewhere within the domain. In other words, you cannot set differing password policies at the domain and OU levels; the domain policy will override the OU policy.

Domain account policies consist of three policy sections: password, lockout, and Kerberos restrictions. If you look at Figure 3.6, you will see the sections as found in the Default Domain Policy. When the domain is created, a security template is imported into the Default Domain Policy. Every domain member will be controlled by the policy.

Password Policy

Password restrictions can be set to control exactly how passwords are used within the domain. If you open the Password Policy node, you will see the following options:

Enforce Password History   This option specifies how many passwords the system will keep track of how many unique passwords a user will have to use before they are allowed to reuse a password.

Maximum Password Age   Specifies how long a password will remain valid before the user is forced to change the password.

Minimum Password Age   Specifies how long a password has to be used before a user is allowed to change it.

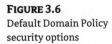

FIGURE 3.6
Default Domain Policy
security options

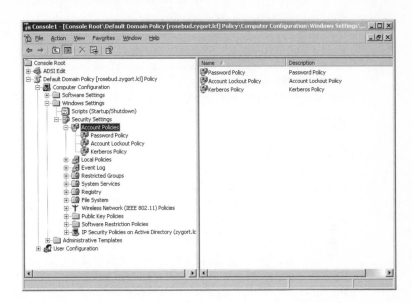

Minimum Password Length Specifies how many characters a password is required to contain.

Password Must Meet Complexity Requirements If enabled, the passwords that users generate will need to contain three of the following four criteria: uppercase character, lowercase character, numeral or special character (i.e., !,@,#,$,%).

Store Password Using Reversible Encryption For All Users In The Domain When enabled, the user's password is stored within Active Directory in a format that can be used to authenticate users when they are accessing websites that use digest authentication.

Account Lockout Policy

The Account Lockout node contains the options that control when a user's account will be locked out, or disabled from use, if too many password attempts fail. This is used to make sure that a user's account is not easily compromised if an attacker is trying to determine what the user's password is. The options contained within this node are:

Account Lockout Duration Specifies how long an account remains in a locked-out state. If it's set to 0, the administrator will have to unlock the account manually. If it's set to any other value, the system will automatically unlock the user's account after the number of minutes specified.

Account Lockout Threshold Defines the number of attempts that can be made to enter the correct password. Once this number is exceeded, the account will become locked out.

Reset Account Lockout Counter After After an invalid password entry is made, the account lockout counter is incremented by 1. If this number is set to 0, the account lockout counter is reset as soon as the password is entered correctly. If this is set to any other number, the counter will be reset after the time in minutes has expired after a successful login attempt or from the last invalid attempt.

Even though every account within the domain will have to follow the rules as set forth under the Default Domain Policy, you can programmatically enforce some options on users. For instance, if you want to ensure that administrative accounts are forced to change their passwords on a 30-day cycle, but the account policy for the domain is set so that users will not have to change their password until 60 days have lapsed, you can write a script that checks when the administrator's password was last changed. If 30 days have passed, the script can force them to update their password.

NOTE For more information on scripting control of Active Directory, see Part 4 of this book.

REPLICATION BOUNDARY

Domain controllers within a domain will share their domain partition, or domain naming context, with one another, but will be selfish with domain controllers from other domains. There is a perfectly good reason for this, though. The domain partition will usually be the largest of the Active Directory partitions and is the one that changes the most frequently. To reduce the amount of replication traffic that has to be sent to each of the domain controllers within your forest, the domain boundary was defined.

If you have two locations that have very poor network connectivity, or you want to control the replication that is sent across WAN links, you can divide the locations into separate domains to reduce the replication traffic. Once you have separate domains, all of the changes to objects within the domain partition are replicated only to the domain controllers within the domain. The other domains do not "see" the changes. If both domains are still within the same forest, they will share global catalog information as well as the Configuration and Schema partitions.

Defining Tree Requirements

Every domain within a tree shares the same DNS namespace. A majority of organizations will only need to use a single namespace to define all the units within their organization. If you need to support two namespaces within your organization, and you do not want to support multiple forests, creating another tree within your existing forest will provide additional administrative advantages over the multiple-forest design. Every tree within the forest will still use the same schema and configuration naming contexts. They will also be under the same Enterprise Admins control. Every global catalog will contain the same information so that users will be able to search for resources anywhere within the forest.

At the same time, the administrative staff from the new tree will have autonomous control over their resources only. This can become a political issue if you are working with separate companies all under the same organizational umbrella. However, the administrative costs of maintaining a single forest with multiple trees will usually outweigh the need for complete isolation of resources between divisions of an organization. Remember, always start simple, and then add complexity to your design only if you have a valid reason to do so.

Multiple Domains: Pros and Cons

Any time you add domains, whether the domains exist within the same tree or if there are multiple trees hosting the domains, you will have additional administrative requirements. Table 3.3 details some of the advantages and disadvantages to having multiple domains.

NOTE   If you add several layers of domains within your forest, the resources required to process resource access through the transitive trusts could hinder performance of your domain controllers.

TABLE 3.3:   Multiple Domains Pros and Cons

ADVANTAGES	DISADVANTAGES
Account policy boundary	Additional administrative overhead
Centralized GPOs, account policies, and administrative delegation	Separate GPOs, account policies, and administrative control at each domain
Active Directory database size reduced	Increase in global catalog size
Reduced domain naming context replication traffic	Increase in global catalog replication
Less file replication service traffic	Moving user accounts to other domains more difficult than moving them within domain

DNS Requirements

The Domain Name System (DNS) design criteria were discussed in the previous chapter; however, any discussion of domains must mention DNS. Active Directory relies on DNS to function, and the domains that make up Active Directory have a one-to-one relationship with DNS. Each of your domains will share a name with a DNS zone. Whenever a domain controller is brought online, SRV records are registered within the DNS zone that supports the AD domain. Figure 3.7 shows the correlation between AD domains and the corresponding DNS zones.

FIGURE 3.7
Active Directory and
DNS domain correlation

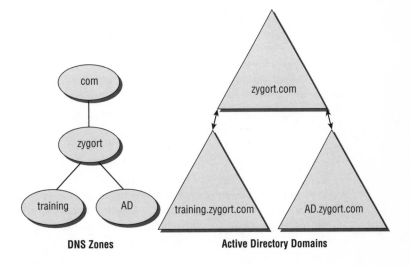

Authentication Options

When a domain is in mixed mode, the authentication options are limited. You will have the ability to use only the standard logon method. Once you have cleansed your environment of the Windows NT backup domain controllers, you can let your remaining Active Directory domain controllers expand their horizons and start taking advantage of some of the new features. For user authentication, this means that the User Principle Name can now be used when authenticating.

Standard Logon   Most users are now familiar with the standard logon method in which you enter your username and password, and then choose the domain to which you are authenticating. Using this method, your username and password are taken and used to create a hash that is sent to the nearest domain controller from the domain that was chosen from the drop-down box.

User Principle Name (UPN)   If you choose to use your UPN instead of the standard logon method, after you enter your UPN and password, a global catalog server is contacted to determine to which domain your logon request should be sent. This approach offers several advantages. If your users become familiar with their UPN, they do not have to be concerned about which domain the workstation is a member of when they sit down at a workstation. As a matter of fact, at that point the user doesn't really need to know in which domain their account is a member.

Using either of the two logon methods produces the same results when the user is authenticated. Kerberos builds the appropriate tickets for the user so that the user can be authenticated and authorized to access all the resources for which they have been given permission. The only difference is that a global catalog server is required when using the UPN in order to determine which domain the user belongs to, or when the domain is in native mode. As we look at global catalog servers in Chapter 4, "Organizing the Physical and Logical Aspects of Active Directory," we'll discuss some of the pros and cons of locating a global catalog server within a site.

Interforest Trusts

Between domains within a forest, you will find trust relationships that define how the users within the domains can access resources within other domains in the forest. By default, when a domain is created, a trust relationship is built between the new domain and its parent. In a single tree, the trust relationships are parent-child trusts. When a new domain tree is created, a tree-root trust is created between the forest root and the root of the new tree. You cannot control this behavior. The Active Directory promotion tool, dcpromo, is responsible for creating the trust relationships and configuring how they will work. When the trust relationships are in place, each domain will allow requests to flow up the tree in an attempt to secure Kerberos access to a resource.

Parent-child trust   A parent-child trust is the most basic of the two trust types due to the fact that all of the domains share the same namespace. Each trust relationship is configured to allow two-way access to resources and is also transitive in nature so that users within every domain can access resources anywhere in the tree structure, if they have been given permissions to do so.

Tree-root trust   Tree-root trusts also share the same behavior as the parent-child, but they are used to allow communication between the two namespaces. Because of their two-way transitive nature, users from any domain within the forest are allowed to access resources anywhere within the forest, assuming that the administrative staff has given them the permissions to do so.

Another interforest trust relationship type exists: the shortcut trust. A shortcut trust is available to reduce the network traffic that is incurred when a user attempts to gain access to a resource within the forest. By default, when a user attempts to connect to an object, and that object resides within another domain, the user's account has to be authorized to access the object. This process has been nicknamed "walking the tree" due to the fact that the trust path through which the user needs to be authorized could take the user to multiple domains within the forest. A domain controller from each domain within the trust path will be contacted to determine whether the user is allowed to access the object in question. If you look at Figure 3.8, you will see that for John, whose account is located in the domain `hr.north.bloomco.lcl`, to access a printer in the `hr.east.zygort.lcl` domain, domain controllers from `hr.north.bloomco.lcl`, `north.bloomco.lcl`, `bloomco.lcl`, `zygort.lcl`, `east.zygort.lcl`, and `hr.east.zygort.lcl` will need to be contacted in order for John's account to receive the appropriate Kerberos authentication and authorization to the printer.

FIGURE 3.8
Trust path

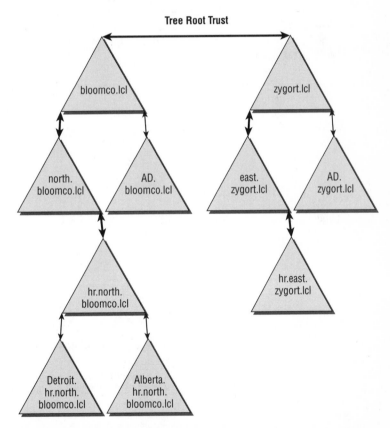

There are a couple of options that you can implement that will reduce the amount of Kerberos traffic as John attempts to access the printer. The first is to place domain controllers from each of the domains within the trust path into the same site as John's account. This will alleviate the need to send the traffic across WAN links. However, you will incur additional costs because you will need additional hardware, and you may also incur additional administrative overhead at that site as a result of the addition of the domain controller hardware at that location. This scenario has a serious drawback. If you have users who frequently access resources from the other domain, yet those users are located in different sites, you may be forced to locate domain controllers at each of the sites to optimize your traffic.

As an alternative, you can create a shortcut trust between the two domains. In doing so, you are essentially cutting a path from one domain to another, thereby allowing the two domains' Kerberos subsystems to work together instead of having to pass the data through intermediary domains. Figure 3.9 shows the shortcut trust created between `hr.north.bloomco.lcl` and `hr.east.zygort.lcl`.

There is an advantage to creating a shortcut trust: you have the ability to dictate how the trust will be used. As long as you have the appropriate credentials, you can create the shortcut trust between the two domains so that it is a two-way trust; in other words, both domains can then utilize the trust path. You can also create the trust as a one-way trust, which will allow only users from one domain to access resources in the other, but not vice versa.

Remember the last line of the opening paragraph for this section; when the trust path is used, the trust path flows up the domain hierarchy. In Figure 3.9, users from `hr.north.bloomco.lcl` and any child domain beneath it can take advantage of the trust path, but the parent domains will still have to take the original trust path.

FIGURE 3.9
Shortcut trust path

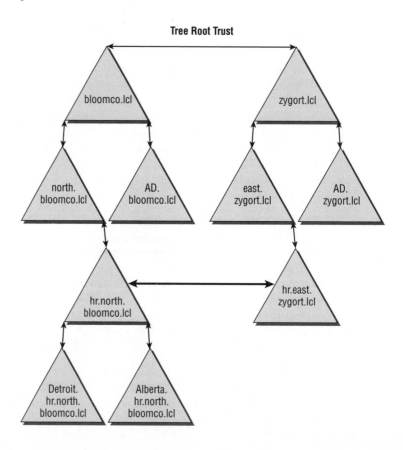

Domain Controller Placement

Domain controllers host the database that is Active Directory. In order for users to log on to the domain, they need to be able to connect to a domain controller. The rule of thumb is to locate a domain controller near any user so that the user can log on even if WAN connections fail. There are instances when you will not want to place a domain controller at a specific location. In the following sections, we look at the options for placing domain controllers within your infrastructure, and in some cases, the reasons why you would not.

PHYSICAL ACCESS TO DOMAIN CONTROLLERS

It is rare to meet a developer who doesn't believe he needs to be a member of the Domain Admins group. As a matter of fact, many developers have rogue domain controllers under their desks to use for testing. This is a bad practice because any domain admin can bring down the entire forest. A simple power-off on the domain controller immediately causes replication problems in Windows 2000, although Windows Server 2003 has a mechanism for just such an occurrence. The solution is to use a separate forest for any developer who either develops on Active Directory or needs elevated privileges. Yes, this increases administrative costs, but it will help secure your forest.

No matter how much time or money you spend securing an environment, it is for naught if someone can physically get to your servers. All bets are off if your server is physically accessible. If someone is in front of your server, it is not *your* server anymore. Especially take this into account if you have branch offices that may not have a room to lock up the domain controller. Protecting your directory service database should take precedence over making sure that the users will be able to log on if the WAN link fails.

SITE AWARENESS

Active Directory–aware clients (such as Windows 2000, Windows Server 2003 and Windows XP), along with operating systems that have Active Directory client software available (such as Windows 98 Second Edition and Windows NT 4) are able to determine whether a domain controller is within the same site as the client. If a domain controller is not located in the same site, the client will connect to a domain controller that is located in a nearby site.

If you have several users within a site, it may be in your own best interests to include a domain controller within the site. Of course, you should take the previous section into consideration; you want to make sure you can physically secure the domain controller. After users authenticate and receive an access token and the appropriate Kerberos tickets, they will be able to access resources until the Kerberos ticket expires. However, users log off during the time a domain controller is unreachable, they will be logged on using cached credentials and will not be able to regain access to resources using their domain account.

If the users require uninterrupted access to network resources within the domain, you should also consider having two domain controllers at their site. Although this is an added expense, you have the peace of mind of knowing that if one domain controller fails, the other will still allow users to authenticate. You also gain the added advantage of having an additional domain controller to take on part of the client load.

GLOBAL CATALOG PLACEMENT

Global catalog servers are domain controllers that take on the additional load of hosting objects from every domain within the forest. You should be familiar with the placement of GC servers within your network. The same basic rule applies to a GC server as does a domain controller; one should be placed within every site. Of course, this could be easier said than done. Budget limitations and security practices may prohibit you from placing GC servers everywhere you want. Follow these guidelines for trade-offs:

- If the global catalog cannot be physically secured, do not place it in the unsecured location.

- If an Exchange 2000 or Exchange Server 2003 system is within a site, place a GC server within the same site.

- If you have only a single domain, make all of your domain controllers GC servers.

- If you have multiple domains, you will need to make sure that the Infrastructure Master role is not on a GC server and the Domain Naming Master is on a GC server.

GC servers provide functionality to users as well as applications within the domain. GC servers are responsible for collecting information about the objects that exist in the domain partition of other domains in the forest. Although this is just a subset of the attributes for the objects, this could still be a considerable amount of information. Once a domain controller is specified as a GC server, additional replication will occur so that information from the other domains will populate the database. You need to determine if this additional replication is going to affect the performance of the network links.

One of the new features of Windows Server 2003 is universal group membership caching. This feature is available only when the domain is in the Windows 2000 native mode or a higher functional level, and only Windows Server 2003 domain controllers provide this functionality. The benefit of using universal group membership caching is that a domain controller does not have to be made a GC server to provide users with their universal group membership, which is required to log on. As users authenticate, the domain controller contacts a GC server from another site to retrieve the required information. The group membership is then cached on the domain controller and is ready to be used the next time the user logs on. Because the domain controller does not have to provide GC services, replication across the WAN link is reduced.

Universal group membership caching is not meant for sites with large user populations, nor is it meant to be used where applications need to access a GC server. A maximum of 500 users is supported using this caching method. Also, the cached data is only updated every eight hours. If you are planning on performing group membership changes on a regular basis, your users may not receive those changes in a timely manner. You can reduce the time frame for updating the cache, but in doing so you will be creating more replication traffic on your WAN link. Make sure you weigh the trade-offs before you decide where you will place a GC server.

When determining if you should have a GC server placed within a site, you should consider how much the GC server will be used and whether applications within the site need to use a GC server. The following questions should be asked to determine whether a GC should be placed within a site:

Are any applications, such as Exchange 2000 Server or Exchange Server 2003, located within the site? If this is the case, you will want to locate a GC server within the same site as the application, because the LDAP queries being posted to the GC server will probably consume more bandwidth than replication. Test the network requirements to determine which will consume more bandwidth. If the WAN link is not 100 percent reliable, you should always have the GC server local; otherwise the application will not function properly when the link goes down.

Are more than 100 users located within the site?   If more than 100 users within a site, you will need to determine if stranding them without having the ability to access a GC server if the WAN link goes down is an acceptable option. You will also need to determine whether the query latency is worth the cost savings of keeping the GC server at another location and not dedicating hardware for the site in question.

Is the WAN link 100 percent available?   If you need application support and the user base consists of fewer than 100 users, you could have those users access a GC server in the remote site if the WAN link is reliable. Although no WAN link will ever be 100 percent available, the higher the reliability of the link, the better your chances of being able to support the user base from a remote site. If the WAN link is not always available and there are no other applications that rely on the GC server, you could implement universal group membership caching to alleviate some of the problems associated with user authentication

Are there many roaming users who will be visiting the site?   If many roaming users will be logging on at the site, you will want to locate a GC server within the site. Whenever a user logs on, the user's universal group membership is retrieved from the GC server. However, if the user population at the site is relatively static, you may be able to implement universal group membership caching on a domain controller.

Another Active Directory technology whose location needs to be determined is the Master Operations roles. Because only specific servers support the Master Operations functions, you should know the criteria for their placement.

Domain Functional Levels

As the engineers behind Active Directory build new and better features, administrators are given more efficient and easier tools with which to work. At the same time, the new features in one operating system are not always supported in legacy operating systems. Windows NT 4 had some serious limitations when it came to secure and efficient administration. Windows 2000 addressed many of the limitations and presented Active Directory as the next generation of directory services.

Moving from the original Security Accounts Manager–based directory service within Windows NT 4 to Active Directory was embraced by thousands of organizations once they realized the level of control and security that was built in. The only problem was that the thousands and thousands of Windows NT 4 installations could not simply roll over to Active Directory overnight. There had to be a means of interoperability between the directory services. To complicate matters, some of the features introduced with the Windows Server 2003 version of Active Directory are not supported under the Windows 2000 version of Active Directory.

To help with the interoperability issues between the differing directory services, Microsoft created functional levels that essentially put restrictions in place on the newer versions of Active Directory so that they play by the rules of the earlier operating systems. These functional levels come in various flavors: Windows 2000 mixed mode, Windows 2000 native mode, Windows Server 2003, and Windows Server 2003 Interim.

Windows 2000 mixed mode   If you need at least one each of Windows NT 4 and Windows 2000 domain controllers within your domain, you will need to maintain a mixed-mode environment. In mixed mode, the domain controllers work under the NT 4 rules for backward compatibility. This is the most restrictive mode, and you do not get all of the functionality of Active Directory. However, you can still utilize your Windows NT 4 Backup Domain Controllers (BDCs) to authenticate users until you have a chance to upgrade all of the BDCs.

NOTE Note that the functional levels apply only to domain controllers. You can still have Windows NT 4 and Windows 2000 member servers within domains of any functional level.

Windows 2000 native mode   When you decide that you are ready to move to native mode, you manually set off the update through the appropriate Active Directory snap-ins. How do you know if you are ready? You are ready if you no longer need to have NT 4 BDCs as part of Active Directory. This could mean application needs, political needs, or timidity from moving from NT 4. Basically, if an NT 4 BDC has to be a part of an Active Directory domain, then you are not ready to go to Windows 2000 native mode. Moving to Active Directory native mode is a one-time, permanent move. Once you are here, replication to Windows NT BDCs no longer occurs and you cannot add any new BDCs to the network.

Windows Server 2003   This is the utopia for Windows Server 2003 domain controllers. Once you have raised the domain to this level, they no longer need to share their databases with any of the Windows NT–based or Windows 2000–based domain controllers. As with native mode, once you have set the functional level to Windows Server 2003, there is no going back and you cannot install a Windows 2000–based domain controller into your Active Directory infrastructure.

Windows Server 2003 Interim   The Interim functional level assumes that you are migrating directly from Windows NT 4 to Windows Server 2003 without ever introducing Windows 2000–based domain controllers into the mix. You can still implement a Windows 2000–based workstation or server into the infrastructure; they will work perfectly. The major advantage to moving directly from Windows NT 4 to Windows Server 2003 is that the Windows Server 2003 Interim functional level allows you to take advantage of linked value replication (LVR) when replicating the membership of groups. This means that every member of a group is seen as a separate attribute. If you do not choose the Windows Server 2003 Interim level during the upgrade of the PDC to the forest root, or you do not have the forest root domain at the Windows Server 2003 Interim level when you upgrade PDCs to their own domain within the forest, group membership values will be replicated as a single attribute. LVR also removes the 5,000-member limit on groups.

Depending on the version of Active Directory you are currently running, you will have different methods of changing the functional level of the domain. If you are running Windows 2000's Active Directory, meaning that you have not added any Windows Server 2003 domain controllers, you can change to native mode as seen in Figure 3.10. If you have added a Windows Server 2003 domain controller, you can change to native mode by raising the functional level within Active Directory Users and Computers by right-clicking on the domain and selecting Raise Domain Functional Level, as seen in Figure 3.11. The same procedure can be performed through Active Directory Domains and Trusts. The screen seen in Figure 3.12 will appear after you have chosen to raise the functional level of the domain. Notice that you do not get an option to change to any other levels except for Windows 2000 native mode and Windows Server 2003.

You may have noticed from the previous two functional level options that you cannot raise the functional level to Windows Server 2003 Interim. You do have the option to set the functional level when you upgrade the domain's PDC. To set the functional level to Windows Server 2003 Interim after the PDC has been upgraded, you will have to use either the LDP.exe tool or the ADSI Edit MMC snap-in. Using either of these tools, connect to the domain controller that holds the Schema Master role and connect to the configuration naming context. The fully qualified path is CN=Partitions,

CN=Configurations, DC=*ForestRootDom*, *DC=tld object*, where *ForestRootDom* is the name of the root domain for your forest and *tld* is the name of the top-level domain that you are using within your forest. The attribute you need to change is the msDS-Behavior-Version attribute. Setting this attribute to a value of 1 will place the forest in Windows Server 2003 Interim. Figure 3.13 shows the ADSI Edit utility being used to change the msDS-Behavior-Version attribute.

FIGURE 3.10

Changing to Windows 2000 native mode

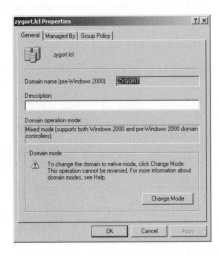

FIGURE 3.11

Choosing to raise the functional level in a Windows Server 2003 Active Directory domain

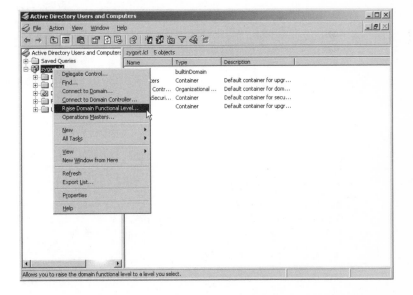

FIGURE 3.12

Changing to the Windows 2000 native mode functional level

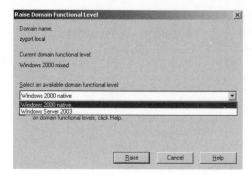

FIGURE 3.13

Using ADSI Edit to change the functional level to Windows Server 2003 Interim

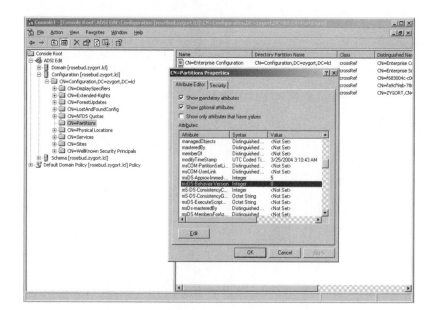

SETTING THE FOREST FUNCTIONAL LEVEL

You can set the forest functional level to any of the three levels by using LDP.exe or ADSI Edit. When you attach to the msDS-Behavior-Version attribute, you have the ability to set the level by entering one of the following values:

◆   Value of 0 or not set=mixed level forest

◆   Value of 1 = Windows Server 2003 Interim forest level

◆   Value of 2 = Windows Server 2003 forest level

BENEFITS OF NATIVE MODE

Native mode gives you the best options that Windows 2000 has to offer. Once at this level, you will have the ability to use security groups to your advantage. Global and domain local groups can be nested and universal security groups are available to make administering large organizations easier. Native mode and higher allows for the following group functions and features:

◆ Domain local groups

◆ Universal groups

◆ Group nesting

◆ Switched-off NETLOGON synchronization

◆ SIDHistory

◆ ADMTv2

Domain Local Groups

All of the servers within a Windows NT 4 domain, and member servers within Active Directory, have local groups to access local resources. Using local groups became cumbersome to use because you had to re-create the group on every server where you wanted to allow users to access similar resources. Now you can share local groups across the entire domain in Windows 2000 native mode. Domain local groups membership can include universal groups, global groups, user accounts, and computer accounts from any domain within the forest, in trusted forests, or in trusted Windows NT 4 domains. Domain local groups are able to grant permissions only within their own domain.

Universal Groups

Universal groups were created to address the limitations of global groups within a large environment. Just as local groups had the negative side effect of duplicate groups on multiple servers, which domain local groups alleviated, universal groups alleviate the need to manage several global groups when adding membership to domain local groups.

For instance, consider an organization that has 10 domains. Each of these domains has printers for which users from every domain will need to have print permissions. Creating domain local groups and assigning print permissions to the domain local groups is the logical starting point. Then you need to create the global groups and add user accounts that have the same resource access needs to the global groups. For simplicity's sake, let's say you have 20 domain local and 20 global groups. If you were to then add the global groups to the domain local groups, the users would have the ability to print, but if you added one more domain local group, you would have to add in all 20 of the global groups to the new domain local. Inversely, if you created a new global group, you would have to add it in to 20 domain local groups.

The universal group would simplify your administrative overhead by minimizing the number of groups with which you would have to work. After you have assigned permissions to the domain local group and added the users to the global groups, you can create a universal group and add all of the global groups to it. Then by adding the universal group to the domain local group, all of the users will have access to the printers. If you add another printer and create a domain local group for access, all you would have to do is add the universal group to the domain local group's membership and all of the users will have access. Of course, the inverse works. If you create a new global group, you can add it to the universal group to give the users access to all printers.

There are a couple of caveats to using universal groups. First, you should make sure all domains in the forest are in native mode. Native-mode functionality is controlled on a domain-by-domain basis. Users logging on to domains that are in native mode will have their universal group membership enumerated before they log on, but if they log on to a computer in a mixed-mode domain, the universal group membership is ignored. This can cause problems with the access token when accessing resources because a user could be denied access to a resource due to their universal group membership.

Another caveat is the universal group membership replication that occurs. Global catalog servers within the forest will receive the universal group's membership through replication. Whenever there is a change to the group's membership, the changes have to be replicated to all of the other global catalogs throughout the forest. Within a Windows 2000 Active Directory domain, the group membership is a single attribute within the Universal Group object. Unfortunately, if you change a single member of the group, all of the members have to be replicated, and a group with a large number of members will cause a considerable amount of replication. Your best bet is to include global groups as the only members of a universal group. Doing so will allow you to add and remove members from the global group, thus not directly affecting the universal group.

Group Nesting

Nesting groups is immensely helpful. Putting global groups into other global groups can really simplify matters for an administrator. This feature is available once you have moved to Windows 2000 native mode. Windows 2000 has a group limitation of 5,000 members—Windows 2003 has no such limitation. Using nested groups in Windows 2000 helps alleviate the 5,000-member limit by allowing a single group object (which may contain thousands of members) to count as one object in the group in which it is put.

Group nesting also allows you to apply the "most restrictive/most inclusive" nesting strategy to make administration of resources easier. In most organizations, you will find that there are employees who need access to the same resources. These employees may have different levels of authority within the organization, yet they have similar resource access needs. After you determine what resources they will need to access, you can develop a nesting strategy that will allow you to control the resource access easily.

Take for instance the typical accounting division. Within the division, you usually have at least two departments, accounts payable and accounts receivable. Within each of these departments, you usually find employees who have differing job responsibilities and different resource access needs—yet there will be those resources to which they will all need access. Managers from all of the departments will need to have access to resources that the other employees need to access, such as employee performance reviews. If you create a global group for the accounts payable managers and another for the accounts receivable managers, you can add the appropriate user accounts into the groups so that they can access the confidential resources.

Because accounts payable employees have different resource access needs than accounts receivable employees, global groups should be created for each and the appropriate user accounts should be added to the global groups. Now, this is where group nesting and the most restrictive/most inclusive method of group creation comes into play. Instead of adding all of the managers from each department to the employees global groups, simply add the managers' global group to the employees' global group. This has the same effect as adding the managers' accounts into the employees' global groups, but it simplifies group administration later. If you hire a new manager, you simply add the new manager's account into the managers' global group and the new manager will have access to all the resources from both global groups. Taking this one step further, if there are resources that all the users from both accounts payable and accounts receivable need, you could create an All Accounting global group and add the Accounts Payable and Accounts Receivable global groups to it.

NETLOGON Synchronization Is Switched Off

Don't worry about this; it isn't as bad as it seems. It just means that you will not be able to add additional Windows NT 4 BDCs to your domain. Once you have made the commitment to move to Active Directory, you should not need to install additional Windows NT 4 domain controllers to your network. There are always cases where this may not be true, but if you have eliminated all of the Windows NT 4 BDCs from your domain, you can safely make the move to native mode. Windows NT 4 member servers can still be part of the Windows 2000 Active Directory domain.

SIDHistory

Moving user accounts between organizational units (OUs) is a relatively painless operation. Because they are still within the same domain and retain the same security identifier (SID), you only need to be concerned about the effects of group policy objects (GPOs) during the move. Moving the user between domains is another issue altogether. A special utility needs to be used to move the user accounts, and when the account is moved, the SID is changed. In order for the user to continue accessing the same resources they had access to within the original domain, you would need to rebuild the access control for every resource.

Active Directory accounts within native mode have an additional attribute, SIDHistory. When an account is moved from a domain, Windows NT 4 or Active Directory, to a native mode or higher Active Directory domain, the SIDHistory attribute is populated with the SID from the previous domain. Almost as if by magic, the user has access to all the resources that were granted to the user's previous account. Every time you move the account to another domain, the previous SIDs are included in the SIDHistory to make the move easy on administrators and users alike.

WARNING   There is a catch to the SIDHistory attribute; it is deemed as a security risk in some environments. See Chapter 7, "Managing Access to Active Directory," for more information on how you can limit the use of the SIDHistory attribute.

ADMTv2

The Active Directory Migration Tool version 2 is the best free migration tool around. You can find it on the Windows 2003 CD under the i386\ADMT directory or as a free download from the Microsoft website. This is the tool you want if you are moving users between domains. It will allow you to migrate users from a Windows NT 4 domain as well as move users between Active Directory domains. It is also the tool that populates the SIDHistory attribute, but you need to be in native mode in order to do so. Make sure you get version 2. It has lots of upgrades, including password migration.

Coming Up Next

Designing the domain structure will force you to have a good grasp of how the organization administers resources. Usually this is not the full story when it comes to administering the resources, however. Nearly every domain will be broken down into smaller administrative boundaries so that the organization does not have to supply every administrator with high-level domain rights and permissions. Instead, smaller administrative fiefdoms are created to allow a fine level of control over resources.

In the following chapter we are going to take a look at how the resources are organized for administrative control as well as how the physical side of Active Directory can be organized to control the replication that occurs within a domain and throughout the forest.

Chapter 4

Organizing the Physical and Logical Aspects of Active Directory

At this point, you have had a chance to take a good look at designing some of the most common aspects of Active Directory (AD). As we move on, we will be working with some of the important technologies that make up our Active Directory infrastructure but that sometimes go ignored until they start causing problems within the organization.

This chapter covers how to use sites for the physical organization of Active Directory, and you'll learn some of the criteria you should consider when creating sites. The second part of this chapter discusses organizing Active Directory objects logically by using organizational units (OUs).

NOTE Some of the material in this chapter is also found in Chapter 10 because it's relevant to both topics.

Determining the Site Topology

Active Directory employs a multimaster replication technology that allows nearly every aspect of the directory service to be modified from any of the domain controllers within a domain. Changes that are made to one domain controller within the domain are replicated to all the other domain controllers within the domain. This replication allows all the domain controllers to act as peers and provide the same functionality. However, this same replication can cause problems when you are trying to keep WAN traffic to a minimum.

To reduce the amount of WAN traffic generated by replication, you will need to create sites within Active Directory that define the servers that are considered "well connected." The domain controllers that are all members of the same site will update quickly, whereas replication to domain controllers in other sites can be controlled. You will be able to control when and how often the replication will occur.

Another advantage to using sites is that client traffic can be contained within the site if there are servers that provide the service the user needs. If there is a domain controller for the appropriate domain in that site, user authentication will occur with domain controllers that are located in the same site as the computer that the user is logging onto. In addition, you can make queries to a global catalog server and access the *Distributed File System (DFS)* shares within the same site as the user's computer.

Within a site, the *Knowledge Consistency Checker (KCC)*, a background process that runs on all domain controllers, creates connection objects that represent replication paths to other domain controllers within the site. These connection objects are created in order to produce an efficient replication path to all the domain controllers within the site. When the site topology is analyzed, the KCC will determine which domain controllers should replicate to one another and build the connection objects so that no more than three hops are necessary to deliver a new object or updated attribute. This allows for fast and efficient replication within the site, with very little latency.

An administrator can also create connection objects manually. If a connection object is created manually, the KCC will build other connections around the manual connection to allow for replication redundancy. Do note, however, that if you create a connection object that does not allow for efficient replication, the KCC will not override your efforts. As domain controllers are brought online or sites are created, the KCC is responsible for creating the connection objects to allow replication to occur. If a domain controller fails, the KCC will also rebuild the connection objects to allow replication to continue. Figure 4.1 shows two connection objects, one that was automatically created by the KCC, the other a manual connection object created by the administrator.

The KCC is also responsible for generating the intersite connection objects. When a site connector is created to allow replication between two sites, one domain controller is identified as the *Intersite Topology Generator (ISTG)*. The ISTG is responsible for determining the most efficient path for replication between sites. Windows 2000's version of the ISTG did not have a very efficient algorithm for building intersite connection objects, which left many large companies with 100 or more sites creating their own connection objects between those sites. If you have the ability to put your forest in the Windows Server 2003 Forest Functionality level, a new algorithm is used by the ISTG to calculate and build the intersite connection objects. You can identify which domain controller is functioning as the ISTG by using the Active Directory Sites and Services snap-in and displaying the properties of the site, as seen in Figure 4.2.

Domain controllers that are placed in different sites do not automatically replicate to one another. Unless a mechanism is put into place to allow replication, changes made to domain controllers in one site do not get replicated to domain controllers in other sites. To give them the ability to replicate objects to one another, you have to configure a site connector. Once the site connector is created, the domain controller that is defined as the bridgehead server for the site will poll the bridgehead server from the other site to determine if any data needs to be replicated. Because data that is replicated between sites is compressed to conserve network bandwidth, you may want to designate a server to be the bridgehead server. Bridgehead servers should have enough available resources to perform the compression and decompression of data as well as send, receive, and redistribute the replicated objects.

NOTE A new feature of Windows Server 2003 is that intersite replication compression can be toggled in order to favor WAN utilization versus CPU overhead on the bridgeheads. See Chapter 15, "Troubleshooting Problems Related to the Active Directory Database," for more information.

Bridgehead servers are chosen according to their *globally unique ID (GUID)*. If you do not select a domain controller to be a preferred bridgehead server, then the domain controller with the highest GUID is selected. The same holds true if you have multiple domain controllers that are configured to be preferred bridgehead servers; the one with the highest GUID is selected. The remaining domain controllers will wait until the bridgehead server goes offline, and then the ISTG will appoint one of the remaining domain controllers according to the GUID value.

Only one domain controller in each site will become the ISTG. Initially, it is the first domain controller within the site. As systems are added to the site, rebooted, and removed from the site, the ISTG will change. The domain controller with the highest GUID in the site will become the ISTG for the site. It is responsible for determining the bridgehead server and maintaining the connection objects between bridgehead servers in each of the other sites.

FIGURE 4.1
Connection objects

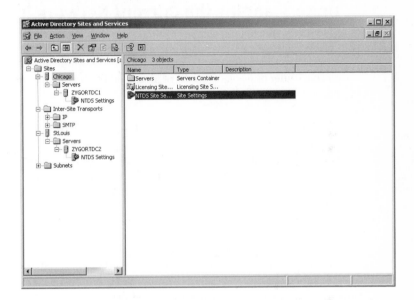

FIGURE 4.2
Site properties
showing the ISTG

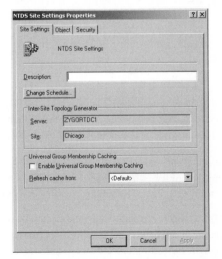

In the following section, we look at the options and strategies you need to consider when designing the site topology to support your Active Directory design. You will need to be comfortable with and knowledgeable about all aspects of your current infrastructure before you can implement a stable Active Directory infrastructure.

Understanding the Current Network Infrastructure

Very few organizations will be starting fresh with Windows Server 2003. Unless it is a brand-new business, some type of network will already be in place. To build an effective site topology for the Active Directory design, you will also need to know how the current infrastructure supports the user and computer base. Once you have identified the current network infrastructure, you can create the site and site link design.

Identifying the Current Network Infrastructure Design

Networks are made up of well-connected network segments that are connected through other less-reliable or slow links. For a domain controller to be considered "well connected" to another domain controller, the connection type will usually be 100Mbps or greater. Of course, that is a generalization. Some segments on your network may have 100Mbps or higher links between systems, but if the links are saturated, you may not have enough available bandwidth to support replication. The inverse is also true; you may have network connections that are less than 100Mbps that have enough available bandwidth to handle the replication and authentication traffic.

Look over the existing network and draw up a network map that defines the subnets that are well connected. Some organizations have a networking group that is responsible for the network infrastructure and a directory services group that is responsible for the Active Directory infrastructure. If this is the case, you have to make sure that the two groups work closely together. From the group that is responsible for maintaining the network infrastructure, find out the current physical topology of the network. Gather information about the location of routers, the speed of the segments, and the IP address ranges used on each of the segments. Also note how many users are in each of the network segments and the types of WAN links that connect the locations. This information will prove useful as you design the site topology.

As an example, consider a company that has a campus in Newark with four buildings and two remote locations: Albuquerque and New Haven. All of the buildings in Newark are connected via a fiber distributed data interface (FDDI) ring. The two remote locations are connected to Newark via T1 connections. Figure 4.3 shows the network map, which also lists the user population at each location.

For those organizations that have more than one domain, you will need to determine where the user accounts reside. A site can support users from multiple domains as long as those domains are members of the same forest. On your network map, if you have more than one domain, designate the number of users from each domain. In our previous example, if the Research and Development department has its own domain for security purposes, the network map may look like Figure 4.4.

NOTE Don't confuse the logical representation of your network with the actual physical entities. You could still have domain controllers from multiple forests within the same physical subnet, but the Active Directory objects that define the resource can exist only within one forest.

FIGURE 4.3
Network map

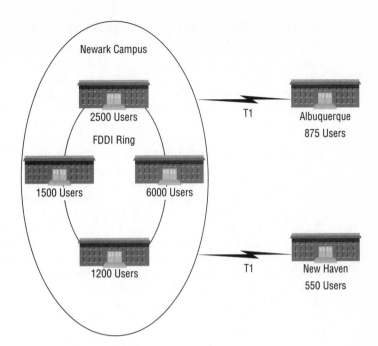

FIGURE 4.4
Multiple-domain
network map

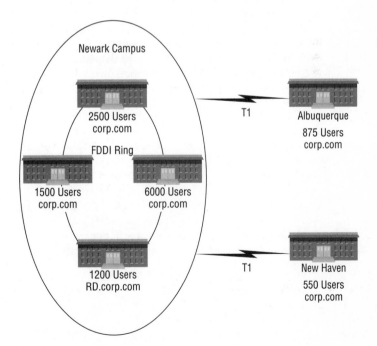

Setting Your Sites to Support the Active Directory Design

Once you have created the network map, you can begin designing the required sites. Sites are collections of well-connected subnets that are used to control Active Directory replication or manage user and application access to domain controllers and global catalog servers. As with every other Active Directory object, you should determine a naming strategy for sites and site links. A site's name should represent the physical location that the site represents. The location could represent a geographic location for organizations that have regional offices (the buildings within an organization's campus or distinct portions of a building). Once you have defined the naming strategy, make sure all the administrators who have the ability to create sites understand the strategy and follow it.

You need to create a document that details the sites that will be used within the design. This document should include the name of the site, the location that the site represents, the IP subnets that are members of the site, and the WAN links that connect the sites.

If you look at Figure 4.4, you can see that the information that was gathered about the current infrastructure is shown in the network map. You need to use this information to create the site design, as shown in Figure 4.5. Notice that the primary locations are identified as sites within the design. Newark, New Haven, and Albuquerque are all identified as sites. Each of the IP subnets from the buildings at the Newark campus is shown as included within the Newark site, the IP subnets from the office in Albuquerque are included in the Albuquerque site, and the IP subnets from the office in New Haven are included in the New Haven site.

The WAN links that connect Albuquerque and New Haven to the Newark campus are shown on the site design layout. But because the Newark campus is considered a single site, the FDDI connections between the buildings are not considered WAN links at this point. Later when you address the replication needs, this may change.

You should also consider including information about the WAN links on the site layout. This information should include the locations that the WAN link connects, the speed of the link, the available bandwidth on the link during normal operation, and how reliable the link is. You may also want to consider including information concerning when the link is used the most, when the off-peak hours are, and whether the link is persistent or a dial-up connection. This information will help you determine the replication schedule.

FIGURE 4.5

Site design layout

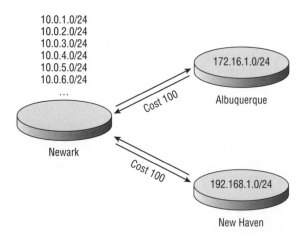

Once the initial site choices are made based on the network requirements, determine whether you should create sites to support user and application requirements. Users sitting at workstations that are Active Directory–aware will authenticate to a domain controller from their domain if there is one within their site. If their site does not have a domain controller for their domain, they will authenticate with a domain controller within another site. All domain controllers determine whether any sites exist that do not contain domain controllers from their domain when they are brought online. If some sites match these criteria, the domain controller then determines whether it is located within a site logically near the site without a domain controller. The domain controller determines this based on the cost of the site link or site link bridges that connect the two sites. If it is determined that the domain controller is close to the site, it registers a service locator (SRV) record for the site. Microsoft refers to this as *Automatic Site Coverage*.

TIP For more information on how to configure domain controllers to register their services to other sites, see Knowledge Base articles 200498 and 306602.

As an example, Company G has two domains: `corp.com` and `RD.corp.com`. Five sites exist within their environment: A, B, C, D, and E. Figure 4.6 shows the site layout and the site links that connect them. Within the sites are domain controllers for each of the domains. Note that Site C does not contain a domain controller for `RD.corp.com`. In this case, as domain controllers start up, they will check the configuration of the domain to determine whether a site exists without a domain controller from their own domain. When domain controllers from `RD.corp.com` start up, they will recognize that Site C does not have a domain controller. They will then determine whether they should register SRV records for the site based on whether they are in a site that is considered to be the nearest. Because Site B has the lowest cost value over the site link to Site C, `RDDCB1.RD.corp.com` will register SRV records on behalf of Site C. When users from the `RD.corp.com` domain authenticate from a computer in Site C, they will authenticate with the nearest domain controller, `RDDCB1.RD.corp.com`.

TIP New to Windows Server 2003 is a Group Policy setting that will allow you to configure whether domain controllers will participate in Automatic Site Coverage.

Active Directory replication can consume a considerable amount of network resources within a site. Replication traffic is not compressed between domain controllers that exist within the same site. If the available network bandwidth will not support the replication traffic that you are anticipating, you may want to look into dividing up IP segments so that you can control the replication moving between the domain controllers. Once additional sites are created, site links can then be configured. Replication traffic that passes across site links is compressed to conserve bandwidth if the data exceeds 50KB.

Another consideration is application support. Applications such as Exchange Server 2003 require access to a global catalog server. If you want to control which global catalog server an Exchange server will use, you could create a site and place the two servers within the site to control the traffic between them. For example, within the `corp.com` domain, the Exchange Server 2003 server is located within Building 1 of the Newark campus. We have specified that a domain controller within Building 2 is to be used by the Exchange server when it sends queries to a global catalog server. In order to control the requests, we create another site that includes Building 1 and Building 2. Figure 4.7 represents the site design once the change has been made to support the decision.

FIGURE 4.6
Determining the
nearest site

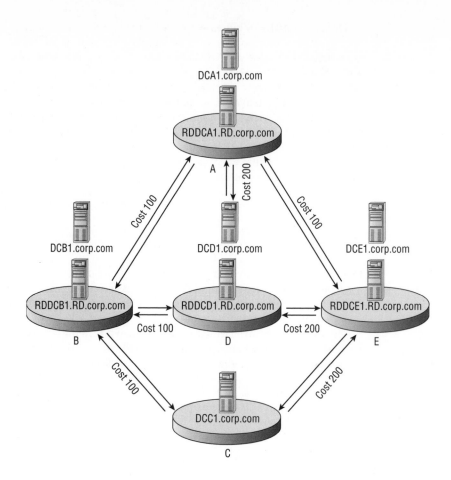

FIGURE 4.7
Site design to
support application
requirements

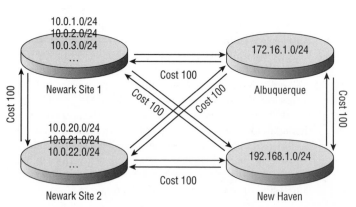

Designing Site Links and Site Link Bridges

Because you have identified the WAN links that connect the sites within your design, you can decide easily on the site links that you will need to support the design at this point. *Site links* are objects that are created to connect sites so that replication can be controlled. You also need to address other considerations such as replication, logon authentication control, and application support.

Site link bridges are collections of site links that allow replication traffic from domain controllers in one site to pass to domain controllers in another site when no explicit replication partners exist in the intermediary site that connects them.

In the following sections, we spend some time reviewing the options available for sites and site link bridges.

Site Links

By default, one site link is created when the first domain controller is installed. This site link is called DEFAULTIPSITELINK, but it can be renamed to conform to your naming strategy. This site link uses remote procedure calls (RPCs) for replication. You could take advantage of using this site link for all the sites that you have within your infrastructure if they all have the same replication requirements. For example, if all the sites are connected by WAN links that have approximately the same available bandwidth and they all use RPC for replication, then simply rename this site link to conform to your naming strategy and make sure all the sites are included.

Another reason you may want to create additional site links is to control when the replication can occur. You may have some sites that need to have objects updated at different schedules. Using site links, you can create a replication schedule between sites. You cannot define which physical connection a site links uses in order to control the replication traffic over specific network links. For instance, if you have a T1 connection and an integrated services digital network (ISDN) connection to a branch office and the ISDN connection is used only as a backup communication link if the T1 goes down, you cannot create two site links with two different costs, one for each of the communication links.

When creating the site link, you can choose between the following options:

Protocol used for replication   Two protocols (IP and SMTP) can be used for replicating objects. When selecting IP, you are specifying that you want to use RPCs to deliver the replicated objects. You can select SMTP if the domain controllers that you are replicating data between are not within the same domain. If the domain controllers are within the same domain, the file replication service (FRS) has to use RPCs to replicate the Sysvol data. Because FRS requires the same replication topology as the domain partition, you cannot use SMTP between the domain controllers within a domain. You can use SMTP if you want to control the replication between global catalog servers or domain controllers that are replicating the schema and configuration partition data between domain controllers.

Name of the site link   The name should follow your naming strategy and should define the sites that are connected using the link.

Connected sites   These are the sites that will explicitly replicate between bridgehead servers in each listed site.

Schedule The schedule consists of the hours when replication can occur and the *interval*, or how often you want to allow replication to occur during the hours that replication data is allowed to pass between the bridgehead servers.

Cost of the connection This value determines which link will be used. This cost, or priority, value is used to choose the most efficient site link. You will use the combination of site links with the lowest total cost to replicate data between any pair of sites.

Note the replication patterns when you are trying to determine the schedule. You could cause a good deal of latency to occur if the schedule is not compatible. For example, a company may have a central office that acts as the hub for the regional office. The regional offices are responsible for replication to the branch offices in their region. Figure 4.8 shows the schedule for the Atlanta central office, the Sydney and Chicago regional offices, and the Exmouth, Peoria, and Bloomington branch offices. Because all of the domestic U.S. links have approximately the same bandwidth availability, you could create a single site link that uses a 15-minute interval. You could then create a separate site link between Atlanta and Sydney for which the replication interval is set to every two hours so that replication does not adversely affect the WAN links. Between the Sydney and Exmouth sites, another site link uses a one-hour interval to control traffic. Depending on the connection objects that are created by the KCC, the total propagation delay for an update in Chicago to reach Exmouth could be three and a half hours—and that is only considering the replication interval. The schedule on the site link could be configured to allow replication traffic to flow only during the evening hours. If you have a schedule that is closed off for a portion of time, the propagation delay will increase even more. You need to make sure that this will be acceptable within your organization.

You should also plan the cost of site links carefully. The default site link cost value is 100. If all of the communication links have the same available bandwidth, you could leave the default cost on all links. However, if different bandwidth constraints occur on any of the communication links, you will need to adjust the cost values. One method of determining a valid cost for site links is to divide 1,024 by the base 10 logarithm of the available bandwidth as measured in kilobits per second (Kbps). In doing so, you will find cost values that correspond to the entries in Table 4.1.

FIGURE 4.8
Replication schedules based on site links

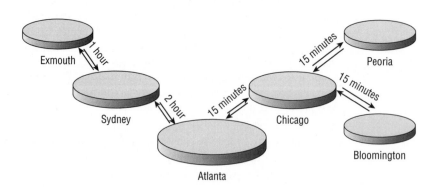

TABLE 4.1: Example of Costs for Available Bandwidth

AVAILABLE BANDWIDTH IN KBPS	COST VALUE
4,096	283
2,048	309
1,024	340
512	378
256	425
128	486
64	567
56	586
38.4	644
19.2	798
9.6	1,042

Site Link Bridges

In Windows Server 2003 Active Directory, site link bridging is enabled for all site links by default, making replication transitive throughout sites. In Figure 4.9, note that domain controllers are in all three sites from corp.com. Site B is the only site that does not have a domain controller from RD.corp.com. With site link bridging enabled, replication from domain controllers for RD.corp.com in Site A will pass to RD.corp.com domain controllers in Site C.

If you have a network infrastructure that is fully routed and all the locations can communicate directly with one another, then you can leave this default setting turned on. However, if you have locations where not all the domain controllers are able to communicate directly to one another—for instance, if they are separated by firewalls—you may want to turn off the site link bridging. You may also want to turn it off if you want to manually control where it is allowed. If you have a large, complex network, you could turn off the bridging and create your own site link bridges by defining which site links will be included in a bridge.

Firewalls that exist within your organization's network infrastructure could also pose challenges. Rules could be in place that will only allow specific servers to communicate with internal resources. If you do have a firewall in place, you may need to turn off site link bridging so that you can control the site links that will pass replication traffic from site to site.

Remember that the site link does not define any physical network links. The physical connections are determined by how the domain controllers are connected to one another. A site link cannot detect if a physical link is down and, therefore, will not reroute the traffic immediately. Determine your site link's costs based on the paths on which you would like replication to occur when using bridging.

FIGURE 4.9
Site link bridge

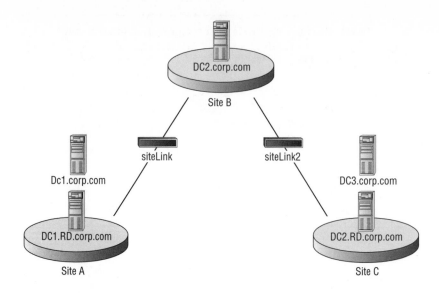

Organizational Unit Design

Before we start looking at the organizational unit (OU) design options, we should make one thing clear: the highest priority when designing OUs is the administrative control. OUs can be used for a myriad of purposes, but the basic design philosophy should be to ease the administrative burden. As we continue through this chapter, you will find that it is divided into two main sections. The first section deals with designing for administrative control, and the second section discusses how to enhance the administrative design with Group Policy.

When you are determining how the OU structure will be designed, you must understand how the organization is administered. If you do not understand how the organization is administered, the OU structure you create might not be as efficient as it could be and it might not remain effective over time. An unwieldy or faulty design could create more administrative problems than it helps alleviate.

Designing OUs for Administrative Control

To have complete control over an OU, you must first be delegated Full Control permission. This delegation is provided by the domain owner and can be granted to users or groups. For efficiency's sake, create a group that will manage the OU and delegate permissions to this group. You can then add user accounts that need to manage the objects, otherwise known as the OU *owners,* to the group with Full Control permissions.

OU owners control all aspects of the OU that they have been given authority over, as well as all the objects that reside within the OU tree. Like the domain owner, they will not be isolated from outside influences, because the domain owner will have control if the need arises. However, this autonomy of control over the resources allows the OU owner to plan and implement the objects necessary to effectively administer their OU hierarchy. This includes delegating administrative control to those users who need to be OU administrators.

OU administrators are responsible for the specific objects within their OU. Usually, they will not have the ability to create child OUs. Their control will more than likely be limited to working with a specific object type within the OU. For example, the OU owner could delegate permissions to create and delete computer objects to the technical support staff. This would allow the technical support staff to create and delete computer objects within the OU, but they would not be able to control or modify user objects within the OU. Controlling user objects could be delegated to a human resources employee who is responsible for creating user objects when a person is hired and disabling and deleting objects when a person is discharged.

In the following sections, we look at some of the design options available when creating OUs. These include the choices that should be made so that changes within the organization will not adversely affect the OU structure.

Understanding the OU Design Options

The OU design should be predicated on the administrative structure of the organization, not the departmental organization as seen on the company's organization chart. Most companies do not base the administration of resources on the organization chart. Usually, the IT department is responsible for objects within the company no matter which department is using the resource.

Although this centralized approach is the most basic method of controlling the objects within Active Directory, some organizations cannot utilize one single administrative group that has power over all the objects. Other organizations will not have a centralized administrative team; instead they will have decentralized control over objects. In such cases, design decisions will have to be made that will dictate where the objects will reside within the OU structure. Microsoft has identified five design options when developing the OU design. These five allow the OUs to be designed by location, organization, business function, location and then business function, or organization and then location.

OUs Based on Location

If an organization has resources that are centralized but the administrative staff is based at different geographic locations, the OU design should take on a location-based strategy. Using this strategy, the OU structure is very resistant to reorganizations, mergers, and acquisitions. Because all the objects are located beneath the top-level OU, which is based on company location, as seen in Figure 4.10, the lower-level OUs can be modified and the objects moved within the OUs to accommodate the changes. Consider the alternative: having domains that are used to host the objects. Moving objects between domains has many more implications because the security ID of the objects will have to change as will the domain owners.

However, some disadvantages to the location-based strategy exist. Unless the inheritance of permissions has been blocked, administrative groups that are granted authority at an upper-OU level will have the ability to affect objects in the lower-level OUs. This could create unwanted administrative control over objects as well as pose security concerns. You might not want to allow some administrative personnel to have the ability to control some of your resources.

The location-based strategy works well within organizations that are using the departmental model but have geographically dispersed resources. In this manner, administrators located at the site where the resources are will have control over the objects that represent them in Active Directory.

FIGURE 4.10
OU structure based
on location

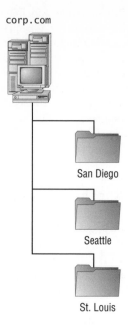

OUs Based on Organization

If the administrative structure has an administrative staff that reports to divisions and is responsible for the maintenance of the resources for that division, the OU structure can be designed so that it takes advantage of the departmental makeup of the company, as seen in Figure 4.11. Using this design strategy makes the OU structure much more vulnerable to change within the organization should a reorganization occur. However, it does allow departments to maintain autonomy over the objects that they own.

This strategy is usually employed whenever the cost center–based, product/service-based, or project-based business models are employed. This allows the resources to be grouped so that the cost centers are separate OU structures. The product, service, or project resources can likewise be isolated within an OU tree, and those administrators who are responsible for the resources can be delegated the ability to control the objects within Active Directory.

OUs Based on Function

Smaller organizations that have an administrative staff who have specific functions they provide to the organization typically use an OU design strategy based on job functions, as seen in Figure 4.12. In these smaller organizations, the administrators will have several job responsibilities. Building the OU structure based on the job responsibilities allows the controlled objects to be grouped together based on the tasks that have to be administered. This type of OU deployment is resistant to company reorganizations, but due to the way the resources are organized, replication traffic may be increased.

This strategy can be employed with any of the business models. Because it is usually implemented in smaller companies, a single administrative group such as IT is responsible for maintaining all the objects. The functions can be broken out based on the staff responsible for maintaining user objects, group objects, shared folders, databases, mail systems, and so on. Of course, the administrative staff will have to be trusted by all divisions if this model is employed, but this is usually not as much of an issue in smaller companies.

FIGURE 4.11
OU structure based
on organization

FIGURE 4.12
OU structure based
on function

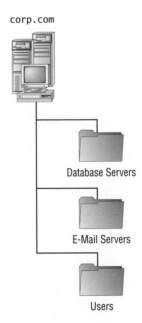

OUs Based on Location and Organization

Two hybrid methods of organizing resources exist. Each one is based on a combination of the location of resources and the method the company uses to organize the objects.

OUs based on location, then organization When you use an OU design strategy that is first based on location and then organization, the upper-level OUs are based on the location of the objects within the directory, and the lower-level OUs are broken out by the organization's departmental structure, as seen in Figure 4.13. This strategy allows the organization to grow if necessary, and it has distinct boundaries so that the objects' administration is based on local autonomy. Administrative staff will need to cooperate if administrative groups are responsible for the departments within the OU structure, because if this is the case, OU owners will have control over all the objects within the OU tree.

Large companies that employ the departmental business model might have several locations within the company that have administrative staff controlling the resources. If this is the case, the OU owner for the location can control all the accounts that are OU administrators for the individual departments within that location. This allows the OU owner to control users within the location for which they are responsible, while still maintaining control over their location. OU administrators would only be able to affect objects within their department at that location.

FIGURE 4.13
OU structure based on location, then organization

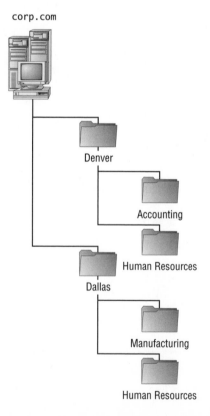

OUs based on organization, then location   With an OU design strategy that is first based on organization and then location, the OU trees are based on the organization's departmental makeup with the objects organized based on location, as seen in Figure 4.14. Using this strategy, the administrative control of objects can be delegated to administrative staff responsible for objects at each of the locations, whereas all the resources can be owned by a department's own administrative staff. This allows a strong level of autonomous administration and security; however, the OU structure is vulnerable to reorganization because the departmental design of the company could change.

Very large companies using the cost center–based, product/service-based, or project-based business models may create an OU tree that is based on the organizational makeup of the company and then have a decentralized administrative staff that is responsible for the resources within different geographic regions. This allows more efficient control of the resources while still allowing the OU owners to have a level of autonomy over the objects that represent their resources within the company.

FIGURE 4.14
OU structure based
on organization, then
location

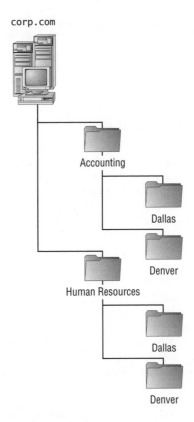

corp.com

Accounting

Dallas

Denver

Human Resources

Dallas

Denver

CHOOSING THE BEST ADMINISTRATIVE OU DESIGN

You will notice that each of the design options has its own unique set of advantages and disadvantages. To choose the best design for your company, weigh the pros and cons of each strategy so that you come up with the design that is the best fit for your environment. If your company is not going to undergo many reorganizations or mergers and acquisitions, you may want to choose a design that makes the delegation of control easiest for your current administrative model. Company reorganizations could force a reevaluation of the departmental makeup within the organization, therefore forcing the OU hierarchy to change. Projects that are completed or abandoned will also force the OU structure to change. You might not want to rework the OU structure every time management decides it wants to try running the business in a new fashion.

The adage "The only constant is change" will probably ring true no matter what strategy you employ, so try to employ the strategy that appears to be the least likely to change but that reflects the way the administration is provided.

Understanding OU Design Criteria

As you build your organization's OU hierarchy, design the OU structure so that it uses the most efficient layout possible. Designing the OU hierarchy can prove a very challenging endeavor. If you build too many OUs with several child OUs beneath them, you could create problems when trying to apply Group Policies. If you create too few, you may find that you have to perform special actions against the Group Policies so that you are not applying them to the wrong accounts.

OUs are built based on three criteria: autonomy over objects, control object visibility, and efficient Group Policy application. The following sections describe controlling the visibility of OUs and how to control autonomy over OUs. Once we finish this section, we discuss designing with Group Policies in mind.

OPTIONS FOR DELEGATING CONTROL

Object autonomy should be the primary criterion by which most organizations design their OUs. Giving the OU owners the ability to control the objects for which they are accountable allows them to perform their job functions. At the same time, they will feel comfortable knowing those objects are not controlled by other OU owners or administrators from outside their OU structure, with the exception of the forest's and domain's service and data administrators. Once a group is identified as the OU owner, they can control the accounts to which administrative control within the OU tree can be granted.

Users do not usually have the ability to view OUs. They use the global catalog to find objects that give them access to the resources within the network. OUs are designed to make administration easier for the administrative staff within the company. Keep this in mind when you are creating your OU structure. Build it with administration as the top priority; you can address other issues later.

Because so much power can be wielded when a user is allowed to become an OU owner, they should be trained on the proper methods of delegation. This means that anyone who is allowed to delegate control to another user should understand the two methods of delegating permissions—object-based and task-based—as well as how inheritance affects the design. If OU owners are not properly trained on how to delegate control, the OU structure could be at a security risk with users who have too much power or, on the opposite extreme, with users who do not have the proper amount of authority to administer the objects they are supposed to control.

The OU owners are responsible for making sure that the appropriate users and groups have the ability to manage the objects for which they are responsible. In the following sections, we look at the options available to make sure those users and groups are properly configured for the access they need.

Understanding Delegation Methods

Object-based delegation grants a user control over an entire object type. Objects within Active Directory include users, groups, computers, OUs, printers, and shared folders. If a user needs to have control over computer accounts, you can use the Delegation of Control Wizard to allow Full Control permission only over computer objects within the OU. You might have another user who administers the User and Group objects within the OU. This level of control can be delegated as well.

Task-based delegation grants a user the ability to perform specific functions against objects within the OU. Controlling objects at this level is more difficult to manage and maintain, but sometimes you may find it necessary. Take, for instance, a case where a company has a help desk department and one of its job duties is to reset passwords for users. However, you don't want them to modify any of the user properties. If you delegate the ability to work with user objects, the help desk personnel will have too much power. Instead, you can delegate the ability to reset passwords at the task level, locking them out of having the ability to affect the objects in any other way.

As mentioned earlier, however, it is much more difficult to manage the permissions granted at the task level than it is the object level. You will need to document the groups to which you are delegating permissions. Otherwise, you may find it problematic to track down where permissions are applied and troubleshoot access problems. As a best practice, design the OU structure so that you can take advantage of object-based delegation as much as possible.

Understanding Account and Resource OUs

In some Windows NT 4 directory service structures, the user accounts and resources are divided into their own domains, based on the administrative needs of the domain owners. Because the domain is the administrative boundary within NT 4, the user account administrators have control over the account domain. Resource administrators have domains that are made up of the resources they are responsible for maintaining—usually systems that provided database, e-mail, file, and print services, to name a few.

Depending on the administrative needs of the organization, delegation of the sublevel OUs should follow a few rules:

The OU owner will have full control.   The OU owner will have the ability to work with any object within the OU tree for which they are the owner. Once the domain owner delegates full control to the top-level OU for the OU owner, the OU owner will be able to take ownership of any object within that OU tree.

The OU admin can control only objects for which they have been granted permissions.   The OU owner should only delegate the ability to work with the object types that the OU owner needs to modify. If the OU administrator is an account administrator, then only user and/or group object permissions should be granted. If the administrator is a resource administrator, only the appropriate object type should be delegated to them. OU administrators should not have the ability to affect OUs, but only the objects within them.

Account OUs and resource OUs can provide the same functionality that account and resource domains provided under NT 4. Account OUs will hold the user and group accounts that are used when accessing the resources. Resource OUs will host the resources that users will need to access within the domain. These could be computer accounts, file shares, shared folders, and contacts. You can build an OU structure that allows the user, group, and resource objects to be separated based on the staff that needs to have administrative control over them.

Understanding Inheritance

Inheritance allows the permissions set at a parent level to be assigned at each child level automatically. The inheritance of object permissions from the parent object to the child object eases some of the administration headaches. Permissions set at the parent level are propagated to the child levels by default. Any object created within an OU will inherit the applicable permissions from the OU. With this being the case, whenever an account is granted permissions at the OU level, all of the child OUs and objects within those OUs inherit the settings. OU owners have the ability to control all the objects within their OU tree after the domain owner delegates the appropriate permissions to the top-level OU.

Occasionally the permissions set at higher levels within Active Directory are not the proper permissions needed at a lower level. If this is the case, inheritance can be blocked, which means that permissions set at the parent level will no longer pass to the child objects. When blocking the inheritance of permissions, the administrator who is initiating the block can choose whether to copy the inherited permissions to the object or remove them completely. If the inherited permissions are removed from the object, only the permissions that are explicitly set at the object level will apply. This could restrict an upper-level OU owner, OU administrator, domain owner, or forest owner from being able to perform actions against the object. If this happens, the OU owner, domain owner, or forest owner has the ability to reset the inheritable permissions on the object or objects that were affected.

The blocking of inheritance could be problematic for those users or groups who do not have the power to change the inheritable permissions setting. If inheritance is blocked to objects that a group needs to have control over, they will not be able to effectively maintain those objects. At this point, the OU owner could step in and change the inheritance on the OU or object, or change the effective permissions on the objects that the group needs to control. Trying to troubleshoot inheritance issues can be time consuming and difficult, so limit the amount of inheritance blocking you use within your design.

Creating an OU structure for a brand-new design can be challenging. Developing a design that allows the administrative functions to be performed easily is of the utmost priority. However, few organizations have the option of creating a brand-new design. An existing infrastructure probably already exists. If the organization is using a Windows NT 4 domain environment, you need to consider several design options.

CONTROLLING VISIBILITY

When controlling object visibility, OUs can be used to hide objects from users when they are searching within Active Directory. By hiding the objects that users do not need to access, you can add a level of security to those objects. If users do not have the List Contents permission to an OU, they will not be able to view any of the objects within the OU. In this manner, you can hide printers that they do not need to use and shares that should not appear in search results. You can also hide user and group objects from other administrators.

When you design the OU structure, always start with designing for administrative control, and then take visibility of objects into consideration. The primary goal of the OU design is to make administration of objects as efficient and easy as possible. Once you have completed the administrative design, you can address visibility requirements.

For example, take a company that has a printer that is restricted from users being able to print to it with the exception of a few authorized users. This printer is used to print accounts payable and payroll checks. Only a few accounts payable employees are allowed to send print jobs to this printer. Also, some shares on the accounts payable server are exclusive for use by the accounts payable staff.

Because these resources need to be isolated from the rest of the organization, they should not show up when users from other departments perform searches within Active Directory.

The accounts payable department is part of the accounting division of the company. Because the company has all of the accounting resources located at the corporate office, the corporate IT department is responsible for maintaining the objects in Active Directory. Other departments have staff located at other offices, and each of those offices has administrative staff responsible for maintaining the resources.

During the design phase, the design team decides to use the "location, then organization" design approach. This allows them to assign control over all resources to the administrative groups that need to be owners of the OU hierarchy, and then to grant other levels of control at the departmental level for those administrators who control a subset of resources. The initial design looks like Figure 4.13.

The objects that were initially identified as needing to be hidden from users should be placed within an OU that will not allow users to view its contents. For users to be able to "see" the objects within an OU, at the very least they will need the List Contents permission granted to them. If they do not have this permission, the objects contained within the OU will not show up in their searches. Because this permission is included in the standard Read permission, accounts with Read permission will be able to list the contents of the OU.

FIGURE 4.15

OU design for administrative purposes

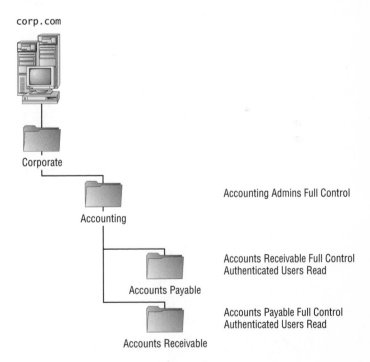

Because users need to view objects within the accounts payable OU, the permissions to that OU cannot be changed. Instead, a child OU is created to control visibility of the objects. The users within the accounts payable department who need to work with the objects will be able to see them when they access Active Directory tools or perform searches, but no one else will. It should be noted that the accounts payable administrators still need to be able to maintain the objects within the OU, so either their permissions will have to be re-added to the access control list, or the existing permissions will need to be copied directly to the OU with the unnecessary accounts and permissions then removed. The final OU design for accounting will look like Figure 4.16.

As we have mentioned, the primary reason to create an OU structure is to have the ability to control administrative abilities and make resource administration more efficient. Because there is only one way to delegate administration of resources and there are many options to control Group Policies, as you will see in the next section. You should remember though, the administrative design should take precedence.

FIGURE 4.16
OU design with OU
created to control
visibility

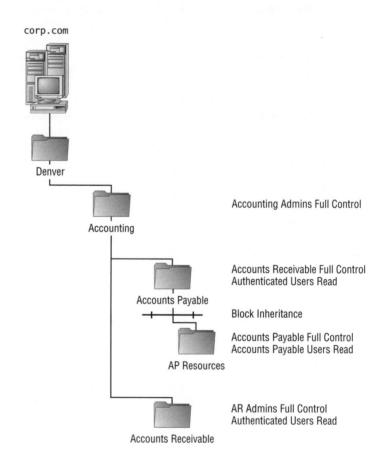

Designing OUs for Group Policy

Group Policy has proven to be one of the most widely used Active Directory technologies and, at the same time, one of the most misunderstood and misused. Many administrators who have taken advantage of Group Policy Objects (GPOs) in order to control the security of systems and to distribute software to users and computers do not fully understand the options available when using GPOs.

Understanding the settings that can control security, restrict user sessions and desktops, deploy software, and configure the application environment should be given top priority when you are using GPOs. Options that affect how the GPOs are applied must be understood as well; some of the options we will discuss include blocking inheritance, enforcing settings, applying settings to specific users or systems, and filtering out the accounts that do not need to have settings applied to them.

To make your job much easier, Microsoft has introduced a freely downloadable utility: the Group Policy Management Console (GPMC). The GPMC simplifies the task of administering the GPOs used within your organization. From one location, all the GPOs from any domain in any forest of the organization can be controlled and maintained. You can download the utility from Microsoft's website. As you can see in Figure 4.17, once this utility is installed on a system, the Group Policy tab on the property page of a site, domain, or OU will no longer show the GPOs linked at that object. Instead, a button to open the GPMC appears there. The GPMC is added to the Administrative Tools menu also.

NOTE For more information about the Group Policy Management Console and how to download your copy of this tool, go to www.microsoft.com/windowsserver2003/gpmc/default.mspx.

The GPMC will function only on Windows XP and Windows Server 2003 operating systems. Any administrators within the organization who need to use this utility will need a workstation running Windows XP or else they will need to work from a server where the GPMC has been added. Figure 4.18 shows the GPMC. Notice how the Group Policies are all organized beneath the Group Policy container. This allows you to go to the container and work with any of the GPOs that you are using in Active Directory. Also note that the domain and all the sites and OUs are organized within the console so that you can see at which level GPOs are linked.

NOTE To run the Group Policy Management Console on a Windows XP–based system, you will need to load Windows XP Service Pack 1 and the .NET Framework 1.1 or later.

Of course, the real power of the GPMC is the ability to run sample scenarios and to determine which GPOs are being applied to a user or computer. As you design the GPOs that will be used within your organization, take the time to test the effects the GPO will have on users and computers when applied in conjunction with other GPOs. Figure 4.19 shows an example of the GPMC's Group Policy Modeling section.

FIGURE 4.17
The Group Policy tab after the Group Policy Management Console is added

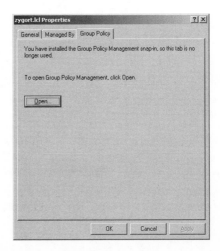

FIGURE 4.18
Group Policy Objects
within the GPMC

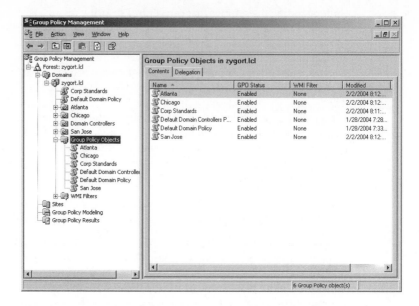

FIGURE 4.19
Group Policy Modeling

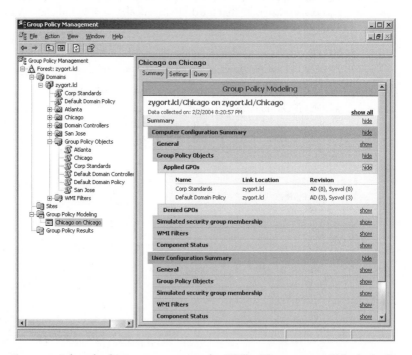

In the following sections, we take a look at company uses for GPOs. These uses will include the security needs, software installation options, and user restrictions that will be used to control the user's environment.

NOTE   For more information on Group Policies and the GPMC, see Chapter 9, "Managing Group Policy."

Understanding Company Objectives

Before designing the OUs that you will use for implementing GPOs, you need to understand the needs of the organization. Although every Active Directory rollout will have password requirements, lockout restrictions, and Kerberos policies applied, that is usually where any similarities between organizations end. The first thing you should do is document the administrative structure of your organization. This will give you a better understanding of how administration of resources is applied within the organization.

Base your Group Policy design on this administrative design as much as possible. Most organizations find that if they create their OU structure on the administrative functions, the Group Policy requirements follow along pretty well. Although you may still have to build OUs for special purposes, the basic design should already be put into place. The special purposes could include special software that a subset of users from a department need to use, or restrictions on the systems that temporary employees will have.

A good Group Policy design starts with defining exactly what actions GPOs will perform for your organization. Because GPOs are primarily an administrative tool, you can ease the administrative staff's load and allow the system to control users' environments. Some of the areas that can be controlled are security, software installation, and user restrictions.

IDENTIFYING SECURITY NEEDS

The security settings that will be enforced for users and the systems to which they connect will be the first types of settings that have to be determined. When Windows Server 2003 is configured as a domain controller, the security policy for the domain requires users to use *strong passwords*, which are passwords that do not use words that can be found in a dictionary and that utilize several types of characters. Microsoft has identified strong passwords as those that follow these guidelines:

- ◆ They are at least seven characters long.

- ◆ They do not contain your username, real name, or company name.

- ◆ They do not contain a complete dictionary word.

- ◆ They are significantly different from previous passwords. Passwords that increment (*Password1*, *Password2*, *Password3*...) are not strong.

- ◆ They contain characters from at least three of the following four groups:

  - ◆ Uppercase letters, such as *A, B,* and *C*

  - ◆ Lowercase letters, such as a, *b,* and *c*

  - ◆ Numerals, such as *0, 1, 2,* and *3*

  - ◆ Symbols found on the keyboard (all keyboard characters not defined as letters or numerals), including the following: ` ~ ! @ # $ % ^ & * ( ) _ + - = { } | [ ] \ : " ; ' < > ? , . /

Training users on the proper methods of creating and using passwords can prove to be difficult. For instance, turning on the complexity requirements that force a user to have strong passwords usually ends up with the user writing their password down on a piece of paper or a sticky note and placing it close to their computer. You should implement corporate standards that identify how passwords should be protected and the ramifications of not following the policy. Of course, training the users and explaining the reason passwords are a vital defense mechanism can aid in the acceptance of the password policy.

Account lockout restrictions are another defense mechanism that should be used. Any time a brute-force attack is made against an account, the account lockout policy prevents the attackers from being able to make too many attempts at discovering the password. Most companies have this setting configured to allow between three and five attempts before the account is locked. Once it is locked, the attacker does not have the ability to try any additional passwords against the account for as long as the account is locked. This brings us to the second part of account lockout restrictions: you should always leave the accounts locked until an administrator unlocks it. Although this increases the administrative load to some extent, and more times than not the lockout is due to the user forgetting their password or having the Caps Lock key turned on, at least the administrator is notified of the possible attack. Just to make sure that you are not allowing an unauthorized user access to another user's account, put procedures in place that will help you identify the user who needs their account unlocked. This is especially true if they call to have their account unlocked and they mention that they cannot remember their password. Before changing the password, authenticate the identity of the user.

Aside from the account policies that can be set, other requirements also need to be identified. For instance, you may have users who need access to servers that hold confidential information. If users need to use an encrypted connection when accessing the data, you can specify the Internet Protocol Security (IPSec) (Secure Internet Protocol) policies that will be enforced by using GPOs. For example, if a user within the payroll department needs to modify the salary and bonus structure for an employee, and the employee data is hosted on a server that you want to make sure is only accessed when IPSec communication is used, you can create an OU, IPSec Servers, for the payroll department's server and any other servers that require IPSec communication. You can then create a Group Policy for the IPSec Servers OU that enforces the Secure Server IPSec policy and apply it to all servers in the IPSec Servers OU. Another OU, Payroll Clients OU, can be created for the workstations within the payroll department. The Group Policy that is defined for the Payroll Clients OU could have the Client IPSec policy assigned to it, which would turn on IPSec communication whenever connecting to the payroll servers.

IDENTIFYING SOFTWARE INSTALLATION NEEDS

Using GPOs to roll out software can drastically reduce the administrative efforts required to install and maintain software within the organization. At the same time, it can increase the load on the network to a point that is not acceptable. You need to determine whether the benefits gained from having automated installation of software outweigh the network overhead required. Of course, no matter how much you may want to use GPOs to push software to client machines, some instances will occur when the network infrastructure will not allow it. This is especially true if you use WAN links between locations and the software distribution point is located on a server on the other end of the slow link.

A service-level agreement (SLA) could affect the rollout of software. SLAs are contractual obligations that dictate the amount of service availability that is required for servers or workstations. In some cases, software can take several minutes to install. If SLAs are in place and they restrict the amount of time that it takes to install an application, you may be forced to manually install the application for the user during times when they are not using the system. Another alternative is to link the GPO after hours and have the software installation assigned to the computer. Because the software installation client-side extension is not included in the periodic refresh of GPOs, any changes you make to the software installation options within a GPO are not processed on the client. Using remote access tools, you could then restart the user's computer, which would initiate the installation of the software.

If you determine that you are going to assign or publish applications to users or computers, identify which applications are required. Most applications written by commercial software vendors within the last few years take advantage of Microsoft's IntelliMirror technology and are supported by Group Policy. Make sure the software is stamped with Microsoft's seal of approval. If Microsoft has certified the software to run on Windows Server 2003, the application will support IntelliMirror.

Work with each department within the organization to determine their software requirements. Understanding the software needs of the organization helps you identify which software packages need to be rolled out through a GPO. You may need to make some trade-offs. If every user within the organization needs to have a specific application such as antivirus software, it may be easier to create a system image that includes that operating system and the software. Using a third-party disk imaging utility, you can create a generic image of a system that includes all the software and the appropriate system settings for the organization. Whenever the tech staff builds a new client system, the image is placed on the hard drive of the new computer, and when the computer is rebooted, it is configured with the default settings and software. This is a very quick and usually painless method of getting systems online in short order. However, you will encounter some drawbacks.

If devices on the new hardware are not supported at the time the image was originally created, the new hardware may not start up correctly and you will be left trying to install the correct drivers. As new software packages are identified, as required for the organization, you may have to rebuild the image to support the software, which then brings us back to the advantages of Group Policy software deployment. Although operating systems cannot be deployed through a policy—that is, a function of Remote Installation Services (RIS)—new and updated software can be. Of course, Microsoft Systems Management Server (SMS) will also roll out software to client machines and will do so with more efficient management options. One of the benefits of SMS that Group Policy has yet to implement is the ability to push the software package out at a predetermined time.

After determining which of the deployment options you are going to use, determine which software packages are to be rolled out with Group Policy and how you will accomplish this.

IDENTIFYING USER RESTRICTIONS

User restrictions limit what actions users can perform on their workstations or control the applications that are allowed to run. For some companies, not many settings are required. The users have control over their workstations and the administrators may only control the security policies that are put into effect with the Default Domain Policy, which is where the password requirements, account lockout settings, and Kerberos policy settings are configured. Other companies take full advantage of using GPOs to restrict their users from being able to access any of the operating system configuration options. Some companies even force all the systems to have the corporate background.

As extreme as it may sound, the fewer configuration options that a user is allowed to access, the less the user can affect, and possibly change for the worse. Desktop restrictions can remove the icons for My Computer and My Network Places, or they can change what the user sees from the context menu when the user right-clicks these icons. The Display properties can be locked out so that the user cannot choose a monitor refresh rate or screen resolution that is not supported by the video subsystem. Start menu items can be restricted so that the user does not have the ability to open the Control Panel and modify settings within the operating system.

NOTE For more information about Group Policy and the settings that you can use to control a user's environment, see the Group Policy section within the Windows Server 2003 Technical Reference on the Microsoft website, www.microsoft.com/resources/documentation/WindowsServ/2003/all/techref/en-us/default.asp.

Identify which operating system configuration settings the users within the organization need to work with, and how much power they need to wield over their workstations. It may take you a little longer to plan out the Group Policy settings that should be applied to groups of users, but avoiding the administrative headaches that these restrictions will alleviate is worth the trouble. As you design the Group Policy settings that will be used to control and assist the administrative structure, remember the golden rule: keep it simple.

Creating a Simple Design

The underlying design goal, aside from supporting the organization's objectives, should be to create a Group Policy design that is as simple as possible. A simple design will allow more efficient troubleshooting and processing of Group Policy settings. The fewer Group Policy settings that need to be applied to a computer or user, the faster the computer will start up, the quicker the users will be able to log on to their systems, and because a small GPO can be 1.5MB in size, network traffic will also be reduced. If problems arise due to Group Policy conflicts or inappropriate settings, it is easier for an administrator to troubleshoot the problem if the design is simple.

When determining the best and most efficient use of GPOs, review the requirements of the users who will be affected and then consolidate settings into the fewest GPOs possible. Then make sure you are taking advantage of the natural inheritance of Active Directory and are not using too many options that change the inheritance state.

IDENTIFYING USER REQUIREMENTS

Determine what you need to provide for the users and their computers. Every company's requirements will be different. Understanding how employees function on a day-to-day basis and what they need to perform these functions will aid you in determining the Group Policy settings you need to enforce. Determine which settings need to be applied based on employees' job functions and job requirements, and identify the corporate standards that should be put in place.

Corporate Standards

Corporate standards are usually the easiest settings to figure out. These are the settings that should be set across the board for every employee and computer. Corporate standards are settings that you define in order to control the environment so that no employee is allowed to perform actions that are prohibited. Settings that make up these standards include the password policy, account lockout policy, software restrictions, Internet Explorer Security Zone settings, and warning messages that appear when someone attempts to log on.

Corporate standards are settings that should be applied as high in the Group Policy hierarchy as possible. The Group Policy hierarchy consists of the three levels at which a GPO can be linked; site, domain, and OU. Because the GPO settings are inherited from each of these levels, by linking the GPO at the highest level within the hierarchy where it applies you will be able to enforce the settings over a large number of objects with the fewest GPOs.

Most designs apply the corporate standards at the domain level so that every user logging on and every computer starting up will have the policy applied to it. To ensure that these settings are imposed on every user and system, enable the Enforced setting on the GPO that represents the corporate standards. This way, if another administrator configures a GPO with settings that conflict with the corporate standards and links the new GPO to an OU, the corporate standards will still take precedence.

Don't modify the Default Domain Policy to include the settings for the corporate standards. Although this may seem like a logical place to enforce the settings because the Default Domain Policy affects all users and computers within the domain, the new Default Group Policy Restore Command (`dcgpofix.exe`) found in Windows Server 2003 will not retain the settings that have been modified since the domain was created.

NOTE   For more information about the Default Group Policy Restore Command utility (`dcgpofix.exe`), see the section "Options for Linking Group Policies" later in this chapter.

If multiple domains exist within the organization, chances are the corporate standards will apply to them also. The GPMC will allow you to copy a GPO from one domain to another. Using this functionality, you can create a duplicate GPO that can be linked to a domain. This will alleviate having to link a single GPO to multiple domains. Whereas this is not an issue when you have domain controllers within a site that host the GPOs, if you have to pull the GPO from across a WAN link, you could increase the user's logon time considerably.

Job Function

Employees have specific functions that they provide for the company. An employee within the human resources department provides different functions than a temporary employee providing data entry for the marketing department. Identify what the employees require to perform their jobs. Document your findings, and then compare what is the same among all employees within an OU and what is different. You may be able to create a single GPO for a department that applies to all the users and computers and then link it at the parent OU for the department. Those settings that are specific to a subset of users or computers can then be added to a GPO that is linked to the child OU where the user or computer accounts are located.

Organize all the settings required by employees within a department and create a GPO named after the department. That GPO can then be linked to the department. Other settings that are specific to a subset of the users within that department can either be linked to the OU and configured so that only those users receive the settings, or linked to a child OU if the users and computers are distributed for administrative purposes.

Job Requirements

There may be specific job requirements that must be met by users or computers that are different even though the job functions may be very similar. Whereas all members of the human resources department will need to access the training materials and benefits documents so that they can assist employees when necessary, a subset of human resources personnel may have access to the employee database. If this database resides on a server that requires IPSec-encrypted communication, only the appropriate human resources personnel should fall under the control of the GPO that provides the appropriate IPSec policy settings. By linking a GPO to the server's OU that enforces the servers to require IPSec for communication and another GPO linked at the human resources' client OU that uses the IPSec client policy, the human resources personnel will communicate securely with the servers.

System requirements may be different for users depending on their job requirements. You may have users who need to use modems to connect to remote systems. Other users may need to have access to administrative tools. Exceptions to restrictions that are applied at the domain or parent OU may have to be overridden for these users. Make sure you document the special needs of every user.

MINIMIZING GROUP POLICY OBJECTS

If you use as few GPOs as possible, you will be able to troubleshoot problems that arise much more easily than if several GPOs could affect users and computers. Policy settings that are related, such as software restrictions that affect a large group of users, should be added to the same GPO. By adding settings to a single GPO instead of using multiple GPOs to enforce the settings, you reduce the GPO processing time.

SLAs are starting to become more widespread. As systems become more vital to company operations, having these systems online becomes mandatory. Although we think of SLAs controlling servers and server maintenance, SLAs that affect workstations are also being put into place. Some of these dictate the amount of time that a user will have to spend for applications to load and the amount of time spent waiting for logon to complete. This may sound picky to some individuals, but some financial institutions, brokerage firms, and other organizations require their workstations to be available at all times so that they can perform their duties.

If your organization falls under an SLA, determine how long it takes to process the GPOs you are planning. By combining settings into a single GPO, you decrease the amount of processing time required to process the settings. If the settings are spread among several GPOs, all of the settings for each of the policies will have to be processed.

Determine whether you can condense the settings into a single policy, and if you cannot, condense to the fewest policies possible. Of course, this is a practice that you should follow whether or not you are working under an SLA. Users do not like to wait to access their systems. The faster they are able to see their logon screen and access their desktops, the happier they are. The happier the users are, the better your day will be.

Another method of making your GPOs more efficient is to disable part of GPO from processing. Each of the two sections that you can configure settings in, computer and user, can be disabled. When you do so, you are essentially telling the system to ignore any of the settings in that section. Because the client-side extensions do not have to parse through the GPO to determine what needs to be enforced or disabled, the GPO will process faster, thereby reducing the time it takes for the computer to reach the logon screen or the users to log on to their system.

IDENTIFYING INTEROPERABILITY ISSUES

Windows XP and Windows Server 2003 are the only operating systems that can take full advantage of the new Group Policy settings in a Windows Server 2003 Active Directory environment. Windows XP Professional can take advantage of all the new client-specific settings, whereas Windows Server 2003 can take advantage of all the new server-based settings. For users running Windows 2000 Professional or servers running Windows 2000 Server, over 200 possible settings will not be processed on those platforms. When you edit the settings for a GPO, make sure each setting specifies to which operating system platform it will apply.

Windows Management Instrumentation (WMI) filters provide additional functionality to a Group Policy application. By specifying operating system or system options, you can control to which computers a GPO will apply. For instance, if you want to make sure that a system has enough free space on a partition or volume in order to install software, you can specify that the free space must exceed the minimum requirement for the application. Figure 4.20 is an example of a WMI filter that is used to control the installation of software to partitions or volumes with enough free space. If the requirement is not met, the application installation setting is ignored. Again, Windows XP and Windows Server 2003 can take advantage of WMI filters, but Windows 2000 cannot. If a WMI filter is in place that controls whether a GPO is applied and the computer is running Windows 2000, the WMI filter is ignored and the settings are applied.

Other operating systems, such as Windows NT 4, Windows 95, and Windows 98, will not process GPOs. To control computers running these operating systems, you have to use System Policy Editor. This means that you have to support two different technologies when trying to set user restrictions. Another drawback comes from the fact that only a small subset of settings is supported by System Policies. To efficiently control the systems and users within your environment, determine an upgrade path for the older operating systems.

FIGURE 4.20
WMI filter for detecting adequate drive space

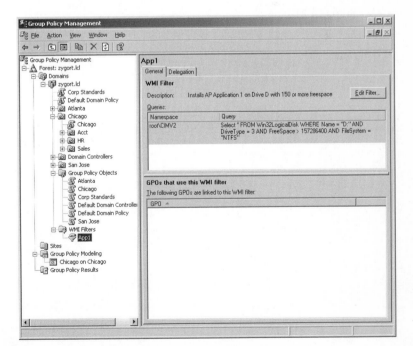

DESIGNING FOR INHERITANCE

Just as permissions are inherited from a parent OU to the child OU, Group Policy settings will also pass down through the hierarchy. Taking advantage of *inheritance*, you will be able to create a Group Policy hierarchy that allows you to efficiently apply GPOs to your organization and make it easy for your staff to troubleshoot issues arising from GPOs. You have several options when you are using inheritance. Implement best practices that will allow inheritance to work as it should and then use the options that change the default behavior only when necessary. The more the options for enforcing (referred to as No Override if you are not using the GPMC), blocking, and filtering you use, the harder it is to troubleshoot the design.

Organizing OUs

Use the OU structure that is based on the administrative requirements as much as possible. Create additional OUs only if it makes the application of Group Policy easier to maintain and troubleshoot. For instance, in Figure 4.21, an OU structure has been created that allows the engineering department administration to be broken out into two departments: graphic design and model shop. Each of the departments has a different internal administrative staff responsible for maintaining the user and computer accounts. Within the model shop, some employees work with the research and development (R&D) department to build prototypes. For users to access the plans from the R&D servers, which are placed in an OU that has the required IPSec policy applied, they need to use IPSec-encrypted communication. The GPO that allows the IPSec client policy is applied to the R&D Model Shop OU, where the user accounts are located, giving them the ability to access the plans from which they need to build. The rest of the model shop employees' accounts are placed with the Users container.

FIGURE 4.21
OU structure
enhanced for
Group Policy
application

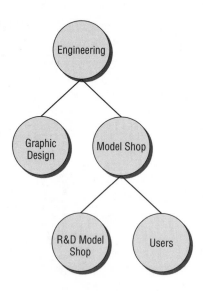

Define Corporate Standards

Once the settings for corporate standards have been identified and configured within a GPO, they should be linked high within the hierarchy, preferably at the domain level. Once linked, the Enforced option should be set so that lower-level GPOs do not override any of the standards. Figure 4.22 shows a domain with the Default Domain Policy and the Corporate Standards policy. Notice that the Corp Standards GPO has the Enforced option turned on. Figure 4.23 shows the inheritance of GPOs at the Accounting OU. Notice that the Corp Standards GPO is the GPO with the highest priority within the list due to its Enforced setting.

FIGURE 4.22

Corporate Standards GPO enforced at the domain level

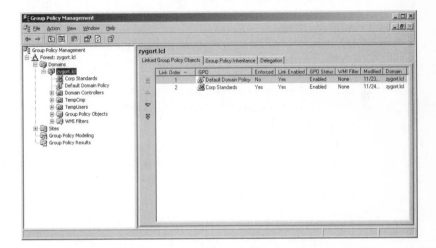

FIGURE 4.23

Corporate Standards affecting the Accounting OU

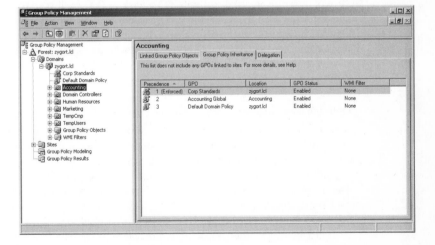

Use Blocking and Filtering Sparingly

The Block Inheritance option stops the natural inheritance of settings from GPOs higher in the hierarchy. When you use this option, you will block every GPO setting from any parent object with the exception of the domain account policies. Once blocked, the only way that a GPO's settings will override the Block Inheritance option is if you apply the Enforced option. The Enforced option takes precedence over any Block Inheritance option that it encounters, but it is only applied to an individual GPO. Set the Enforced option for every GPO that needs to override the blockage.

Filtering is the process of specifying to which accounts the GPOs will apply. By default, the Authenticated Users group will have the GPO applied to it at the location where the GPO is linked. This may work in some instances, but for most applications, you will not want every account to be under the GPO's control. For instance, if the user account that has administrative rights to the OU is located within the OU and the GPO restricts the use of administrative tools, administrative users will not have access to the tools they need to perform their job. Determine which accounts will need to have the GPOs applied to them and create a group based on that need. Do not add the administrative users to the group for the user accounts; instead, create another group so that the administrators can be members of it. Configure the Security Filtering option to include the group to which the GPO will be applied.

TIP   If you are changing the permissions for a user or group so that the GPO is not applied to them, make sure you remove the Read permission if the accounts do not need to work with the GPO. If you simply remove the Apply Group Policy permission, the accounts will still process the GPO settings, resulting in longer logon delays.

Prioritizing

If more than one GPO is attached to a site, domain, or OU, determine the processing priority for each. As the GPOs are processed, the GPO with the lowest processing number, which is the highest priority, will override any of the other GPO's settings that are linked to the same location (with the exception of those GPOs that have the Enforced options enabled). Compare Figure 4.21 to Figure 4.24. In Figure 4.24, the processing priorities of the three GPOs linked at the Accounting OU are set so that the Accounting Registry & File GPO has the lowest processing priority. Yet because the Enforced option is set, you can see in Figure 4.25 that the Group Policy Inheritance tab lists it with a higher priority than the other two GPOs.

Enabling Loopback

Some computers within an organization should be used only for certain purposes. Kiosks will have access to public information, but because they are usually accessible to the general public, you may not want such computers to have the ability to access sensitive corporate information. You may encounter other computers that need to have user settings applied to the computer no matter which user is logged on. To enforce these settings, use the loopback feature. Once enabled, the settings from the User Configuration portion of the Group Policy object that is applied to the computer's OU will take precedence instead of the User Configuration settings at the user's OU.

There are two methods of applying the settings once loopback processing has been enabled. The first, Merge, consolidates all the settings from the user's and computer's GPOs; if any settings conflict, the computer's setting will apply. The second is Replace. When Replace is chosen, the user's settings are not processed. Instead, the computer's settings are applied, thereby restricting the user account to just those settings that are allowed by the computer's GPO settings.

FIGURE 4.24
FIGURE 4.24
Priorities for
GPOs attached to
the Accounting OU

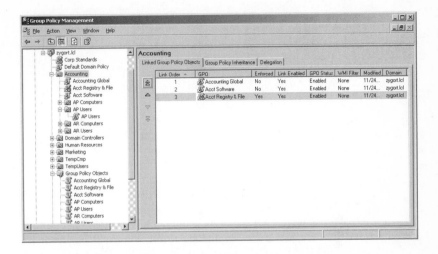

FIGURE 4.25
Processing order
for GPOs at the
Accounting OU

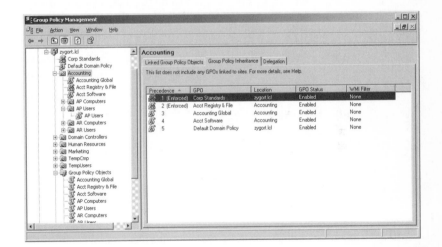

OPTIONS FOR LINKING GROUP POLICIES

At this point, you should know that GPOs can be linked at the site, domain, or OU level. Although you might want to link at the site or domain level, doing so is usually not suggested. Linking at the OU level allows you to efficiently control the GPOs and how they are applied to users and computers. Of course, there are always exceptions.

The primary exception is for the security settings that are applied at the domain level. You'll recall that the Default Domain Policy is where the password requirements, account lockout settings, and Kerberos policy settings are configured. These settings are then applied throughout the domain and cannot be overridden. This is the reason that a separate domain needs to be created if any settings within these options need to be different between user accounts.

As a general rule, you should not make changes to the Default Domain Policy, with the exception of setting the security policy options settings. If any settings will define corporate standards other than the security policy settings and you want to apply them at the domain level, create a new policy for these settings. Although this goes against the recommendation that you use the fewest GPOs possible, it will allow you to have a central point to access the security policies for the domain and separate any other policy settings that are applied. Another reason is that this gives you the ability to re-create the Default Domain Policy if it becomes damaged.

Included with Windows Server 2003 is a utility called dcgpofix.exe. This command-line utility will re-create the Default Domain Policy and the Default Domain Controller Policy if necessary. It will not create either policy with any modified settings; it will only re-create the policy with the initial default settings that are applied when the first domain controller in the domain is brought online. Keeping this in mind, only make changes to the security settings that are applied to either of these two policies, and make sure the settings are documented. After running dcgpofix.exe, the settings that define the corporate security standards can then be reset.

If you were to add settings to the Default Domain Policy and then run dcgpofix.exe, the settings would be lost and you would have to re-create them. However, if you were to create a new Group Policy and add the settings to it instead, when the Default Domain Policy is re-created, the new Group Policy would not be affected. The same rule holds true for the Default Domain Controllers Policy. Because some settings should be applied to domain controllers to ensure their security, do not edit the settings on this Group Policy. The dcgpofix.exe utility can be used to regenerate this policy as well.

NOTE For more information on dcgpofix.exe and how to regenerate the Default Domain Policy and Default Domain Controllers Policy, look at Chapter 9, "Managing Group Policy."

As a general rule of thumb, when you plan where the policies should be linked, if the policy applies to a large number of users, link it at the parent OU. If the policy applies to a specific subset of users, link the policy at the child OU. This should alleviate the need to have elaborate filtering and blocking schemes that will affect the natural inheritance of GPOs.

Creating the OU Structure

When creating the OU structure, you need to base it primarily on administrative needs. Although we keep hitting on that point, it cannot be stressed enough. You should build the OU structure to make the administration of the domain as easy and efficient as possible. You can create GPOs to take advantage of the administrative structure of the OUs, and you can create additional OUs if the Group Policy requirements dictate it, but do so sparingly.

Two containers exist within Active Directory: the Users container and the Computers container. If a user or computer account is created and an OU membership is not specified, then the user account is created in the Users container and the computer account is created in the Computers container. GPOs cannot be set on these containers. The only GPOs that will apply to these users are the settings applied at the site or domain level. If you are following the recommendation that GPOs be applied at the OU level as much as possible, these users and computers will not be under the jurisdiction of GPOs that would otherwise control what the accounts can do.

To avoid this scenario, Microsoft has included two utilities with Windows Server 2003: redirusr.exe and redircmp.exe. As you can probably tell from their names, these utilities redirect the accounts to OUs that you specify instead of the default containers. However, there is one caveat to using these utilities: the domain has to be at the Windows 2003 functional level. Unfortunately, not many organizations are ready to move to this functional level. Those that have had the good fortune to change their domain functional level to Window 2003 will find that they can take advantage of creating new OUs for controlling those new user and computer accounts.

NOTE For more information about the `redirusr.exe` and `redircmp.exe` commands, see Chapter 6, "Managing Accounts: Computer, Group and User."

IDENTIFYING OU STRUCTURAL REQUIREMENTS

After redirecting new accounts to the new OUs, you can identify the rest of the OU structure needs. Most of the OU structure should already be designed because it is based on the administrative structure of the organization. In the first part of this chapter, we discussed creating the top-level OUs based on a static aspect of the organization. This still holds true for Group Policy design. If the top-level OUs are based on either locations or functions, the structure is resistant to change. The child OUs can then reflect the administrative requirements. This allows for the administrative staff to have efficient control of those objects they need to manage.

GPOs will use this structure, but other OUs may have to be created to further enhance the Group Policy requirements. Be careful when you create additional OUs to implement Group Policy. The more layers in the hierarchy, the harder it is to manage the objects within. Remember, the key to the OU structure is to make administrative tasks easier. Investigate all the possible options when you are determining how to apply GPOs.

New OUs should be added to the OU structure only if they enhance the application of GPOs and make the assignment of settings and restrictions to a group of users or computers easier than if they were linked at an existing OU. Use the Group Policy Modeling wizard within the GPMC to determine whether the application of policies is going to work as you expect it to. Experiment with the linkage of GPOs at those OUs that you already have defined. View the results and see which accounts are adversely affected before determining that an additional OU is required. You may find that filtering the GPO to a new group that you create allows you to assign settings to those users within that group while keeping the users within the OU instead of creating a new OU to host them.

Those users who have to create and link the OUs will need the appropriate rights delegated to them. You should also identify how you are going to maintain the GPOs and monitor how the GPOs are administered. Once the OU structure has been identified for applying Group Policy, the staff who will be responsible for the creation and maintenance of the GPOs will need rights delegated to them and training provided. If you are delegating the ability to perform specific functions to those users who are working with GPOs, you can give them the ability to create, edit, and link GPOs. One user could have the ability to perform all three functions, or you could separate the functions so that only certain users can perform an individual task. The following section describes how you can design your GPO management for delegated administration.

IDENTIFYING ADMINISTRATIVE REQUIREMENTS

In smaller organizations, the same administrator who creates user accounts will maintain the servers and work with the GPOs. Such an administrator, sometimes known as the Jack-of-All-Trades administrator, does it all. For this type of administration, identifying who is going to perform the tasks is simple. That administrator has to make sure that they are trained to perform the tasks at hand. In larger environments, however, one administrator cannot do it all. Usually specific tasks are assigned to users, and they are responsible for their own little piece of the organization. In this case, the users who are delegated the tasks of maintaining GPOs have to be trained on the proper methods of maintaining the Group Policy infrastructure.

Training Users

Different users can be assigned to create GPOs than those who are allowed to link the GPOs. In larger organizations where specialized job functions are assigned to employees, or in organizations that use the hybrid administrative model, users who are in charge of corporate standards can be allowed to create unlinked GPOS and modify GPOs with the settings determined by the corporate administration. The domain and OU owners are then responsible for linking the appropriate GPOs to their OUs or domains.

When you delegate the permission to perform actions on GPOs to users other than administrators who already have that ability, make sure that you are giving the user permission to do so only for the portion of Active Directory for which they are responsible. Within the GPMC, you can delegate the ability to link GPOs at the site, domain, or OU level. By changing permissions within the discretionary access control list for the GPO, you can control who is able to edit the GPO. When you grant someone the Read and Write permissions, that user could modify settings within the GPO. Figure 4.26 shows the Delegation tab within the GPMC for an OU.

A special group exists to make the task of delegating the creation of GPOs easier: the Group Policy Creator Owners group. When a user is added to this group, they will be able to modify any GPO that they create but they will not be able to link the GPO anywhere within Active Directory unless they have been delegated the right to do so at a site, domain, or OU.

When employees are granted the ability to create, modify, or link GPOs, they should be trained on the proper methods of handling their responsibilities. Guidelines for the functions that can be performed should be explained to the OU owners, domain owners, and forest owners. Without a basic set of guidelines, users could inadvertently make changes or create GPOs that will not function properly within your environment. Document the guidelines that you want to use and make sure everyone involved understands them.

The Group Policy administration training methodology should include best practices for the following topics:

◆ Creating GPOs

◆ Importing settings

◆ Editing settings

◆ Linking GPOs

◆ Setting exceptions for inheritance

◆ Filtering accounts

◆ Using the Group Policy Modeling Wizard

◆ Using the Group Policy Results Wizard

◆ Backing up and restoring GPOs

◆ Learning which settings apply to specific operating systems

◆ Using WMI filters

◆ Handling security templates

FIGURE 4.26

Delegation tab for an OU

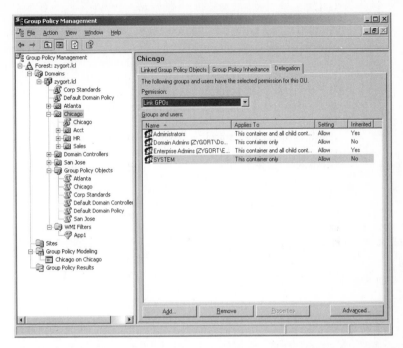

FIGURE 4.26

Delegation tab for an OU

If users understand how each of these work, they will have a better understanding of why GPOs should be implemented the way they are, and as a result, the troubleshooting required to determine problems should ease. The more training and understanding that goes on before the users are allowed to create and maintain GPOs, the less time will be spent troubleshooting later in the life cycle of Active Directory.

Identifying Required Permissions

For the most part, GPOs should be linked at the OU level. This allows you to use the most versatile method of controlling how the settings are applied. Sometimes you will find that the best method of applying policies is performed if the policy is linked at the site or domain level. As mentioned previously, the account policies are always set at the domain level. You may also find a reason to link them at the site level, such as when all computers at the site need to have an IPSec policy applied to them.

In order for a GPO to be linked at the site level, the administrator who is performing the linking has to have enterprise-level permissions or have the permission to link to the site delegated to them. Adding an account to the Domain Admins global group or Administrators domain local group at the root domain or Enterprise Admins universal group is not a recommended practice unless that administrative account is the forest owner.

Administrative staff responsible for linking at the domain level will need to be members of the Domain Admins global group, or they will need to have the Manage Group Policy Links permission delegated to them. Members of the Domain Admins global group will also be able to use the GPMC and edit any GPOs for their domain. To have access to GPOs for any other domain, they will need permissions delegated to them for the objects within the other domains, or they will have to be members of the Enterprise Admins universal group.

Policies linked at the OU level require the administrative staff to be members of the Domain Admins global group for the domain or have the proper permissions delegated to them to work with GPOs.

Coming Up Next

There are certain functions within Active Directory that are so important you will only have a single domain control running those functions. These are known as the Flexible Single Master Operations (FSMO) roles. Understanding what these roles do for you as well as understanding where you should place these roles will help you when designing your domain controller placement, as you'll learn in the next chapter.

Chapter 5

Flexible Single Master Operations Design

Certain tasks should only be carried out by a single entity. When adding chemicals to a pool, for example, you should make sure that only one person is measuring and dumping them in. You don't want more than one person doing the work, because one of them could throw off the chemical balance by making changes the other didn't know about.

And so it is with Active Directory (AD). For the most part, Active Directory has fail-safes in place that allow changes to be made on any domain controller. However, certain functions should be provided by only one domain controller at a time; otherwise, you could introduce instability into your Active Directory infrastructure. These functions are collectively known as the Flexible Single Master Operations (FSMO).

Even though this may be the shortest chapter in this book, the information is still highly relevant to the successful functioning of your Active Directory domain. Later, in Chapter 11, "Managing Operation Masters," we take a look at some of the troubleshooting methodology that you will put into place when you have problems with one of these roles, or with the domain controller that hosts them. Right now, though, we'll concentrate on introducing the roles and discuss what you need to consider when designing their placement.

What Are the FSMO Roles?

As we mentioned, the FSMO roles are specialized services within Active Directory that should be performed only on a single domain controller. If you are wondering what the word *flexible* stands for, although only one domain controller can provide the functionality provided by the FSMO role, the role can be transferred to any other domain controller. Because of this flexibility, not only do you have the option of transferring the role to another domain controller if the original role holder goes down, but you can also plan which domain controller will hold the role, thus optimizing your network.

Five roles make up the FSMO: Schema Master, Domain Naming Master, Infrastructure Master, Relative Identifier (RID) Master, and Primary Domain Controller (PDC) Emulator. All five of these roles can coexist on one domain controller, or you can move them so that they all run on their own independent domain controller. Before transferring a role, you should take into consideration the interaction between some of the roles as well as how they interact with other Active Directory services.

Schema Master

As we discussed earlier in this book, all of the domain controllers within the domain allow administrators to create and make changes to the objects contained within the domain. As an administrator creates an object, such as a computer or user account, the schema controls how the object is built. Since all the domain controllers within the forest share the same schema, every object that is created from an object class contains the same attributes. Domain controllers work as peers to one another; as changes are made to attributes within the objects, the changes are replicated to other domain controllers. The only problem with this model is that two administrators can make changes at the same time and cause a replication problem.

The designers of Active Directory, when presented with the challenge of making all the domain controllers members in the multimaster replication model, realized that if they allowed two or more administrators to change schema information, they could potentially render objects, and possibly the entire domain or forest, completely useless.

To protect the schema from the corruption that could be caused by more than one administrator attempting to make changes to the schema on multiple domain controllers, the Schema Master was introduced. The Schema Master is the one domain controller within the forest that is allowed to access and modify the portion of the Active Directory database that holds the schema. The schema partition, sometimes known as schema naming context, resides on every domain controller within the forest, but can only be modified on this one domain controller, the Schema Master. The schema partition can be accessed through an LDAP call to `LDAP://cn=schema,cn-configuration,dc=`*domainname*`,dc=`*TLD*.

NOTE For more information on issuing LDAP commands and what you can do when you access an LDAP-based directory, see the Scripting section at the end of this book.

By default the Schema Master is the first domain controller that is promoted within the forest. As a matter of fact, all five of the FSMO roles are held on this system until you transfer them. For most installations, the first domain controller can continue to participate as the Schema Master until you decide to decommission the system at the end of the hardware or system life cycle. Because the Schema Master is not utilized heavily, it does not have large resource requirements.

Besides being the central location for changes to the schema, the Schema Master is required to be online when the Forest Functionality level is raised. Keep this in mind as you are in the process of adding Active Directory–based applications such as Exchange, System Management Server, Microsoft Operations Manager, and others, or you are in the process of decommissioning the Windows NT 4 and Windows 2000-based domain controllers. If the Schema Master is not online, you will not be able to perform certain necessary functions.

NOTE For more information on transferring and seizing the Schema Master role, consult Chapter 11, "Managing Operations Masters."

Domain Naming Master

As with the Schema Master, there is only one Domain Naming Master within the forest. The Domain Naming Master is the system that is responsible for making sure that domain names are unique and available when you're adding or removing domains from your forest. Typically this is not an FSMO role that is utilized very often once the organization's forest structure has been built and stabilized.

Because there is only one Domain Naming Master, it is important that the role be available as domains are created and removed, yet it does not consume very much in the way of resources on the system where it resides. And just as you can with the Schema Master, you can leave this FSMO role on the first domain controller within the forest for as long as necessary. Once you deem it necessary to decommission the server running this role, determine which server will be responsible for hosting the Domain Naming Master role.

Since this is another role that is not utilized very often once your forest structure has become stabilized, if the domain controller that is holding this role fails, you can usually go without the role until you can bring the domain controller online again. If you do need to create a new domain, or decommission an existing domain, you can seize this role on another system.

NOTE For more information on transferring and seizing the Domain Naming Master role, consult Chapter 11, "Managing Operations Masters."

Infrastructure Master

Whereas the Schema Master and the Domain Naming Master can reside on only one domain controller within the entire forest, the Infrastructure Master, Relative ID Master, and PDC Emulator roles can be found within every domain in the forest. When you install the first domain controller for the forest, these roles are installed. When you add additional domains to your forest, each one will have these roles installed on the first domain controller within each domain.

The Infrastructure Master is an interesting role. Its job is to check other domains in the forest for changes to objects. If it finds a change to an object in another domain, it will update the attributes for any instances of that object, and then the changes are replicated to other domain controllers from its domain. You are probably asking yourself, "Why would the object be contained in more than one domain?" If an object is used within an access control list, or as a member of a group, changes to the object within the other domain will not replicate to any other domains by default. The global catalog will pick up the change due to the intradomain replication that global catalogs participate in, but the non–global catalog domain controllers will not receive any domain partition updates.

The Infrastructure Master is not deemed a service that is needed all the time. If you are making several changes to objects within your forest on a daily basis, you may miss this function because the changes will not propagate correctly. However, if you are not making many changes, you may not miss this role for several days.

NOTE For more information on transferring and seizing the Infrastructure Master role, consult Chapter 11, "Managing Operations Masters."

RID Master

The RID Master, as mentioned earlier, is one of the roles that is available in each domain. The RID Master is responsible for making sure that each security principle within the domain has a unique identifier. This identifier is actually a number that is incremented for each object that can be created within the domain. Since each object takes on the security identifier (SID) of the domain for identification purposes, the relative identifier (RID) uniquely identifies the security principle within the domain.

It is important to note that the RID Master is not contacted for each RID that is handed out when an account is created. Instead, domain controllers contact the RID Master when they are promoted, and the RID Master allocates a large block of RIDs to the domain controller. When the domain controller is close to depleting the RIDs it has been allocated, the domain controller contacts the RID Master once again to replenish its RID pool.

With the original implementation of Active Directory in Windows 2000, the RID pool allocation was 500 RIDs per domain controller, and the domain controllers would contact the RID Master when 20 percent of their RID pool remained. There were implementations in which this scenario caused problems. If an import utility such as csvde or ldifde were in use, or if the Active Directory Migration Tool was used, the RID pool could potentially become depleted before the domain controller would receive a new allocation of RIDs. To solve this problem, Windows 2000 Service Pack 4 changed the allocation request limit to 50 percent. Windows Server 2003 and Windows Server 2003 R2 both adhere to the same criteria.

If the domain controller hosting the RID Master fails, you could have problems. Because all the domain controllers responsible for creating accounts need to obtain their allocation of RIDs from the RID Master as their RID pool becomes depleted, if the RID Master is not available, the domain controllers will not be able to get any new RIDs.

NOTE   For more information on transferring and seizing the RID Master role, as well as changing the default RID allocation amount, consult Chapter 11, "Managing Operations Masters."

PDC Emulator

The final FSMO role that we'll cover is another role that is available in each domain within your forest, the Primary Domain Controller (PDC) Emulator. The name of this role is a little misleading because there are several other functions that this role provides besides acting as the PDC for Windows NT 4 domain controllers; time synchronization and password changes are controlled here as well.

Whenever a domain is in mixed mode and Windows NT 4 Backup Domain Controllers (BDCs) exist within the domain, the PDC Emulator is responsible for keeping the Windows NT 4 BDCs and all other Windows 2000 Server or Windows Server 2003 domain controllers updated. The PDC emulator is also responsible for accepting password change requests from pre–Active Directory clients. If the domain is placed in Windows 2000 native mode or the Windows Server 2003 functional level, the PDC emulator becomes the clearinghouse for password changes within the domain. Any time another domain controller receives a password change from a client, the PDC emulator is passed the change so that the other domain controllers can be notified of the change. If a user has entered a bad password, the authentication request is passed to the PDC emulator in order to validate that the user's password was not changed on another domain controller prior to the authentication attempt.

By default the PDC Emulator is the domain controller that is responsible for making updates to group policies, and the master replication point when changes are made. Group Policy Objects (GPOs) consist of two parts: the Group Policy Container, which is an object that exists within Active Directory, and the Group Policy Template, which is the configuration date for the GPO that resides within the Sysvol directory. As changes are made by an administrator, the changes are effected on the PDC Emulator, and then replicated to the PDC Emulator's replication partners. At any time, an administrator can choose another domain controller to work with GPOs, but you should have a good reason to do so.

NOTE   For more information on working with GPOs, see Chapter 9, "Managing Group Policy."

Another important function of the PDC Emulator is time synchronization. All members of the domain, whether they are running Windows 2000, Windows XP, or Windows Server 2003 as their operating system, synchronize their clocks according to the time on the PDC emulator and use the timestamp to authenticate clients. This timestamp is then used with the Kerberos service to authenticate clients. If the timestamp is off by more than 5 minutes, the Kerberos service will reject the authentication attempt.

The PDC Emulator is the one service that relies on having decent hardware resources for it to function. Without the PDC Emulator in place, you could have serious issues arise within your domain. For instance, without the PDC Emulator, Windows NT 4 domain controllers will not receive updates to accounts, Windows NT and Windows 98 systems will not be allowed to authenticate, time synchronization will not work, and accounts could be locked out due to password changes not being replicated in time.

NOTE For more information on transferring and seizing the PDC Emulator role, consult Chapter 11, "Managing Operations Masters."

STANDBY SERVERS

As we start discussing the placement of the FSMO roles within the forest and domains, you are going to read about standby servers. For any of the FSMO roles, you should consider which domain controllers will act as a standby system if the original role holder fails for any reason. There are no configuration settings on a domain controller that say "I am a standby server for a FSMO role." Instead, just make sure that all administrative personnel are aware of your preference to use a specific server as the standby in case the first fails. Then, if a failure of the first server does occur, you can quickly seize the master operations on the second server. Make sure that the two systems are located close to one another and connected via a high-speed connection. You could even create connection objects between the two systems so that they replicate directly to one another, ensuring that their directories are as identical as possible.

Choosing Flexible Single Master Operations Placement

Because of the importance of the FSMO roles, you should carefully choose where the domain controllers holding each of these roles are placed. Certain functions don't play well together, and depending on the functional level of the domain and forest, you may want to choose wisely where you place the FSMO roles. The following sections discuss the guidelines you should take into consideration.

Operations Masters in a Single-Domain Forest

Within a single domain forest, the infrastructure master does not play a very important role. As a matter of fact, its services are not used at all. Because you don't have any remote domains for the infrastructure master to compare domain information to, it doesn't matter whether the domain controller is a global catalog server. In fact, in a single-domain environment, all domain controllers could be enabled as global catalog servers because there will be no additional replication costs. By default, the first domain controller within the domain will hold all the Master Operations roles and will also be a global catalog server. You should also designate another domain controller as a standby server. You do not have to configure anything special on this domain controller.

Operations Masters Site Placement in a Multiple-Domain Forest

The five Master Operations roles will have to be placed on domain controllers where they will be the most effective. You should take certain criteria into consideration when you are deciding on which site these domain controllers will be placed.

FORESTWIDE ROLES

The two forestwide roles don't have a lot to do after the forest is stabilized, so they don't really require the "horsepower" that some of the other roles require, nor do they need to be highly available.

Schema Master

The Schema Master role is not one that is used very often. Typically, the only time the Schema Master needs to be online after the initial installation of Active Directory is when you are making changes to the schema or the functional level of the forest is raised. When you are planning the placement of the Schema Master, place it in a site where the schema administrators have easy access to it. You want to make sure that the changes made to the schema are done on a domain controller that is accessible within the same LAN-based infrastructure as the administrator making the change. Doing so makes sense from both an administrative as well as a security standpoint. For security reasons, you don't want the schema changes that you are making traveling across a potentially vulnerable network connection. Any information that attackers can glean from information that you are working on could give up vital information about your Active Directory infrastructure.

Also, consider the replication that will be incurred when a change is made. For this reason alone, you may want to place the Schema Master within a site that has the most domain controllers within the forest. As replication is initiated due to schema changes, if you have the Schema Master located close to a majority of the domain controllers within the domain, you incur the replication cost on the LAN segments and reduce the amount of traffic that needs to be sent across the WAN links. Of course, you need to weigh the replication costs against the administrative requirements. If security is the highest concern, you may want to design your placement so that the domain controllers are close to the administrator, even though it may mean that you incur additional replication across the WAN links.

Domain Naming Master

As with the Schema Master, the Domain Naming Master is not used very often. Its role is to guarantee the uniqueness of domain names within the forest. It is also used when removing domains from the forest. For the Domain Naming Master to perform its function, it must be able to check in with a global catalog server. The global catalog server holds information from every domain within the forest, and when a new domain is added to the forest, or a domain is decommissioned, the Domain Naming Master is responsible for identifying the domain information, making sure it is unique, and then updating the configuration information.

If the domain controller holding the Domain Naming Master role is a Windows 2000–based server, you should locate it on a global catalog server. Microsoft made changes to Windows Server 2003–based domain controllers to allow them to contact a global catalog server instead of having the Domain Naming Master reside on a global catalog server.

The Domain Naming Master can be located on the same domain controller as the Schema Master because neither of the roles impacts the way the domain controller functions. As with the Schema Master, it should be located close to where the administrative staff has access, even though this role does not incur the replication costs that the Schema Master does.

DOMAINWIDE ROLES

The domainwide roles have a tendency to be utilized a little more often, and require that the domain controller holding the roles be highly available. When planning the hardware that will be used for these domain controllers, make sure that the hardware is highly reliable.

Infrastructure Master

The Infrastructure Master holds a very important role within a multiple-domain forest. If users from one domain are added to the membership of groups from a second domain, the Infrastructure Master is then responsible for maintaining any updates when changes occur within the remote domain.

For instance, if a user from Domain A is added to a group in Domain B, and the user's name changes because she gets married, the user account name in Domain A will not match the entry within the group membership of Domain B. The Infrastructure Master is responsible for reviewing the information from Domain A and checking for discrepancies. If it finds that a change has been made, the Infrastructure Master updates the information in Domain B so that the new name information within the group can be replicated to all the domain controllers.

If the Infrastructure Master is located on a global catalog server, it checks for differences between Domain A and Domain B, but it won't notice any discrepancies because the global catalog server hosts information from Domain A. Other servers that are not global catalog servers in Domain B won't have the correct information for the group, and the Infrastructure Master won't update the other domain controllers. So, in a multiple-domain forest, move the Infrastructure Master to a domain controller that is not a global catalog server. Of course, if you make every domain controller a global catalog server, you don't have to worry about the Infrastructure Master placement because every domain controller hosts information from every domain and replicates changes whenever they are made.

When you are choosing the placement of the Infrastructure Master, place it within a site that also contains domain controllers from most, if not all, of the other domains in the forest. This ensures that the queries and updates are performed on the local network infrastructure.

Relative Identifier (RID) Master

The RID Master is responsible for generating and maintaining the RIDs used by the security principles within the domain. Each domain controller will contact the RID Master to obtain a group of RIDs to be used as the accounts are created. If your domain is in native mode or higher, you should place the RID Master in a site that has domain controllers where administrators are creating a majority of the accounts. This allows the RID Master to efficiently hand out allocations of RIDs to the domain controllers performing most of the account creation work. If your domain is in mixed mode, consider placing the RID Master on the same server as the PDC emulator. The PDC emulator is the only domain controller that can create accounts within the domain when the domain is in mixed mode.

Since the RID Master is responsible for handing out the RIDs for all the accounts that are created within the domain, you should designate a standby server so that you can seize the role quickly if necessary. As mentioned earlier, the standby server should be a direct replication partner to the original RID Master so that any updates to the RID Master are known to the standby server.

Primary Domain Controller (PDC) Emulator

The RID Master is a highly utilized FSMO role, but the PDC Emulator is the busiest role of all. The domain controller hosting this FSMO role should be highly available and definitely have a standby server available. When a PDC Emulator goes down, you want to make sure you can seize the role quickly so that you do not lose the functionality it provides.

If you are making several changes to group policies, position the role close to the administrators responsible for making the updates to GPOs. This keeps the updates local for the administrators. However, if you have a majority of your domain controllers within a site other than where the administrators are located, you have to decide whether the replication cost of GPO updates outweighs local administration.

Keep in mind that whenever a user changes their password, the PDC Emulator is immediately notified of the change. When a user's credentials are sent to a domain controller that has not been updated with the new password, the domain controller will check with the PDC Emulator before incrementing the account lockout counter and potentially locking out the user. Because of this additional traffic, consider placing the PDC Emulator close to a majority of the user accounts within the domain.

Another placement factor is the time synchronization function. In an attempt to keep the traffic generated from this function to a minimum within the domain, identify the site that contains the most computer accounts and determine whether the PDC Emulator should be positioned within that site. If that site also contains the domain controller that supports the most user authentication, you won't have anywhere else to look. However, if the domain controllers that provide the authentication are in a site other than where most of the computers are located, you have to test the traffic that is generated by each function to decide the best placement for this role.

Another consideration is domains in mixed mode. Some administrators like to move each FSMO role to its own domain controller. This way, if one domain controller fails, the other roles are not affected. When a domain is in mixed mode, you may not want to separate the RID Master and the PDC Emulator. As mentioned earlier, when a domain is still in mixed mode, where Active Directory assumes that there are still Windows NT 4 backup domain controllers that it has to support, the only domain controller that creates security accounts is the domain controller holding the PDC Emulator role. All the RIDs from the RID Master are handed over to the PDC Emulator and no other domain controller. If these two functions are held on the same domain controller, then the allocation is very simple and does not incur any additional network traffic.

Coming Up Next

After looking at the FSMO roles and the placement options for each one, we can move on to a subject that is at the heart of the RID Master role: user, group, and computer creation. We also take a look at managing these accounts within an Active Directory–based environment. This moves us out of the planning phase of the book and into the management section.

Part 2

Active Directory Management

In this part:

Chapter 6

Managing Accounts: User, Group, and Computer

One of the most common administrative duties is working with user, group, and computer accounts. On any given day you will find that user accounts need to have their passwords reset, have attributes or names changed, or have additions and deletions performed. Group accounts will need to have users added and deleted. Computer accounts will need to be reset from time to time or added as new workstations and servers are introduced to the network.

You can choose from several methods when you are working with these accounts. Depending on your comfort level with the scripting options available, you could automate some of your tasks instead of having to manually manipulate the accounts. Once you start working with the scripting options, you will find that you can usually perform your administrative tasks faster when using a script. What many administrators find as the drawback to the scripting options is the learning curve. One of our goals in this chapter is to make you feel more at ease with scripting.

First, let's look over the different accounts that are available within Active Directory, and then we will discuss the methods of management and maintenance.

Account Types

You will need to create accounts in order to differentiate each of your users on the network, and to grant the appropriate permissions so that those users can access the resources they need to perform their jobs. You will also need to create accounts for the computers that are going to act as members of your domain. The final type of account you will need to create is used for users and computers within your domain that require the same rights and permissions granted to them.

Of course, you will also have accounts that will not need any rights or permissions granted to them, but you may have to represent them within your domain. For each of these accounts, you can create the account and use it within your domain, but then not have to worry about the accounts being used as security principles within the domain.

Security Principle Accounts

Each account that needs access to resources must be assigned a unique security identifier (SID). The domain controller that is responsible for creating the account will build the SID from its Relative Identifier (RID) pool. If you have looked over Chapter 5, "Flexible Single Master Operations Design," you know that the RID Master is responsible for allocating the RIDs to each domain controller. These RIDs, combined with the SID from the domain, make up the account's SID. If you take a moment to think about this methodology, you will soon realize that an account's SID identifies the domain in which the account resides, as well as uniquely identifying the account within the domain.

NOTE For more information on the RID Master and how it allocates RIDs to domain controllers, see Chapter 5, "Flexible Single Master Operations Design," and Chapter 11, "Managing the Flexible Single Master Operations Roles."

So why do we need to have RIDs? Why not just use the account's name? In short, names change. If we want to have an identifier that can be used for the lifetime of the account, we need to make sure that the identifier will not change. Having an identifier that changes makes more work for the administrator. If you were to change a user's name from Angela Jones to Angela Smith, and the account's permissions and rights were associated with the account's name, you would have to go into all the resources that the account was associated with and make the change. By using the account's SID (which should never change), you do not have to go into access control lists or group memberships and make a change when you alter the account's name.

There are several accounts that are already created within a domain and they have SIDs that are considered well known. Table 6.1 lists some of these well-known SIDs and the security principles that they are associated with. These are the SIDs that are used in every domain and are controlled by the operating system.

Table 6.2 shows the well-known security principles that are created for each domain. These are accounts that your users will utilize when logging on to the domain, or accounts your computers will use when authenticating to domain resources. Note that each of these security principles' SIDs includes the domain identifier. Because these accounts could have access to resources within other domains, there has to be a way to uniquely identify them.

NOTE These tables are not comprehensive lists of well-known SIDs. For more information about well-known SIDs, see Knowledge Base article 243330 at http://support.microsoft.com.

TABLE 6.1:   Well-known system controlled SIDs

SID	ACCOUNT
S-1-1-0	Everyone
S-1-3-0	Creator Owner
S-1-5-1	Dialup
S-1-5-2	Network
S-1-5-3	Batch
S-1-5-4	Interactive
S-1-5-7	Anonymous
S-1-5-9	Enterprise Domain Controllers
S-1-5-11	Authenticated Users
S-1-5-13	Terminal Server Users

TABLE 6.2:   Well-known administrator controlled SIDs

SID	ACCOUNT
S-1-5-{Domain}-500	Administrator
S-1-5-{Domain}-501	Guest
S-1-5-{Domain}-512	Domain Admins
S-1-5-{Domain}-513	Domain Users
S-1-5-{Domain}-514	Guests
S-1-5-{Domain}-515	Domain Computers
S-1-5-{Domain}-516	Domain Controllers
S-1-5-{Domain}-518	Schema Admins
S-1-5-{Domain}-519	Enterprise Admins
S-1-5-{Domain}-544	Administrators
S-1-5-{Domain}-545	Users

In the following sections, we discuss the accounts that you can create that will allow you to assign rights and permissions to the users and computers within your domain. The three accounts we start off with—Users, Computers, and Groups—are all known as security principles. A security principle is an account that has a SID associated with it; it can be assigned access to resources and can also be granted the ability to perform special functions within the forest. The other two accounts that we examine are not security principles, but they provide other functionality within the forest.

USER-BASED ACCOUNTS

There are actually two account types that can represent a person who needs access to resources within your network infrastructure: the user account and the InetOrgPerson account. Both of these account types will grant users access to resources, but the InetOrgPerson account is an industry-standard Lightweight Directory Access Protocol (LDAP) account type that is interoperable with other X.500 directory services.

User Account

User accounts can be created for each of the users that you have within your organization and is necessary to uniquely identify the user. Once created, user accounts can be used to grant access to resources to the individuals that they represent. You can also use these accounts to represent your users by populating the attributes on each one to further identify the person.

For instance, if you have a user who is a member of the Human Resources department, and their manager is Tom Avery, you could put this information within the user's properties and then use it to locate or group the user in the future. If you look at Figure 6.1, you will see that there are several property pages ready for you to populate with information. The information that you supply will go a long way toward identifying the user within your domain. The more data you supply, the better off you will be when you are setting up and issuing your queries.

Informational Property Pages

All of these property pages are used to either configure the user's account, or to aid in identifying the user within the directory. Although most of the property pages are used to configure how the user account will be used within the directory, or the options that define the account, some are simply informational. If you take a look at Figure 6.2, the Address property page has several attributes that can be populated, but none of the information on this property page is required. The Telephone and Organization property pages work the same way; the fields don't have to be populated to affect the account's access to resources; however, all of the fields can be populated, and once populated, can be targets of a query.

FIGURE 6.1
User properties

FIGURE 6.2
Address property page
for user accounts

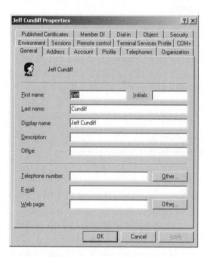

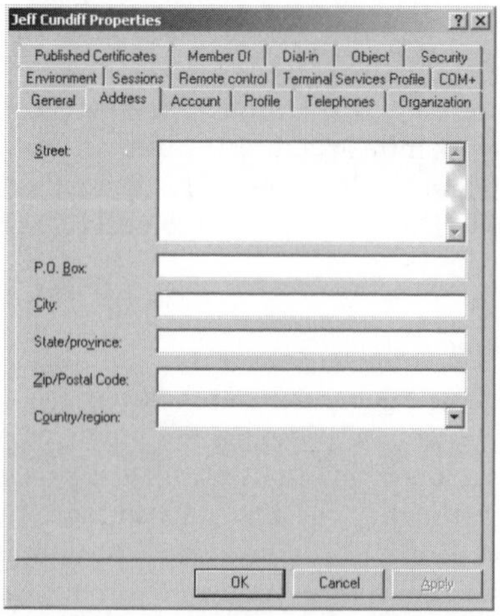

Account Property Page

The rest of the property pages all contain fields that affect access to resources within the domain. The first, and one of the most important property pages, seen in Figure 6.3, is the Account property page. This is a very busy tab, as there are several options that control the account itself, including password information.

Although a user's account has a specific "personality," it is known under a few different names. On the Account property page, you will find these names listed near the top. The first name is the user logon name. You will notice that this name is broken up into two parts: the user account's alias and the user principle name (UPN). When the account is created, you have to specify what the user's alias will be. Once created, it can be changed here. The UPN, by default, takes on the domain name of the forest root domain. You can create other UPNs to match the naming conventions for your user accounts.

The second name that is used is known as the user logon name (pre–Windows 2000). This name is used for backward compatibility with operating systems that still rely on NetBIOS. When your domain is in Windows 2000 mixed mode, you will need to authenticate using this name. You can still log on to the domain using this method when you are in the Windows 2000 native mode or higher, but you do gain an advantage when you use the UPN version instead. In Figure 6.4, notice the typical logon screen as it appears when you are using the pre–Windows 2000 logon; you have to enter your username and password, and pull down the domain name that you wish to authenticate. Once you click OK, the authentication request will be sent to a domain controller for the domain you specified. This is the same no matter which functional level your domain is in.

In Figure 6.5, notice that once you specify the UPN, the domain pull-down list is no longer accessible. When you click OK at this point, and your domain is in the Windows 2000 native mode or higher, the authentication request is passed to the nearest global catalog server for processing. The global catalog server locates the user account based on its UPN, processes the authentication request, and enumerates the account's universal group membership.

FIGURE 6.3

Account property page

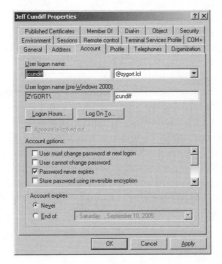

FIGURE 6.4
Logging on using
pre–Windows 2000
logon name

FIGURE 6.5
Logging on using UPN

To change the UPN to fit your organization's naming conventions, right-click the Active Directory Domains and Trusts label within the snap-in of the same name and select Properties. You will find a property page that looks like the one shown in Figure 6.6. Entering additional name suffixes in the page will allow you to associate a user with a suffix. This comes in especially handy when you want to create a shorter UPN for domains that have a long namespace. For instance, you could create a UPN suffix `atl.int` and use that for the user's UPN instead of `hr.atlanta.na.zygort.lcl`.

Next on the Account property page are the two buttons that help you define when and where the user account can log on. The Logon Hours button leads you to a dialog box like the one in Figure 6.7. You can define the hours that a user is allowed to log on with this account by clicking in the boxes to select them and clicking the Logon Permitted radio button. For those hours you want to restrict the user from having the ability to log on, you simply select the boxes that represent the appropriate times and click the Logon Denied radio button.

The Log On To button will lead you to a dialog box, shown in Figure 6.8, that gives you the ability to define which workstations the user is allowed to use when logging onto the domain. Note that when you take advantage of this option, you will need to make sure that you still have NetBIOS running within your infrastructure. Each workstation will also need to have NetBIOS enabled if you want to control the accounts that will have the ability to log onto that system.

FIGURE 6.6
Defining new UPNs

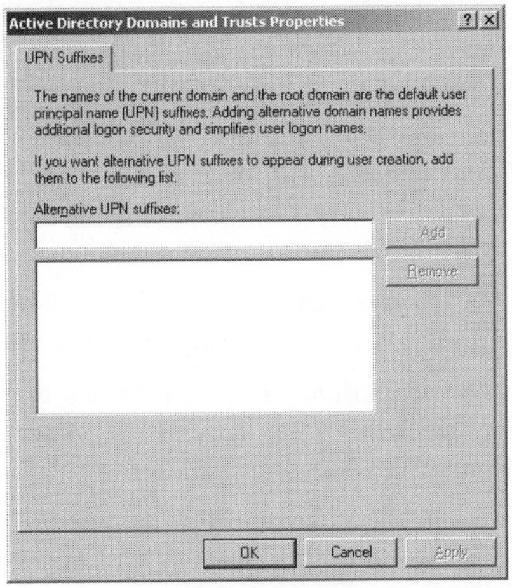

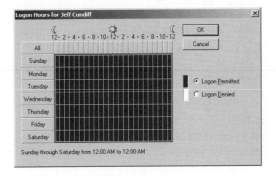

FIGURE 6.7
Logon hours

FIGURE 6.8
Log On To dialog box

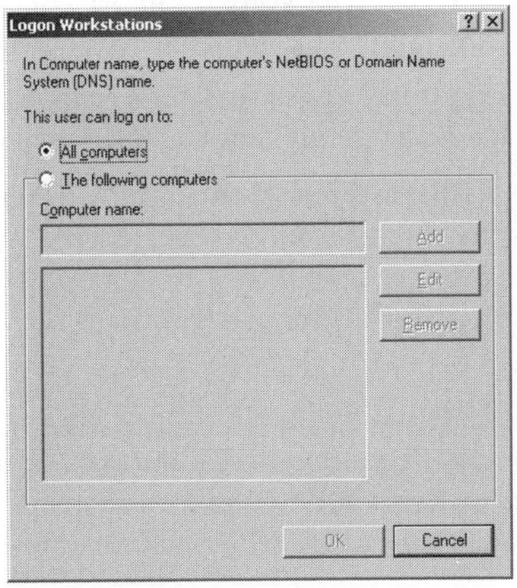

Back on the Accounts property page, notice that there are several options within a scroll box. Most of these options are password control options. Let's take a look at each one:

User Must Change Password At Next Logon Selecting the User Must Change Password At Next Logon check box forces the user to change their password the next time they log on to their account. This is a good option to enable when you first create an account or when an authorized individual changes a user's password. This way, the user can be certain that whoever changed their password no longer knows what the user's password is.

User Cannot Change Password There are some rare cases where users are not in control of their password, and only administrative personnel have the ability to change the password.

Password Never Expires If you are trying to maintain secure passwords, do not select this option. This check box essentially overrides the Maximum Password Age setting within the effective domain group policy.

Store Password Using Reversible Encryption If you are using Digest authentication, enable this option so that Active Directory can store a version of the user's password that can be used for authentication purposes.

Account Is Disabled Once this option is selected, the account cannot be used. This is a good alternative to deleting the account when it is no longer needed in cases where you may want to keep the SID associated with the account, or where the account will be used sometime in the future.

Smart Card Is Required For Interactive Logon Selecting this option guarantees that the user will authenticate using a smart card instead of the traditional authentication that uses a username and password.

Account Is Trusted For Delegation This option only appears in a Windows 2000 native mode domain; it will not appear in a Windows 2003 functional mode domain.

Account Is Sensitive And Cannot Be Delegated When an account has a high level of access to resources, you may want to select this option so that the account cannot be misused when compromised. Usually, delegated access is used by services and applications that need to be impersonated so that another system can act on behalf of the user. If you have accounts that have a high level of access to resources, you should consider selecting this option so that the account cannot be impersonated by another system; instead it can only be used directly by the account itself.

Use DES Encryption Types For This Account Select this option if you need the account to use one of the Data Encryption Standard (DES) security protocols.

Do Not Use Kerberos Preauthentication If the account is using another Kerberos implementation, such as one of the versions supplied with Unix, ticket-granting tickets may not be used during the authentication process. If they are not used, the time synchronization check may not allow the authentication of the user unless this check box is selected.

Profile Property Page

The Profile property page allows an administrator to define information that is used when the user's profile is created on a computer. This property page, shown in Figure 6.9, is divided into two sections: User Profile and Home Folder. The first line of the User Profile section displays the Profile Path, where the user's roaming profile is stored. User profiles come in a couple of flavors: standard and roaming. The standard profile is created and stored on the local computer. Whenever a user logs on for the first time and no entry is listed in the Profile Path box, the user's profile is generated from the Default User profile that is stored on the local computer. If an entry is listed in the Profile Path box, the profile is downloaded from the location specified.

The Logon Script option defines the logon script name that will be processed when the user logs on. When you specify a script in this line, you only need to enter the name of the script. It is assumed that the script will be run from the NETLOGON share, which is located in *%systemroot%*\SYSVOL\ sysvol*domain_name*\scripts, where *%systemroot%* is the location where the system files were loaded during setup and *domain_name* is the name of the domain for which the domain controller functions.

A home folder is a directory that is used to store data files that the user works with. Usually this is a folder on a network file server in your domain, but it doesn't have to be. In the Home Folder section, you can identify where the user's home folder will be located: either on a server within the network or on the local computer. If you want to define a path on the user's local system, you simply click the Local Path radio button and type the path that will be used on the computer where the user is logged on. As we mentioned earlier, the home folder is usually a network location. If you are using a file server, click the Connect radio button and then type the UNC path to the folder that will host the user's files.

There is a neat little function that is built into Windows domain-based operating systems. If you create a shared folder on a file server and assign the Users group Full Control permissions to the folder, you can automate the creation of each user's home folder. When you enter the path to the home folder for the user in the format \\server\share\%username%, the user's home folder is created in the share and the user's account is granted Full Control permissions to the folder.

FIGURE 6.9
Profile property page

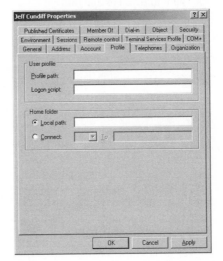

COM+ Property Page

COM+ partition sets can be used to group applications within Active Directory and then control which users have access to the applications. You can use COM+ partition sets to add another level of security to your applications by defining which users are allowed to use an application or set of applications.

NOTE   For more information on COM+ partition sets, see Chapter 7, "Managing Access to Active Directory Resources."

Published Certificates Property Page

When a certificate is issued to a user account, whether the certificate is used for authentication purposes or for encrypting files, the certificates will appear in the Published Certificates property page for the user, as shown in Figure 6.10. This property page, which is available only in Advanced mode, can then be used to see which certificates are associated with the user.

Member Of Property Page

All of the groups that the user is a member of are displayed on the Member Of property page, shown in Figure 6.11. From here you are able to add and remove the user from groups. If you are going to add the user to several groups, you'll want to take advantage of this property page. If on the other hand you want to add several users to a single group, you would be better served to go to the group's properties and use the Members property page.

Dial-in Property Page

The Dial-in property page, shown in Figure 6.12, allows you to define the options that control whether a user is allowed to dial into a RAS server, and if so, the options that control the access to the RAS server.

FIGURE 6.10
Published Certificates
property page

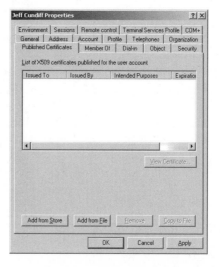

FIGURE 6.11
Member Of
property page

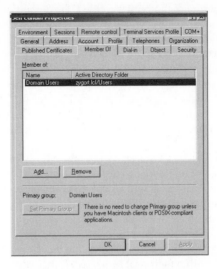

FIGURE 6.12
Dial-in property page

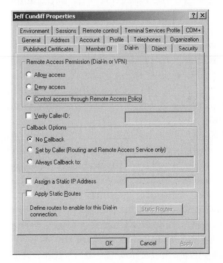

Starting at the top of this property page, notice that there are three options that let you control whether the user can dial into the RAS server. The first two options explicitly control the level of access for the user. As you can probably tell, Allow or Deny will either grant you access or stop you from being able to connect. The third option is a little less clear, however. When you select the Control Access Through Remote Access Policy radio button, you are removing control of the dial-up permissions from the user's account to a policy that is stored on the RAS server. While the domain remains in Windows 2000 mixed mode, the Control Access Through Remote Access Policy option is not available due to the fact that Windows NT 4 domain controllers could be authenticating the user. Windows NT 4 domain controllers do not know how to process RAS policies, so you will have to use the user account permissions.

When a user account is created, the default option that is selected for the user depends on the functional level of the domain. In Windows 2000 mixed mode, the Deny Access radio button is selected. In Windows 2000 native mode or higher, the Control Access Through Remote Access Policy option is selected.

Many organizations like to control access to their RAS servers by using some type of RAS server-based preauthentication. Usually this is performed by using a phone number that is associated with the user who is allowed to dial in. The Verify Caller-ID option sets a phone number that the user has to use when connecting to the RAS server. Once you select the check box and enter a phone number, the account can only be used for dial-in purposes if the user is calling from that one specific phone number.

The Callback Options section also allows phone number–level control if you set it correctly. The default option for this section is No Callback, which means that the user will dial into the RAS server and the RAS server will accept the connection. The other two options in this section control how the RAS server will handle the initial connection by the user. When the user dials in to the RAS server, the RAS server will prompt the user for their credentials. After the user enters their credentials, the server will disconnect the session and then call the user back. If the Set By Caller (Routing And Remote Access Service Only) option is set, the phone number that is specified in the user's telephony entries within their profile is used. If the Always Callback To option is selected, the phone number that is entered in the text box is used to call the user back.

The Always Callback To option is used as a security mechanism, allowing only the predetermined phone number to be used when accessing the RAS server. This helps safeguard the system in case someone has compromised a user's account; they will not be able to connect to the RAS server unless they are using the predetermined phone number to dial in. The Set By Caller option comes in handy when you have users who travel from location to location and need to connect to the organization's resources but you do not want them to incur hefty long-distance charges. The system will dial back on the number that they choose, putting the bulk of the long-distance charges on the company's accounts.

The last two options allow you to control how the user's system interacts with the RAS server and the network beyond it. Microsoft's Routing and Remote Access Server (RRAS) allows you to choose how the user's system will obtains its IP address. If the server is set to allow the user's computer to choose its own IP address, you will need to select the Assign A Static IP Address check box and enter the address the user's computer will use.

The Apply Static Routes check box should be selected if you need to create a special routing table for the user's computer when it connects to the RAS server. Once you select this option, you can click the Static Routes button and enter routes that you want the system to use. This may come in handy if you want to control how the user's computer accesses resources on the organization's network, or if you have a specific route that you want to restrict the system to take advantage of while connected.

NOTE   For more information about controlling user account dial-in access and how to configure Routing and Remote Access, see our sister publication *Mastering Windows Server 2003 R2*.

Environment Property Page

The last four property pages that we are going to discuss all pertain to terminal services and remote desktop connections. Any time a user connects to another system and starts a Terminal Services session, settings that control those sessions should be configured. Microsoft has taken care to make sure that the default settings will work in most environments, but if yours is like many organizations, you will find that you will need to tweak some of the user accounts to work optimally and correctly.

The Environment property page, shown in Figure 6.13, specifies the available resources when the session is started. In the Starting Program section you have the option of specifying a program that will start when the session initializes. Usually this option is selected if you have a special application that the user needs to use during the session and nothing else. Once specified, when the user starts their session, the application will start, and when the user closes the application, the session is ended.

In the Client Devices section you can specify which of the user's local devices are accessible within the terminal session. If you select the check box beside each one, the device setting will be applied. Connect Client Drives At Logon will allow the user's local drives to be accessible from the terminal session. This allows the client to use and save files on their local hard drives as though they were located on the server where their session is running. The same goes for the Connect Client Printers At Logon. Each of the printers that are configured in the user's profile become part of the session profile. And finally, the Default To Main Client Printer sets the user's default printer to the same printer in their session as in their local profile.

Sessions Property Page

The Sessions property page controls how the user's session runs on the server. As seen in Figure 6.14, you have options to control how the user's session is handled if it has not been active and what to do when the user tries to reconnect to their session. The first option, End A Disconnected Session, gives you the ability to set a time limit for a disconnected session to remain running on the server. Disconnected sessions are sessions where the user's client software is no longer accessing the session but the session is still running on the server. The pull-down list for this option, seen in Figure 6.15, allows a wide range of timeout values to be chosen.

FIGURE 6.13
Environment
property page

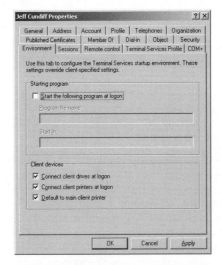

FIGURE 6.14
Sessions property page

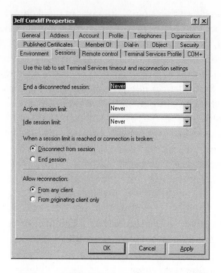

FIGURE 6.15
Timeout values for
ending a disconnected
session

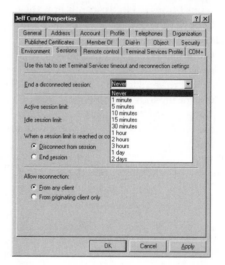

The next section controls how long sessions can remain active and what happens when those timeouts occur. The Active Session Limit setting allows you to control how long a user's session is allowed to remain running. This option comes in very handy if you have several users who need to use a terminal session and you do not want them to remain connected to the terminal server for long periods of time, denying others the opportunity to connect. The Idle Session Limit setting specifies how long a session can remain inactive. For both of these options, the same timeout values that appeared for the disconnected session pull-down list apply.

The two radio buttons beneath the session limits control how the session is handled when the timeout value is reached. The first option, Disconnect From Session, will disconnect the client from the session, but it will not close out the session. The End Session option will end the session entirely.

The last section on the Sessions property page is the Allow Reconnection section. You can see two radio buttons here: From Any Client and From Originating Client Only. When a session is disconnected, the session itself remains running on the server, but there is no interaction with any client. When the user starts the client and authenticates, by default the user is reconnected to their existing session. If the From Any Client option is selected, the user could move to another computer and start up the Terminal Services client software and reconnect to their existing session. If the From Originating Client Only option is selected, the user can only connect to their session from the same computer where the session had been initiated. For this option to work, NetBIOS needs to be running on the client and server.

Remote Control Property Page

Whenever a user is running a terminal services session, the session can be viewed, and sometimes controlled by anyone who has permissions to do so. The level of remote control can be configured using a group policy setting, or you can set each user individually on the Remote Control property page, shown in Figure 6.16. Once you select the Enable Remote Control option, you are allowing the user's session to be managed or viewed, depending on the other options set on this page.

Require User's Permission, when selected, sets the user's session to warn the user that someone wants to interact with their session, either by just viewing it or controlling it. The user then has the power to deny the interaction, or allow it if they want. Before you deselect this check box, make sure that company policies, current legislation, and union rules allow you to connect to a session without the user's knowledge.

The Level Of Control section allows you to specify how much control you have over the session. View The User's Session allows the session itself to be watched and monitored, but the user who has connected to the session will not be able to take over the session and control the mouse and keyboard. The Interact With The Session option gives the user who has connected to the session full access to control the session. Note that if you are trying to work with the session and the user who is logged on to the session is also trying to perform actions, you will fight over the mouse movement and both users' keystrokes will be entered in the session.

FIGURE 6.16
Remote Control
property page

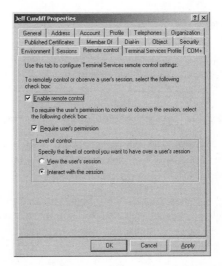

Terminal Services Profile Property Page

The Terminal Services Profile property page, shown in Figure 6.17, allows you to set alternate profile settings to be used during a terminal session than what the user typically uses when logging on to a computer. The options on this page work the same way that the Profile options work for a user's local login. Note that if a Profile Path option is not set for a roaming profile, the user's terminal session profile will be initially generated from the Default Profile on the server running Terminal Services.

The only option on this property page that is not available from the Profile property page is the check box Deny This User Permissions To Log On To Any Terminal Server. Selecting this check box does exactly what it sounds like. If you have a user that you don't want to use Terminal Services at all, select this option.

FIGURE 6.17
Terminal Services
property page

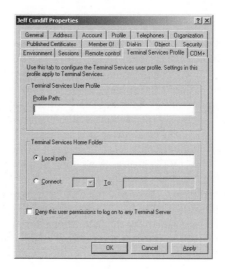

InetOrgPerson Account

The InetOrgPerson account can take the place of a user account within Active Directory. The biggest advantage to using an InetOrgPerson account over a user account is the interoperability with other directory services that the InetOrgPerson account gives you. If you take a look at other directory services, such as Novell's eDirectory, you will find that they include the InetOrgPerson account type as well. Any time you need to have an account that will easily interoperate with other LDAP-based directory services, you should consider creating the user's account using this account type.

TIP   If you are lucky enough to be able to raise your directory service to the Windows Server 2003 Forest Functionality level, you can convert a user account to an InetOrgPerson account at any time, and vice versa.

If you look at the property pages that are available from the InetOrgPerson account, you will see several options that are very similar to the user account type. Figure 6.18 displays the object property page that shows that the account is an InetOrgPerson account.

FIGURE 6.18

InetOrgPerson account
object property page

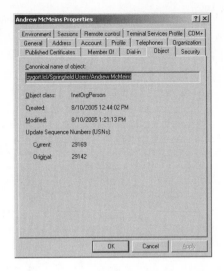

SECURITY GROUP

Security groups are used to organize accounts that need to have the same level of access to resources. Each security group has its own security identifier (SID) that is included with the user's SID when the user's access token is generated. After the access token is generated, the user will have the same level of access to resources as the other members of the group. Because the user's access token is only generated when the user logs on, whenever a user is added or removed from a security group, the user will have to log off and log back on for the new group membership to take effect.

Security groups have several property pages that you can configure. Starting with Figure 6.19, you will note that just like any other account type that we have discussed, groups have names that help an administrator identify them when they are managing their environment, as well as users when they are accessing them for use in applications such as Microsoft Exchange Server, which uses groups as distribution lists. The name that you can alter here is the pre–Windows 2000 name, or NetBIOS name that is used with older operating systems such as Windows 98 and Windows NT. Other options on this property page include the group type and group scope options. You are able to change the group type at any time. Note, however, that when you change a security group to a distribution group, the group will lose its SID and will no longer have the rights and permissions that had been assigned to the group. If you are going to change the group to a distribution group, check to make sure that all the users who are members of the group no longer need access to the resources, or that they no longer need to perform the functions granted to them through the group. If they do need to have their rights and permissions preserved, you should reconsider changing the group type.

There are specific rules about the types of accounts that can populate each of the group scopes, and the rules change depending on the functional level of the domain. Table 6.3 defines the group membership rules.

FIGURE 6.19
General property page
of a security group

TABLE 6.3: Group Membership rules

GROUP SCOPE	WINDOWS 2000 MIXED	WINDOWS 2000 NATIVE/2003
Domain Local	User accounts and global groups from any domain in the forest	Universal groups; user accounts and global groups from any domain in the forest; domain-local groups from the same domain
Global Groups	User accounts from the same domain	User accounts and global groups from the same domain
Universal Groups	Do not exist within Windows 2000 mixed mode	Universal groups; user accounts and global groups from any domain in the forest

The group scope can also be changed, but you will need to understand the limitations of changing the scope. The functional level the domain is in will determine what changes you can make. For instance, if your domain is still in the Windows 2000 mixed mode, you will not be able to change a global group to a domain-local group if the global group is a member of any domain-local groups. This is due to the fact that a domain-local group cannot be nested within another domain-local group in mixed mode. Once you raise the functional level of the domain to Windows 2000 Native mode or higher, you will be able to perform this change since domain-local groups are allowed to be nested within other domain-local groups.

Universal groups cannot be changed to any other group scope if the universal group contains another universal group as a member. If you need to change the scope of a universal group, you will need to make sure that you have removed any nested universal groups from the membership list. That is the only restriction imposed by the universal group.

As mentioned earlier, a global group can be converted to a domain-local group as long as the global group is not a member of any other domain-local groups, unless the domain functional level is in Windows 2000 native mode or Windows Server 2003 functional level. There is another limitation to global groups, however. If the global group is nested within another global group, you will not be able to convert the global group to a universal group. This is due to the fact that a universal group cannot be a member of a global group.

Domain-local groups can be converted to either a global group or universal group. The only caveat is that the domain-local group cannot have another domain-local group as a member.

The second tab, Members, allows you to view the accounts that are members of the group. As you can see in Figure 6.20, there isn't a lot you can do from this tab with the exception of adding and removing accounts. A handy feature is built in to this property page; if you double-click on any groups that are members of this group, it will take you to the group membership of the included group. You can do the same thing with user accounts and have the user account properties appear.

The Member Of property page, shown in Figure 6.21, displays the group nesting that has been configured. As previously mentioned, you can nest groups based on the functional level of the domain. Just like the Members property page, it looks like the only thing you can do from the Member Of property page is add or remove accounts, but you can double-click on a member group and trace all the group memberships back to the first group in the group nesting line.

The Managed By property page, shown in Figure 6.22, allows you to define who is responsible for maintaining the group. This property page contains four options: the Change, Properties, and Clear buttons and the Manager Can Update Membership List check box. When you want to define the manager of the group, you can click the Change button, which brings up a dialog box that allows you to define the manager. Once you have defined the manager, click the Properties button to view and change the account's properties, much like you could do if you right-clicked on the user's account. You will notice that there are some fields from the manager's properties appearing on this property page. They are populated from the information that has been added to the user's properties. To change them, you will need to click the Properties button and make the changes. To remove the manager, click the clear button.

FIGURE 6.20

Members property page

FIGURE 6.21
Member Of
property page

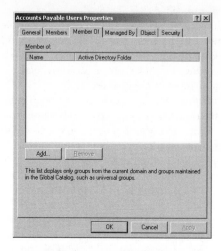

FIGURE 6.22
Managed By
property page

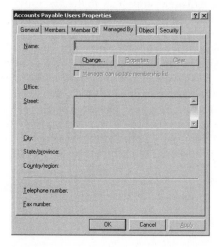

The Manager Can Update Membership List check box allows you to delegate some administrative control over the membership of the group. When you define the manager, you can select the check box to grant the manager the ability to modify the accounts on the Members property page. Where you will find this the most useful, however, is when you have distribution groups that have been mail-enabled for use with Exchange Server.

COMPUTER

Computers that become members of your domain need a computer account within Active Directory. These computer accounts are then used for the computer to have access to resources. Each computer account will be known by two different names: the host name and the NetBIOS name, sometimes referred to as the pre–Windows 2000 name.

If you look at the tabs that are available from the computer properties, you will see several options you can work with. Figure 6.23 shows the General properties page, which has the computer names listed along with the computer role.

The Operating System property page, shown in Figure 6.24, shows the operating system name, the version of the operating system that is installed, and the service pack that is currently installed.

To view the groups that the computer is currently a member of, select the Member Of property page. This property page, shown in Figure 6.25, allows you to add and remove the computer account to and from groups just as you would a user account.

FIGURE 6.23

General property page
for a computer account

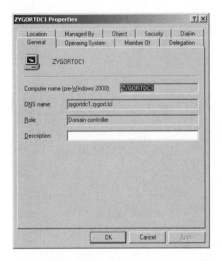

FIGURE 6.24

Operating System
property page

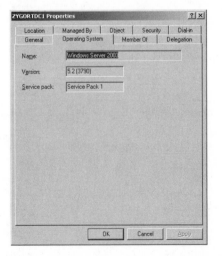

The Delegation property page appears for domain controller by default because they are used in authentication of accounts and need to access other services on behalf of other computers as well as users. This property page, shown in Figure 6.26, works the same way as the Delegation property page for a user account.

You can define the Active Directory location for a computer within the Location property page as shown in Figure 6.27. This allows you to specify where within Active Directory the computer account is located and acts as the default location specifier for any printers that are installed on the computer.

FIGURE 6.25
Member Of
property page

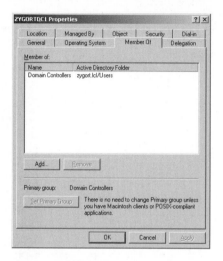

FIGURE 6.26
Delegation
property page

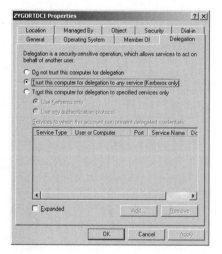

The Managed By property page simply identifies who is responsible for maintaining the computer account. Some organizations use this property page, shown in Figure 6.28, to identify the user who "owns," or is responsible for maintaining, the computer itself, not the account in Active Directory.

Finally, the Dial-in property page, shown in Figure 6.29, controls the computer account's ability to gain access using a remote access session. The computer account can be used to authenticate to a RAS server in the same manner that a user account can. The settings on this property page work the same way as those shown on a user account.

FIGURE 6.27
Location property page

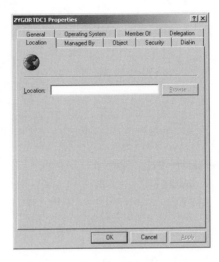

FIGURE 6.28
Managed By
property page

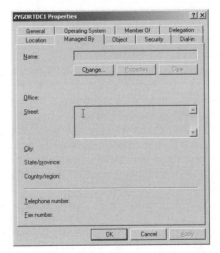

FIGURE 6.29

Dial-in property page

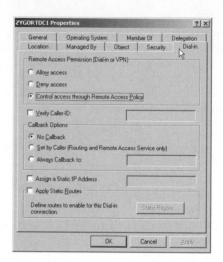

Nonsecurity Principle Accounts

There are times when you will want to represent people and groups within Active Directory even though they will not need to have access to any of your resources. There are two types of accounts that you can create that are not considered security principles: contacts and distribution groups. Both of these accounts are used primarily with the Microsoft Exchange Server e-mail server.

CONTACT

Contacts accounts do not have access to resources in your domain, but are instead used as an identifier for accounts that you want to catalog information on within Active Directory. The most common use for a contact account is e-mail. When Exchange is used within your Active Directory infrastructure, you can mail-enable contacts. Doing so will assign several new attributes to the account and allows the account to be shown in the Global Address List and any other address lists that you have configured. By mail-enabling a contact, you allow your Exchange users to easily choose the account that they want to e-mail from their contacts instead of having to type in the user's e-mail address each time.

As mentioned, the contact accounts will not have access to any of your domain resources. If you want to give a person access to domain resources you will have to configure a user account. However, if all you want is an object that will identify a person and it is not necessary for that individual to use any of the resources that you administer, you can create the contact account and populate the attributes.

The General property page, shown in Figure 6.30, contains attributes that are similar to those on the user account's General property page.

In fact, all of the property pages of a contact object look surprisingly similar to those of a user account. As with a user account, the information on the Address, Telephones, and Organization property pages is used primarily to further identify the contact.

FIGURE 6.30
General property page
for a contact object

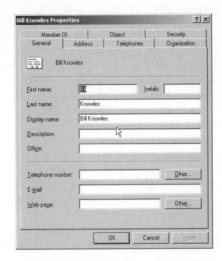

The one property page that seems to be a little out of place is the Member Of property page. As we mentioned, a contact does not have the ability to access resources due to the lack of a SID. So why would you need to add a contact to a group if the contact cannot be used to grant someone access to resources? Within an Active Directory environment, groups can be used as distribution lists. Any contact that has been mail-enabled can be added to a group and can therefore become a member of an e-mail distribution list.

DISTRIBUTION GROUP

As with the contact, distribution groups are used primarily with Exchange e-mail servers. Because distribution groups are not security principles, they do not have to be evaluated during a user's logon. If you are creating a group for the sole purpose of being used as a distribution list for e-mail, you should create a distribution group instead of a security group. The property pages for a distribution group are the same as you will find within a security group.

Utilities

Instead of restricting administrators to one tool, Microsoft offers several methods you can use to create and manipulate accounts. As far as graphical tools are concerned, the Active Directory Users and Computers snap-in is installed on domain controllers when they are promoted, by installing the Admin Pack, or registering the `dsa.dll` dynamic link library The command-line utilities are also added to a domain controller when it is promoted, but can be included on a workstation by installing the Admin Pack. To install the Admin Pack, run the adminpak.msi file from the Windows Server 2003 CD or from a network share. You can find this file in the i386 directory.

Active Directory Users and Computers

Active Directory Users and Computers (ADU&C) is the primary tool of choice for most administrators when they want to work with domain-based accounts. This utility is another MMC snap-in that can be added to any Windows 2000/XP/2003 system as long as the appropriate libraries are installed and registered. During the promotion to a domain controller, the ADU&C link is added to the domain controller's Administrative Tools, and you can also install it by running the adminpak.msi file that is found in the I386 directory of the Windows Server 2003 installation CD. Once added to the system, you will find that the link beneath the Administrative Tools menu will bring up the stand-alone version of ADU&C, but you can also add ADU&C to any MMC that you create. So if you want to have your own customized administrative console that holds several different snap-ins that you use on a regular basis, you can add it to your collection of tools.

Once it's opened, you will see a view that looks much like Figure 6.31. Your domain will be listed within the containers pane along with a container called Saved Queries. You can double-click the domain to view the containers and organizational units (OUs). Figure 6.32 shows the view once you have expanded the domain to shows these additional containers. For the most part this is the view that you will probably use throughout your administrative lifetime, but there is more to this tool than meets the eye. If you click the View menu at the top of the MMC, you have the option to control how the ADU&C snap-in looks and works. The Advanced Mode option allows you to see all the containers that are part of ADU&C, and the Users And Computers As Containers option allows you to view the additional objects that are part of the object not normally considered to be containers.

FIGURE 6.31
Default view of Active
Directory Users and
Computers

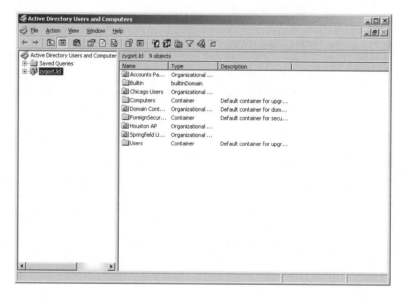

ADVANCED MODE

Advanced mode gives you a little more information about the objects that appear within ADU&C. Figure 6.33 shows the ADU&C containers that become available once you select this option. If you take a look at Figure 6.34, which displays the normal view of user account properties, and compare the property pages that are available when in Advanced mode, shown in Figure 6.35, you will notice that some additional property pages become available.

FIGURE 6.32
Expanded view of Active Directory Users and Computers

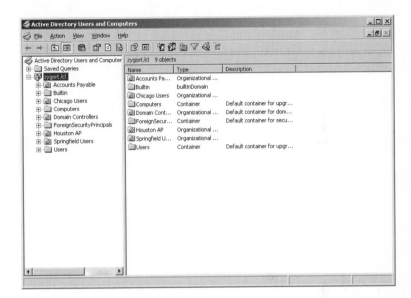

FIGURE 6.33
Additional containers become available in Advanced mode.

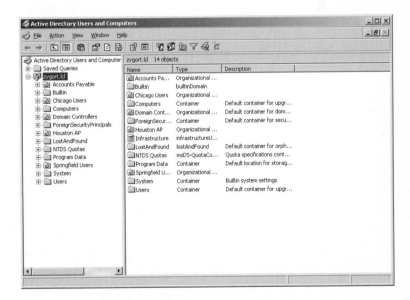

FIGURE 6.34
Normal view of
a user account

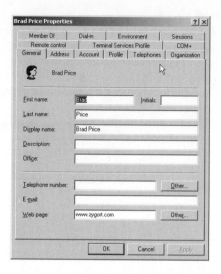

FIGURE 6.35
Advanced view
of a user account

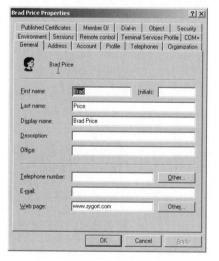

Notice that a container named Lost And Found is available when you use Advanced mode. This container holds objects that have been orphaned when the container they are a member of is deleted when they are being created or moved into the container. How does that happen? Remember that Active Directory is a multimaster replication model. Two administrators can perform administrative duties, each on a different domain controller. If one administrator were to delete an OU on DC1 while another administrator is creating an account on DC2, when replication occurs between the two systems, the OU will be deleted, and since the user account has nowhere to be created during replication, the account is created in Lost And Found. You may want to periodically check this container to make sure that there are no orphaned accounts lying around.

USERS GROUPS AND COMPUTERS AS CONTAINERS

There are times when you may want to see the objects that are associated with accounts. One example would be the printer objects that are associated with computer accounts. From the normal view of ADU&C, these objects do not show up, so you will have to use another method to view the information.

Under the View menu in ADU&C, you will find the menu item Users, Groups And Computers As Containers. Selecting this menu item will alter the information that is displayed so that each of the account types will show the objects associated with them. Normally, if you were to click on an OU, you would see each of the objects contained within that OU appearing in the details pane on the left side of the MMC console. If you select Users, Groups And Computers As Containers, each of the account objects appear in the navigation pane in the MMC, and the objects that are associated with them appear in the details pane. Figure 6.36 shows the appearance of the accounts once Users, Computers And Groups As Containers is selected.

QUERIES

In small organizations, you can usually open ADU&C, take a look at the accounts, and find exactly what you need to work with without too much trouble. Medium-sized and large organizations are another matter altogether. Finding a user account in the directory can be a time-consuming chore. Finding accounts that meet specific requirements can seem nearly impossible.

Microsoft has added in a handy node to the ADU&C interface called the Queries node. This node allows you to create queries that you commonly issue. It will also save queries that will help you cut down on some of your administrative chores. For instance, let's say that you wanted to find out how many of your user accounts were configured so that their passwords will not expire. You could create a simple query that would then return the results to you within the ADU&C snap-in. When you first open the Queries node, you will notice that there are no predefined queries. Most queries are very easy to create, and you can even create some very complex queries once you become more familiar with LDAP syntax.

FIGURE 6.36
Users, Computers And Groups As Containers

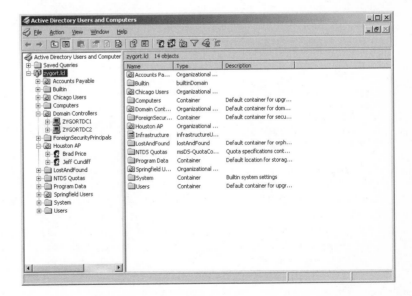

To create a query, start by right-clicking the Queries node and selecting New Query. This presents you with the New Query creation utility, as shown in Figure 6.37. This utility allows you to create some common queries as well as generate some very complex queries. The easiest of the queries to create include finding accounts based on the account name or description or the attributes that are defined. Once you define the query name, you can click the Define Query button to open the Find Common Queries dialog box.

Figure 6.38 shows the options on the Users tab of the query utility when the Common Query option is used. Notice that two check boxes are available that allow you to quickly create a query that will display accounts that do not have passwords that expire and disabled accounts. Figure 6.39 shows the query that is generated from selecting the Accounts With Non-expiring Passwords check box.

If you select the Computers or the Groups tab, you will see options identical to those on the Users tab, except that the Non-expiring Passwords check box is not available on either of these two tabs and the Disabled Accounts check box does not appear on the Groups tab.

If you pull down the query types, you will see that other options are available to you if you don't like the limitations set in the Common Queries. If you select the Users, Computers And Groups option, you will have the ability to create a query that can search based on any of the attributes within the accounts. You can make these queries as simple or as complex as necessary to fit your needs. If you want to create a query that shows you every user who is a member of the Accounts Payable department, you can select the Advanced tab and click the Field button to view the options, as shown in Figure 6.40.

FIGURE 6.37
New Query creation
utility

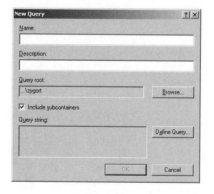

FIGURE 6.38
Common Query options

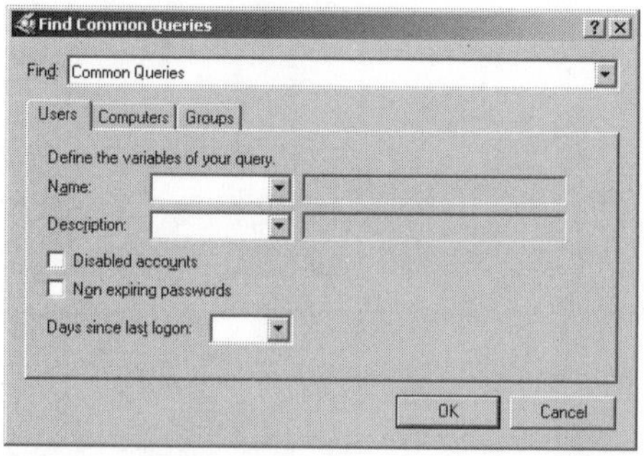

FIGURE 6.39
Query definition

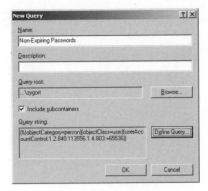

FIGURE 6.40
Account types for which
you can define queries

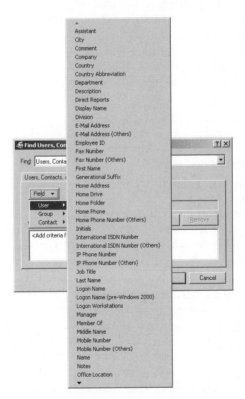

When you hover the mouse over the account type, such as User, another menu appears with all the available attributes that you can include in your query. This menu scrolls so that you can review the entire list to see all the attributes available. Once you select Department, you then define how you want to search. The next pull-down list, shown in Figure 6.41, allows you to set the conditions for the query. Six options are normally available:

FIGURE 6.41

Conditions for the query

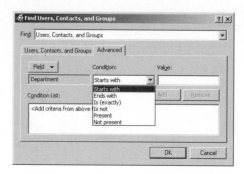

Starts With   Choosing Starts With allows you to define the initial characters of a string that you want to search for. If you wanted to include all the users from the Accounts Payable and Accounts Receivable departments, you can enter **Accounts** and both departments would be included in the results.

Ends With   The Ends With option is just the opposite of Starts With. You enter the characters at the end of the string so that you can search for specific information. If you want to include only the users who have Payable as the last part of the field, you choose Ends With and then type **Payable** in the box.

Is (Exactly)   The Is (Exactly) option allows you to completely define the string that you want to base the query on. For example, you can enter **Accounts Payable** in the text box after selecting the Is (Exactly) option and only those accounts that have the exact phrase entered will be returned in the results.

Is Not   This is pretty much the opposite of the Is (Exactly) option. When using the Is Not option, you enter the exact word or phrase that you do *not* want results returned from. For this option, if you want to find all the accounts that are not part of the Marketing department, you choose User ➤ Department, pull down the option for Is Not, and then type **Marketing**. The query returns all the user accounts that are not members of the Marketing department.

Present   When you use the Present option, you are specifying that you do not care what is populated in the field you have chosen and that you only want results returned for accounts that have data entered in the attribute. While not as popular as the Not Present option, you may still use this option to check for accounts that have data entered into attributes. For example, you may want to know which accounts have data entered into the Custom Attribute 10 field. When building the query, if you choose User ➤ Custom Attribute 10 and then select Present from the pull-down list, all the appropriate accounts appear when you run the query.

Not Present   The most popular reason for using the Not Present option is to discover the accounts that do not have data in attributes that you normally populate. Remember, Active Directory searches and queries are only as good as the data that is populated in the accounts. If accounts are created and the attributes are not populated according to your standards and practices, you have the ability to find accounts that are missing critical information by using this query option. For example, if you want to find all the users that do not have their Manager attribute populated, you select User ➤ Manager and then pull down the option for Not Present. Once you run this query, you see all the user accounts with missing Manager attribute information.

You are allowed to enter as many query options as you would like. If you want to create a query that displays all the user accounts that are members of the Accounts Payable department and their manager is Tom Timmons, you can define the first criterion by selecting the options, adding the query option, and then defining the second criterion and adding it to the list, as shown in Figure 6.42. There is a limitation to this, however. All the criteria that you add are considered a logical And. You do not have the option to select a Not or an Or operator. If you want to define a query that allows you to specify that the results are returned based on one set of criteria or another, you have to write your own query to do so.

To write your own query statement, first select Custom Search from the query types pull-down list. Of course, at this point you do not have the luxury of simply choosing a few options and filling in a few fields in order to generate a query—you will need to know LDAP syntax. You can begin by creating a query using the graphical tools and then copy and paste the query statement into the custom query dialog box. As shown in Figure 6.43, each query that you create will appear in the Query String dialog box for the query. You can highlight the query, right-click it, and then click Copy. Then open the Custom Search option from the query types pull-down list and paste in the query. You then have the ability to make changes to the query. Note that if you make a mistake in the query, it will not process or return results to you.

FIGURE 6.42

Multiple query options

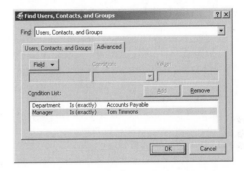

FIGURE 6.43

Query string

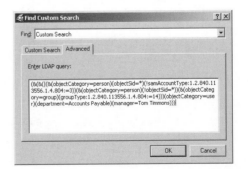

MANAGING ACCOUNTS

When it comes to time-consuming administrative tasks, managing accounts has to be right at the top of the list. And if you ask most administrators, they will tell you that they tire of the administrative overhead that is involved with this task. But, as I have heard one administrator say, "Users are the bane of my existence, but if it weren't for users, I wouldn't have this job." Between the creation and deletion of an account, you will find yourself making some type of changes to it during its lifetime.

So what is involved with account administration? The list includes creating, deleting, adding accounts to groups, modifying account properties, unlocking locked accounts, resetting account passwords, and much more. In the following sections we look at ways to manage user, group, and computer accounts.

Managing Users

Most administrators and users who have been delegated administrative control over user accounts will use Active Directory Users and Computers to manage and manipulate accounts. Others swear by the command-line utilities, but using the graphical utilities has become a natural extension to the Windows interface.

Before someone can access resources in your organization, they need to have a user account created for them. The user account is responsible for controlling access to resources and granting rights to perform tasks in the organization. Once you determine that you want to create a user account for someone, you have a couple of options at your disposal. Most administrators use Active Directory Users and Computers to create the account, but you could just as easily have a script written that will allow you to create the account from outside the built-in Active Directory administrative tools.

Whenever you are preparing to create an account, you should take into consideration where you will create the account. Active Directory has different containers that can hold a user account. Decide where the user account needs to be located, and then right-click on the container and select New➢ User from the context menu. This brings up the dialog box where you can enter the user's identifying information, as shown in Figure 6.44. As you enter the user's first name, middle initial, and last name, the display name is generated for you. You need to provide the username for the user according to your organization's naming conventions.

FIGURE 6.44
Add User dialog box

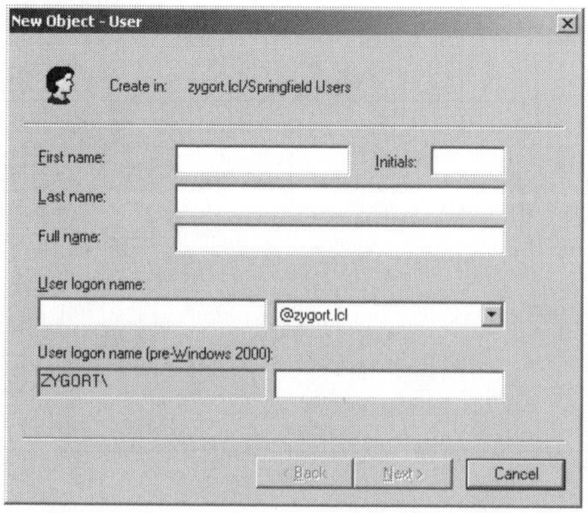

Notice that the username is just part of the user principle name (UPN). If you take the default options, the UPN consists of the username and the forest root name in what appears to be an e-mail address. If you wanted to, you could have the user's e-mail address and their UPN use the same format, but then you are running the risk of making your users' logon available to anyone who knows what their e-mail address is. This can be considered a security risk.

So what are all the options that you have available to you when managing a user account? As you probably have already deduced, a user account has several attributes that you can work with to help identify the person the account represents. Everything from the user's name to the cell phone used to the person's manager can be entered in the account properties. As we move forward in this section, we'll look at the properties available in the user account, and discuss ways to manipulate those properties. Along the way, we'll also point out the command-line options that are available for managing user accounts.

NOTE   Everything we mention in this section is also accessible using various scripting methods. For more information on scripting access to Active Directory, check out the last three chapters of this book as they concentrate on managing Active Directory through scripting.

Let's first take a look at the options available from the context menu when you right-click on a user account in Active Directory Users and Computers. Figure 6.45 shows the menu that appears when you do not have any other applications altering the default options. Applications such as the Exchange System Manager snap-in alter the options. When added, the Exchange Tasks menu item becomes available, which allows you to manipulate the user's Exchange configuration.

Let's start with the options that you will need to use the most. First is Reset Password, which does exactly what the name suggests: It allows an administrator to change the password on an account. As you can see in Figure 6.46, not only do you have the choice of changing the user's password, but you can also specify whether the user needs to change their password after they successfully log on after your password reset.

FIGURE 6.45
The default
context menu

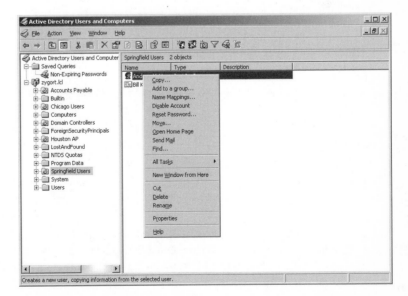

FIGURE 6.46
Password Reset
dialog box

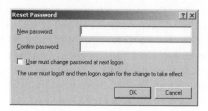

The Copy option lets you copy the current user object settings to a new user object. Not all the object properties will copy over, but those that are not specific to an individual user will copy over. For instance, the username and password will not copy over to the new account, but the group membership will copy over.

If you right-click on an active account, you will see an option called Disable Account. If the account is disabled, you see an option for enabling the account. This is a fast and easy way to make sure you can either enable or disable an account without having to go into the account properties and selecting or deselecting the check box on the Account property page.

Another option on the context menu is Move. If you come from a Windows 2000 Active Directory environment, this is the only option you have to move an account from one OU to another. Figure 6.47 shows the dialog box that appears when you choose this option. To move the account, all you have to do is select the OU or container in which you want to place the account and click OK. For any Windows 2003 or later domain environment, you can simply drag and drop the account to any OU or container you want.

NOTE   You can only move accounts into OUs or containers within the same domain using this option. If you need to move an account to a location in another domain, you need to use another utility, such as the Active Directory Migration Tool (ADMT).

The final two options that appear in the top portion of the context menu are Open Home Page and Send Email. These two options perform these two actions depending on whether the account has a default web page or e-mail address associated with it.

FIGURE 6.47
Move dialog box

If you hover the mouse pointer over the All Tasks menu item, you will see the same options that appear at the top of the context menu, but two other options are available from here as well: Resultant Set Of Policy (Planning) and Resultant Set Of Policy (Logging). If you have been granted the ability to run these two wizards (which is granted either from the Group Policy Management Console or the object's Security property page), you can check to see what Group Policy Objects (GPOs) were applied to the user or the user's computer the last time the user logged in, or you can see what GPOs will be applied to a user if you move that user to another location within Active Directory.

NOTE For more information on using the Resultant Set of Policy wizards, see Chapter 9, "Managing Group Policy."

Managing Groups

As shown in Figure 6.48, you don't get many options to work with when you right-click a group. Send Mail is the only option that appears at the top of the context menu. If the group has been assigned an e-mail address, you will be able to open your default e-mail application from here and compose a message to be sent to the members of the group. Of course, members will receive the e-mail only if they have also been mail-enabled.

Managing Computers

Computer accounts act similar to user accounts. They are needed in order to authenticate the computer account in the domain and allow access to resources in that domain. The context menu for a computer account does not have as many options as you would find with a user account, but there are still some important and useful options. Figure 6.49 shows the available options.

The first option is Reset Account. If you select this option, the account's password is reset and you will need to add the computer account back into the domain in order for a new password to be generated between the computer and Active Directory.

The second option is Move, which works the same way as the Move option under a user object's context menu. And just as with a user account, the drag-and-drop functionality that has been added to Active Directory Users and Computers is easy and intuitive to use.

FIGURE 6.48
Group context menu

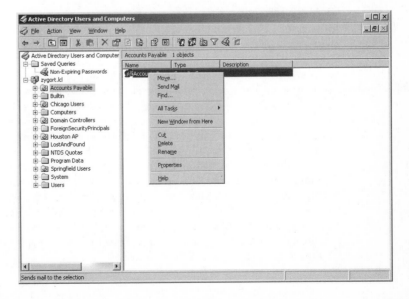

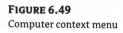

FIGURE 6.49
Computer context menu

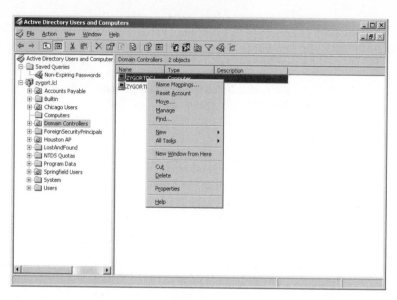

The final option is Manage. This is a very handy option to have available to an administrator. Once you locate the computer that you want to work with, you can choose Manage from the context menu and the Computer Management console will appear. Although you could do the same thing by opening the Computer Management console directly and then choosing which computer you would like to manage, if you are already within Active Directory Users and Computers, or if you cannot remember the full name of the computer that you want to manage, you have the ability to start the management console from here.

CREATING TASKPADS

As you will see in Chapter 9, you can delegate rights and permissions to users so that they can perform actions in Active Directory even if they are not a member of any of the default administrative groups. This makes it easy for the domain owners and domain administrators to delegate administrative control to other users without giving those other users too much power in the domain. For example, if you want to give help desk users the ability to change passwords for users but you do not want them to have the ability to change other user properties, such as group membership or address and phone attributes, you can give them just that amount of power.

Even if you do give a user some level of administrative control, they need to have an interface in which to perform their functions. By copying the dsadmin.dll file from a Windows Server 2003 domain controller, or extracting the file from the adminpak.msi file on the Windows Server 2003 CD into the system32 directory on the user's computer, you could give them access to the snap-in required for the taskpad. You could register the dynamic link library (DLL) that is used for Active Directory Users and Computers entering **regsvr32 dsadmin.dll** at a command prompt and then add the snap-in to an MMC, but then you would need to train each of the users on performing their functions in the ADU&C interface, and probably have to explain why they cannot use many of the functions that they find in the interface.

Instead, you can create a taskpad that can be used for specific tasks. A taskpad is a web-based interface that allows you to perform the same tasks that you can from in a full version of a snap-in, but you can tailor it to your own needs, having it display only the functions you want to use. In our example of the help desk employee who needs to have the ability to change user's passwords, you could create a taskpad that gives the employee that ability but nothing else from the ADU&C snap-in.

You still need to register the DLL on the computer where the user will be performing their duties. Other than that, there is nothing that you have to specifically do to the user's computer. You do need to create the taskpad, however. The process is very simple, but you can get sophisticated with task-pads if you want. The first thing you need to do is add the snap-in that is normally used to perform the administrative task that is going to be performed in the taskpad. Note that the default utilities that are added to the Administrative Tools will not allow you to create taskpads from them.

Once you've added the snap-in, navigate to the node where you would normally perform the function. For our example, you navigate to an OU that contains user accounts. Figure 6.50 shows the context menu that appears when you right-click the OU. Choosing Create Taskpad View from the menu brings you to a wizard that is used to create the taskpad. When the wizard starts, you are allowed to define how the taskpad will be identified and used. On the last page of this wizard is a prompt to launch another wizard that allows you to define the tasks that can be performed in the taskpad.

This second wizard starts by asking what the task is you are defining. You have the options Menu Command, Script, or Navigation. A menu command is any command that is available from the context menu of an object. If you select the Script option, you can define a command or script that will run when you select the option in the taskpad. Selecting the option Navigation allows you to create a navigation link so that you can allow that user of the taskpad to jump to a predefined node.

For our example we will create a simple taskpad that allows us to change passwords for users. We are going to assume that the help desk personnel will have the ability to change passwords for users in two different OUs, Chicago Users and Springfield Users. Once the wizard starts, we define the taskpad appearance by following the wizard as shown in Figures 6.51 through 6.55.

FIGURE 6.50

Context menu with the option to create a taskpad

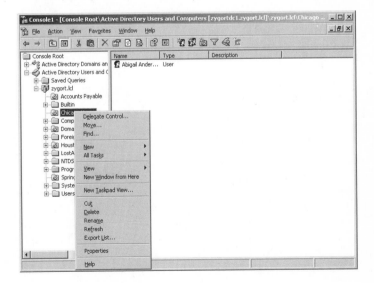

FIGURE 6.51
Start of taskpad wizard

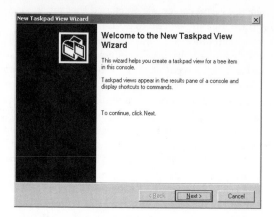

FIGURE 6.52
Choosing the look
of the taskpad

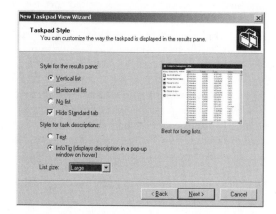

FIGURE 6.53
Selecting the scope
of the taskpad

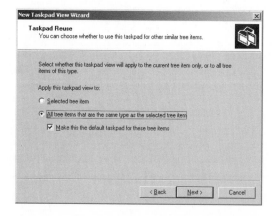

FIGURE 6.54

Naming the taskpad

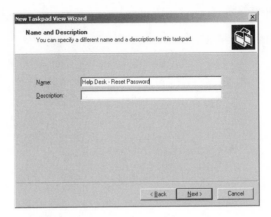

FIGURE 6.55

Choosing to add new
tasks using the tasks
wizard

Once you reach the final page of the wizard, you can start the second wizard to create the individual tasks. The first task we will create is the Navigation option. Selecting the Navigation radio button and clicking Next takes you to the wizard page shown in Figure 6.56. When creating a navigation link, make sure that you have added the OUs or containers that you will reference to the Favorites list of the MMC. The wizard prompts you for the favorites link you want to use, as shown in Figure 6.57, and then asks you for a name to be associated with the link. You also have the opportunity to choose an icon to be used next to the link, as shown in Figure 6.58. For each task you add, you are prompted to add another task, as shown in Figure 6.59.

After the navigation task is finished, you define the change password task. This is going to be a menu command, so select that radio button from the list. Figure 6.60 displays the available menu options. There are two different menu sets that you can work with: the container options or the details option. If you choose the container options, you will see all the menu items.

FIGURE 6.56
Selecting the
Navigation option

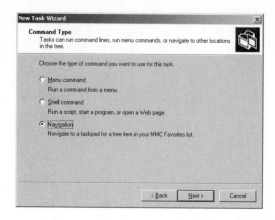

FIGURE 6.57
Selecting a favorite
to link to

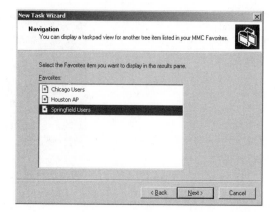

FIGURE 6.58
Choosing an icon

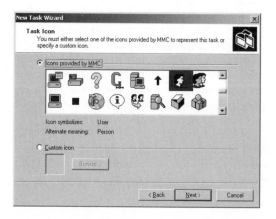

FIGURE 6.59
Choosing to create
another task

FIGURE 6.60
Menu command options

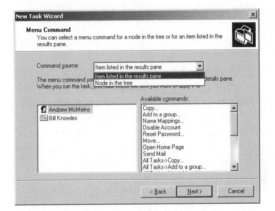

Choosing the Reset Password option and clicking Next takes you to a screen that allows you to name the task. As with the navigation tasks we added, you are presented with a screen that allows you to add an icon to the task link. Once you've added tasks to the taskpad, you will have a nice-looking administrative view that allows you to limit the functions that can be performed by a user. Figure 6.61 shows the taskpad. Notice the task links for navigation and resetting passwords on the left side of the taskpad.

Command-Line Utilities

If you like typing your commands, or you would like to script the administrative control of accounts, command-line utilities have been included for you to manipulate the Active Directory–based accounts. There are limitations to the Active Directory Users and Computers interface. If you want to create several accounts, you have to right-click on the container or OU where you wish to create the account, and as shown in the Active Directory Users and Computers section, you can only enter the user's authentication information in the wizard that appears. You then have to find the account you just created, right-click the account, choose Properties, and then add any additional attributes for the account.

FIGURE 6.61
Navigating the taskpad

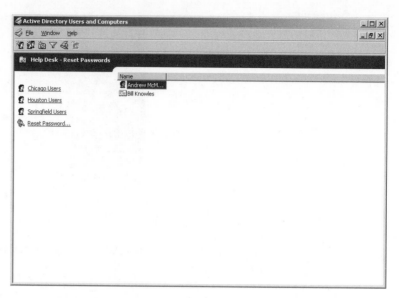

Another benefit to these utilities is that they can be used in a batch file or script. The batch file can then be altered for new accounts and scripts can be written to allow for a prompt to appear. The administrator running the script could then enter the data when prompted.

Whether you are typing commands at the command line or including them in a script, you must have the appropriate rights to create the account. By default, any person who logs in with an account who is a member of the Administrators, Domain Admins, Enterprise Admins, or Account Admins groups, or who logs on using the Administrator account will be able to use any of these utilities. You can also delegate the right to create object types in Active Directory. If the account that you are logged in with has been delegated the ability to create an account, you could use these utilities to create an account of that account type.

NOTE For more information on delegating administrative access to nonadministrator accounts, see Chapter 8, "Managing Organizational Units."

DSADD

The DSAdd utility can be used to create accounts in Active Directory. When using DSAdd, you have the option to populate any of the attributes that are available from the account's properties when using Active Directory Users and Computers. The advantage to using DSAdd is that you can populate the attributes when the account is being created instead of modifying the account after it already exists in the directory service.

Any of the account types can be created when using DSAdd. If you take a look at the syntax of the command in Figure 6.62, you will notice the account options you have if you enter **dsadd /?** at the command prompt. If you want to further drill down and look at the options for any of the account types, such as a user account, you can enter **dsadd -user /?** at the command prompt and receive the results shown in Figure 6.63.

FIGURE 6.62

Syntax for the
DSAdd utility

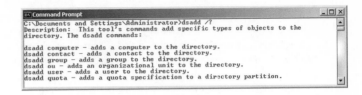

```
Command Prompt                                                    _ | □ | X
C:\Documents and Settings\Administrator>dsadd /?
Description:  This tool's commands add specific types of objects to the
directory. The dsadd commands:

dsadd computer - adds a computer to the directory.
dsadd contact - adds a contact to the directory.
dsadd group - adds a group to the directory.
dsadd ou - adds an organizational unit to the directory.
dsadd user - adds a user to the directory.
dsadd quota - adds a quota specification to a directory partition.
```

FIGURE 6.63

Syntax when using
DSAdd to create a
user account

```
Command Prompt                                                    _ | □ | X
C:\Documents and Settings\Administrator>dsadd user /?
Description:  Adds a user to the directory.
Syntax:    dsadd user <UserDN> [-samid <SAMName>] [-upn <UPN>] [-fn <FirstName>]
          [-mi <Initial>] [-ln <LastName>] [-display <DisplayName>]
          [-empid <EmployeeID>] [-pwd (<Password> | *)] [-desc <Description>]
          [-memberof <Group ...>] [-office <Office>] [-tel <Phone#>]
          [-email <Email>] [-hometel <HomePhone#>] [-pager <Pager#>]
          [-mobile <CellPhone#>] [-fax <Fax#>] [-iptel <IPPhone#>]
          [-webpg <WebPage>] [-title <Title>] [-dept <Department>]
          [-company <Company>] [-mgr <Manager>] [-hmdir <HomeDir>]
          [-hmdrv <DriveLtr:>] [-profile <ProfilePath>] [-loscr <ScriptPath>]
          [-mustchpwd {yes | no}] [-canchpwd {yes | no}]
          [-reversiblepwd {yes | no}] [-pwdneverexpires {yes | no}]
          [-acctexpires <NumDays>] [-disabled {yes | no}]
          [{-s <Server> | -d <Domain>}] [-u <UserName>]
          [-p {<Password> | *}] [-q] [{-uc | -uco | -uci}]

Parameters:

Value                         Description
<UserDN>                      Required. Distinguished name <DN> of user to add.
                              If the target object is omitted, it will be taken
                              from standard input <stdin>.
-samid <SAMName>              Set the SAM account name of user to <SAMName>.
                              If not specified, dsadd will attempt
                              to create SAM account name using up to
                              the first 20 characters from the
                              common name <CN> value of <UserDN>.
-upn <UPN>                    Set the upn value to <UPN>.
-fn <FirstName>               Set user first name to <FirstName>.
-mi <Initial>                 Set user middle initial to <Initial>.
-ln <LastName>                Set user last name to <LastName>.
-display <DisplayName>        Set user display name to <DisplayName>.
-empid <EmployeeID>           Set user employee ID to <EmployeeID>.
-pwd {<Password> | *}         Set user password to <Password>. If *, then you are
                              prompted for a password.
-desc <Description>           Set user description to <Description>.
-memberof <Group ...>         Make user a member of one or more groups <Group ...>
-office <Office>              Set user office location to <Office>.
-tel <Phone#>                 Set user telephone# to <Phone#>.
-email <Email>                Set user e-mail address to <Email>.
```

Notice in Figure 6.63 that you have a long list of attributes that you can take advantage of when using DSAdd. This means that as you create the user account, you can immediately populate the account attributes instead of having to go back later and enter them.

DSMod

If you already have an account created, you can use the DSMod utility to make changes to the account's attributes. This is an easy way to make changes to several accounts at once. For example, let's examine a company that has relocated part of its employees to another office building. When they move to the new location, you could assign someone to open all of the affected accounts using Active Directory Users and Computers and change the address attributes, or you could write a quick batch file that reads a list of user account names and then modifies the address attributes on those accounts. The second method might take a few minutes to write, but you could potentially save a lot of time and reduce the amount of typographical errors over changing the accounts manually. Figure 6.64 shows the syntax of the DSMod command when you enter **dsmod /?** at the command prompt.

DSQuery

Just as the name suggests, `DSQuery` allows you to locate accounts as well as other object types in Active Directory by issuing a command. Figure 6.65 shows the object types that you can search for using `DSQuery`. You can then find the syntax of each object type by retrieving the help on each object type; for example, type **dsquery user /?** to find the query options for a user account.

When you use `DSQuery`, you will get the results returned to you based on the query parameters. If you want to find all the users who have the name Rebecca, you can issue the command **dsquery user -name Rebecca***. With the asterisk acting as a wildcard, all of the user accounts who have the first name Rebecca will appear on the screen. If you want to create a file from the results, you could enter **dsquery user -name Rebecca* > *d:\queryresultspath\queryfile.txt*** where *d:* is the drive where you want to place the results, *queryresultspath* is the folder path, and *queryfile.txt* is the filename you want to use.

DSGet

`DSGet` will return attribute information when you specify an account as the target of the command. When issuing this command, you will need to know which attributes you want returned in the results. Figure 6.66 shows the syntax of the `DSGet` command used to display the user information.

FIGURE 6.64
DSMod syntax

```
C:\Documents and Settings\Administrator>dsmod /?
Description:  This dsmod command modifies existing objects in the directory.
The dsmod commands include:

dsmod computer - modifies an existing computer in the directory.
dsmod contact - modifies an existing contact in the directory.
dsmod group - modifies an existing group in the directory.
dsmod ou - modifies an existing organizational unit in the directory.
dsmod server - modifies an existing domain controller in the directory.
dsmod user - modifies an existing user in the directory.
dsmod quota - modifies an existing quota specification in the directory.
dsmod partition - modifies an existing quota specification in the directory.
```

FIGURE 6.65
Syntax for the `DSQuery` command

```
C:\Documents and Settings\Administrator>dsquery /?
Description: This tool's commands suite allow you to query the directory
according to specified criteria. Each of the following dsquery commands finds
objects of a specific object type, with the exception of dsquery *, which can
query for any type of object:

dsquery computer - finds computers in the directory.
dsquery contact - finds contacts in the directory.
dsquery subnet - finds subnets in the directory.
dsquery group - finds groups in the directory.
dsquery ou - finds organizational units in the directory.
dsquery site - finds sites in the directory.
dsquery server - finds domain controllers in the directory.
dsquery user - finds users in the directory.
dsquery quota - finds quota specifications in the directory.
dsquery partition - finds partitions in the directory.
dsquery * - finds any object in the directory by using a generic LDAP query.

For help on a specific command, type "dsquery <ObjectType> /?" where
<ObjectType> is one of the supported object types shown above.
For example, dsquery ou /?.

Remarks:
The dsquery commands help you find objects in the directory that match
a specified search criterion: the input to dsquery is a search criterion
and the output is a list of objects matching the search. To get the
properties of a specific object, use the dsget commands (dsget /?).

The results from a dsquery command can be piped as input to one of the other
directory service command-line tools, such as dsmod, dsget, dsrm or dsmove.

Commas that are not used as separators in distinguished names must be
escaped with the backslash ("\") character
(for example, "CN=Company\, Inc.,CN=Users,DC=microsoft,DC=com"). Backslashes
used in distinguished names must be escaped with a backslash (for example,
"CN=Sales\\ Latin America,OU=Distribution Lists,DC=microsoft,DC=com").
```

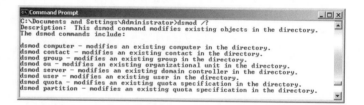

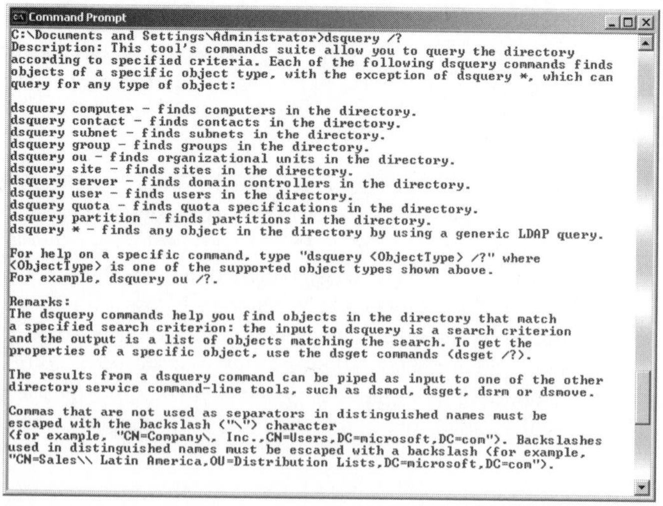

DSRM

If you wish to remove accounts, you can use the DSRm command. Figure 6.67 shows this command; note that there are few parameters for this command, but a couple do come in handy. The -noprompt switch puts the command in silent mode, deleting the objects without prompting first. The -subtree switch deletes the entire tree structure, including the tree level you specified in the command. If you want to leave the tree level that you included in the command but just delete the subtrees, you have the -exclude switch.

FIGURE 6.66

Syntax of the
DSGet command

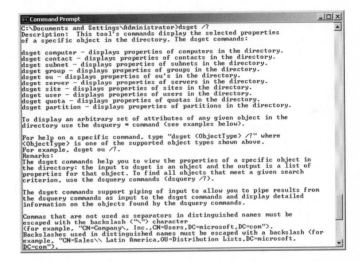

FIGURE 6.67

Syntax of the
DSRm command

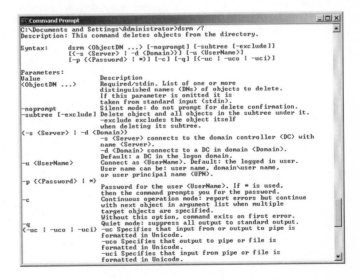

DSMOVE

DSMove is another utility that is pretty easy to figure out. To change the location in Active Directory, you can use this command and specify the new location for an existing object. The syntax of this command is shown in Figure 6.68. Note that during the move from one Active Directory location to another, you can also specify a new name for the object. This comes in especially handy when you already have an object with the same relative distinguished name in that directory location.

One of the benefits you will find with the directory service command-line utilities is its ability to send the results of command to one of the other utilities for processing. When you add the pipe symbol (|)between two commands, the results from the first will be used as input arguments for the second. For example, let's assume you are trying to move several users to an OU. You can create the OU either manually or by issuing the DSAdd command, and then use DSQuery to move the users to the new OU instead of moving them manually or using the DSMove command alone. For this example, let's move all of the users from the Accounts Payable OU to the new Houston AP OU that we have created. To do so, all you have to do is issue the following command:

```
dsquery -user "ou=Accounts Payable,dc=zygort,dc=lcl" | dsmove
➥-newparent "ou=Houston AP,dc=zygort,dc=lcl"
```

LDAP UTILITIES

Active Directory can be accessed by using LDAP commands and utilities that used LDAP-based access. Two utilities have been available since the first version of Active Directory with Windows 2000. With the arrival of the aforementioned directory service utilities that were introduced with Windows Server 2003, the two LDAP utilities seem to have lost popularity, but there are several organizations that still use them to some extent.

FIGURE 6.68
Syntax of the
DSMove command

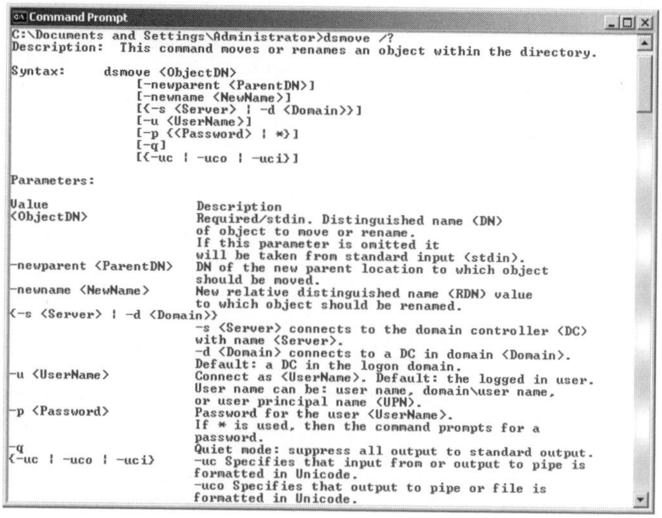

CSVDE

CSVDE is used to populate Active Directory from a comma-separated value file. If you already have a file that contains information about the user, group, or computer accounts that you want to use when populating Active Directory, you can quickly modify the file to fit the needs of CSVDE and then quickly import the data. You will find that this utility is most commonly used when a company is importing account information from an existing Exchange 5.5 implementation.

Each file that you want to import will need to be formatted correctly. For CSVDE, you will need to make sure that the import file has all of the attributes separated by commas. You will also need to make sure that the first line of the file is the header line, which defines each of the attributes that you are importing into the new accounts. Each account will have a separate line in the import file, and when imported, the Active Directory location and all of the attributes defined in the file will be used to create and define the account.

NOTE   For more information on the attributes available for use in the CSVDE import file, see Knowledge Base article 281563.

Once the file has been created and saved to a location where it can be accessed by the user who has permissions to create accounts in the Active Directory locations specified in the import file, all that is required to run the tool is to open a command line and enter

```
csvde -i -f file_location
```

When you specify the -i option, you are specifying that you are performing an import function. The -f specifies the filename is the next item in the command line. One other option is available, -k, which informs CSVDE that it needs to ignore errors that are generated from the import file and continue with the remaining entries in the file.

The limitation that you have with CSVDE is that it cannot be used to modify existing accounts. The only options available are exporting existing accounts to a file, or importing new accounts from a file. If you want to modify existing accounts, you will need to use a tool like LDIFDE.

LDIFDE

Like CSVDE, LDIFDE allows you to populate Active Directory with account information included in a file. The advantage to using LDIFDE over CSVDE is the ability to modify and delete entries in Active Directory. The file format is a little different also. CSVDE uses commas to separate the attributes; LDIFDE uses line breaks to separate the attributes.

DEFAULT FOLDER REDIRECTORS

When you initially install Active Directory, there are two containers that are used to hold user and computer accounts. If you open Active Directory Users and Computers, you will see these two containers directly beneath the domain node, as shown in Figure 6.69. You can tell immediately that these are containers instead of OUs by the icon used to represent them. An OU is shown by an icon that has the directory symbol in the center of a folder, whereas containers are simply shown as a folder.

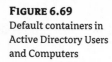

FIGURE 6.69

Default containers in
Active Directory Users
and Computers

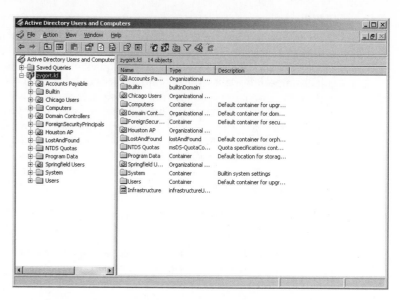

These two containers are used primarily for interoperability with Windows NT 4–based domains. When you upgrade Windows NT 4 domains, you upgrade the Primary Domain Controller first, and in doing so, the dcpromo utility moves all of the user and group accounts in the domain to the Users container, and the computer accounts are moved to the Computers container. Although this doesn't initially seem as if it should be a problem, you must remember that these are containers and not OUs.

Since containers are used for interoperability with Windows NT 4 domains, they cannot utilize group policies. OUs, on the other hand, were designed to be used with group policies. With that in mind, you probably realize that the only GPOs that can be applied to users or computers in Active Directory are those that are applied at the domain or site levels. Later, in Chapter 9, we are going to take a look at some of the reasons you want to link GPOs to OUs instead of at the domain or site level. If you do follow the reasons and suggestions that you find in Chapter 9, you will realize that you become very limited if you only have the options of linking at the domain or site level. OUs give you better control over how you apply the GPOs to users and computers.

Due to the fact that the Users and Computers containers are protected from deletion, you cannot remove these containers. You can, however, rename them and then create OUs to take their place. There are two utilities that you can use that will allow you to change the default location of users, computers, and computers when they are created. Once you run one or both of these utilities, whenever an account is created and a location for the account is not specified, the account will be created in the new default location that you specify.

So now you are probably asking yourself, "Why do I need to redirect where the users, groups, and computers are created if all I have to do is choose the OU where I would like to create the accounts?" It is true that you can simply right-click on any of the OUs in your domain and choose New and then select either User, Group, or Computer to create the account. If you are using a script to create the accounts, however, you may not have the luxury of specifying where the account is created. If that is the case, the default locations will be used. To change the default locations, use the following utilities.

redirusr

By default, the Users container is used as the default location for user and group accounts. In order to create a new OU that will take over as the new default location, you will need to use the `redirusr` utility. If the new OU will also be called Users, you should first rename the Users container to something else that fits the naming standards for your Active Directory implementation. You can then create a new OU named Users. Once you have the new OU created, you can redirect the creation of new accounts by opening a command prompt and using the following syntax:

```
%systemroot%\system32\redirusr container_distinguished_name
```

If you have created a new OU and named it Users, and the system files are installed in the WINNT folder on the D: drive, and the domain name is `zygort.lcl`, your command would look like the following:

```
d:\winnt\system32\redirusr ou=users,dc=zygort,dc=lcl
```

redircmp

By default, the Computers container is used as the default location for computer accounts, with the exception of domain controllers. In order to create a new OU that will take over as the new default location, you will need to use the `redircmp` utility. If the new OU will also be called Computers, you should first rename the Computers container to something else that fits the naming standards for your Active Directory implementation. You can then create a new OU named Computers. Once you have the new OU created, you can redirect the creation of new accounts by opening a command prompt and using the following syntax:

```
%systemroot%\system32\redircmp container_distinguished_name
```

If you have created a new OU and named it Computers in the `zygort.lcl` domain, and the system files are installed in the WINNT folder on the D: drive, your command would look like the following:

```
d:\winnt\system32\redircmp ou=computers,dc=zygort,dc=lcl
```

Coming Up Next

After looking at the ways to manage accounts, we are going to take a step forward and discuss the options that are available to you for managing access to Active Directory resources. There are different authentication mechanisms in place to help secure your Active Directory infrastructure, but you will need to know which methods to use depending on how users connect to your environment.

Chapter 7

Managing Access with Active Directory Services

Creating an Active Directory–based infrastructure is a good first step in controlling user access to resources within your organization. But even though you have Active Directory in place, it doesn't mean that gaining access to those resources is going to be easy for some of your users. Once you have planned out how you are going to implement Active Directory for your organization's users, you may still need to enable other user accounts to have access to your resources.

A good case in point is when you are working with another organization, as either a business partner, or possibly in a manufacturer/supplier relationship. In both cases, the Active Directory environment may be composed of two or more Active Directory forests. One of the organizations may not even have an Active Directory infrastructure, opting to use a Unix-based solution instead.

There have been tools available that allow Unix accounts to have access to Active Directory resources for some time. Services for Unix have included mechanisms that allow accounts from a Unix Kerberos realm to have access to objects within an Active Directory domain. Microsoft is rolling some of the Services for Unix functionality into the Windows Server 2003 R2 release.

Active Directory forests are truly the security boundary for the entire Active Directory infrastructure. Prior to Windows Server 2003, if you wanted to allow resource access to accounts that resided within another Active Directory forest, you had to create an explicit trust relationship, known as an *external trust*, between the domains where the account and the resources resided. Windows Server 2003 changed the rules by including a forest trust relationship, thereby granting resource access to accounts within any domain of the neighboring forest. With the release of Windows Server 2003 R2, a new feature known as Active Directory Federation Services (ADFS) is available to grant an "application-level" trust. Using ADFS, you can specify which applications a user has available to them when they access your forest, as well as enable a single sign-on (SSO) environment for them.

In this chapter we take a look at the new features that are included with Windows Server 2003 R2. First, we are going to present ADFS. ADFS has piqued several administrators' curiosity, since it allows you to control access to resources on a user-by-user basis if you want, but can also control based on other criteria, such as group membership. Following ADFS, we are going to delve into Identity Management for Unix and see how you can manage access to resources when your user accounts are Unix-based, as well as synchronizing passwords between their Active Directory and Unix accounts.

Active Directory Federation Services

As we just mentioned, there are traditional methods of allowing access to resources between forests. Windows 2000 and Windows Server 2003 will let you create a trust relationship, known as an external trust, with domains that are outside of your Active Directory forest. These domains can be in another Active Directory forest, a Windows NT 4.0 domain, or a Unix Kerberos realm. The drawback to using an external trust is that the trust relationship is restricted to the two domains that are linked with the trust. The nontransitive nature of the external trust makes it difficult when trying to grant resource access to a user account that resides in a domain in one forest and the resources reside in several domains in another forest. If that is the case, you need to create an external trust relationship between every domain where the resources reside and the domain where the account resides.

Windows Server 2003 made things a little easier by providing a forest trust. The forest trust creates a transitive trust between two forests, allowing any account in any domain in one forest to have resource access to any domain in the other forest. Having only one trust relationship to manage made it much easier for administrators to allow two Active Directory forests to interoperate. Once the forest trust is created, the enterprise administrators for each forest can control how access is granted within their forest. They have the option to allow all users the ability to authenticate to all of the servers within their forest, or they can limit the authentication to specific servers, thus controlling object access to a finer degree.

NOTE For more information about external and forest trust relationships, see Chapter 3, "Active Directory Forest and Domain Design."

Although these options allow administrators to have control over their resources while allowing another organization to control their user accounts, there are some drawbacks to using trust relationships between forests. First, a trust relationship assumes that the two Active Directory infrastructures are going to interoperate. Usually when a trust relationship is created, the two divisions of an organization, or the two organizations that are involved, will have a distinct business need for the two directory services to be linked. If we're talking about two divisions within the same organization, they usually need to have separation of administrative control as well as maintain a security boundary between the two directory services. If the trust relationship interconnects two separate organizations, it is usually due to a business merger or acquisition, although trusts between business partners are not uncommon.

Maintaining trust relationships between two organizations can be troublesome. When the trust relationships are created, the proper communication channels have to be created that will allow both organizations to pass the appropriate directory service information so that users can gain access to the resources that they need to use in order to perform their duties. Some organizations have very specific rules as to the type of traffic that they will allow outside their organization and are leery of allowing sensitive directory service information to be accessible outside their own network infrastructure.

As companies start partnering with other companies to form business relations, one of the highest concerns is the security and reliability of their data. They need to make sure that they are allowing access to the right data so that their business partner can do their job, while also making sure that they restrict access to the sensitive data that the business partner should not have access to. Although trust relationships have made progress in allowing access to resources, many organizations do not allow the trust relationships due to organizational standards or limitations in technology, or they would rather create an application-level trust that allows access to specific applications and application features.

Application-level trusts are usually created by the development staff of the organization so that they can allow external users to access applications and view, and possibly even manipulate data. A typical example of this is a company that creates a web-based front-end to a database. They make the interface available on their web servers, but to gain access to it, the external users have to authenticate. Once authenticated, the external user can access the data, and the organization has control over what data is viewed. Controlling the user accounts then becomes tricky for the administrator. If the administrator is responsible for maintaining the account, then the administrator has to remain in constant contact with the business partner to make sure the user account is still valid. Otherwise, if the external user leaves the business partner's organization, they may still have access to data within the administrator's organization. The external user is also inconvenienced. When they gain access to the data that they need from the business partner, they are more than likely going to have to maintain another user account that will probably have a different password, and possibly a different naming convention. The two companies could agree on a method of controlling user access, such as certificate mapping, but then it becomes difficult to control which users have access to which set of data.

Microsoft and IBM, along with other organizations, have been developing another method of access control between organizations. Known as the Web Services (WS-*) architecture, its goal is to allow the secure exchange of data between organizations while maintaining a simple method of data access to users. Ideally, the users should be able to access data from the partner organization using their existing Windows-based account, and the administrators should be able to map the accounts to the level of application access that the user needs. Specifically, ADFS falls under the WS-Federation (WS-F) subheading beneath the WS-* specifications.

Once the ADFS trust is created, the administrator of the data will not have to be as concerned about the user accounts, because when a user leaves the partner organization, their account should be disabled or removed by the administrators at the partner organization. Users should be able to access the resources or applications from the partner organization using their existing account without having to provide authentication credentials.

How It Works

ADFS creates trust relationships between entities through a web-based interface. Let's say we have two companies, Zygort and BloomCo. When the two companies work out a business relationship, the information technology group from each will determine the resources that will have to be made available to the other company. Using ADFS and other web technologies, each company could create a web interface for the users to access, and based on their account attributes, they will have access to just the data that they need to work with. All of this can be provided by using an SSO solution so that the user will not have to authenticate again once they have accessed the partner's website.

Once the web applications are built, you can use ADFS to provide access to the applications and control the sign-on capabilities. Both organizations have to support ADFS to make this work seamlessly, but once it is implemented, the administrative support is greatly reduced due to the fact that you will no longer have to control access on a user-by-user basis. Future partnerships are also easier to establish once an ADFS solution is implemented because you can add the new partnership rules into ADFS instead of building an entirely new solution for the new business partner.

For a high-level overview of ADFS, let's consider the two companies from our earlier example. Zygort is a manufacturing company and BloomCo provides preassembled parts for Zygort's products. BloomCo needs to be able to view the production schedule that Zygort has planned, as well as the specifications of the parts that they will need to provide. All of this data is contained within the

Zygort internal network utilizing several servers and databases. Zygort, on the other hand, wants to view the current inventory levels and the production schedules that BloomCo has planned.

Once the business arrangement was finalized, the two companies set about trying to decide the best method of sharing information. Traditionally, a trust relationship or a custom application would be created to allow the two companies to interact. If a forest level trust is created between the two organizations, then the trust, and a method of communication, needs to be maintained. Usually some type of VPN connection is created between the two organizations so that they can share their information.

But what if one of the companies is not using Active Directory within their environment? Or there are company standards in place that will not allow the appropriate firewall ports open to maintain the trust relationship? And if those ports are not open, what are you going to do if one of the companies has a policy in place that will not allow the clients from another organization to access their internal network? The solution might be to create an application that is run through a web page. The web server that the user connects to can reside within the company's perimeter network, safely seated behind an external firewall, yet sitting on the outside of the company's internal network, the two separated by a firewall also.

The firewall that sits between the internal network and the perimeter network will have rules in place that allow the web server to access data within the internal network. The firewall that sits between the web server and the external clients will allow just the standard web ports. Applications can then be written that will allow an external client to have access to the data that is necessary, but nothing else. So when a user from BloomCo connects to the Zygort website, they are presented with an authentication dialog box. The user authenticates and is then presented with the applications necessary to view the production schedule and schematics for the parts they are producing.

So you ask yourself, "What is wrong with that scenario?" Granted, it does get the job done. The user from BloomCo can get the data that is necessary for BloomCo's production needs. But what if the user leaves BloomCo? A Zygort administrator is responsible for removing or disabling the user's account. If the Zygort administrator is not notified of the employee leaving BloomCo's employ, the account could remain active—a security breach. Also, the users from each company will need to remember not only the username and password that they use for their own company's resources, but also another username and password to gain access to the business partner's resources.

With ADFS, the user accounts that are used to gain access to the resources in either forest are maintained by the administrators of each respective company. So when the user leaves BloomCo, the administrator of the BloomCo accounts either disables or deletes the user's account. Using a method of mapping accounts between forests, the user's account is used to gain access to the applications so that they will not have to use another account and remember another password.

When you start thinking about deploying ADFS, you will need to identify which organization needs to access web resources from their partner. Once you have determined which user accounts will need to access those resources, either from one organization, or possibly both, you can then start making choices as to how the federation trust needs to be created. The organization that is responsible for maintaining the web resources is known as the resource partner. The organization that hosts the user accounts that need to use those resources is known as the account partner.

In comparison, if you create a trust within Active Directory, you need to make the same design decisions. If you create an external trust or a forest trust, you need to decide where the user accounts are located in conjunction with the resources they need to have access. The trust relationship that you build can be created so that users in only one forest have access to resources in another, or you could allow users from both forests to access resources in both. The trust relationship, once created, controls access to the resource based on the trust settings.

NOTE   For more information on Active Directory external and forest trusts, see Chapter 3.

ADFS trust relationships are not Active Directory constructs, however. Essentially, you are designing rules and settings that control how the company's websites, and the applications within those websites, are accessed.

ADFS Services

To get all of this working, you will need to make sure that you are utilizing an Active Directory or WS-F infrastructure in both organizations and your servers that are going to take on the Federation Server roles are Windows Server 2003 R2–based. Since any Active Directory environment can be used, even Windows 2000, you do not have to upgrade your existing infrastructure to take advantage of ADFS. You will need to decide how you are going to implement your ADFS solution, however. Since there are different uses for ADFS, you will need to make sure you have the appropriate services installed so that your solution will work, yet meet your security requirements. Let's look at the services that are part of an ADFS solution.

FEDERATION SERVICE

The Federation Service is responsible for retrieving account information from an account store and building access tokens based on the rules created for the federated trust. In a typical solution, each entity within the federated trust, which we will refer as the business partners, will create a Federation Service system. When a Federation Service is responsible for contacting the user store, in this case Active Directory, it is known as the account-side Federation Service, or FS-A. When a Federation Service is responsible for building the access token that is used to grant access to a resource, that Federation Service is known as the resource-side Federation Service, or FS-R. The FS-A is responsible for accessing the user's account from the account store and determining what claims are to be used within the token that is passed to the FS-R.

Claims

Claims are assertions that are used to determine what level of access a user will have when accessing an application. A claim can be as simple as a user's account name, or as complex as the groups the user is a member of and Active Directory attributes that you can populate for the account. For instance, Jim's user account is named jimc and the UPN for the account is `jimc@bloomco.lcl`. When Jim logs on using his UPN and then accesses Zygort's partner web page, his UPN is the claim that is used to identify Jim. Jim's level of access to the applications that are available from the web page are dependent on the access that has been granted to his UPN. Zygort's administrative staff can also specify that the applications are available based on the user's group membership. Someone within the HR Administrators group can be granted access to more functionality than users who are members of the HR Users group.

Claims have to be agreed on before either partner can configure their trust policies for claims. A map of outgoing claims from the account partner has to be configured for the incoming claims at the resource partner. Once the claims have been mapped between partners, they can be entered into the trust policy so that the users can be granted the appropriate level of access to the web applications. Claims come in three flavors:

Identity Claim   The identity claim type allows you to identify an account based on information that should uniquely identify the user account. The information that is used within the claim can take the following forms:

UPN   Each user account within an Active Directory forest will have a UPN assigned to it. The UPN uniquely identifies the user within the forest, regardless of which domain the user's account is created in.

E-mail   E-mail addresses are assumed to be unique. When you assign an e-mail address to a user account, the address should be unique on the Internet, as well as unique to the account and resource partners.

Common name   Common name is not usually seen as a unique name type. Several objects could contain the same common name data. When using the common name option, you will need to make sure that you are identifying the accounts by another means also.

Group claim   Group claims are seen as a means of identifying which groups the user is a member of. However, the groups that are used on each side of the ADFS trust do not have to be identical. You can create rules that allow you to define which groups are analogous to one another on each side of the trust.

Custom claim   Custom claims allow you to make assertions about an account that do not fit into the other two claim types. You can use a custom claim to expose attributes from the account side of the trust to the resource side. A custom claim could be used to extract attribute information from an account, such as department, manager, and description, and then pass that data to the resource side.

Tokens

Claims are included within a token that is passed to the resource side of the trust relationship and are used to grant access to the applications. Tokens are encrypted so that their contents cannot be viewed when intercepted, and signed so that their authenticity can be proven. If they are intercepted and manipulated before arriving at the resource side, they will be invalidated by the FS-R. When the token is received on the resource side, the FS-R reviews the claims and then passes the token to the Federation Web Component, which in turn creates the view that is appropriate to the user from the account side.

FEDERATION SERVICE PROXY

The Federation Service Proxy (FSP) is used as an intermediary pass-through system so that you do not have to place your Federation Service system within the company's perimeter network. As with the Federation Service, there is an account- and resource-side Federation Service Proxy, known as the FSP-A and FSP-R, respectively. Unlike the FS-A and FS-R, the FSP is an optional service. A system configured as a Federation Service can perform its own account and resource duties without the FSP, but if you want to have another level of security, you should place the FSP in the company's perimeter network where it can intercept ADFS requests and pass them to the appropriate FS-A or FS-R.

SSO AGENT

The SSO agent is an ISAPI extension that you can install and enable on an IIS 6.0 web server. This agent is responsible for accepting access tokens and managing the authentication cookies. The SSO agent on the account side of the trust is responsible for building and delivering cookies to the user accounts so that they can access all web resources on the resource side without have to authenticate again. On the resource side, the SSO agent is responsible for building and delivering cookies to the user account so that the user account does not have to return to the FS-A every time it accesses an ADFS-enabled site.

AUTHORIZATION MANAGER

Authorization Manager is actually a service that was included with the original release of Windows Server 2003. The primary function of the Authorization Manager is to provide role-based access control (RBAC) to applications. In other words, you can use Authorization Manager to control who will have access to specific applications based on rules that you create within the Authorization Manager interface. Since this access control is performed from the Authorization Manager, you are not required to hard-code authorization into each individual application.

ACTIVE DIRECTORY

Within a Windows Server 2003 environment, Active Directory or Active Directory Application Mode (ADAM) can be used as the account store. When a user attempts to access an application on the resource side, the user's account information is extracted from Active Directory by the Federation Service. The Federation Service then compiles the user's account information into a token, which includes the attributes of the user account that have been converted to claims.

Federated Web Single Sign-On

So the decision has been made to allow users from BloomCo to have access to resources within your domain. However, you do not want to set up a VPN connection because they do not need to have access to very much of your data. Instead, you have decided to allow them to access your website and use web applications. These applications will be configured to give the BloomCo users access to the data that they need in order to manufacture the subcomponents.

Once the decision is made to create the website for BloomCo users, you determine that the applications should be created that will give users access to the production schedule and the schematics for the subcomponents that they will be manufacturing. Since the two web applications are going to be used by different groups of users at BloomCo, you determine that you will need to have different access permissions so that the users will only be able to view the information that they need.

PREPARE YOUR INFRASTRUCTURE

The first step is to make sure that your current infrastructure meets the requirements for ADFS. At this point you are only concerned with your infrastructure and not the partner's infrastructure. Since ADFS can interoperate with other WS-F compliant systems, your partner's organization could be running another operating system entirely. You will need to make sure that your organization has Active Directory deployed before you can take advantage of ADFS. There are also other services that will be needed:

Active Directory   Active Directory or Active Directory Application Mode can be used as your account store. Since either of these account stores holds user account authentication mechanisms, they provide the Federation Server with authentication information that can be used as claims to populate the tokens that are sent to the resource partner.

DNS Any time you are using web-based applications, you must have a mechanism in place that allows you to find the servers that host those applications. ADFS is no different; it relies on DNS for name resolution to find the web servers that are used in the federation trust.

Certificate services In order for your ADFS solution to function, you will need to obtain certificates that allow you to secure your website as well as the ADFS tokens that you will be passing to your partner's organization. On the resource side, you are going to be securing your website so that all access to the website uses SSL. This will guarantee that the data passing from your site to the users on the account side are secure. On the account side, tokens will be generated that will include the claims that will be used to authenticate the user to resources. These tokens will need to be signed so that the resource partner can validate the authenticity of the token.

FEDERATION SERVER PREREQUISITES

Before you can install the Federation Server, make sure that you have all of the required services and software installed on your Windows Server 2003 R2 system. IIS 6.0 is required for the Federation Server, and for this reason alone it is recommended that the Federation Server not reside on a domain controller. Domain controllers should have as few services as possible running on them so that they do not have a very large attack footprint for hackers.

IIS IIS 6.0 needs to be installed with some of the most common options for a web server, but you also need to add in a few options that you may not enable on any of your web servers. To install IIS, open Add/Remove Programs and click the Add/Remove Windows Components icon. Once the Add/Remove Windows Components dialog box appears, select Application Server and click the Details button. This brings up the options for the application server services, of which IIS is a part. Select the IIS check box along with the ASP.NET and COM+ check boxes.

Microsoft .NET Framework 2.0 The .NET Framework 2.0 can be selected from the Add/Remove Windows Components dialog box at the same time you add IIS. You can also perform the installation of either option separately, but no matter which approach you choose, both need to be installed prior to installing the Federation Server.

Certificates During the installation of the Federation Server you will be required to provide token signing certificates for the federation to use when it generates a token to be passed to the partner's forest. These token signing certificates are used to validate the security tokens that contain the claims used for authentication in the remote forest. For testing purposes you can use certificates that are generated by programs such as SelfSSL, which comes with the IIS 6.0 Resource Kit, or other third-party programs. These types of certificates should not be used in production, however; you should implement some type of Public Key Infrastructure (PKI).

NOTE For more information on how to create certificates for use in web page SSL and token signing, see the Microsoft website: https://www.microsoft.com/windowsserver2003/technologies/pki/default.mspx.

COMMON FEDERATION SERVER INSTALLATION OPTIONS

Once the prerequisites have been met, you will be able to install the Federation Server within each of the partner forests. In this section we are going to look at the installation requirements that are the same for both forests. In the sections that follow, we will look at the installation options and requirements that are unique to the resource and account forest.

The initial steps that start the installation of the Federation Server are the same between the two forests. As long as all of the prerequisites have been met, you can install the Federation Service by opening Add/Remove Programs ➤ Add/Remove Windows Components and selecting Active Directory Services and then clicking the Details button. The dialog box shown in Figure 7.1 shows the options that are available.

Select the Active Directory Federation Services option and click the Details button. The only option we will need at this point is the Federation Service. Select the check box for Federation Service and then click OK. At this point you will be presented with a wizard that will lead you through the initial configuration of the Federation Server. In the Windows Component Wizard page, click Next.

The Federation Service page, shown in Figure 7.2, will appear requesting the token signing certificate. Specify the location of the certificate, either explicitly or by browsing for it. In the lower portion of this page you need to specify whether this is the first Federation Server that is installed, or if it is another Federation Server within an existing Federation Server farm. If it is the first, you will need to select the Create A New Trust Policy option and name the trust policy. If you are joining this server to an existing server farm, you will need to select the Use An Existing Trust Policy option. After making your selections, click the Next button, then click the Finish button.

FIGURE 7.1

Active Directory Services

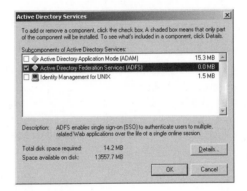

FIGURE 7.2

Federation Service token signing certificate request page

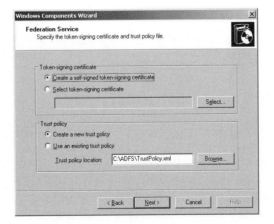

Once the Federation Service has been successfully installed, you will need to define the trust policy that will be used by all of the Federation Servers within the server farm. The trust policy contains the information required to locate the federation's organization name as well as the URL required to locate the Federation Servers.

To edit the information that is used within the trust policy, open the Active Directory Federation Services snap-in from Administrative Tools or your own custom MMC. Double-clicking the Federation Service node will allow you to gain access to the Trust Policy node shown in Figure 7.3. Right-click on Trust Policy and select Properties. Figure 7.4 shows the properties pages available for the Trust Policy. On the General tab, you will need to replace the generic entries with identifying information for your side of the federation.

FIGURE 7.3

Trust policy node

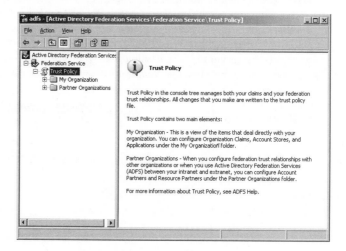

FIGURE 7.4

Trust policy properties

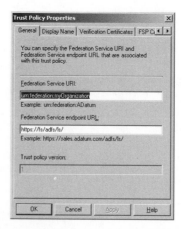

On the Federation Service Uniform Resource Identifier (URI) line, replace MyOrganization with the name of your domain. On the Federation Service Proxy URL, the computer name that you specified when installing the Federation Service will appear. Notice that the name is not fully qualified.

For the Federation Service to work correctly, you will need to supply the fully qualified domain name of the server. In our example, you would replace `https://fs/adfs/ls/` with `https://fs.zygort .lcl/adfs/ls/`.

NOTE In a test environment, if your Federation Service is running on a domain controller, you should change the ADFS application pool identity to run as the Local System account. This is not necessary on a member server. As a best practice, do not install the Federation Service on a domain controller in a production environment.

CONFIGURING THE ACCOUNT FEDERATION SERVER

The account forest side of the federation is responsible for maintaining the user accounts that will have access to the web pages on the resource side of the trust. Since the account partner is sending tokens to the resource partner, the Federation Server is not restricted to only Active Directory as the account store. ADAM can also be used as an account store, but you will not have the ability to use Kerberos as the authentication mechanism.

To add an account store, you will need to open the Active Directory Federation Services snap-in from the Administrative Tools or from your own custom MMC. Expand Federation Service ➤ Trust Policy ➤ My Organization to see the view shown in Figure 7.5. Right-click on Account Stores and select New ➤ Account Store from the context menu. The Add Account Store Wizard will appear. Click Next and you will be presented with the options Active Directory and Active Directory Application Mode (ADAM). Selecting Active Directory and clicking Next will take you to a page that has a check box that allows you to enable the account store for use by the Federation Service. If you do not select the check box, the account store will be added but not used for authentication purposes. Clicking Next will take you to the final screen, the Completing The Add Account Store Wizard page, on which you can click Finish to see your account store appear in the snap-in.

For each Active Directory group that you want to map to claims that are sent to the resource partner, you will need to create an organization claim. Expanding Federation Service ➤ Trust Policy ➤ My Organization and then right-clicking on Organization Claims will bring up a context menu from which you can choose New ➤ Organization Claim.

FIGURE 7.5
Account stores in the
Federation Service

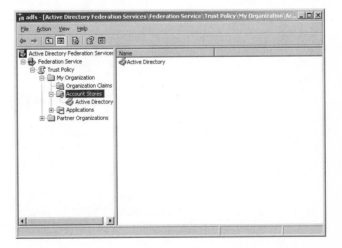

The dialog box that appears, shown in Figure 7.6, allows you to type in a claim name and specify whether it is a group claim or custom claim. Use the group claim to map an Active Directory group, and use the custom claim to map user attributes.

The claims will then need to be associated with user account information. The FS-A can determine the group memberships of user accounts and discover Active Directory attributes from the user accounts, but until those groups and attributes are mapped to claims, the claims will not be usable. To perform the Active Directory to claim mapping, you will need to identify the properties that are associated with the claim. To do so, expand Federation Server ➤ Trust Policy ➤ My Organization ➤ Account Stores and then right-click on the account store. From the context menu, shown in Figure 7.7, select New ➤ Group Claim Extraction or New ➤ Custom Claim Extraction.

Figure 7.8 shows the Create A New Group Claim Extraction dialog box and Figure 7.9 shows the Create A New Custom Claim Extraction dialog box. To map a group, click Add and select the group from the Select Users Or Groups dialog box. Once the group has been selected, use the Map To This Organization Claim pull-down menu to associate the group to the appropriate claim.

The custom claim mapping works similar to the group mapping. In the Create A New Custom Claim Extraction dialog box, type in the attribute that you want to map to a claim and then use the Map To This Organization Claim pull-down menu to associate the attribute to the appropriate claim.

FIGURE 7.6

The Create A New Organization Claim dialog box

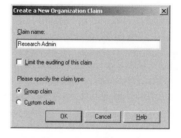

FIGURE 7.7

Extracting account information

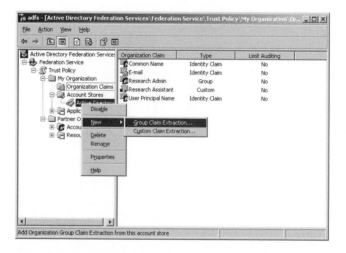

Once the organization claims have been created and the Active Directory mappings have been configured, you will need to add in the resource partner that will be part of this trust relationship. Expanding Federation Service ➢ Trust Policy ➢ Partner Organization, right-clicking on Resource Partner, and selecting New ➢ Resource Partner from the context menu will present you with the Welcome To The Add Resource Partner Wizard. Click Next to start the wizard at the Import Policy File page.

If the resource partner has provided you with a policy file, you can click Yes and enter the path to the policy file, but if not, you will need to select No and click Next to manually enter the information. On the Resource Partner Details page, enter the URI and URL for the FS-R as shown in Figure 7.10.

FIGURE 7.8
New group
claim extraction

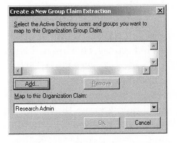

FIGURE 7.9
New custom
claim extraction

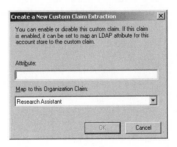

FIGURE 7.10
Resource Partner
Details page

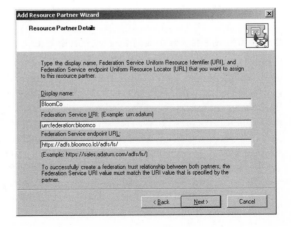

After clicking Next, you are presented with the Resource Partner Verification Certificate page. This is where you will need to make sure that you have obtained the token signing certificate from the partner. Without the token signing certificate, you will not be able to move forward and add the account partner to the trust policy, and you will not be able to create a trust relationship with the account partner. Either enter the path or browse for the certificate and click Next.

The final step is to configure the outgoing claims that will be sent to the FS-R. Expand Federation Service ➤ Trust Policy ➤ Partner Organizations ➤ Resource Partners and right-click the resource partner. From the context menu, select New and then choose either Outgoing Group Claim Mapping or Outgoing Custom Claim Mapping. If you are mapping a user's group membership to a group claim, you can use the Outgoing Group Claim Mapping, but if you are mapping any type of attribute that is associated with the user's account you will have to use the Outgoing Custom Claim Mapping option.

When you select the Outgoing Group Claim Mapping option, you will be presented with a dialog box, as shown in Figure 7.11. This will allow you to type in the group name claim that will be generated from the FS-A. Make sure you type this information correctly; if the claim is misspelled, the mapping will fail and the user will lose access to the resources. Once you have typed in the group name, you can select the organization claim name from the pull-down menu. If you do not see the correct entry in the pull-down menu, the organization claim has not yet been created.

Before moving on to configuring the Resource Federation Server, the FS-A server authentication certificate should be exported to a file that can be used when the FS-R's trust policy is created. Have an administrator who is responsible for your PKI export the certificate and then send the certificate file to the administrative staff responsible for creating the trust policy at the FS-R.

FIGURE 7.11
Outgoing claim mapping

CONFIGURING THE ACCOUNT FEDERATION SERVER PROXY

When the users access our web server to gain access to their partner website, the resource ADFS systems will request authentication of the user account. If your Federation Server is to be protected in your internal network and you do not want it sitting in the perimeter network, you will need to configure a server to appear as the Federations Server to the partner organization, otherwise known as the Federation Server Proxy. This service is not required for an ADFS solution; you could have your users access the Federation Server directly, but that decreases the security level of your ADFS infrastructure. As with any solution, the smaller the attack vector you have available, the better off you are.

The Federation Server Proxy role can be added by going into Add/Remove Programs, but you will need to make sure that you have the prerequisites in place before you can add the role. First, you will need to have IIS 6.0 installed and you should make sure that you have configured SSL for the default website. If you have not done so, you will not be allowed to install the Federation Server Proxy.

In much the same way that you added the Federation Server, you add the Federation Server Proxy. From the Active Directory Federation Services option in Add/Remove Windows Components, you will select to add the Federation Server Proxy. Note that you cannot install this role on a server that is already configured as a Federation Server. The Federation Server will accept requests that are sent to it directly and does not need to have a Federation Server Proxy in place, but if you decide to place the Federation Server within the internal network so that external users cannot access it, you will have to make sure the Federation Server Proxy is available in the perimeter network instead.

CONFIGURE RESOURCE FEDERATION SERVER

You create the Federation Server on the resource side in much the same way that you did the account side. There are some specific differences, however. The FS-R cannot use ADAM for an account store; it is restricted at this point to using Active Directory.

Add Applications

You will also need to add any claims-aware or traditional Windows applications to the FS-R so that the FS-R knows what applications are available and how the claims are to be used. Using Windows SharePoint Services, you can control access to the traditional Windows applications.

When adding claims-aware applications, you have the option to enable claim types so that the claim can be extracted from the tokens sent by the FS-A used to authenticate the user to the application. The application's logic will determine what the user is allowed to perform at that time. You can configure the applications to allow specific levels of access to users based on the claims that are presented.

Add Account Partner

The account partner information will need to be entered into the FS-R so that the trust can be built. You must perform two steps to enable the account partner to be trusted by the resource partner: obtain the account partner's token signing certificate and add the account partner using the trust policy node.

There are several methods of obtaining the account partner's token signing certificate. You could have an administrator from the account partner organization e-mail it to you. You could have it sent on digital media through a courier. You could even connect to a secure website and download it. No matter which method you choose, you should make sure that any transmission method you use is secure.

Once the certificate is obtained, you can add the account partner to the trust policy. In the Active Directory Federation Services snap-in, you will need to open Federation Service ➤ Trust Policy ➤ Partner Organization. Right-click on the Account Partners node and select New ➤ Account Partner from the context menu. The Add Account Partner Wizard will start, and you will need to click Next to continue. On the Import Policy File page shown in Figure 7.12, you have the option to provide the path to policy file that was provided by the account partner, or you can click No and enter the information manually. If you select No and then click Next, you will be prompted for the account partner details. On the Account Partner Details page shown in Figure 7.13, you will need to enter a display name as well as the URI and URL of the account partner's Federation Server.

FIGURE 7.12
Import Policy File page

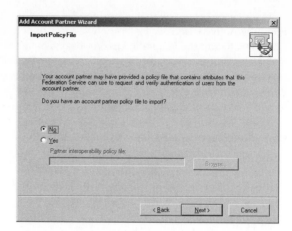

FIGURE 7.13
Account Partner
Details page

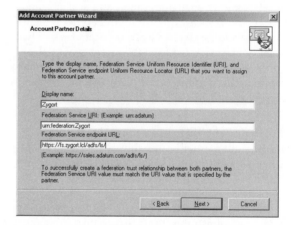

After clicking Next, you are presented with the Account Partner Verification Certificate page. This is where you will need to make sure that you have obtained the token signing certificate from the account partner. Without the certificate, you will not be able to move forward and add the account partner to the trust policy, and you will not be able to create a trust relationship with the account partner. Either enter the path or browse for the certificate, and then click Next.

As shown in Figure 7.14, the Federation Scenario options include Federated Web SSO and Federated Web SSO with Forest Trust. If you have configured a forest trust between the resource and account partners, you can select the second option, but most companies will use the first option. Partner organizations that are taking advantage of ADFS typically will not have Active Directory trust relationships built; they will be relying on ADFS for access to the web apps instead.

With that said, you could have a scenario where your organization hosts both the resource and account partner sides of the trust relationship. This could be due to you having a perimeter network that has a separate Active Directory infrastructure than your internal network. To allow users to access web applications, you could configure ADFS to use the existing trust relationships for authentication purposes.

To follow along with our example, select Federated Web SSO and click Next. The Account Partner Identity Claims page appears. On this page you have the option of specifying which type of claims you are going to enable for the account partner. As described earlier, the claim types of UPN, E-mail, and Common Name are available from this page. If you choose either the UPN or E-mail claim types, you will be presented with the Accepted UPN Suffixes, shown in Figure 7.15, or Accepted E-mail Suffixes, respectively. After entering the suffixes that you want to allow, or if you selected Common Name, you will be presented with the Enable This Account Partner page. The Enable This Account Partner check box is selected by default. Deselect it if you are not ready to enable the trust between the partners.

Once you click Finish on the final page of the wizard, you will find that the account partner appears beneath the Account Partners node in Active Directory Federation Service snap-in. The claim type that you have enabled, in this case UPN, appears in color with the claims that you did not enable grayed out.

FIGURE 7.14
Federation
Scenario page

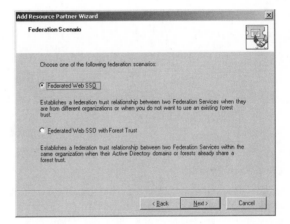

FIGURE 7.15
Accepted UPN suffixes

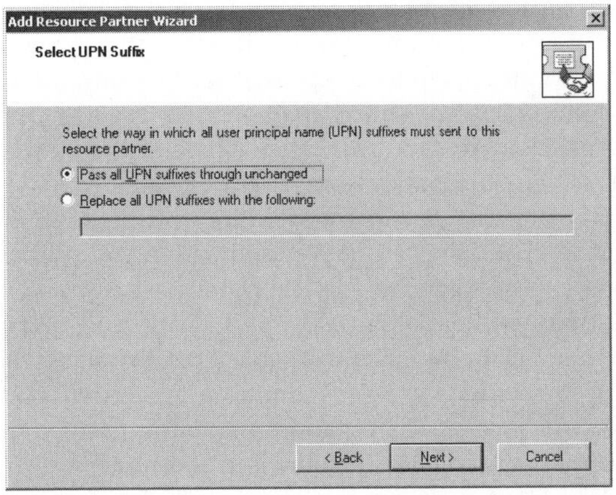

Add Additional Token Signing Certificates

If you are only configuring one Federation Server, you can move on to creating claims, but if you have additional Federation Servers within the server farm, you should add the token signing certificates from each one to the Verification Certificates tab in the account partner's properties sheet. To do so, right-click on the account partner within the Account Partner's node and select Properties. Once the properties sheet appears, select Verification Certificates, as shown in Figure 7.16. Then click Add and enter the path to the token signing certificate.

FIGURE 7.16
Verification
Certificates tab

Claim Configuration

Claims need to be configured so that the access entries within the claims-aware applications have the correct entries passed to them from the account partner. When we configured the initial trust policy settings, we selected to enable the UPN claim and entered a UPN suffix. This was assuming that the application used UPN criteria to grant access to an application. Other claims can be added in so that when a user attempts to access a website, the claims that are passed on behalf of the user account can be processed and the appropriate application access can be granted.

To configure a claim, you will need to open the Trust Policy within your Active Directory Federation Service snap-in and right-click on Organization Claims. From the context menu select New ➤ Organization Claim. The Create A New Organization Claim dialog box appears, which allows you to name the claim and select the type of claim, either Group or Custom. At this point you will need to make sure that you are coordinating your efforts with the application development team so that you know what claims they have used within the application. For each claim that you want to use, create it as either a Group or Custom claim type. If you no longer need a claim, you can delete it from the list, but the original three claims, UPN, E-mail, and Common Name, cannot be removed.

Once all of the claims have been created, they will need to be mapped to the claims that will be arriving within the tokens sent from the account partner. To configure this mapping between the account partner's claims and the resource partner's organization claims, right-click on the account partner's entry in the Account Partners node in the Trust Policy and select either Incoming Group Claim Mapping or Incoming Custom Claim Mapping under the New menu item. If you are mapping a user's group membership to a group claim, you can use the Incoming Group Claim Mapping option, but if you are mapping any type of attribute that is associated with the user's account you will have to select Incoming Custom Claim Mapping.

When you choose the Incoming Group Claim Mapping option, you will be presented with the dialog box shown in Figure 7.17. Here you can type the group name claim that will be generated from the FS-A. Make sure you type this information correctly; if the claim is misspelled, the mapping will fail and the user will lose access to the resources. Once you have typed the group name, you can select the resource partner's organization claim name from the pull-down menu. If you do not see the correct entry in the menu, the organization claim has not been created yet.

After the claims have been configured, you can select the application from within the Applications node and view the claims that are available. Right-clicking any of these claims presents a context menu that allows you to enable the claim for use with the application. If at any time you wish to limit access by a claim, you can disable it.

The FS-R server authentication certificate should be exported to a file that can be imported into the Trusted Root Certification Authorities store on the web server. Have an administrator who is responsible for your PKI export the certificate and then send the certificate file to the administrative staff responsible for managing the web server.

FIGURE 7.17
Incoming Group
Claim Mapping

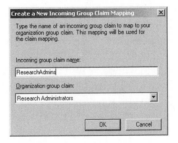

CONFIGURE WEB SERVER

Your web servers that are going to be responsible for hosting the ADFS-enabled applications will need to understand how ADFS is incorporated into the ADFS solution. To make them ADFS-aware, you must add in ADFS web agents that will be used to interpret the claims and allow access to the web applications. There are two agents available to install: the claims-aware agent and the Windows NT token-based applications agent. Depending on the application types that you are using, you may have to install one or both of the agents on your web servers.

Claims-aware applications can take advantage of using Authorization Manager's (AzMan) built in role-based authorization. Windows NT token-based applications are used with Windows SharePoint Services, which control the access to the applications based on a security token generated from Active Directory. If you are using traditional web applications and want to control the level of access that users have, you can use SharePoint's role-based control, limiting users to specific levels of control over the website.

NOTE   For more information about using Authorization Manager, see the MSDN website at `http://msdn.microsoft.com/library/en-us/secauthz/security/authorization_manager_model.asp`

NOTE For more information about using Windows SharePoint Services, see the Microsoft website at http://www.microsoft.com/windowsserver2003/technologies/sharepoint/default.mspx

ADFS Web Agents

The ADFS web agents can be installed from the Active Directory Services ➤ Active Directory Federation Services ➤ ADFS Web Agents from within the Windows Components node in Add/Remove Programs. Selecting the check box for the application type that you will be using and clicking OK three times will take you back to the Windows Components dialog box, where you can click Next to install the components.

NOTE When you install the ADFS Web Agents on a web server, you will need to install Microsoft .NET Framework 2.0, COM+, and the World Wide Web service.

Web Site SSL

The website that you will be using will need to have an SSL certificate installed. Make sure that you coordinate with the PKI team to obtain a valid web SSL certificate and associate it with the website. To do so, open Internet Information Services (IIS) Manager and open the properties sheet of the website. Click the Directory Security tab and then click the Server Certificate button in the Secure Communications section.

The wizard that appears will step you through creating a new certificate for the website. Depending on how your PKI is configured, you will either generate a request and send it to the certification authority, or you will send the request immediately. If you have automatic enrollment of certificates enabled, you may be able to do the latter, but most organizations want to have finer control over the certificates that they issue.

TIP For testing purposes, the IIS 6.0 Resource Kit has SelfSSL, which can be used to generate a self-signed SSL certificate. Although this comes in very handy in a test environment, you should not use these certificates in a production environment.

As you step through the wizard, you will specify information about the website, and then a certificate request file will be generated that should be unique. Save the text file to a secure location and then have your PKI team generate a certificate from the data. After the certificate has been generated, you can go back to the Directory Security tab of the website and install the certificate for use. Start by clicking the Server Certificate button again, but this time choose Process The Pending Request And Install The Certificate.

NOTE For more information about requesting certificates and configuring your public key infrastructure, see the Microsoft website at https://www.microsoft.com/windowsserver2003/technologies/pki/default.mspx.

Claims-Aware Applications

Windows Server 2003 Service Pack 1 included an update to AzMan that made it claims-aware. The purpose of this update was primarily so that AzMan could be used with ADFS and thus become the primary authorization mechanism for claims-aware applications. When applications are written to take advantage of claims, AzMan is used to check the roles that are available to each of the claims that are presented and then allows access to the applications if the claim matches one or more of the roles.

If you determine that you want to use claims-aware applications with AzMan, be sure that your development team understands how the application relies on AzMan to authorize access. You can find information on Microsoft's MSDN website that will aid the development staff when creating these applications.

SharePoint Services Access

SharePoint can control the level of access a user has when accessing a traditional web application. Windows SharePoint Services must be installed, and once it is, you can add applications and configure the level of access users have to the application. The access that you grant through SharePoint Services is based on the Active Directory accounts that you create. The accounts are then tied to incoming claims sent from the FS-A.

NOTE   As with the claims-aware applications, Microsoft has provided more information about how to manage SharePoint Services at the MSDN website.

Configuring the web.config File

The website's `web.config` file needs to be edited to include the location of the FS-R. Once this has been accomplished, requests sent to the website will use the `web.config` file and pass the data contained in the token to the FS-R. You must add the following code to your `web.config` file:

```
<compilation defaultLanguage=""c#"" debug=""true"">

<assemblies>

<add assembly=""System.Web.Security.SingleSignOn, Version=1.0.0.0,
➥Culture=neutral, PublicKeyToken=31bf3856ad364e35, Custom=null"" />
<add assembly=""System.Web.Security.SingleSignOn.ClaimTransforms, Version=1.0.0.0,
➥Culture=neutral, PublicKeyToken=31bf3856ad364e35, Custom=null"" />
</assemblies>

</compilation>

<customErrors mode=""Off"" />

<authentication mode=""None"" />

<httpModules>
<add name=""Identity Federation Services Application Authentication Module""
type=""System.Web.Security.SingleSignOn.WebSsoAuthenticationModule,
➥System.Web.Security.SingleSignOn, Version=1.0.0.0, Culture=neutral,
PublicKeyToken=31bf3856ad364e35, Custom=null"" />
</httpModules>

<websso>
```

```
<urls>
<returnurl>https://apppath </returnurl>
</urls>

<cookies writecookies=""true"">
<path>/ apppath </path>
<lifetime>240</lifetime>
</cookies>

<fs>https://federationservername /adfs/fs/federationserverservice.asmx</fs>

<authenticationrequired>
</authenticationrequired>

<loghttpevent>1</loghttpevent>

<auditlevel>255</auditlevel>

<tokenCacheSize>1</tokenCacheSize>

<tokenCacheEntryLifetime>5</tokenCacheEntryLifetime>

<tokenCacheScavengePeriod>5</tokenCacheScavengePeriod>

</websso>

</system.web>
```

In the preceding example, the entries for the path to the application and the Federation Service need to reflect your environment. For example, if your domain name is `zygort.lcl`, the application is called `researchapp` and it is hosted on the web server `fsweb`, you would replace the line `<returnurl>https://apppath </returnurl>` with `<returnurl>https://fsweb.zygort.lcl/ researchapp </returnurl>`.

If your Federation Server is named `fs` the line `<fs>https://federationservername /adfs/fs/ federationserverservice.asmx</fs>` will need to show `<fs>https://fs.zygort.lcl /adfs/ fs/federationserverservice.asmx</fs>`.

Configuring Clients

Each client that will be used to access the website will have to use a secure channel. After the website has been configured to use SSL, the client will then have to use an HTTPS call through the web browser to make the connection. The client may also have to connect to a specific port number to make the connection if host headers are not used. The following options should be taken into consideration for the user to have a positive experience when using the partner's website.

Installing SSL Certificates on Clients

Each of the client systems that will operate within the federation will need to trust the certificates that are used by both the FS-A and the FS-R. The easiest method of configuring the client to trust the Federation Servers is to install the root certificate for both into the Trusted Root Store. To do so, you could use a Group Policy that contains the root certificates that need to be installed on the client. When the client logs into the computer, the certificates will already be installed and they will then be able to connect to the Federation Servers without being prompted to trust them.

To use a Group Policy to install the certificates, open the Group Policy Management console, navigate to the Group Policy container in your domain, and then right-click the Group Policy that you want to modify and select Edit. Once the Group Policy Object Editor opens, navigate to Computer Configuration ➤ Windows Components ➤ Security Policy ➤ Public Key Policies. Right-click Trusted Root Certification Authorities and select Import. Once the wizard starts, enter the path to the certificate that you wish to import and choose the Place All Certificates In The Following Store option. Once the wizard is complete, the Group Policy will install the certificates on the clients as the computer is started or the refresh interval for the computer is reached.

TIP   If you want to immediately install the certificates after the group policy has been modified, run `gpupdate /force` from a command prompt at the client computer.

If the client's computer is not a member of your domain, Group Policies will not apply to them. If this is the case, you can instruct the users to open a web page that prompts them to install the root certificate for the company. If you are using a third party for your trusted root certificate, you could direct the users to install the root certificate from the third party by accessing the third party's website that hosts the root certificate.

Configuring Internet Explorer

Once you have the certificates installed, you can configure Internet Explorer to trust the FS-A and the FS-R. To do so, open the Internet Options dialog box and select the Security tab. From the Security tab, select the Trusted Sites icon and click the Sites button. Each of the federation server's URLs should be entered in this dialog box. If the users access the FS-A and the FS-R directly, the URL to the Federation Servers should be entered here, but if you are using a Federation Server Proxy, the URL to the proxy should be entered here. In any case, the URL that is used within the trust policy to identify the Federation Server to the clients should be the one that you have entered into the trusted sites.

Once the entire configuration is complete, users who need to access resources that are managed by administrators on the other side of the federation will be able to do so, and they won't have to enter their username and password when connecting. The advantage for the administrators is that they won't have to manage individual accounts for each user who needs to access the website. It becomes a win-win situation and makes the user's experience a pleasant one. And as we all know, the happier users are, the more real work we administrators can perform.

The other side to Active Directory Services allows users to have Unix and Windows accounts that they use to access resources. For some companies, the administrative staff may want to centralize and simplify their user administration. For others, the users actually have two accounts—one used with Unix or Linux, the other used with Windows—and they would like to keep the passwords synchronized between the two operating systems. In the next section we'll look at both Server for NIS and Password Synchronization to see how they can ease some of your administrative overhead.

Identity Management for Unix

There are two parts to Identity Management for Unix: Server for NIS (Network Information Service) and Password Synchronization. Identity Management for Unix allows you to configure an Active Directory domain controller as the master NIS server for one or more NIS domains. In this way you can manage the user accounts for Active Directory as well as the NIS-based accounts within a Unix NIS domain from one location. Domain controllers can then be configured to act as subordinate NIS servers and function alongside Unix subordinate NIS servers, or you could retire the Unix NIS servers and have the Unix accounts authenticate using the same accounts they have been using, only through Active Directory domain controllers instead.

The Password Synchronization component allows you to configure the accounts that will have their passwords synchronized automatically, and will keep the Active Directory accounts' and the Unix accounts' passwords in sync.

While these utilities have been available when you install Microsoft's Services for Unix, they have not been included as part of the operating system. Up until Windows Server 2003 R2, you had to download Services for Unix 3.5 and install the utilities separately. Now that they are included as part of the operating system, you can install them from the Active Directory Services link within the Add/Remove Windows Components option.

The primary thrust behind Identity Management for Unix is to have a central location in which to manage user accounts. Due to the fact that both Unix and Linux operating systems are used in many organizations, a need exists to make an administrator's job a little easier. With this in mind, having one unified interface in which to control the user accounts does indeed make an administrator's life a little easier.

Server for NIS

Server for NIS works in conjunction with other NIS systems, either running on a Windows platform or Unix and Linux platforms. NIS was originally known as Yellow Pages, and you will notice that a lot of the commands that are used with NIS have the "yp" designation at the beginning of them. For instance, the command that is used to replicate the changes made on the master NIS server to the subordinate servers is yppush.

Just as in the Windows NT domain model, NIS-based systems use a master server and subordinate servers to host the authorization data. In Windows NT, the domain controllers were divided into the single master, known as the Primary Domain Controller (PDC), and multiple subordinates, known as Backup Domain Controllers (BDCs). NIS-based servers are known as master and subordinates. The master is the only system where updates to the directory database can be made, and the subordinates host read-only versions of the database and accept the updates as they are sent out from the master.

Master NIS servers process updates to accounts and then use the yppush command to send the updates to the subordinate servers, but if the subordinate servers are not online, or there is a communication breakdown, they may not receive the updates. Using Active Directory as the central repository for the account information, one domain controller can act as the master NIS server and other domain controllers can act as the subordinates. The updates are sent through Active Directory replication, so all of the domain controllers will receive the updates. Unix and Linux-based clients that use NIS for authentication purposes can utilize a Windows Server 2003 R2 domain controller for authentication because the domain controller appears as a standard NIS server.

WARNING   If a domain controller is configured as a subordinate and then later the service is removed, the domain controller will still receive the updates through Active Directory replication; they will simply not respond to NIS authentication requests any longer.

INSTALLING SERVER FOR NIS

Server for NIS is installed just as the other Active Directory Services that we have discussed in this chapter. Open Add/Remove Programs, click Add/Remove Windows Components, then select Active Directory Services and click Details. From the Active Directory Services component options, select Identity Management for Unix and click the Details button. Notice that when you select Server for NIS, the Administrative Components option is automatically selected. Click OK twice and then click Next to install the components.

Once installed, the Identity Management for Unix menu item will appear on the Start menu under All Programs. When you select this option you will be presented with the Microsoft Identity Management For Unix console, where you can specify the servers that will act as the NIS servers within the domain as well as the NIS maps that define the objects used within the NIS domains.

Once the service is installed, the domain controller on which it is installed will assume that it is going to be the master NIS server, but it cannot do anything until the NIS map data from a domain has been migrated to it. Note that a domain controller can act as a master NIS server to other systems within the Active Directory domain as well as the Unix domains, but domain controllers will not act as subordinate NIS servers to a Unix master NIS server.

SETTING THE ENCRYPTION TYPE

Either before or after the migration has occurred, you can set the encryption type that will be used between the Unix clients and the NIS servers. Two types of encryption exist: crypt and MD5. Of the two, crypt is used with all flavors of Unix as well as Linux. MD5 can be used with any of the implementations of Linux that support the MD5 encryption algorithm. If you are setting up Server for NIS to interoperate with domains that include only Linux systems that support MD5, you can select the option by right-clicking on the domain node within Microsoft Identity Management for NIS and selecting Unix Password Encryption. The dialog box that appears, shown in Figure 7.18, shows the default option of crypt, but you can use the Encryption Scheme pull-down menu to change that to MD5.

FIGURE 7.18
Unix Password Encryption dialog box

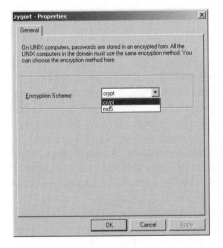

MIGRATING DATA

When Server for NIS is installed on a domain controller, the server assumes that it will become the master NIS server for a domain. If you already have a Unix or Linux system that is acting as the master NIS server, you will need to migrate the NIS data. There are two options for migrating the data: you can use the NIS Data Migration wizard or the nis2ad command-line utility. Either option allows you to extract data from the existing NIS server and populates Active Directory with the appropriate user account information. NIS maps are stored on Unix servers as text files, so you will need to make sure that you have access to the files when you go to migrate them.

After the migration is complete, the domain controller can then be used as the master NIS server and the other NIS servers can be made subordinate servers by transferring the new maps from the domain controller. In order to do so, you will have to use the ypxfr command to transfer the maps to the Unix or Linux systems. Other domain controllers from your Active Directory domain can be added as subordinate servers by using the Microsoft Identity Management for Unix snap-in. Expand Server for NIS ➢ *yourdomain* ➢ NIS Servers to view the NIS servers. If you have not added any subordinates, the first domain controller you installed the service on will appear in the list as the master. To add subordinates, right-click on the NIS Server node and select Add Server. After adding the domain controller's name, click OK and the server will appear as a subordinate server.

If you wish to make one of the subordinate servers the new master, you can right-click on the server in the details node and select Promote. This will force the server to become the new master NIS server for the domain and the original master will become a subordinate if it is still online. After performing this transfer of power, you will have to transfer the maps to the Unix subordinates so that they recognize the new master NIS server.

One of the biggest benefits of using Server for NIS is that you can merge multiple Unix NIS domains into a single NIS domain under Active Directory. When you are merging the domains, you will be restricted to a maximum of 960 maps. For example, you could have 96 domains with 10 maps each or 64 domains with a maximum of 15 maps each.

To start the migration of your NIS maps, go to Start ➢ All Programs ➢ Identity Management for Unix ➢ Microsoft Identity Management for Unix, or open an MMC console that you have added the snap-in. When you expand the Server for NIS node, you will find the domain listed for the domain controller that is acting as your master NIS server, as shown in Figure 7.19. Right-click the Server for NIS node and select NIS Data Migration Wizard. You will be presented with a wizard that starts by prompting you for the Unix domain that your master NIS server will control, as shown in Figure 7.20.

After you click Next, you will have the opportunity to authenticate with a user account that can manage Active Directory. You must have an account that has the ability to create objects within Active Directory. If you are already logged on as the administrator, you can click Next, or you can enter credentials that you want to use and click Next.

As you can see in Figure 7.21, the NIS Maps Selection page allows you to select the maps that you want to migrate from your Unix domain to Active Directory. Select the maps and click Add. If there are any nonstandard maps within your Unix domain, you can click the New button and define the map name, the separator that is used to separate the values within the map, and the column number where the key field starts. After defining the nonstandard map and adding all of the standard maps, click Next.

After selecting the maps, you will be prompted to enter the location of the maps. If you have copied the text files to your domain controller, specify the path. If the maps are located on another system, you will have to enter the network location of the files so that the domain controller can read the files and populate Active Directory. Once you click Next, the Destination Domain page appears, prompting you to provide the name of the domain where the accounts will be migrated. Either choose an existing domain, or enter a new name if you are creating a new domain for the NIS accounts. Once you click Next, the wizard will prompt you for conflict resolution terms. As you can see in Figure 7.22, the options are Overwrite, Rename, and Preserve. You also have the option to create a log file that will detail the conflicts.

Overwrite   Replaces existing Windows accounts with the NIS account names.

Rename   If the accounts are the same type, the Windows account names will be changed in Active Directory. If the accounts are different types, both of the accounts will be renamed. For example, if one account is a user account and the other is a group account, they will be renamed to unique names.

Preserve   The Windows account will not be renamed within Active Directory.

FIGURE 7.19
Domain listing

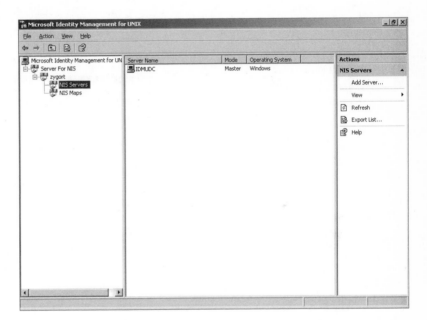

FIGURE 7.20
NIS Data Migration Wizard prompting for Unix domain name

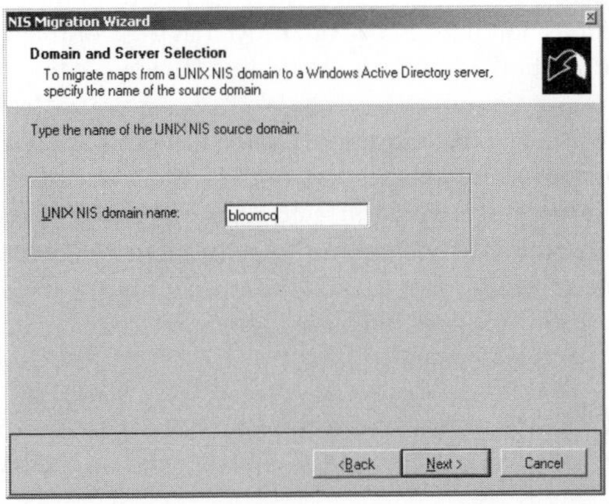

FIGURE 7.21

NIS Maps Selection page

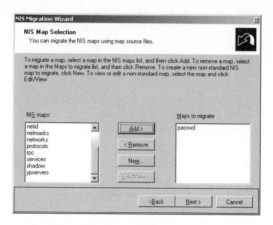

FIGURE 7.22

The Managing Conflicts
During Migration page

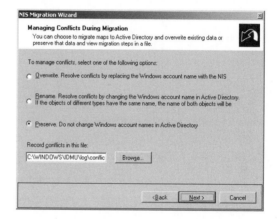

The Migration Behavior page allows you to choose between a test migration and a live migration. The first option shown on this page and in Figure 7.23 is Do Not Migrate (Log Only). As it implies, this option will test the entries to make sure there are not any conflicts between the Unix domain and Active Directory. The Migrate And Log option will migrate the accounts according to the conflict options you had chosen on the Managing Conflicts During Migration page. Of course, you can enter the location where you would like the log file to be located, and when you click Next, the migration summary is shown. Clicking Next once more will start the migration according to your settings. If you chose to test the migration, the log locations are displayed and you will have the option to click Next and perform the migration, or click Close in order to not migrate the maps.

After you have performed your migration, open Active Directory Users and Computers to view the accounts. If you did not specify a location, the accounts will be created in the users container by default. Notice that all of the new accounts are disabled by default. This is due to the fact that the passwords for these migrated accounts are now blank and you should apply a password to each one before you enable it.

NOTE   If you have redirected your default location for user accounts by using the `redirusr` command, the accounts will be located to the new default location.

If you look at the properties of the accounts you will notice a new tab that is available with Windows Server 2003 R2, the Unix Attributes tab, as shown in Figure 7.24. The attributes on this tab map to the information that was included in the original NIS maps for the Unix domain. The NIS Domain attribute specifies the domain that you selected when you migrated the account. You can change it to any existing domain by using the pull-down menu. The UID is the user identification attribute associated with the Unix domain. The Login Shell specifies the interface that the user uses. Home Directory specifies the location of the user's home directory where they save files on the network. Primary Group Name/GUID specifies the group that is default group that the user is associated with when accessing Unix resources.

FIGURE 7.23
The Migration
Behavior page

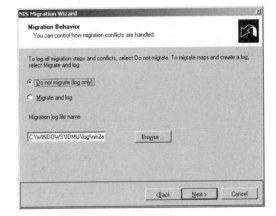

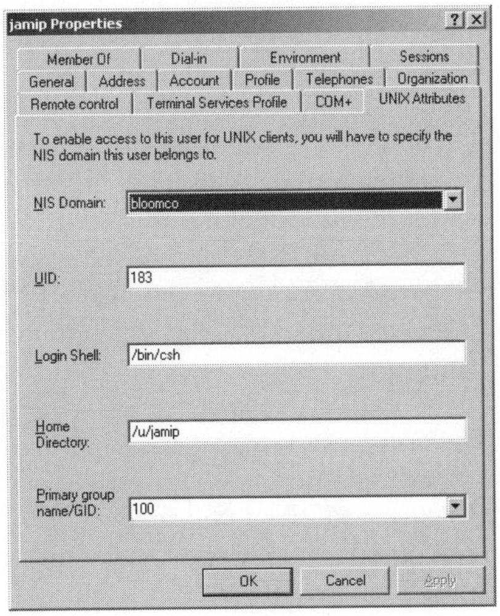

FIGURE 7.24
The Unix Attributes tab

MANAGING SUBORDINATES

You can have Windows domain controllers as well as Unix and Linux systems acting as NIS servers. Each of these systems needs to receive updates in order to allow users to authenticate and successfully access resources. The Active Directory domain controllers have the advantage insofar as they participate in Active Directory replication. All of the Unix attributes that are used as NIS map data are replicated between all of the domain controllers any time there is a change. Unix systems do not have that luxury. Unix systems that are going to act as the subordinate NIS servers must have the maps pushed to them after updates are made. Fortunately you will not have to manually push the updates; you can automate the task. There are methods to push the updates manually if you want to make sure they are sent out when you decide to send them.

Adding Subordinates

Unix NIS servers will need to "see" the master NIS server for their domain. After you have migrated the maps from the existing master NIS server, the existing subordinates must be informed. On each of the subordinates you should transfer the maps from the new master to the subordinate using the ypxfr command. The syntax for the command is: ypxfr -h *newmaster map* where *newmaster* is the name of the domain controller acting as the new master NIS server, and *map* is the name of the map to be transferred.

Windows domain controllers have to be added to the NIS server list. If you right-click the NIS Servers node within the Microsoft Identity Management for Unix snap-in, you can select the option Add Server. After entering the domain controller's name on the dialog box shown in Figure 7.25, you will note that the domain controller will appear within the server list and will show as Subordinate in the Mode column.

Controlling Transfers

All of the subordinate servers will receive updates to the maps, but the method of transfer depends on which operating system you are sending the updates to. As we mentioned, domain controllers will receive updates through Active Directory replication. Unix systems will receive an update through the yppush command, either manually or from an automated task. Built into Server for NIS is an automatic propagation routine. You can configure how often the updates are propagated to the Unix subordinates by right-clicking the Server for NIS node and selecting either Map Updates or Properties from the context menu. Both options will present you with the Server for NIS – Properties dialog box shown in Figure 7.26. Changing the entries for the Days, Hours, and Minutes settings will change the frequency that the maps are propagated to the Unix subordinates.

FIGURE 7.25
Selecting domain controllers to act as subordinate NIS servers

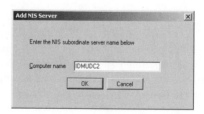

FIGURE 7.26

Changing the map
update frequency

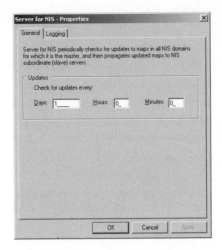

Promoting

When you put Server for NIS in place, only Windows domain controllers can take on the master NIS server role. With that in mind, make sure you plan which domain controller will start acting as the master NIS server in case you decommission the original master or when you lose the master due to a system failure or a disaster. To promote another domain controller, open the NIS Servers node and right-click on the server you wish to take on the master role. From the context menu you can select Promote to force the promotion. The existing master will demote itself to a subordinate. For all of the Unix servers to now notice the new master, you will have to run the ypxfr command as shown in the "Adding Subordinates" section earlier.

MANAGING MAP DATA

Once the maps have been migrated, you will no longer have to rely on the text files that act as maps in the Unix realm. All of the map data will reside within Active Directory, and you can update the information from the Unix Attributes tab of an account's properties. For most Windows administrators, working within the graphical environment is much easier. There are command-line options for many of the tasks that you will need to perform when working with the map data, but some of the tasks can be performed only from the Windows GUI.

Users

The user's name that is used in NIS is pulled from their account. Whereas Windows allows for an account to have a long username, Unix only allows for eight characters for the username. If you are going to use an Active Directory account to allow Unix or Linux users to authenticate, you will need to make sure the account is renamed with a name containing eight characters or less.

The information contained on the Unix Attributes tab for a user account allows you to identify the account to the Unix realm. You can change any of the attributes shown in Figure 7.27 by right-clicking on the user's account within Active Directory Users and Computers and selecting Properties, then selecting the Unix Attributes tab. The attributes that appear are:

NIS Domain   The name of the domain that the user account will use.

UID   The Unique Identifier for the users account. Access to resources in the Unix domain is controlled by the user's UID.

Login Shell   This is the path to the shell that runs when the user logs into the Unix domain.

Home Directory   This directory becomes the default location where users store data on the network or the local computer.

Primary Group Name/GID   Becomes the group that the user is associated with when accessing POSIX-based applications.

As you make changes to the user account, especially if you change the account's domain membership, you will need to make sure that you configure the UID to be unique within the domain. The user's access to resources is based on their UID and their GIDs. If you make changes to these IDs, you could cause the user to lose access to resources.

When setting the user's Primary Group Name/GID, make sure that you go to the properties sheet of the group and verify that the user is a member of the group. If the user is not included in the Unix Attributes tab of the group's properties sheet, add the user account.

Groups

Groups need to be identified by a Group Identifier (GID) just as user accounts need to have a UID. When you open the Unix Attributes on the group's properties sheet, you will see that there are not many attributes. Figure 7.28 shows the NIS map attributes that you can work with.

NIS Domain   The name of the domain that the group account will use.

GID (Group ID)   The numeric identifier that is used when granting members of the group access to resources.

Members   List of accounts that use the group's GID when accessing resources.

FIGURE 7.27
Unix Attributes for
a user account

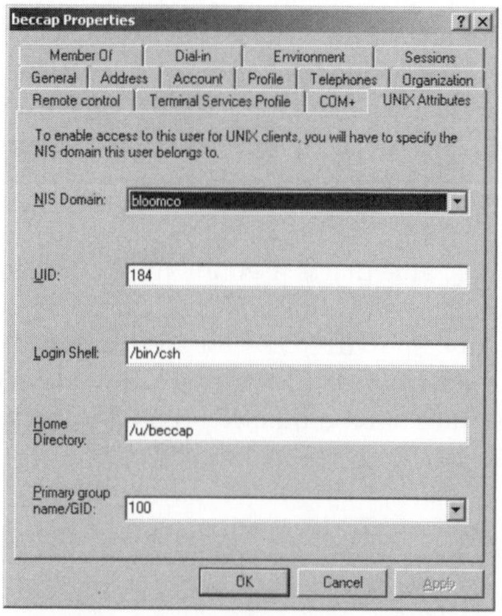

Computers

Computers are identified in an NIS domain by their IP address and alias names. When you open the Unix Attributes tab of the computer's properties sheet, as shown in Figure 7.29, you will find that you can select the domain in which the computer will be used, along with the addressing information for the computer.

NIS Domain   The name of the domain where the computer account will be used.

IP Address   Network address that will be used by the computer.

Alias   Hostname that the computer will be known by.

List of Aliases   All of the aliases that are associated with the computer.

FIGURE 7.28
Unix attributes
for a group

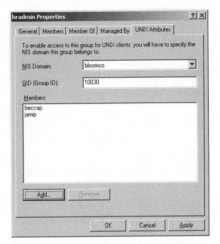

FIGURE 7.29
Unix attributes for
a computer

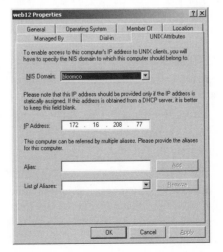

Configuring the Unix Clients

After you have migrated the maps and configured all of the systems to use the new master NIS server, the clients that will use the master server will need to be configured. Each of the Unix and Linux systems is bound to an NIS server. To force the system to renew its domain binding information, use the command kill -9 ypbindpid. Then start the process by running the command ypbind.

If you merged Unix domains, or you changed the domain when you migrated the maps, run the command domainName *domain* where *domain* is the new domain for the client computer, before you stop and restart ypbind.

Changing Passwords

Once Active Directory hosts the NIS map data, the user's password should be changed using Windows-based password utilities when at all possible. For the Unix and Linux accounts, users should not try to use the NIS yppasswd command to change the password unless the Password Synchronization utilities are installed.

Command-Line Options

Unix and Linux administrators are usually very comfortable with using commands from the command line instead of using a graphical user interface (GUI). As you will find, you can perform most of your administrative tasks from the command line, and sometimes you can do things from the command line that are not possible when using the GUI. Server for NIS has commands available for administrative use also.

nis2ad   You can migrate your NIS maps using the migration wizard that is built into Server for NIS, or you can use the command nis2ad. The same cautions apply with this utility as they did with the migration wizard; make sure you know which maps you want to migrate and where you want to migrate them. The user running nis2ad needs to have the appropriate permissions to create the objects within Active Directory. The syntax for nis2ad is:

```
nis2ad.exe -d directory_name [-s server_name] [-u user_name -p password]
➡[-f logfile_path] [-c conflict_file_path] [-r (yes|no)] [-n]
➡[-t target_container_name] [-m] [-h -?]
```

-d *directory_name*   Defines the path to the location of the NIS map files.

-s *server_name*   Specifies the name of the domain controller where you are importing the NIS maps.

-u *user_name*   Specifies the name of a user account that has permissions to write objects within the Active Directory location specified by the -t option.

-p *password*   Specifies the password for the user account used in the -u option.

-f *logfile_path*   Specifies the location where the log file will be created.

-c *conflict_file_path*   Specifies where the conflict file will be created if there are conflicts between Active Directory and the NIS maps.

-r (yes|no)   Specifies whether an existing Active Directory object should be replaced if there is a conflict between Active Directory and the NIS maps.

-n   Changes the Active Directory account name if there is a conflict between Active Directory and the NIS maps.

-t target_container_name   Specifies the name of the Active Directory container where the user accounts will be migrated.

-m   Performs the migration. Omitting this option will perform a trial migration.

-h or -?   Opens the help file for the nis2ad utility.

NOTE   The -u option will only apply to permissions within Active Directory, therefore you will need to make sure that the context the user is currently authenticated with has access to the directories where the log files will reside when using the -f and -c options.

nisadmin   The nisadmin utility is a command-line version of the Server for NIS MMC snap-in. If you issue the command nisadmin from the command prompt without any options, the current settings for Server for NIS will be displayed. The syntax of the command is:

```
nisadmin computer [-u user_name] [-p password] function
```

where *computer* is the name of the remote NIS server that you are performing the action on, *user_name* is the name of a user that has administrative control over the NIS server, *password* is the password of the user account defined in the -u option, and *function* can be one of the following:

```
[mkmaster -d domain_name]
[mkslave -d domain_name -m server_name]
[config [pushint=[[days:]hours:]minutes]]|[logging=(n|v)]
[syncall]
[start]
[stop]
[pause]
[continue]
[encryptiontype (md5|crypt)]
```

mkmaster   In the preceding options, when using the mkmaster command, you would connect to the domain controller that you want to promote to a master NIS server and specify the domain that it will become a master of by using the -d *domain_name* option. For example, if server1 is going to become the master NIS server for the domain bloomco, you would enter:

```
nisadmin server1 mkmaster -d bloomco
```

mkslave   The mkslave option allows you to specify that the server you are currently running the command against will become a slave and the server that you identify in the -m *server_name* option will be promoted to the master NIS server. If you are demoting server1 and server7 is to be promoted, you would use the command:

```
nisadmin -server1 mkslave -d bloomco -m server7
```

config   Two options are available when using `config`: `pushint` and `config`. `pushint` defines the interval that is used when the server checks for changes in the configuration information and pushes the new map data to the Unix or Linux subordinate servers; `logging` specifies the logging level that is used for troubleshooting purposes. When using `pushint`, you have the option to specify the days, hours, and minutes that you want to wait before checking and pushing changes. The days setting must be numeric, hours must be numeric and in the format 0–23, and minutes must be numeric and in the format 0–59. For example, if you want to set the interval to every five hours and 30 minutes, you enter:

```
nisadmin -server1 config pushint=5:30
```

When setting the logging level, the value n specifies normal logging, which only logs failures, and the v, or verbose, level will log all failure, warning, and success events. You should only enable verbose logging for troubleshooting purposes. If you want to enable verbose logging you enter this command:

```
nisadmin -server1 config logging=v
```

syncall   Using the `syncall` option will force all changed maps to be immediately synchronized with the subordinates. Enter the following command:

```
nisadmin -server1 syncall
```

start   This option will start the Server for NIS service.

stop   This option will stop the Server for NIS service.

pause   This option will pause the Server for NIS service.

WARNING   When you `stop` or `pause` the Server for NIS service, changes to accounts will still replicate to domain controllers within Active Directory, but any subordinate servers that are running Unix or Linux operating systems will not receive map updates.

continue   This option will resume the Server for NIS service after it has been paused.

encryptiontype   Two types of encryption are available for NIS servers: MD5 and crypt. If all of the client systems are running a Linux operating system that supports MD5 encryption, you can enable MD5 by using the command line:

```
nisadmin server1 encryptiontype -d bloomco md5
```

However, if any of the clients are running a Unix operating system, or the version of Linux that they are using does not support MD5, you should use the default setting of `crypt`. To use crypt, you do not have to enter any special command-line option unless the domain was instructed to use MD5 and you need to revert back to using crypt. To do so enter:

```
nisadmin server1 encryptiontype -d bloomco crypt
```

nismap   You can manage the NIS maps by using the `nismap` command instead of working with the Active Directory Users and Computers administrative snap-in. There are four primary options when using the `nismap` command; `add`, `mod`, `del`, and `create`. As the options imply, you can add a map entry using the add option, modify an existing entry using the mod option, delete an existing entry from the map using the del option, and create the structure for a new nonstandard map using the create option. The syntax for each follows:

```
nismap add [-a domain_name] [-f logfile_path] [-s server_name]
➥[-u user_name] [p password]] -e map_entry [-r (yes|no)] [-c conflict_file_path]
```

-a *domain_name*   Name of the NIS domain for the map that is to be modified

-f *logfile_path*   Specifies the location where the log file will be created.

-s *server_name*   Specifies the name of the domain controller where you are importing the NIS maps.

-u *user_name*   Specifies the name of a user account that has permissions to write objects within the Active Directory location specified by the -t option.

-p *password*   Specifies the password for the user account used in the -u option.

-e *map_entry*   Specifies the data that is to be added to the map as a new map entry. This data must be surrounded by quotation marks (" ").

-r (yes|no)   Specifies whether an existing Active Directory object should be replaced if there is a conflict between Active Directory and the NIS maps.

-c *conflict_file_path*   Specifies where the conflict file will be created if there are conflicts between Active Directory and the NIS maps:

```
nismap mod [-a domain_name] [-f logfile_path] [-s server_name]
➥[-u user_name] [p password]] -k key -e map_entry
```

-a *domain_name*   Name of the NIS domain for the map that is to be modified.

-f *logfile_path*   Specifies the location where the log file will be created.

-s *server_name*   Specifies the name of the domain controller where you are importing the NIS maps.

-u *user_name*   Specifies the name of a user account that has permissions to write objects within the Active Directory location specified by the -t option.

-p *password*   Specifies the password for the user account used in the -u option.

-k *key*   Specifies the key search criteria for the key to be modified.

-e *map_entry*   Specifies the map data that is used to modify the entry. This data must be surrounded by quotation marks (" " " ").

```
nismap del [-a domain_name] [-f logfile_path] [-s server_name]
➥[-u user_name] [p password]] -k key
```

-a *domain_name*   Name of the NIS domain for the map that is to be modified.

-f *logfile_path*   Specifies the location where the log file will be created.

-s *server_name* Specifies the name of the domain controller where you are importing the NIS maps.

-u *user_name* Specifies the name of a user account that has permissions to write objects within the Active Directory location specified by the -t option.

-p *password* Specifies the password for the user account used in the -u option.

-k *key* Specifies the key search criteria for the key to be deleted.

```
nismap create [-f logfile_path] [-s server_name]
  ➥[-u user_name] [p password]] -i field_number -g separator -y
```

-a *domain_name* Name of the NIS domain for the map that is to be modified.

-f *logfile_path* Specifies the location where the log file will be created.

-s *server_name* Specifies the name of the domain controller where you are importing the NIS maps.

-u *user_name* Specifies the name of a user account that has permissions to write objects within the Active Directory location specified by the -t option.

-p *password* Specifies the password for the user account used in the **-u** option.

-i *field_number* Identifies the field that acts as the key to the map.

-g *separator* Identifies the character that is used as the separator within the file.

-y Indicates that the key is not part of the value for the map.

ypcat To view all of the keys within an NIS map, you can use the ypcat command to specify which map you want to view, and then have the keys displayed so that you can find possible duplicate keys or missing, null value entries within the map. The syntax is as follows:

```
ypcat ([-k] [-t] [-h server_name] [-d domain_name] map | -x)
```

-k Displays all of the key values within the map specified by *map_name*.

-t Will disable the map nickname table, thereby preventing map nicknames from being used.

-d *domain_name* Specifies the NIS domain where the map is used. If -d is not specified, the default NIS domain is selected.

NOTE The default NIS domain is the domain named within the DEFAULT_NIS_DOMAIN environment variable.

-h *server_name* Using the -h option, you can define which servers will receive the request for the map file. If you do not specify a computer name for *server_name*, the request will be broadcast to all NIS servers for the domain used in the -d option.

map Name of the map that will be used to extract the key values from.

-x This option will display all entries within the map nickname table.

ypclear   There are times when the NIS servers will not update their cached map information. If Active Directory hosts the correct map data, you can force the other NIS servers to clear their cache by issuing the ypclear command. The syntax is:

```
ypclear ([-d domain_name] [-t] -h server_name] map | -x)
```

-d *domain_name*   Specifies the NIS domain where the map is used. If -d is not specified, the default NIS domain is selected.

NOTE   The default NIS domain is the domain named within the DEFAULT_NIS_DOMAIN environment variable.

-t   Will disable the map nickname table, thereby preventing map nicknames from being used.

-h *server_name*   Specifies the name or names of the NIS servers that will be directed to clear their cache. If -h is not specified, the default NIS server will be directed to clear its cache.

NOTE   The default NIS server is the server named within the NIS_SERVER environment variable.

map   Name of the map that needs to have its data cleared from the cache.

-x   This option will display all entries within the map nickname table.

ypmatch   Whereas you could use ypcat to print the values of all the keys within an NIS map, ypmatch is used to display the values of specific keys within a map. The syntax to this command is:

```
ypmatch ([-d domain_name] [-t] [-h server_name] [-k] keys map | -x)
```

-d *domain_name*   Specifies the NIS domain where the map is used. If -d is not specified, the default NIS domain is selected.

NOTE   The default NIS domain is the domain named within the DEFAULT_NIS_DOMAIN environment variable.

-t   Will disable the map nickname table, thereby preventing map nicknames from being used.

-h *server_name*   Using the -h option, you can define which servers will receive the request for the map file. If the NIS_SERVER environment variable is set, the request will be sent to the server defined for that variable. If you do not specify a computer name for *server_name* and the NIS_SERVER variable is not set, the request will be broadcast to all NIS servers for the domain used in the -d option.

-k   Prints the key name as well as the key value.

keys   One or more keys that you want to display the value.

map   Name of the map that will be used to extract the key values from.

-x   This option will display all entries within the map nickname table.

yppush   The yppush utility is used to send notifications to the subordinate NIS servers when changes have been detected to the NIS maps. The subordinate servers will then accept the changes and update the maps that they host. To use this command to force propagation of the maps, the syntax is:

```
yppush [-d domain_name] [-q] [-t timeout] [-h host_names]
```

-d *domiain_name*   This option allows you to select a domain other than the default NIS domain.

NOTE   The default NIS domain is the domain named within the DEFAULT_NIS_DOMAIN environment variable.

-q   Allows the yppush utility to run in quiet mode and will not wait for a response.

-t *timeout*   The default timeout that yppush will wait for a response from the subordinate server is 30 seconds. If you want to change the timeout value, enter the timeout duration in seconds.

-h *host_names*   You can specify one or more subordinate servers that will receive the yppush command, separating them by spaces. If you do not specify the –h option, yppush will use the ypservers map, which contains the hostnames of all of the NIS subordinate servers in the domain.

WARNING   For the yppush command to work correctly, the ypservers map must contain only the hostnames of the subordinate servers. If there are any aliases used within this file, delete the alias and enter the actual hostname of the server.

Password Synchronization

The Password Synchronization components that are included within the Active Directory Services on Windows Server 2003 R2 allow accounts that reside within a Unix system to synchronize their passwords with Windows accounts, and vice versa. When you implement Server for NIS and configure one of your domain controllers to act as the master NIS server for the domain, password changes need to pass to the master. Once the master NIS server has processed the password change request, the password change will propagate through the other domain controllers by way of Active Directory replication, and then subordinate NIS servers will receive a propagation request from the master.

For the Password Synchronization component to work, you will need to do more than just add a service or program to your Active Directory environment. The entire solution is composed of Windows components and modules that need to be installed on the Unix systems. The components that need to be installed on each side depend on the platforms you are running.

To add the Password Synchronization component to your Active Directory domain controllers, you will need to open the Active Directory Services option from Add/Remove Windows components just as you have with each of the other services in this chapter. Once added, you will notice that the Microsoft Identity Management for Unix console will contain a new node called Password Synchronization, as shown in Figure 7.30. This is where you will need to configure the settings to allow password synchronization.

FIGURE 7.30
Password Synchronization node

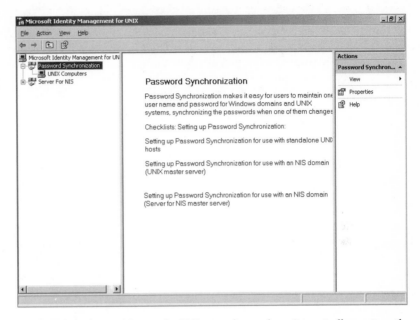

When you have installed and configured Server for NIS, one of your domain controllers acts as the master NIS server and is responsible for updating the Unix-based subordinate NIS servers. Because the domain controllers perform this role, you will have to update the user account passwords in Active Directory. Users that use Unix and Linux as their operating system do not have the same utilities that are used by Windows clients and do not have access to Active Directory tools that allow them to change the user account's password.

To alleviate this problem, you can configure the Password Synchronization component to accept password changes from the Unix and Linux clients and forward those changes to the domain controller. The domain controller will then update the appropriate NIS maps and propagate the changes to any Unix-based subordinate servers.

SETTING THE ENCRYPTION KEY VALUE

The first thing you need to take into account is the encryption key that is used to encrypt the password information as it is passed between the clients and the server. The encryption key must meet the following requirements to be used:

◆ Must be at least 16 characters, up to a maximum of 21 characters.

◆ Must contain at least one character from each of the following four options: uppercase letters, lowercase letters, numerals, and special characters. Valid characters include A–Z, a–z, 0–9, and ` ~ ! @ # $ % ^ & * - _ = + \ | [ ] { } ; : ' " < > . ?

◆ Cannot contain a blank space or any of the following characters: ( ) ,

Once you have decided what you will use for the encryption key, open the Microsoft Identity Management for Unix console and right-click on the Password Synchronization node. Selecting Properties will present you with the Password Synchronization Properties as shown in Figure 7.31. On the Settings property page, you can enter the new encryption key in the Encryption/Decryption Key text box. Once you do, click Apply or OK to set the key. Notice that there is a handy New Key button that allows you to generate a random key. This is very nice to have if you don't want to come up with a key on your own.

FIGURE 7.31
Setting the
encryption key

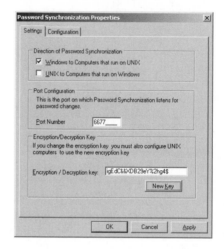

CONFIGURING THE SYNCHRONIZATION DIRECTION

Because the clients will be sending the password synchronization to your domain controllers, you will need to set the synchronization direction so that the Password Synchronization component knows to accept the change and pass it on to the domain controller. This is another setting that you will find on the Settings property page of the Password Synchronization Properties. As shown in Figure 7.31, the top configuration section has a section titled Direction Of Password Synchronization. For this scenario, we want to select the check box Unix To Computers That Run On Windows and make sure that the Windows To Components That Run On Unix is not selected.

PORT TO BE USED

By default, password changes are sent on port 6677. Most implementations will not have other applications that conflict with this port, but if you do, you may have to decide on a different port to use. If you determine that you want to use a different port for the password changes, you can change the port number in the Port Number text box in the Port Configuration section of the dialog box shown in Figure 7.31.

ADDING COMPUTERS TO SYNCHRONIZE

Each of the Unix computers participating in password synchronization need to be identified. Using Server for NIS, the NIS clients already communicate with the master NIS server and do not have to be defined, so only Unix computers that are not NIS clients will need to be added. To do so, right-click on the Computers node within Password Synchronization and select Add Computer. The dialog box that appears, shown in Figure 7.32, allows you to define the name of the Unix computer, the direction that synchronization will occur, the port number the computer uses, and the encryption key that is used when encrypting and decrypting the password when it is sent across the network.

FIGURE 7.32
Computer Properties
when adding a Unix
system

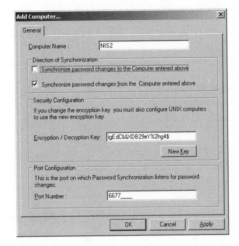

As shown in Figure 7.32, you can specify to allow synchronization either from Windows to Unix or from Unix to Windows. Because the password request is coming from a Unix client, you should select the Synchronize Password Changes From check box.

Configuring Other Domain Controllers

Once the settings have been determined and configured on the first domain controller, install the Password Synchronization component on each of the remaining domain controllers in your environment, making sure that the settings on each one are identical to the first. Once all of the domain controllers have been configured, you can configure the user accounts that will be able to synchronize their passwords.

Configuring User Account Password Synchronization

The Password Synchronization component checks for the existence of two global groups before allowing a password to be changed: `PasswordPropAllow` and `PasswordPropDeny`. As you can probably tell by the names of these groups, the `PasswordPropAllow` group will include users who are allowed to synchronize their passwords, and the `PasswordPropDeny` group will contain those who are restricted from synchronizing their passwords. These groups do not exist by default; you will have to create them using Active Directory Users and Computers. Of course, you don't have to create these groups; if neither group exists, then all users are allowed to synchronize their passwords. Take into account the rules in Table 7.1 to determine how you want to use these groups.

On the Unix side of the equation, you can configure the `sso.conf` file on the user's computer to include a deny option for the user's account by the line SYNC_USERS= and specifying the user's account name with a minus sign (-) sign preceding it. For example, if the user's name is `charlesf`, you would use SYNC_USERS=-`charlesf`. At this point, even if the user is allowed to synchronize the account password on the Windows side, the Unix side will stop the synchronization.

TABLE 7.1:   Password Group Rules

EXISTS	DOESN'T EXIST	RESULT
PasswordPropAllow	PasswordPropDeny	Any account within the allow group will be able to synchronize their password.
PasswordPropDeny	PasswordPropAllow	Any account will be able to synchronize their account as long as they are not in the deny group.
PasswordPropAllow PasswordPropDeny		Any account that is in the Password PropAllow group that is not included in the PasswordPropDeny group will be allowed to synchronize their passwords.
	PasswordPropAllow PasswordPropDeny	All accounts will be allowed to synchronize their passwords.

CONFIGURING THE PASSWORD SYNCHRONIZATION SETTING ON THE CLIENT

NIS clients need to know which server is going to accept the password change requests. Editing the sso.cfg file to include the master NIS server in the SYNC_HOSTS line, the NIS clients will then direct password changes to the domain controller. Once the domain controller acting as the master NIS server receives the request, it will replicate the changes to other domain controllers and send updates to the Unix-based subordinate NIS servers.

NOTE   No additional configuration needs to be performed on the Windows clients because they already update Active Directory when changing their passwords.

The clients cannot use the yppasswd command to change the password, however. Server for NIS does not support it. Instead, the client must be configured to use the passwd command. Editing the nsswitch.conf file to reflect this change will make the client believe that yppasswd is used when changing the password, when in reality the passwd binaries are called. When editing the nsswitch .conf file, the passwd and shadow lines should appear as:

```
passwd: files [NOTFOUND=continue] nis
shadow: files [NOTFOUND=continue] nis
```

Once all of the Identity Management for Unix components are configured, users will be allowed to change passwords when they are logged into a Windows-based system and the changes will be propagated to the Unix subordinate NIS server. When they log on to their Unix systems, they can use the same password they set on the Windows side. When they change their password while logged on to their Unix-based system, the password is forwarded to the domain controller acting as the master NIS server; when they log on to their Windows-based system, they use the same password that they just set from the Unix side.

Coming Up Next

Now that we have configured the interoperability options and methods of access to resources using the new Active Directory Services, we need to make sure that all of the resources are accessible to the appropriate clients. In the next chapter, we will look at how to control access to Active Directory resources so that only the appropriate staff members can update object properties, yet still allow users to connect and search for objects they need to perform their duties.

Chapter 8

Maintaining Organizational Units

Active Directory functions as a central repository of objects. These objects represent users, groups, computers, printers, and other items. You can control who has access to these objects and the scope of operations that may be performed upon the objects once that access is allowed. There is also one special object within Active Directory that was designed to make an administrator's life a little easier: organizational units, or OUs. By using OUs, you can organize other objects, as well as control administrative access to these objects. This chapter will help you control and manage the resources you choose to put within OUs.

Organizational Units

OUs have specific purposes within Active Directory. First and foremost, they are used for managing administrative control to resources. If you look back at Chapter 3, "Active Directory Forest and Domain Design," you will find a lengthy discussion on the creation of OUs and the criteria you should take into consideration when you are designing your OU structure. OUs should not be created to conform to the company's organizational chart. OUs should be created in such a way that they answer the question "Who manages what?" Once you have determined who is responsible for the objects within Active Directory, you will have a much easier time planning your OU structure.

The other OU design criterion is the efficient implementation of Group Policies. Once you have designed the administrative structure of OUs, then you should enhance the design so that you can use Group Policies to control user environments and manage security settings. Taking both administrative control and Group Policies into account when designing your OU infrastructure can be a daunting task, but once you have successfully deployed your OU structure, the administrative overhead will be reduced.

Components of Resources

OUs organize resources. That is a plain and simple statement, but it gets right to the point. Once we have the OU structure in place, the Active Directory resources can be added to their respective OU. Some of the more common resources you can create in Active Directory and place within OUs are computer, group, organizational unit, printer, shared folder, or user objects. Depending on how you manage your resources, you could have an OU that is dedicated to printer objects, and then the users who are responsible for maintaining those printers could be granted the permissions required to do their jobs.

Before we can take advantage of using OUs, the first thing we will need to do is create the OU structure. Creating OUs works in much the same way as creating the accounts we worked with in Chapter 6, "Managing Accounts: User, Group, and Computer." You can use Active Directory Users and Computers to create OUs, you can use the command-line utility DSAdd, or you can write a script. Whichever method you are most comfortable with is the method you should use. Do seriously consider the scripting solutions, though, because they are very powerful.

NOTE For more information on creating administrative scripts, see the last part of this book, which covers scripting and managing Active Directory using scripts.

Once created, the OUs can then be populated with objects. We have covered user, contact, InetOrgPerson, and computer accounts in Chapter 6. The other two object types that are commonly grouped within OUs are printer and shared folder objects.

PRINTER OBJECTS

A printer becomes a *printer object* when you publish the printer in Active Directory. When you install and share a printer on a server running either Windows 2000 or Windows Server 2003, it is automatically published in Active Directory. There is an option to remove a printer from Active Directory by going to the properties of the printer and clearing the List In The Directory check box as shown in Figure 8.1.

The property fields of a printer are populated when the printer is created and published in Active Directory. This allows users to search for printers by name, capabilities, or other criteria. A user can also search for printers by printer location. If you have Printer Tracking Location enabled and properly configured, then a user can find a printer based on location and not have to hunt for the closest printer. We will discuss this feature further in the Printer Tracking Location section. Users typically search for printers by using the Find Printer option in the Start menu or by performing a search in Active Directory.

You will not find a printer if you are searching the Active Directory console itself. Printers that are published are not directly visible because they appear beneath their computer objects and computer objects themselves are not usually treated as containers. If you want to view a printer, you will have to change the view of the Active Directory and Users console to Users Groups And Computers As Container. Once you do this, you can view printers (see Figure 8.2).

FIGURE 8.1
Property for listing the printer in Active Directory

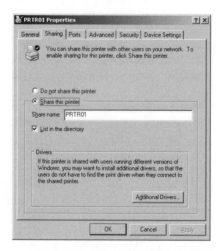

You should control access to your printers for security, cost, and departmental requirements. Some printers simply cost more than others to operate, and you may want to limit which and when users have access to these printers. Three permission levels are available (besides special permissions): Print, Manage Documents, and Manage Printers, as you can see in Figure 8.3. When you install a printer on the network, the default permission of Print is assigned. As with other areas of your network, you will want to plan what permissions are assigned to users and groups. Spending some time doing this will help maintain greater control over your printers and limit costs. You assign permissions to a printer the same way you do any other resource—through the Security tab on the properties sheet. Let us use the newly installed printer object Office Printer and assign our manager John Smith Manage Document permissions for our new printer.

FIGURE 8.2

Enabling the View Users Groups And Computers As Containers option

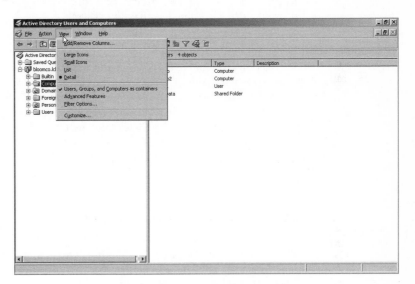

FIGURE 8.3

Printer permissions

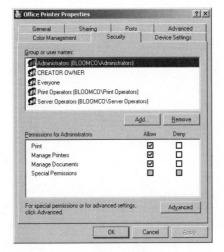

NOTE One thing to keep in mind when multiple permissions are applied to a group of users is that the effective permissions for a given printer will be the least restrictive of all assigned permissions. This does not hold true with the Deny permission, as Deny will take precedence over all other assigned permissions.

We have determined what permissions we are going to assign the printer and have applied them. What we need to do now is look at the Advanced tab on the properties sheet for a printer. Through the settings in the Advanced tab you can specify what hours a printer will be available and can control how a printer is accessed based on printer priorities. You can also specify how printer spooling will be handled, if and how separator pages will be used, as well as other options. In Figure 8.4, we have specified the printer is only available from 7 AM until 6 PM. So along with the normal permissions applied, the printer also has limited availability as well.

Printers and Group Policy

Group Policy is a powerful tool that you as an administrator can use to secure and control your network. This holds true with your printers and printing as well. You can use Group Policy to manage and control access to your printers once you have published your printers in Active Directory. (As you'll recall, a printer is published in Active Directory once it is created and shared). In the Group Policy Object Editor are a number of policies that you can use to streamline printing and facilitate control in your network, as you can see in Figure 8.5. Printer policies are found in the `computer configuration/administration templates/printers` section of the Group Policy Object Editor. We will take a closer look at these policies and implement methods for utilizing printing in an Active Directory environment to include web-based printing and printer tracking location.

Printing Policies for Accessing and Controlling Printers

A couple of the policies we will take a closer look at are Automatically Publish New Printers In Active Directory and Allow Printers To Be Published. These two policies are actually mutually exclusive as Allow Printers To Be Published takes precedence over Automatically Publish New Printers In Active Directory. So, if you disable the Allow Printers To Be Published policy, then users will not be able to use Active Directory to find printers. If you disable the Automatically Publish policy, then users will have to manually add printers.

FIGURE 8.4
Advanced settings
for printers

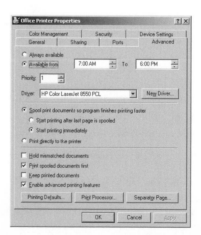

FIGURE 8.5

Group policy settings
for printers

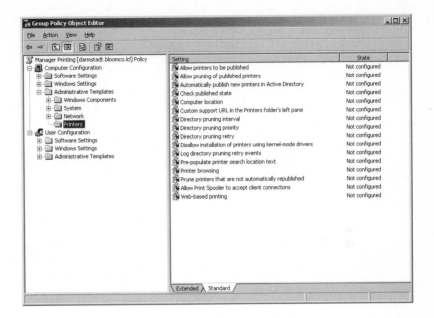

Web-Based Printing

This feature allows users to connect to a printer via an HTTP connection, such as `http://printer-servername/printers`. Some configuration on your part is required for this to function properly, namely setting up IIS to accommodate web-based printing. Web-based printing uses the Internet Printing Protocol (IPP) within HTTP to allow printing. You can control access to web-based printing through the directory security on the IIS server for the web-based printer website.

NOTE For more information on web-based printing and a white paper that goes into more detail on IPP, see www.`microsoft.com/windowsserver2003/techinfo/overview/` `internetprint.mspx`.

Printer Location Tracking

This new feature allows a user to find printers based on the user's location in the network. This is accomplished by implementing a systematic naming convention for the logical sites in your network. You then use the naming convention from your logical sites in the Location field in the properties sheet of the printer when initially created or at a later time. You will also need to create subnet objects in Active Directory Sites and Services for each site location. After establishing a naming convention and creating the requisite objects in Active Directory Sites and Services, you need to enable the Pre-populate Printer Search Location text policy in the `computer configuration/administrative templates/printers` settings in the Group Policy Object Editor for the container as shown in Figure 8.6.

FIGURE 8.6
Enabling printer
location tracking

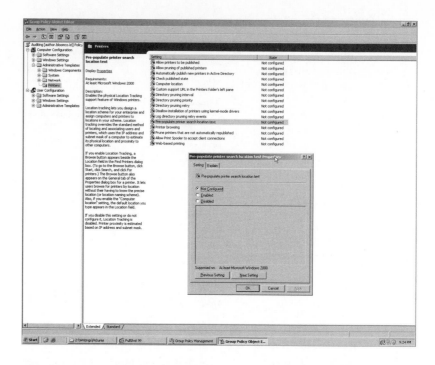

SHARED FOLDER OBJECTS PUBLISHED IN ACTIVE DIRECTORY

The last Active Directory object we are going to discuss is *shared folder* objects that have been published in Active Directory. A folder that has been published in Active Directory is accessible to all users with the appropriate permissions. The advantage for your users is that once a folder has been published, users can search AD for the object and don't have to know where the folder is stored or its share name , and they can use a Universal Naming Convention format (*server**share*).

You must first decide what container will host your newly created shared folder. Once you have decided on the container, you follow the steps you used earlier for creating users and groups, except you are going to choose Shared Folder instead. You must specify a correct Universal Naming Convention for the location of the share in the form *serve_ name**share_name*. The two remaining fields are optional and the information contained there only helps facilitate searches of Active Directory by users for these shared folders. You can enter a description of the shared folder and also use keywords by clicking the Keywords tab and typing what is needed.

One point to consider with shared folders is that if users have mapped a drive to the shared folder and you move the share to another server, then users will have to re-create the mapped drives based on the new location for the shared folders.

NOTE   You will not be able to see either the Security or the Object tab in the default view settings for the shared folder. To view these tabs, you need to go to the View tab in Active Directory Users and Computers and click the Advanced Features tab.

Granting Administrative Control

An object in Active directory is accessed by a security principal. A security principal can be a computer, group, service, or user. Every security principal is automatically assigned a security identifier. The security identifier uniquely identifies the specific security principal in Active Directory and is specific to a domain. Every object you create in Active Directory has an associated security descriptor. In fact, any object you create or store on an NTFS partition has an associated security descriptor. An object's security descriptor states who owns the object, who is allowed to access it and to what degree, and what—if any—auditing is enabled for the object. The accessibility level of an object is controlled by the Discretionary Access Control List (DACL), which is itself composed of an access control list and access control entries. Auditing for Active Directory objects is handled by the System Access Control List (SACL).

User Rights and Permissions When Accessing Resources

In the preceding sections I have used the terms *rights* and *permissions* interchangeably. In fact, it is quite common for people to interchange these two terms, but they do have their own specific meanings and applications. Rights, or user rights, are privileges that you assign to users or groups. Permissions are used to control access to objects.

How do Active Directory and NTFS work together using rights and permissions to ensure only authorized individuals gain access to approved resources? This is accomplished through the use of security descriptors, security principals, DACLs, SACLs, SIDs, and access tokens.

User Rights

A right, also called a user right, is a privilege that allows the designee to perform certain tasks. Rights can be assigned to users and groups. Rights can be very specific and detailed or can be broad in scope. User rights can be used to deny actions as well as permit actions. Rights can implicitly deny actions—for example, if you don't grant rights to a group, that group cannot perform a task—as well as explicitly deny rights by categorically denying someone permission. Assigning rights can have either very broad or very narrow scope. Other rights could potentially impact multiple domains—for example, if you had a site with multiple domains and applied an action to that site. If you had users or computers from two different domains in the same site, when the policy is applied to the site, then the users or computers would have to get their policies from both domains.

Security Descriptors

Every object you create in Active Directory or on an NTFS partition that can be secured has a security descriptor that is created when the object itself is created. A security descriptor is used to control access to the object and is composed of several parts: the DACL, the SACL, and information about the object's owner.

COMPONENTS OF A SECURITY DESCRIPTOR

An object's security descriptor states who owns the object, who is allowed to access the object, and to what degree and what, if any, auditing is enabled for the object. The accessibility level of an object is controlled by the DACL, and auditing of any accessed objects is handled by the SACL. A user's access token is compared with the requested action and if a match is found within the DACL, then the user is granted access. There are five fields contained in the DACL that are used together, as shown in Table 8.1.

TABLE 8.1: Structure of a Security Descriptor

FIELD	ENTRIES
Header	Identity Information
Owner	Owner's SID
Group	Group's SID
DACL	Access Control Entries for rights or access permissions
SACL	Access Control Entries for Auditing

Access to resources in Active Directory is set at the object level and is determined by the different permissions or levels of access. You can set the security for an object when it is created. If you don't make any security settings at the time you create an object, the object inherits settings from the parent object. The parent object can be the OU, folder, hard drive, or other container that the object was created in. If the parent object doesn't have security set, the object will use the default levels.

SECURITY PRINCIPALS

As we mentioned earlier, security principals are accounts that have permissions applied to them that allow them to access objects. When you create a security principal in Active Directory, that account or security group will then have access to resources contained in the domain once they have been properly authenticated by a domain. But what permits or denies a security principal access to resources? This is accomplished through a unique security identifier, or SID, which is generated at the time same time you create a security principal. We track security principals by name, whereas Active Directory tracks them by their SID. A security principal's SID is unique for a domain, so no two security principals will ever have the same SID in a domain. We will spend more time with SIDs later in this chapter.

We know that security principals can consist of computer, group, or user objects; user and group objects are typically the ones you will spend the most time administering. This is due to the fact that companies and their corresponding networks are dynamic. Employees come and go, have name changes, are promoted, reassigned, and so forth. Groups don't usually require as much time administering as users except for changes in membership.

DACL

The security descriptor is the basis for access to objects within Active Directory. Access to objects is determined by the access token of the security principal accessing the object and the ACL of the object.

The access control list (ACL) is composed of four parts: an ACL size, an ACL revision number, an access control entry (ACE) count, and the ACEs themselves. The ACL size is the amount of memory space, in bytes, that the ACL will occupy. An ACL can accommodate about 1820 ACEs based on maximum memory usage. The ACEs themselves are stored in the ACL in the order in which they were added following a canonical pattern. The canonical order is listed as Explicit Deny, Explicit Allow, Inherit Deny, and then Inherit Allow. This ensures that if there is an Explicit Deny, it will take precedence over an Explicit Allow.

When an object is accessed, a check is made to see if a DACL is present. If a DACL is not present, then access is automatically granted. If a DACL is present, then the ACEs are examined to see if any are applicable for the security principal accessing the object. If an Access Denied ACE is found first, then access is denied to the object requesting access.

SACL

You use a System Access Control List (SACL) to log any attempts to access an object that has been configured. When you configure auditing, those events that are enabled will be written to the security log, whether as a success or a failure. When configuring the SACL, you will specify the accounts upon which you want to perform auditing and the rights and permissions that you wish to audit. For example, if you want to audit who changes permissions on a printer, you would add in the Everyone group and specify that you want to audit the Success and Failure options on the Change permission.

An SACL only generates entries in the log on the domain controller where the actual access attempt occurred and not on every replicating domain controller. This is a situation in which using Microsoft Audit Collection System (MACS) or Microsoft Operations Manager would be beneficial.

SID

A security identifier (SID) is a unique identifier that is assigned to each and every security principal or security group upon creation. Every SID is composed of two parts: a relative identifier (RID) and the SID of the domain. Thus, each SID in a domain and any other domain in your enterprise network is unique and never repeated. The SID of a domain account is stored as part of the domain user or group account attributes, and is used as part of the authentication and authorization process when generating an access token.

As part of the object creation process, a globally unique identifier (GUID) is generated at the same time the SID is created and is one of an object's attributes that is published in the global catalog. The GUID is used by Active Directory to locate and identify objects, not just users and groups.

SID History

A SID is unique within a domain, but what happens to an object if it is moved to a new domain? If a user account is moved to a new domain, a new SID is generated. The value of a SID will change when it is moved. The losing domain will store the SID in the SID history property of the user object and the gaining domain will create a new SID for the object. When a user logs onto the network and an access token is generated for the user, the current SID and all SIDs in the SID history are placed in the access token. Thus, a user object maintains a listing or history of these SIDS if the domain functional level is set at Windows 2000 native or to Windows Server 2003.

So, what happens to the GUID if the SID changes for an object? Nothing; the GUID of the object does not change, but remains the same throughout the lifetime of the object, as long as that object is moved within the forest. The GUID only changes if the object is moved to another forest.

NOTE   A script is available to clear the SID history on an object. See "How to Use Visual Basic Script to Clear SidHistory," available at `http://support.microsoft.com/default.aspx?scid=kb; en-us;295758` for more information.

SID Filtering

Because Microsoft gives us the ability to move user objects across domains and even forests, there is the potential to misuse this capability and gain unauthorized access to resources. To help control this, you can use SID filtering. SID filtering is mainly used with external domain trusts and trusts between forests. SID filtering prevents the use of SIDs from outside the forest from gaining access to any resource within the forest. You can allow access to resources within the forest to users outside your forest by including the user's SID in the permission list on the resource. You can use the LDP.exe utility in the Support Tools to perform actions on SIDs.

NOTE   The LDP utility available in the Support Tools can be used to view information about Active Directory objects to include SID data. More information on LDP can be found at `www.microsoft .com/technet/prodtechnol/windowsserver2003/library/TechRef/4efcf47f-e3eb- 46e4-9c6c-842b39eca201.mspx`.

Access Token

This is the last of the items we will discuss when accessing objects and their permissions. An access token is generated at the time a user logs on to the domain and is authenticated by a domain controller. The access token has a listing of all the SIDs that contained in the user's SID history field (see the previous sections "SID History" and "SID Filtering") and SIDs for all the groups that the user belongs.

When a user attempts to access a securable object, the user's SID is verified against the DACL to ensure the user is authorized to have access. This is where the ACL and ACEs we talked about earlier are used.

If a user is made a member of a new group, the user does not inherit any of the permissions from that group until the user logs off and then back on again. The reason for this is that the access token of the user will be updated with new group membership access.

Permissions

Objects in Active Directory and on NTFS partitions have permissions assigned to them either through inheritance from a parent container or directly applied by the owner of the object or another user who has been granted or delegated permissions. Access to the object is controlled through the object's DACL. This list shows what users or groups have access to the object and what they are allowed to do with the object. In some cases, you might deny permissions.

You assign permissions to control access to resources in your network. In some situations you will grant limited access; in others you might grant full control; and in a few limited situations, you might explicitly deny access to resources. If you want to change permissions on an object, you must either be the owner of the object or have been granted the right to change permissions by the owner of the object.

Implicit and Explicit Permissions

Assigning permissions is one of the first steps in granting or denying someone access to resources. You can grant someone permissions, deny them access, or just not grant them permissions at all. If you grant someone access, they get the access level granted, plus any that they might inherit (more on that later). If you do not grant someone access, you have *implicitly denied* them access. If you select the Deny box for a permission, then you have *explicitly denied* them access, as shown in Figure 8.7. The Deny permission has the potential to cause problems with shares, so it is generally best to just not grant them access (Implicit Deny), rather than deny access (Explicit Deny).

You are the owner of an object because you created the object, were given ownership, or clicked the Take Ownership button. If you are the owner of an object, then you can grant permissions to others to your object. Generally, explicit permissions will take precedence over inherited permissions—for example, if an object inherits a Deny permission from a parent object it will not prevent access to an object if there is an Explicit Allow permission assigned to that object.

FIGURE 8.7

Explicitly denying permissions for an object

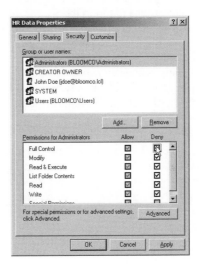

Permissions Inheritance

When you assign permissions to a container, those permissions will affect that container and any objects contained in that container *by default*. Known as permissions inheritance, this is a very useful tool for ensuring that permissions are applied systematically to all objects; it also helps to reduce administrator error when assigning permissions and is more efficient than manually assigning permissions.

Inheritance is enabled by default, but can be changed according to your administrative or security requirements. In some situations, you want to ensure that corporate-approved permissions are applied but need to change what permissions are applied at lower levels. To see if a specific permission is inherited, check the security properties sheet for the object; if the Allow or Deny box is unavailable, then that specific permission is inherited from the *parent* container, as you can see in Figure 8.8. A parent container holds the object in question. This can be another folder or even the domain itself.

To change the permissions inheritance of an object, you must go to the properties sheet of the object, click the Security tab, and then click the Advanced button. To change permissions inheritance, you will have to deselect the option "Allow inheritable permissions from the parent to propagate to this object and all child objects. Include these with entries explicitly defined here," as shown in Figure 8.9. When you deselect this box, another dialog box will appear that asks you how you want to handle the current inherited permissions that the window in Figure 8.10 displays:

◆ You can specify that permissions be copied to all child objects.

◆ You can specify that inherited permissions be removed from all child objects, and then later explicitly define what permissions will be applied.

◆ You can click the Cancel button.

Special Permissions

You can apply special access permissions to files or folders that will provide a more granular control or access of objects to meet specific security or corporate concerns. These are a further refinement of the basic permissions found in the Securityproperty page.

Assigning special permissions is done through the Advanced tab on the Security properties sheet. Click the user or group you need to assign special permissions to and click Edit. This will open the Permission entry box for the object, where you can modify the permissions. You can specify what objects the permissions will be applied to: This Folder, Subfolder And Files, or one of six other options, from the This Folder Only option to Files Only option, as shown in Figure 8.11. Once you are done and have clicked the OK button, the Permissions entry for the user or group will change to Special under the Permission tab.

FIGURE 8.8
Changing permissions inheritance

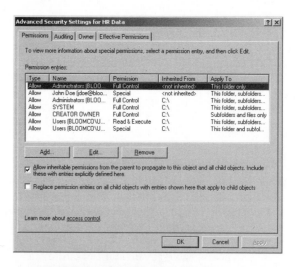

FIGURE 8.9
Changing inherited permissions

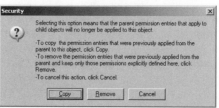

FIGURE 8.10
Permissions inheritance from a parent container

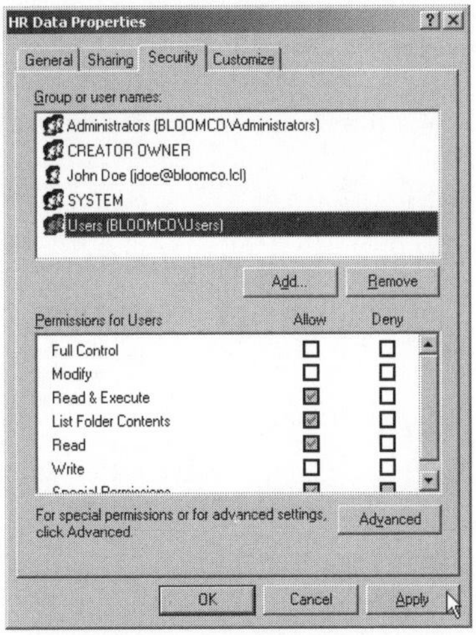

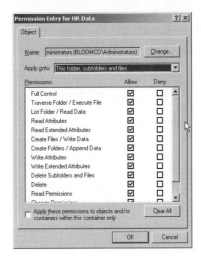

FIGURE 8.11
Special permissions

Effective Permissions

As you have seen, permissions can be directly assigned to a user (though you usually want to avoid this option) or to a group, or they can be inherited from parent containers. Trying to ascertain what permissions a user or group has applied or inherited can be a daunting task. Recall John Smith, our user from our earlier example. John Smith has permissions directly assigned to him; he is also a member of a group that has permissions applied to it and inherits permissions from another container. What are John Smith's overall permissions? This can be determined using Effective Permissions.

Effective Permissions is a new feature that allows an administrator to quickly determine what the overall permissions are for a user or group on an object. To access effective permissions, select the Advanced tab in the Security Settings dialog box for the object. Click Effective Permissions and pick the user or group you want to check. The Effective Permissions for the selected entity will be displayed, as shown in Figure 8.12.

Taking Ownership

There will be instances when an object (such as a printer or shared folder) was created by an employee who is no longer with the company and immediate access is required. How do you go about rectifying this situation? There is a nice feature in Windows Server 2003 that allows an administrator or someone who has been granted permission through a GPO to take ownership of the object.

Every object that is created has an owner—somebody created that object either on an NTFS partition or in Active Directory. The owner of that object has the ability to set permissions on this object to include the Take Ownership right. If the owner of an object assigns this permission to another user, that user can, in turn, either take ownership of the object for themselves or can assign ownership rights to other groups to which the user is a member. By default, administrators are granted the Take Ownership Of Files Or Other Objects right.

Delegation of Control

One feature in Windows Server 2003 that enhances our ability to administer networks is *delegation of control*. What this means to us is that we now have the capability of delegating administrative tasks to specific nonadministrator users or groups as well as limiting the functionality of other administrators. We can delegate control to practically all levels in our network: sites, domains, or OUs. Because we have this granularity of delegation capability, we can assign or delegate what are normally considered administrative tasks without giving up complete administrative authority for our network. No longer is it necessary to give someone administrative privileges, or make them a member of an administrators group, just to enable them to change user properties or reset passwords. We will discuss creating a delegation strategy as well as the mechanics of delegating administrative control. The tool that is useful for viewing or removing permissions is DSREVOKE.

FIGURE 8.13

Granting of Take Ownership rights

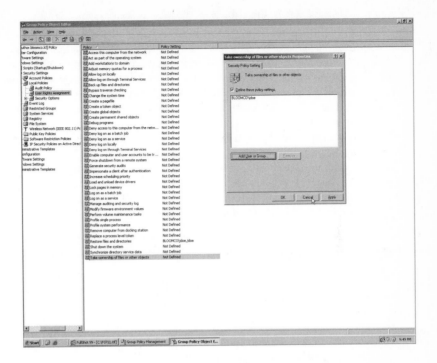

NOTE DSREVOKE is a new tool you can download from Microsoft that enables you to view or revoke the permissions on a user or group in Active Directory. If you want more information see www.microsoft.com/downloads/details.aspx?FamilyID=77744807-c403-4bda-b0e4-c2093b8d6383&DisplayLang=en.

Designing Delegation of Control

As with any other aspect of network design, you should carefully plan your delegation of control policies before implementing them on the network. This is especially true when you are talking about granting administrative or partial administrative access and control to parts of your network to other people. You are, in effect, giving "keys" to the network to those you delegate permissions. As part of your delegation strategy you should incorporate auditing, which we will talk more about later, to ensure you have a record of what others are doing on your network.

There are several factors to consider when designing your delegation of control strategy. First you need to determine what task or tasks you are going to delegate. Once you have done that, you need to decide to whom you are going to delegate. Is there a group already created or do you need to create one? What users will be a member of the group? Having decided on what is delegated and to whom, you need to determine how the permissions will be assigned and whether these permissions will be generic or property-specific. Included in this is whether the delegated group will be allowed to create and delete any child objects. One of the final things to decide is at what level you are going to assign control. Is this something you are going to allow for the entire domain, or just a site or an OU? Are you going to create an OU just for control purposes?

As we discussed earlier with groups, you want to avoid, as much as possible, assigning permissions directly to a user. This applies to delegated permissions as well. By assigning permissions to a group instead of directly to a user, you limit potential administrative problems and security holes. You can always add a user to a group and have the user log off and log on to receive the Effective Permissions of the group. There is the potential to forget that you assigned permissions directly to a user and, if the user is reassigned, the permissions will follow the user.

You have identified the group to whom you are going to delegate; now you have to decide on the level of delegation. This is a critical part of your delegation. Assigning of permissions can assist the administration of your network or become a security nightmare. Careful planning, coordination, and design sessions need to take place to ensure that the delegation will occur according to design, that corporate objectives are met, and that security is maintained.

The level of delegation for an object can run the gamut from Full Control of an OU to the granting of only one specific, limiting task. There are a number of scenarios that are typically employed in an organization for delegation.

◆ You can delegate permission to modify only one specific property in an OU. This would be applicable in a help desk scenario or for a new administrator in a controlled OU environment.

◆ You might delegate partial control of an OU to a group who might administer parts of an OU. In this case it could be an OU that is remote to the rest of your organization and the administrators require further control than the help desk can provide, such as creating or deleting child objects, adding or removing users to groups, and so on.

◆ In some cases you might assign full control of an OU to a group. This might be due to legal, political, or corporate concerns.

Another aspect of designing a delegation of control strategy is to decide if you need to create OUs for optimizing management and administration of your network; that is, creating OUs only for administration or management. This requirement could be the result of management wishes for delegation or to give control over OUs to specific administrators based on corporate policies, governmental regulations, or due to the acquisition of other companies.

Implementing Delegation of Control

Once you have decided on the level of control and who is going to receive the delegation, the next task is to actually delegate control. You do this through the Delegation of Control wizard.

USING THE DELEGATION OF CONTROL WIZARD

To delegate control of an OU, go through the Active Directory users and Computers and right-click the OU you want to delegate; then click Delegate Control. There are four steps in the delegation process:

1. Choosing which users or groups are going to receive delegated permissions

2. The actual tasks to delegate and whether they are

   ◆ Common tasks

   ◆ Creating a custom task

3. Active Directory object type

4. Permissions

   ◆ General

   ◆ Property specific

   ◆ Creation/deletion of specific child objects

In the first step, you will choose the users or groups that are going to have permissions delegated to them. This should have followed some sort of coherent design strategy to ensure that another group could not have been used or that the group would constitute a security risk.

You must next decide whether to select Delegate The Following Common Task or Create A Custom Task To Delegate, as shown in Figure 8.14. If you choose a common task(s), then you are finished. If you choose to create a custom task to delegate, you have a few extra steps. In the next screen you will have to choose between This Folder, Existing Objects In This Folder And Creation Of New Objects In This Folder, or Only The Following Objects In The Folder, as shown in Figure 8.15. Also in this screen, you will have to specify whether these are applicable for creating or deleting selected objects in this folder.

FIGURE 8.14
Delegation of tasks

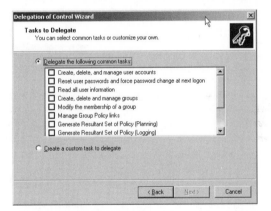

FIGURE 8.15
Scope of delegation

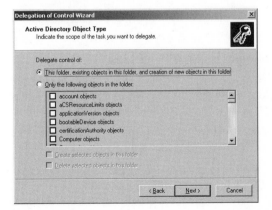

In the last step you must choose what permissions you wish to delegate and at what level, as Figure 8.16 shows.

From this you can see just how far you can delegate and to what granularity of control you can delegate. After deciding who will receive the delegation, you must decide what will be delegated. Some tasks that are commonly delegated include the following:

◆ Create user accounts

◆ Delete user accounts

◆ Manage user accounts

◆ Reset passwords on user accounts

◆ Read all user information

◆ Create, delete, manage groups

◆ Modify the membership of a group

◆ Manage Group Policy links

In the next section we will take a look at some best practices for implementing and employing delegation of permissions in a networked environment

FIGURE 8.16
Delegation of
permissions

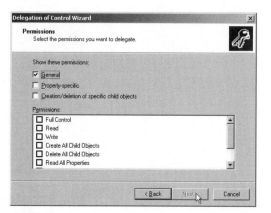

Delegation Best Practices

Delegation is a powerful tool for administering your network. If it is used carefully, then it will prove quite useful. So far in this section we have mentioned a few good practices to use when delegating; now let us expand on these and give more examples:

◆ Create groups and OUs that will have delegation applied to them. This facilitates security as well as administration.

◆ Try to avoid assigning permissions directly to a user. Create a group (see our earlier discussion) and place the user in that group. Creating a group to house one user is not as burdensome as it might seem initially; in fact, it will make your administrative life much easier than trying to track down why this one individual can still perform actions that they shouldn't.

- Least is most: Assign the *least* amount of permissions to users and groups. This will help make your network *most* secure. Users might think they are entitled to Full Control for everything, but they rarely if ever require it.

- Speaking of Full Control—use it sparingly! Full Control can backfire on you when users or groups start taking advantage of your largesse. Full Control gives the opportunity for a user to work with the permissions of an object. In this case they could give themselves greater permissions than were intended by the administrator. In addition, if someone gains control of this account, then they could potentially have a chance to cause more mayhem than they would otherwise.

- To further enforce security and enhance good administration techniques, you should delegate object creation and object management to different groups. This is known as TPI: Two Person Integrity. If you split the responsibility between two separate individuals or groups, then there is less likelihood of mismanagement by either. Think of this as splitting the create backup and restore permissions between two groups or a bank safety deposit box.

- Create Taskpad views. Taskpad views are great when you want to delegate tasks to help desk personnel or other groups that require some permissions but you don't want them to have access to the full console. This might a technique to help train new administrators before you give them the "keys" to the domain.

- You can delegate at levels higher than an OU, but avoid doing this as a rule. If you delegate permissions at the domain level, then that group could have a potentially far greater impact on your network than you anticipated.

NOTE For more information about Taskpad views, see www.microsoft.com/technet/ prodtechnol/windowsserver2003/library/ServerHelp/3d0c783c-7789-4400-953b-d22a501ae535.mspx.

Auditing

So far we have talked about enabling access to Active Directory objects and resources and controlling access to these objects. Another important aspect of controlling access and improving security is auditing. This section will not cover all aspects of auditing, but only those areas relevant to object and Active Directory access.

As with delegation, you want to spend some time planning your audit strategy. Auditing involves deciding which server and what actions will be recorded. Yes, you can audit every server for every listed action, but this would be too much information to sort through in an organized manner, especially in a large network. Not all objects or machines require auditing for both success and failure of those actions. If you suspect one of your administrators or delegated users of misusing their permissions, then you should audit the container that the administrator has been delegated permissions to control.

Once you have set up and are using an audit policy, you need to review the events that are recorded. Audit events are recorded in the Security log found in the Event Viewer. Of all the logs in the Event Viewer, the Security log has the tightest controls limiting access. By default, only administrators have access to this log, and you might consider limiting even that access to only a few individuals. The Security log will list all success and failed events that you have configured auditing to monitor. Some of those you are monitoring might have access to the Security log and can potentially remove evidence of their actions. As a result, you want to limit access to this log.

A consideration to keep in mind is that event logs are server-specific: actions that occur on server A440 are only listed on server A440 and not replicated throughout the network. This means you will have to check the logs and filter events on each server. Another option is to use Microsoft Operations Manager (for more information on MOM, see Chapter 16, "Troubleshooting Active Directory with Microsoft Operations Manager") or wait for the release of Microsoft Audit Collection System (MACS). MACS will collect the security event logs from your servers and stores them in a centralized SQL database. As of this writing, it is still in beta.

Though there are a total of ten audit categories events, we are mainly concerned with only a few of these as they pertain to accessing objects in Active Directory. The events we are interested in are as follows: Auditing Account Logon events, Auditing Account Management events, Auditing Directory Service Access events, Auditing Logon events, Auditing Privilege Use events, and Auditing Object Access events. Of these, only Auditing Object Access is done at the object level; the rest are handled through Group Policy.

Auditing of Security Events

Having decided what events you want to audit, you now need to configure your Group Policies in support of your auditing. Configuring an audit policy is done through the Group Policy Management MMC on the specific object level (site, domain, or OU). For our example in Figure 8.17, we will use the Personnel OU in our `bloomco` domain. The audit policy configuration settings are located in the Computer Configuration/Windows Settings/Security Settings/Local Policies tab in the Group Policy Object Editor.

FIGURE 8.17
Configuring an audit policy

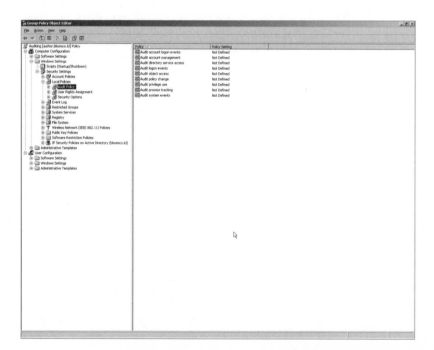

AUDIT ACCOUNT LOGON EVENTS

This policy tracks when users log on to the domain and when the logon is validated by a specific domain controller. The log is updated at the domain controller that authenticated the user. This is very useful for verifying and recording when a user actually logs on to the network or fails to log on.

AUDIT ACCOUNT MANAGEMENT EVENTS

Account management is concerned with tracking actions that affect user accounts, groups, and computer accounts. Any time a user account is created, deleted, disabled, enabled, or modified, the log is updated. Any time groups are created, deleted, or the membership changes, an entry is made in the log. If passwords are reset or changes made to security policies, these actions will be recorded in the event log.

AUDIT DIRECTORY SERVICE ACCESS

Directory service access occurs any time an object is accessed or changed in Active Directory. Use this policy to track when objects are accessed of if someone tries to access an object.

AUDITING PRIVILEGE USE

This is logged every time a user tries to exercise almost any right. Enable this for failure to detect possible network permissions problems or when someone is trying to gain access to resources that are not granted to them. This is typically seen when someone tries to *take ownership* of a resource. If set for *success* auditing, your log will grow very quickly.

Audit Object Access

Object Access is the only auditing event we are going to discuss that is not handled through the object editor in Group Policy. This auditing is handled on a per-object basis and is configured in the Advanced Security Settings properties sheet of the object you wish to audit.

To enable auditing on a folder or any other object, you need to open the properties sheet for that object, click the Security tab, and click the Advanced button in the Security Properties window. In the Advanced Security Settings window for the object, click the Auditing tab, as shown in Figure 8.18. In the Auditing window you will specify which users and/or groups you want to audit by clicking the Add button and choosing whether you want to audit Success, Failure, or both in the Auditing window, as shown in Figure 8.19. Other options you have available in this window are to specify at what level you are going to apply auditing, i.e., whether it will apply to This Folder, Subfolders And Files, or one of six other settings dependent on your auditing needs.

We've only discussed applying auditing to a folder, though you can apply it to other Active Directory objects in the same way. Auditing can be enabled for objects in Active Directory by going through Active Directory Users and Computers. Before you can view the Security tab for objects in the Active Directory Users and Computers MMC snap-in, you need to enable them for viewing. By default, you cannot view the Security tab on Active Directory objects; you enable this by clicking the View button and then select the Users, Groups And Computers As Containers or Advanced Features listing in the View drop-down box. This also applies to any printers you might have listed in Active Directory. They will not be visible unless you select the Users, Groups And Computers As Containers tab as well.

FIGURE 8.18
Enabling auditing
of an object

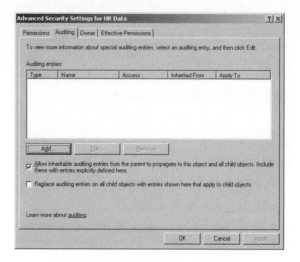

FIGURE 8.19
Configuring auditing
of an object

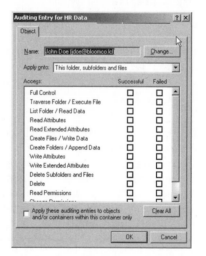

Auditing Printers and Printing

As with other objects, you should audit printer access to see who has been printing or is *trying* to print to the new high-resolution color printer or high-speed duplex printer. Our first step is determining who has access; we can do this through Effective Permissions. We talked before about Effective Permissions, but not with printers. We will use the same interface for printers as well as we did with objects. To access the Effective Permissions, right-click the printer in the Printers and Faxes tab, select Properties, and select the Security tab. Then, click the Advanced tab and click Effective Permissions.

At this point you can choose what users or groups you want to check for permissions, as shown in Figure 8.20. This will tell you who has the potential access but not who is accessing the printer. To determine who is accessing the printer and when, you will use auditing.

You enable auditing on a printer in the same way as you do for other objects. The Auditing window is accessed through the Advanced tab under Security Settings. Select what users or groups you want to audit; then specify what events and whether it is for success, failure, or both, as shown in Figure 8.21.

FIGURE 8.20
Viewing Effective Permissions on a printer

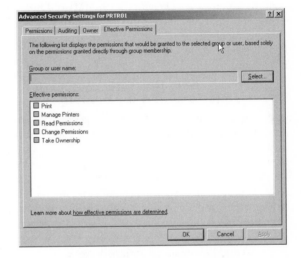

FIGURE 8.21
Viewing audit permissions of a printer

Moving Objects in Active Directory

Certain assumptions were made about the growth of the network and its structure in the initial design of the Active Directory network. A network is rarely static; it will grow and contract. You may add child domains or create new trees or even add forests. Within the domains you may add or remove OUs to facilitate administration, and you will definitely have to move users, computers, printers, and other objects. This is especially true if you are taking over a network from someone else and need to reorganize. If you need to move objects between domains or between forests, you will have to use tools other than Active Directory Users and Computers. If you have to move object between domains, you can use the movetree command-line utility or the Active Directory Migration Tool. If, however, you need to move objects between forests, you can again use the Active Directory Migration Tool or if you are just moving security principals, the clonepr tool. We will discuss all of these tools later in this section.

Moving Objects within the Domain

Several methods are available for moving objects in Active Directory. You can use a script to move large numbers of objects. The dsadd command mentioned earlier is always available, though you must be careful when using dsadd due to typos and syntax errors. The method you are most likely to use when moving objects will be the Active Directory Users and Computers console. When using the Active Directory Users and Computers console, you can either drag and drop an object to a new container, or you can use the move command. Either approach will accomplish the same purpose.

The drag-and-drop feature is quite handy for moving computer objects. Just click and hold the computer object you want to move and drag it to its new container. When using this method, a dialog box will appear telling you that "Moving objects in Active Directory can prevent your existing system from working the way it was designed. Are you sure you want to move this object?", as shown in Figure 8.22.

If you plan to use the move command, you will right-click the object, click the Move tab, and specify the new container in which you want to place the object, and then click the OK button. You will not receive the warning as you did when using the drag-and-drop method.

Moving of objects is not confined to just computers. You can move printers, users, and shared folders using the same methods as we used with computers. If you are moving a printer to a new container you will need to *connect* it so it can be used. You connect a printer by right-clicking the printer and selecting Connect.

Moving Objects between Domains

You cannot directly move objects between domains as readily as you can within a domain. If you need to move objects between domains, use the movetree command-line utility included in the Support Tools on the Windows Server 2003 CD.

FIGURE 8.22
Moving an object
within a domain

MOVETREE

The `movetree` command-line utility allows you to move Active Directory objects, organizational units, computer, user accounts, and other to other domains *within* the same forest. That is the caveat with `movetree`—all movement must be in the same forest. There are some requirements that must be met before you can successfully use `movetree`. The destination domain must have the domain functional level of Windows 2000 native or higher. You must have proper permissions on both source and destination computers. There must be proper DNS name resolution with source and destination domains.

What Contents Are Moved?

What is moved and what is not? Computer accounts are moved, but not valid; if you need to have valid computer accounts use the `netdom` command-line utility, which we will discuss next. Users and organizational units are moved completely. Users' passwords will be moved with the user accounts. Groups, however, are a special case. Universal groups and their members can be moved to a new domain without any problem. Domain local and global groups can be moved to the new domain only if the groups are empty. You will have to re-create all the group memberships in the new domain.

If you are planning to move any organizational units, you should be aware that all associated Group Policy object links will remain intact from the original (source) domain. These links will remain in effect and continue to be applied and updated to the OU across your WAN links. This cross-domain linkage of Group Policy objects could have a detrimental impact on your network performance, especially for slower WAN links. In this scenario, create new Group Policy objects in the destination domain.

Syntax

The syntax of `movetree` is:

```
Movetree /[/start | /continue | /check | /startnocheck] /s /d /sdn /ddn
```

The options are:

- `/start` will initiate the move and includes the `/check`. The command will continue until either it is finished or there is an interrupt.

- `/continue` will resume the move if there is an interrupt.

- `/check` will conduct a practice run without moving any objects—great for testing a move first.

- `/s` is the fully qualified primary DNS name of the server in the source domain.

- `/d` is the fully qualified primary DNS name of the server in the destination domain.

- `/sdn` is the distinguished name of the source subtree.

- `/ddn` is the distinguished name of the destination subtree.

Remember that the distinguished name is the complete LDAP name for the object or tree you wish to move. If you want to move the Managers OU in the Operations child domain of `AcmeEnterprises.com`, then the complete distinguished name (DN) would be `ou=managers, dc=operations, dc=acmeenterprises, dc=com`.

Let us move our Managers OU from before to a new domain, planning. What would it look like?

```
Movetree /start /s opserver1 /d planserver1 /sdn ou=managers,dc=operations,dc=acme
enterprise,dc=com ~CA/ddn ou=managers,dc=planning,dc=acme enterprise,dc=com
```

TIP For more information on movetree, see http://support.microsoft.com/default
.aspx?scid=kb;en-us;238394.

NETDOM

As I mentioned earlier, if you want to move a computer account to a different domain, you will have to use the netdom command-line utility. This powerful tool has many purposes beyond just moving a computer account. You can use it to create one-way and two-way trusts between domains; query the domain for trust information; add, join, and remove computers to the domain; reset secure connections between a workstation and computer; and many other tasks. The netdom utility is in the Support\Tools folder on the Windows Server 2003 CD and can be installed with the suptools.msi command.

If you wanted to join the ws053 computer to the AcmeEnterprises domain in the planning OU, the syntax would look something like this:

```
Netdom join /d:acmeenterprises.com ws053 /ou:ou=planning, dc=acmeenterprises,
dc=com
```

TIP For more information on netdom, see www.microsoft.com/technet/prodtechnol/
windowsserver2003/library/TechRef/954cf9bf-e152-4b82-a342-10db4b016cd7.mspx.

Moving Objects between Forests

There may be times as your network grows when you need to reorganize and create new domains in a new forest or maybe migrate older domains to a new Windows Server 2003 forest. In either case, you can use the Active Directory Migration Tool for these purposes. This tool can be used to copy users, groups, and computers between two forests. There is another utility that can be used to copy only security principals: the clonepr tool.

ACTIVE DIRECTORY MIGRATION TOOL

The Active Directory Migration Tool (ADMT) is used to move users, groups, and computers between forests and within forests. If you use ADMT to migrate objects within the forest, it will move the objects to the new domain and is a destructive process.

There is more work in configuring the domains when using ADMT than is required with the other methods we have talked about so far. To install ADMT, double-click the admigration.msi file in the i386\admt folder on your Windows Server 2003 CD. ADMT is installed in your Administrative Tools by default. Once it's installed, you can then begin the process of configuring permissions, migration groups, and computers for migration.

How you set up ADMT is dependent on whether it will be used for migrating objects within a forest or between forests. If you are going to migrate objects within a forest, you should create account migration groups and resource migration groups (if applicable) in both the source and destination domains. Within each of these groups, create the migration accounts necessary.

If you are planning on using ADMT to migrate objects to a different domain, you will need Administrator rights in the source domain and on every computer you want to migrate. You will also have to configure the source domain to trust the target domain. You must ensure that the computer you have installed ADMT on is a member of either the target or the source domain.

The actual process of moving is simplified using the wizards in the ADMT. Open the ADMT console in your Administrative Tools and click the Actions tab at the top of the console. Then click the Migration wizard, as shown in Figure 8.23. Once you have opened the wizard, you will have to choose whether you want to migrate now or test the migration. In the next screen you will specify the source and destination domains involved in the migration. Next you will specify the user and the group computer you are going to migrate, and then the target OU that will receive the migrated object. The last two screens contain the user and naming conflicts options you can configure.

NOTE For more information on ADMT version 2, see www.microsoft.com/technet/ prodtechnol/windowsserver2003/library/DepKit/c1caaadf-0f66-4c9b-a26f-2f707f7 ded49.mspx.

NOTE To download ADMT, go to www.microsoft.com/downloads/details.aspx?FamilyID =788975b1-5849-4707-9817-8c9773c25c6c&DisplayLang=en.

FIGURE 8.23
Accessing a
migration wizard

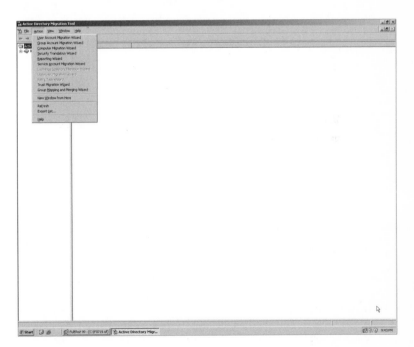

CLONEPRINCIPAL OR CLONEPR

The clonepr and movetree tools are similar in function: they both can be used to migrate users from one domain to another. However, movetree can only be used inside a forest for moves, whereas clonepr can migrate users to different forests. Another major difference is that clonepr *copies* the users to the new domain without their passwords, maintaining the integrity of the source domain. movetree, on the other hand, *moves* the users to the new domain, maintaining their passwords, and thus removing those objects from the source domain.

Coming Up Next

In this chapter, as well as in Chapter 3, we have mentioned how you should build your OU design to accommodate administrative control as well as group policies. In the next chapter, we are going to delve into the world of Group Policies. Within this world you will find the magical tools that allow you to control your user's environments and maintain the security levels of your systems. We will also cover the utilities that are used to maintain the myriad Group Policy settings as well as keep track of all of the Group Policies that you may be implementing.

Chapter 9

Managing Group Policy

Microsoft offers a very powerful way of managing user and computer settings in a domain without having to visit each system or make changes to each user account. This centralized control is available by using Group Policies in Active Directory. Essentially, Group Policies are a collection of configurable user and computer settings consolidated into a single Active Directory object, called a Group Policy Object (GPO).

The benefit of using GPOs is that an administrator can make a settings change in a single location, and those changes are then applied to all objects that the GPO manages. Imagine a company that has 20,000 computers that need a single change applied—such as a proxy setting for Internet Explorer. The administrator can visit each computer and make the change manually, or create a GPO for those 20,000 computers, make the change in a single location, and then have it automatically applied to the 20,000 systems.

Group Policies are not new. Even before they were introduced in Windows 2000, similar policies were available in NT 4, when they were called System Policies. In Windows 2000, Microsoft extended the functionality of these System Policies, created Group Policies, and gave administrators the ability to configure user and computer settings on the domain, site, or organizational unit (OU) level in Active Directory.

Microsoft improved Group Policies in Windows Server 2003 by increasing the number of configurable settings, providing the ability to filter these settings using Windows Instrumentation Management (WMI) filters, and offering better management tools for Group Policies with the Group Policy Management Console and Resultant Set of Policies (RSoP).

Although Group Policies provide a comprehensive set of configurations for administrators to use, many companies have yet to leverage the benefits of Group Policies fully in their environment. Sadly, many companies simply use the default settings created during the implementation of Active Directory.

By leveraging Group Policies, companies can realize a quick return on their investment, and they can reduce their overall administrative effort—and cost—associated with the management of users and computers significantly.

Group Policy Management Tools

Before we dive into the details of Group Policies and explain some practical usages of them, we need to first start with the tools that are used to manage them. Microsoft offers the same tools available with Windows 2000—Active Directory Users and Computers, and Active Directory Sites and Services—as well as new tools that allow administrators to fully leverage new features in Windows Server 2003: Group Policy Management Console, and Resultant Set of Policies.

Working with ADU&C or ADS&S

Even with the release of Windows Server 2003 and all of the new management tools that became available, administrators are still able to use the Group Policy dialog box in Active Directory Users and Computers (ADU&C) and Active Directory Sites and Services (ADS&S) to manage Group Policy Objects, shown in Figures 9.1 and 9.2.

ADU&C and ADS&S Differences

Although the user interface for both ADU&C and ADS&S are similar, their reach is far different. ADU&C can manage Group Policies that target either the domain level in Active Directory or any OU in the directory structure. When using ADS&S, administrators can manage Group Policies that specifically target Active Directory sites.

FIGURE 9.1

Viewing Group Policy from Active Directory Users and Computers

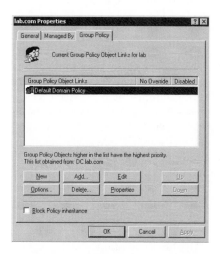

FIGURE 9.2

Viewing Group Policy from Active Directory Sites and Services

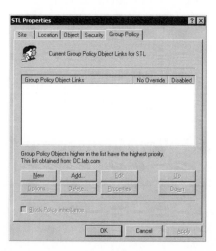

Sometimes you may have overlap, where settings in an organizational unit GPO are different from the settings in a site GPO. It's important to remember that when using both ADU&C and ADS&S, it may become difficult to effectively manage numerous GPOs that are targeting OUs and sites. As this task becomes more difficult, it's best to install the Group Policy Management Console (GPMC). GPMC provides administrators with a consolidated management tool for all GPOs: domain level, OU level, or site level.

Group Policy Management Console (GPMC)

GPMC is a great tool for complete Group Policy management, and it can be used to manage Windows Server 2003 as well as Windows 2000–based Group Policy implementations. GPMC simplifies the deployment, management, and troubleshooting of Group Policy implementations. Several key features are available with the GPMC:

- Single-seat Group Policy administration
- Backup/restore of GPOs
- Import/export and copy/paste of GPOs
- Management of security related to Group Policy
- Reporting for GPO settings and RSoP data
- Scripting of Group Policy–related tasks available in the GPMC

GPMC is not built in to Windows 2000, Windows XP, or Windows Server 2003, but it can be downloaded from www.microsoft.com/technet/prodtechnol/windowsserver2003/technologies/featured/gp/default.mspx.

As you can see in Figure 9.3, the Group Policy Management Console displays information about all of your group policy settings in a single clear, concise utility.

Group Policy Management Tasks

Group Policies are a collection of hundreds of settings that can be applied to either computers or users. When you look at a GPO, you'll notice that it is divided into computer and user categories, with settings that are specific to each. Although these settings are contained in a single GPO, they are processed at different stages. Computer settings are processed when the computer starts up, and the user settings are processed when the user logs on.

Understanding each setting in a GPO can be a very daunting task. Even though the intent of this chapter is not to break out each setting and explain what it does and why, we will talk about the components of a GPO and how you can leverage them in your environment.

Software Settings

Active Directory allows an administrator to control software settings on client computers. Using IntelliMirror technology, an administrator can remotely install software to client computers and control how that software will appear to the user. All of these settings are configured in the portion of a Group Policy Object titled Software Installation.

FIGURE 9.3

Group Policy Management Console

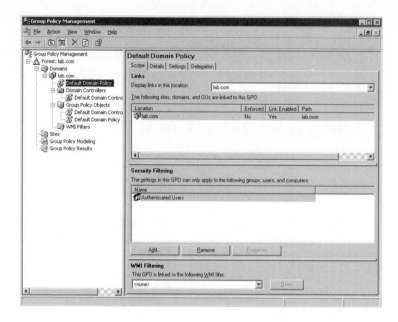

SOFTWARE INSTALLATION

When talking about leveraging Group Policy to reduce the cost associated with administrative overhead, we need to talk about using Group Policy to deploy software. Application life cycle management is one of the biggest tasks that administrators have to deal with, so if we can reduce the number of hours associated with this chore, we can focus on more important administrative duties and lower cost in the process.

Any application that has an `.msi` extension can be installed using this technology, and you can manage the entire life cycle from the installation of the software, upgrades to it, or the removal of it.

There are a couple of approaches when deploying software using Group Policy. You can deploy the software to a user if you want a user to receive an application no matter where they log on. Or you can deploy the software to a computer if you want to make sure that everyone who logs on to the computer will get that application.

Publish/Assign Software to a User

You can deploy software to users if you want to make sure that they receive the software independent of the computer they log on to. This is useful if you have users who always need a certain application available regardless of the computer they log on to.

There is some flexibility when deploying software to users. You can either *publish* the application to the user, or *assign* the application to the user. Each method acts differently when a user logs on:

♦ **Published**. When you publish an application, the application doesn't actually install when the user logs on. Instead, the application is made available in Add/Remove programs in the Control Panel. You can also set the application to install if the user opens a file that is associated with the application. For example, if you deploy Microsoft Word using this approach, and the user opens a .doc file, the Microsoft Word application would automatically install and open the file.

◆ **Assigned**. Assigning an application works a bit differently. When you assign an application, it will be added to the Start menu and/or to the desktop. Unless you configured the Group Policy to install the application during logon, it still doesn't actually install the software until a user attempts to use it for the first time. Additionally, whenever a user attempts to use this application, Windows will check to make sure that the application hasn't been damaged. If any files or settings are missing, they will be replaced.

Assign Software to a Computer

Assigning software to a computer is very similar to assigning software to a user. The differences are that it will take effect when the computer starts up, and that the application will actually install.

Unless there is a specific reason to publish software, consider the option to assign all software that will be deployed using Group Policy. The benefit to this is that users do not need to go to Add/Remove Programs to install the software.

Deploying Software Using a GPO

You can use the following steps to install an application using a GPO:

NOTE All steps are performed using the GPMC snap-in and assume that a GPO has already been created, and permissions have been given to a network share where the MSI package resides.

1. In the left pane, expand the Forest container, expand the Domains container, browse to the domain of the target GPO, and expand the Group Policy Objects container.

2. Right-click on the target GPO and select Edit.

3. Under Computer Configuration or User Configuration, expand Software Settings.

4. Right-click on Software Installation and select New ➢ Package.

5. Browse to the network share that has the MSI package for the application and click OK.

6. Select Assign (to assign the application) or Publish (to publish it) and click OK.

Deploying software using Group Policy is great, but there are some things to keep in mind. Group Policy software deployment is absolute, so make sure the package that you are deploying is configured correctly and that you've tested it. Group Policy will try to install the package almost immediately after you configure the GPO, and it doesn't care so much about available bandwidth. If your package is big, you'll probably see a hit on the network, as well as a hit on computer resources.

If you use a product like Systems Management Server (SMS) 2003 to deploy software packages, it's still a good idea to leverage the power of Group Policy for software installation. A good blend of these two tools would be to use Group Policy to do the initial install of software packages to new computers, and then use SMS to management the software—to include reporting, patching, and updating.

Create an OU specifically for systems deployment and link a GPO with all the necessary software to it. Once the computer drops in the OU, it will install the software and become available for management through SMS. This approach will ensure that software is installed immediately, without user or administrator involvement, and is still managed by SMS.

Windows Settings

The section of a Group Policy Object titled Windows Settings contains many settings that give an administrator a lot of power over how a client computer behaves. Keep this in mind as you are planning your settings changes in this area. It is a very good idea to test these settings on a few computers or in a lab environment before making changes to many clients.

SCRIPTS

Scripts are a valuable tool that administrators can use to further extend the capabilities of Group Policies. If you have experience scripting using batch files, VBScript, or JScript, you can add those scripts to your GPO and have them run as part of your Group Policy process.

Scripts can run at four different times using Group Policy:

Logon/Logoff There are two times a script can run when targeting users: logon and logoff.

Startup/Shutdown These two scripts are specific to computers, and they run independently of the user logging in.

Assigning Scripts in a GPO

To assign scripts in a GPO, follow these steps:

NOTE All steps are performed using the GPMC snap-in and assume that a GPO has already been created, and permissions have been given to a network share where the MSI package resides.

1. Open the GPMC snap-in.
2. In the left pane, expand the Forest container, expand the Domains container, browse to the domain of the target GPO, and expand the Group Policy Objects container.
3. Right-click on the target GPO and select Edit.
4. For computer startup or shutdown scripts, browse to Computer Configuration ➢ Windows Settings ➢ Scripts. For user logon or logoff script, browse to User Configuration ➢ Windows Settings ➢ Scripts.
5. In the right pane, double-click on the type of script you want to add.
6. Click the Add button.
7. Select the script by typing the name of it in or browsing to its location.
8. Type any script parameters in the Script Parameters field.
9. Click OK twice.

You can accomplish much using Group Policy scripts. If you are fortunate enough to have scripting gurus working with you—or if you are one yourself—the possibilities are endless.

For example, if you are using a product that requires an agent to be installed on all computers, and you need a way to get the agent installed quickly and efficiently, Group Policy scripts may just be your answer. As an example, deploying the SMS 2003 Advanced Client to all workstations in the domain is much more effective if you create a script that points each workstation to a network share, and starts the install process.

If you don't have an enterprise systems management solution in place, but you need to determine hardware inventory for all computers in your company, you can create a script that queries this information, place it into a GPO, and link it to your domain. Have the script run, create a `.txt` file of the hardware inventory, and copy the `.txt` file to a network share.

SECURITY SETTINGS

You can define a security configuration in a GPO that consists of settings applied to one or more security areas supported on Windows 2000, Windows XP, or Windows Server 2003. The specific security configuration is then applied to computers as part of the Group Policy application.

Be very careful when you make changes to these settings, as a wrong configuration could render your domain inoperable. Make sure that you test all security changes by linking a new GPO to a test OU, or filtering a GPO using security groups or WMI. These types of filtering are explained in detail later in this chapter.

Account Policies

Account policies consist of password policies, account lockout settings, and Kerberos policies. Although these policies are available in GPOs at all levels in Active Directory, they are only effective at the domain level. This means that even if you set these policies in a GPO at a second-level OU, they will not apply.

Password policies define the age, length, and uniqueness of passwords that are used for domain authentication. Account lockout settings include how Active Directory treats failed logon attempts. The Kerberos policy defines Kerberos ticket duration and Kerberos synchronization.

Local Policies

Audit policy, User Rights Assignment, and Security Options are found in the Local Policies section of GPOs. There are a vast number of settings that can be configured in these components of Group Policy.

Successful and failed events can be logged into the security log by configuring any of the nine events found in the Audit Policy. Windows Sever 2003 has some security auditing enabled by default, depending on the policy.

The Default Domain Controller Policy has the following categories that are set to audit successful events:

- Audit account logon events
- Audit account management
- Audit directory service access
- Audit logon events
- Audit policy change
- Audit system events

Policies that apply to stand-alone servers and member servers have the following categories set to audit successful events:

- Audit account logon events
- Audit logon events

User Rights Assignment settings and Security Options settings make up over 100 configurable settings in Local Policies. These settings include the ability to change the administrator and guest accounts, and LAN Manager authentication levels. Be aware that some of these security settings may have an adverse affect on the computers that communicate with systems configured by these policies. Specifically, legacy systems—Windows 9x and NT—may cease to communicate if certain settings are configured without proper planning.

Event Log

Within Security Settings of GPOs, settings can be defined for application, security, and system logs. These settings include increasing or decreasing the log size, specifying what to do when they reach their maximum size, and settings for overwriting logs after a specific number of days. Also, you can prevent guests who log on to the machine from seeing the logs.

Restricted Groups

Restricted Groups are used to configure membership in groups in Active Directory or in local groups of systems that have joined the domain.

The Members list defines who belongs to the restricted group. When you enforce a Restricted Groups policy, any current member who is not on the Members list is removed. Any user on the Members list who is not currently a member of the restricted group is added to that group.

The Member Of list specifies which other groups the restricted group itself belongs to. This setting allows you to control which other groups the specified group has membership in.

Restricted Groups are very useful, but they can become difficult to manage if you are trying to leverage them too much. Stick with using Restricted Groups for important accounts, like administrators accounts.

Some of the common uses of Restricted Groups are to restrict membership for the local Administrators group on corporate systems, and to restrict membership for the Domain Admins group. When using them for local Administrators group membership, remember that only the users or groups defined in the Restricted Groups policy will be added to the local Administrators group on the system.

Equally, any user or group that is a member of the local Administrators group will be removed. Keep this in mind when planning your Restricted Group deployment, as an incorrect implementation could cause access problems.

System Services

This setting allows you to configure the state of a service when the computer starts. Services can be configured as Automatic, Manual, or Disabled, and permissions can be applied to each service as well.

The best services to disable are FTP, Trivial FTP, Telnet, Computer Browser, and WWW Publishing. Unless there is a need for any one of these services on a client computer, it's best to just disable them to avoid security risks that are inherent with these services.

Registry

Another valuable collection of configurable settings found in Group Policy relates to the Registry. Using GPOs, you can define the permissions and audit settings for Registry keys. This is especially useful if you want to lock down access to computer resources, including the Registry.

Be careful not to remove all access to Registry keys for specific users or groups unless you are confident that access to these Registry keys will not be required by the user, or an application run by the user.

If you remove access to Registry keys and users are having problems using applications, you can run Registry monitoring tools to determine the keys that the application needs to access. Then, you can make the appropriate access adjustments in the Registry settings of Group Policy.

File System

Similar to the Registry settings, File System settings allow you to define the permissions and audit settings for files and folders. Be certain you understand the impact of these settings before removing access to files or folders for users or groups.

Wireless Network

This section is used to restrict computers from accessing wireless networks. By using these settings, you can permit the following networks to access:

Wireless Access To Any Available Network   With this choice, computers will connect to any 802.11 access point. The computer can also make a connection to wireless-enabled computers if no access point is available.

Access Point (Infrastructure) Networks Only   With this choice, computers will connect to access points only.

Computer-To-computer (Ad Hoc) Networks Only   With this choice, the computer can connect to wireless-enabled computers only.

This section also contains settings for designating preferred network, and key types for encryption and authentication. Smart cards and certificates can also be used by enabling access control through IEEE 802.1x.

Public Key Policies

The Public Key Policies include the following sections:

Encrypting File System   Settings that allow specified users the ability to decrypted files or folders that have been encrypted by other users. This is useful if the files are needed when a user leaves a company or when a user is unavailable and the files are needed immediately.

Automatic Certificate Request Settings   Settings that define the types of certificates that computers can automatically request. By using automatic certificate settings in public key policies, you can have computers that are targeted by this policy automatically enroll for certificates.

Trusted Root Certificates Authorities   Authorities that are automatically trusted by systems targeted by this policy. This is common for web pages that require secure communication.

Enterprise Trust   Settings that allow you to specify certificate trust lists (CTLs). A CTL is a list of self-signed certificates for the certificate authorities that are trusted by systems targeted by the policy.

Software Restriction Policies

This section is used for controlling which applications are allowed to run on the machines that are targeted by this policy. When creating a new software restriction policy, settings can be configured for the default security level. If Unrestricted is set as the default, everything is allowed. If Disallowed is set as the default, nothing is allowed. After configuring the default settings, you can create additional rules, as detailed here:

Hash Rule   A hashed value is created for the executable file. This value is calculated and compared to the stored value before it is allowed to run—or not run—based on the default security level. If the values do not match, the file will not open.

Certificate Rule   These rules use digital certificates to determine if a file should be allowed to open.

Path Rule   These rules use a specific location for permitting an executable to launch. If this rule is created, only executables located in this location will be allowed to run.

Internet Zone   These rules use the zones defined in Internet Explorer to determine whether a file can be executed.

Make sure you thoroughly test Software Restriction policies. If you set your default as Disallowed, you'll need to choose what you want to allow. This can become very difficult to manage, especially if one application calls another application. Many times you'll get denied errors even if you choose to allow an application because the application has dependencies that are not allowed. It can become cumbersome to keep up with all the applications that are needed.

As a best practice, create a new GPO for Software Restriction policies. This is important because you can disable this policy if necessary without disabling the Default Domain Policy.

Also, if you accidentally lock down a workstation with Software Restriction policies, restart the computer in Safe Mode. Software Restriction policies do not apply in safe mode. Log into the affected computer as a local administrator, modify the policy, run `GPUpdate`, and restart the computer.

IP Security Policies

These settings are used to enable authenticated and/or encrypted data communication between computers. Three IPSec policies are defined by default, and it's best to create new IPSec policies and use the predefined ones only as reference.

With these policies, filter lists can be created based on ports, protocols, and direction of traffic (inbound/outbound). When traffic matches a filter, specified actions can be carried out. These actions include blocking, permitting, and requesting or requiring encryption.

As with any security setting, thoroughly test your desired configurations. Since IPSec policies deal with network traffic, incorrectly configuring these policies can result in access problems, authentication errors, and application issues.

Folder Redirection

Certain folders can be redirected from user profiles to a central location. This is very useful in order to back up all this data centrally. The following folders in the user profile can be redirected to a specified file server:

◆ Application Data

◆ Desktop

◆ My Documents

◆ My Pictures

◆ Start menu

Different UNC paths can be defined for each of these folders, and users can have their folders redirected to different locations based on the security group(s) that they belong to.

NOTE When configuring Folder Redirection, allow the system to create the folders. If you create the folders manually, the permissions will not be correct.

If you want to remove the settings for Folder Redirection so that the folders are set back to the local profile location, make sure to use the Redirect To The Local User Profile policy setting. If you try to set the redirection option to Not Configured, it will continue to redirect to the location defined when configuring Folder Replication.

Remote Installation Services

Remote Installation Services (RIS) is a very useful way of deploying Windows 2000, XP, and Server 2003 operating systems to bare metal computers (computers that do not have an OS). Although the planning and implementation process for RIS configuration is comprehensive and requires DHCP, DNS, and Active Directory, RIS can be a very valuable tool for administrators.

The Choice Options can be set to define setup options for users. These settings, along with customizable screen settings on the RIS server, give administrators very granular control over the RIS operation.

RIS is one of the most underused and underappreciated tools available to administrators. By leveraging RIS, administrators can see a dramatic decrease in the number of hours spent deploying operating systems, patches, and software to machines. If you use both RIS and Group Policy software installation, you can fully build a system—with the operating system, patches, service packs, and software—in under an hour without any user involvement.

Internet Explorer Maintenance

These policies help you control Internet Explorer. The following settings can be configured with this section of the group policy:

Browser User Interface Settings that change the way the interface looks.

Connection

Connection Settings Use these settings to automatically set the connections settings for Internet connectivity.

Proxy Settings Use these settings to specify the proxy server IP and ports. These settings are very useful for companies that want to centralize these settings.

Automatic Browser Configuration These settings are useful for checking for updates.

User Agent String These settings are used mainly for tracking statistics.

URLs

Important URLs Settings for the Internet Explorer's home page, the search engine URL, and the online support page URL.

Favorites And Links These settings are useful if you want to predefine favorites for company users targeted by this policy.

Security

Security Zones and Content Rating   Settings for controlling which sites are allowed.

Authenticode Settings   These settings allows Internet Explorer to download and automatically install ActiveX and other types of components when supplied by trusted sources.

Programs   Settings that can be defined to identify which program Windows automatically uses for each Internet services.

The Internet Explorer Maintenance extension can be tricky for administrators who don't deal with it often. The most common settings configured here are Proxy Settings. Regardless of what is configured, it is important to remember that Internet Explorer Maintenance settings can be set in two modes: Preference mode and Policy mode.

Preference mode   All settings will be applied only once, and unless there is change to the policy, they will not apply again, even if you forcefully apply the policy again.

For example, the proxy settings for HTTP are configured as 192.168.0.100 Port 8080. After the policy applies to a computer, the user changes the proxy settings to 10.10.10.1 Port 80. The settings will stay 10.10.10.1 Port 80 until the Group Policy has been changed.

Policy mode   All settings are applied every time Group Policies are processed or updated.

For example, the proxy settings for HTTP are configured as 192.168.0.100 Port 8080. After the policy applies to a computer the user changes the proxy settings to 10.10.10.1 Port 80. The settings will go back to 192.168.0.100 Port 8080 the next time Group Policies are refreshed or reapplied.

If you need to switch from Preference mode to Policy mode, you'll need to reset the browser settings, which will clear all browser settings that were previously configured. As a rule, configure the settings in Internet Explorer Maintenance and leave them alone. It will save you a lot of heartache.

Administrative Templates

Administrative Templates are a collection of over 1300 Registry-based settings that are available using the Group Policy snap-in. These templates have the extension `.adm`, and give options to modify the registry for either the machine (HKEY_LOCAL_MACHINE) or the user (HKEY_CURRENT_USER).

By default, five templates are built in and available in Windows Server 2003, and they are stored in `%System Root%\inf`. These are shown in Table 9.1.

Additional templates are available in the `%System Root%\inf` folder, and they include settings for Windows 9x and NT systems, as well as additional settings for Internet Explorer. These templates are `Common.adm`, `Inetcorp.adm`, `Inetset.adm`, and `Windows.adm`.

All Registry-based settings that are modified using Group Policy are stored in the follow four Registry keys:

HKEY_CURRENT_USER\Software\Policies
HKEY_LOCAL_MACHINE\Software\Policies
HKEY_CURRENT_USER\Software\Microsoft\Windows\CurrentVersion\Policies
HKEY_LOCAL_MACHINE\Software\Microsoft\Windows\CurrentVersion\Policies

You can create additional `.adm` templates, but it's best to stay with settings that are stored under these keys. If Group Policy changes the Registry in a location other than those listed here, the changes will be persistent. This means that the changes will not be removed when the user logs off the computer or when the computer is shut down. This is often referred to as "tattooing" the Registry.

"Tattooing" the Registry can be a very frustrating situation, especially when troubleshooting Group Policy problems. The common scenario that causes the most grief is when an administrator creates an .adm template incorrectly and applies it to a computer. Removing the template from the Group Policy does not change the settings back, and this can be very painful if the administrator doesn't realize it.

If you get into a situation where an incorrectly configured .adm template has caused you problems, don't delete the template from the GPO. Instead, configure the settings in the template as Disabled and allow the settings to propagate completely. After the settings have been disabled on all target systems, change the settings to Not Configured. After these settings propagate, you can safely remove the .adm template from the GPO.

TABLE 9.1:   Default Policy Templates

TEMPLATE	DESCRIPTION	OS VERSIONS
Conf.adm	Policy settings for Microsoft NetMeeting	2000/XP/2003
Inetres.adm	Policy settings for Microsoft Internet Explorer	2000/XP/2003
System.adm	Policy settings for core OS GUI features	2000/XP/2003
Wmplayer.adm	Policy settings for Windows Media Player	XP/2003
Wuau.adm	Policy settings for automatic updates	2000 with SP3/XP with SP1/2003

Group Policy Inheritance

Within Active Directory, Group Policy settings are inherited from the parent container down the tree to the objects in the child containers. The complete inheritance model that Group Policy uses works like this:

1. Local computer GPOs are applied first to any user logging on to the system.

2. Site GPOs are applied and overwrite the settings specified in local computer GPOs.

3. Domain GPOs are applied and overwrite settings specified in local GPOs or site GPOs.

4. Organization unit GPOs are applied (from parent to child), and overwrite all other GPOs.

If any conflicts exist between the GPOs, the settings in the GPO closest to the object will apply. If conflicts exist between user settings and computer settings, the computers settings will usually apply.

Blocking Inheritance

Group Policies can be blocked so that child containers are not affected by GPOs in parent containers. This is useful if there is a container that needs to be unaffected by any other GPOs. A common example of this is an organizational unit that contains users and/or computers for testing purposes. By blocking inheritance from parent GPOs, these objects will be completely isolated from parent container settings.

The thing to remember with the Block Inheritance setting is that you cannot block specific settings in a GPO. Either the entire GPO is blocked, or it is allowed. If there is a specific setting that you do not want to inherit, consider creating a separate GPO with only that setting, and block that GPO at the lower-level container.

Enforcing Inheritance

Blocking inheritance is useful, but sometimes certain GPOs need to be enforced. This is true of GPOs that contain settings for every object in the domain, and is linked at the domain level. This is common for companies that use a tiered administrative model. Top-level administrators can apply GPOs to all lower-level objects, and by enforcing these GPOs, these settings will apply to the targeted objects even if Block Inheritance has been configured.

Be very careful how you use Block Inheritance and Enforce Inheritance. If you don't keep a close eye on these settings, troubleshooting will become very difficult.

Policy Filtering

Group Policies can be linked to the site, the domain, or to organizational units. This is good, if you want to apply the GPO to every object contained in each of those locations. But what commonly happens is that administrators need to apply certain settings to just a specific computer or user, or to a group of computers or users. And sometimes it's important to apply a GPO to a computer based on certain criteria, like Windows XP systems with at least 500MB of free space on the primary partition.

GPOs can be filtered in two ways: security group filtering, and WMI filtering.

SECURITY GROUP FILTERING

Linking a GPO to an OU with 500 computers will apply all the settings in the computers section of the GPO to all 500 computers. If you want to apply these settings to a selected group of computers, you can create a security group and add only the desired computers into that group. Then, you can add that group to the Security tab of the Group Policy Object Properties dialog box and give the group Read and Apply Group Policy. This will ensure that the policy applies to the security group you created.

If you did this, you'd soon realize that the policy still applies to all computers in the OU. This is because every new GPO is applied to the Authenticated Users group by default—which contains all security principals that have been authenticated by Active Directory. This includes all user accounts as well as all group accounts.

In order to ensure that the GPO only applies to the selected security group, deselect Apply Group Policy in the Security tab of the Group Policy Object Properties dialog box. Optionally, you can remove the Authenticated Users from the list.

WMI FILTERING

Windows Management Instrumentation (WMI) filtering is an addition to Group Policy in Windows Server 2003. Administrators can choose the filter they want, create a new filter, or edit an existing one.

Each GPO can be linked to one WMI filter, although the same filter can be linked to many GPOs. The WMI filter is evaluated on the targeted computer during Group Policy processing. If the filter evaluates to TRUE, the GPO will apply.

One thing to keep in mind is that WMI filters are ignored on Windows 2000 computers. If a GPO is linked to an OU containing Windows 2000 computers, it will apply to all Windows 2000 computers even if there is a WMI filter specifying that the policy only apply to Windows XP computers.

Although Windows 2000 computers ignore WMI filtering, you can still leverage WMI to target GPOs to Windows 2000 computers. For example, if you had a GPO with settings that you wanted to apply to Windows 2000 computers only, you can create a WMI filter that looks something like this:

```
Root\CimV2; Select * from Win32_OperatingSystem where Caption =
""Microsoft Windows 2000 Professional""
```

You can see that this WMI filter is targeting systems with the Operating System Caption of "Microsoft Windows 2000 Professional."

When the GPO is processed on all Windows XP computers, it will see that the GPO is configured to target only Windows 2000 Professional computers, and it will ignore the policy. Since Windows 2000 systems cannot understand WMI filtering, it accepts the policy and processes the settings. So although Windows 2000 ignores WMI filters, you can eliminate Windows XP so that Windows 2000 is the only operating system that the policy can be applied to.

Group Policy Storage

There are two kinds of Group Policy objects: local and non-local. Non-local Group Policy objects are used in Active Directory. Local Group Policy objects are stored on each computer.

Local

Local group policies are stored on the local system in the `%SystemRoot%System32\GroupPolicy` directory. They function differently than GPOs applied to Active Directory in that they do not replicate to other computers, and they have limited settings.

The `GroupPolicy` folder also contains subfolders. Two subfolders are always present: `Machine` and `User`. Here is a description of each folder:

Machine   This `Registry.pol` file contains the Registry settings that are applied to computers and are specific to the HKEY_LOCAL_MACHINE key.

User   This `Registry.pol` file contains the Registry settings that are applied to users and are specific to the HKEY_CURRENT_USER key. The `Gpt.ini` file contains version information.

Non-Local

Non-local Group Policy objects store Group Policy information in two locations: a Group Policy container and a Group Policy template. Each Group Policy is given a globally unique identifier (GUID) to keep them synchronized.

GROUP POLICY CONTAINER

The Group Policy container is stored in Active Directory and includes information for both computers and users. The properties that are specific to the Group Policy container include Version Information, Status, and Extensions for the Group Policy.

GROUP POLICY TEMPLATE

The Group Policy template is stored in the `System Volume` folder of Domain Controllers (SYSVOL) in the `\Policies` subfolder. The Group Policy template contains Administrative Template settings, Security Settings, Software Installation applications, and scripts.

Since each Group Policy object is stored partly in SYSVOL on each Domain Controller and partly in Active Directory, replication of changes can sometimes get out of sync. It's important to understand that these two components of a GPO rely on different replication mechanisms.

The part of the GPO that is stored in SYSVOL is replicated through the File Replication Service (FRS), independently of Active Directory replication.

If you are experiencing problems with GPO replication, use the `GPOTool` in the Windows Server 2003 Resource Kit to check the health of the GPOs and make sure they are replicating to all domain controllers. `GPOTool` is explained later in this chapter.

Group Policy Processing

Group Policies are processed in the following order:

1. **Local Group Policies:** Each computer processes a single GPO regardless of whether or not the computer is part of a domain. This local GPO cannot be blocked by domain GPOs, but the settings can be overwritten by domain GPOs during processing.

2. GPOs linked to the site.

3. GPOs linked to the domain.

4. GPOs linked to an organization unit: This includes all nested GPOs. As mentioned earlier, OU GPOs are processed from the parent down to the child, and settings in child OUs will overwrite the settings from parent OUs.

There are a few conditions that can change the way GPOs are processed. These include:

Filtering   By using WMI or Security group filtering, GPOs linked to a location can be set to target only specific objects in that location.

Enforce   GPOs can be enforced in the domain so that the settings contained in the policy are applied regardless of settings in lower-level GPOs. The highest GPO in the domain hierarchy will take precedence if multiple GPOs are enforced.

Block Inheritance   If a domain or organizational unit is set to Block Inheritance, higher-level GPOs will not process for objects in that location. The exception to this is if a higher-level GPO has been enforced. If this happens, the enforced GPO will apply even if lower-level locations are set to Block Inheritance.

Initial Group Policy Processing

Group Policies are processed initially when a computer starts up, and when a user logs on. The way they are processed depends on the operating system of the computer that the GPO is processed on, whether Fast Logon Optimization (see the upcoming section) has been configured, and if the GPO is set to process synchronously or asynchronously.

Synchronous processing means that each process must complete before the subsequent process can begin. Asynchronous means that different processes can run without having to wait for an earlier process to complete.

SYNCHRONOUS VS. ASYNCHRONOUS

Windows 2000 and Windows Server 2003 processes Group Policy synchronously. This means that the computer policy is applied before the logon dialog box is presented, and the user policy is applied before the shell is available to the user.

Windows XP can process Group Policies either synchronously or asynchronously. When processing is done synchronously, the boot process is considered complete only when computer policy has been applied successfully, and the user logon process is considered complete only when user policy has been applied successfully. When processing is done asynchronously, the user can be presented with the shell even if the computer policy has not completed. This will happen when there haven't been any changes to the policy that require synchronous processing.

FAST LOGON OPTIMIZATION

By default in Windows XP Professional, the processing of Group Policies has been changed to speed up the logon process. Both computer and user policies are processed asynchronously in the background as the network becomes available. Existing users are logged on using cached credentials. This process is called Fast Logon Optimization.

For Windows XP Professional computer, this process is turned on by default. However, because this is a background refresh using cached credentials, there are a few conditions where this process cannot run asynchronously:

◆ When a user first logs on to a computer

◆ When a user has a roaming user profile or a home directory

◆ When a user has synchronous logon scripts

You'll notice that these conditions are specific to users. Computer processing can still be completed asynchronously, even if these conditions are present.

Background Group Policy Refresh

In addition to the initial processing of Group Policies for computers during startup and users during logon, Group Policies are also refreshed in the background on a periodic basis, and are always applied asynchronously.

By default, this background refresh is set for 90 minutes, and is offset randomly for up to 30 minutes. These defaults can be changed by using a setting in Administrative Templates, but it's important to understand the impact of increasing or decreasing this refresh interval before they are changed.

To change the policy refresh interval setting, edit the Default Domain Controllers Group Policy object, which is linked to the Domain Controllers organizational unit. The Group Policy Refresh Interval For Computers setting is located under the Computer Configuration ➢ Administrative Templates ➢ System ➢ Group Policy node.

For domain controllers, the default period is every five minutes. The Group Policy Refresh Interval For Domain Controllers setting is available under the Computer Configuration ➢ Administrative Templates ➢ System ➢ Group Policy node.

Manual Group Policy Refresh

Group Policy can be refreshed manually with the following commands:

◆ Windows 2000:

`SECEDIT /REFRESHPOLICY MACHINE_POLICY` for machine settings
`SECEDIT /REFRESHPOLICY USER_POLICY` for user settings
Use `Secedit` for an entire list of options.

◆ Windows XP/Server 2003:

`GPUPDATE`
Use `GPUPDATE /?` for an entire list of options. Here are the common switches:
`/target:computer or /target:user`: Applies only the user or computer section of your policy
`/logoff`: For settings that do not apply until the user logs on again
`/boot`: For configurations that need the computer to restart
`/force`: Reapplies all settings

Slow Link Processing

When Group Policy detects a slow link, it communicates to client-side extensions that a policy setting is being applied across a slow link. Certain policies should not run over slow connections, so this mechanism allows processing of only those settings that should applied over slow links.

Security should not be compromised, even if network connections are slow. Slow link processing can scale back the processing of certain settings in Group Policy, while still applying security settings to target objects.

Table 9.2 contains the default settings when a slow link is detected.

TABLE 9.2:   Default Settings for Slow Link

SETTING	DEFAULT
Security Settings	On (cannot be changed)
IPSec	On
EFS	On
Software Restriction Policies	On
Wireless	On
Administration Templates	On (cannot be changed)
Software Installation	Off
Scripts	Off
Folder Redirection	Off
IE aintenance	Off

Client-Side Processing

The Group Policy infrastructure consists of a Group Policy engine and client-side components that plug into the infrastructure. Group Policy components allow you to enforce and maintain a wide variety of configurations, and allow your Group Policy infrastructure to be flexible and extensible.

The Group Policy architecture includes both server-side and client-side components. The server-side component includes the user interface that can be used to configure a policy. Once the policy is applied to a user or a computer, the client-side component translates the policy and applies the changes to the environment. These are known as client-side extensions.

A unique 128-bit number, known as a globally unique identifier (GUID), is assigned to each extension. When Group Policy is processed, a list of GPOs is passed to each Group Policy client-side extension for processing. The extension uses the list to process the right policy when applicable.

Loopback Processing

Loopback processing can be used to enforce user settings at a computer regardless of who logs on to the computer. Normally, user settings are applied to a site or OU with users. When a user logs on to a computer, the user settings defined in the GPO at the site or OU level will apply to each user.

Sometimes it's necessary to apply user settings to a computer, so that any user who logs on to the computer will be affected by the policy. Kiosks are a great example of this. Settings need to be consistent for each user that logs on to the kiosk. Loopback allows this to be configured.

Two modes are available with loopback processing. In Replace mode, the user settings defined in GPOs are applied to the computer. In Merge mode, user settings from GPOs that would normally apply to the user are processed, provided they do not conflict with user settings that apply to the computer. User settings that are applied to the computer will always apply over conflicted user settings that are applied to the user. This ensures that only the user settings targeted to specific computers are always applied.

Group Policy Troubleshooting

There are several tools that can be used for troubleshooting Group Policy problems. Three of the common Group Policy troubleshooting tools are Resultant Set of Policy, `GPResult`, and `GPOTool`.

Resultant Set of Policy (RSoP)

Resultant Set of Policy (RSoP) is an addition for Group Policy that makes the process of implementing a policy and troubleshooting a policy easier. RSoP offers the ability to determine existing results of policy application as well as planned results that can be used for testing and troubleshooting.

RSoP is a query engine that polls existing policies based on site, domain, domain controller, and organizational unit. It gathers this information through Windows Management Instrumentation (WMI), and then reports the results of the queries.

RSoP is a powerful administration tool because it gives administrators a detailed look into the policy settings that are being applied to users or computer. If policies are applied on multiple levels, RSoP can help to determine what settings are finally being applied to the object, and the order by which they are being applied.

RSoP has two modes: Planning and Logging. Logging gives insight into the existing policy settings for a computer and user that is currently logged on. Planning is for simulating the effect of policy settings applied to computers and users before the Group Policy is actually linked in Active Directory.

RSoP is a great improvement to Group Policy management. With this tool, the process of determining if policy settings are actually being applied to a computer or a user takes just a few seconds.

Included with RSoP is a helpful wizard that assists in the creation of RSoP queries. You can get to this wizard from the Microsoft Management Console (MMC), Active Directory Users and Computers, or Active Directory Sites and Services.

GPResult

GPResult.exe is a great tool that helps determine the Group Policy settings that were applied during Group Policy refresh. The version in the Windows 2000 Resource Kit runs only locally on Windows 2000. The version included in Windows Server 2003 can run locally or remotely on Windows XP or Windows Server 2003 computers. Figure 9.4 shows the results of a GPResult query on a Windows 2003 server.

GPOTool—Group Policy Verification Tool

GPOTool can be used to check the health of GPOs on domain controllers. GPOTool will check each GPO for consistency on each domain controller in the domain, and will determine if the policy is valid. The tool also displays detailed information about replicated GPOs, as shown in Figure 9.5.

For a more detailed look at group policy troubleshooting, see *Group Policy, Profiles, and IntelliMirror for Windows XP, 2003, and Windows 2000* by Jeremy Moskowitz (Sybex, 2004).

FIGURE 9.4
Output screen of a
GPResult query

FIGURE 9.5
Results of the
GPOTool utility

```
Command Shell                                                    _ □ ×
C:\Program Files\Windows Resource Kits\Tools>gpotool
Validating DCs...
Available DCs:
DC.lab.com
DC-2K.lab.com
DC2-2K.lab.com
Searching for policies...
Found 2 policies
=================================================================
Policy {31B2F340-016D-11D2-945F-00C04FB984F9}
Friendly name: Default Domain Policy
Policy OK
=================================================================
Policy {6AC1786C-016F-11D2-945F-00C04FB984F9}
Friendly name: Default Domain Controllers Policy
Policy OK
=================================================================

Policies OK

C:\Program Files\Windows Resource Kits\Tools>_
```

Practical Uses of Group Policy

There are countless ways that Group Policy can be leveraged. With over 900 configurable settings in Group Policy, every company can see real benefit from Software Installation, Remote Installation Services, and Software Update Services.

The biggest problem I had when administering large Active Directory environments was the time spent rebuilding computers with the operating system, security patches, services packs, and software. I needed a solution that would completely build a computer without me having to sit at the system and click through each install screen. I leveraged existing technologies available in Windows Server 2003 to accomplish this.

1. I used Remote Installation Services (RIS) to deploy the operating system with a current list of patches. I configured RIS to join the computer to the domain and place the computer in a New Computers organizational unit.

2. I then configured a GPO for this OU that included settings for Software Installation, and configured deployment of all the standard desktop software that we used throughout our organization. Microsoft Office 2003, Adobe Reader, and WinZip are examples of the types of software that we used.

3. Finally, I configured a GPO for this OU that included settings for Windows Update. I configured Windows Update to use an internal update server for new patches.

Once all of that was complete, I was able to build a new computer with the operating system, patches and service packs, and all software. I was able to do this without a minimal amount of involvement (just press F12 for RIS and type in my username and password), and had the computer up and running in under an hour.

Server OU Design

This chapter is focused specifically on Group Policy, so it may seem strange that I'm mentioning the server OU design in this section. But the way your OUs are structured servers in Active Directory can help with how you deploy GPOs.

What many companies do is join all their computers to the domain—workstations and servers—and then keep them in the default location. Or, they create an OU called Servers and move all of the servers into that OU, and create an OU called Workstations and move all the workstation in there. Then they apply a very weak policy to each OU and call it a day.

A better suggestion is to create an OU structure that allows for the application of GPOs that are configured specifically for each type of server. The OU structure in Figure 9.6 is a good place to start.

With this design, you can create a General Servers GPO and link it to the Servers OU. Then you can create specific GPOs for each type of server. If you want to create GPOs specific to each server type, follow the recommendations in the Windows Server 2003 Security Guide located at `www.microsoft` `.com/technet/security/prodtech/windowsserver2003/W2003HG/SGCH00.mspx`. This guide is very comprehensive and will help you determine the best security approach for your servers.

FIGURE 9.6
OU structure

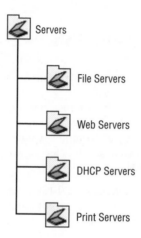

Creating a Test OU with Test Computers and Test Users

After months of changing Group Policy settings and breaking computers in the process, it finally became clear that I could benefit from an OU dedicated solely to testing GPO settings. It also became clear that many of the applications used throughout the company were constantly breaking because of incorrect settings.

A good recommendation is to create an OU for testing, and move test computers and test users into the OU. Load the test computers with applications used throughout the company, and be sure to configure the test users with the same settings given to standard users.

The benefit of this design is that any time you want to configure a Group Policy you can have it apply to test users and computers that are configured identically to users and computers in the production environment.

From this test OU, can you pilot the deployment of GPOs to a small group of users and computers, and then on to full-scale deployment.

Service Accounts

Here is an example of how you can secure service accounts in your environment by leveraging Group Policy. Service accounts are normally user accounts that have been created in the domain to be used by applications to run tasks. Many times, these accounts have elevated permissions and are immediately considered a security risk.

Take the situation where a service account is a member of Domain Admins. Because of the elevated permissions given to this account through the Domain Admins group, a user may feel the need to log into a workstation and perform some actions. It is possible that a person with enough knowledge can retrieve the username and password that may have been cached on the workstation. At this point, this user has enough information to become a rogue Domain Admin.

A good way to solve this problem is to first deny the ability of the service account to log on locally to any computer in the domain. Realistically, a service account does not need to log on locally anyway. By doing this, a user will be unable to log on to a machine with this account, and the likelihood of this account getting hacked is diminished. Additionally, the service account should be given access to log on to systems as a service, which will ensure that applications can still use them.

Before using this approach completely in a production environment, make sure you test the applications or systems that rely on these service accounts. Apply these settings to all of your service accounts only after extensive testing and verification.

Within Group Policy, you can configure both of these settings.

Denying Log On Locally Right to Service Accounts

Service accounts are often a necessary evil. Many times service accounts are used by administrators to perform certain automated tasks. Some of these accounts can have elevated permissions and rights. To keep people from using these accounts to log in to a server or a computer on the network, follow these steps. Figure 9.7 shows what the configuration screen will look like.

NOTE All steps are performed using the GPMC snap-in and assume that a GPO has already been created.

1. Open the GPMC snap-in.

2. In the left pane, expand the Forest container, expand the Domains container, browse to the domain of the target GPO, and expand the Group Policy Objects container.

3. Right-click on the target GPO and select Edit.

4. Browse to Computer Configuration ➢ Windows Settings ➢ Security Settings ➢ Local Policies ➢ User Rights Assignment.

5. Double-click on Deny Log On Locally.

6. Click Add User Or Group.

7. Type in the name of the user or group, or click Browse to search for the object.

8. Once the user or group has been chosen, close all windows.

FIGURE 9.7
Deny log on
locally setting

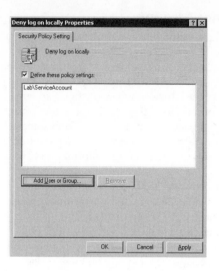

GIVING RIGHTS TO LOG ON AS A SERVICE TO SERVICE ACCOUNTS

After creating the service account and configuring the account so it cannot be used to log on locally to a server or workstation, you must now give it the "Log On as a Service" right. The following steps explain how to do this. Figure 9.8 shows what the configuration screen will look like.

NOTE All steps are performed using the GPMC snap-in and assume that a GPO has already been created.

1. Open the GPMC snap-in.

2. In the left pane, expand the Forest container, expand the Domains container, browse to the domain of the target GPO, and expand the Group Policy Objects container.

3. Right-click on the target GPO and select Edit.

4. Browse to Computer Configuration ➢ Windows Settings ➢ Security Settings ➢ Local Policies ➢ User Rights Assignment.

5. Double-click on Log On As A Service.

6. Click Add User Or Group.

7. Type in the name of the user or group, or click Browse to search for the object.

8. Once the user or group has been chosen, close all windows.

IPSec Between Root Domain Controllers and Child Domain Controllers

For companies that have multiple domains, here is a good approach to locking down access to root domain controllers (DCs). It's likely that only a couple of administrators will ever have access or the need to log on to DCs in the root. The root domain is very important for many reasons, so access should be limited.

FIGURE 9.8

Log on as a
service setting

One Group Policy way to do this is to create an IPSec filter that allows only communication between the subnet of all child DCs to the subnet of the root DCs. Configure it so that anything can communicate with child DCs, but only DCs in the child can communicate with DCs in the root.

Again, thoroughly test this in your environment to ensure that business systems and applications are still functional, and that users and computers can still communicate with necessary network systems.

Message Title and Text for Users Attempting to Log On

This Group Policy tip isn't earth shattering, but it can be useful. When users are attempting to log on to the domain, you can configure two settings to present them with a dialog box that displays a message of your choice. The two configurable settings for this include one for the title of the message (Message Title For Users Attempting To Log On), and one for the message itself (Message Text For Users Attempting To Log On).

An organization may require that all users who about attempting to log on to the domain are notified that their actions can be monitored, or that only approved use of the network is authorized.

CONFIGURING A LOGON MESSAGE TITLE

With the onslaught of legal issues and regulatory compliance issues that have come up in the last few years, it is a good idea to configure a logon message that warns users that they should not attempt to use the system if they are not authorized. To configure a logon message title, follow these steps:

NOTE   All steps are performed using the GPMC snap-in and assume that a GPO has already been created.

1. Open the GPMC snap-in.

2. In the left pane, expand the Forest container, expand the Domains container, browse to the domain of the target GPO, and expand the Group Policy Objects container.

3. Right-click on the target GPO and select Edit.

4. Browse to Computer Configuration ➢ Windows Settings ➢ Security Settings ➢ Local Policies ➢ Security Options.

5. Double-click on Interactive Logon: Message Title For Users Attempting To Log On.

6. Click Define This Policy Setting.

7. Type in the title for this message box.

8. Click OK and close out windows.

CONFIGURING A LOGON MESSAGE TEXT

The text of the message should include warnings about illegal activity and information about system monitoring. Follow these steps to configure the logon message text:

NOTE All steps are performed using the GPMC snap-in and assume that a GPO has already been created.

1. Open the GPMC snap-in.

2. In the left pane, expand the Forest container, expand the Domains container, browse to the domain of the target GPO, and expand the Group Policy Objects container.

3. Right-click on the target GPO and select Edit.

4. Browse to Computer Configuration ➢ Windows Settings ➢ Security Settings ➢ Local Policies ➢ Security Options.

5. Double-click on Interactive Logon: For Users Attempting To Log On.

6. Click Define This Policy Setting.

7. Type in the text for this message box.

8. Click OK and close all windows.

Coming Up Next

Now that we have a firm grasp of managing Group Policy, we will take a look at site boundaries in Active Directory. The next chapter discusses Active Directory replication and the tools and utilities that are required to manage site boundaries.

Chapter 10

Managing Site Boundaries

Replication is vital to the health of Active Directory. Every domain controller on your network contains a copy of the Active Directory database. Proper replication is important, not only to make sure every domain controller can communicate with every other domain controller, but also to ensure that it communicates and replicates in an efficient manner.

This replication is controlled by the Active Directory Sites and Services utility. As you define sites in Active Directory, you also control all aspects of AD replication.

NOTE Some of the material in this chapter is also found in Chapter 4 because it's relevant to both topics.

Replication within Active Directory

Active Directory employs a multimaster replication technology that allows nearly every aspect of the directory service to be modified from any of the domain controllers within a domain. Changes that are made to one domain controller in the domain are replicated to all the other domain controllers in the domain. This replication allows all the domain controllers to act as peers and provide the same functionality. However, this same replication can cause issues when you are trying to keep WAN traffic to a minimum.

To reduce the amount of WAN traffic generated by replication, you will need to create sites within Active Directory that define the servers that are well connected. The domain controllers that are all members of the same site will update quickly, whereas replication to domain controllers in other sites can be controlled as to when and how often the replication will occur.

Another advantage to using sites is that client traffic can be contained within the site if there are servers that provide the service the user needs. User authentication will occur with domain controllers that are located in the same site as the computer that the user is logging onto if a domain controller for the appropriate domain exists in that site. In addition, you can make queries to a global catalog server and access the Distributed File System (DFS) shares within the same site as the user's computer.

Replication Topology

Two protocols (IP and SMTP) can be used for replicating objects in Active Directory. When selecting IP, you are specifying that you want to use Remote Procedure Calls (RPCs) to deliver the replicated objects. You can select SMTP if the domain controllers between which you are replicating data are not within the same domain. If the domain controllers are in the same domain, the File Replication Service (FRS) has to use RPCs to replicate the Sysvol data. Because FRS requires the same replication topology as the domain partition, you cannot use SMTP between domain controllers in the same domain. You may choose SMTP if you want to control replication between global catalog servers or domain controllers that are replicating the schema and configuration partition data between domain controllers.

THE KNOWLEDGE CONSISTENCY CHECKER

Every domain controller on your network runs a process called the Knowledge Consistency Checker (KCC). The KCC is responsible for automatically identifying the most efficient replication topology for your network. The KCC uses information that is defined in the Active Directory Sites and Services (ADSS) snap-in. As you make changes in ADSS, the KCC will recalculate the replication topology and make adjustments accordingly.

Active Directory will automatically create connection objects that will produce an efficient replication path to all the domain controllers within the site. An administrator can also create connection objects manually. If a manual connection is created, the KCC will build other connections around the manual connection to allow for replication redundancy. Keep in mind, however, that if you create a connection object that does not allow for efficient replication, the KCC will not override your efforts. As domain controllers are brought online or sites are created, the KCC is responsible for creating the connection objects to allow replication to occur. If a domain controller fails, the KCC will also rebuild the connection objects to allow replication to continue.

The KCC is also responsible for generating the intersite connection objects. When a site connector is created to allow replication between two sites, one domain controller is identified as the Intersite Topology Generator (ISTG). The ISTG is responsible for determining the most efficient path for replication between sites.

Only one domain controller in each site will become the ISTG. Initially it is the first domain controller within the site, but as systems are added to the site, rebooted, and removed from the site, the ISTG will change. The domain controller with the highest GUID in the site becomes the ISTG for the site. It is responsible for determining the bridgehead server and maintaining the connection objects between bridgehead servers in each of the other sites.

Each domain controller stores data in the directory store, which is logically divided into specific directory partitions. Every domain controller within a forest contains a replica of the schema as well as configuration partitions for the forest. Every domain controller in a domain contains a replica of the domain partitions for that domain. Certain applications store directory data specific to that application in application directory partitions.

WINDOWS 2003 REPLICATION IMPROVEMENTS

With the introduction of Windows Server 2003, Microsoft has introduced many enhancements to Active Directory replication. These enhancements not only improve efficiency, but also make replication much more scalable to a very large network.

Most of these improvements come from enhancements to the spanning tree algorithm. If you are running a mixed-mode forest, you can take advantage of improvements of the Windows 2000 spanning tree algorithm by placing Windows Server 2003 domain controllers in each of your sites. By default, a Windows Server 2003 domain controller will become the ISTG for your site, and you can take advantage of the new spanning tree algorithm.

If your domain is at a Windows 2003 Forest Functional level, then you are treated to a completely new spanning tree algorithm. Under the old spanning tree algorithm, your domain was limited to 300 sites. With the new spanning tree algorithm, you can expand your domain to 3000 sites.

DETERMINE WHICH DOMAIN CONTROLLER HOLDS THE ROLE OF ISTG

To learn which domain controller is the ISTG, follow these steps:

1. Open the Active Directory Sites and Services MMC snap-in.

2. Navigate to the site you would like to check, expand the site, and select NTDS Site Settings.

3. Right-click NTDS Site Settings and select Properties.

4. Look for Inter-Site Topology Generator on the Properties page. If the server is the ISTG for that site, it will be listed here.

The new ISTG also greatly improves the process to determine bridgehead servers. It is a randomized selection process that improves the distribution of the workload. This process takes place when a new connection object is added to the site. You can, however, trigger the process with a utility called `adlb.exe`.

`adlb.exe` is a utility that is included with the Windows Server 2003 resource kit tools, and is a free download from Microsoft. When you run the `adlb.exe` utility, you must enter a site name and a server name to configure load balancing. The site name you enter will determine the name of the site whose inbound and outbound connections to balance. The server name is the name of the LDAP server used to read and write directory objects.

Optional command-line parameters used with `adlb.exe` are:

/commit   Until you specify this parameter, all changes are written in LDAP Data Interchange Format (LDIF) format to standard output. Only when you use the `/commit` parameter will changes be written to the directory.

/ldif: <filename.ldif>   This option allows you to specify an LDIF output file instead of using standard out.

/log: <filename.log>   Used to redirect the utility's output to a log files, specified as `filename.log`. If no filename is specified, the output is written to standard out.

/verbose   Specifies that that output is given in verbose mode.

/perf   Indicates that performance statistics should be written to the log file.

/showinput   All objects read from the directory will be written to the log file.

/maxbridge:<n>   Specifies the maximum number of connection objects that will be modified due to bridgehead load balancing.

/maxsched:<m>   Specifies the maximum number of schedules that will be staggered due to schedule staggering. If this option is not specified, the `stagger` option must be specified in order to stagger schedules.

/stagger   This option must be specified in order to stagger the schedules.

/disown   Any schedules previously staggered by this tool are disowned. Control of the schedules is relinquished back to the KCC. This option requires the schedule staging be disabled with the option `/maxsched:0`.

/maxperserver:<mps>   Specifies the maximum number of changes to be moved onto a given Domain Controller at any one time. Defaults to 10. A setting of 0 disables the limit.

Another improvement introduced with Windows Server 2003 is the change in the way multivalued attributes are replicated between domain controllers. In a mixed-mode forest, any change made to group memberships triggers replication of the entire membership list. This approach encounters problems when two administrators make changes to the same group on different domain controllers before replication occurs. Administrator Joe adds a user named HallieM to a group. At relatively the same time, administrator Paul adds a user to the same group named ScottB. When replication occurs, changes made by Paul will overwrite the changes made by Joe.

If the Forest Functional level is Windows 2003 Forest Functional Level, then only the individual value is replicated to other domain controllers. Only changes made to the group membership are replicated instead of the entire membership list.

FORCE THE KCC TO RUN

To force the KCC to run, follow these steps:

1. Open the Active Directory Sites and Services MMC snap-in.

2. Navigate to the site that holds the server that you would like to run the KCC on, expand the Servers container, and expand the server that you would like to run the KCC on.

3. Right-click on NTDS Settings, select All Tasks, and then select Check Replication Topology.

Replication performance is enhanced by using sites. By creating a site topology you can define how Active Directory replication communicates between sites.

Creating the Site Topology

The definition of a site is a well-connected network. A well-connected network is considered a network that has a connection of at least 10Mbps. Active Directory uses information stored in sites and site link objects to generate the most efficient replication topology. This information is defined in the ADSS snap-in. Sites are the physical representation of your network. This is different from domains, which represent the logical design of your network.

Networks are made up of well-connected network segments that are connected through other less-reliable or slow links. For a domain controller to be considered "well-connected" to another domain controller, the connection type will usually be 10Mbps or greater. Of course, that is a generalization. Some segments on your network may have 10Mbps or higher links between systems, but if the links are saturated, you may not have enough available bandwidth to support replication. The inverse is also true; you may have network connections that are less than 10Mbps that have enough available bandwidth to handle the replication and authentication traffic.

Look over the existing network and draw out a network map that defines the subnets that are well connected. Find the current physical topology of the network. Gather all information about location of routers, the speed of the segments, and the IP address ranges used on each of the segments. Also note how many users are in each of the network segments and the types of WAN links that connect the locations. This information will prove useful as you design the site topology.

As an example, consider a company that has a campus in Newark with four buildings and two remote locations: Albuquerque and New Haven. All of the buildings in Newark are connected via an FDDI ring. The two remote locations are connected to Newark via T1 connections. Figure 10.1 shows the network map, which also lists the user population at each location.

For those organizations that have more than one domain, you will need to determine where the user accounts reside. A site can support users from multiple domains as long as those domains are members of the same forest. On your network map, if you have more than one domain, designate the number of users from each domain. In our previous example, if the R&D department has its own domain for security purposes, the network map may look like the one shown in Figure 10.2.

FIGURE 10.1
Network map

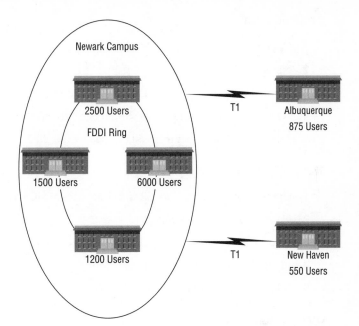

FIGURE 10.2
Multiple domain
network map

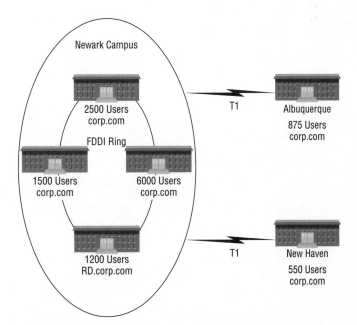

NOTE Don't confuse the logical representation of your network with the actual physical entities. You could still have domain controllers from multiple forests within the same physical subnet, but the Active Directory objects that define them can only exist within one forest.

CREATING SITES

1. Open the Active Directory Sites and Services MMC snap-in.

2. Navigate to the Sites container.

3. Right-click on the Sites container and select New Site.

4. Name the new site. The name should be a "friendly" name that accurately describes the site.

5. Select a site link object that will be used by the site.

MOVING SERVERS TO THE NEW SITE

1. Open the Active Directory Sites and Services MMC snap-in.

2. Navigate to the Sites container.

3. Find the server that you would like to move to the new site.

4. Right-click on the server and select Move.

5. Select the destination site and click OK.

CREATING SUBNETS

1. Open the Active Directory Sites and Services MMC snap-in.

2. Navigate to the Subnets container.

3. Right-click on the Subnets container and select New Subnet.

4. Enter the network address and subnet mask of the subnet you would like to add.

5. Select the site to associate with the new subnet and click OK.

CREATING SITE LINKS

1. Open the Active Directory Sites and Services MMC snap-in.

2. Navigate to Sites ➤Inter-Site Transports ➤ IP.

3. Right-click on the IP container and select New Site Link.

4. Select the sites that will be included in the site link and click Add.

5. Click OK.

Setting Your Sites to Support the AD Design

Once you have created the network map, you can begin designing the required sites. Sites are collections of well-connected subnets that are used to control Active Directory replication or manage user and application access to domain controllers and global catalog servers. As with every other Active Directory object, you should determine a naming strategy for sites and site links. A site's name should reflect the physical location that the site represents. The location could represent a geographic location for organizations that have regional offices (the buildings within an organization's campus or distinct portions of a building). Once you have defined the naming strategy, make sure all of the administrators who have the ability to create sites understand the strategy and follow it.

You need to create a document that details the sites that will be used within the design. This document should include the name of the site, the location that the site represents, the IP subnets that are members of the site, and the WAN links that connect the sites.

If you look at Figure 10.2, you can see that the information that was gathered about the current infrastructure is shown in the network map. You need to use this information to create the site design, as shown in Figure 10.3. Notice that the primary locations are identified as sites within the design.

Newark, New Haven, and Albuquerque are all identified as sites. Each of the IP subnets from the buildings at the Newark campus is shown as included within the Newark site; the IP subnets from the office in Albuquerque are included in the Albuquerque site; and the IP subnets from the office in New Haven are included in the New Haven site.

The WAN links that connect Albuquerque and New Haven to the Newark campus are shown on the site design layout. But because the Newark campus is considered a single site, the FDDI connections between the buildings are not considered WAN links at this point. Later when you address the replication needs, this may change.

You should also consider including information about the WAN links on the site layout. This information should include the locations that the WAN link connects, the speed of the link, the available bandwidth on the link during normal operation, and how reliable the link is. You may also want to consider including information about when the link is used the most, when the off-peak hours are, and whether the link is persistent or a dial-up connection. This information will help you to determine the replication schedule.

FIGURE 10.3

Site design layout

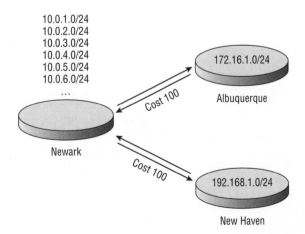

Once the initial site choices are made based on the network requirements, determine if you should create sites to support user and application requirements. Users sitting at workstations that are Active Directory–aware will authenticate to a domain controller from their domain if there is one within their site. If their site does not have a domain controller for their domain, they will authenticate with a domain controller within another site. All domain controllers determine if any sites exist that do not contain domain controllers from their domain when they are brought online. If some sites match these criteria, the domain controller then determines if it is located within a site logically near the site without a domain controller. The domain controller determines this based on the cost of the site link or site link bridges that connect the two sites. If it is established that the domain controller is close to the site, it registers a service locator (SRV) record for the site. Microsoft refers to this as Automatic Site Coverage.

TIP For more information on how to configure domain controllers to register their services to other sites, see Microsoft Knowledge Base articles 200498 (http://support.microsoft.com/default .aspx?scid=kb;en-us;200498) and 306602 (http://support.microsoft.com/default.aspx ?scid=kb;en-us;306602).

As an example, Company G has two domains: `corp.com` and `RD.corp.com`. Five sites exist within their environment: A, B, C, D, and E. Figure 10.4 shows the site layout and the site links that connect them. Within the sites, there are domain controllers for each of the domains. Note that Site C does not contain a domain controller for `RD.corp.com`. In this case, as domain controllers start up, they will check the configuration of the domain to determine whether or not a site exists without a domain controller from their own domain. When domain controllers from `RD.corp.com` start up, they will recognize that Site C does not have a domain controller. They will then determine whether they should register SRV records for the site based on whether or not they are in a site that is considered to be the nearest. Because Site B has the lowest cost value over the site link to Site C, `RDDCB1.RD.corp.com` will register SRV records on behalf of Site C. When users from the `RD.corp.com` domain authenticate from a computer in Site C, they will authenticate with the nearest domain controller, `RDDCB1.RD.corp.com`.

Active Directory replication can consume a considerable amount of network resources within a site. Replication traffic is not compressed between domain controllers that exist within the same site. If the available network bandwidth will not support the replication traffic that you are anticipating, you may want to look into dividing up IP segments so that you can control the replication moving between the domain controllers. Once additional sites are created, site links can then be configured. Replication traffic that passes across site links is compressed to conserve bandwidth if the data exceeds 50KB.

Another consideration is application support. Applications such as Exchange Server 2003 require access to a global catalog server. If you want to control which global catalog server an Exchange server will use, you could create a site and place the two servers within the site to control the traffic between them. For example, within the `corp.com` domain, the Exchange Server 2003 server is located in Building 1 of the Newark campus. We have specified that a domain controller in Building 2 is to be used by the Exchange server when it sends queries to a global catalog server. In order to control the requests, another site is created that includes Building 1 and Building 2, as shown in Figure 10.5.

FIGURE 10.4
Determining the nearest site

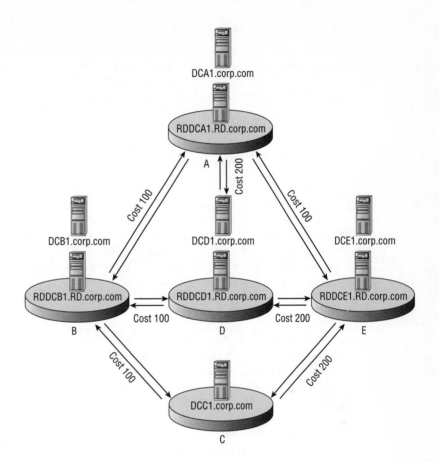

FIGURE 10.5
Site design to support application requirements

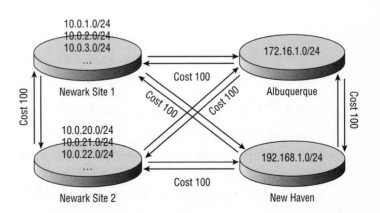

Designing Site Links and Site Link Bridges

Because you have identified the WAN links that connect the sites within your design, you can decide easily on the site links that you will need to support the design at this point. Site links are objects that are created to connect sites so that replication can be controlled. You also need to address other considerations such as replication, log-on authentication control, and application support.

Site link bridges are collections of site links that allow replication traffic from domain controllers in one site to pass to domain controllers in another site when no explicit replication partners exist in the intermediary site that connects them. In the following sections, we are going to spend some time reviewing the options that are available for sites and site link bridges.

SITE LINKS

By default, one site link is created when the first domain controller is installed. This site link is called DEFAULTIPSITELINK, but it can be renamed to conform to your naming strategy. This site link uses RPCs for replication. You could take advantage of using this site link for all the sites that you have within your infrastructure if they all have the same replication requirements.

For example, if all the sites are connected by WAN links that have approximately the same available bandwidth and they all use RPC for replication, then simply rename this site link to conform to your naming strategy and make sure all the sites are included.

Another reason you may want to create additional site links is to control when the replication can occur. You may have some sites that need to have objects updated at different schedules. Using site links, you can create a replication schedule between sites. You cannot define which physical connection a site links uses in order to control the replication traffic over specific network links. For instance, if you have a T1 connection and an ISDN connection to a branch office and the ISDN connection is used only as a backup communication link if the T1 goes down, you cannot create two site links with two different costs, one for each of the communication links.

CONFIGURE SITE LINK COST

Configure site link costs to establish a priority for replication routing. By defining a cost for each site link, you can manually define replication traffic in your environment.

1. Open the Active Directory Sites and Services MMC snap-in.

2. Navigate to Sites ➢ Inter-Site Transports ➢ IP.

3. Right-click the site link object you would like to configure and select Properties.

4. In the Cost box, enter the number you would like to associate with the site link.

5. Click OK.

CONFIGURE SITE LINK INTERVAL

Use the site link interval setting to determine how often during the available replication schedule you want bridgehead servers to poll their intersite replication partners for changes.

1. Open the Active Directory Sites and Services MMC snap-in.

2. Navigate to Sites ➢ Inter-Site Transports ➢ IP.

3. Right-click the site link object you would like to configure and select Properties.

4. In the Replicate Every ____ Minutes box, enter the number of minutes that replication polling will occur.

5. Click OK.

Site links consist of the following configurable parameters:

Cost   Cost is associated with site links and defines whether a particular route is favorable or not. The higher the cost, the less favorable the route. Lower numbers are associated with faster connections.

Schedule   You can control site link availability by configuring a schedule on site links. The site topology owner defines the schedule and specifies when site links are available. The default schedule allows availability 24 hours a day. You can block certain peak hours of the day, but keep in mind that this can cause replication latency. To ensure that all sites can replicate at all times, you must review the schedules of other site links that replication must travel. If replication between two site links must traverse many site links, the schedules of all site links in the path must be calculated and the schedules must overlap at some point. If the schedules never overlap, replication will never occur.

Interval   This value determines how often domain controllers will poll other domain controllers across the site link during your schedule window. A lower number represents a smaller time interval and will decrease latency but will also increase traffic across the site link.

When creating the site link, you have the options of choosing the following:

Protocol used for replication   Two protocols can be used for replication of objects: IP and SMTP. When selecting IP, you are specifying that you want to use RPCs to deliver the replicated objects. You can select SMTP if the domain controllers that you are replicating data between are not within the same domain. If the domain controllers are within the same domain, the File Replication Service (FRS) has to use RPCs to replicate the Sysvol data. Since FRS requires the same replication topology as the domain partition, you cannot use SMTP between the domain controllers within a domain. You can use SMTP if you want to control the replication between global catalog servers or domain controllers that are replicating the schema and configuration partition data between domain controllers.

Name of the site link   The name should follow your naming strategy and should define the sites that are connected using the link.

Connected sites   These are the sites that will explicitly replicate between bridgehead servers in each listed site.

Schedule   The schedule consists of the hours when replication can occur and the interval—how often you want to allow replication to occur during the hours that replication data is allowed to pass between the bridgehead servers.

Cost of the connection   This value determines which link will be used. This cost, or priority, value is used to choose the most efficient site link. You will use the combination of site links with the lowest total cost to replicate data between any pair of sites.

Note the replication patterns when you are trying to determine the schedule. You could cause a good deal of latency to occur if the schedule is not compatible. For example, a company may have a central office that acts as the hub for the regional office. The regional offices are responsible for replication to the branch offices in their region. Figure 10.6 shows the schedule for the Atlanta central office, the Sydney and Chicago regional offices, and the Exmouth, Peoria, and Bloomington branch offices. Because all of the domestic U.S. links have approximately the same bandwidth availability, you could create a single site link that uses a 15-minute interval. You could then create a separate site link between Atlanta and Sydney for which the replication interval is set to every two hours so that replication does not adversely affect the WAN links. Between the Sydney and Exmouth sites, another site link uses a one-hour interval to control traffic. Depending on the connection objects that are created by the KCC, the total propagation delay for an update in Chicago to reach Exmouth could be three and a half hours—and that is only considering the replication interval. The schedule on the site link could be configured to allow replication traffic to flow only during the evening hours. If you have a schedule that is closed off for a portion of time, the propagation delay will increase even more. You need to make sure that this will be acceptable within your organization.

You should also plan the cost of site links carefully. The default site link cost value is 100. If all of the communication links have the same available bandwidth, you leave the default cost on all links. However, if different bandwidth constraints occur on any of the communication links, you need to adjust the cost values. One method of determining a valid cost for site links is to divide 1024 by the base 10 logarithm of the available bandwidth as measured in kilobits per second (Kbps). In doing so, you will find cost values that correspond to the entries in Table 10.1.

TABLE 10.1:   Example of Costs for Available Bandwidth

AVAILABLE BANDWIDTH IN KBPS	COST VALUE
4096	283
2048	309
1024	340
512	378
256	425
128	486
64	567
56	586
38.4	644
19.2	798
9.6	1042

SITE LINK BRIDGES

In Windows Server 2003 Active Directory, site link bridging is enabled for all site links by default, making replication transitive throughout sites. In Figure 10.7, note that domain controllers are in all three sites from `corp.com`. Site B is the only site that does not have a domain controller from `RD.corp.com`. With site link bridging enabled, replication from domain controllers for `RD.corp.com` in Site A will pass to `RD.corp.com` domain controllers in Site C.

If you have a network infrastructure that is fully routed and all of the locations can communicate directly with one another, then you can leave this default setting turned on. However, if you have locations where not all of the domain controllers are able to communicate directly with one another—for instance, if they are separated by firewalls—you may want to turn off site link bridging. You may also want to turn it off if you want to manually control where it is allowed. If you have a large, complex network, you could turn off bridging and create your own site link bridges by defining which site links will be included in a bridge.

FIGURE 10.6
Replication schedules
based on site links

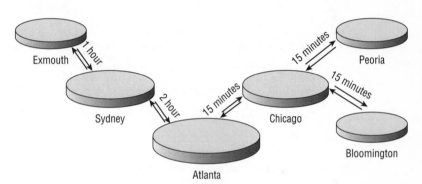

FIGURE 10.7
Site link bridge

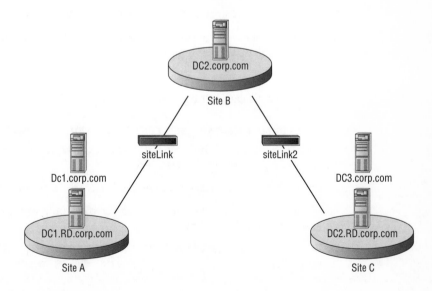

Firewalls that exist within your organization's network infrastructure could also pose challenges. Rules could be in place that only allow specific servers to communicate with internal resources. If you do have a firewall in place, you may need to turn off site link bridging so that you can control the site links that will pass replication traffic from site to site.

Remember that the site link does not define any physical network links. The physical connections are determined by how the domain controllers are connected to one another. A site link cannot detect if a physical link is down and, therefore, will not reroute the traffic immediately. Determine your site link's costs based on the paths on which you would like replication to occur when using bridging.

It is a best practice to let the KCC determine the preferred bridgehead server, but you can manually create a preferred bridgehead server in ADSS.

CREATING SITE LINK BRIDGES

Site link bridges are important for intersite communication. If site link transitivity is disabled, you must manually bridge sites so that replication can complete and the KCC can create the necessary connection objects.

1. Open the Active Directory Sites and Services MMC snap-in.

2. Navigate to Sites ➤ Inter-Site Transports ➤ IP.

3. Right-click on the IP container and select New Site Link Bridge.

4. Select the sites links that will be included in the site link bridge and click Add.

5. Click OK.

DISABLE DEFAULT BRIDGING OF SITE LINKS

Before you can create new site link bridges, you must disable the default bridging of site links.

1. Open the Active Directory Sites and Services MMC snap-in.

2. Navigate to Sites ➤ Inter-Site Transports ➤ IP or SMTP (depending on which site transport you would like to disable bridging).

3. Right-click the transport and select Properties

4. Clear the box labeled Bridge All Site Links.

CONFIGURE A DOMAIN CONTROLLER TO BE A PREFERRED BRIDGEHEAD SERVER

Rather than letting the KCC choose the bridgehead server, you might prefer to nominate a domain controller to be a preferred bridgehead server.

1. Open the Active Directory Sites and Services MMC snap-in.

2. Navigate to the site that contains the server you would like to define as the preferred bridgehead server for the site link.

3. Right-click the domain controller that will become the preferred bridgehead server and select Properties.

4. Highlight the intersite transport or transports (IP or SMTP) that this server will become the preferred bridgehead server for and click Add.

5. Click OK.

CONFIGURE A DOMAIN CONTROLLER TO NOT BE A PREFERRED BRIDGEHEAD SERVER

1. Open the Active Directory Sites and Services MMC snap-in.

2. Navigate to the site that contains the server you would like to remove as a preferred bridgehead server.

3. Expand the Servers node and view the server currently configured for that site.

4. Right-click the server you would like to remove and select Properties.

5. If the IP transport is listed in the box labeled This Server Is a Preferred Bridgehead Server for the Following Transports, highlight IP, and click Remove.

Optimizing Replication for a Large Network

Generally, the following section is recommended only for very large networks consisting of hundreds if not thousands of sites and domain controllers. Small to medium-sized networks will probably never see the performance problems associated with these networks. Replication problems experienced on smaller networks are discussed further in the troubleshooting section of this book.

Knowledge Consistency Checker Optimization

Earlier we discussed the function of the Knowledge Consistency Checker (KCC). It is the KCC's job to create connection objects based on the network topology defined in the Active Directory Sites and Services snap-in. In a large environment, there are many things you can do to alter its performance. Every 15 minutes, the KCC performs the following tasks:

◆ Defines replication to domain controllers within the same site. This is an inbound connection to the server running the KCC.

◆ Defines replication to domain controllers in different sites. This includes inbound connections to the servers running the KCC that is also the domain controller that was elected the ISTG.

◆ Converts the ntdsConnection objects into a configuration that is understood by the Directory Service replication engine. ntdsConnection objects are Microsoft Windows NT Directory Service Connection objects that are defined automatically by the KCC, and manually by the Active Directory administrator.

The KCC can become overwhelmed and consume too much CPU time if you have a very high number of sites and domain controllers. There are a few things you can do to help streamline the KCC.

REDUCE THE NUMBER OF POTENTIAL ROUTES BETWEEN SITES

You can reduce the number of potential routes between sites by limiting the number of site-link bridges in your configuration. Automatic site-link bridging is a feature that makes the entire network fully routed, making every computer in a given site able to communicate with any computer in any other site.

You can disable automatic site linking and define site-link bridges only where needed. A site-link bridge is needed only if a particular site does not have a domain controller for a domain but is adjacent to a site that does have a domain controller for the domain. In this example, an adjacent site would be defined as a site that is connected via a site link to that site.

Most networks are configured in a way that will put a site holding a domain controller adjacent to at least one other site that holds a domain controller for a given domain. Chances are your network is configured in this way, and site-link bridges will not be needed. If you do not need site-link bridges, you can disable automatic site linking.

To disable automatic site linking:

1. Open the Active Directory Sites and Services snap-in.

2. Navigate to the IP transport object.

3. Right-click and select Properties.

4. In the properties page of the Inter-Site Transports container, uncheck the box.

5. Click OK.

DISABLE THE KCC'S INTERSITE TOPOLOGY CALCULATION

You can configure the KCC to disable its intersite topology calculation. The KCC will still respond to changes to the network made in the Active Directory Sites and Services snap-in. You can then reenable the intersite topology calculation during off-peak hours so the KCC can run the intersite check. You can then disable it again.

This practice has one ramification; the site that is changed will not respond to changes to the intersite topology. If either of the replication partners for the intersite connection is available, the KCC cannot automatically adapt the new source or destination until the domain controllers come back online, or until the intersite transport portion of the KCC is run again.

MANUALLY CONFIGURE CONNECTIONS

There is always the option of completely disabling the KCC and configuring the connection objects manually. This option is generally used for networks that use a hub topology and have grown very fast to a very large number of branch office sites.

While a manual configuration may help ease the processing time and performance of the KCC, it can be an administrative nightmare. Consider the following when making the decision to turn off the KCC entirely:

♦ Redundant connections to each site must be configured. Branch1 has a manual connection to Server1 at MainOffice1. If the KCC were still enabled, it would automatically determine another route for the replication to occur. Since you have manually created the connections, and only one has been defined, Server1 and Branch1 are no longer able to replicate Active Directory information. Unless the redundant connections are configured properly, replication problems could occur. If different domain controllers in a site are configured for inbound connections, some Active Directory updates could be replicated more than once.

♦ Global catalog servers must remain synchronized. At least one global catalog in a site must have a connection to and from another site with a global catalog.

◆ If sites contain domain controllers from more than one domain in the forest, the domain controllers from each domain must have a connection to another domain controller of the same domain in a different site. For example, Site1 contains domain controllers for Domain1, Domain2, and Domain3. It will not be sufficient to simply connect one domain controller from one site to a domain controller in another site. Domain controllers from all three sites must have connections to domain controllers from their same domain in the other site.

◆ Consider load balancing your inbound and outbound connections. If you have a corporate site with 100 domain controllers and 1500 branch sites with one domain controller at each site, you do not want to configure all 1500 branch domain controllers to replicate to one server at the main office. Create 15 connection objects on each domain controller in the main office to share the load.

DISABLE AND ENABLE REPLICATION ON A DOMAIN CONTROLLER

There may be an instance when you would need to disable replication on a particular domain controller. Such an instance would be for testing or if you were running a restore procedure.

1. Open a command prompt.

2. From the command prompt, type the following command: **<repadmin /options +disable_ outbound_repl>**.

3. To enable replication, go to a command prompt and type the following: **< repadmin /options -disable_outbound_repl>**.

CONFIGURE SITE LINK REPLICATION SCHEDULE

In intrasite replication, replication occurs frequently and without a schedule. In intersite replication, you can use a schedule to determine how often replication can occur. If you provide a schedule, you can allow replication to occur as frequently as possible, without impacting bandwidth during peak network hours.

1. Open the Active Directory Sites and Services MMC snap-in.

2. Navigate to Sites ➤ Inter-site transports ➤ IP or SMTP.

3. Select the site whose schedule you would like to adjust, right-click, and choose Properties.

4. Select Change Schedule.

5. Highlight the timeframe you would like to schedule.

6. Select either Replication Not Available or Replication Available, whichever you would like to configure.

Securing Active Directory Replication

If one or more firewalls separate domain controllers in a network, the firewalls must be configured to allow secure communication with other domain controllers in other networks. Common communication ports used by active directory replication include the ones shown in Table 10.2.

If you deploy Active Directory in an environment with firewalls separating networks in this manner, you will need to configure the domain controllers as well as the firewalls that separate them. The ports listed in Table 10.2 will need to be opened on the firewall.

In this chapter, we concentrate on domain controller replication across firewalls. We recommend using IPSec to secure replication between domain controllers that reside in separate domains, or in the same domain. This configuration allows for more secure communication and requires only a small set of ports to be opened on the firewall. (See Table 10.3.)

TABLE 10.2:   Active Directory Replication Ports

SERVICE	PORT NUMBER
RPC Traffic	Configurable
LDAP	TCP 389
LDAP over SSL	TCP 686
Kerberos	TCP and UDP 88
DNS	TCP and UDP 53
SMB over IP	TCP and UDP 445

TABLE 10.3:   Ports Used by Active Directory in an IPSec Configuration

SERVICE	PORT NUMBER
IPSec Encapsulated Security Payload (ESP)	IP Protocol 50
Internet Key Exchange (IKE)	UDP 500
Kerberos	TCP and UDP 88
DNS	TCP and UDP 53
IPSec Authentication Header (AH)	IP Protocol 51

Table 10.4 contains a list of ports that Active Directory commonly uses for replication, mutual authentication, and domain controller location mechanism.

You will notice that the RPC static port for Active Directory replication port is configurable. You can configure each domain controller to replicate active directory traffic using a single port. You can accomplish this by editing the following Registry key:

```
[HKEY_LOCAL_MACHINE\SYSTEM\CurrentControlSet\Services\NTDS\Parameters]
```

Change the value of the entry `<""TCP/IP Port"" = dword:>`.

You can also limit the range of ports that RPC uses. By default, RPC uses a dynamic range of ports. If you do not define a fixed RPC port, you can allow a smaller well-known range of ports.

A starting port number of at least 5000 is recommended. It is also recommended that the range consists of at least 20 ports. The change can be made in the following Registry key:

```
[HKEY_LOCAL_MACHINE\SOFTWARE\Microsoft\Rpc\Internet]
```

Change the value <""Ports"" = REG_MULTI_SZ:5000-5020>.

TABLE 10.4:   Common Ports Used by Active Directory

SERVICE	PORT NUMBER
RPC Endpoint Mapper	TCP and UDP 135
PRC Static Port for AD Replicaiton	Configurable
Kerberos	TCP and UDP 88
LDAP	TCP 389
LDAP over SSL	TCP 686
Global Catalog LDAP	TCP 3268
Global Catalog LDAP over SSL	TCP 3269
SMB over IP	TCP and UDP 445
DNS	TCP and UDP 53
Network Time Protocol (NTP)	UDP 123

Coming Up Next

Now that you have a pretty good understanding of how Active Directory replication works, how to manage it, and how to tweak it to perform better, we can start looking at how to manage the different Flexible Single Master of Operations (FSMO) roles in your environment.

Chapter 11

Managing the Flexible Single Master Operations Roles

As you saw in Chapter 5, the Flexible Single Master Operations (FSMO) roles play an important part of the Active Directory infrastructure. Since these roles can only be held by one domain controller at a time, the placement planning that you initially performed during the design and planning phases plays an important role. If you do not place these roles where they can be used effectively and efficiently, you could potentially cause your Active Directory infrastructure to perform slowly or introduce unnecessary network traffic.

At this point we are going to assume that you have taken our recommendations and have already configured your FSMO role holders. So what happens if you lose the domain controller that holds one, some, or all of your FSMO roles? And what are your options if you want to take the domain controller holding those roles offline, or move the roles to another system? This chapter answers these questions.

We start off by discussing how you can locate each of the five roles. Then we take a look at how and why you would want to transfer each of the roles to another domain controller and the options available if you have lost the role-holding domain controller.

Identifying the Role Holders

As with many things in the Windows environment, there are several ways to find out which domain controller holds a FSMO role. Some ways are easier than others, but it depends on your familiarity with the built-in utilities that ship with Windows Server 2003 and the tools that are part of the support tools.

One of the easiest ways to find out which domain controller is hosting a FSMO role is to use the built-in Active Directory utilities. Most of the Active Directory utilities are easy to find and work with, but one of them is hidden from view. Let's take a look at each one of these utilities and what they have to offer.

Active Directory Users and Computers

You can use the Active Directory Users and Computers utility to find the domain controllers that hold the roles that are domain specific. If you remember the discussion of the role holders in Chapter 5, each domain has an Infrastructure Master, RID Master, and PDC emulator. So it only makes sense that in order to find the role holders of these FSMO roles, you consult a utility that helps you maintain aspects of your domain.

When you open up Active Directory Users and Computers, it is not immediately obvious that the FSMO role holders can be found in this utility. However, if you right-click on the domain node, you see the option Operations Masters in the context menu, as shown in Figure 11.1. Clicking this option presents you with the Operations Masters dialog box shown in Figure 11.2.

Notice that you have tabs at the top of this dialog box, one for each of the domain-based roles: RID, PDC, and Infrastructure. As you select each of these tabs, two domain controllers appear in the window. If you target the Active Directory Users and Computers snap-in on the domain controller that is holding the FSMO role, you will see that domain controller listed in both spots. If you are not focused on the role holder, you will see the current role holder listed first in the Operations Master text box, and the domain controller you are focused on listed in the transfer text box.

FIGURE 11.1
Domain node
context menu

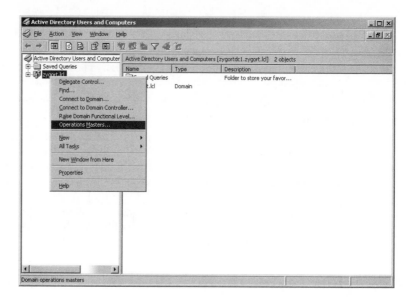

FIGURE 11.2
Operations Masters
dialog box

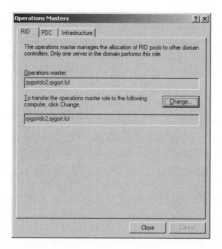

To transfer roles, you need to make sure that you target the Active Directory Users and Computers snap-in on the domain controller you want to take over the role. When you have decided to which domain controller you want to transfer the role, all you have to do is open Active Directory Users and Computers, right-click on the domain, and select Connect To Domain Controller, as shown in Figure 11.3. Once the dialog box appears, as shown in Figure 11.4, you can enter the name of the domain controller you want to host the role.

FIGURE 11.3
Context menu that lets you choose a domain controller

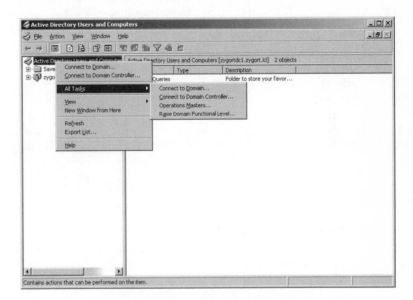

FIGURE 11.4
Changing the domain controller

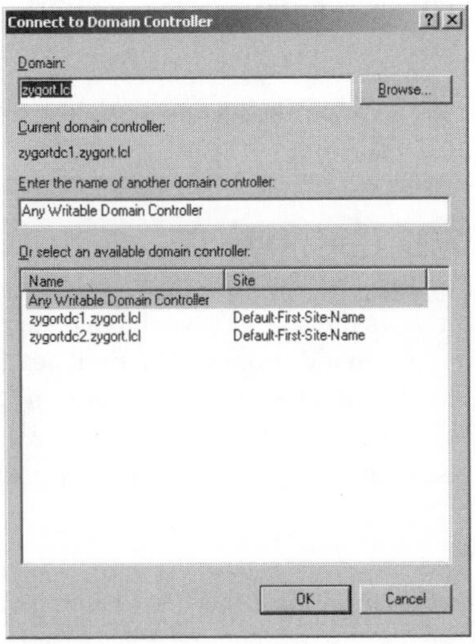

Active Directory Domains and Trusts

The first of the two forest-based roles is easy to locate using the Active Directory Domains and Trusts snap-in. The Domain Naming Master role can be found using the same method as the domain-based roles. Right-click on the domain node in the Active Directory Domains and Trusts snap-in and select Operations Master. The dialog box that appears, shown in Figure 11.5, displays the current role holder as well as the domain controller that you want to become the role holder. Just as with Active Directory Users and Computers, you can choose which domain controller will take over the role by selecting it from the context menu that appears when you right-click the domain node in the snap-in.

FIGURE 11.5

Active Directory Domains and Trusts Operations Master

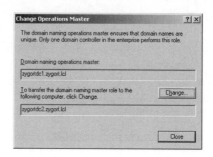

Active Directory Schema

This is the one snap-in that is not available to administrators unless they choose to register the dynamic link library (DLL) necessary for it to be displayed and used. The designers of Active Directory did this intentionally. The reason they decided to "hide" this snap-in is because the designers did not believe the tool should be available to every administrator within the forest. Instead, Microsoft forces anyone who wants to use this tool to research how to get to the schema. Because the schema should not be altered unless there is a valid business case to do so, this snap-in would not be used very often anyway.

NOTE   To gain access to the Active Directory Schema snap-in, you will need to register it using the command line `regsvr32 schmmgmt.dll`.

Command-Line Options

Some command-line utilities allow you to identify the role holders. Although these utilities may not be as intuitive as the snap-ins we have been discussing, they can come in very handy when you are already at a command prompt. The first, `netdom`, shows you all the role holders at the same time. The second, `dsquery`, allows you to find individual roles when you ask for them. The DCDiag utility shows you all the roles. The final utility, `dumpfsmos.cmd,` displays the FSMO roles that the domain controller knows about. You can find this utility in the Resource Kit.

REPLMON

The replication monitor utility (`ReplMon`) included with the support tools on the Windows Server 2003 CD can identify the current FSMO role holders as well as send a query against them in order to see if they are up and running. To start `ReplMon`, type **ReplMon** at the support tools command line.

When the tool opens, you will need to add a domain controller to the console. Right-click the Monitored Servers node, and then select Add Monitored Servers from the context menu, as shown in Figure 11.6.

The resulting dialog box allows you to type the domain controller's name, or you can search Active Directory for the domain controller you want to use. Figure 11.7 displays the dialog box that you use to choose the monitored server, and Figure 11.8 shows the methods you can use to search for the domain controller's name.

Once you have added the domain controller to the monitored servers list, you can look at the properties of the domain controller to learn which domain controllers hold the FSMO roles by right-clicking on the server and selecting Properties. After opening the properties, you can click the FSMO Roles tab to view the current role holders, as Figure 11.9 shows. Notice the Query button next to each role. Clicking this button causes Replication Monitor to check the current role holder to see if it is online. If it is online, the message shown in Figure 11.10 appears. If the role holder cannot be contacted, you see the message shown in Figure 11.11.

FIGURE 11.6

Choosing to monitor a server in Replication Monitor

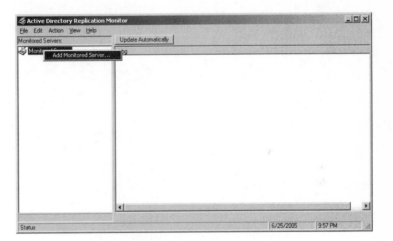

FIGURE 11.7

Choosing the monitored server

FIGURE 11.8
Searching for the domain
controller's name

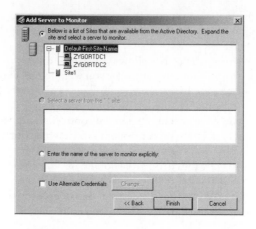

FIGURE 11.9
Domain controller prop-
erties FSMO Roles tab

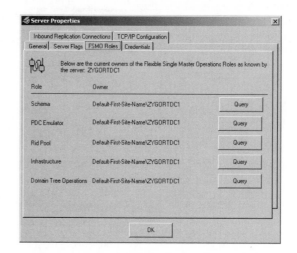

FIGURE 11.10
Positive result from
FSMO query

FIGURE 11.11
Negative result from
FSMO query

NETDOM

The `netdom` command syntax that reports the role holders is as follows:

```
netdom query fsmo /domain:zygort.lcl
```

Of course, you replace `zygort.lcl` with your domain name. This returns a list of all the role holders. The results appear in the command prompt window, as shown in Figure 11.12.

FIGURE 11.12
The netdom command lists the FSMO roles.

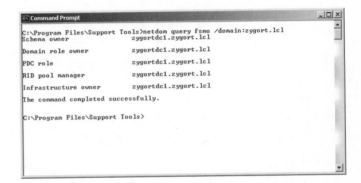

DSQUERY

To find individual role holders with the `dsquery` command, use the following commands:

◆ To find the Schema Master:

```
dsquery server -hasfsmo schema
```

◆ To find the Domain Naming Master:

```
dsquery server -hasfsmo name
```

◆ To find the Infrastructure Master:

```
dsquery server -hasfsmo infr
```

◆ To find the RID Master:

```
dsquery server -hasfsmo rid
```

◆ To find the PDC emulator:

```
dsquery server -hasfsmo pdc
```

This command-line utility also presents the results in the command prompt window. Figure 11.13 shows an example of what you receive when you issue one of the commands.

FIGURE 11.13
dsquery results for the
Schema Master

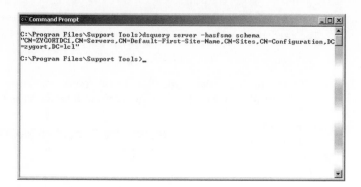

DCDIAG

The DCDiag utility is used as follows:

```
dcdiag /test:knowsofroleholders /v
```

Because we included the verbose switch (/v), this command returns the role holders and provides information on each. Figure 11.14 displays a portion of the information you receive when you issue this command at a command prompt.

FIGURE 11.14
DCDiag results

DUMPFSMOS.CMD

The `dumpfsmos.cmd` utility from the Resource Kit is a small script that actually starts NTDSUTIL and issues the appropriate commands to return a list of the role holders. The syntax for this command is as follows:

```
dumpfsmos.cmd zygort.lcl
```

Of course, you replace `zygort.lcl` with the name of the domain you are querying against. Figure 11.15 shows the information returned when you issue this command at the command prompt.

FIGURE 11.15

`dumpfsmos.cmd` results

Maintaining the Role Holders

There are reasons why you would want to move a role from one domain controller to another. Many organizations need to move at least one of these roles because they have more than one domain in their forest. The Infrastructure Master cannot work effectively on a global catalog server when there are two or more domains. Other reasons to make changes to the location of your FSMO roles are addressed in the following sections.

Depending on your situation, you can transfer the role to another domain controller if the original role holder is still online, or you can seize, which is forcibly taking the role, if the original role holder has failed. Transferring the role is the preferred method because it performs a controlled switch-over from one domain controller to the next. You should only consider seizing a role if the original role holder cannot be brought back online. Of course, safeguards are in place that protect the forest or domain from data corruption should the original role holder come back online, but you shouldn't take a chance. If the original role holder has failed and you have seized the role on another domain controller, do not attempt to bring the original role holder back online just yet.

TRANSFERRING THE ROLE TO ANOTHER DOMAIN CONTROLLER

If you are demoting a role holder, make sure that you transfer the role to another domain controller, preferably the domain controller you have designated as the standby role holder. Doing so guarantees that you are transferring the role to the appropriate domain controller instead of allowing Dcpromo to choose another domain controller on its own. Remember, it is always better to have control over these things than to allow random chance to control your organization.

SEIZING THE ROLE ON THE STANDBY DOMAIN CONTROLLER

You should have already designated another domain controller as the standby server in case a role holder becomes unavailable. If you have configured the original role holder and the standby as replication partners, there is a very good chance that they are completely synchronized with one another. If the original role holder becomes unavailable and you deem it necessary to have the standby server become the role holder, you can seize the role on the standby server. Again, this is a drastic measure and should be performed only if you are certain the original role holder is not going to be reintroduced on the network.

NOTE   If you are permanently taking a domain controller offline, whether it is a role holder or not, you should demote it so that the references to the domain controller are removed from Active Directory.

In the following sections, we cover each of the roles and the steps necessary to transfer or seize each role. We start with the two forest-level roles, and then discuss the domain-level roles. We also cover the ramifications of not moving a role to another domain controller when the original domain controller is offline.

Maintaining the Schema Master

The Schema Master role is not one that you will have to worry about if the domain controller holding it goes offline. The Schema Master is used whenever you have to make a change to the forest's schema and when the Forest Functional level is raised. Otherwise, the Schema Master does not have a lot to do, and just waits for changes to be made by a member of the Schema Admins group or an administrator who is responsible for raising the Forest Functional level. Obviously, neither of these options is performed very often. The Forest Functional level can only be raised one time, and cannot revert to its previous level, so schema changes should be kept to a minimum.

You would want to move the Schema Master to another system for a couple of reasons. A controlled move, or transfer, may be necessary if you are planning on decommissioning the domain controller that holds the Schema Master role. If this is the case, it is much easier to transfer the role to the domain controller that is taking over the Schema Master responsibility than to seize it later on.

Another reason to transfer the role lies in how companies maintain their FSMO roles. Many companies prefer to have all of the roles held on one domain controller. This way, they know which domain controller is performing these functions, they can control the services that are operating on the domain controller, and they can isolate the domain controller for security purposes.

TRANSFERRING THE SCHEMA MASTER ROLE

The Schema Master is not readily transferable using the standard administrative tools. As a matter of fact, Microsoft intentionally hid the Active Directory Schema snap-in so that people would not have easy access to it. To make it accessible, you must register the DLL that it uses on the system where you will administer the changes. To register the DLL, open a command prompt or at the Run line type **regsvr32 schmmgmt.dll**.

Using the Active Directory Schema Snap-In

Once you have registered the snap-in, you can open it by creating your own MMC and adding the snap-in to it. Once you add the snap-in, you can connect to the domain controller that you want to take over the role responsibility by right-clicking on the Active Directory Schema node and selecting Change Domain Controller. Notice that for the Schema Master the dialog box for connecting to another domain controller (Figure 11.16) is different than the one for the other snap-ins. Once you have focused on another domain controller, you can change the Operations Master by right-clicking the same node and choosing Operations Master.

The current role holder appears in the top text box, and the domain controller you are focused on appears in the lower section, as shown in Figure 11.17. When you click the Transfer button, the entry in the upper text box reflects the change, and now matches the name of the domain controller in the lower section.

FIGURE 11.16
Connecting to the
Schema Master

FIGURE 11.17
Schema Master
Operations Master

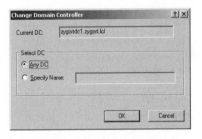

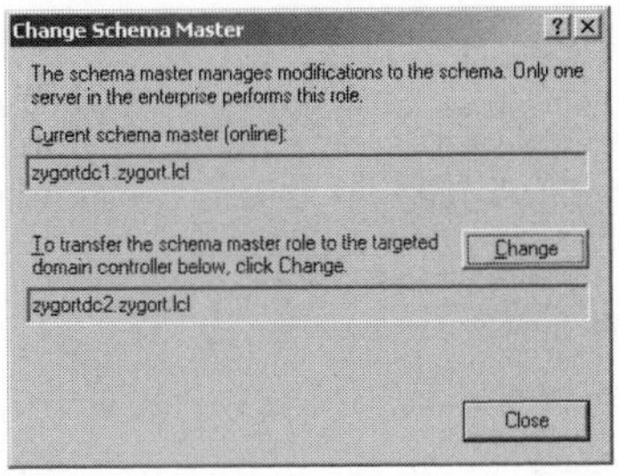

That's all there is to it. The transfer of the role is usually a very quick process. One domain controller is told to take the token that identifies it as the one that can perform schema updates, and the other has the token taken from it. If the original role holder is not available, it may take a minute or two for a dialog box to appear that states the original role holder could not be contacted. If the original role holder has failed, you have to seize the role on the new domain controller. Otherwise, if it is still up and running, you must troubleshoot to learn why the original role holder could not be contacted by the potential role holder.

Using NTDSUtil

You can also transfer the role by using NTDSUtil. This command-line utility allows you to perform many functions in Active Directory, including transferring and seizing the FSMO roles if necessary. After you open a command prompt and type **NTDSUtil**, perform these steps to transfer the Schema Master:

1. At the `ntdsutil:` prompt, type **roles** to enter `fsmo maintenance`.

2. At the `fsmo maintenance:` prompt, type **connections** to enter `server connections`.

3. At the `server connections:` prompt, type **connect to server *domain_controller***, where *domain_controller* is the name of the domain controller to which you are going to transfer the role.

4. At the `server connections:` prompt, type **quit** to enter `fsmo maintenance`.

5. At the `fsmo maintenance:` prompt, type **transfer schema master**.

After you have transferred the role, type **quit** twice to exit NTDSUTIL. You can then use one of the utilities listed earlier to verify that the role was transferred to the appropriate domain controller.

SEIZING THE SCHEMA MASTER ROLE

If you have lost the original Schema Master and you want to designate another domain controller as the Schema Master, you must use NTDSUtil. This allows you to force the new domain controller to take on the responsibility. Open a command prompt and enter **NTDSUtil**; then follow these steps:

1. At the `ntdsutil:` prompt, type **roles** to enter `fsmo maintenance`.

2. At the `fsmo maintenance:` prompt, type **connections** to enter `server connections`.

3. At the `server connections:` prompt, type **connect to server *domain_controller***, where *domain_controller* is the name of the domain controller to which you are going to transfer the role.

4. At the `server connections:` prompt, type **quit** to enter `fsmo maintenance`.

5. At the `fsmo maintenance:` prompt, type **seize schema master**.

After you have transferred the role, type **quit** twice to exit NTDSUTIL. You can then use one of the utilities listed earlier to verify that the role was transferred to the appropriate domain controller.

Maintaining the Domain Naming Master

The Domain Naming Master role is used just slightly more than its forest-level brethren, the Schema Master. Whenever a domain is created or removed from the forest, the Domain Naming Master is queried to make sure everything is valid in the request. If a domain exists that has the same name as the domain being created, the Domain Naming Master halts the creation of the new domain. If an attempt is made to remove a domain and the Domain Naming Master finds anything about the request that is not valid, it will stop the removal of the domain.

As with the Schema Master, you don't have to worry about the resource requirements for the Domain Naming Master. It can continue to run on the original domain controller for the remainder of the lifetime of that server. If you do lose the server, or you want to decommission it, you can move the role to another machine by either transferring or seizing the role.

TRANSFERRING THE DOMAIN NAMING MASTER ROLE

Transferring the Domain Naming Master role using a graphical interface requires fewer steps than transferring the Schema Master. This is because the interface that you use is already available on domain controllers and is one of the snap-ins made available when you load the administrative tools onto your workstation. The snap-in that you will be using for this procedure is Active Directory Domains and Trusts.

Using Active Directory Domains and Trusts

To perform the transfer you must be a member of the Enterprise Admins group. Once you open the snap-in in an MMC, you need to connect to the domain controller to which you are going to transfer the role. To do so, right-click the domain node and select Connect To Domain Controller, as shown in Figure 11.18.

FIGURE 11.18
Selecting the domain controller

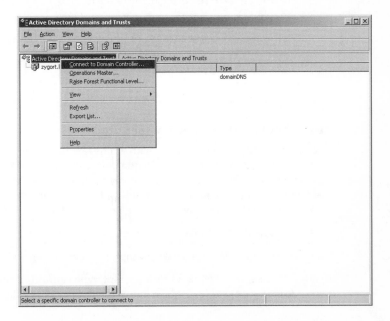

Once you have targeted the snap-in on the domain controller that will be taking over the Domain Naming Master role, you can right-click the domain once again and select the Operations Masters option. This takes you to a screen that displays the current role holder in the top pane, and the domain controller you are transferring the role to in the bottom, just like the one shown in Figure 11.19.

FIGURE 11.19

Transferring the role

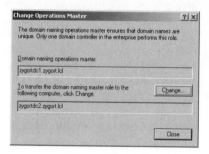

Using NTDSUtil

You can also transfer the role by using the NTDSUtil command-line utility. Open a command prompt and type **NTDSUtil**. When the NTDSUtil interface appears, issue the following commands to transfer the role to the desired domain controller:

1. At the `ntdsutil:` prompt, type **roles** to enter `fsmo maintenance`.

2. At the `fsmo maintenance:` prompt, type **connections** to enter `server connections`.

3. At the `server connections:` prompt, type **connect to server** *domain_controller*, where *domain_controller* is the name of the domain controller to which you are going to transfer the role.

4. At the `server connections:` prompt, type **quit** to enter `fsmo maintenance`.

5. At the `fsmo maintenance:` prompt, type **transfer domain naming master**.

After you have transferred the role, type **quit** twice to exit NTDSUTIL. You can then use one of the utilities mentioned earlier to verify that the role was transferred to the appropriate domain controller.

SEIZING THE DOMAIN NAMING MASTER ROLE

The Domain Naming Master can remain offline for quite some time before you will have miss it. Since its main role is to check and approve domain additions and deletions, you will not need it online unless you are making a critical change to your forest. If you do want to sieze the role, either due to needing the Domain Naming Master online or determining that the original role holder is not going to be restored, you can follow the instructions that follow.

1. At the `ntdsutil:` prompt, type **roles** to enter `fsmo maintenance`.

2. At the `fsmo maintenance:` prompt, type **connections** to enter `server connections`.

3. At the `server connections:` prompt, type **connect to server** *domain_controller*, where *domain_controller* is the name of the domain controller to which you are going to transfer the role.

4. At the `server connections:` prompt, type **quit** to enter `fsmo maintenance`.

5. At the `fsmo maintenance:` prompt, type **seize domain naming master**.

After you have transferred the role, type **quit** twice to exit NTDSUTIL. You can then use one of the utilities mentioned earlier to verify that the role was transferred to the appropriate domain controller.

Maintaining the Infrastructure Master

If you are working in a multiple-domain environment, the Infrastructure Master can be your best friend or your worst enemy. It is the Infrastructure Master's job to make sure that accounts from other domains that are members of a group are kept up-to-date. You do not want an account to have access to resources that it is not supposed to, and if changes are made to users and groups in other domains, you need to make sure that the same changes are reflected in your domain. For instance, let's say the administrator of `bloomco.lcl` has just added two accounts to a global group and removed one from the group. Within the `bloomco.lcl` domain, the changes are replicated throughout. In your domain, there is a domain local group that contains the global group. Because the changes are not replicated to domain controllers in your domain, the user who was removed from the group might still have access to resources in your domain and the two new accounts might not.

The Infrastructure Master needs to be able to maintain the differences between domains so that the correct group membership can be applied at all domain controllers. This is why the Infrastructure Master should not be on a domain controller that is acting as a global catalog. The Infrastructure Master will contact a global catalog and compare the member attributes for the groups with the attributes that are contained in its domain. If there is a difference, the Infrastructure Master updates the attributes to keep everything synchronized. If you want to change the default scanning interval for the Infrastructure Master, set the following Registry value from two days to whatever value works best in your environment:

```
HKEY_LOCAL_MACHINE\System\CurrentControlSet\Services\
NTDS\Parameters\Days per database phantom scan
```

NOTE For more information on the Infrastructure Master and how to control the scanning interval, see Knowledge Base article 248047 at `http://support.microsoft.com/default.aspx?scid=kb;EN-US;248047`.

Loss of the Infrastructure Master is a little more severe than the previous two Master Operations roles. If the Infrastructure Master is offline for an extended period of time, the data cannot be synchronized and users could have access (or be denied access) to the wrong objects. If you cannot resolve the problem with the Infrastructure Master, you may want to seize the role on the standby server.

TRANSFERRING THE INFRASTRUCTURE MASTER ROLE

As with all of the domain-level Operations Masters, you can transfer the role to another domain controller by using the Active Directory Users and Computers snap-in. This snap-in is available when you promote a domain controller and when you add the administrative tools to another system such as your workstation.

Using Active Directory Users and Computers

To initiate the transfer, open Active Directory Users and Computers, and then connect to the domain controller that will become the Infrastructure Master by right-clicking on the domain name and choosing Connect to Domain Controller. Of course, this assumes that you are working with domain controllers from the domain in which your user account resides. You could very easily be an administrator for another domain within your forest and need to perform a transfer of a role in another domain. If that is the case, choose the Connect to Domain option from the context menu, and then select Connect to Domain Controller to connect to the domain controller that will become the Infrastructure Master.

Remember that the Infrastructure Master should not reside on a global catalog server unless you are in a single-domain environment, or all of your domain controllers are also global catalog servers. Then, to transfer the role, you will again right-click on the domain and choose Operations Masters. The dialog box that appears, shown in Figure 11.20, has three tabs representing the domain-level FSMO roles. Click Infrastructure; you should see the current Infrastructure Master listed at the top and the domain controller you are focused on at the bottom. Clicking the Change button transfers the role to the new role holder.

FIGURE 11.20
Operations Masters
transfer dialog box

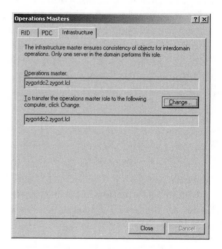

Using NTDSUtil

You can also transfer the role by using the NTDSUtil command-line utility. Open a command prompt and type **NTDSUtil**. When the NTDSUtil interface appears, issue the following commands to transfer the role to the desired domain controller:

1. At the `ntdsutil:` prompt, type **roles** to enter `fsmo maintenance`.

2. At the `fsmo maintenance:` prompt, type **connections** to enter `server connections`.

3. At the `server connections:` prompt, type **connect to server *domain_controller***, where *domain_controller* is the name of the domain controller to which you are going to transfer the role.

4. At the `server connections:` prompt, type **quit** to enter `fsmo maintenance`.

5. At the `fsmo maintenance:` prompt, type **transfer infrastructure master**.

After you have transferred the role, type **quit** twice to exit NTDSUTIL. You can then use one of the utilities mentioned earlier to verify that the role was transferred to the appropriate domain controller.

SEIZING THE INFRASTRUCTURE MASTER ROLE

The Infrastructure Master is not as critical to the functionality of the domain so you will probably not have to sieze the role. However, if you deem that the original Infrastructure Master is not going to be brought back online, or if there are changes going on in other domains, you will want to sieze the role using the following instructions.

1. At the `ntdsutil:` prompt, type **roles** to enter `fsmo maintenance`.

2. At the `fsmo maintenance:` prompt, type **connections** to enter `server connections`.

3. At the `server connections:` prompt, type **connect to server *domain_controller***, where *domain_controller* is the name of the domain controller to which you are going to transfer the role.

4. At the `server connections:` prompt, type **quit** to enter `fsmo maintenance`.

5. At the `fsmo maintenance:` prompt, type **seize infrastructure master**.

After you have transferred the role, type **quit** twice to exit NTDSUTIL. You can then use one of the utilities mentioned earlier to verify that the role was transferred to the appropriate domain controller.

Maintaining the RID Master

Whenever a security principal, such as a user, group, or computer account, is created within a domain, it has an associated security identifier (SID). An account's SID consists of the domain's SID and a relative identifier (RID) that is unique to the security principle. Allocating and keeping track of all of the RIDs for the domain is the RID Master's responsibility. Having the RID Master online allows you to sleep better at night knowing that a duplicate SID will not be generated within the domain. Even if the security principle associated with a RID is deleted, the RID will still not be regenerated and used again.

If you take a look at a SID, you will notice that it is an alphanumeric combination that is not easy to understand. There is logic behind the madness, however. If you take a look at the SID or a user account it may look like this:

```
S-1-5-21-1068514962-2513648523-685232148-1005
```

Broken down, the sections that make up the RID fall into these categories:

S   The initial character S identifies the series of digits that follow as a SID.

1   This is the revision level. Every SID that is generated within a Windows environment has a revision of 1.

5   This third character is the issuing authority identifier. A majority of the SIDs will have the Windows NT issuing authority number of 5, but some of the well-known built-in accounts will have other values.

21   The fourth character set represents the sub-authority. The sub-authority identifies the service type that generated the SID. SIDs that are generated from domain controllers will contain the characters 21, while built-in accounts may have other characters, such as 32.

1068514962-2513648523-685232148   This long string of characters is the unique part of the SID for a domain. If you are working with local accounts, it represents the unique SID for the computer.

1005   The last set of characters represents the RID for the account. The RID Master starts at 1000 and increments by 1 for every RID it allocates to the domain controllers.

Since any domain controller within a native mode domain can generate a RID to an account, you must make sure that only one domain controller is allocating and controlling the RIDs. For this reason, make sure that you do not seize the RID role on a domain controller when the original role holder is just temporarily unavailable. You could create a nightmare for yourself trying to troubleshoot permission problems.

This is a role that you might miss sooner than some of the others. The RID Master allocates blocks of RIDs to the domain controllers within the domain. If a domain controller uses up its last RID while creating a security principle, it will no longer be able to create security principles. Another drawback to losing the RID Master is you cannot promote another domain controller without the RID Master online. For these reasons, you should attempt to recover the original RID Master role holder as quickly as possible, or you will have to seize the role on the standby server as the RID pools on the domain controllers start to become depleted.

TRANSFERRING THE RID MASTER ROLE

Transferring the RID Master to the standby server is another very easy task. When you deem it necessary to move the role to another domain controller, you can use the Operations Masters dialog box from Active Directory Users and Computers or NTDSUtil. Your utility of choice should be based on the method you are most comfortable using.

Using Active Directory Users and Computers

This is another domain-level role that can be found within Active Directory Users and Computers. When you select the Operations Masters menu item and select the RID tab, click the Change button to move the role to another domain controller just as you did with the Infrastructure Master.

Using NTDSUtil

You can also transfer the role by using the NTDSUtil command-line utility. Open a command prompt and type **NTDSUtil**. When the NTDSUtil interface appears, issue the following commands to transfer the role to the desired domain controller:

1. At the `ntdsutil:` prompt, type **roles** to enter `fsmo maintenance`.

2. At the `fsmo maintenance:` prompt, type **connections** to enter `server connections`.

3. At the `server connections:` prompt, type **connect to server *domain_controller***, where *domain_controller* is the name of the domain controller to which you are going to transfer the role.

4. At the `server connections:` prompt, type **quit** to enter `fsmo maintenance`.

5. At the `fsmo maintenance:` prompt, type **transfer RID master**.

After you have transferred the role, type **quit** twice to exit NTDSUTIL. You can then use one of the utilities mentioned earlier to verify that the role was transferred to the appropriate domain controller.

SEIZING THE RID MASTER ROLE

The RID Master role is one that you can get by with for a short period of time. The amount of time it can remain down depends on the number of accounts that you are creating. Since each of the domain controllers receive an initial allotment of 500 RIDs, you can probably get by for some time before you run out of RIDs.

If your domain is still in Windows 2000 mixed mode, you may have a shorter time frame for your RID Master, however. The PDC emulator is the only domain controller that can create accounts in mixed mode. Therefore, you do not have the option to connect to another domain controller in order to create an account. To seize the role, follow these steps.

1. At the `ntdsutil:` prompt, type **roles** to enter `fsmo maintenance`.

2. At the `fsmo maintenance:` prompt, type **connections** to enter `server connections`.

3. At the `server connections:` prompt, type **connect to server *domain_controller***, where *domain_controller* is the name of the domain controller to which you are going to transfer the role.

4. At the `server connections:` prompt, type **quit** to enter `fsmo maintenance`.

5. At the `fsmo maintenance:` prompt, type **seize RID master**.

After you have transferred the role, type **quit** twice to exit NTDSUTIL. You can then use one of the utilities mentioned earlier to verify that the role was transferred to the appropriate domain controller.

Maintaining the PDC Emulator

The PDC emulator is probably the busiest of the master operations, and yet it is the only one that is not known by the name "master." This is also the role that confuses new administrators, because they think that this role is needed only until all of the NT 4 BDCs are taken offline. This is far from the truth. Microsoft should consider changing the name of this master operation to reflect the other functions it provides.

First off, the PDC emulator allows for replication of directory information to Windows NT 4 BDCs while the domain is still in mixed mode. This is also the only domain controller that will create security principles while the domain is in mixed mode, because it has to act like a Windows NT 4 PDC. You should make sure that you place this role holder in a location that will create the most accounts.

This is also the only domain controller that is allowed to change passwords for legacy operating systems, such as Windows 98 and Windows NT. They will look for the PDC of the domain, and the PDC emulator fulfills that roll. Another password function that this role holder provides is that it has the final say when there is a password change. When an account's password is changed, the PDC emulator is notified immediately. After a user types in their password for authentication, the domain controller that is attempting to authenticate the user will check with the PDC emulator to make sure the user's password has not been changed before notifying the user that they typed in the wrong password.

Two other functions, time synchronization and global policy centralization, are also functions of the PDC emulator. All the other domain controllers within the domain will look to this role holder as the official timekeeper in the domain. You should set the PDC emulator to synchronize with an external time source so that all the other domain controllers will have the correct time. This is also the domain controller that is used as the default location for changing group policies. Making one domain controller the default GPO holder allows you to control policy changes and minimize conflicting changes within the domain.

NOTE In a multiple-domain forest, the PDC emulator for the forest root becomes the Time Master for all PDCs within the forest.

Due to the amount of responsibilities that the PDC emulator has, it will probably be the master operation that you will miss the most if it fails. When it fails, you should immediately assess how long it is going to take to recover the domain controller holding this role. If it looks as if the domain controller is going to be offline for an extended period of time—let's say more than a couple of hours—you should seize the role on the standby server. Although the other roles may cause problems for administrators, users will be affected by a loss of the PDC emulator, and they will let you know that they see something wrong!

TRANSFERRING THE PDC EMULATOR ROLE

This is yet another of the domain-level roles. As with the Infrastructure Master and RID Master roles before it, you will find that the Active Directory Users and Computer snap-in is the tool to use. This, as well as NTDSUtil, allows you to connect to the domain controller that you want to become the PDC emulator, and to transfer the role.

Using Active Directory Users and Computers

Following the same steps that were outlined in the "Transferring the Infrastructure Master Role" section, you can take the change token away from the existing PDC emulator and allow another domain controller to take its place as the role holder.

Using NTDSUtil

You can also transfer the role by using the NTDSUtil command-line utility. Open a command prompt and type **NTDSUtil**. When the NTDSUtil interface appears, issue the following commands to transfer the role to the desired domain controller:

1. At the `ntdsutil:` prompt, type **roles** to enter `fsmo maintenance`.

2. At the `fsmo maintenance:` prompt, type **connections** to enter `server connections`.

3. At the `server connections:` prompt, type **connect to server** *`domain_controller`*, where *`domain_controller`* is the name of the domain controller to which you are going to transfer the role.

4. At the `server connections:` prompt, type **quit** to enter `fsmo maintenance`.

5. At the `fsmo maintenance:` prompt, type **transfer PDC**.

After you have transferred the role, type **quit** twice to exit NTDSUTIL. You can then use one of the utilities mentioned earlier to verify that the role was transferred to the appropriate domain controller.

SEIZING THE PDC EMULATOR ROLE

This is the one role that you may need to seize very quickly after the original role holder has failed. You may be able to go for a short period without it; however, all of the password changes, account lockout information, time synchronization, and group policy updates are made on this system. With that in mind, you will probably need to seize this role on the standby system almost immediately.

WARNING   If you are working in a Windows 2000 mixed mode domain, the PDC emulator is the only domain controller that is allowed to create user accounts. To create accounts after the PDC emulator has gone offline, you need to seize the role on another machine.

To seize the role on another domain controller:

1. At the `ntdsutil:` prompt, type **roles** to enter `fsmo maintenance`.

2. At the `fsmo maintenance:` prompt, type **connections** to enter `server connections`.

3. At the `server connections:` prompt, type **connect to server *domain_controller***, where *domain_controller* is the name of the domain controller to which you are going to transfer the role.

4. At the `server connections:` prompt, type **quit** to enter `fsmo maintenance`.

5. At the `fsmo maintenance:` prompt, type **seize PDC**.

After you have transferred the role, type **quit** twice to exit NTDSUTIL. You can then use one of the utilities mentioned earlier to verify that the role was transferred to the appropriate domain controller.

Failed Role Holders

When a role holder fails, you need to seize the role using NTDSUtil because transferring the role won't be possible. You will realize this when you are first attempting to open the Operations Masters dialog box for any of the roles. The initial connection takes a considerable amount of time, and then the dialog box appears with the word ERROR in the Operations Master section. Figure 11.21 shows the dialog box with the error message that you receive. Figure 11.22 shows the error message that appears if you attempt to transfer the role while the original role holder is not online.

FIGURE 11.21
Operations Master dialog box showing original role holder problem

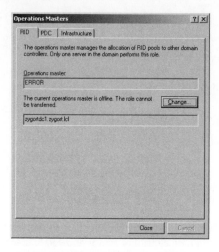

FIGURE 11.22
Error message when attempting to transfer the role

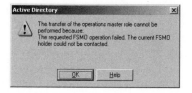

Coming Up Next

Although Microsoft has done a very commendable job of developing a stable directory service, things happen with any type of file, service, or database that can cause problems and, ultimately, corruption. In the next chapter, we investigate the troubleshooting steps and tools that help you assess and repair your directory service.

Chapter 12

Maintaining the Active Directory Database

The term *database* has many interpretations. The most common is "a collection of persistent data." Microsoft leverages an object-oriented database to store, or persist, Active Directory (AD) data currently. There is little doubt Microsoft will leverage relational database technology in future versions of Active Directory. This begs the following questions: what is the difference, and why should you care? Let's start with how they differ.

The object-oriented database paradigm is simply the extension of object-oriented programming languages to support a persistent state of the transient data found in executing code. The process of storing and using data in the same format has been used since the dawn of computing and is still in wide use today. Object-oriented databases are nothing more than large, structured files linked by indexes that are themselves structured files.

Relational database management systems (RDBMSs) are based on E. F. Codd's relational database theory, which is founded on relational algebra and calculus. The greatest deviation from earlier storage models, like object-oriented, is the concept of tables or entities and their relationships to each other. Each record in a table represents a unique instance of the entity described. An RDBMS uses matching values in multiple tables to relate the data in one table to other tables. Gone is the concept of storing data as methods use it. Data structure is now defined by the business rules that govern it and the interdependence of the entities stored.

Consider for a moment a file cabinet full of various human resource forms. The object-oriented model is only concerned with storing the form. As data is manipulated and persisted, forms are created or altered and placed in the file cabinet. The same file cabinet is used for all forms: hirings, promotions, and terminations.

In a relational model, the data elements of a given form are reorganized into tables or entities and stored. A single record in a table, or piece of paper in a folder, describes one instance of the entity defined by the table. Following the example above, all three forms contain attributes of employees, the job they are fulfilling, and their current employment status; thus employee, job, and employment status tables might be created in a relational model, each storing an employee ID so the data set could be reconstructed when needed.

Why should you care? Relational databases are easier to understand. This opens the door for administrators, programmers, and business users to leverage the corporate data assets embedded within Active Directory.

The Active Directory Database

Active Directory stores its data in a file named `ntds.dit`. By default, this file is located in the `%systemroot%/NTDS` folder. In addition to the database file, Active Directory uses log files that store information prior to committing it to the database.

This self-maintained system does not require daily maintenance. There are a few reasons that you may need to maintain the database:

◆ Low disk space

◆ Hardware failure

◆ Need to recover disk space

During day-to-day operation, objects will get deleted from Active Directory on a somewhat regular basis. As your Active Directory environment grows, the database grows as needed. The reverse is not true, however. As you delete objects from Active Directory, the database will not automatically shrink itself as objects are removed.

This process creates "white space" (or unused space) in your database. Think of it like this: you have a row of pop cans (or soda cans, if you prefer) on a table. If you have a row of 20 cans of pop in a single-file line, and you put another in line, either in the beginning or end, or squeeze it into the middle, the line grows as you add pop cans. If you take a few pop cans out of the middle, the line is still just as long as it was before, but now you have some empty spaces in there.

You can add cans back to the empty space (or white space). On a regular basis, Active Directory will defragment the database to reorganize the data. This is done through a process called the Garbage Collection Agent. This process runs every 12 hours, and will defrag the white space to help with performance, but it does not do anything for the unused space that could be returned back to the disk partition where the database resides. By performing an online defragmentation, you do not actually reclaim any drive space. This process is performed only to enhance performance. To reclaim the unused white space, you must perform an offline defragmentation.

Defragmenting the Active Directory Database

You may experience a high amount of white space if you performed a bulk deletion or the size of your system state backup is significantly increased due to the white space. Often, removing the Global Catalog role from a domain controller will result in large amounts of white space.

You can determine how much space is recoverable by changing the logging level of the Garbage Collection Agent. Two levels of logging are available:

◆ 0—Only critical events or error events are logged in the directory service log.

◆ 1—High-level events are logged. Event ID 700 is recorded when defragmentation begins, and event ID 701 is recorded when defragmentation ends. Event ID 1646 reports the amount of free space (white space) in the database and the total amount of allocated space.

If you find from this process that you can recover a significant amount of data, you may want to perform an offline defragmentation of the Active Directory database file. To do so, follow these steps.

Changing the Garbage Collection Logging Value

1. Click Start, click Run, type **regedit**, and then press Enter.

2. In Registry Editor, navigate to the Garbage Collection entry in HKEY_LOCAL_ MACHINE\SYSTEM\CurrentControlSet\Services\NTDS\Diagnostics.

3. Double-click Garbage Collection, and for the Base, click Decimal.

4. In the Value data box, type **1**, and then click OK.

Backing Up the System State

1. Click Start ➢ Run ➢ Programs ➢ Accessories ➢ System Tools ➢ Backup.

2. On the Welcome To The Backup Or Restore Wizard page, click Next.

3. Select Back Up Files And Settings, and then click Next.

4. Select Let Me Choose What To Back Up, and then click Next.

5. In the Items to Back Up window, double-click My Computer.

6. In the expanded list below My Computer, click the box labeled System State, and then click Next.

7. Select a location to store the backup.

8. Type a name for this backup, and then click Next.

9. On the last page of the wizard, click Advanced.

10. Keep the default settings for in the Type Of Backup screen. Normal should be selected, and the check box should remain cleared for Backup Migrated Remote Storage Data. Click Next.

11. Select Verify Data After Backup, and then click Next.

12. In the Backup Options dialog box, select a backup option, and then click Next.

13. If you are replacing the existing backups, select the option to allow only the owner and administrator access to the backup data and to any backups that are appended to this medium, and then click Next.

14. In the When To Back Up box, select the appropriate option for your needs, and then click Next.

15. Click Finish to perform the backup operation according to your selected schedule.

Taking the Domain Controller Offline

1. Restart the domain controller.

2. When the screen for selecting an operating system appears, press F8.

3. From the Windows Advanced Options menu, select Directory Services Restore Mode.

4. When prompted, log on as the local administrator.

PERFORMING AN OFFLINE DEFRAGMENTATION

In Directory Services Restore mode, compact the database file to a local directory or remote shared folder, as follows:

1. For a local directory:

   ◆ At the command prompt, enter **ntdsutil** and press Enter.

   ◆ At the ntdsutil: prompt, type **files** and press Enter.

   ◆ At the file maintenance: prompt, type **compact to** *drive:\LocalPath,* where *drive:\LocalPath* is the path to a location on the local computer—for example, e:\NTDS.

2. For a remote directory:

   You must map a drive to the shared folder that you are copying the files to. Because you are logged on as a local administrator, you will probably not have permissions to your remote share. To map the drive, and authenticate, you must supply domain administrator credentials when mapping the drive:

   ◆ Open a command prompt.

   ◆ Type the command **net use** *drive:* *server**share*/user:*DomainName\Username*, where *drive:* is the drive letter you would like to use for the mapping, *server* is the remote server name, *share* is the name of the shared folder, *DomainName* is the name of your domain, and *Username* is the name of a user that has rights to that folder.

   ◆ Type the password for \\server\share that corresponds to the username defined in the command line.

   ◆ At the command prompt, enter **ntdsutil** and press Enter.

   ◆ At the ntdsutil: prompt, type **files** and press Enter.

   ◆ At the file maintenance: prompt, type **compact to** *drive:\MappedDrive* where *drive:\MappedDrive* is the path that was created in the steps listed above—for example, p:\NTDS.

Figure 12.1 shows a screenshot of defragging the Active Directory database.

WHAT COULD GO WRONG?

If errors appear when you restart the domain controller:

1. Restart the domain controller in Directory Services Restore mode.

2. Check the errors in Event Viewer.

   You may find Event ID 1046 or 1168 in the Event Viewer. If you find these events, you should respond to them accordingly:

   Event ID 1046 "The Active Directory database engine caused an exception with the following parameters." You cannot recover from this error, and you must restore from backup media.

Event ID 1168 "Internal error: An Active Directory error has occurred." If you see this error message, Active Directory is missing information in the Registry and you must restore from backup media.

3. Check database integrity and then proceed as follows:

   If the integrity check fails, copy the original version of the `Ntds.dit` file that you preserved to the original database location and repeat the offline defragmentation procedure.

   If the integrity check succeeds, perform semantic database analysis with `fixup`.

4. If semantic database analysis with `fixup` succeeds, quit `Ntdsutil.exe` and restart the domain controller normally.

5. If semantic database analysis with `fixup` fails, contact Microsoft Product Support Services.

   If the database integrity check fails, perform semantic database analysis with `fixup`.

   When you run semantic database analysis with the `Go Fixup` command instead of the `Go` command, errors are written into `Dsdit.dmp.xx` log files. A progress indicator reports the status of the check.

FIGURE 12.1
Defragging the Active
Directory database

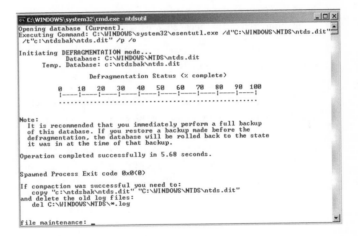

TO PERFORM SEMANTIC DATABASE ANALYSIS WITH *FIXUP*

Figure 12.2 shows semantic database analysis with `fixup`.

1. Open a command prompt.

2. Type the command `ntdsutil:` and then press Enter.

3. At the `ntdsutil:` prompt, type **semantic database analysis** and then press Enter.

4. At the `semantic checker:` prompt, type **verbose on** and then press Enter.

5. At the `semantic checker:` prompt, type **go fixup** and then press Enter.

FIGURE 12.2

Semantic database
analysis with `fixup`

```
C:\WINDOWS\system32\cmd.exe - ntdsutil

C:\Documents and Settings\Administrator>ntdsutil
ntdsutil: semantic database analysis
semantic checker: verbose on
Verbose mode enabled.
semantic checker: go fixup
Fixup mode is turned on

Opening DIT database... Done.

Done.

Opening database [Current].......Done.

Getting record count...3165 records
Getting security descriptor count...82 security descriptors

Writing summary into log file dsdit.dmp.1
SDs scanned:            82
Records scanned:       3165
Processing records..Done.

semantic checker: _
```

If errors are reported during the semantic database analysis with `fixup` phase, perform a directory database recovery.

NOTE The `recover` and `repair` commands are not to be confused. Never use the `repair` command in `ntdsutil`, because forestwide data loss can occur.

If semantic database analysis with `fixup` is successful, close `Ntdsutil.exe`, and then restart the domain controller normally.

Using *ntdsutil* for Active Directory Database Troubleshooting and Repair

The Active Directory database is the same type of database that is used within Exchange servers. If you are familiar with the utilities used with an Exchange server, you should be familiar with some of the utilities used with Active Directory. A benefit of using `ntdsutil` is that the cryptic commands needed to manage the Exchange databases are encapsulated into easier-to-understand commands.

Upcoming chapters will introduce some of the other utilities, such as `dsastat` in Chapter 14, and `dcdiag` in Chapter 15; however, for now let's concentrate on the tool that is used to manage the consistency of the Active Directory database, `ntdsutil`. Using this tool, you can perform the following actions:

- Check database integrity
- Recover the database
- Compact the database
- Move the database
- Move the log files
- Remove orphaned objects
- Maintain security accounts

In the following sections, I detail the steps required to perform each of these actions. Although you may rarely have to perform most of these actions, you should understand when and how to use ntdsutil to perform each one.

The ntdsutil utility is included on Windows 2000 and Windows Server 2003 domain controllers. There are very few differences between the two versions, so most of what is presented within this chapter applies to any of your domain controllers. I point out the differences as we go along.

COMMITTING TRANSACTIONS TO THE DATABASE

Due to the nature of the ESE database, all the transactions are processed in memory and written to log files before they are committed to the database on the hard drive. If the server were to fail, the transaction logs would still contain all the information necessary to bring the database back to a consistent state.

Before performing most of the actions that follow, commit the transactions to the database, which is also known as performing a recovery procedure. Just follow these steps:

1. When starting the computer, press F8 to enter the Startup Selection screen.

2. Select Directory Services Restore Mode.

3. Once you log on with the Directory Services Restore Mode administrator account, open a command prompt.

4. At the command prompt, type **ntdsutil** and press Enter.

5. From the ntdsutil: prompt, type **Files** and press Enter.

6. From the file maintenance: prompt, type **Recover** and press Enter.

As shown in Figure 12.3, the screen will display information about what is taking place as the recovery is running. After the recovery is complete, the database will be consistent and you will be able to run other utilities as necessary.

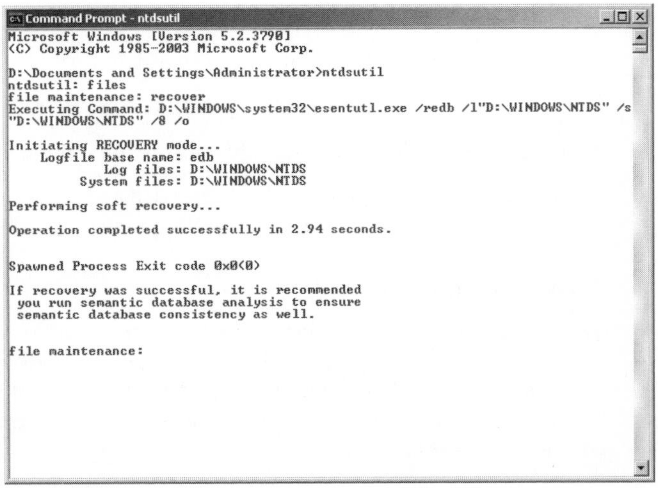

FIGURE 12.3
ntdsutil is used to commit the transactions.

```
Microsoft Windows [Version 5.2.3790]
(C) Copyright 1985-2003 Microsoft Corp.

D:\Documents and Settings\Administrator>ntdsutil
ntdsutil: files
file maintenance: recover
Executing Command: D:\WINDOWS\system32\esentutl.exe /redb /l"D:\WINDOWS\NTDS" /s
"D:\WINDOWS\NTDS" /8 /o

Initiating RECOVERY mode...
    Logfile base name: edb
        Log files: D:\WINDOWS\NTDS
      System files: D:\WINDOWS\NTDS

Performing soft recovery...

Operation completed successfully in 2.94 seconds.

Spawned Process Exit code 0x0(0)

If recovery was successful, it is recommended
 you run semantic database analysis to ensure
 semantic database consistency as well.


file maintenance:
```

If errors crop up while running the recovery on a Windows 2000–based domain controller, and the recovery option does not repair them, you may need to repair the database. Exercise caution before you run this command against your database because you could lose data in the process.

Make sure you have a good backup of your domain controller. You might want to contact Microsoft Product Support Services to make sure that you have covered all your bases; they may have another option for you to try before you run a repair.

Once you are committed to running the repair process, follow these steps:

1. When starting the computer, press F8 to enter the Startup Selection screen.

2. Select Directory Services Restore Mode.

3. Once you log on with the Directory Services Restore Mode administrator account, open a command prompt.

4. At the command prompt, type **ntdsutil** and press Enter.

5. From the ntdsutil: prompt, type **Files** and press Enter.

6. From the file maintenance: prompt, type **Repair** and press Enter.

CHECKING DATABASE INTEGRITY

When you are checking the integrity of the database, every single byte of data within the database is analyzed for corruption. This procedure can take a great deal of time if your database is large. This is not something you should run just because you feel like you want to see what happens. Before starting an integrity check, make sure you have performed the recovery option as detailed in the previous sections. The steps to perform an integrity check are as follows:

1. When starting the computer, press F8 to enter the Startup Selection screen.

2. Select Directory Services Restore Mode.

3. Once you log on with the Directory Services Restore Mode administrator account, open a command prompt.

4. At the command prompt, type **ntdsutil** and press Enter.

5. From the ntdsutil: prompt, type **Files** and press Enter.

6. From the file maintenance: prompt, type **integrity** and press Enter.

As you can see in Figure 12.4, the utility will perform the check against the database. If any errors are reported, contact Microsoft Product Support Services to determine how you should proceed.

COMPACTING THE DATABASE

During normal operations, the Active Directory database will not need to be compacted. Every domain controller will perform its own garbage collection every 12 hours by default. During this garbage collection, the database will be defragmented, but the database size will not be reduced. This usually does not present a problem, because databases tend to grow over time to take up the additional free space.

FIGURE 12.4
ntdsutil integrity
check

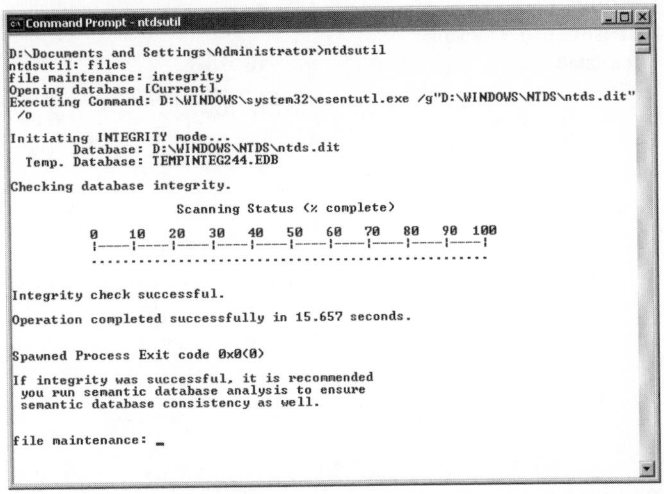

```
Command Prompt - ntdsutil

D:\Documents and Settings\Administrator>ntdsutil
ntdsutil: files
file maintenance: integrity
Opening database [Current].
Executing Command: D:\WINDOWS\system32\esentutl.exe /g"D:\WINDOWS\NTDS\ntds.dit"
 /o

Initiating INTEGRITY mode...
        Database: D:\WINDOWS\NTDS\ntds.dit
   Temp. Database: TEMPINTEG244.EDB

Checking database integrity.

                    Scanning Status (% complete)

        0    10   20   30   40   50   60   70   80   90  100
        !----!----!----!----!----!----!----!----!----!----!
        ...................................................

Integrity check successful.

Operation completed successfully in 15.657 seconds.

Spawned Process Exit code 0x0(0)

If integrity was successful, it is recommended
 you run semantic database analysis to ensure
 semantic database consistency as well.

file maintenance: _
```

With that being said, there are times when you may want to recover disk space with an offline defragmentation and compaction. If you have just deleted a large number of objects from Active Directory, have removed the Global Catalog role from a domain controller, or have just moved several accounts to another domain, you may want to reduce the size of your database.

TIP   To log an event to the Directory Services event log that will tell you the amount of space that you can free up during an offline defragmentation, you can change the Registry entry at HKEY_LOCAL_MACHINE\SYSTEM\CurrentControlSet\Services\NTDS\Diagnostics\6 Garbage Collection to a value of 1.

To compact your database, follow these steps:

1. When starting the computer, press F8 to enter the Startup Selection screen.

2. Select Directory Services Restore Mode.

3. Once you log on with the Directory Services Restore Mode administrator account, create an empty directory to store the new compacted database.

4. Open a command prompt.

5. At the command prompt, type **ntdsutil** and press Enter.

6. From the ntdsutil: prompt, type **Files** and press Enter.

7. From the file maintenance: prompt, type **compact** and press Enter.

After the compact command finishes, copy the new compacted database file, ntds.dit, to the location of the original database file. The utility will let you know where to copy the database if you are unsure, as seen in Figure 12.5.

FIGURE 12.5
ntdsutil after moving
the database

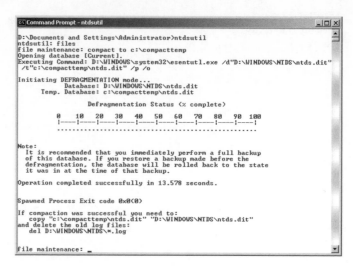

You should also delete the old log files that were associated with the original bloated database file. Again, if you are unsure of the location of the log files, the Compact utility will let you know where they are located.

MOVING THE DATABASE

As databases age, they have a tendency to grow. Even with our best intentions and attempts to create partitions and volumes large enough to hold databases, there are times when they grow too large. There are also times when you may want to take a database off a spindle that may be showing signs of having problems. Being proactive and moving the database to another drive may save you headaches later on.

To move the database, follow these steps:

1. When starting the computer, press F8 to enter the Startup Selection screen.

2. Select Directory Services Restore Mode.

3. Once you log on with the Directory Services Restore Mode administrator account, open a command prompt.

4. At the command prompt, type **ntdsutil** and press Enter.

5. At the ntdsutil: prompt, type **Files** and press Enter.

6. At the file maintenance: prompt, type **move DB to <*directory*>** and press Enter. The <*directory*> can be any location on a partition or volume that has enough space to hold the database, and that preferably has room for the database to continue growing. If the directory to which you are moving the database does not already exist, the utility will create it for you.

The utility will also configure the system to use the new location so that you do not have to perform any other steps to tell the operating system where to locate the database. However, you should perform a backup of the domain controller after moving the database so that your backup files reflect the new location of the database.

MOVING THE LOG FILES

The same issues hold true for the transaction log files that affect the database. You may not have enough room on a partition or volume to hold the logs, but more than likely you will either have a failing drive or you will simply want to separate the transaction log files and the database. As a matter of fact, I recommend that you move the transaction logs off the same physical disk as the database files. Place them on their own physical disk so that they do not have to compete for disk time with any other service. Once you do so, the system will actually perform better.

The steps to move the transaction logs are basically the same as moving the database:

1. When starting the computer, press F8 to enter the Startup Selection screen.

2. Select Directory Services Restore Mode.

3. Once you log on with the Directory Services Restore Mode administrator account, open a command prompt.

4. At the command prompt, type **ntdsutil** and press Enter.

5. At the `ntdsutil:` prompt, type **Files** and press Enter.

6. At the `file maintenance:` prompt, type **move logs to *\<directory\>*** and press Enter.

Again, *\<directory\>* does not have to previously exist; the system will create the directory for you. You should back up the system after performing the move so that the files can be restored if necessary.

REMOVING ORPHANED OBJECTS

Typically, when you decommission a domain controller, the entries for the domain controller are removed from the database. The same holds true when you remove the last domain controller for a domain. If you select the check box that identifies the domain controller as the last domain controller for the domain, all of the metadata for the domain should be removed from all the other domain controllers within the forest.

Removing Orphaned Domain Metadata

In a perfect world, you would not have to concern yourself with the metadata stored in the database—but as we know, nothing is perfect. You may encounter instances when the metadata for domain controllers or domains is not correctly removed from the database. This could be due to the unsuccessful demotion of a domain controller or because a domain controller failed and you cannot restore it. If this happens, services might try to connect to domain controllers that they think still exist. This can cause problems with replication as well as the Knowledge Consistency Checker (KCC).

To remove a domain's orphaned metadata, follow these steps:

1. Log on to the domain using an account that is a member of the Enterprise Admins group.

2. Make sure that all the domain controllers have been demoted or taken offline. Also, verify that all of the remaining domain controllers within the forest have successfully replicated.

3. Identify which domain controller holds the Domain Naming Master Operations role. You can do this by opening Active Directory Domains and Trusts, right-clicking on the root node, and selecting Operations Master. You will find the Domain Naming Master domain controller within the Current Operations Master box.

4. Open a command prompt, type **ntdsutil**, and press Enter.

5. At the ntdsutil: prompt, type **metadata cleanup** and press Enter.

6. At the metadata cleanup: prompt, type **connections** and press Enter.

7. Type **connect to server *servername*** where ***servername*** is the name of the domain controller holding the Domain Naming Master Operations role.

NOTE If you have not logged on using an account that is a member of the Enterprise Admins group, you can set your credentials at this point by typing **set creds *domainname username password*** and then pressing Enter.

8. Once you have received confirmation that the connection has been made, type **quit** and press Enter.

9. Type **select operation target** and press Enter.

10. Type **list domains** and press Enter.

11. From the list of domains that appears, locate the domain where you want to remove the metadata and the number with which it is associated.

12. Type **select domain number** and press Enter.

13. Type **quit** and press Enter.

14. Type **remove selected domain** and press Enter.

15. Once you receive confirmation that the domain metadata has been removed, type **quit** and press Enter.

16. Once you receive confirmation that the connection to the Domain Naming Master has been disconnected, type **quit** and press Enter.

Removing Orphaned Domain Controller Metadata

To remove Domain Controller metadata, you begin by using the same method you used to remove the domain; however, you need to remove additional data with other utilities to complete the removal. After running ntdsutil, you have to remove the computer account, the File Replication Service (FRS) member, and the trustDomain object using ADSI Edit. The DNS entries using the DNS snap-in and the domain controller object within Active Directory Sites and Services will also need to be removed. The steps for all these procedures are given in the following sections.

We will start with Metadata Cleanup. To remove Domain Controller metadata, you will need to follow these steps from the ntdsutil command line utility.

1. Log on to the domain using an account that is a member of the Enterprise Admins group.

2. Verify that all the domain controllers within the forest have successfully replicated.

3. Open a command prompt, type **ntdsutil**, and press Enter.

4. At the `ntdsutil:` prompt, type **metadata cleanup** and press Enter.

5. At the `metadata cleanup:` prompt, type **connections** and press Enter.

6. Type **connect to server *servername***, where ***servername*** is the name of the domain controller holding the Domain Naming Master Operations role.

NOTE   Note: If you have not logged on using an account that is a member of the Enterprise Admins group, you can set your credentials at this point by typing **set creds *domainname username password*** and then pressing Enter.

7. Once you have received confirmation that the connection has been made, type **quit** and press Enter.

8. Type **select operation target** and press Enter.

9. Type **list domains** and press Enter.

10. From the list of domains that appears, locate the domain that the domain controller is a member of and note the number associated with the domain.

11. Type **select domain number** and press Enter.

12. Type **list sites** and press Enter.

13. From the list of sites that appears, locate the site the domain controller is a member of and note the number associated with the site.

14. Type **select site number** and press Enter.

15. Type **list servers in site** and press Enter.

16. From the list of domain controllers that appears, locate the domain controller and note the number associated with the domain controller.

17. Type **select server number** and press Enter.

18. Type **quit** and press Enter.

19. Type **remove selected server** and press Enter.

20. Once you receive confirmation that the domain metadata has been removed, type **quit** and press Enter.

21. Once you receive confirmation that the connection has been disconnected, type **quit** and press Enter.

Using ADSI Edit to View Directory Service Partitions

ADSI Edit is a utility that is part of the support tools. Once you add the support tools, ADSI Edit is available from Start Menu ➢ Programs ➢ Support Tools. The Windows Server 2003 version is an MMC snap-in. With either version, you can connect to domain controllers and view the Directory Service partitions.

Figure 12.6 shows the dialog box that appears when you choose the Connect To option from the ADSI Edit context menu. From here, you can name the connection you are making to anything that will help you identify the naming context you are accessing. Within the Connection Point text options, you can enter the fully qualified name of the naming context to which you are connecting, or you can choose one of the four well-known naming contexts. If you are connecting to one of the new Application Partitions, identify it by its fully qualified name.

In the Computer section, choose a domain controller to connect to, or default to the domain controller you are logged onto if you are running ADSI Edit from a domain controller.

Once you choose the naming contexts to which you are connecting and the server to which you are connecting, you see them reflected within the ADSI Edit window, as shown in Figure 12.7. You can now expand the appropriate naming context to locate the objects you need to manipulate. Later in this chapter, and in other chapters in the book, we show you how to use ADSI Edit to perform some of your administrative troubleshooting.

FIGURE 12.6
ADSI Edit connections
dialog box

FIGURE 12.7
ADSI Edit with naming
contexts added

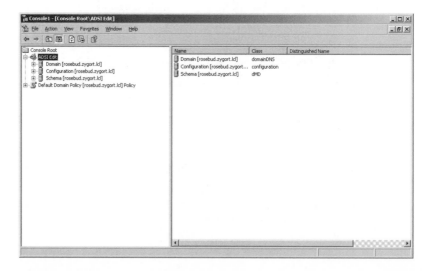

USING ADSI EDIT TO REMOVE A COMPUTER ACCOUNT

If you are unsuccessful removing a computer account by using Active Directory Users and Computers, you can use this method:

1. Open ADSI Edit.

2. Expand Domain NC.

3. Expand DC=domain,DC=tld.

4. Expand OU=Domain Controllers.

5. Right-click CN=domain controller and click Delete.

Figure 12.8 displays the Domain Controllers node within ADSI Edit and the menu items you can choose.

USING ADSI EDIT TO REMOVE THE FRS MEMBER

To remove a file replication system member, use these steps:

1. Open ADSI Edit.

2. Expand Domain NC.

3. Expand DC=domain,DC=tld.

4. Expand CN=System.

5. Expand CN=File Replication Service.

6. Expand CN=Domain System Volume.

7. Right-click the FRS Member you are removing and click Delete.

FIGURE 12.8
ADSI Edit dialog box

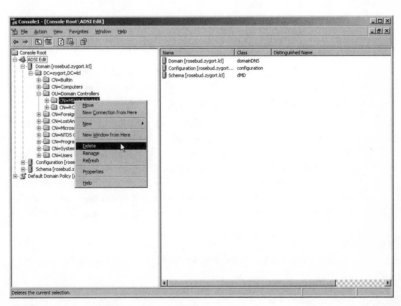

USING ADSI EDIT TO REMOVE THE TRUST DOMAIN OBJECT

If you need to remove a trust due to a failure of the GUI utilities to perform the operation, use these steps:

1. Open ADSI Edit.

2. Expand Domain NC.

3. Expand DC=domain,DC=tld.

4. Expand CN=System.

5. Right-click the Trust Domain object and click Delete.

USE THE DNS SNAP-IN TO REMOVE DNS RECORDS

DNS records may need to be manually removed. If so, follow these steps:

1. Locate the A record within the zone, right-click the A record, and click Delete.

2. Expand the _msdcs container, locate the CNAME record, right-click the CNAME record, and click Delete.

3. If the server was a DNS server, right-click the zone, choose Properties, and then remove the server's IP address from the Name Servers tab of the resulting dialog box.

USING ACTIVE DIRECTORY SITES AND SERVICES TO REMOVE THE DOMAIN CONTROLLER OBJECT

After you have removed the domain controller references, you may have to remove the replication object from Active Directory Sites and Services:

1. Open Active Directory Sites and Services.

2. Expand Sites.

3. Expand the server's site.

4. Expand the Servers node.

5. Right-click the domain controller and click Delete.

MAINTAINING SECURITY ACCOUNTS

For all of the safeguards that Microsoft has taken to ensure that identical SIDs are not introduced into a domain, there is still the possibility that two accounts could have the same SID. This could occur when an administrator seizes the RID Master role while the original RID Master is offline but still operational. If the original RID master did not have an opportunity to receive updated replication information and is brought online, it could generate identical RIDs and allow them to be used within the domain. Any time you seize the RID Master role, you should run this check.

To check for accounts that may be using identical SIDs, follow these steps:

1. Open a command prompt.

2. Type **ntdsutil** and press Enter.

3. Type **security account management** and press Enter.

4. Type **check duplicate SID** and press Enter.

The log file that is created from this check is placed within the directory path where you had started ntdsutil. If you had changed directories to the root of the D: partition and then started ntdsutil, you would find the dupsid.log residing there. If you are lucky, you will not have any entries within the files. If there are entries, note them and delete the duplicate.

To delete the duplicate SID, follow these steps:

1. Open a command prompt.

2. Type **ntdsutil** and press Enter.

3. Type **security account management** and press Enter.

4. Type **cleanup duplicate SID** and press Enter.

The object with the newer GUID is removed from the database. You will then need to re-create the account that was removed during this process.

BEST PRACTICES FOR OPTIMIZING ACTIVE DIRECTORY

Active Directory is the heart of your organization's infrastructure and you need to make sure that is it performing optimally. If you are having problems, you should be familiar with some of the tools you have at your disposal to troubleshoot and treat the ailment:

◆ When troubleshooting the Directory Services, increase the logging level gradually to isolate the problem if the problem isn't apparent.

◆ Always use the Recover utility in ntdsutil to commit all transactions to the database prior to running any other utilities.

◆ Don't run an offline defragmentation on the database unless you have deleted a large number of objects or are planning to move the database and want to reduce its size.

◆ If any domain controller fails during demotion, make sure you remove the associated metadata from the database and remove all of the object information using ADSI Edit.

◆ If the last domain controller for a domain fails during demotion, make sure you remove the associated metadata from the database.

◆ Move the transaction log files to their own drive to increase the domain controller's efficiency.

◆ If the RID Master role is inadvertently seized while the original is still functioning but offline, check for duplicate SIDs when the original is returned to the network.

The Active Directory Schema

The Active Directory database is made up of attributes and object classes that form the Active Directory Schema. Some of the object classes include users, groups, computers, domains, organizational units, and security policies.

You can modify the schema by defining new object types and attributes associated with them, or by adding new attributes to existing objects. This is accomplished by using the ADSI Edit MMC snap-in.

This may sound very confusing. Here is a brief description of each component:

Object classes   Define the objects that can appear in the Active Directory. Classes are collections of attributes. These attributes store the actual information stored in the directory.

Class derivations   Define a method for building new object classes out of existing object classes.

Object attributes   Define the available attributes. This includes extended attributes that govern actions that can be taken on object classes. Attributes are the pieces of information that an object can hold.

Structure rules   Determine possible tree arrangements.

Syntax rules   Determine the type of value an attribute that can be associated with a given class.

Content rules   Determine the attributes that can be associated with a given class.

Extensible schema   Additions can be made to the list of available classes and attributes.

Dynamic class assignments   Certain classes can be dynamically assigned to a specific object rather than an entire class of objects.

To keep the database clean and in order, rules must be established to keep the schema behaving properly. These rules fall into three categories:

Structure rules   Each object class has only certain classes that can be directly above it, called Possible Superiors. This structure rule is very important because classes inherit attributes from their parents. Structure rules prevent putting a User class object under a totally unrelated container class, like IPSEC-Base or NTDS Settings.

Content rules   Every object class has certain attributes with values that cannot be left blank when an object is instantiated. These are called *must-contain* attributes. Other attributes are optional and are designated *may-contain* attributes.

Only attributes with values are stored in the database. This greatly reduces the size and complexity of the database. Because attributes can be added after an object is created and then later removed if they are set to null, the database engine must constantly pack and repack the data. This is done by the garbage collection service that runs every 12 hours.

Syntax rules   Attributes store data. Data must have a data type to define the storage requirements. Real numbers have a different form from integers, which are different from long integers, which are different from character strings. An attribute can have only one data type. It cannot hold a string when associated with one object class and an integer when associated with another. The syntax rules in the schema define the permissible values types and ranges for the attributes.

For each class in Active Directory, there is a `classSchema`. For every object attribute in the database, there is an `attributeSchema` object.

The `attributeSchema` attributes provide information about attributes of another Active Directory object. The `attributeSchema` mandatory attributes are:

`attributeID`   Identifies the attribute with a unique value.

`attributeSyntax`   Identifies the object that defines the attribute type.

`cn`   Provides the Unicode string name of an attribute.

isSingleValued   This attribute is set to either `true` or `false`. When it is set to `true`, it indicates that there is only one value for the attribute. When set to `false`, the attribute can have several values.

LDAPDisplayName   Contains the LDAP Unicode name string used to identify the attribute.

NTSecurityDescriptor   Contains the object security descriptor.

ObjectClass   This attribute is always `attributeSchema`.

OMSyntax   Identifies the object syntax specified by the open object model.

SchemaIDGUID   Contains the unique global ID value of the attribute.

The `classSchema` attributes provide information about another Active Directory object. The `classSchema` mandatory attributes are:

Cn   Contains the Unicode string name of the object.

DefaultObjectCategory   Contains a distinguished name of where the object belongs.

GovernsID   Contains a unique number identifying the class.

LDAPDisplayName   Contains the LDAP Unicode name string used to identify the object.

NTSecurityDescriptor   Contains the object security descriptor.

ObjectClass   This setting is always `classSchema`.

ObjectClassCategory   This setting is an integer that describes the object class type. The values that this attribute will hold are:

- 0—Type 88 class: These are classes that don't have a type and they are class types created before 1993, before class types were established in the X.500 standard.

- 1—Structural class: These classes can have objects created from them and are the class type that is contained as objects in the directory.

- 2—Abstract class: This is a class that cannot be an object, but is used to pass attributes down to subclasses.

- 3—Auxiliary class: This is a class that is used to provide structural or abstract classes with attributes.

SchemaIDGUID   Contains the unique global ID value of the class.

SubClassOf   Contains the identifier of the class parent class.

Modifying the Schema

The schema should only be modified when absolutely necessary. Changes to the schema must be made from the domain controller that holds the Schema Operations Master FSMO role. This server must have the ability to update the schema. Each schema object has permissions set through the Windows 2003 security model.

By default in Windows 2003 AD, the schema is already enabled for updates. Nothing more must be done, unless the registry has specifically been locked down to keep schema updates from occurring on that domain controller.

To edit this registry setting, perform the following steps.

1. Navigate to Start ➢ Run

2. In the Open dialog box, type <regedit> and press ENTER.

3. Navigate to the following registry key: HKLM\SYSTEM\CurrentControlSet\Services\NTDS\Parameters

4. On the Edit menu, click New, then click the DWORD Value.

5. Enter the following information:

   Value Name: Schema Update Allowed

   Data Type: REG_DWORD

   Base: Binary

   Value Data: Use a value of 1 to enable schema updates, 0 to disable schema updates.

6. Close the registry editor.

There are many ways to modify the schema:

◆ Application programming interfaces (APIs)

◆ Lightweight Directory Interface Format (LDIF) scripts.

◆ The LDIFDE bulk schema modification tool

◆ The CSVDE bulk schema update tool

When the schema is modified, Active Directory performs consistency and safety checks to ensure Active Directory database availability.

Consistency is checked to verify that identifiers are unique and mandatory attributes exist. The existence of superclasses in the schema is also checked.

Safety checks ensure Active Directory functionality is not disrupted. Category1 and Category2 object types are checked.

Since both classes and attributes are represented in the directory as objects, you simply need to add a new `class-definition` or `attribute-definition` object with the necessary attributes. If you would like to instead modify a class or attribute, modify the `class-definition` or `attribute-definition` object.

Before you can modify the schema, you must add a value to the Registry. Open the Registry editing program, navigate to HKLM\System\CurrentControlSet\Services\NTDS\Parameters, and add a Registry value called Schema Update Allowed. Make it of type `REG_DWORD` and give it any nonzero positive integer value.

Coming Up Next

The next section of the book deals with troubleshooting. We start with a discussion about overall troubleshooting methodology, and then advance into more detailed discussions about tools, utilities, and troubleshooting techniques for network infrastructure, resources, and the Active Directory database.

Part 3

Troubleshooting Active Directory

In this part:

Chapter 13

Microsoft's Troubleshooting Methodology for Active Directory

Microsoft employs a standard troubleshooting practice with every problem that it diagnoses. This standard methodology helps find the answer to problems in a structured way. In this chapter, we'll examine this troubleshooting methodology.

High-Level Methodology

Figure 13.1 illustrates the six-step plan Microsoft Product Support Services engineers use as a basis for all troubleshooting situations.

You can follow this method to help you track down your problem and find a solution. By using this strategy, you'll cut your troubleshooting time because you're using a structured approach to your troubleshooting efforts.

Discover the Problem

This step is often reactive as opposed to proactive. Usually you discover a problem with Active Directory either by receiving a phone call to alert you of a problem, by viewing messages in Event Viewer, or by identifying a problem with some performance counters you are monitoring. Document as much information as you can so you can reproduce the problem at will. Gather information about symptoms, the rate of occurrence, the servers involved, the sites involved, the communication mechanisms between computers or sites, and so forth.

Typically, a problem is reported to the help desk by a user. A Microsoft best practice for Active Directory is to use a monitoring system to monitor services related to Active Directory's health.

Information about the problem collected from a user or from the monitoring system should include the following:

- Date and time of occurrence
- Error message number and text
- Client information, including:
    - Computer name for the client
    - User ID being used when the problem occurred
    - TCP/IP configuration

- ◆ List of DNS servers that the client is configured to use
- ◆ Operating system version, service pack, and any hotfixes
- ◆ Server information, including:
  - ◆ Computer name for the server
  - ◆ TCP/IP configuration
  - ◆ Operating system version, service pack, and any hotfixes
- ◆ Network information, including:
  - ◆ Domain name of the client
  - ◆ Domain name of the server
  - ◆ Application name and related settings
  - ◆ The service involved in the problem, such as network BIOS (NetBIOS), DNS, Server Message Block (SMB), or Lightweight Directory Access Protocol (LDAP)

FIGURE 13.1

Microsoft troubleshoot-
ing methodology

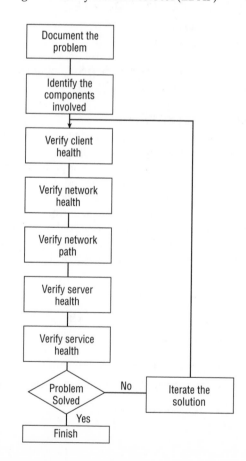

In addition, identify whether any of the following are true:

◆ The problem is repeatable. If so, include the steps taken to reproduce the problem.

◆ Others are having the same problem.

◆ The help desk is able to duplicate and verify the issue. Include any troubleshooting steps already taken by the help desk, such as using Ping to verify network connectivity to the client or server.

Often, the source of a problem is related to some aspect of the system configuration, such as an outdated software component, a service that has not been properly tested, or an incompatible hardware component. Recording the details of the system configuration is an important part of gathering information about the conditions that surround the occurrence of a problem.

You can create a text file that contains important system configuration information. This text file can be created in one of two ways: either by a GUI utility or by a command-line utility.

To create the system configuration file by using a GUI:

1. Click Start ➢ Run.

2. Type **msinfo32** in the Run box and click OK.

3. Open the File menu and select Save.

4. Enter a name for the file and click Save.

You can now use the System Information tool to view the NFO file that is created by this process. The file is in XML format.

To create the system configuration file by using command-line utilities:

1. Click Start ➢ Run.

2. Type **cmd** and click OK.

3. Execute these commands:

```
systeminfo > c:\folder\filename.txt
tasklist > c:\folder\filename.txt
openfiles > c:\folder\filename.txt
```

DOCUMENT THE PROBLEM

Documentation is an important part of your troubleshooting plan. Not only can documenting all your changes reduce misunderstandings, but it will also provide an accurate history that you can reference if Microsoft Technical Support personnel have to get involved.

You will reference and update this documentation as you follow the next steps in the troubleshooting process.

Explore the Conditions

If you have ever worked the help desk at a company, during your first week of work you probably learned two key phrases: "Have you tried rebooting?" and "What changed?" While you may be asking yourself the first question, we're going to explore the second question in this section.

Review the affected system(s) event logs, error logs, and history to determine what configuration changes (if any) took place since the affected system(s) last worked correctly. Have new hardware, software, service packs, hotfixes, or other updates been installed on the affected system(s) or supporting infrastructure?

Except for hardware failures, you can usually narrow down this list to service packs, hotfixes, or security updates that were recently applied. A stable system will remain stable as long as it is untouched, except for a hardware failure. Unfortunately, you cannot get a server to a stable point, lock it in a cabinet, and never touch it again. In today's world you have to deal with updates, which often come out at a steady pace.

Start your search with recent updates to the system. Check your documentation to see what was changed, and when, and then determine what effect the update may have had on your system. Often, many problems are caused by recently installed software, especially unsigned drivers or beta applications. Unsigned drivers have not been "approved" by Microsoft and can cause instability issues.

Some common Active Directory events that appear in the event logs are listed in Table 13.1.

TABLE 13.1: Common Active Directory Events Recorded in the Event Viewer

EVENT SOURCE	EVENT ID	REFERENCE
FRS	13508, 13509, 13512, 13522, 13567, 13568	Chapter 14
Netlogon	5774, 5775, 5781, 5783, 5805	Chapter 14
NTDS	1083, 1265, 1388, 1645	Chapter 15
UserEnv	1085	Chapter 15
W32Time	13, 14, 52-56, 60-64	Chapter 14

IDENTIFY THE COMPONENTS INVOLVED

Identify the specific components that are involved in the problem, including the clients, network paths, and services. This can quickly narrow down where your problem is, and with what service you are having a problem.

VERIFY CLIENT HEALTH

Start with the client defined in the previous step. Because all client/server communication begins with the client, start the troubleshooting process there. Verify the health of your client computer by checking to see whether it is configured correctly, is connected to the network, and is communicating properly. Some tests you can perform to check client health include the following:

◆ Verify network connections. Make sure the client is actually connected to the network by checking network cables, link status indicators on your card and hub and or switch, or connection status in your wireless network card settings.

◆ Use Performance Monitor to ensure that the client's CPU usage is not too high.

◆ Verify network configuration for the client. Verify that the client's IP configuration settings are correct. This includes the IP address, subnet mask, default gateway, and any DNS or WINS settings that may be defined.

VERIFY SERVER HEALTH

To verify server health, start by following the same troubleshooting pattern as the client health check. More often than not, the client has received its settings from a DHCP server, while the server is often assigned with static information. When a server has static settings, the chance for human error always exists. While I was typing that last sentence I hit the Backspace key at least three times.

Human error can cause any number of problems with static mappings. An administrator can "fat finger" or transpose numbers in any one of the IP settings on the client. A server on a class C subnet with a subnet mask of 255.255.225.0 is going to have a hard time talking to other servers on the subnet defined as 255.255.255.0.

VERIFY NETWORK PATH

Verify that the network path between the client and server is properly working. If the server health check turns out okay, the problem may lie at either the client or the path between the client and the server. If you then perform a client health check and it also turns out okay, you may want to run Network Monitor (`NetMon`) to perform traces at both the client and the server.

VERIFY SERVICE HEALTH

To verify the health of the service, follow these steps:

◆ Verify that the service is installed properly on the server.

◆ Verify that the service is running.

◆ Verify that the user has permissions to make the request.

Regularly review the application event log. The log is where services usually record their events, and indicate whether they are error, warning, or informational events. If you find a warning or error event in the event log, determine the source and search knowledge base information (internal or external to your company) for that particular error, EventID, and Event Source.

Explore Possible Problems with Microsoft Operations Manager

Microsoft Operations Manager (MOM) with the Active Directory Management Pack (ADMP) provide you with a comprehensive overview for a proactive approach of monitoring your network for possible problems.

MOM has built-in monitoring alerts that give you an idea of problems that may occur in your network. Along with the theme of this chapter, this will give you a proactive approach for troubleshooting your network.

The following monitoring alerts are included in the Active Directory Management Pack for MOM 2005. Monitor the following events daily:

A domain controller has received a significant number of new replication partners.   This can happen when a server is in the process of becoming a global catalog server or bridgehead server. It can also happen when new domains or domain controllers are added to the network. Site link problems or replication problems can cause this alert to trigger.

Active Directory Essential Services has detected (message).   This is a high-priority alert that indicates that the domain controller is unusable for the reason specified in the message. This can sometimes indicate that a service is not running on the server. Sysvol problems may indicate problems with the file replication service (FRS), and problems with a domain controller not advertising may indicate problems with the Domain Name System (DNS).

Active Directory global catalog search failed.   This high-priority alert warns you that a global catalog server cannot be reached.

Active Directory - lost objects warning.   This alert warns you of a high number of objects in the LostAndFound directory.

Active Directory replication is occurring slowly.   This indicates that replication times have exceeded set time thresholds.

Failed to ping or bind to the `<operations master>` role holder.   This alert indicates that there may be network connectivity problems with the server in the error message.

High CPU alert.   This alert indicates that an application or server is consuming a high amount of CPU.

Replication is not occurring, all AD replication partners failed to synchronize.   This alert may be triggered occasionally, but extended failures indicate a problem. Investigate problems that occur for more than a few hours.

Time skew detected.   The system time on the server indicated in the alert is not synchronized.

Identify Possible Approaches

After you have gathered as much information about the problem as you can, the next step is to determine a possible plan of attack. This is the research portion of the plan. Your findings in this stage will determine the approach you will take to implement your fix.

At this stage, Microsoft recommends you take the following direction for resolving the problem:

1. Submit an error report, if prompted, and study the analysis.

2. Review problem-tracking databases internal to your organization.

3. Read the Microsoft Knowledge Base articles.

4. Escalate the problem to Microsoft technical support.

This is great in a perfect world, or if you work for Microsoft. Not many organizations have an up-to-date problem-tracking database. I've seen many companies that have an internal knowledge base, and almost just as many companies with administrators who laugh when you suggest looking up the error in their own database first. In the "real world," the search for a fix goes a little something like this:

1. **Help and Support Center:** Okay, all of you old-schoolers can stop chuckling now. I will admit that I would have laughed at this statement three or four years ago. The online help guides (for the most part) are a very good starting point now. The Help and Support Center not only provides information and links about 2003 Server, but it also includes troubleshooting tools and wizards that can come in very handy.

   Microsoft's Knowledge Base articles: Microsoft has a wealth of information on its website. You can use keywords to locate all the type of information you gathered in the previous step. For example, you can search for Event IDs, exact error messages, and so forth. To become familiar with how to get the best results from your search, read KB article 242450, "How to Query the Microsoft Knowledge Base Using Keywords."

2. **Internet newsgroups:** Well-known or favorite newsgroups are often a "first check" for many administrators. Newsgroups offer very technical discussions on subjects that are similar to your problem. There are many Active Directory newsgroups, including Microsoft public newsgroups that many Microsoft employees and Microsoft Valuable Professionals (MVPs) visit on a daily basis to discuss problems and answer questions.

3. **Google and other websites:** Intuitive search engines and web-based forums are quickly becoming more popular than newsgroups. You will find the same type of interaction as with newsgroups, often with a friendlier interface. One of the more popular forums is Expert Exchange (www.experts-exchange.com).

4. Escalate the problem to Microsoft technical support.

Of course, everyone is different and each situation is different. I usually follow the path listed directly above, but I have also skipped steps 1 and 3, and a few times I have gone directly to step 4.

Attempt a Solution

By this time, you should have many possible approaches that could resolve the problem. Determine which items from your list are most likely to fix the problem. For example, say you recently upgraded the Network Interface Card (NIC) driver on a server in a remote site. Using the troubleshooting steps listed earlier, you first find that information in Active Directory is not being replicated to one remote site. You then find that the server at that remote site, which is a replication partner for your main site, is not working correctly. You perform a diagnosis of that server, and discover that it is not communicating properly. Once you realize that the NIC driver was recently updated, you decide to roll back the driver to a previous version.

Always back up your system state data and other vital service files for that domain controller. Execute the plan that is most likely to resolve the problem, documenting all steps along the way. "Real-world" admins like the ones listed above are kindly asked to refrain from snickering at this comment.

Check for Success

Reproduce the conditions that caused the problem to determine whether your plan was successful. If the error or problem continues to occur, return to step 3 and use a different approach.

ITERATE THE TROUBLESHOOTING PROCESS

If the steps listed earlier do not locate the problem for you, you must take additional measures to track down the problem. This could involve identifying the next client, server, or service that might be involved in the problem and verifying the health of each of those components until you reach the actual source of the problem.

Tie Up Loose Ends

Once the problem is fixed, you're done, right? You can walk away and simply forget about everything you've done to this point? If you stopped here, you would be missing out on a valuable opportunity to cut down troubleshooting time if similar problems should arise in the future.

DOCUMENT YOUR FINDINGS

This is where your documentation will come in handy. You're still documenting at this point, right? How many times, while troubleshooting, have you tried one approach only to find that you were going down the wrong road and your changes or "fix" didn't change or fix anything? After the unsuccessful attempt, did you then roll back your changes so the system was in the same state it was in before you started your tests?

Documentation is very important; it gives you a clear path of what has been changed on a system in case a rollback procedure is required. It also provides you with a quick reference to view information about your systems that can come in handy when reviewing potential system changes or updates.

You can then turn this information into detailed information about your current environment, modifying it as you change your systems. You can use the documents to reduce the chance of redundant work and can possibly avoid future problems by using the information in the document to take preventive action.

Periodically verify, update, and back up this documentation so you will not have to document everything again should you lose the information. Items to note in the documentation include the following:

◆ Changes made to the system

◆ Time and date of changes

◆ Reasons for the change

◆ Name and contact information of the administrator who made the change

◆ Positive and negative effects the change had on system stability and/or performance

◆ Information found through research to back up reasoning for making the change

◆ Your contact information (so you can be contacted with specific questions about the changes you made to the system or network)

If you do not already have baseline documentation for your servers, you can use this document to create a baseline. After you have created a baseline, keep track of all information listed here and add it to the baseline document.

When you have finished troubleshooting, you may want to document other findings that came as a result of the troubleshooting process, such as:

- What changes resulted in improvements?

- What changes made the problem worse?

- What downtime occurred while implementing the solution, and how did it affect users?

- Was system performance restored to expected levels?

- What actions were redundant or unnecessary?

- How effectively were technical support resources used?

- What tools or information not used might have helped?

- What unresolved issues require further testing?

CREATE A CUSTOM TROUBLESHOOTING GUIDE

Some of the "discovery" portions of the troubleshooting process can be eliminated if you create very detailed information about your environment and past troubleshooting results. Use this document as a starting point, and compare notes from the custom troubleshooting guide against information you find during the discovery phase.

Keep the following information available to the personnel performing Active Directory troubleshooting:

- Active Directory configuration, including replication-related configuration information

- DNS, DHCP, and IP configurations

- Application and service documentation (such as Exchange)

- Administrative model

- Server placement and configurations

Personnel performing Active Directory troubleshooting should have a basic understanding of the following:

- Name resolution, including DNS and NetBIOS name resolution with broadcasts, LMHOSTS files, and WINS

- Replication

- Time synchronization

- Group Policy and FRS

- Core Active Directory, including an understanding of the global catalog, domains, and forests

◆ Authentication (both Kerberos authentication and LAN Manager)

◆ Active Directory Microsoft Management Console (MMC) snap-ins and Active Directory-related tools

◆ Operations master roles: PDC emulator, relative identifier (RID) master, domain naming master, schema master, and infrastructure master

◆ Key Distribution Center (KDC)

◆ Knowledge Consistency Checker (KCC)

◆ Intersite Topology Generator (ISTG)

◆ Time Reference Server (TRS)

Because Active Directory interacts with so many external services and protocols, a broad range of knowledge is required for this type of troubleshooting. Ultimately determining the cause of a problem and applying a solution becomes more complex.

BE PROACTIVE

The best time to take care of problems is when they are still considered "potential" problems. There are a lot of things you can do to prevent outages:

◆ Consistently back up system state data and configuration settings. Regular backups of the system state will give you a good restore point in case you need to restore to a previous state. It is also a good idea to back up the system state or configuration settings if you feel that changes you make while implementing a possible solution may have an adverse effect on your system, or you are unsure of the results.

◆ Periodically test troubleshooting and recovery plans. Recovery plans are great, if you know that they have been tested and known to work. Many companies back up the system state on a regular basis because it is a best practice. But ask them how to restore system state if it's lost completely, or ask them if they would feel comfortable actually performing the steps themselves, and you may get some blank looks. If someone told me I could safely land a plane by pressing a series of ten buttons in a certain order, I would feel pretty safe and think it would be pretty easy to do. If the plane started going down, I wouldn't feel quite as comfortable unless I had actually performed the task and felt comfortable about the process and seen success in the past.

◆ Rapidly evaluate and deploy updates. To ensure updates are deployed in a relatively timely manner, implement a process to test and deploy updates in your environment. In an ideal world, the testing portion would be done in a lab environment. (We discuss this later in the list.) After the update has been tested, it must be quickly and efficiently deployed to all the affected servers in your network. This could prove to be a time-consuming process. Microsoft has helped this process with the introduction of Windows Server Update Services (WSUS).

◆ Use antivirus software. Antivirus software has traditionally been viewed as a requirement for client computers and application and data servers on networks. As malicious software becomes more prevalent, smarter, and more damaging, it is just as important to protect your domain controllers as well as all other devices. Use an antivirus package that is Windows 2003 compatible.

◆ Improve the computing environment. Servers are happy in nice, clean, cool, quiet rooms. When I say "quiet," I'm not talking about sound volume; I'm talking about traffic volume. The more traffic, the better the chances of some type of impact damage. Make these checks periodically in your server room:

   ◆ Test uninterruptible power supply (UPS) batteries.

   ◆ Check room temperature, humidity, and air circulation.

   ◆ Check server fans and system boards for a buildup of dust.

◆ Monitor performance and event logs. Often, warnings in the Event Viewer will notify you of impending doom. Check the event logs daily, looking for warnings and errors that do not seem familiar. I know that sounds odd to think that there may be warnings or errors that should look familiar, but some warning messages may appear on a daily basis that may have no effect on your system's health. Use the Performance Console (`perfmon.msc`) to compare current settings and results to the baseline you created when the server was running at optimal health.

◆ Document hardware and software changes. Along with recording system changes, you should record information regarding the computer operation, such as Group Policy and network infrastructure changes.

◆ Plan for hardware and software upgrades. As "beefy" as your system is when you purchase it, at some point in its life cycle a piece of hardware or software on the system will require an update. This could be due to an increased demand for computing resources or discontinued support for a device or software.

◆ Test changes in a lab environment before implementing them on production systems. As I mentioned earlier, in a perfect world all testing would be done in a lab environment that mimics your live environment. Change your lab environment as you change your live environment so the lab will remain a "mirrored" environment.

◆ Use compatible and tested hardware.

◆ Use compatible software.

◆ Condense legacy software to eliminate conflicts and increase fault tolerance.

Become Comfortable with Active Directory Tools

The following list of tools will help you in your troubleshooting methodology. Become familiar with the tools to make your troubleshooting efforts easier.

Tool	Function	Chapter
Active Directory Domains and Trusts	Administer domain trusts, add user principal name suffixes, and change the domain mode.	14, 15
Active Directory Sites and Services	Administer the replication of directory data.	14, 15
Active Directory Users and Computers	Administer and publish information in the directory.	14
ADSI Edit	View, modify, and set access control lists (ACLs) on objects in the directory.	15
Backup Wizard	Back up and restore data.	14
Control Panel	View and modify computer, application, and network settings.	14
Dcdiag.exe	Analyze the state of the domain controllers in a forest or enterprise.	14, 15
DNS snap-in	Manage DNS.	14
Dsastat.exe	Compare directory information on the domain controllers and detect differences.	14
Event viewer	Monitor events recorded in event logs.	14
Ipconfig.exe	View and manage network configuration.	14
Ldp.exe	Perform Lightweight Directory Access Protocol (LDAP) operations against Active Directory.	14, 15
Linkd.exe	Create, delete, update, and view the links that are stored in junction points.	14
MMC	Create, save, and open administrative tools that manage hardware, software, and network components.	14, 15
Netdiag.exe	Check end-to-end network connectivity and distributed services functions.	14, 15
Netdom.exe	Allow batch management of trusts, joining computers to domains, and verifying trusts and secure channels.	14
Net use, start, stop, del, copy, time	Perform common tasks on network services, including stopping, starting, and connecting to network resources.	14
Nltest.exe	Verify that the locator and secure channel are functioning.	14

Tool	Function	Chapter
`Ntdsutil.exe`	Manage Active Directory, manage single master operations, remove metadata.	14
Performance Monitor	View system performance data, performance logs and alerts, and trace log files.	14
`Pathping.exe`	Trace a route from a source to a destination on a network, show the number of hops, and show packet loss.	14
`Ping.exe`	Verify network connectivity.	14
`Regedit.exe`	View and modify Registry settings.	14
`Repadmin.exe`	Verify replication consistency between replication partners, monitor replication status, display replication metadata, and force replication events and topology recalculation.	14, 15
`Secedit.exe`	Manage Group Policy settings.	14
Services snap-in	Start, stop, pause, or resume system services on remote and local computers, and configures startup and recovery options for each service.	14
`Setspn.exe`	Manage security principal names.	14
Task Manager	View process and performance data.	14
Terminal Services	Access and manage computers remotely.	14
`W32tm`	Manage Windows Time Service.	14
Windows Explorer	Access files, web pages, and network locations.	14

Coming Up Next

We have now discussed a general "road map" for your troubleshooting efforts. An understanding of the tools listed in this chapter will help with your troubleshooting efforts, and reduce your troubleshooting time frame.

In the next chapter, we will discuss troubleshooting techniques relating to network infrastructure.

Chapter 14

Troubleshooting Problems Related to Network Infrastructure

Understanding how the various elements in your network function and work together is important when you're trying to diagnose network communications problems. This chapter will introduce you to some useful troubleshooting tools, various components of your network infrastructure, and how you can troubleshoot problems with these services.

Components of Network Infrastructure

A generic computer network has two basic parts: software and hardware. The software runs on the hardware and, in some cases, controls how the hardware will run and communicate. The hardware provides the means of conveyance for the software to communicate—think of the seven layers of the OSI model. The network infrastructure falls into both the hardware and software categories. When we talk about our hardware network infrastructure, we mean the cables, routers and switches, servers, workstations, and other physical items. The software networking infrastructure consists of the operating systems, services, and other applications that run and use the cables, routers, and switches. Here, we are concerned with the services that run on these servers.

The types of services that form your infrastructure will vary somewhat and are dependent on your own network configuration and any specific network requirements imposed by management. Typically, though, you are going to have an operating system (Windows Server 2003 R2 in this case), some method of name resolution (DNS, BIND, or WINS), Dynamic Host Configuration Protocol (DHCP) for address assignment, and remote connectivity via RRAS, IAS, VPN, and so on.

In a typical TCP/IP-based network you need to have some address issuance mechanism—DHCP—and some method to provide name resolution, either Windows Internet Name Service (WINS) or Domain Name System (DNS). Yes, WINS is mentioned as there are legacy computers and applications that require WINS.

Name Resolution Methods

Name resolution is the process that occurs when you're trying to find a device on the network by either an address or a name. All computers, servers, printers, and other networking devices have names. These devices also have an address that has been assigned them as well. Name resolution ensures that you can find a device by either name or address when required. The two methods we are concerned with here are DNS and WINS.

WINS

Windows Internet Name Service (WINS) has been around for a long time and is due to remain around even longer—and just when you thought it was safe to finally decommission those old WINS servers. There are still valid requirements for continued use of WINS in your network, so don't retire those old WINS servers quite yet. There are still older legacy clients, servers, or applications that require this service, and this requirement extends to Windows Server 2003 R2 as well.

The WINS service provides a dynamic address registration service that is used to register clients and resolve NetBIOS names to IP addresses on your network to enable clients to find other computers and resources. NetBIOS names were developed to provide a mechanism for applications and computers to communicate in a networked environment. Each NetBIOS name is composed of a 16-byte address. The first 15 bytes represent the name of the computer, with the 16th byte representing the service provided by the computer or application.

INSTALLING WINS

As I said earlier, WINS is still needed in Windows Server 2003 R2 for much the same reason as it is still needed in Windows 2000—for the resolution of NetBIOS names. You install WINS by opening Add/Remove Programs and then clicking Add/Remove Windows Components. When the Windows Components dialog box appears, select the Network Services options, click the Details button, and select Windows Internet Name Service. Once the installation is complete, open the WINS console from Administrative Tools and click on the name of the server; the green up arrow appears, as you can see in Figure 14.1. In most cases, installing the WINS service and using the default settings with the installation will suffice in providing name resolution for your network.

You will need to add some static mappings to your WINS server for proper connection to servers and possibly some clients. If you need to create a static mapping, right-click the Active Registrations tab, select the New Static Mapping tab, and fill in the information fields as shown in Figure 14.2. There is the potential for problems with static mappings, which we will cover later in the section "Troubleshooting Tools and WINS."

FIGURE 14.1
Installation of WINS

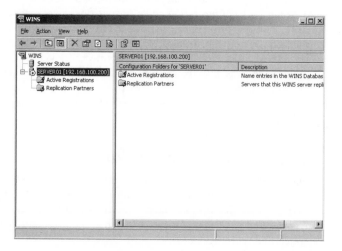

FIGURE 14.2

Creating a static
mapping in WINS

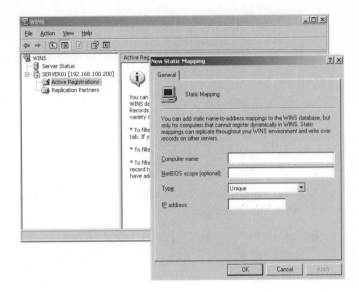

CURRENT USES AND APPLICATIONS FOR WINS

The need for WINS still exists in Windows Server 2003 R2, mainly for Network Load Balancing (NLB) as it uses NetBIOS names. NLB enables you to enhance the scale and availability of IP-based servers. Using NLB with several servers running the same program, for example, ADFS-enabled web servers in an NLB cluster, will provide a redundant environment for critical applications. The functionality of WINS can be met by using another NetBIOS Name Service (NBNS) or an LMHOSTS file.

DNS

The Domain Name System (DNS) is another name resolution service that is used to find resources on a network. These resources are stored in a hierarchical database that lists all of the computers and other resources contained within this database. In order for Active Directory to function properly, you must have DNS configured and running properly. Once this is done, then clients can find resources by querying the DNS database, and they can find a domain controller by searching the DNS database and other servers.

NOTE   Active Directory requires a name resolution method to function properly. You do not have to use Windows DNS server to support Active Directory. You can use BIND (Berkeley Internet Name Domain) as long as you are using version 8.1.2 or later and it supports SRV and dynamic updates.

INSTALLING DNS

The DNS service can be installed as part of the process in creating a domain controller or separately. When you create a domain controller, the `dcpromo` process queries the network to hunt for a DNS server; if none are found, then a dialog box will appear asking if you want the Active Directory Installation Wizard to create a DNS server for you (or fix the problem later), as you can see in Figure 14.3.

Installing DNS when you do not have Active Directory installed is straightforward. You install the DNS service through Add/Remove Programs and click on the DNS tab in Administrative Tools. Where this is different is that you have the option of creating one of three types of zones: primary, secondary, or stub, as shown in Figure 14.4. Though you can create them at this point, you just cannot store them in Active Directory—yet.

RESOURCE RECORDS

The DNS database is composed of one or more zone files. These zone files are composed of resource records, which contain the actual information that is used by the domain. Each resource record is a reference to specific computers, servers, and the services in a domain. There are 25 different types of resource records available in DNS; Table 14.1 lists the 6 most commonly used.

TIP   For more information about DNS records, see RFCs 1035, 1183, and 1886, 2052 and 2782, which can be found at www.faqs.org.

FIGURE 14.3
Installing DNS through the Active Directory Installation Wizard

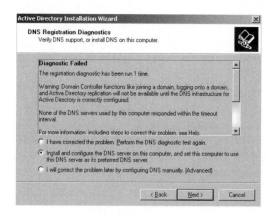

FIGURE 14.4
Creating a zone in DNS

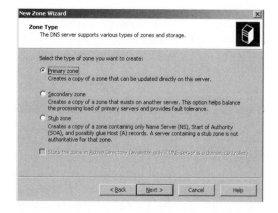

TABLE 14.1: Common Resource Record Types

RECORD	PURPOSE
Host (A)	Specifies the IP address of a computer to a specific hostname.
Alias (CNAME)	Is used to map another name to a specific host.
Mail Exchanger (MX)	The name of a server that is used for messaging.
Name Servers (NS)	Specifies the name servers for a specific domain.
Pointer (PTR)	Specifies the hostname of a specific computer given the IP address. This record is stored in the reverse lookup zone.
Service (SRV)	Specifies the name of a computer and the service it provides, e.g., SRV records to locate a domain controller.

SERVICE LOCATOR RECORDS (SRV)

One of the main purposes of DNS is to provide a service for clients to find resources. In the case of service locator (SRV) records, the resources referenced are domain controllers. The SRV record enables a client to find a domain controller on the network and can be viewed through the DNS console, as you can see in Figure 14.5.

The actual SRV record informs a client of where a particular server can be found based on the domain name of the client. The format used by SRV resource records is described in detail in RFC 2782. The actual format for SRV records has 10 parts:

```
Service Protocol DomainName TTL Class SRV Priority Weight Port Target
```

Service Specifies the service that the server is running. For Active Directory, the service setting will be kerberos or ldap.

Protocol Specifies the protocol used by the client to connect to the service: UDP or TCP.

FIGURE 14.5
Viewing SRV record in the DNS console

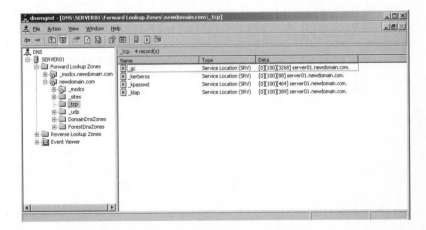

DomainName The fully qualified name of the domain where the domain controller is running.

TTL The amount of time in seconds that the record can be cached on the client.

Class The class of the record, which in the case of SRV records is always the Internet class, IN.

SRV Identifies this record as a service locator record.

Priority Identifies the priority for this record. If the priority setting is a lower value than the other SRV records for the same service in the same domain, this will be the preferred record.

Weight When other records for the same service and domain have the same priority, the weight determines the preferred record. If multiple records have the same priority and weight, they are used equally by the clients.

Port The TCP or UDP port that is used by the service.

Target Identifies the domain controller's fully qualified domain name that is hosting the service.

When a domain controller name DC5 registers its SRV resource records, the Kerberos record would appear as:

```
_kerberos._tcp.zygort.lcl. 600 IN SRV 0 100 88 dc5.zygort.lcl
```

When you run **dcpromo** on a server to create a domain controller, a file called `Netlogon.dns` is created in the `%systemroot%\system32\config` folder. The `Netlogon.dns` file contains all the resource records needed by Active Directory, as shown in Figure 14.6.

When you make changes to a DNS server, you might have to re-register SRV records. You can do this one of two ways: either through a command line or through the Services snap-in. To use a command line, open a command prompt and type **net stop netlogon** and then **net start netlogon**. If you are going to use the interface, open the services interface (either through Administrative Tools or by typing **services.msc** in the Start ➤ Run box) and right-clicking the Netlogon tab and stopping or starting the service.

DNS ZONES

When creating your DNS structure, you will have the option of creating different types of zones depending on the purpose of the zone. Normally you can create primary, secondary, or stub zones. If you create a primary or stub zone, then you will have the option of storing the zone in Active Directory. We will discuss these zones and their options in this section. Active Directory–integrated (AD-I) zones need to be covered as well. We will point out the difference between AD-I zones and standard zones, especially the benefits.

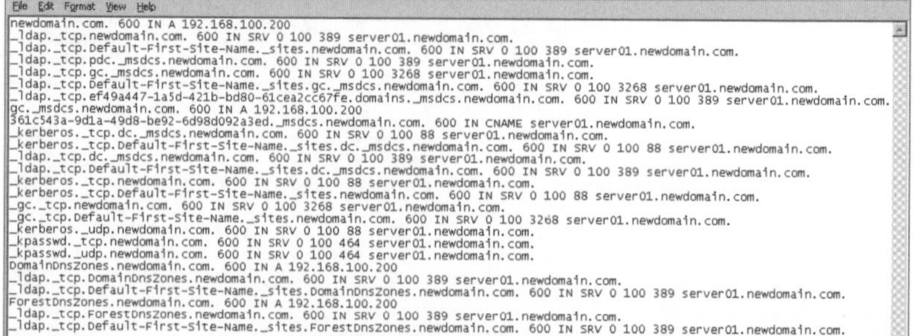

FIGURE 14.6
Contents of the
`Netlogon.dns` file

Primary Zones and Secondary Zones

When you create your DNS zone, you have the option of deciding what type of zone you will create. In this case, the primary zone represents the initial point where you will create and update all records for your domain and whether they are stored on only one domain. This does make for ease of use—you only have one server to work with—but it does not provide for any fault-tolerance in case of server failures.

If you want to spread the work of name resolution and provide fault tolerance with DNS, then create a secondary server. A secondary server will receive updates from the primary server through zone transfer and will still respond to name queries of clients even if the primary server is offline. You will still need to create new records and manage updates from the primary server as this is the only copy of the zone file that can be modified. Any changes or modifications will automatically be replicated to the secondary servers.

Active Directory–Integrated Zones

There are a few drawbacks associated with a standard zone, namely replication and latency. To ensure effective name resolution and provide access to resources, you will need to create a secondary zone that will replicate with the primary zone. What if there was a better way to accomplish this replication and provide better service for clients? This is accomplished by creating Active Directory–integrated (AD-I) zones.

Creating an AD-I Zone

It is now time to create an AD-I zone in DNS. To begin, right-click the name of the DNS server, and specify New Zone, and click Next. The next screen is where you will specify what type and where the zone will be stored. At the bottom of the Zone Type screen is a box that reads Store The Zone In Active Directory (Available Only If DNS Server Is A Domain Controller), as you can see in Figure 14.7. Checking this box means that the zone file will be stored in Active Directory and will be replicated when Active Directory replicates to the domain controllers or DNS servers you specify. The next screen will determine how and where zone replication will occur. There are three choices here: To All DNS Servers In The Active Directory Forest *<domain name>*, To All DNS Servers In The Active Directory Domain *<domain name>*, or To All Domain Controllers In The Active Directory Domain *<domain name>*. The last choice is the default choice, as shown in Figure 14.8.

An AD-I zone improves the whole replication process by removing zone replication from the primary and secondary zones to Active Directory. Moving the database and replication to Active Directory makes sense for a number of reasons, including security. The benefits for allowing Active Directory to handle replication include the following:

◆ It ensures timely updates to the zones, since replication occurs through Active Directory and not from a standard primary server to secondary servers.

◆ Because all domain controllers that have DNS installed are in effect primary DNS servers, there is increased replication.

◆ You can limit what is replicated—only changes are replicated, not the entire database.

◆ Updates are secure; you have greater control over what servers will receive updates.

FIGURE 14.7
Storing zone information in Active Directory

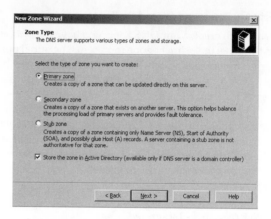

FIGURE 14.8
Choosing replication scope in Active Directory

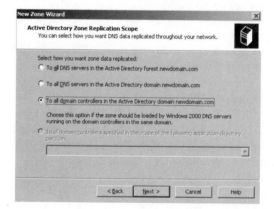

Application Directory Partitions

One of the new features in Windows Server 2003 is the introduction of Application Directory partitions. With application directories, you will only replicate to specific domain controllers whereas with domain partitions you would replicate with all domain controllers. This will allow you to have more control over where replication will occur in your network.

When you initially created a domain controller, you had the chance to install DNS at the same time (if there wasn't a DNS service available) as we talked about in the "Installing DNS" section earlier. When you installed DNS, two new directory partitions were created: the DomainDnsZone and the ForestDnsZone, which are stored in Active Directory. These two directories enable you to specify where replication will occur: either to DNS servers in the domain or to DNS servers in the forest.

If you installed DNS first and then promoted a server to become a domain controller, the two directory partitions will not be created. You can create these later by right-clicking the DNS server name and choosing the Create Default Application Directory Partitions option.

DHCP

The Dynamic Host Configuration Protocol (DHCP) is used to automatically assign IP addresses and other required networking information to DHCP-enabled hosts on your network from a central location. You configure and authorize a DHCP server in Active Directory to respond to requests from clients for configuration information. There is always the possibility of assigning duplicate addresses or incorrect addresses to clients if you manually configure them on your network. Since the assignment of these addresses is done automatically, there is little chance for human typing errors to affect your network. This also ensures that only the information you want the hosts to receive actually reaches them. Other benefits include the ability to handle quickly handle changes of IP addresses for hosts such as laptops and the ability to use DHCP relay agents.

The DHCP server service can be installed on a domain controller, a domain member server, or a stand-alone server. Generally, you will install DHCP on a domain controller or a domain member server. Once you have the service installed, you will need to create a scope or a range of addresses. Included in this scope will be any *options* you wish to have assigned to hosts. These options can include subnet masks, DNS and WINS servers, default gateways, and domain names as well as other services used within the TCP/IP protocol stack.

Authorizing DHCP Servers

Each and every DHCP server is authorized in Active Directory to prevent unauthorized or rogue servers from either issuing new IP address leases or renewing existing IP address leases. This authorization will occur before any leases are issued or renewed. For a DHCP server to be authorized in Active Directory, it must either be configured as a domain controller or be a member server that is in the domain. The actual authorization process is done through the DHCP console. To authorize a server, right-click on the on the server name in the console and click on the Authorize tab, as shown in Figure 14.9. You might have to refresh the console by either pressing the F5 key or selecting the Refresh option after right-clicking the console in order for the red down arrow to change to the green up arrow, which indicates the server has been authorized.

FIGURE 14.9
Authorizing a DHCP in
Active Directory

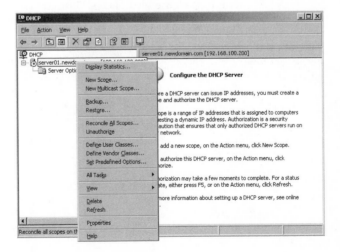

Most of the problems you will encounter with a DHCP server are usually related to either authorization or network connectivity issues such as connectivity between segments rather than with the servers themselves. As stated earlier, a DHCP server must be authorized in Active Directory to issue addresses. If you have a server that is not responding to client requests for new or renewed addresses and there is connectivity to the server, check to see if the server is authorized. If it is not authorized, use the steps outlined earlier and authorize the server.

Once you have your server authorized and you have created a scope, you must activate the scope for it to issue addresses. Activating a scope enables the server to respond to requests from clients on that segment. If you need to activate a scope, you go to the DHCP console, right-click on the scope, and click Activate. The scope is successfully activated when the red down arrow changes to a green up arrow, as you can see in Figure 14.10.

In some scenarios, you might have your DHCP server configured to support clients on multiple segments. In this case, if clients on one segment are not receiving addresses, then you should check the default bindings for the network connections. If your DHCP server is multihomed, the DHCP service will bind to the first IP address that is statically configured for each network connection. If the first network connection is configured dynamically, then the connection is disabled in the server bindings. However, if the first connection is configured statically, then the connection is enabled in the server bindings.

There is a helpful command line included in the Support Tools called dhcploc that is useful for detecting any DHCP servers on a specific network segment and for discovering if there are any unauthorized servers. Usage for dhcploc is dhcploc -p machine-ip-address. The -p switch will preclude authorized DHCP servers from this query, and machine-ip-address is used to specify the machine from which the utility is actually run from, as shown in Figure 14.11.

DHCP Relay Agent

Now that we have our DHCP server authorized, we must look at DHCP relay agents. A DHCP relay agent requests a DHCP address on behalf of a client on network segments that do not have DHCP servers. DHCP relay agents are created in the Routing and Remote Access console and not through the DHCP interface, as Figure 14.12 shows. Once configured, it is transparent to users where the address comes from—all they know is that they have an address.

FIGURE 14.10
Activating a scope
on a DHCP server

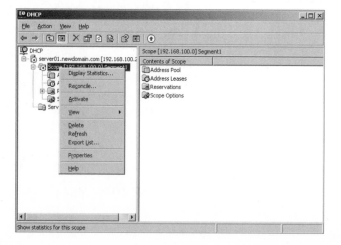

FIGURE 14.11
Using dhcploc

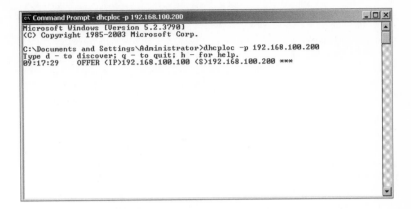

FIGURE 14.12
Configuring a DHCP
relay agent

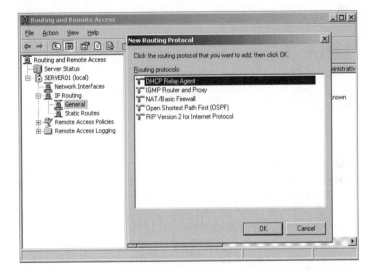

If you have a DHCP relay agent configured but clients on a segment are not receiving addresses, check the Routing and Remote Access server and ensure that the service and interfaces are running. You should also ensure that the Relay DHCP Packets box is checked on the interface in question.

DHCP DATABASE

The DHCP database can be backed up one of three ways: through a normally scheduled backup of the system using Windows Backup or your preferred backup solution, synchronously through automatic backups that occur every 60 minutes, or through asynchronous or manual backups through the DHCP console. If either the synchronous or manual backups have been performed, you can recover the database through the DHCP console (right-click the server name and click Backup), as you can see in Figure 14.13.

FIGURE 14.13

Backing up a
DHCP database

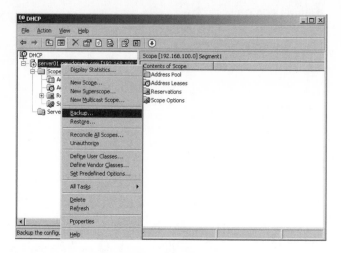

Methodologies of Network Troubleshooting

One of your most important tasks will be to troubleshoot problems on your network. Troubleshooting is as much an art as a science and is network dependent. All networks have their own quirks and issues that affect performance and reliability. These can be environmental, people (users), technology, or outside influences.

There are numerous troubleshooting models and methodologies available for your use. Eventually you will find what works for you, your network, and your users. Most troubleshooting will follow a systematic approach to isolating and repairing the problem. There will be occasions when a more intuitive approach is required; sometimes it will be a combination of the two. Experience will help you learn when to choose between a systematic over an intuitive approach as you gain more practice and learn your network. As you saw in Chapter 13, the Microsoft methodology helps make troubleshooting less stressful.

Other Issues with Troubleshooting

As I mentioned earlier, when troubleshooting you should try to isolate the problem. While you are trying to fix the network problem, do not make too many changes at once—preferably only one or two at a time. The logic behind this is if you make too many changes, you might accidentally inflict more harm to your network while trying to fix the problem. The other consideration is that if you need to undo any or all of your previous actions, you might not remember what you did.

You might consider writing down the changes you make to the network as you make them—a checklist of actions performed. This will help you remember what troubleshooting and repair actions you have performed on the network, and you can readily undo them if required. This will also serve as a roadmap for anybody who has to perform the same task again in the future.

The last thing we need to discuss is priorities. The priority of your actions will be determined by a number of factors: how critical the problem is, whom the problem affects, who has "interest" in the problem, and how long the outage will last. Any one of these factors can influence the order in which you will try to fix network outages.

TOOLS FOR TROUBLESHOOTING

Learning how to successfully and quickly troubleshoot is important, and knowing what tools to use in given situations will assist you in this immensely. There are a large number of tools that can be used for basic troubleshooting of your network infrastructure, and we will cover some of the basic ones in this section.

IPCONFIG

The IPCONFIG command-line utility is used for displaying current TCP/IP configuration for a client, troubleshooting DHCP issues with a client, and as a basic client-side DNS tool. One of the most common uses of IPCONFIG is the display of the basic IP address information of a client. When you type **ipconfig** at a command prompt, the IP address, subnet mask, and default gateway for a client will be displayed, as shown in Figure 14.14. The IPCONFIG command has a number of common switches that are used for gathering information used in troubleshooting.

When you use the basic ipconfig command and get an address returned in the 169.254.*x.x* range, then you know that for some reason the client cannot contact a DHCP server to receive or renew an IP address. You might consider trying the /release and /renew switches to release the current address and then contact a DHCP server to get a new address, as shown in Figure 14.15.

FIGURE 14.14
Display results for
IPCONFIG

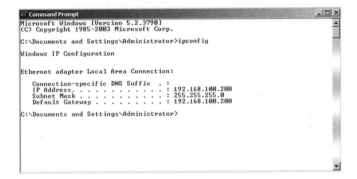

FIGURE 14.15
Releasing and renew-
ing an IP address

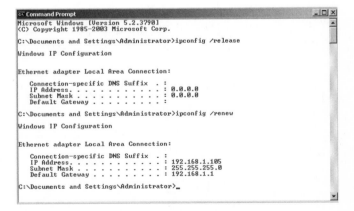

Another switch you can use is /flushdns, which will clear and reset the DNS client resolver cache, as shown in Figure 14.16. This is useful when verifying proper DNS resolution for a client.

Two last switches we will talk about are /registerdns and /displaydns. The register DNS switch is used to manually update dynamic DNS name and IP address registrations, as shown in Figure 14.17. This switch is extremely useful when verifying name resolution with a DNS server. The last switch we will talk about with ipconfig is /displaydns. This switch will display the contents of the local clients' DNS resolver cache, including all preloaded entries from a local Hosts file and any entries newly added, as shown in Figure 14.18. This command is useful for seeing what has been resolved—especially when used in conjunction with the /registerdns command.

NSLOOKUP

This is a command we will discuss in much greater depth later in this chapter. This command can be used for a variety of useful and powerful tasks. For our basic troubleshooting concerns at the moment, it can be used to diagnose DNS issues and check for name resolution by querying a DNS server, as shown in Figure 14.19.

FIGURE 14.16

Clearing and resetting the client resolver cache

FIGURE 14.17

Using the /registerdns switch

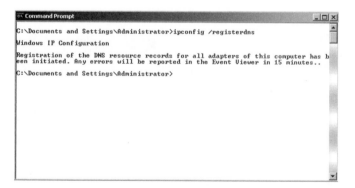

FIGURE 14.18
Verifying the contents of
the client resolver cache

FIGURE 14.18
Verifying the contents of
the client resolver cache

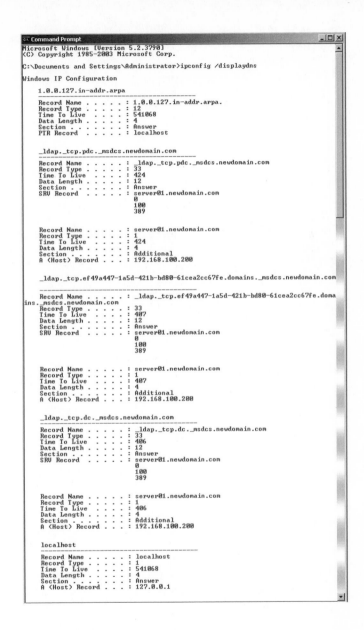

Netdiag

This command-line tool can be used to help diagnose and isolate connectivity issues in your network. It does this by performing a number of tests on the system and displaying network and configuration information. The information that is generated, as shown in Figure 14.20, can be used to start troubleshooting connectivity issues.

FIGURE 14.19
Using the basic
NSLOOKUP command

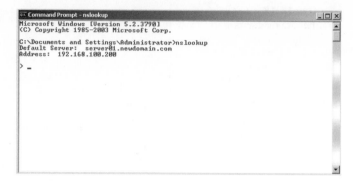

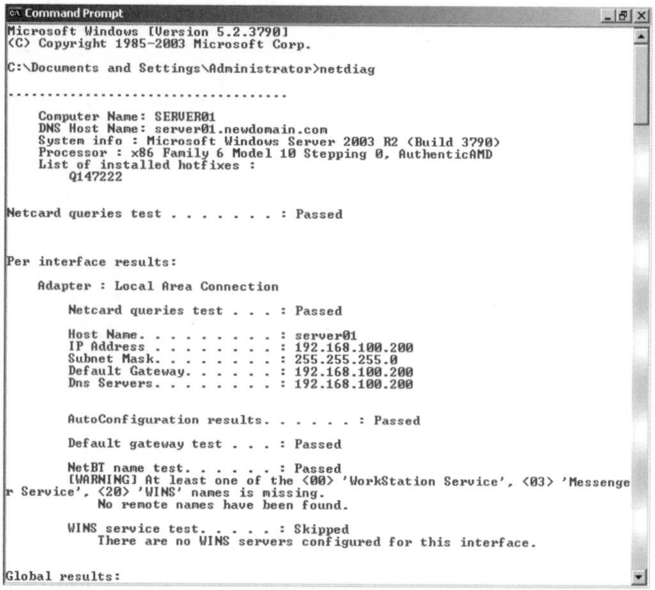

FIGURE 14.20
Displaying the results
of Netdiag

ping

This command-line utility is used for testing connectivity between systems. Using ping in its basic form, you can determine whether you can "see" the distant end or not. A complete syntax for ping is listed as follows.

```
ping [-t] [-a] [-n Count] [-l Size] [-f] [-i TTL] [-v TOS] [-r Count] [-s Count]
➥[{-j HostList | -k HostList}] [-w Timeout]
➥[-R] [-S SrcAddr] [-4] [-6] TargetName
```

You use this command-line utility to test connectivity between two systems by using either the name or IP address of the target system, as shown in Figure 14.21. A new feature with ping in Windows Server 2003 is the ability to specify that IPv6 is used by ping to identify the name of target host.

You do this by using the -6 switch in the command line. If you know the IP address, but not the host-name, you can use the -a switch in the command line to find the hostname.

```
Command Prompt                                                          _ □ X
Microsoft Windows [Version 5.2.3790]
(C) Copyright 1985-2003 Microsoft Corp.

C:\Documents and Settings\Administrator>ping 192.168.100.200

Pinging 192.168.100.200 with 32 bytes of data:

Reply from 192.168.100.200: bytes=32 time<1ms TTL=128
Reply from 192.168.100.200: bytes=32 time<1ms TTL=128
Reply from 192.168.100.200: bytes=32 time<1ms TTL=128
Reply from 192.168.100.200: bytes=32 time<1ms TTL=128

Ping statistics for 192.168.100.200:
    Packets: Sent = 4, Received = 4, Lost = 0 (0% loss),
Approximate round trip times in milli-seconds:
    Minimum = 0ms, Maximum = 0ms, Average = 0ms

C:\Documents and Settings\Administrator>ping -a 192.168.100.200

Pinging server01.newdomain.com [192.168.100.200] with 32 bytes of data:

Reply from 192.168.100.200: bytes=32 time<1ms TTL=128
Reply from 192.168.100.200: bytes=32 time<1ms TTL=128
Reply from 192.168.100.200: bytes=32 time<1ms TTL=128
Reply from 192.168.100.200: bytes=32 time<1ms TTL=128

Ping statistics for 192.168.100.200:
    Packets: Sent = 4, Received = 4, Lost = 0 (0% loss),
Approximate round trip times in milli-seconds:
    Minimum = 0ms, Maximum = 0ms, Average = 0ms

C:\Documents and Settings\Administrator>_
```

pathping

Knowing the path that data packets take in a network can help with troubleshooting communications problems. The pathping command-line utility is a very useful tool in finding the path that packets take in a network as well as determining the latency involved with each intervening router, switch, and subnet.

The syntax for pathping is as follows:

```
pathping [-n] [-h MaximumHops] [-g HostList] [-p Period] [-q NumQueries]
➡[-w Timeout] [-T] [-R] [TargetName]
```

When you initiate the pathping command, it sends echo requests as ICMP packets out to each intervening hop that a data packet traverses and displays the information it collects concerning the latency at each subsequent level. In this way you will have information that will help you identify the source of the bottleneck on the network. As part of the testing process, pathping tests each segment or hop, and as such, there can be a delay in the test completing, as shown in Figure 14.22. Because pathping uses ICMP, there is the potential for firewalls to block these packets and have incomplete data displayed for a specific segment.

tracert

This command-line utility functions in a similar manner as pathping but with a few exceptions. tracert, like pathping, uses ICMP echo packets to display the path a packet takes from source to destination. But unlike pathping, tracert does not display the latency of the packets as they traverse the network or of communications—it only displays the path it takes, as shown in Figure 14.23. Also like pathping, tracert will be affected by firewalls since it uses ICMP echo packets and many fire-walls block ICMP packets.

FIGURE 14.22
Switches available
for `pathping`

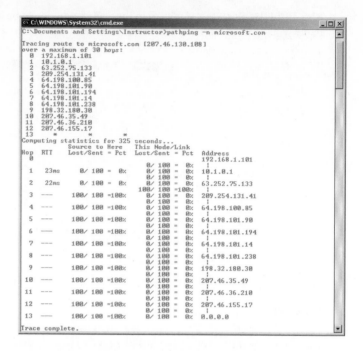

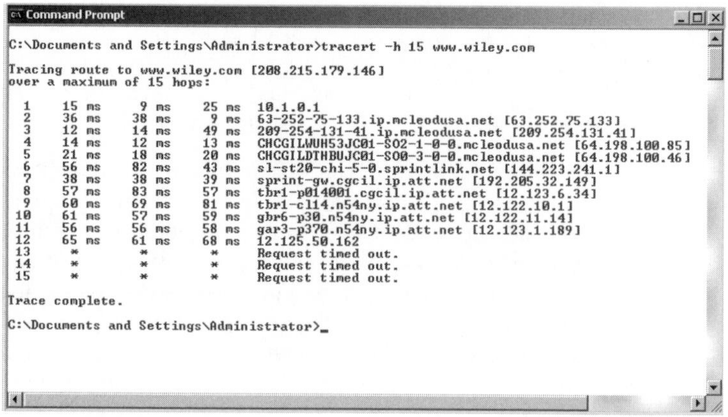

FIGURE 14.23
Display results
from `tracert`

The syntax for `tracert` is as follows:

```
tracert [-d] [-h MaximumHops] [-j HostList] [-w Timeout]
➡[-R] [-S SrcAddr] [-4][-6] TargetName
```

There are two switches of interest in `tracert`. As in `ping`, `tracert` also has the capability of using only IPv6 for testing purposes. By using the -6 switch, `tracert` will only use IPv6 for this test. The -d switch is useful for improving performance; it will prevent `tracert` from resolving the names of intervening routers. By default, `tracert` has a maximum hop count of 30, though you can change this by using the -h switch.

DNS TROUBLESHOOTING TOOLS

Knowing what tools are in your troubleshooting arsenal is important when deciding how to tackle a problem with DNS. There are several command-line utilities you can use, such as the popular Nslookup, to manage your DNS server with DNSCMD. We will discuss the most common tools in this section and give some examples on how you can use them for troubleshooting.

The first step in troubleshooting is ensuring that you have the proper permissions for using the tools, that is, you are a member of the administrators group or have been delegated permission to use the tools. If you are using a secondary logon, make sure you specify the proper account. Permissions tend to be one error that is overlooked initially when troubleshooting.

Debug Logging

Another place you can look for information on the performance of your DNS server is the event logs, and if you have DNS Debug logging enabled, you can use this log as well. To enable DNS Debug logging, right-click on the name of the server, click Properties, and click the Debug Logging tab. Enabling the debug logging feature is achieved by clicking the Log Packets For Debugging box, as shown in Figure 14.24. Once you are in the debug console window, you can specify logging for packet direction, transport protocol, packet contents, packet type and other options. The actual log file is stored in the C:\Windows\System32\DNS folder, but you can change the location to suit your needs.

Domain Information Groper (dig)

This command-line utility is derived from Unix. There is a version available for Windows from www.isc.org. The query feature is what makes dig more powerful than nslookup. When you initiate a query in dig, you must specify what you want to query and any associated records or switches. dig can also be used to make zone transfers in the same way as nslookup.

NOTE   You can be downloaded dig by clicking the link Bind9.3.1.zip at the www.isc.org site at ftp://ftp.isc.org/isc/bind/contrib/ntbind-9.3.1/.

FIGURE 14.24
Enabling debug logging for DNS

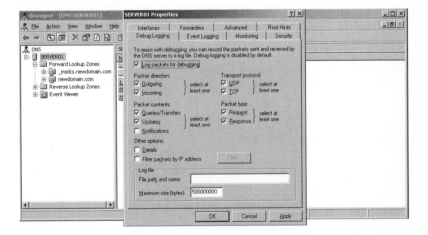

DNSCMD

This command-line tool is found in the Support Tools and enables you to display and modify settings for your DNS server. It can be used to create, modify, and delete resource records and zones. If you want to view the DNS information and statistics of a server, you type **dnscmd <server name> info** at a command prompt, as shown in Figure 14.25. By typing **dnscmd** at a command prompt, you will get a listing of all the commands you can use, as you can see in Figure 14.26. One thing to keep in mind with this utility is that it is usually run on one computer, but is used to act upon another system.

Other useful switches with DNSCMD are:

/Zoneinfo This will display information about the target zone.

/DirectoryPartitionInfo This command will display the directory partition information for the target partition.

DNSlint

This is a new command-line utility in Windows Server 2003 and is located in the Support Tools. It can be used to check for and verify DNS records and server functionality and generate a report in HTML, as you can see in Figure 14.27. The syntax for `dnslint` is as follows:

```
dnslint /d domain_name | /ad [LDAP_IP_address] | /ql input_file [/c]
➥[smtp,pop,imap]] [/no_open] [/r report_name] [/t] [/test_tcp]
➥[/s DNS_IP_address] [/v] [/y]
```

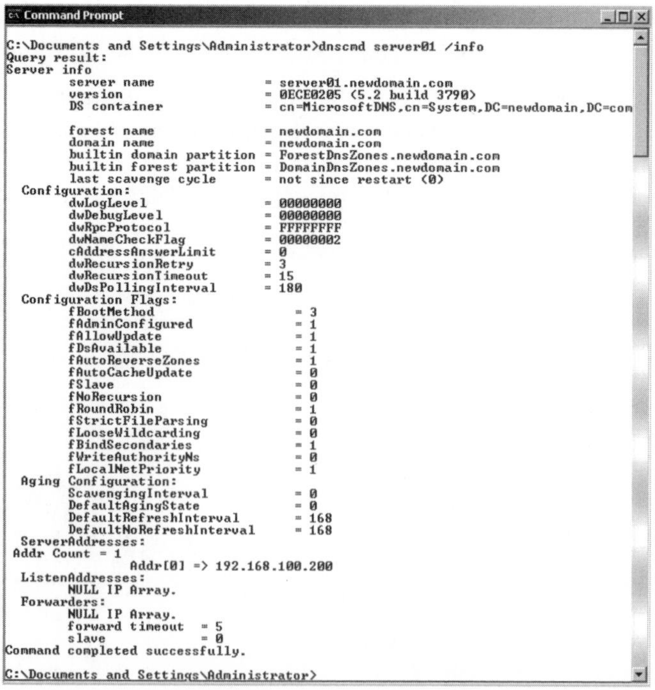

```
C:\Documents and Settings\Administrator>dnscmd server01 /info
Query result:
Server info
        server name                 = server01.newdomain.com
        version                     = 0ECE0205 (5.2 build 3790)
        DS container                = cn=MicrosoftDNS,cn=System,DC=newdomain,DC=com

        forest name                 = newdomain.com
        domain name                 = newdomain.com
        builtin domain partition    = ForestDnsZones.newdomain.com
        builtin forest partition    = DomainDnsZones.newdomain.com
        last scavenge cycle         = not since restart (0)
  Configuration:
        dwLogLevel                  = 00000000
        dwDebugLevel                = 00000000
        dwRpcProtocol               = FFFFFFFF
        dwNameCheckFlag             = 00000002
        cAddressAnswerLimit         = 0
        dwRecursionRetry            = 3
        dwRecursionTimeout          = 15
        dwDsPollingInterval         = 180
  Configuration Flags:
        fBootMethod                   = 3
        fAdminConfigured              = 1
        fAllowUpdate                  = 1
        fDsAvailable                  = 1
        fAutoReverseZones             = 1
        fAutoCacheUpdate              = 0
        fSlave                        = 0
        fNoRecursion                  = 0
        fRoundRobin                   = 1
        fStrictFileParsing            = 0
        fLooseWildcarding             = 0
        fBindSecondaries              = 1
        fWriteAuthorityNs             = 0
        fLocalNetPriority             = 1
  Aging Configuration:
        ScavengingInterval            = 0
        DefaultAgingState             = 0
        DefaultRefreshInterval        = 168
        DefaultNoRefreshInterval      = 168
  ServerAddresses:
 Addr Count = 1
                Addr[0] => 192.168.100.200
  ListenAddresses:
        NULL IP Array.
  Forwarders:
        NULL IP Array.
        forward timeout  = 5
        slave            = 0
Command completed successfully.

C:\Documents and Settings\Administrator>
```

FIGURE 14.25
Information display results for `dnscmd`

FIGURE 14.26

List of commands available for `dnscmd`

When using `dnslint`, you must specify one of three switches—`/d`, `/ql`, or `/ad`—in the command line, as shown in Figure 14.28. Each switch is further explained:

/d Diagnosis problems with "lame delegation." You cannot use the `/ad` switch with the `/d` switch, and you must specify a domain to test.

/ql Verifies user-defined set of DNS records on multiple servers.

/ad Verifies DNS records specifically used for Active Directory replication. You must use the `/s` switch with the `/ad` switch. The `/s` switch specifies the IP address of a DNS server that is authoritative for the _msdcs zone in the Active Directory forest. When using the `/ad` switch, `DNSLint` will compare the domain controller's canonical name (CNAME) record that is registered within the domain's zone in DNS with the alias that is found as an attribute of the domain controller's computer object.

A switch that is commonly overlooked is `/test_tcp`. When running `dnslint` tests, only UDP port 53 is tested. By using this switch, TCP port 53 will be tested to see if it is responding to queries. Another switch that is not usually utilized to its fullest is `/s`. When the `/s` switch is used with `/d`, it will not start testing at the InterNIC whois lookup site that is performed by default. This allows private networks to be tested or for you to determine which DNS server is queried.

FIGURE 14.27
Running DNSlint with the /AD switch displayed in HTML format

FIGURE 14.28
DNSlint command line

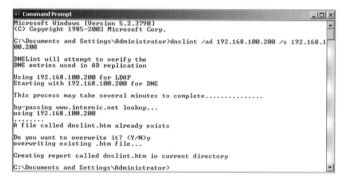

NSLOOKUP

This is, perhaps, the most important tool at your disposal for troubleshooting DNS issues. There are two modes available for nslookup: interactive and noninteractive. Which mode you will use depends on the location and type of information you are seeking.

The noninteractive mode is used for searching for only one record or other specific information. To use nslookup in noninteractive mode, you type the following:

```
Nslookup [name or IP address of target] [name or IP address of a DNS server]
```

If you need to search for a number of different records, then you would use the interactive mode of nslookup. If you only type **nslookup** at a command prompt, you will get a result similar to what you see in Figure 14.29. In this case we see the FQDN and IP address for server01. This is the basic form of the interactive mode.

You can use `nslookup` to search for detailed records. If you need to search for a specific record type, then you would specify through a `set type=`*`resource_record_type`* command what resource record type you are looking for, as shown in Figure 14.30.

You can use `nslookup` for zone transfer. You do this by using the `ls` command. The syntax for this command is:

```
Ls [-a | d | t type] domain [> filename]
```

-a   Will display all the aliases and canonical names.

-d   Will display all data from target domain.

-t   Will filter data by specific type.

TROUBLESHOOTING TOOLS AND WINS

The WINS server itself is fairly robust, but as with all servers, some problems might arise. We will go through some of these troublesome areas now and discuss a few of the tools we have available to use when troubleshooting.

Before performing too much work on the WINS database, you should back up the database by right-clicking the server, clicking the Backup Database option, and specifying the backup location.

FIGURE 14.29
Display using `nslookup`

FIGURE 14.30
Displaying a specific
record with `nslookup`

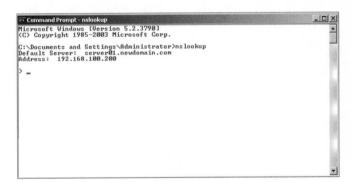

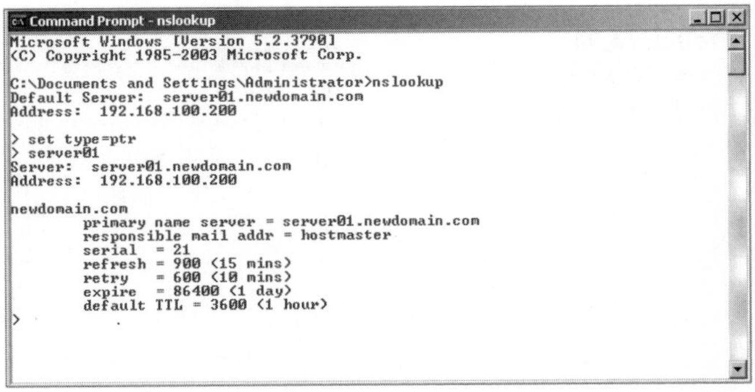

One of the most basic problems is a WINS server not giving out addresses. In this case, ensure the WINS server is started and on the proper subnet. If you need to start the WINS server, right-click the server name, select All Tasks, and then click the Start option.

Eventually you will need to use static mappings in WINS, but you should use them judiciously, as they can adversely impact your network if you have duplicate names. When a client connects, it will attempt to register its name with an NBNS. The NBNS will check its database to see if the name is unused. If a client attempts to register a name and the requested name is in use, the NBNS server will query the first machine to see if the name is still being used. If it is still in use, then the requesting machine will be sent a negative name registration response. Otherwise, the NBNS will register the name for the client.

Another issue associated with static mappings is updating. If you have made changes to the network or if you have made modifications to any servers (for example, a server name, address, or type) and have not updated your static mappings, then clients or other servers may not be able to connect. You will need to devise a strategy to ensure you keep your static mappings current to avoid these pitfalls.

Netsh WINS

This tool is mainly used for configuring your WINS server from the command line, but can be used for viewing potential problems and troubleshooting. By typing **netsh wins server**, you get the results shown in Figure 14.31. If you type only **netsh wins**, then you will just get the help screen. From this console you can check, set, show, or choose from other options. The information displayed can be used to start the diagnoses of your WINS server.

Nbtstat

The Nbtstat tool is used to display information about NetBIOS functions on your server. It can be used to display protocol statistics with NetBIOS over TCP/IP (NetBT), display or purge the NetBIOS name cache, and release and refresh the name of the local machine if it is registered with a WINS server.

Following is the syntax for nbtstat:

```
nbtstat [-a RemoteName] [-A IPAddress] [-c] [-n] [-r] [-R]
➥[-RR] [-s] [-S] [Interval]
```

FIGURE 14.31
Showing the output of
netsh wins server

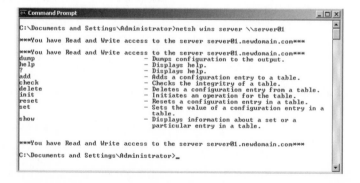

While you have many capabilities available with `nbtstat`, in most cases you are going to use it to view the cache and to purge and refresh the cache. To view the name cache, open a command prompt and type **nbtstat -c**, as shown in Figure 14.32. If you need to purge and reload the #PRE-tagged entries (the entries that are loaded first from the LMHOSTS file), use `nbtstat -r`, as shown in Figure 14.33. The -RR switch will clear and refresh the cache on the local computer from which it is run, as shown in Figure 14.34.

FIGURE 14.32
Displaying the NetBIOS name cache with nbtstat

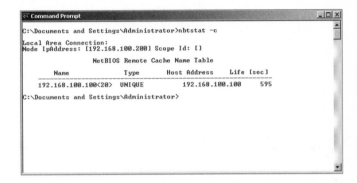

FIGURE 14.33
Purging and reloading the #PRE-entries

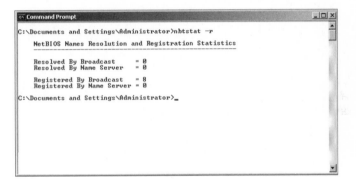

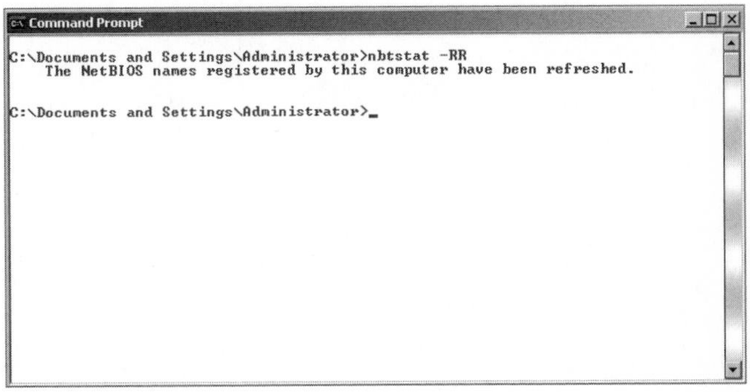

FIGURE 14.34
Clearing and refreshing the name cache with the -RR switch

Coming Up Next

Now that we have taken a look at troubleshooting the network infrastructure and services that the Active Directory services rely upon, it is time to move on to troubleshooting Active Directory itself. As with most of the Windows Server 2003 services, there are several tools available for you to use when trying to isolate problems related to Active Directory. We will introduce those tools and cover how they are used in the next chapter.

Chapter 15

Troubleshooting Problems Related to the Active Directory Database

The Active Directory database consists of database files and log files, and the overall health of these files is key to Active Directory's stability. In this chapter, we discuss problems related to these files, such as corrupted files or inconsistent data due to replication problems.

Active Directory Files

The key to a successful Active Directory backup is the system state. The Active Directory file system is built to handle full and complete restoration even when time has elapsed since the backup occurred. The files that make up the system state are:

- NTDS.DIT: This file is the Active Directory database file.

- EDB.LOG: This log file contains the transactions that have occurred since the last backup.

- EDB001.LOG, EDB002.LOG, etc.: These log files are similar to the EDB.LOG file; they are created when the EDB.LOG is full.

- EDB.CHK: This file contains an authoritative list of all transactions contained in the EDB files.

- RESn.LOG: These files are created when the EDB.LOG file creation fails. When the NTDS.DIT file is backed up, the current EDB.LOG file is deleted and a blank 10MB EDB.LOG file is created. If there is not enough disk space for the new file creation, RESn.LOG (where n is a number, assigned in sequence to each file) files are created. One file is created per transaction. This allows more transactions to be recorded.

- *.PAT: These files are created when a transaction is split between log files. During a restore, these files are used to patch transactions that happen to span more than one log file.

The Guts of NTDS.DIT

For the true database geeks out there, let's take a quick look inside the NTDS.DIT file. Earlier, we defined this file simply as the Active Directory database file. Well, there is a little more to it than that.

NTDS.DIT is the heart of Active Directory. It holds information about Active Directory, including user accounts, computer accounts, and so on. A deeper look into how this information is stored reveals the following tables:

◆ Schema table: This table contains data about the types of objects that can be created in Active Directory, the relationships between then, and the attributes (both mandatory and optional) that exist on each type of object. This table only changes when changes are made to the Active Directory schema.

◆ Link table: This table contains data about linked attributes, which contain values referring to other objects in Active Directory. A prime example of this is the MemberOf attribute on a user object. That attribute contains values that reference groups to which the user belongs.

◆ Data table: This is the largest table in the database. Users, groups, application-specific data, and any other data stored in Active Directory is contained in this table. Think of this table as having rows, where each row represents an instance of an object (such as a user), and columns, where each column represents an attribute in the schema, such as GivenName.

What Happened to NTDS.DIT?

In Chapter 12, we talked about how to perform an offline defrag of the NTDS.DIT file. This is a great procedure that you should run to reclaim "white space" from the database file.

What would happen if we ran into an instance where the file either is corrupted, has been deleted, or is missing? The restore process is the same for each of these instances.

To restore NTDS.DIT from backup, perform the following steps:

1. Reboot the domain controller.

2. Press F8 at the appropriate time to display the Advanced Options menu.

3. Select Directory Services Restore Mode and press Enter.

4. Log on using the administrator account and password you specified when you were installing Active Directory on that server.

5. When prompted, click OK at the warning screen that says you will be entering safe mode.

6. Click Start ➢ Programs ➢ Accessories ➢ System Tools ➢ Backup.

7. Select the Restore tab.

8. Click the + button to expand each of the following items:

   ◆ File

   ◆ Media Created

   ◆ System Drive (assuming default installation)

   ◆ Winnt

   ◆ NTDS

9. Click the NTDS folder to display the files in the folder.

10. Click the check box to select the NTDS.DIT file.

11. Leave the Restore Files To box set to Original Location. If you select to restore to an alternate location, you will have to copy the NTDS.DIT file to the location where it is supposed to exist.

12. Click Start Restore.

In some instances, you will want to move a database or log file. To perform this task, follow these steps:

1. Reboot the domain controller.

2. Press F8 at the appropriate time to display the Advanced Options menu.

3. Select Directory Services Restore Mode and press Enter.

4. Log on using the administrator account and password you specified when you were installing Active Directory on that server.

5. Start a command prompt.

6. Type **ntdsutil.exe**.

7. At the `ntdsutil:` prompt, type **files**.

8. At the `file maintenance:` prompt:

    ◆ To move a database, type **move db to %s**, where **%s** is the drive and folder where you want the database moved.

    ◆ To move log files, type **move logs to %s**, where **%s** is the drive and folder where you want the log files moved.

    ◆ To view the log files and database, type **info**.

    ◆ To verify the integrity of the database at its new location, type **integrity**.

    ◆ Type **quit**.

    ◆ Type **quit** to return to a command prompt.

9. Restart the computer in Normal mode.

CIRCULAR LOGGING

This feature is turned off by default, which I happen to highly recommend. It also follows best practices. Circular logging turns the EDB.LOG file into a first-in, first-out (FIFO) bucket. The data in the file is constantly up to date.

Sequential log files grow until they reach a specified size. After that, another log file is created, and so on until all transactions are committed to the database. Every 12 hours, the garbage collection process deletes unnecessary log files.

If your server cannot run for 12 hours between reboots, these files cannot be deleted, eventually consuming valuable disk space. Enabling circular logging will help minimize the amount of logged data the physical disk must store.

Do I recommend this? No, definitely not! In very few instances, such as the one listed earlier, circular logging makes sense. The negatives definitely outweigh the positives.

The main reason that circular logging is turned off is for disaster recovery purposes. If a restore should become necessary, the system will restore the NTDS.DIT from tape, and look at the EDB.CHK file to get a list of all the transactions that occurred since the last backup. The system will then pull in the EDB log files to restore all the changes that occurred since the NTDS.DIT was last backed up.

If circular logging is turned on and the Active Directory database hasn't been backed up in a while, transactions will be lost. Since we are working with a FIFO bucket, transactions can be overwritten before they have a chance to be backed up. The resulting changes defined in those transactions will be lost forever.

Database Capacity Planning

You must consider many factors when planning an Active Directory implementation. One very important step is to plan for proper placement and sizing of the partition where your Active Directory database will reside.

On an Active Directory domain controller, database file access will probably consume the most processes on that server. Keeping the database on a different partition than the system and boot files will help with performance. By default, the Active Directory database installs itself in the %systemroot%\ntds folder.

When planning your Active Directory implementation, use the ADSizer utility to plan for disk space requirements that may be needed by Active Directory. ADSizer will automatically estimate the size of the database for you, based on the following number estimates. Each security principal (users, groups, and computers) will consume about 3600 bytes each, while other items such as share files may only take around 1100 bytes each.

Figure 15.1 shows the ADSizer utility, which will lead you through a series of questions and give you recommendations based on your answers.

FIGURE 15.1

The ADSizer utility

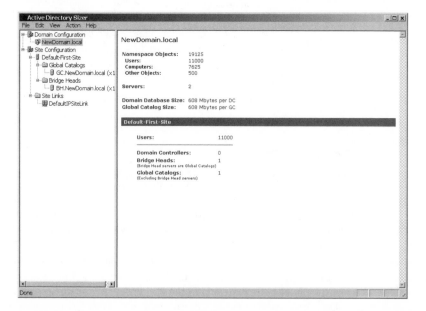

Troubleshooting Active Directory Replication

Nothing is more stressful than having domain controllers that are not sharing information. By their very nature, domain controllers are supposed to be multimaster replicas of one another, and you should have identical information on every domain controller within a domain. However, some issues can rear their ugly heads and cause you to have a nightmarish day of troubleshooting.

Replication Overview

Understanding how something works is the first part of knowing how to troubleshoot a problem. Whereas having troubleshooting methodology will help you ascertain the problem, you will have a better "feel" for where to start looking for problems if you understand the way something works and behaves.

Active Directory replication is probably one of the most obscure things that you will have to learn. Most administrators know why they need it, but they don't know how it gets the objects from one domain controller to another. A quick review of the process is in order before we move on to troubleshooting replication problems.

If your DNS infrastructure has issues, Active Directory replication may not work. Verify that your DNS infrastructure is stable and that name resolution is working correctly. Chapter 14, "Troubleshooting Problems Related to Network Infrastructure," covers some of the options you have when maintaining and troubleshooting your DNS infrastructure.

If DNS is working correctly, domain controllers will have a better chance at replicating the objects between one another. The first thing a domain controller does when replicating objects is to examine the connection objects to other domain controllers. The domain controller will not be concerned about domain controllers other than those to which it has a connection.

Within the Configuration partition, the domain controller will find the domain controllers to which it is connected. Active Directory will return the GUID that is associated with the domain controller defined on the connection object. Each domain controller registers the SRV records for the Active Directory services it supports and its GUID. If you open the _msdcs zone for the domain, you will find the domain controller GUID. Figure 15.2 shows the GUID for the domain controllers within the zygort.lcl domain. The GUIDs appear as the last two lines within the details pane.

After the domain controller has obtained the GUID for the partner domain controller, it sends a query to DNS to locate the hostname; then using the hostname, it queries for the IP address. Once the domain controller has the IP address of the partner domain controller, it can initiate an RPC connection to the partner and begin the replication process.

Determining DNS Problems

When domain controllers are brought online, they register records within the DNS server they are configured to use. This registration includes the GUIDs that are registered within the _msdcs zone. If the domain controller fails to update its GUID, other domain controllers will not be able to locate it in order to replicate Active Directory objects. To troubleshoot DNS issues, you can use the DNSLint command.

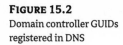

FIGURE 15.2
Domain controller GUIDs
registered in DNS

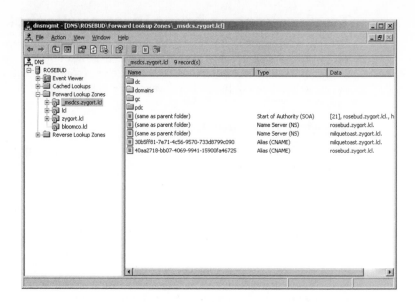

NOTE The DNSLint command can be used to perform other troubleshooting tasks. See Chapter 14, "Troubleshooting Problems Related to Network Infrastructure," for more information on the additional uses of DNSLint.

When using DNSLint to troubleshoot Active Directory issues, you need to use the /ad switch. This will force DNSLint to compare the GUIDs within the DNS server to the domain controllers for the domain. The command is issued at the command prompt in the form

```
Dnslint /ad domain_controller_ip_address /s dns_server_ip_address
```

The /s switch informs DNSLint that you are not going to attempt name resolution to the Internet root domains; instead, you will work with specific DNS servers to validate the name resolution information. For instance, if your domain controller is using IP address 10.23.74.1 and the DNS server that you are testing against is using IP address 10.23.77.5, your command line would appear as

```
Dnslint /ad 10.23.74.1 /s 10.23.77.5
```

Once issued, DNSLint will attempt to bind to the domain controller to retrieve the GUIDs for all of the domain controllers within the domain. If successful, it will then compare the GUIDs to those within DNS by issuing queries to the _msdcs zone looking for the CNAME records. At this point, the DNS server that you identified when using the /s parameter will need to be authoritative for the _msdcs zone. If it is not, the DNS server must have an entry listed within it that will allow DNSLint to locate a DNS server that is authoritative for the zone.

Once the DNS server is located and the GUIDs are queried, if a positive response is returned, DNSLint will attempt to locate the A record for the domain controller based on the hostname that is returned from the CNAME record. If everything is successful, you will not receive any errors on the HTML output that DNSLint provides. Otherwise, you will notice errors and have a starting point when trying to determine why replication is not working correctly. Figure 15.3 is an example of the first half of the HTML report that is generated; it shows the GUIDs that were found. Figure 15.4 shows the bottom half of the same report; it details the domain controller entries that were discovered within DNS.

FIGURE 15.3
DNSLint report
showing GUIDs of
domain controllers

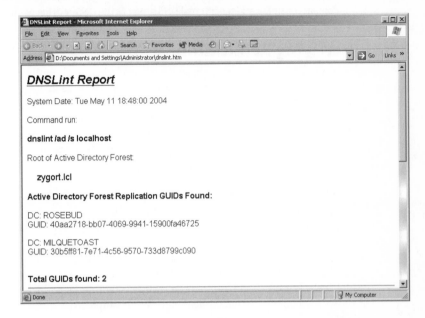

FIGURE 15.4
DNSLint report showing
domain controller entries
within DNS

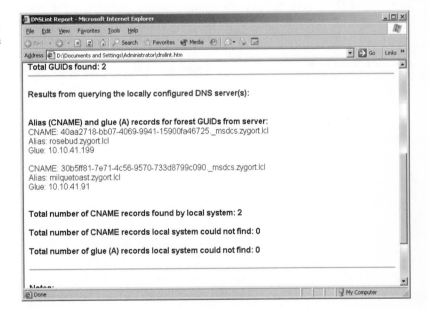

NOTE To check a domain controller that is configured as a DNS server also, you can issue the command `dnslint /ad /s localhost`. Doing so will cause `dnslint` to use `127.0.0.1` as the IP address of the domain controller and the internal DNS server as the DNS starting point.

Verifying Replication

You may want to verify that objects have been completely replicated throughout the domain before you attempt to run applications or perform administrative management of the domain controllers. In order to do so, you can use the `dsastat.exe` utility from the Support Tools. This utility will allow you to compare the contents of the Active Directory database so that you can determine whether replication has completed. In its most basic form, you can issue the command and specify only the domain controllers you want to compare, separated by semicolons, such as

```
Dsastat -s:domaincontroller1;domaincontroller2
```

When issuing the command in the `zygort.lcl` domain for the domain controllers `rosebud` and `milquetoast`, the command line would look like this:

```
dsastat -s:rosebud;milquetoast
```

The utility will attempt to make LDAP connections to each of the domain controllers and query the partition information. It will compare both directory databases and return whether or not they are identical. Figure 15.5 shows the response that is returned if the databases are identical, and Figure 15.6 shows the response when replication has not completed.

NOTE The `dsastat.exe` utility can also be used to verify that specific portions of the Active Directory structure are synchronized. For more information on the switches available for use with `dsastat.exe`, enter **dsastat /?** at the command prompt.

FIGURE 15.5
Response from
dsastat.exe if
replication has
completed

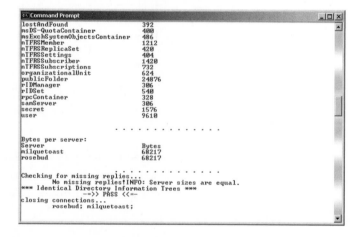

FIGURE 15.6

Response from dsastat.exe if replication has not completed

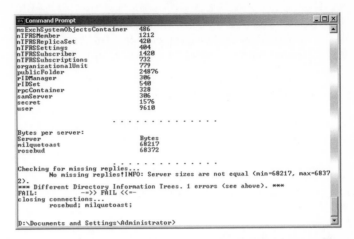

Other tools are available that can also provide information about your Active Directory directory service and tell you whether or not the replicas are up-to-date. The first is the command-line tool repadmin, which can be found in the Support Tools. If you are more comfortable using the GUI-based tools, the ReplMon utility is available to perform the same functions. The final tool we will discuss is the DCDiag utility.

Using RepAdmin

The RepAdmin utility can assist you when you are trying to determine the cause of replication problems. Some of its more popular options include checking the status of the Knowledge Consistency Checker (KCC), viewing the replication partners for domain controllers, and viewing which domain controllers have not replicated. If you want to view the KCC status, you can enter this command:

    repadmin /kcc

If you want to view the replication status of the last replication attempt from a domain controller's replication partners, enter this command:

    repadmin /showreps

Windows 2000 and Windows Server 2003 will both use the /showreps option, but the RepAdmin utility that is included with Windows Server 2003 Support Tools can also use the /showrepl switch to do the same thing. Windows Server 2003 also uses the /replsummary switch, sometimes abbreviated as /replsum, to allow you to view the failures and replicated objects. You should see a minimum of three connections per domain controller, one connection for each of the directory partitions. If the /showreps or /showrepl options do not display any connections to other domain controllers, you should run the KCC by using the ReplMon utility. If you are working within a Windows Server 2003 environment, you can open Active Directory Sites and Services, right-click the NTDS Settings object, and select All Tasks ➢ Check Replication Topology. If you still receive errors because the KCC did not create the appropriate connection objects, manually create a connection object between the domain controllers.

NOTE If you use the Check Replication Topology option on the domain controller that is the Inter-site Topology Generator, you will recalculate the intersite and intrasite replication topology. If you run it from any other domain controller, you will recalculate the intrasite topology.

You can force synchronization for any of the partitions with RepAdmin tool by using the /sync switch. This will force replication for a specific partition from a replication partner that you use in the command. If you want to force replication between all domain controllers, you can use the option /syncall. By default, the Active Directory replication is *pull replication,* meaning that the domain controller will request the data from its partners. You can change that behavior by using the /P switch, which forces the domain controller to push its objects to it partner domain controllers. The command looks like this:

```
repadmin /syncall domain_controller_FQDN directory_partition /P
```

Using *ReplMon*

ReplMon is the graphical utility that will allow you to view the connections between domain controllers and troubleshoot issues with Active Directory replication. It will also enable you to view the Update Sequence Number (USN) of the replication partners and the last successful replication time.

ReplMon is not installed on Windows 2003 Server by default. It is included in the Windows 2003 Support Tools, located on the Windows 2003 Server CD at \Program Files\Support Tools\.

As shown in Figure 15.7, you can add the domain controllers that you want to monitor within the contents pane of the utility and perform tests on them. Beneath the domain controller, all of the directory partitions are listed. When you expand the partition, you will be shown the replication partner and the replication results for the last replication attempt for that partition.

FIGURE 15.7
ReplMon interface

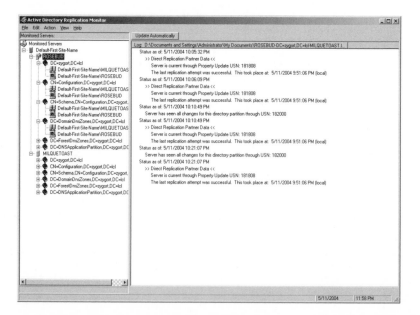

The menu that is shown in Figure 15.8 shows the options that are available when working with a domain controller. You can perform the same functions from this menu that you can from the RepAdmin command-line utility.

In order to push the changes from one domain controller to another, you need to enable push mode on the directory partition that you want to force to the partners. To do so, right-click on the partition that you want to push and select the Synchronize This Directory Partition With All Servers option. In the dialog box that appears, you can select the Push Mode option. The other options in this dialog box can also come in handy. The option Disable Transitive Replication will force replication to the partner domain controllers only and will not cause them to send out notifications to their partners. The option Cross Site Boundaries will allow you to replicate the data to all domain controllers regardless of the site in which they are located.

Using *DCDiag*

DCDiag is a command-line utility that will run diagnostic tests against the domain controller. It runs several tests, and the output can span many screens. If you want to perform specific tests against the domain controller, use the /test: switch. For instance, if you want to make sure that the replication topology is fully interconnected, issue the following command:

```
dcdiag /test:topology
```

To test that replication is functioning properly, issue the command

```
dcdiag /test:replications
```

To view the status of global catalog replication, use the command

```
dcdiag /v /s:domain_controller_name | find "%"
```

You may have to issue this command a few times from the command line to monitor the progress. As soon as DCDiag has no more output to show, the replication is complete.

FIGURE 15.8

ReplMon menu options

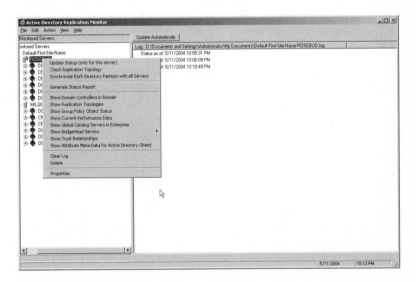

Controlling Replication in Large Organizations

In a large organization where you have several domain controllers, you could experience CPU and memory performance problems on bridgehead servers as they attempt to compress the data that needs to be sent between sites. The KCC and ISTG functions run every 15 minutes to calculate and repair the replication topology, which adds an additional load on the domain controller.

In a Windows 2000–based Active Directory forest, even though each directory partition can have a different bridgehead server assigned to replicate it, the KCC can assign only a single bridgehead server to replicate a partition. Windows Server 2003 improved upon this design by allowing the KCC to randomly assign a bridgehead server from the list of available bridgehead servers to replicate a partition. All of the partitions must still be replicated at the same time, however, so the network could still take on a large load if data from all of the partitions were replicated.

The Active Directory Load Balancing (ADLB) tool will allow you to perform advanced load-balancing tasks within the forest. Even though the tool has limitations, it does allow you to load-balance Windows 2000 domain controllers, as well as set time staggering on Windows Server 2003 domain controllers.

The limitations are few. However, if you do not specify that you want to retain the ADLB settings, the next time the KCC runs, it will reset the connection objects that ADLB had modified. If you do specify to keep the settings, you will need to make sure that the changes are replicated to the other domain controllers that are acting as partners.

Running ADLB without using the /commit parameter will allow the administrator to view the settings that ADLB would like to put into effect. When specifying the bridgehead server that you are running ADLB against, you can use the hostname or the NetBIOS name of the server, depending on the name resolution methods that your network supports. To view the changes for the bridgehead server rosebud.zyort.lcl within the Chicago site, you would enter this command:

```
adlb /server:rosebud /site:Chicago
```

The output will detail the connections and changes that ADLB would make if the /commit parameter were specified. The ADLB utility can be used by any user who has loaded it from the Windows Server 2003 Resource Kit tools. However, if you want to allow ADLB to make the changes to your replication topology, you must have Enterprise Admin privileges.

If you want to view the changes that ADLB is recommending, but you want to print them out instead of viewing them at a command prompt, you can specify a log file by using the /log parameter and specifying the path to the log file. You can also view additional performance statistics that ADLB uses to make its recommendations by including the /perf parameter.

If you are running your domain within the Windows Server 2003 functional level, you can stagger the replication schedule by using the /stagger parameter. This will allow you to stagger the updates for each of the directory partitions so that they are not sent at the same time.

The command to create a log file that will allow you to view the performance statistics and recommendations of ADLB when it is set to stagger settings would look like the following command:

```
adlb /rosebud.zygort.lcl /site:Chicago /log:d:\logfiles\adlbtest.log /stagger /perf
```

The /stagger option will not modify the connection objects of bridgehead servers in remote sites; you will need to run the utility on each bridgehead server. If you have administrative rights on the remote bridgehead server, and you have Terminal Services configured for administrative use, you can open a session and run the utility. Otherwise, you will have to work in conjunction with an administrator for the remote site.

Best Practices for Troubleshooting AD Replication

If your domain controllers are not replicating objects correctly, users will not be able to gain access to the objects that they need, and may fail to log on at all. The following are tips that you should keep in mind when troubleshooting replication issues:

◆ Use the tool you are most familiar with when troubleshooting replication problems.

◆ Verify the replication topology to make sure all of the domain controllers from all sites are interconnected.

◆ Urgent replication, such as account lockouts, will occur within the site, but will not be replicated to other sites until the site link allows it to replicate. Use `RepAdmin` to force the change.

◆ Create connection objects between domain controllers that hold FSMO roles and the servers that will act as their backup if the FSMO role holder fails. Make sure replication is occurring between the two servers.

Troubleshooting FSMO Roles

Back in Chapter 5, "Flexible Single Master Operations Design," we discussed the Flexible Single Master Operations (FSMO) roles and where you should place each one. Because there can be only one domain controller holding each of the roles, you need to make sure that you keep them operational. Of course, with some of these roles, getting them up and operational is more important than it is with others; however, you should still know what is required to get them into an operational state.

This chapter is going to deal with making sure you know which of the FSMO roles you need to repair immediately, and which ones you can probably leave offline for a while. It will also look at how you can move the roles to other domain controllers and how you can have another domain controller take over the role in case of an emergency.

FSMO Roles and Their Importance

Each of the FSMO roles is important within the forest. Without them, you will not have a means of identifying objects correctly, and data corruption can occur if two or more administrators make changes to objects within the forest. As we move through this section, I am going to introduce each of the FSMO roles and how important it is to get each one back online immediately. If you are familiar with the FSMO roles, you may want to skip this section and head directly to the "Transferring and Seizing FSMO Roles" section later in this chapter.

For efficiency's sake, you should identify another domain controller that could be used as the role holder if the original role holder were to fail. You have to do very little to configure another system to become the standby server. Realistically, you should have the role holder and the standby on the same network segment, and they should be configured as replication partners of one another. This will give you a higher probability that all of the data is replicated between the two systems in case there is a failure of the role holder.

Schema Master

The Schema Master controls all of the attributes and classes that are allowed to exist within Active Directory. Only one Schema Master can reside within the forest. The domain controller that holds the Schema Master role is the only domain controller that has the ability to make changes to schema objects within the forest. Once changes are made to a schema object, the changes are replicated to all other domain controllers within the forest.

You should not be too concerned if the Schema Master goes offline. The only time that you will need the Schema Master is when you have to make changes to the schema, either manually or when installing an application that modifies the schema. The forest can exist and function for an extended period of time without the Schema Master being online. If you cannot repair the Schema Master and you need to make a change to the schema, you can seize the role on the standby domain controller.

Domain Naming Master

As with the Schema Master, there can be only one Domain Naming Master within the forest. This is the domain controller that is responsible for allowing the addition and deletion of domains within the forest. When Dcpromo is executed and the creation of a new domain is specified, it is up to the Domain Naming Master to verify that the domain name is unique. The Domain Naming Master is also responsible for allowing deletions of domains. Again, as Dcpromo is executed, the Domain Naming Master is contacted, and the domain that is being deleted will then be removed from the forest by the Domain Naming Master.

Losing the Domain Naming Master should not affect the day-to-day operations of the organization. The only time the Domain Naming Master is required to be online is when a domain is added or removed from the forest. As with the Schema Master, you can allow the Domain Naming Master to remain offline as you try to recover the domain controller. If the Domain Naming Master is still offline when you need to add or remove a domain, or if the original role holder is not recoverable, you can seize the role on the domain controller that has been identified as the standby server.

Infrastructure Master

If you are working in a multiple-domain environment, the Infrastructure Master can be your best friend or your worst enemy. It is the Infrastructure Master's job to make sure that accounts from other domains that are members of a group are kept up-to-date. You do not want an account to have access to resources that it is not supposed to, and if changes are made to users and groups in other domains, you will need to make sure that the same changes are reflected in your domain. For instance, the administrator of bloomco.lcl has just added two accounts to a global group and removed one from the group. Within the bloomco.lcl domain, the changes are replicated throughout. Within your domain, there is a domain local group that contains the global group. Because the changes are not replicated to domain controllers within your domain, the user who was removed from the group might still have access to resources within your domain and the two new accounts might not.

The infrastructure master needs to be able to maintain the differences between domains so that the correct group membership can be applied at all domain controllers. This is why the Infrastructure Master should not be on a domain controller that is acting as a global catalog. The Infrastructure Master will contact a global catalog and compare the member attributes for the groups with the attributes that are contained within its domain. If there is a difference, the Infrastructure Master updates the attributes to keep everything synchronized. If you want to change the default scanning interval for the Infrastructure Master, you can set the following Registry value from two days to whatever value works best in your environment.

```
HKEY_LOCAL_MACHINE\System\CurrentControlSet\Services\
NTDS\Parameters\Days per database phantom scan
```

NOTE   For more information on the Infrastructure Master and how to control the scanning interval, see Knowledge Base article 248047 at `http://support.microsoft.com/default.aspx?scid=kb;EN-US;248047`.

Loss of the Infrastructure Master is a little more severe than the previous two Master Operations roles. If the Infrastructure Master is offline for an extended period of time, the data cannot be synchronized and users could have access, or be denied access, to the wrong objects. If you cannot resolve the problem with the Infrastructure Master, you may want to seize the role on the standby server.

Relative Identifier Master

Whenever a security principal, such as a user, group, or computer account, is created within, it has an associated security identifier (SID). A SID consists of the domain's SID and a relative identifier (RID) that is unique to the security principal. Allocating and keeping track of all of the RIDs for the domain is the RID Master's responsibility. Having the RID Master allows you to sleep better at night knowing that a duplicate SID will not be generated within the domain. Even if the security principal associated with a RID is deleted, the RID will still not be regenerated and used again.

If you take a look at a SID, you will notice that it is an alphanumeric combination that is not easy to understand. There is a logic behind the madness, however. If you take a look at the SID or a user account it may look like this:

```
S-1-5-21-1068514962-2513648523-685232148-1005
```

Broken down, the sections that make up the RID fall into these categories:

S   The initial character S identifies the series of digits that follow as a SID.

1   This is the revision level. Every SID that is generated within a Windows environment has a revision of 1.

5   This third character is the issuing authority identifier. A majority of the SIDs will have the Windows NT issuing authority number of 5, but some of the well-known built-in accounts will have other values.

21   The fourth character set represents the subauthority. The subauthority identifies the service type that generated the SID. SIDs that are generated from domain controllers will contain the characters 21, while built-in accounts may have other characters, such as 32.

1068514962-2513648523-685232148   This long string of characters is the unique part of the SID for a domain. If you are working with local accounts, it represents the unique SID for the computer.

1005   The last set of characters represents the RID for the account. The RID Master starts at 1000 and increments by 1 for every RID it allocates to the domain controllers.

Due to the fact that any domain controller within a native mode domain can generate a RID to an account, you must make sure that only one domain controller is allocating and controlling the RIDs. For this reason, make sure that you do not seize the RID role on a domain controller when the original role holder is just temporarily unavailable. You could cause yourself a nightmare trying to troubleshoot permission problems.

This is a role that you might miss sooner than some of the others. The RID Master allocates blocks of RIDs to the domain controllers within the domain. If a domain controller uses up its last RID while creating a security principal, it will no longer be able to create security principals. Another drawback to losing the RID Master is you cannot promote another domain controller without the RID Master online. For these reasons, you should attempt to recover the original RID Master role holder as quickly as possible or seize the role on the standby server.

Primary Domain Controller Emulator

The PDC emulator is probably the busiest of the master operations, and yet it is the only one that is not known by the name "master." This is also the role that confuses new administrators, because they think that this role is needed only until all of the NT 4 BDCs are taken offline. This is far from the truth. Microsoft should consider changing the name of this master operation to reflect the other functions it provides.

First off, the PDC emulator allows for replication of directory information to Windows NT 4 BDCs while the domain is still in mixed mode. This is also the only domain controller that will create security principals while the domain is in mixed mode, due to the fact that is has to act like a Windows NT 4 PDC. You should make sure that you place this role holder in a location that will create the most accounts.

This is also the only domain controller that is allowed to change passwords for legacy operating systems, such as Windows 98 and Windows NT. They will look for the PDC of the domain, and the PDC emulator fulfills that roll. Another password function that this role holder provides is that it has the final say whenever there is a password change. Whenever an account's password is changed, the PDC emulator is notified immediately. After a user types in their password for authentication, the domain controller that is attempting to authenticate the user will check with the PDC emulator to make sure the user's password has not been changed before notifying the user that they typed the wrong password.

Two other functions, time synchronization and global policy centralization, are functions of the PDC emulator. All of the other domain controllers within the domain will look to this role holder as the official timekeeper within the domain. You should set the PDC emulator to synchronize with an external time source so that all of the other domain controllers will have the correct time. This is also the domain controller that is used as the default location for changing group policies. Making one domain controller the default GPO holder allows you to control policy changes and minimize conflicting changes within the domain.

NOTE   In a multiple-domain forest, the PDC emulator for the forest root becomes the Time Master for all PDCs within the forest.

Due to the amount of responsibilities that the PDC emulator has, it will probably be the master operation that you will miss the most if it fails. When it fails, you should immediately assess how long it is going to take to recover the domain controller holding this role. If it looks like the domain controller is going to be offline for an extended period of time—let's say more than a couple of hours—you should seize the role on the standby server. Although the other roles may cause problems for administrators, users will be affected by a loss of the PDC emulator, and they will let you know that they see something wrong!

Transferring and Seizing FSMO Roles

Transferring a FSMO role to another system is a rather painless process. Because all of the domain controllers within a domain have identical data within the Active Directory database, when you transfer a FSMO role, you are simply changing a flag that specifies that one domain controller can control the master operation and the other cannot.

Seizing a FSMO role has serious implications. If you are going to take this drastic step, you must commit yourself and make sure that the original role holder is never reintroduced onto the network. Doing so could cause serious problems within your Active Directory infrastructure.

In the following sections, you will find the methods you can use to identify the systems that currently hold the Master Operations roles and the methods you can use to make sure the domain controller that is identified as the standby server can take over the role.

Identifying the Current Role Holder

There are several ways that you can identify which domain controller is holding a FSMO role. With some of these options, you will be able to see all of the role holders at one time; with others, you are forced to view them separately.

BUILT-IN ACTIVE DIRECTORY TOOLS

You can view the roles for four of the five roles by using the Active Directory Users and Computers (ADU&C) and Active Directory Domains and Trusts (ADD&T) snap-ins. Using ADU&C, you can identify the PDC emulator, RID Master, and Infrastructure Master role holders. ADD&T will allow you to identify the Domain Naming Master. In order to get to the screen shown in Figure 15.9, you need to open ADU&C and right-click on the domain name and select Operations Masters.

Figure 15.10 shows the Domain Naming Master when you choose the Operations Masters option from the context menu that is available when you right-click the Active Directory Domains and Trusts label within the ADD&T snap-in.

FIGURE 15.9

FSMO roles listing in Active Directory Users and Computers

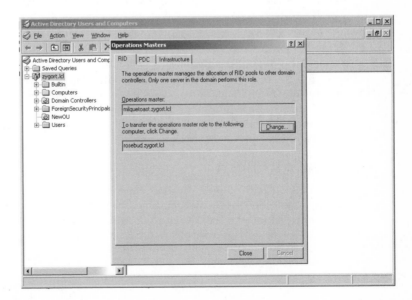

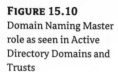

FIGURE 15.10
Domain Naming Master
role as seen in Active
Directory Domains and
Trusts

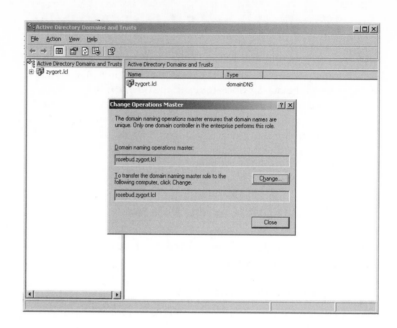

ACTIVE DIRECTORY SCHEMA

The Active Directory Schema snap-in is listed separately because it is not available by default. In order to access this snap-in, you must register its associated DLL. To do so, type **regsvr32 schmmgmt.dll** at the run line or a command prompt. After you receive a message stating that the DLL is registered, you can add the snap-in to an MMC. You can view the Schema Master role holder, as shown in Figure 15.11, by right-clicking the Active Directory Schema container within the MMC and selecting Operations Master.

REPLMON

This tool was discussed in Chapter 13, "Microsoft's Troubleshooting Methodology for Active Directory." In addition to the benefits that we introduced in that chapter, Rep1Mon has the ability to view the role holders within the domain. When you add a monitored server to the console, you can view its properties by right-clicking on the server and choosing Properties. As shown in Figure 15.12, you can view all five of the role holders from the FSMO Roles tab. Note the naming convention for the RID Master and Domain Naming Master.

COMMAND-LINE OPTIONS

Some command-line utilities will allow you to identify the role holders. The first, netdom, will show you all of the role holders at the same time. The second, dsquery, will allow you find individual roles when you ask for them. The DCDiag utility will show you all of the roles. The final utility is from the Resource Kit, dumpfsmos.cmd.

netdom

The netdom command syntax that will report the role holders is as follows:

```
netdom query fsmo /domain:zygort.lcl
```

Of course, you would replace *zygort.lcl* with your domain name. This will return a list of all of the role holders.

FIGURE 15.11
Schema Master role as seen in Active Directory Schema snap-in

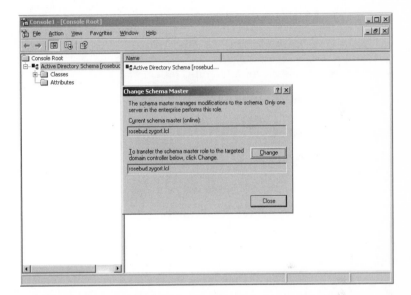

FIGURE 15.12
Identifying the roles using Replication Monitor

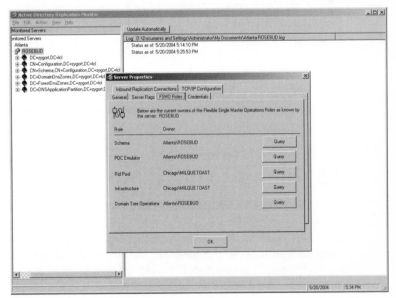

dsquery

In order to find individual role holders with the dsquery command, you would use the following commands:

- ◆ To find the Schema Master:

  ```
  dsquery server -hasfsmo schema
  ```

- ◆ To find the Domain Naming Master:

  ```
  dsquery server -hasfsmo name
  ```

- ◆ To find the Infrastructure Master:

  ```
  dsquery server -hasfsmo infr
  ```

- ◆ To find the RID Master:

  ```
  dsquery server -hasfsmo rid
  ```

- ◆ To find the PDC emulator:

  ```
  dsquery server -hasfsmo pdc
  ```

DCDiag

The DCDiag utility is used as

```
dcdiag /test:knowsofroleholders /v
```

Because the verbose switch (/v) is used, this command will return the role holders and give you information on each.

dumpfsmos.cmd

The dumpfsmos.cmd utility from the resource kit is a small script that actually starts NTDSUTIL and issues the appropriate commands to return a list of the role holders. The syntax for this command is

```
dumpfsmos.cmd zygort.lcl
```

Of course, you would want to replace *zygort.lcl* with the name of the domain you are querying against.

Transferring the Role to Another Domain Controller

If you are demoting a role holder, you should make sure that you transfer the role to another domain controller, preferably the domain controller you have designated as the standby role holder. Doing so will guarantee that you are transferring the role to the appropriate domain controller instead of allowing Dcpromo to choose another domain controller on its own. Remember, it is always better to have control over these things than to allow random chance to control your organization.

NOTE If you are permanently taking a domain controller offline, whether it is a role holder or not, you should demote it so that the references to the domain controller are removed from Active Directory.

Transferring the role to another domain controller is a very simple process. Using the snap-ins that we discussed in the "Identifying the Current Role Holder" section, you can simply connect to the domain controller that you want to be the new role holder, choose the Operations Master option to view the role holder, and click Change. Look back at Figure 15.9 and note that the snap-in is currently connected to the domain controller rosebud.zygort.lcl. The RID Master role is currently held by milquetoast.zygort.lcl. When you click the Change button, the role will be transferred to milquetoast.zygort.lcl.

You can also use NTDSUTIL to transfer the roles. To do so, you need to start a command prompt and enter the ntdsutil command. Once the ntdsutil: prompt appears, enter the following commands:

1. At the ntdsutil: prompt, type **roles** to enter fsmo maintenance.

2. At the fsmo maintenance: prompt, type **connections** to enter server connections.

3. At the server connections: prompt, type **connect to** *server domain_controller*, where *domain_controller* is the name of the domain controller to which you are going to transfer the role.

4. At the server connections: prompt, type **quit** to enter fsmo maintenance.

5. At the fsmo maintenance: prompt, type one of the following to transfer the appropriate role:

   ◆ To transfer the Schema Master:

      transfer schema master

   ◆ To transfer the Domain Naming Master:

      transfer domain naming master

   ◆ To transfer the Infrastructure Master:

      transfer infrastructure master

   ◆ To transfer the RID Master:

      transfer rid master

   ◆ To transfer the PDC emulator:

      transfer PDC

After you have transferred the role, type **quit** twice to exit NTDSUTIL. You can then use one of the aforementioned utilities to verify that the role was transferred to the appropriate domain controller.

Seizing the Role on the Standby Domain Controller

You should have already designated another domain controller as the standby server in case a role holder becomes unavailable. If you have configured the original role holder and the standby as replication partners, there is a very good chance that they are completely synchronized with one another. If the original role holder becomes unavailable and you deem it necessary to have the standby server become the role holder, you can seize the role on the standby server. Again, this is a drastic measure and should be performed only if you are certain the original role holder is not going to be reintroduced on the network.

In order to seize a role, you need to follow steps 1 through 4 as outlined in the previous section, "Transferring the Role to Another Domain Controller." Once you have connected to the domain controller that will become the role holder, use one of the following commands from the NTDSUTIL `fsmo maintenance:` prompt:

◆ To seize the Schema Master:

```
seize schema master
```

◆ To seize the Domain Naming Master:

```
seize domain naming master
```

◆ To seize the Infrastructure Master:

```
seize infrastructure master
```

◆ To seize the RID Master:

```
seize rid master
```

◆ To seize the PDC emulator:

```
seize PDC
```

Now that the role has been seized, type **quit** twice to exit NTDSUTIL. Verify that the role has been taken over by the new role holder. If the original system is repaired and could be used again, make sure you reformat the system and reinstall the operating system. This will guarantee that you will not introduce problems within your Active Directory from having a rogue role holder in place.

NOTE   The PDC emulator and Infrastructure roles are designed for "graceful seizure." This means that the old role holders can be brought back online after a seizure with no ill effects.

NOTE   If a domain controller does go offline and you are not going to reintroduce it to the network, make sure you remove all references to the domain controller within Active Directory. See Chapter 12, "Maintaining the Active Directory Database," for information on removing orphaned objects.

Best Practices for Troubleshooting FSMO Roles

Just a few pointers here, but they are good tips to remember:

◆ Do not seize a role unless you are absolutely positive that you will never reintroduce the original role holder to the network.

◆ If demoting a role holder, transfer the role to another domain controller first.

◆ Keep documentation that identifies the role holders and the domain controllers that are designated as the standby servers.

Troubleshooting Logon Failures

Nothing is more frustrating for users than to attempt to log on first thing on a Monday morning, only to receive an error. Immediately their workweek is off to a bad start, and they are on their way to having a bad day. Troubleshooting is your realm, so it's up to you to determine what is causing the problem and set things back on track. Within an Active Directory domain, several things could be at fault.

If you are using a Windows Server 2003–based domain, the default password policy uses complex passwords. Although this is a good policy to use from the standpoint of most of your security auditors, you will find that it can cause additional headaches. Complex passwords, while more secure, are also more difficult for users to remember. You will probably end up unlocking users' accounts and changing their passwords for them more often than you would with simpler passwords. You will also run into the problem of users writing their passwords down and leaving them close to their systems where they are readily available. Controlling passwords, monitoring authentication, and maintaining a sensible password and lockout policy will help you minimize logon problems, but you will still be forced into troubleshooting these issues.

Auditing for Logon Problems

As with any troubleshooting, you should start with checking out the event logs on the client system and the domain controllers within their site. Although many administrators criticize the event logs, you can find out some interesting and useful information from them. If you have enabled auditing of account logon and logon events, you will receive events in the security log that pertain to accounts as they authenticate, or fail to authenticate. In order to watch for failures, you will need to start auditing the failure of authentication within an audit policy. Once you do, you can peruse the audit log for specific entries if users start having difficulty authenticating.

Figure 15.13 shows an example of a GPO that is being used to implement auditing for the domain. When you choose the options to audit and you want to see information concerning authentication, you should set the options shown in Table 15.1.

Setting Failure for Account Logon will tell the system to send an event to the security log any time a domain user account fails to authenticate. Doing the same thing for Logon will audit a local account authentication failure. Successful changes to any account, whether it is a password reset or the unlocking of an account, will be registered by the Audit Account Management setting.

Once these settings are enacted, you will be able to view the security logs for common events. On domain controllers, you can look for information concerning account lockouts and changes to the accounts. Event ID 675 will show you the IP address of a client computer from where the bad password originated. If this IP address is not the computer from which the client normally authenticates, it may be an indication of an attack on the account. Event ID 644 will appear if the Audit Account Management auditing option is set for Successful. This event is generated any time an account is locked out due to improper credentials.

You can also view the security logs on client systems and search for common Event IDs. Event 529 is recorded if the system does not have the user account that is attempting to log on. This could be due to the user accidentally pressing the wrong keys when they are logging on, but it could also be an indication of someone trying to hack into a system by guessing an account name. Event ID 531 indicates that the account that was attempting to authenticate is locked out, or has been disabled by an administrator.

TABLE 15.1:   Audit Settings for Monitoring Domain Logon Problems

AUDIT OPTION	SETTING
Account Logon	Failure
Account Management	Success
Logon	Failure

FIGURE 15.13
Audit Policy in GPO

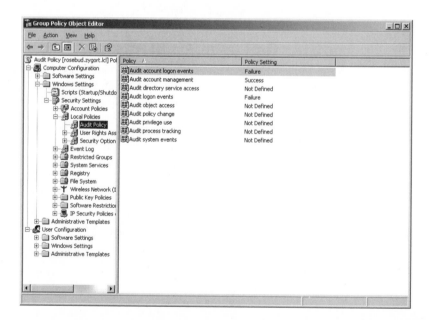

Table 15.2 is a list of the Event IDs that you will encounter as you troubleshoot logon failures and account lockouts.

TABLE 15.2:   Logon Event IDs

EVENT ID	DESCRIPTION
528	Successful interactive logon.
529	Failed logon. Due to either unknown account or bad password.
530	Failed logon. Time restrictions prohibited authentication.
531	Failed logon. Account disabled.
532	Failed logon. Expired account.
533	Failed logon. Computer restrictions do not allow logging on to the chosen computer.
534	Failed logon. Disallowed logon type.
535	Failed logon. Expired password.
536	Failed logon. NetLogon is not available to accept authentication request.
537	Failed logon. The logon attempt failed for other reasons. The reason for the logon failure may not be known.
538	The logoff process was not completed.
539	Failed logon. Account locked out.
540	Successful network logon.
541	The local computer and its partner completed the main mode Internet Key Exchange (IKE) authentication or quick mode has established a data channel.
542	Data channel terminated.
543	Main mode was terminated.
544	Main mode authentication failed due to invalid certificate or the signature was not validated.
545	Main mode authentication failed due to Kerberos failure or invalid password.
546	IKE security association establishment failed due to invalid proposal.
547	IKE handshake failure.
548	Failed logon. The security identifier (SID) from a trusted domain does not match the client's account domain SID.

TABLE 15.2:   Logon Event IDs *(CONTINUED)*

EVENT ID	DESCRIPTION
549	Failed logon. `SIDFiltering` filtered out all SIDs that correspond to untrusted namespaces during an authentication across forests.
550	A denial-of-service (DoS) attack may have occurred.
551	User logged off.
552	A user successfully logged on to a computer using explicit credentials while currently logged on as a different user.
672	Kerberos successfully issued and validated an authentication service (AS) ticket.
673	Kerberos successfully granted a ticket-granting service (TGS) ticket.
674	An AS ticket or TGS ticket was renewed.
675	Preauthentication failed. The KDC generates this event if an incorrect password is entered.
676	Authentication ticket request failed. This event is not generated in Windows XP or in the Windows Server 2003 family.
677	A TGS ticket was not granted. This event is not generated in Windows XP or in the Windows Server 2003 family.
678	An account was successfully mapped to a domain account.
681	Failed logon. A domain account logon was attempted. This event is not generated in Windows XP or in the Windows Server 2003 family.
682	A user has reconnected to a disconnected terminal server session.
683	A user disconnected a terminal server session without logging off.

Figure 15.14 shows an example of an event that was generated as a user attempted to log on to a system. Take note of the data within the event, especially the Logon Type entry. You can determine the kind of logon attempt that was attempted. Table 15.3 describes the logon types and the code that is entered into events.

Acctinfo.dll

The `acctinfo.dll` file is actually part of the Account Lockout and Management Tools that you can download from Microsoft, which we discuss later in the "Account Lockout Problems" section. Once added into your system, `acctinfo.dll` includes an additional property page with the user account properties. As shown in Figure 15.15, this additional property page will allow you to determine when the account's password was set, when the password expires, when the user last logged on or off the domain, as well as other lockout information.

TABLE 15.3: Logon Type Codes

TYPE	REASON RECORDED	CODE
Interactive Logon	User logged on directly on a computer.	2
Network Logon	User connected to the computer from a remote computer.	3
Batch	Account was authenticated when used from a batch queue.	4
Service	Account used by a service when the service was started by a service controller.	5
Unlock	Credentials entered in order to unlock a locked account.	7
NetworkClearText	Account was authenticated with a cleartext password.	8
NewCredentials	Account connected to the system after password was changed.	9
RemoteInteractive	Account authenticated from a remote system, but the account is used interactively through a terminal services session.	10
CachedInteractive	The user was logged onto the computer using cached credentials.	11

FIGURE 15.14
Logon event

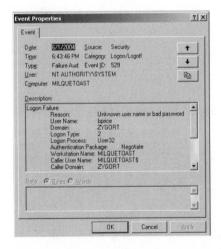

One of the best features of `acctinfo.dll` is that it allows you to change a user's password on a domain controller within the site where the account is used. This allows you to make the change on a domain controller close to the user so that you do not have to wait until replication passes the password change across the site links. Figure 15.16 shows the screen that appears once you have clicked the Set Password On Site DC button. You'll still have the option to reset the password normally, but you will also have the additional site-level options.

FIGURE 15.15
`Acctinfo.dll`
property page

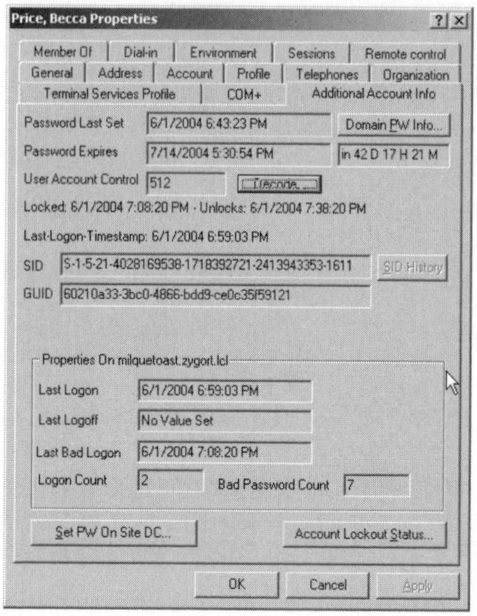

FIGURE 15.16
Set Password On
Site DC

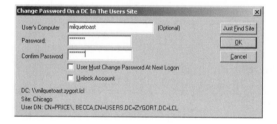

Kerberos Logging

You can have the system present more detailed information concerning authentication by turning on Kerberos logging. To do so, you can either edit the Registry manually or run a script provided within the Account Lockout and Management Tools (see the "Account Lockout Problems" section for more information). If you plan to edit the Registry on a domain controller in order to enable Kerberos logging, you will need to open `regedt32` and navigate to the following Registry key:

`HKLM\System\CurrentControlSet\Control\LSA\Kerberos\Parameters`

You will need to add the `REG_DWORD` entry `LogLevel`. If you set the value of this entry to 1, you will be able to monitor the system event log for Event ID 4. If Event ID 4 appears in the log, it will indicate that a bad password was sent to the Kerberos service for authentication or the account was locked out. If the error code within this event specifies `0x18 KDC_ERR_PREAUTH_FAILED`, the password was incorrect. An error code of `0x12 KDC_ERR_CLIENT_REVOKED` indicates that the account was locked out.

Native Mode Logon Problems

Once you have switched your domain out of Windows 2000 mixed mode, you will be required to have global catalog servers available. Windows 2000 native and Windows Server 2003 functional levels require that a global catalog server be available so that a user's universal group membership is checked prior to authentication. Universal security groups do not exist within a Windows 2000 mixed mode domain. However, once you have changed your domain to support them, each user's universal group membership is checked to make sure that the user is not a member of a universal group that has been denied permission to a resource.

Problems occur when you have replication issues between domain controllers and the universal group membership is not replicated to the local global catalog. A user who is a member of a universal group could be denied access to a resource since the replicated information has not arrived at the domain controller to which the user is authenticating. The same is true about having access to resources to which the user should be explicitly denied access. If the global catalog has not received the new group membership, the user could access resources that you want to prevent them from accessing.

As important as it is to know which resources the user should be able to access, the requirement of having a global catalog server online can cause logon issues for some administrators. Take, for instance, an organization that has remote offices and due to bandwidth restrictions the administrative staff has decided not to use any of their domain controllers as global catalogs within those offices. Global catalog queries are sent to a nearby site that has a global catalog. However, if the users attempt to log on and they cannot contact a global catalog in the nearby site, whether due to down WAN links or unavailable global catalog servers, those users will not be able to log on to the domain.

Windows Server 2003 has addressed this limitation with a feature known as Universal Group Membership Caching. You enable this feature on a per-site basis and any Windows Server 2003–based domain controller will start using it. As users authenticate, the domain controller servicing the request will query a global catalog server within another site for the user's universal group membership and then cache the details.

WARNING   Global catalog caching will support a maximum of 500 users per site. Also, the cache is only updated once every 8 hours. You should not consider using this option if you have frequent group updates or many users.

If your domain does not have any Windows Server 2003–based domain controllers, you will have to either configure a domain controller within the office as a global catalog server or turn off the universal group membership requirement. The latter is not a recommended solution, however, because the user could be allowed to access resources that they should not have permission to use. The inverse could also occur; the user could be denied access to resources that they need to use. If you want to turn off group membership checking when global catalog servers are unavailable, you can navigate to the following Registry entry:

```
HKEY_LOCAL_MACHINE\SYSTEM\CurrentControlSet\Services\NTDS\Parameters
```

From there, you will need to add a new key by the name of `IgnoreGCFailures`. This will tell the domain controller to authenticate a user even though the universal group membership is not evaluated for the user's access token. Again, let me stress that this is not a secure way to run your organization. However, if you are not using universal groups, or you are desperately seeking a way to allow your remote users to authenticate when WAN link failures occur, you can implement this fix.

Account Lockout Problems

Having the ability to lock out accounts when they are being attacked can be a great security feature, but at the same time, you may find that this policy can cause you some definite headaches. If the settings are too restrictive, users will lock themselves out by mistyping their passwords. If they are not restrictive enough, you potentially open up a security hole that will allow accounts to be attacked. Another potential problem occurs if you have the settings too restrictive and you do not reset the bad password count when the user authenticates; their account could become locked out due to scripts that map drives because the scripts have the wrong password associated with them. The most common causes of account lockouts are discussed here:

Programs   Several programs store a user's credentials so that the program can access resources that it requires. If the user changes their password but the program still has the credentials cached, the user's account could become locked out by the program trying to authenticate.

Reset Account Lockout Counter After Setting   You should consider keeping this setting at the default level of 30 minutes or higher. If this setting is too low, you could cause a false lockout as programs attempt to access resources. Cached credentials, or mapped drives that attempt to connect with invalid credentials, could also cause lockouts if this setting is too low.

Persistent Drive Mappings   If a user has a persistent drive mapping, and that mapping has an incorrect or old password, the account that is associated with the mapped drive could become locked out as the user attempts to access it.

Outlook and Outlook Web Access   If you are using e-mail clients to access mail stored on an Exchange server, and the client has cached the password for the account, the multiple attempts that are made to access the user's mail could result in a locked-out account.

Disconnected Terminal Server Sessions   Terminal server sessions that a user has disconnected from will remain running on the server. If the user changes their password while the session is running, the session still uses the original password. If applications running within the session attempt to access resources, they could cause the account to become locked out.

Microsoft has addressed these issues with Windows 2000 SP4 and Windows Server 2003. Domain controllers are instructed to deny the last two passwords that a user has used; if these two passwords happen to be used, they will not increment the bad password count. Most of the common account lockout problems can be resolved by installing the latest service pack from Microsoft.

If you still have issues with locked-out accounts, Microsoft has released a set of tools that you can use when troubleshooting account lockout problems. These tools are collectively known as the Account Lockout and Management Tools. You can download them from the Microsoft website at the following location:

```
http://www.microsoft.com/downloads/details.aspx?FamilyId=7AF2E69C-91F3-4E63-8629-
B999ADDE0B9E&displaylang=en
```

LockoutStatus.exe   As shown in Figure 15.17, `LockoutStatus.exe` will display information concerning a locked-out account. Use this tool to determine which computers were involved in the lockout by the account and when the lockout occurred. You need to copy this tool to the same directory as `acctinfo.dll` if you want to have access to it from the user account properties. This tool is also available from the Windows Server 2003 Resource Kit.

FIGURE 15.17
LockoutStatus.exe
showing information
about a user account

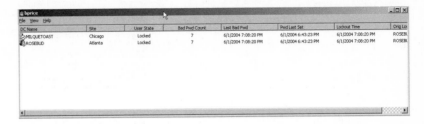

FIGURE 15.17
LockoutStatus.exe
showing information
about a user account

Alockout.dll   This tool, when configured on a system, will monitor the account authentication attempts and deliver the results to a file named Alockout.txt that is stored in the winnt\debug directory. In order to use this tool, you will need to copy the alockout.dll and appinit.reg files that are included in the Account Lockout and Management Tools toolset to the systemroot\ system32 folder. Once they are copied, double-click on the appinit.reg file to embed the Registry entries into the local Registry of the computer and reboot the system to activate the changes.

Aloinfo.exe   If you want to view all of the accounts and the associated password age, you can run this command at the command line. This will allow you to view the accounts that are about to have their passwords expire so that you can anticipate the flood of calls that will occur right after the new passwords go into effect.

Acctinfo.dll   As mentioned previously, acctinfo.dll will add another property page to the user's account properties within Active Directory. Figure 15.18 shows the password policy screen that appears when you click the Domain Password Policy button from the Additional Account Info property page shown in Figure 15.19. To install acctinfo.dll, you will need to type **regsvr32 acctinfo.dll** at a command prompt or from the run line. You will need to close and reopen Active Directory Users and Computers for the change to take effect. You should also have lockoutstatus.exe loaded for the full benefits of this new property page.

EventCombMT   This tool will search through the event logs on several systems looking for events that you have specified. The default events that the tool will search for are 529, 644, 675, 676, and 681. You can add additional Event IDs if you know which events you want to search. You can also control how many threads are used during the search so that you do not consume too many resources within the domain. The fewer threads you specify, the longer the search will take.

EnableKerbLog.vbs   This is a script that changes the Registry in order to enable Kerberos logging. Once it has been run, additional events are sent to the event log so that you can monitor what the Kerberos service is doing during account authentication.

NLParse   NLParse is used to find NetLogon status codes that have been dumped to the netlogon.log file when NetLogon logging has been enabled. It will dump the data that it finds into a comma-separated value file that you can pull into a spreadsheet or database. Several codes can be searched on, but 0X0000006A and 0x0000234 are the default options.

FIGURE 15.18
Domain Password Policy

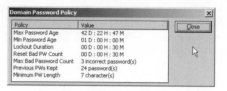

FIGURE 15.19
Property page added by
`acctinfo.dll`

Any time you are troubleshooting logon and account lockout problems, you should start by enabling `NetLogon` logging and then view the logs in an attempt to determine which domain controllers may be involved. `NetLogon` logging has been available since Windows NT 4, and it was used to check the PDC within the domain. You can still use this tool in order to view the interaction between the domain controllers and the PDC emulator. To enable `NetLogon` logging, you will need to open a command prompt and enter the command **nltest /dbflag:0x2080ffff**. This will create a log file within the *systemroot\Debug* directory called `netlogon.log`.

TIP After running the `nltest` command to enable NetLogon logging, if the `netlogon.log` file does not exist, stop and restart the `NetLogon` service.

When you view the `netlogon.log` file on the PDC emulator, you can look for instances of event 0xC000006A for authentication requests that have been passed to the PDC emulator from other domain controllers. You can differentiate between authentication requests that are sent directly to the PDC emulator and those that are passed to it from other domain controllers by the reference within the entries that show transitive network logons and the domain controller that passed the request. Looking at the log file, any line that shows the entry "via" displays the computer where the user was attempting the logon and the domain controller that they were authenticating against. If the password is not valid on the domain controller, the user's credentials are sent to the PDC emulator to verify that the user's password has not been changed recently, but the password has not been replicated to the domain controller yet.

TIP   Due to the additional overhead that is consumed when you are logging the NetLogon service, you should turn off the logging when you have finished troubleshooting. To do so, run the command **nltest /dbflag:0x0**.

Because the netlogon.log files can be up to 10MB in size, you may want to use the NLParse utility to ease your searching woes. With NLParse, you can select the codes that you want to search for and have the utility load the results into a comma-separated value (.csv) so that you can view the results in a spreadsheet. Even though you have several options to choose from, you should start by taking the default options of searching for status codes 0xC000006A and 0xC0000234. These two codes will give you the authentication attempts and the domain controller that locked out the account. Using the resulting CSV file will help you determine whether the lockout was due to a program or service, because they would send several attempts within a matter of a second or two. If the attempts came from a user account, there would be a few seconds in between each attempt. Table 15.4 details the status codes that you will find in a netlogon.log file and that you can search for with NLParse.

TABLE 15.4:   NLParse Status Codes

STATUS CODE	DESCRIPTION
0x0	Successful logon.
0xC0000064	User does not exist.
0xC000006A	Incorrect password.
0xC000006C	Password policy not met.
0xC000006D	Bad username.
0xC000006E	User account restriction prevented successful logon.
0xC000006F	Time restrictions prevented user from logging on.
0xC0000070	Workstation restrictions prevented user from logging on.
0xC0000071	Password has expired.
0xC0000072	The user account is currently disabled.
0xC000009A	Insufficient system resources.
0xC0000193	User's account has expired.
0xC0000224	User must change password before the first logon.
0xC0000234	The user account has been locked.

Remote Access Issues

If you are using Routing and Remote Access Service (RRAS) as a remote access server, you will need to make sure that the remote access policies are configured correctly. Several layers of control are associated with these policies, and a user could be stopped from authenticating even before they connect to the network.

Remote access policies are not stored within Active Directory; they are configured on a per-server basis. With this in mind, you should make sure that all of the RRAS servers to which a user will connect have the same policy parameters. Otherwise, the user's connection attempts could be erratic.

The only way to guarantee that the RRAS servers are using the same policy is to configure an Internet Authentication Service (IAS) server with a policy and make each RRAS server a client of the IAS server. This still does not store a copy of the policy within Active Directory, but you do have a central repository for the remote access policies.

Are You Being Attacked?

Account lockout policies are not simply for administrators to test the patience of their users; they are used to protect an organization's resources against attack. Companies that are very paranoid, or that have very sensitive data, can set the lockout count to between 3 and 5, but most of the companies that I have talked with or worked with have a policy setting that falls between 5 and 7. This should be sufficient when your users mistype their passwords, and at the same time, it should protect the network.

If you are not sure whether you are under attack or if you have a user problem, look through the NetLogon log files on your domain controllers to determine the extent of the problem. Your PDC emulator will be a central location for the events to be recorded. Any time a bad password is entered, the PDC emulator is checked to validate the attempt. If you see several accounts with bad passwords, and there are 15 to 20 attempts on each account, chances are that an attack is occurring, either internal from a virus or Trojan program, or from an external source attempting to hack an account.

Check the computer that appears in the status code to determine if a rogue program is attempting to authenticate. If the computer that is listed within the status code is a remote access server, an external account could be attempting to attack the network.

Controlling WAN Communication

Typically, a user will log on within the same site a majority of the time. At the same time, when a user changes a password, they do not have to worry about logging on to another system within another site prior to their password change replicating to other domain controllers throughout the organization. If your users typically log on to the same site, you could reduce the replication traffic that is sent between remote sites and the site where the PDC emulator is located.

To do so you need to add the AvoidPdcOnWan value under the HKEY_LOCAL_MACHINE\System\ CurrentControlSet\Services\Netlogon\Parameters Registry key. If you set the value to 1, the domain controller will ignore sending password updates as a critical update when the PDC emulator is located in another site. A setting of 0 restores normal operation.

When you turn this value on, the PDC emulator receives the password change during the normal replication cycle. Note that if the user does travel to another site prior to the replication of the password change, they may be denied access to the network if they use the new password.

Best Practices for Logon and Account Lockout Troubleshooting

Nothing frustrates administrators and users alike more than logon issues. The calls that erupt right after a mandatory password change can be frustrating, but if you follow the information in this chapter, and especially these tips, you may be able to reduce some of your headaches.

◆ Only enable Universal Group Membership Caching if you want to reduce the replication across a WAN link and you have a small number of users who will be affected.

◆ Only turn off Universal Group Membership Enumeration for a native mode domain unless you are not using universal security groups.

◆ Turn on auditing for account logon and account management so that you can identify logon failures and can determine the causes.

◆ Take advantage of the new Account Lockout and Management Tools to aid in troubleshooting account lockout.

◆ Monitor the PDC emulator for authentication attempts. All attempts with a bad password are forwarded to the PDC emulator.

◆ Turn off logging when it is not necessary so that it does not consume additional resources.

Coming Up Next

In the next chapter, we will discuss resources you can use to help in your troubleshooting efforts. There are many tools you can use to help troubleshoot Active Directory, such as Microsoft Operations Manager.

Chapter 16

Troubleshooting Active Directory with Microsoft Operations Manager

Whenever you have servers and workstations in your organization, you have a need for monitoring those systems. Monitoring systems can be as simple as logging into the system and checking out the log files in Event Viewer, or as complex as gathering up all the log and system performance data on a group of systems to determine how they are running as individual machines as well as together to serve a business function.

For smaller environments, you may be able to get by with a simple solution that has you checking the event logs and looking at the performance data from time to time. Usually in this type of environment you can get by with comparing the data that has just been collected with a small journal or database of historical information. If your environment does not have very many servers, you could get by with keeping tabs on your systems in this manner. The challenge with this solution is making sure you are monitoring your systems regularly, as well identifying the telltale signs of possible problems.

The larger your organization grows, the harder it becomes to monitor all of the systems within it. Some companies select administrators to watch over certain systems, dividing up the monitoring workload. While this method does allow you to identify the administrative personnel who are responsible for specific aspects of your organization, it still leaves some gaps in your monitoring solution. As events are generated and performance data is collected, you will be able to easily identify what goes on with each system, but you will not have a quick and easy method of identifying distributed issues, such as an attack across many systems. That is where Microsoft Operations Manager 2005 comes in.

About Microsoft Operations Manager

In the last part of this book we introduce some scripting solutions that will assist you in monitoring your systems, but they only go so far and are intended as part of a total monitoring solution. If you want to have a monitoring solution that will automate some of the monitoring and also track data that is distributed among several systems, you will want to take a look at a product like Microsoft Operations Manager (MOM). MOM 2000 was introduced and adopted by several companies, but was somewhat limited in the amount of monitoring and automated management it could perform. Microsoft learned from this initial management solution and added functionality to MOM 2005.

MOM 2005 will not only allow you to monitor the systems in your organization, but it can also perform some automated management of the systems. This chapter isn't meant to act as a comprehensive guide to MOM 2005; instead, it introduces you to the product so that you can see the benefits it can bring to your organization. Other books dedicated to this product are forthcoming. In this section we look at some of the features of MOM 2005 and show you how they can be used to automate some of your system management. In the section that follows we take a look at the Active Directory add-in for MOM 2005, known as the Active Directory management pack.

Microsoft Operations Manager 2005 Features

MOM 2005 is positioned in the Microsoft systems solutions as a monitoring and management tool. MOM 2005 has the ability to parse log files and performance data to determine how well the systems are functioning. Also built into MOM is the ability to automate responses to events. This give you the power to have an action taken as soon as an event takes place or when a system falls out of the normal operating parameters that you have set.

Having an automated monitoring and management solution in your environment will help you become very proactive instead of reactive as issues arise. Most of us are in a continual state of putting out fires instead of looking at performance and event information to try to discern if problems are creeping into the day-to-day operations. MOM 2005 will watch for all the problem indicators and perform actions, whether it is simply notifying an administrator of the problem, or running scripts against the systems that are having problems.

Once you have installed MOM 2005, you will find that there are three separate consoles you can use to work with MOM 2005: the Administrator Console, the Operator Console, and the Web Console. Instead of providing a single console from which you can perform all the tasks associated with MOM 2005, Microsoft decided to deliver separate consoles based on the tasks that are normally performed. The Administrator Console is used to configure the MOM 2005 monitoring solution. The Operator Console is responsible for granting users a view of the events, alerts, and overall health of the monitored infrastructure, and allows them to respond to events and perform some troubleshooting. The Web Console gives administrators the ability to view the same information that is available through the Operator Console, but accessible through a web-based interface. The Web Console does not have as much functionality as the Operator Console does, but it lets administrators see what is happening with their systems while connecting through standard web ports on the firewall. One other console exists, the Reporting Console, which is used to view data collected by MOM 2005 and to allow reports to be easily generated for historical trend analysis or SLA information.

ADMINISTRATOR CONSOLE

If you open the Administrator Console by going to Start ➤ All Programs ➤ Microsoft Operations Manager 2005 ➤ Administrator Console, it appears much the same as any Microsoft supplied snap-in. The containers pane appears on the left, and the details pane appears on the right of the snap-in. As you can see in Figure 16.1, the four top-level containers include Information Center, Operations, Management Packs, and Administration. Of these four, you will probably find yourself working with the latter two containers more than the first two.

Information Center

The Information Center container is simply a page with links to documentation and help files that will aid you in deploying and managing your MOM 2005 infrastructure. Microsoft has done a commendable job presenting information and documenting this product. Many of the links that are present from this container, shown in Figure 16.2, will take you to the Microsoft website. Doing so makes it easy for Microsoft to update the MOM 2005 information, but it also means that the system from which you run the Administrator Console needs to have Internet access. Luckily, you can load the Administrator Console on your Windows XP workstation instead of configuring the MOM 2005 server to have access to the Internet.

FIGURE 16.1
Administrator Console

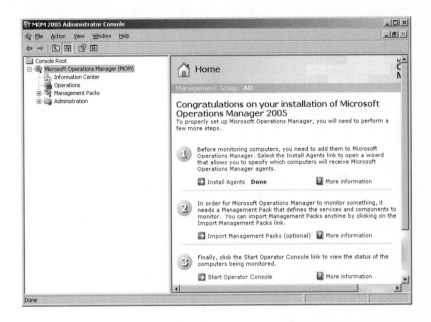

FIGURE 16.2
Information Center container in the Administrator Console

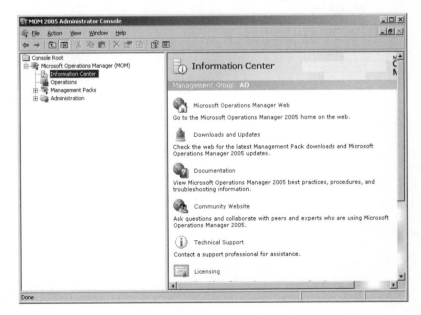

Operations

The Operations container is another page that has links, but these links start the operator-level consoles, as shown in Figure 16.3. Both the Operator Console and the Web Console, discussed later in this section, can be launched from this page, as well as the Reporting Console. This gives the MOM administrator the ability to launch any of these consoles from within the Administrator Console instead of having to leave the console and launch them from another location.

Management Packs

When you install MOM 2005, the initial install does not include the ability to monitor every server type that Microsoft has available. Microsoft made the decision not to include the ability to monitor all the server types so that they would not overburden the MOM 2005 server. Instead, MOM 2005 comes "bare bones," meaning they do not have the ability to monitor many services right out of the box. You are responsible for adding the functionality to the MOM 2005 server. In order to do so, you will need to add management packs.

Management packs consist of collections of settings that define how the MOM 2005 server should respond when a specific event occurs. Management packs exist for nearly all the Microsoft products on the market, and several third parties have created their own so that their products can also be monitored using MOM 2005.

If you take a look at the Management Packs node shown in Figure 16.4, you can see that there are several sublevels beneath it. These nodes are used as follows:

Computer Groups Computer groups allow you to organize your systems according to the services and applications that are running on them. Computers can be added based upon attributes that they possess, or you can add a computer explicitly by name.

FIGURE 16.3
Operations container in the Administrator Console

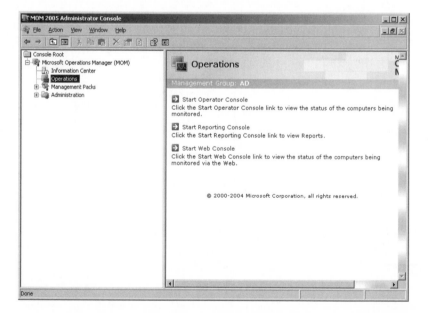

Discovered Groups   Discovered groups are groups of computers that have been created as the computers were found during a discovery process. When you create the discovery rules, you are also defining the discovery group criteria.

Rule Groups   Rule groups contain rules that are organized around a specific criteria. For example, you can create a set of rules that apply to domain controllers. Creating a rule group for these rules allows you to apply the rules to a computer group. Doing so allows you to simplify your administrative overhead by taking several rules and applying them to several computers just by using two objects, the rules group and the computer group. When you need to add a new computer, you can add it to the computer group and the rules will automatically apply to that computer. Changes to rules are automatically applied to all computers in the associated computer groups.

Override Criteria   There are times when you may have a single computer, or maybe a few computers that do not need to have the same settings applied to them as the other systems in the computer group. You can configure settings in the Override Criteria node that will remove the computers from the control of a rules group.

Tasks   Tasks are commands that can be ran against managed computers. When you add a task here, the task appears in the console scopes that you specify.

Notification   The Notification node contains the groups that are used to send notifications when alerts or events are configured to do so. The groups and operators that are configured at this node are not Active Directory–based accounts; instead they are objects that are configured with the e-mail address, pager configuration, or script that is to run as the notification appears.

FIGURE 16.4
Management Packs node

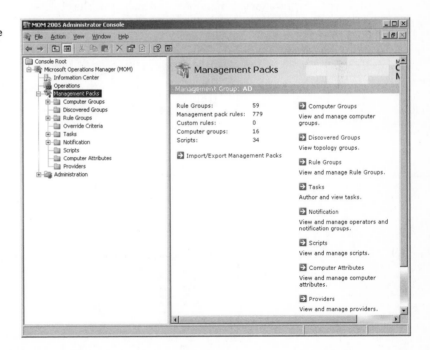

Scripts   Scripts are the Visual Basic scripts that run on the managed systems in order to get information or perform actions on the managed computers. These scripts are usually run as responses to alerts.

Computer Attributes   The rules in the Computer Attributes node define how the attributes are collected from the managed computers.

Providers   Providers specify the data providers that are used to collect information from the managed systems. These include providers such as performance counters and the application log provider.

As you have probably already figured out, there is a management pack for Active Directory. The setting in this management pack will enable you to monitor the domain controllers in your organization as well as the services they rely on. As you can see in Figure 16.5, you can configure several settings in the Active Directory management pack rule group. Later in the section "Active Directory Management Pack," we will look at some of the settings and discuss the benefits they can bring to your monitoring solution.

Administration

Figure 16.6 shows the Administration container expanded to show the main categories. From here you can control how the management servers are configured, as well as the agents that are loaded on the client systems. The four main nodes in Administration are Computers, Console Scopes, Global Settings, and Product Connectors. The Computers node contains objects that define how the systems in your organization are monitored and managed. The objects are as follows:

FIGURE 16.5

Active Directory
management pack

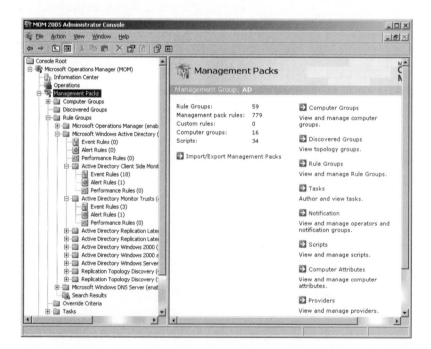

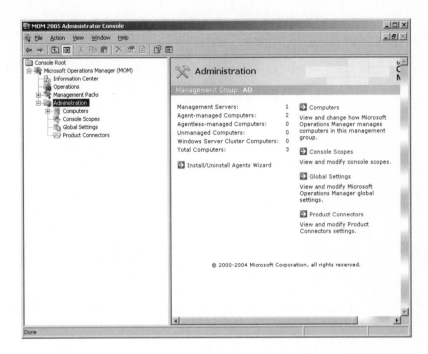

Computers   The Computers node defines the systems that make up the MOM 2005 infrastructure. Computers come in a variety of MOM classifications, each classification broken out into sublevels beneath the Computers node. The Computers node also includes the rules that define which computers become part of the managed infrastructure, and the actions that the administrator needs to approve before they start.

> **All Computers**   Every computer that has been discovered in your MOM 2005 organization will appear in this container. Use this container to view all the systems, whether they are monitored or unmonitored.
>
> **Management Servers**   These are the MOM 2005 servers in your MOM 2005 infrastructure.
>
> **Unmanaged Computers**   Unmanaged computers are computers that have been discovered but are not monitored by any of the MOM 2005 servers in your organization.
>
> **Agentless Managed Computers**   Agentless managed computers do not have an agent installed locally on them, but instead are monitored by the agent that is installed on the MOM 2005 servers. Only limited information can be collected from the computers that undergo agentless management.
>
> **Agent Managed Computers**   Agent-managed computers do have an agent installed on them. They perform their own monitoring, sending data that is collected back to the management servers.
>
> **Windows Server Cluster Computers**   This container allows you to view the virtual servers that the clusters are known by.

Pending Actions Not every action that you perform against a management server or agent is performed immediately. The Pending Actions container will display those actions that need approval before processing.

Computer Discovery Rules You may not want to monitor all of the systems in your organization. There are cases where you may only want to monitor specific types of systems with your MOM 2005 servers. The discovery rules that you define in the Computer Discovery Rules node allow you to specify which systems the MOM 2005 server will try to locate on the network.

Console Scopes Beneath the Computers node you will find the Console Scopes node. The Console Scopes container allows you to configure the computer groups that are available to administrators and users, the accounts that have the ability to use the consoles and what rights they have when they are using the console.

Global Settings Global Settings define the settings that are used by default by the management servers and the agents. Most of the settings you define here can be overridden at the management server and agents, but by default, they will inherit these settings. With the exception of the Management Servers and Agents objects, if you open the properties of any of the Global Settings Types, you will be presented with a group of property pages as shown in Figure 16.7.

Product Connectors Product connectors are conduits that allow your MOM 2005 infrastructure to interoperate with other products such as HP OpenView, Tivoli NetView, and others. Connectors also allow you to connect two or more MOM 2005 organizations together.

OPERATOR CONSOLE

For anyone who needs to view the status of the monitored systems and to find out which alerts and events have occurred, you will need to provide them with the Operator Console. This console presents an overview of the current status of monitored systems in your organization, but does not allow the user to configure any of the administrator-specific options of your MOM 2005 infrastructure. By separating these two functions, you effectively limit the amount of manipulation and misconfiguration that could occur if they had access to other options in your environment.

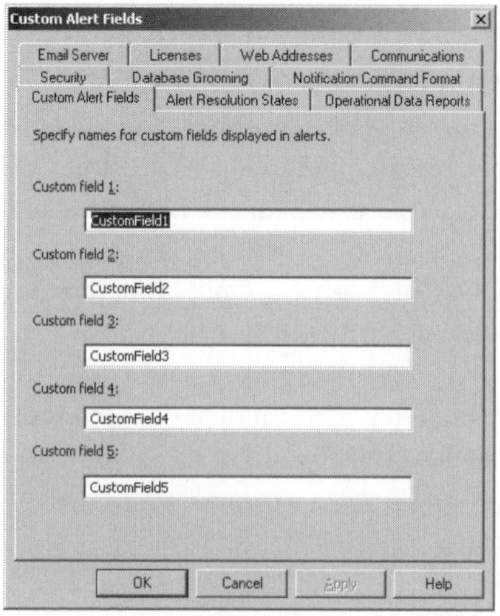

FIGURE 16.7
Custom Alert Fields
shown in the Global
Settings options

Figure 16.8 shows the Operator Console as it appears after you open it for the first time. Notice the navigation controls along the left side of the console. These navigation links will take you to pages that have details on the status of your monitored systems as well as options that you can use to control the systems. The following section list the navigation links can be found in an unmodified Operator Console.

Navigation Pane

Since the Alerts view is the default view that is selected in the navigation pane, we will start by looking at the navigation pane. As you will notice, in Figure 16.8, the Alerts view displays all of the current alerts for the management group. If you click on the Service Level Exceptions node, you can view the current service-level agreements (SLAs) that are in jeopardy. The Microsoft Operations Management node allows you to view the alerts and service-level exceptions that have been generated by the MOM 2005 systems only. For each management pack that you add in, you will have a new node appear. For instance, when you add the Active Directory management pack, an Active Directory node will be added to the Operator Console that will include alerts and service-level exceptions that are specific to domain controllers.

Beneath the Alerts views in the navigation pane is a list of views that you can select. If you take a moment to think about the Operator Console, you realize that it looks very similar to the Outlook 2003 interface. This was a conscious effort by Microsoft. They determined that if the interface was similar to another utility that was commonly used, the learning curve for the new utility would not be so harsh.

Selecting any of the other views allows you to see information about the managed systems that you have been granted access. If custom console scopes have been created, someone using the Operator Console will only be able to view information about the computer groups that they have been granted permission to work with. The views include the following:

State view Whereas the Alerts view shows all of the alerts that have been generated from the managed systems, the State view, shown in Figure 16.9, displays each managed system and its current status.

FIGURE 16.8
Default Operator Console

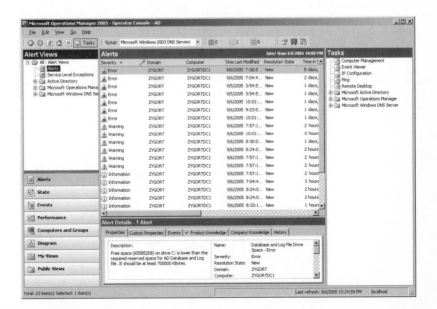

Events view The Events view, shown in Figure 16.10, displays all of the individual events that have been generated by the managed systems. The events that are listed are the individual events that cause alerts to be raised. It depends on the settings in the Administrator Console to determine how many times a specific event needs to be raised before an alert is triggered.

FIGURE 16.9
Operator Console
showing State view

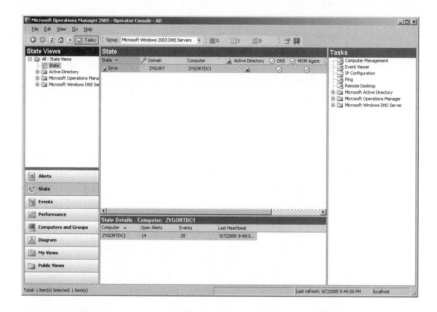

FIGURE 16.10
Operator Console
showing Event view

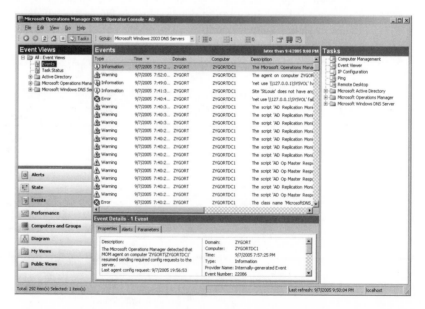

Performance view   Performance counters, the same ones that can be added to performance logs and System Monitor, can be monitored by the MOM 2005 service. You can use the Performance view, shown in Figure 16.11, to display information about the counters. The counters themselves are configured in the Administrator Console, but then an administrator can view a performance graph from the Operator Console.

Computers and Groups view   This view, shown in Figure 16.12, allows you to view the computer groups that are configured, as well as the individual monitored systems.

FIGURE 16.11

Operator Console showing Performance view

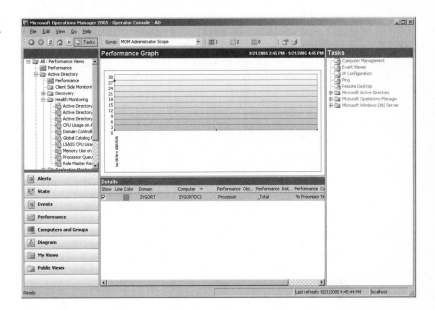

FIGURE 16.12

Operator Console showing Computer and Groups view

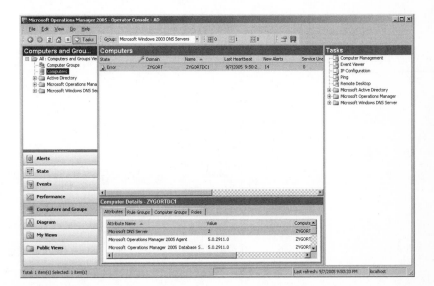

Diagram view   Some management packs will add in diagrams so that you can view the status of the monitored systems in a graphical manner. The Diagram view, shown in Figure 16.13, can make it easy to view your managed systems and identify which computer groups are in an alert state.

My Views view   Depending on the size of your organization, or how you like to view information, you may want to create views that will give you a custom view of the data that is generated from the managed systems. My Views, shown in Figure 16.14, allows you to create views that can be tailored to your own administrative style.

FIGURE 16.13

Operator Console showing the Diagram view

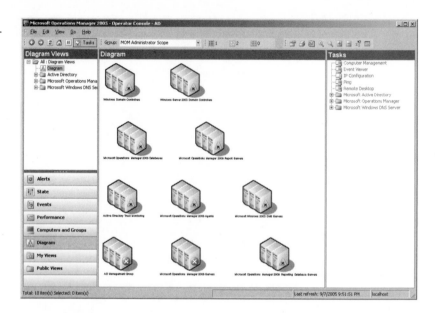

FIGURE 16.14

Operator Console showing the My Views view

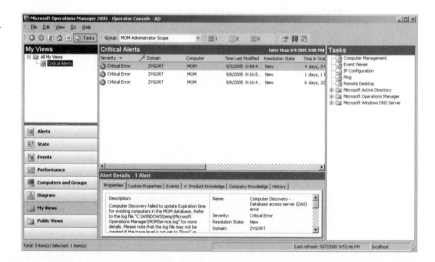

Public Views view   Whereas the My Views view contains customized views for the current user, Public Views, shown in Figure 16.15, has customized views that are available to everyone who has access to the Operators Console.

FIGURE 16.15
Operator Console showing the Public Views view

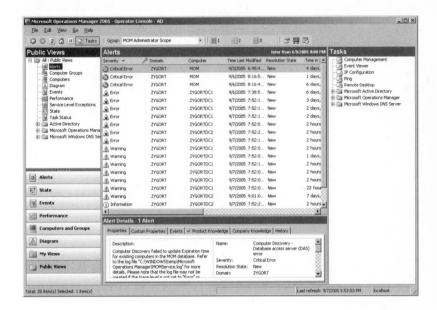

Details Pane

The details pane for the Operator Console is divided into two parts. The upper portion of the pane displays the details of the view that you are currently focused on. If you are in the Alerts view, alerts that are currently raised by one or more of your monitored systems can be found here. If you select an alert, you will see information about the alert appear in the lower part of the details pane. This is where the power of the Operator Console lies.

While you still have your attention on the lower part of the details pane, notice that for each alert, there is additional information you can view. By default, the Properties tab is selected, which gives you a little more information on the alert that you have selected above. This appears to be the same type of information that you will find from the event log on the system that generated the event. However, if you look a little closer at the information (an example is shown in Figure 16.16), you will find more details, including the number of times the event had been raised at the time the alert was generated, known as the repeat count.

If you peruse the other tabs in the details pane, you will find a wealth of information to help you remedy the issues that have arisen. The Custom Properties tab allows you to identify who the owner of the alert is, the ticket ID number, and other information that may be used when others are determining how the alert is being handled. The Events tab displays the individual events that triggered the alert. The History tab shows the actions that have been taken against the alert. If you change the resolution state from New to Acknowledged, the History tab will reflect the change.

FIGURE 16.16
Details of an alert

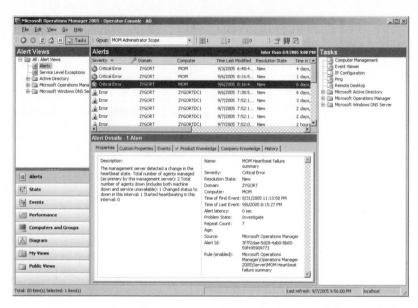

The final two tabs in the details pane are probably the most beneficial from a problem-resolution standpoint. The Product Knowledge and the Company Knowledge tabs display the details that are known about the alert. Microsoft has included a generous amount of information in the Product Knowledge tab for the alerts. This is one of the first places a technician should look when they are trying to resolve an issue. Included in most alert details are hyperlinks to additional data. The Company Knowledge tab can be populated by anyone with access to the Operator Console. As alerts are resolved, the resolution method can be entered in this tab. The next time the alert rears its ugly head, the method of resolution can be viewed before any other step are taken. Using these two tabs can greatly cut down on troubleshooting time and help you stay in service-level compliance.

NOTE The Product Knowledge is already supplied when you add in management packs to MOM 2005. You are responsible for populating the information in the Company Knowledge tab. Remember, the total amount of knowledge base information relies on you and your staff being diligent enough to populate the Company Knowledge information.

Tasks Pane

The final pane that makes up the Operator Console is the tasks pane. Tasks are created using the Administrator Console. Tasks are commands that can be run against managed systems. Depending on what is selected in the details pane, the task that you select from the tasks pane will be run against it. For instance, if you look at Figure 16.17, you will see that the selected alert was raised by the domain controller ZYGORTDC1. When the Ping task was selected, an output window appeared displaying the results from the ping command.

Not all of the tasks will generate a results window as the ping command did. If you select IP Configuration, a wizard will appear asking for the details on the command, and then will process in the background. The results can be viewed by viewing the Task Status in Public Views view, shown in Figure 16.18. Clicking on any of the results in the details pane will allow you to view the results of the task in the Event Details section of the details pane.

Other tasks will perform actions against the managed system. Selecting Computer Management will open the Computer Management snap-in, which allows you to connect to the managed system without having to go to Administrative Tools and starting the snap-in.

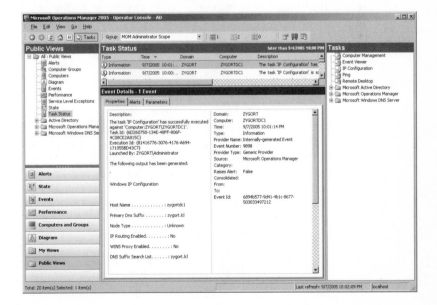

WEB CONSOLE

There are times when you are not sitting at a workstation that has the Operator Console available. You may be sitting at home when you get the call; you know the call, the one telling you that you have to check on something. Or you are sitting at your favorite coffee shop when your cell phone buzzes. There are organizations that will not allow additional firewall ports to be opened up just so that you can run your snap-ins or administrative tools from remote locations. Although there are tools such as Remote Desktop and Remote Assistance, as well as Remote Tools that is included as part of Microsoft's Systems Management Server and third-party tools that allow you to gain access to remote systems, if the company's standards and practices forbid you to have any type of remote access to your internal servers, you will need to have another method of managing and monitoring your systems.

The Web Console provides access to some of the same data that you would have available to you when you run the Operator Console. As you may have already guessed, the Web Console is limited in its functionality, but in a pinch, it will fulfill some of your needs. As you can see in Figure 16.19, some of the same views that were available in the Operator Console are available in a web-based format, but not all of the functionality of the Operator Console is available.

On the left of the console is the navigation pane showing the views that are available. Only three views appear: Alerts, Computers, and Events. These three are very similar to their Operation Console counterparts, showing the same type of information in the details pane, but notice that the tasks pane is missing. You won't be able to run any tasks from the Web Console, which could limit the amount of control that you can exhibit over the managed systems in your environment. The important part of the Web Console, however, is the ability to view the information that is returned from the managed systems and have access to the knowledge base for each alert.

FIGURE 16.19
Web Console

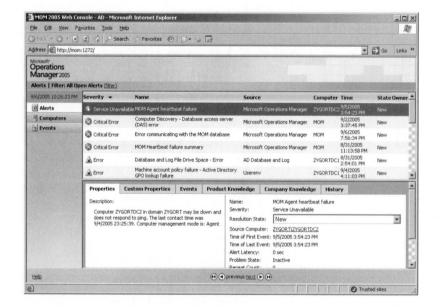

Management Packs

One of the strengths of MOM 2005 is that you can configure your MOM 2005 servers to monitor only the services that you specify. Instead of having a full complement of events, alerts, and performance settings already installed and ready to run, MOM 2005 ships bare-bones, with only the ability to monitor the most basic of settings. In order to add additional functionality, you are required to install management packs. Management packs include additional settings that allow your MOM 2005 systems to monitor other services, such as Active Directory, Exchange Server 2003, SQL Server 2000, and many others.

NOTE   To see a list of the management packs that Microsoft and other third-party companies have made available, go to www.microsoft.com/management/mma/catalog.aspx.

You can obtain management packs by visiting the Microsoft website and downloading them. Once downloaded, you can install them onto the MOM servers that are responsible for monitoring your systems. One word of warning: do not download and install all of the management packs that Microsoft and other third parties offer. The more you add onto your MOM 2005 systems, the more monitoring they will start performing. Make sure that you only install what you need; that way, your servers will perform better.

You should take some time to familiarize yourself with the settings that are supplied with each management pack. While Microsoft has gone to great lengths to ensure that the default settings are appropriate for most environments, you should make sure that they are necessary for your environment, or that the settings that have been turned off are not needed in your environment. You may find that some of the settings are not necessary, whereas others may have a place in your monitoring solution.

Each management pack brings with it a plethora of settings and options that you can take advantage of. However, just because a setting is available does not mean that you should turn it on. Many companies have taken a look at all of the events, alerts, and actions available when you add in a management pack, and decided to turn on just about everything. Of course the MOM 2005 server will not object to the additional monitoring, as long as it has enough resources to handle it. The problem lies with the additional network traffic you will generate due to the monitoring, not to mention the additional space you will consume in your MOM 2005 database.

You are probably asking yourself, "Just what is contained in these management packs?" Good question. When you add in a management pack, you will notice that new groups, Computer and Rule, are created in the Administrator Console along with new tasks and diagram views. The new objects that are created depend on which management pack you install. With each management pack you will also find a comprehensive knowledge base for the alerts that can be generated by the service. Later in this section we take a look at the management packs that are available for Active Directory and DNS.

Computer Groups

To view which computers are members of a computer group, open the properties of the computer group and view the search criteria. You'll see several tabs that define the requirements that must be met in order for a computer to be included as a member of a computer group. Those tabs are as follows:

Included Subgroups   Subgroups can be chosen that define another computer group from which the computers belong and the search criteria will be ran against. In Figure 16.20, notice that the two discovered groups that were created when the domain controllers were discovered are included as subgroups of the Windows Server 2003 Domain Controllers computer group.

Included Computers The Included Computers property page allows you to explicitly define computers that will be included as part of the computer group. If there are computers that are not included in one of the subgroups in the Included Subgroups property page, you can add them in here. Because the domain controllers in the Zygort domain are already included as members of the subgroups, there are no additional computers listed here.

Excluded Computers If you want to explicitly define the systems that you do not want to be included in the computer group, you can add them here. So if there is a domain controller that is included as a member of a subgroup, you can enter it here so that you do not have rules applying to it.

Search For Computers If you have computers that have not been discovered, you can specify the search criteria that you want to use to find additional systems that should be part of your computer group. This property page, shown in Figure 16.21, is very flexible as to how the search should be conducted.

FIGURE 16.20
Included Subgroups

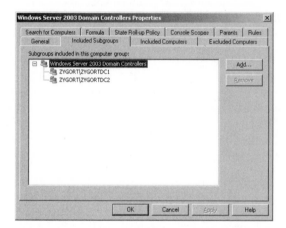

FIGURE 16.21
Search For Computers
property page

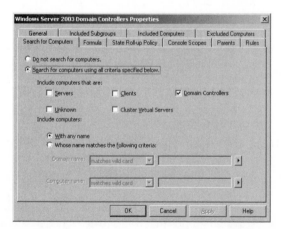

Formula   The Formula property page is used in conjunction with the Search For Computers property page. Any computer that meets the search criteria on the Search For Computers property page is evaluated by the formula that is defined. Figure 16.22 shows the Formula property page and the options you can use to define the formula. You have a full set of operators, and they can be used against attributes as well as systems contained in other computer and discovered groups. If you look at Figure 16.23, you will see just a few of the attributes that can be used to select which computers should be included in the computer group.

The remaining property pages represent how the computer group is represented or controlled in the MOM 2005 infrastructure.

State Roll-up Policy   As shown in Figure 16.24, the State Roll-up Policy property page defines how the computer group will be displayed in the Operator Console when systems start going into alert states.

The Worst State Of Any Member Computer Or Subgroup   Shows the computer group in the state of the included computer that is in the worst condition of any system. When one system goes into a critical or warning state, the computer group appears in that state in the Operator Console.

The Worst State From The Specified Percentage Of Best States In The Computer Group
With this option you are able to select a percentage of the computers in the computer group that will be considered in the best states of the group. For instance, if you have 10 computers included in the group and you select 70%, three systems could be in a critical state and seven in perfect working order and the computer group would not show up as having any problems. As soon as a fourth system went into a warning or critical state, the computer group would then appear in a warning or critical state in the Operator Console.

The Best State Of Any Member Computer Or Subgroup   With this option, the computer group will appear in the state of the computer or subgroup that has the best state. If the best state of 10 systems is a warning state, then that will be the state of the computer group in the Operator Console.

FIGURE 16.22
Formula property page

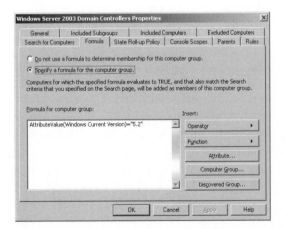

FIGURE 16.23
Attributes available
when creating a formula

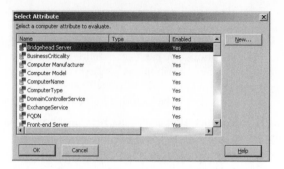

FIGURE 16.24
State Roll-up Policy
property page

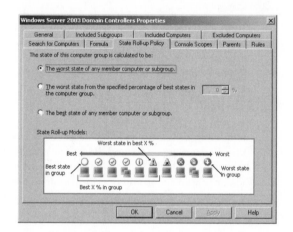

Each of the roll-up policy options has its place. The first option may be used if you have a group of like computers that all need to have the same rules applied to them and you need to know if any of them are having issues. With domain controllers, this will probably be the option that you will want to use. The second option is usually selected if you have a group of like computers that perform the same type of functions, but not all of them need to be online to maintain the functionality of the infrastructure. A good example would be a web server farm that hosts more systems than are necessary to maintain a service level agreement. This option could be selected so that the computer group state does not go into a warning or critical state until a few systems are having problems. The final option may be used to show that at least one system is up and functioning correctly.

Console Scopes   Although you cannot modify the settings on this property page, it is available so that you can easily view which console scopes have the computer group included in them.

Parents   This is another property page that does not have anything that you can configure; it is used for informational purposes only. If the computer group that you are viewing the properties of is a subgroup to another computer group, you will see those computer groups that are its parents.

Rules   As shown in Figure 16.25, the rule groups that are applied to the computer group appear. There are two different types of rule groups that are applied to a computer group: those that are inherited from the parent groups, shown in the top of the property page, and the rule groups that are explicitly applied, which appear in the lower part of the page. You cannot modify the inherited groups, but you can associate rule groups explicitly. You can also disable all rule groups that are associated with this computer group by selecting the check box, but remember that subgroups that have this computer group as a parent will be affected.

Discovered Groups

Although you don't have the ability to make changes to any of the groups that are included in this node, it does come in handy. These groups are created as computers are discovered by the discovery rules and Active Directory OUs are located. As you create new computer groups or modify existing ones, you can use the discovered computer groups as included groups. Doing so can make maintaining computer groups a little easier.

One thing that you can do with the discovered groups is right-click on one and choose Create Replica Computer Group from the context menu. When you do so, you will be creating a new computer group in the Computer Groups node. You can then open the properties of the replica computer group and make any changes necessary.

Rules Groups

As with computer groups, rules groups are used to organize objects, this time rules that are applied to computer groups. When you have a set of rules that all work in conjunction with one another, you should include them in a rules group so that you only have to assign one rules group to a computer group in order to have several rules affecting the included computers.

If you look at Figure 16.26, you will see that rules groups can contain other rules groups. The included management pack for MOM 2005 includes the Microsoft Operations Manager rules group, which in turn includes the Operations Manager 2005 rules group. The Operations Manager 2005 rules group also includes rules groups that are applied to the MOM 2005 systems. If you had MOM 2000 servers in your environment, you could add the MOM 2000 management pack; that would add the Operations Manager 2000 rules group, which would have other rules groups that affect MOM 2000 servers.

FIGURE 16.25
Rules property page

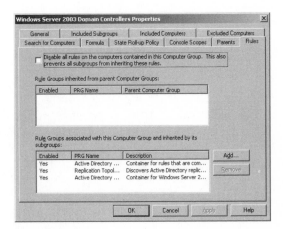

There are not many property pages on a rules group, as you can see in Figure 16.27. The General property page contains the naming and description information, but also includes the Enabled check box that you can use to turn the rules group on and off at any time. For documentation purposes, you should keep track of version information, which can be found on this property page, as well as the Rule Group GUID. As changes are made to the MOM 2005 infrastructure, this information could come in handy for troubleshooting purposes.

FIGURE 16.26

Nested Rules Groups

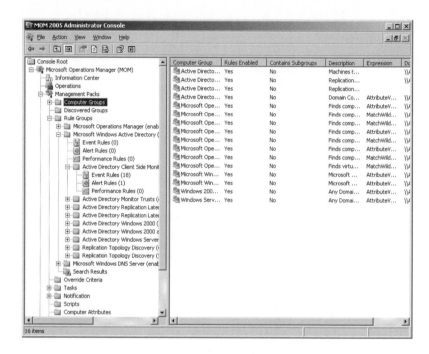

FIGURE 16.27

Rules Group
property pages

The Knowledge Base property page includes information about the rules group and what it is used for. There is also an area that can be used to include company knowledge. If you make any changes to that rules group, you should document it here. That way, anyone that needs to work with the rules group will know what modifications have been made.

The final property page is the Computer Groups property page. You can associate the rules group to a computer group from here. Although you can associate the rules group to computer groups from the computer group's Rules property page, if you want to associate this rule with multiple computer groups, it is easier to do it from here than to open the property pages for each of the computer groups individually.

Any time that you have an Active Directory–based infrastructure, you should monitor the domain controllers and DNS servers that support them. Start by downloading the two management packs from the Microsoft website and installing each into the MOM 2005 servers that will be responsible for monitoring them.

Active Directory Management Pack

When you add in the Active Directory management pack, not only are you are adding in rules for the monitoring of the domain controllers, you are also adding in several tasks that help you troubleshoot and monitor your domain controllers from the Operator Console. If you remember from the other chapters in Part 3, there are several utilities that you can use that will help you diagnose and troubleshoot issues that appear in your Active Directory environment. The Active Directory Management Pack includes some of these utilities as tasks that you can run against managed domain controllers.

In this section we'll take a look at the options that are available in the Active Directory management pack after it is imported into the Administrator Console. Once we have discussed the Administrator Console option, we'll see how the addition of the management pack appears in the Operator Console.

ADMINISTRATOR CONSOLE

The Administrator Console is used to add new management packs and control how they affect the rest of the monitored environment. Once added, the packs provide new settings that will go into effect as soon as the client agents on the managed systems start processing the new rules, based on the groups that the computer belongs to. Of course, as we mentioned earlier, the default settings that are configured in a management pack may work for some organizations, but you should review the settings and make sure they are fine-tuned to work efficiently in your environment.

Computer Groups

The managed domain controllers that you have will appear in these computer groups based on the attributes that are searched for when the computers are discovered. When you navigate to the Management Packs ➤ Computer Groups node in the Administrator Console after adding the Active Directory management pack, you will see six new computer groups:

- Active Directory Client Side Monitoring
- Active Directory Replication Latency Data Collection – Sources
- Active Directory Replication Latency Data Collection – Target

♦ Active Directory Trust Monitoring

♦ Windows 2000 Domain Controllers

♦ Windows Server 2003 Domain Controllers.

Rule Groups

In the Rule Groups node you will find the Microsoft Windows Active Directory rule group shown in Figure 16.28. This rule group contains several other rule groups that have been identified as necessary to monitor domain controllers and the replication that they participate in. The rule groups that make up the Active Directory management pack include Active Directory Client Side Monitoring, Active Directory Monitor Trusts, Active Directory Replication Latency Performance Data Collection – Sources, Active Directory Replication Latency Performance Data Collection – Targets, Active Directory Windows 2000, Active Directory Windows 2000 and Windows Server 2003, Active Directory Windows Server 2003, Replication Topology Discovery (Connection Objects) and Replication Topology Discovery (Site Links).

Notice that all of the rule groups are enabled. You can disable any of them by right-clicking the rule group, choosing Properties from the context menu, and clearing the Enabled check box on the General property page. If you are lucky enough to have Windows Server 2003 domain controllers as the only domain controller type in your environment, you could disable the Active Directory Windows 2000 rule group.

Due to the sheer number of rules that are already available and the different combination of options and attributes that can be used to create new rules, we won't delve too deeply into this topic. If you look at Figure 16.29 you will see that two of the Active Directory Windows Server 2003 rule groups have been expanded to show the number of Event, Alert, and Performance rules that are available in each.

FIGURE 16.28
Active Directory
Rule Groups

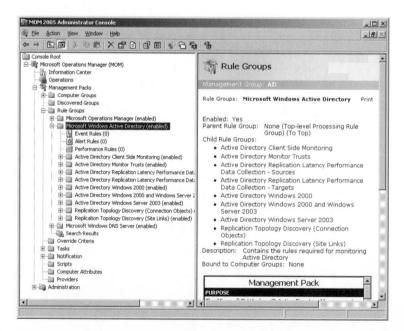

FIGURE 16.29
Expanded Rule Groups

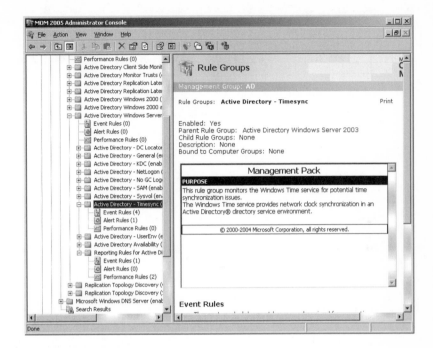

FIGURE 16.29
Expanded Rule Groups

Tasks

When you expand the Microsoft Active Directory task folder under the Tasks node, you will find that there are three subfolders beneath it. These are used to organize the tasks that appear in the Operation Console. The three tasks folders, shown in Figure 16.30, include some of the utilities that have been examined earlier in this troubleshooting section. The Advanced tasks include commands and utilities that run against domain controllers to aid in troubleshooting. The Replication Troubleshooting tasks allow you to view the current status of the replication topology as well as determine the service principle name status of your systems. The Trust Details folder includes a command that will determine the status of the trust relationships in your infrastructure.

OPERATOR CONSOLE

After you've added the Active Directory management pack to the Administrator Console and configured the computer groups, rule groups, and tasks to meet your organization's needs, the Operator Console will reflect the new information. Any time an operator has the ability to work with the domain controllers from within the Operator Console, the information that is shown is available due to the rules that are now part of the MOM 2005 management group.

In Figure 16.31, data that has been collected based on the Active Directory rule groups is shown. An additional piece that is added to the Operator Console when a management pack in added is the Diagram view. When you select the Diagram view from the navigation pane, all of the active computer groups that have collected data appear in this view. Using the Diagram view is an efficient means of viewing the status of the groups in your MOM 2005 infrastructure.

FIGURE 16.30
Active Directory
tasks folders

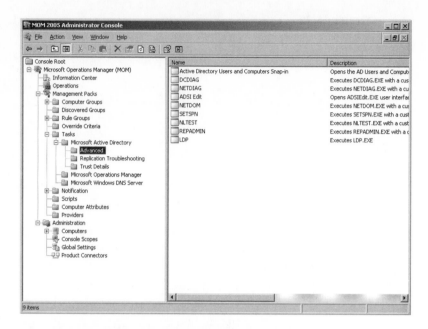

FIGURE 16.31
Details shown in the
Operator Console

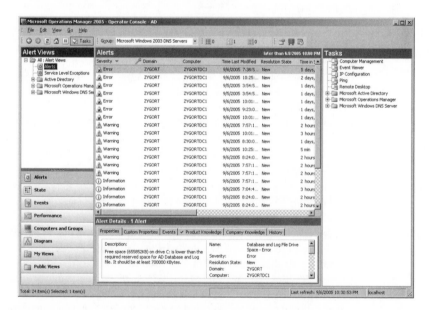

If you choose any other view, you can select a detail line in the details pane and view more information about the alert or event. In Figure 16.32, an alert has been selected from the Alerts details pane. After selecting the alert, the information contained at the bottom of the detail pane will give you plenty of information to start determining where to begin your troubleshooting. You can also select a task to run against the data that you have selected.

FIGURE 16.32

Selecting an alert to run a task against

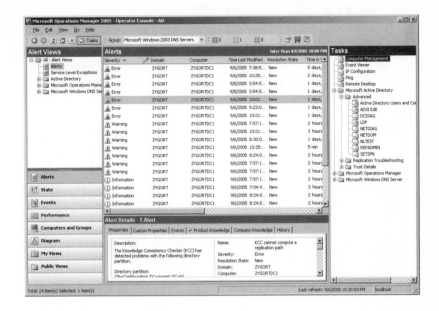

DNS Management Pack

The DNS management pack has a lot in common with all the other management packs; you need to add it into the Administrator Console, and then the new objects can be used from in the Operator Console. Since DNS is a vital part of your Active Directory infrastructure, you should add the DNS management pack to your MOM 2005 infrastructure so that you can start becoming proactive with your DNS monitoring.

ADMINISTRATOR CONSOLE

Shown in Figure 16.33 are the rule groups that are included with the DNS management pack. The top-level rule group container, Microsoft Windows DNS Server, only contains two rules groups beneath it: the Windows 2000 DNS and Windows 2003 DNS rule groups. As you can probably determine from the names, the rules that are included in each one apply to the specific operating system on which the DNS service is running. If you are lucky enough to not have Windows 2000 servers in your organization, you can disable that rule group.

Figure 16.34 shows the Windows 2003 DNS rule group and the rule groups contained in it. Notice that most of the rules in the rule groups are performance rules. When you use the DNS management pack, you will probably need to make sure that the DNS servers are handling the client load efficiently; that is why these rules are in place. As a matter of fact, the only alert that is configured is an alert that will be triggered if the DNS service is unavailable. Other events appear in the rule group, but they are only reporting information into the database and will only raise alerts in the Operator Console as there are not any automated responses configured.

Figure 16.35 shows the tasks that are added when the DNS management pack is installed. Notice that there are not as many tasks included with DNS as there were in the Active Directory management pack, but some of the tasks that are added have significant troubleshooting advantages.

FIGURE 16.33
Rule groups added
with the DNS manage-
ment pack

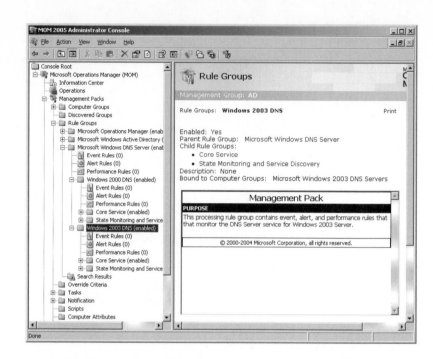

FIGURE 16.34
Windows 2003 DNS
rule group

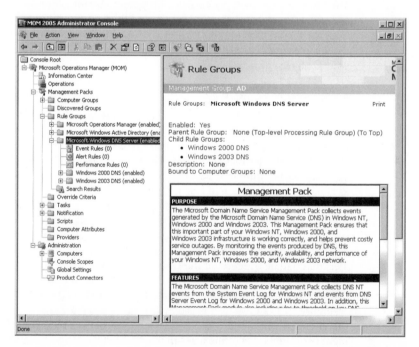

FIGURE 16.35

Tasks included with the Windows 2003 DNS management pack

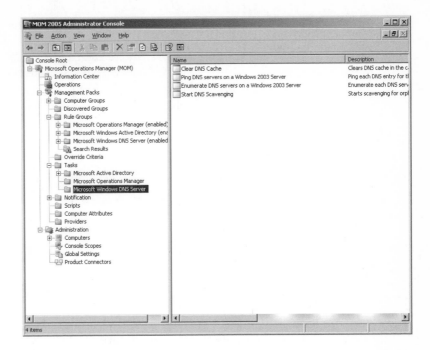

OPERATOR CONSOLE

The Operator Console will contain new tasks and diagrams, as well as groupings of computers that represent the DNS servers and knowledge base information that can be used to assist in troubleshooting DNS issues. In Figure 16.36 you can see the Windows DNS Server Alert view and the tasks that are available in the Tasks pane.

If you double-click on the Ping task, a tasks wizard appears that allows you to define the task that you want to run. Notice in Figure 16.36 that the Ping task will not run against Windows 2000 DNS servers but only the Windows Server 2003–based systems. As with all of the tasks, make sure that they will function the way that you anticipate; otherwise you may not receive the information that you are looking for. You also need to make sure that the appropriate utilities are loaded on each system that will be the target of the task.

Reporting Console

The final section of this chapter focuses on the Reporting Console. As with most applications, there is usually some method of obtaining information in a report format so that you know how the application is functioning. With MOM 2005, the reporting functionality goes one step further by detailing the status of the monitored systems in your MOM 2005 organization.

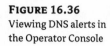

FIGURE 16.36

Viewing DNS alerts in the Operator Console

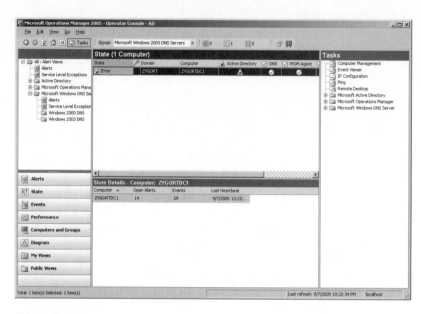

The Reporting Console is based on the SQL Reporting Services. Since SQL is the database for MOM 2005, you already have the prerequisites in place; now you just need to load the SQL Reporting Services before you can load the Reporting Console. Once you have loaded the SQL Reporting Services, you can insert the MOM 2005 CD or run the MOM 2005 setup program, which gives you the option to install the Reporting Console.

Whereas the Operator Console will give you detailed information about the current operational level of your monitored systems, the Reporting Console is used to look at the historical data and possibly use it for trend analysis. When you install the MOM 2005 Reporting Console, an additional task is created that transfers data from the MOM 2005 database to the MOM Reporting database. When you access the reports, you are actually viewing the information contained in the reporting database, not the MOM 2005 database.

After the Reporting Console is loaded, you will have the ability to run the reporting console from in the Administrator Console, or you can access the console directly by accessing the SQL Reporting Server website by entering the URL: `http://reporting_server_name/reports` where `reporting_server_name` is the name of the server that is running the SQL Reporting Services. Figure 16.37 shows an example of what the Reporting Services website looks like when you access it through the MOM 2005 Administrator Console, and Figure 16.38 shows what appears when you go directly through the web address.

The reports that are contained in the default installation of the Reporting Console go a long way in giving you a detailed look at your managed systems. Figure 16.39 shows the Operational Health Analysis reports that are available with the default installation. The Operational Data Reporting reports can be shown in Figure 16.40, and the Microsoft Operations Manager reports can be shown in Figure 16.41. If you are well versed in SQL Reporting Services, you can create custom reports that can give you specific details about your environment in formats that your technical staff can use as well as your organization's management.

FIGURE 16.37

Accessing the Reporting Console through the Administrator Console

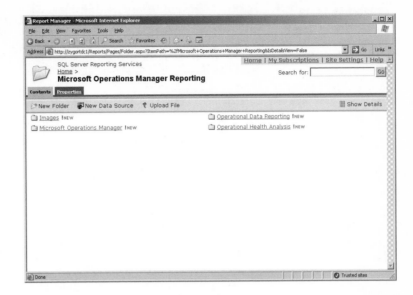

FIGURE 16.38

Accessing the Reporting Console through a web address

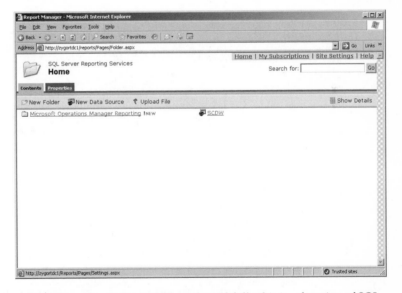

Another nice feature of the Reporting Console (although truthfully this is a function of SQL Reporting Services) is that you can subscribe to reports and have them delivered to you. If you have configured the SQL Reporting Services server to use an SMTP server, you can have the reports delivered through e-mail, or you can have the report uploaded to a file share. Since the reports are in XML format, you could have them uploaded to a file share that is used by a web server. The reports can then be viewed on your intranet by your personnel.

FIGURE 16.39
Operational Health
Analysis reports

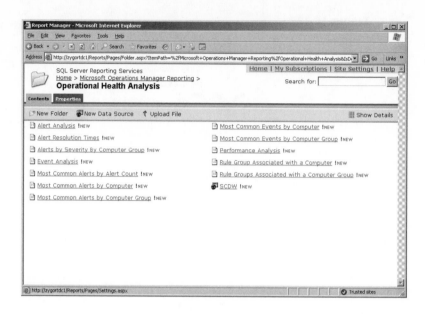

FIGURE 16.40
Operational Data
Reporting reports

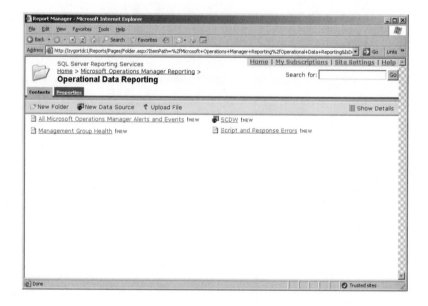

FIGURE 16.41
Microsoft Operations
Manager reports

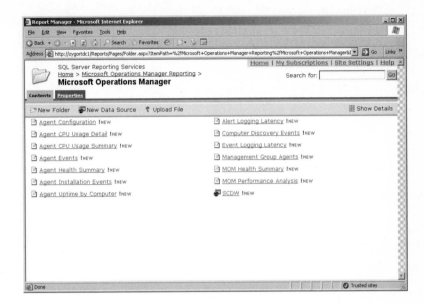

Coming Up Next

So this ends our discussion of Active Directory troubleshooting. Due to the fact that Active Directory is ever evolving, and Microsoft introduces new features from time to time, the troubleshooting topics found in this part of the book will help in most cases, but you will find that new tools and topics become available as Active Directory matures. Make sure you are always checking the Microsoft website for the latest developments.

Next we are going to delve into a topic that many administrators are hesitant to tackle, either because they don't think they have time to learn, or they are unsure whether they have the skill set to tackle it: scripting. No matter what your level of scripting understanding is, it will be in your best interest to take the time to get a better understanding of how scripts function and how they can make your administrative life easier.

Part 4

Streamlining Management with Scripts

In this part:

Chapter 17

ADSI Primer

By this point in the book, you should have a good understanding of Active Directory—what it is and what it can do. You've been working with AD from the outside, using the tools supplied by Microsoft. Now we're going to start working with AD from the inside, where we're going to write the tools. To accomplish this, we need a way to communicate with the directory service itself, and that's where ADSI comes in.

What Is ADSI?

ADSI stands for Active Directory Services Interface, but that name is not entirely accurate. The name implies that it is just an interface for working with Active Directory, when in fact it can work with a number of directory service providers, including Novell's NetWare Directory Services (NDS) and Bindery Services for Netware 3.12 and below.

ADSI vs. Active Directory

It is not uncommon for administrators to confuse ADSI with Active Directory. Active Directory is the Microsoft directory service provider of choice for Windows domains. It holds the objects that define your domain, including sites, subnets, users, computers, printers, and so on. You can consider it a database of sorts and treat it as such. When you create a new user or other object, Active Directory's job is to house it. The task of creating that user, however, falls on the shoulders of ADSI.

ADSI is an object-oriented programming interface, but it is not a language. Rather, it is a toolset for directory services that is used by the programming language. You can think of it as a set of properties and routines focused on doing one job: manipulating a directory service. ADSI is built on Component Object Model (COM) technology, which allows it to work with any programming language that supports COM (and it's tough finding one that doesn't anymore!). The examples in this book and the downloadable samples will be in VBScript, but if you choose to use another language, you are more than welcome to!

COM Interfaces

COM technology gives programming languages the ability to communicate and work with programming objects. You can think of COM as a set of windows that you can look through and open to get access to an object. These sets of windows are called *interfaces*. Each object implements at least one interface for access to the object, and it is not uncommon for Active Directory objects to implement more than one. The individual interfaces themselves are beyond the scope of this book, but if you do further research into ADSI objects you will run into references to them.

By defining a valid set of operations for an object, COM interfaces act like a programming contract. A contract spells out what you can do and sometimes what you cannot do. If we try to do something outside the bounds of that contract, we are very likely going to get errors. Most Active Directory objects implement a standard set of interfaces, allowing you to access the same properties and operations on different types of objects. Some objects will also implement an interface that provides specific functionality unique to that type of Active Directory object.

So how do we know what we can and cannot do? We study the object model that we want to work with. We read the documentation (ADSI is well documented on the Web), and we resort to a little good old-fashioned trial-and-error. As we work through examples in the book, you will see what works and what does not, and we will talk about why some things do not work.

ADSI Providers

One of most endearing qualities of ADSI is its ability to play well with others. I am not just referring to its language independence, but rather to how many directory services it can interact with as well. Active Directory was not the first directory service on the block, and the Active Directory we know today definitely will not be the last version of it. In the ever-expanding corporate world, where companies routinely take over other companies and have to integrate information systems, there's a good chance you might run into another directory service that you will have to work and play with. Not to worry, though—ADSI has you covered.

Active Directory is just one of several directory services that ADSI can communicate with. To provide this kind of support, ADSI implements a provider-based architecture. This means that you, the programmer, specify the directory service provider you want to use, and ADSI takes care of the details. When you tell ADSI to create a user object, it looks at the provider and does exactly what that directory service expects in order to create a new user object.

Think of it like turning on a television. I would be willing to bet that you could walk into any store right now and fire up every make and model of television sitting on the shelf. But, do you know how that television works internally? Probably not, and you probably do not care either. Power circuits will start supplying juice to the tuners, which will get the signal from the cable and feed it into a processor, and sooner or later you wind up with a picture on the tube. Your main concern is that when you press the power button, the picture shows up on the screen. Let the television take care of all the details. This is how we work with ADSI; our concern is working with the objects in Active Directory, and we will let ADSI handle the details.

Let's take a quick look at some of the providers that ADSI supports. Obviously ADSI has support for Active Directory. Since Active Directory is based on the Lightweight Directory Access Protocol (LDAP), we use the LDAP provider to connect to Active Directory. The LDAP provider is used for working with domain controllers, which most of our scripting activity will be focused on, but there is also a provider supplied for communicating with global catalog servers. For working with Microsoft Security Accounts Manager (SAM)-based domains (NT 4 and earlier), ADSI supplies a Windows NT provider. Novell's NetWare Directory Service (NDS) and Bindery Services (NetWare 3.12 and earlier) are supported as well. These are the major players, and a few other providers are available as well, but we will get to them soon enough.

Right now we need to talk about connecting with our provider of choice. To do this, we are going to create a statement, something like a street address. We will specify what object in the directory service we want to work with, and how we want to communicate with it. Take a look at this statement and tell me if it looks familiar:

```
http://www.sybex.com/sybexbooks.nsf/booklist/4305
```

It looks like a URL you would type into Internet Explorer, right? It is basically an address, which says "Using the HTTP protocol, find a web server called www.sybex.com, and on that server look in the sybexbooks.nsf/booklist folder and show me the 4305 file" (I know, that is not exactly what it is doing, but work with me here!). Now look at this statement:

```
LDAP://CN=Scott,CN=Users,DC=zygort,DC=com
```

Following the same basic address idea (but reading the address portion from right to left), this says "Using the LDAP protocol, find the domain named zygort.com, look in the users container and show me object with the common name of 'Scott.'" By specifying LDAP as the protocol to use, I am telling ADSI to communicate with a directory service that supports LDAP (which is probably Active Directory in our case). LDAP is the moniker of the statement, and the moniker is used to specify the protocol.

Table 17.1 lists the ADSI providers and their provider names or monikers. We'll use these provider names when we specify which directory service provider we want to work with.

TABLE 17.1:   ADSI Providers

PROVIDER NAME	DESCRIPTION
LDAP	Used with Windows 2000/2003 Active Directory, as well as other LDAP-compliant sources
WinNT	Used with Windows NT to access information in the SAM database
GC	Used with Windows 2000/2003 Active Directory to access information stored on a global catalog server
NW	Used for Novell Directory Services (NetWare 4.x and later)
NWCOMPAT	Used for Novell Bindery Services (NetWare 3.x and earlier)
IIS	Used for accessing IIS configuration data

As if the list in Table 17.1 were not enough, one more provider is available for accessing a directory service through OLE DB. The name for this provider is ADsDSOObject. However, this is not a moniker; it is not used to reference an individual object in Active Directory. Instead, it is used for writing queries to pull information out of your directory service. When you think of OLE DB, you should think of databases. This provider will let you treat the directory service like a database. A programmer familiar with ActiveX Data Objects (ADO) can query the directory service for information and cycle through the results. This stream of data is read-only, which means you cannot do updates directly through it. If you are not familiar with ADO, rest assured that we will definitely be discussing it later in this chapter.

Now, let's spend some time getting to know the objects in Active Directory that we will be working with. You are probably familiar with most of these objects on a higher level, but now it is time to open the hood and get our hands a little dirty exploring what exactly is inside this data store known as Active Directory.

Active Directory Objects

By now you have created several users and other objects in Active Directory. You are probably so familiar with Active Directory Users and Computers (ADU&C) that you could create a new user in your sleep, right? That's good, but that is also not so good, because what you know about users in ADU&C is not what you're going to see through ADSI. It will take a little getting used to, and some good documentation, but it will be second nature to you soon enough.

Everything in Active Directory is stored as an object. Users are stored as user objects; computers are stored as computer objects; and so on. A user and a computer are obviously different types of creatures, so it only makes sense that they are stored as different types of objects. Another commonly used term for objects is *entity*, but I will use the term *object*. So, what exactly is an object?

An object is basically a programming structure. In a nutshell, an object holds values that describe the object and code that is designed to operate that object. Right now that explanation probably does you very little good, so instead let's use an analogy. Think of an object like a house. What do you know about a house? It usually has windows, it's usually painted one overall color (unless it's the Partridge family house!), and it probably has switches that turn the lights on and off.

Properties

Think about the color of our house for a moment. What color is it? In our object, the color is stored as a *property*, sometimes called an *attribute*. Your house has other properties as well. How many windows does it have? Does it have a fireplace? Now consider a user object and think about the properties it might have. The first name, last name, and account name are all properties of the user object.

These properties have names, and this is where things start to turn tricky during your first foray into ADSI. In ADU&C, you know which field to type in to change a user's first name (I don't have to tell you that field name, do I?). But, in ADSI, you won't find the first name property anywhere. You won't find the last name property anywhere either, because that is simply not what they are named in the object itself.

Nope, you get to learn a whole new set of names that correspond to the fields you see in ADU&C. For example, the first name field corresponds to the `givenName` property in ADSI. The last name field corresponds to the `sn` property (short for surname). We will discuss the property names in more depth when we talk about the specific objects in Active Directory.

And no, I didn't mistype the `givenName` property. That is actually how the property name appears in the schema. When you look at the schema later on, the property name is referred to as the `ldapDisplayName`. The formatting of the name is created using a method of composing programming names known as camel-casing. A variable or property name might be "composed" of several words. Those names can't have spaces in them (trust me, you do not want space in them!), so to visually set each word apart, the first letter of each word is capitalized, with the exception of the very first word. Of course, with every rule, there are the occasional exceptions.

Methods

Going back to our house analogy, we have switches that turn on the lights. Turning on the switches is similar to invoking a method of an object. You might hear the term *function* as well, but the proper term when working with objects is *method*. A method is simply telling the object to do something; in the case of our house, we're turning on the lights. Other methods might be to open the garage door or lower the shades. Think about the things that a user object can do, such as setting its password. There is no password field in the user object, so the only way to set it is through a method call. Objects in Active Directory will have a typical set of methods that you can use, and some will also have more specialized methods. For example, the Organization Unit object, since it is a type of container object, has a method to create new objects in it.

INTERFACES VS. *LDAPDISPLAYNAME*

The properties of objects can be accessed in one of two ways: through an interface or through Get/Put methods with the `ldapDisplayName`. After binding to an object, an interface can be applied to the object (depending on its type) that will associate a "friendly" name for the property to its `ldapDisplayName`. For example, accessing the `User.givenName` is the same property as `User.Get("givenName")`. Not every property is mapped by the interface, and some binding methods will not use the full interface for the object at all.

Which method you use is entirely up to you, but I advise you to choose one and stick with it. I prefer the Get/Put methods for two reasons: consistency and flexibility. I can always use a Get method to retrieve an object property regardless of the applied interface. It is also much easier to use a string variable for the `ldapDisplayName` and change it on the fly in my script than to work around a group of hardcoded property names used by the interface.

Schema

As you probably remember, the Active Directory Schema is where we define what makes up an object. The names that correspond to the fields in our standard administration tools are defined in the schema. To develop scripts that work successfully with Active Directory, we need to look at the schema and get a feel for how it works. Most administrators do not work with Active Directory at this level except when making schema modifications. In fact, most schema modifications have been automated with scripts to some degree to ensure consistent results, so there is even less reason for administrators to open up the schema tools.

Every object in Active Directory, whether it is a user or computer or anything else, was created from information stored in the schema. The schema contains the blueprints for every type of object that can be created in a particular implementation of Active Directory. It describes the properties that an object created from that set of blueprints will have. The blueprint for an object is known as the *class* for that object.

The terms *class* and *object* are used interchangeably all too often. A class is an abstract entity; it cannot actually do anything because it really does not exist as a "physical" object. The class exists only in the schema, and it exists only to create objects. The object is the physical implementation of the class that we can work with in Active Directory. The process of creating the object is referred to as creating an "instance" of an object, or instantiation.

The terms *property* and *attribute* can also be used interchangeably, but in this case the practice is a little more acceptable. When we refer to an attribute, we are usually referring to the name of a property in the class definition in the schema, which has not been instantiated yet. A property is used to refer to the actual value in the instantiated object.

Let's go back to our house analogy for a moment. Have you ever seen two houses that look almost identical, except that one is painted white and the other is painted beige? It is a good bet those houses were built from the same set of blueprints. It is a common practice in the building industry as well as Active Directory. Every object in Active Directory comes from the same set of blueprints for that object, whether it is a user, a computer, or whatever. This means that they are all created with the same attributes and methods. We then change the properties of that object, such as the account name, to make them unique in our domain and to set the appropriate values for that object.

The schema supplied with a standard installation of Active Directory is well documented and available on the Web. You can print the documentation and study it until you are blue in the face, but to really get a feel for how the schema is implemented in Active Directory, you need to see it in action for yourself. We can do this using the tools available either with our Windows Server installation or by downloading the Windows 2003 Server Resource Kit.

Tools

Some of the tools we talk about in this section are designed for modifying the schema itself. Rest assured, we won't perform any updates during the course of this book. You should not need special permissions to view the schema, and you will definitely not need membership in the Schema Admins group!

Let's start with the most basic tool, the `dsquery` utility. The `dsquery` utility is available after installing the `adminpack.msi` from the Windows Server 2003 CD. It will let us view properties of objects in Active Directory as well as the schema. To view the attributes of a class, open a command prompt and run the following command. You will need to replace `<domain>` with the DC elements of your domain (such as `DC=zygort,DC=com`).

```
dsquery * cn=computer,cn=schema,cn=configuration,<domain> -scope base
-attr *
```

It's complete, but definitely not fun to read, as you can see in Figure 17.1.

A friendlier option is the ADSI Edit application. The ADSI Edit utility is a snap-in for the MMC and comes with the Windows Support Tools. Before you can use this snap-in, you must first register the `schmmgmt.dll` with the following command:

```
Regsvr32 schmmgmt.dll
```

After registering the DLL, you can open up an MMC console and add the Active Directory Schema snap-in. Be sure to save the console so you can easily open the ADSI Edit utility later.

One column to pay particular attention to is the Type column; it will tell you if an attribute is mandatory or optional (see Figure 17.2). Mandatory attributes are going to be very important when we begin creating Active Directory objects in our scripts.

My personal preference for developing a script is the Active Directory Viewer, which is available as part of the ADSI Software Development Kit (SDK). The SDK is available as a free download from Microsoft. Be sure to download the SDK, not the ADSI interfaces which should already be installed on your system. To download the ADSI SDK, see http://www.microsoft.com/ntserver/nts/downloads/other/ADSI25/ and download the SDK for Active Directory Services Interface.

The AD Viewer gives you a quick view of an object and its data. You can easily see what data is held by what property, so you can be sure that you are referencing the correct attribute in your script. You should also notice that the data is referred to by the `ldapDisplayName` of the property, not the field that you would see in ADU&C. In addition to the data, you can see what type of data is that is stored in the property, such as an integer or a string. This is extremely useful information to know when you're trying to process the data you retrieve from a property.

FIGURE 17.1
dsquery of computer
class attributes

FIGURE 17.2
The ADSI Edit
application

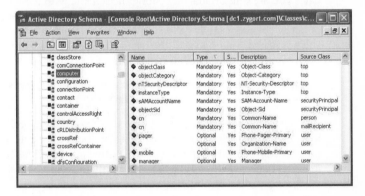

After downloading and installing the SDK, execute the viewer application (`adsvw.exe`). In the New window, select ObjectViewer and click OK. In the New Object window, deselect the User OpenObject check box and enter **LDAP://** along with your domain naming context into the ADsPath field, as shown in Figure 17.3.

FIGURE 17.3
Active Directory Viewer

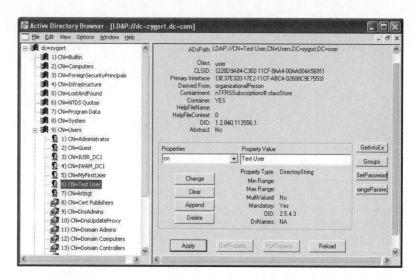

With the Active Directory Viewer, spend some time selecting various objects, especially object types, and cycle through the properties. Make correlations between the actual property names and their friendly names in Active Directory. Print the documentation listing the properties of the objects you will most commonly deal with (users, computers, OUs, etc.) and note the properties that you are most interested in. Even after a brief hiatus from writing Active Directory scripts, it is easy to forget the simplest of property names (like sn).

Inheritance

Once you are comfortable navigating the schema with the tool of your choice, let's get back to the business of mandatory and optional attributes. Mandatory attributes require a value before that object can be successfully created in Active Directory. If an optional attribute is empty, the object can still be created. Take a look at the computer class (cn=computer) using the following dsquery statement. Again, you will need to replace *<domain>* with the DC elements of your domain.

```
dsquery * cn=computer,cn=schema,cn=configuration,<domain> -scope base
➥ -attr * | find "systemMustContain" /I
```

How many mandatory attributes for this class did you find? I'm guessing none. So does that mean that you can just create a computer object without giving it so much as a name? Of course not; just imagine how hard it would be to map a drive to a computer with no name. Every object has some mandatory properties; we just have to find them. Figure 17.4 shows the results from dsquery displaying the mandatory attributes of the computer class.

FIGURE 17.4
dsquery of mandatory
computer class
attributes

Confession time: I asked you to use `dsquery` for a reason; it shows you the definition of the one class and only the one class that was specified. Now try looking at the computer class with the MMC and Active Directory Schema snap-in, and you will get slightly different results, namely some additional attributes that happen to be mandatory. But if those mandatory properties are not defined in the computer class, where did they come from?

The trick lies in understanding the concept of *inheritance*. Just as your kids might inherit your hair color, classes can inherit attributes from parent classes. The use of parent classes makes Active Directory more efficient. By defining attributes in a parent class and then inheriting those attributes into child classes, the class designer does not have to redefine the same attributes over and over for multiple classes. Think about it; why would you want to put an attribute called *"name"* into every single class you might ever create, when you can create it once and let inheritance do the work for you?

The use of inheritance creates a hierarchical set of classes in the schema of Active Directory. One class is inherited into another class until the final child classes are created and ready to be used. The topmost class in the schema is a class known as `top`. The attributes (mandatory and optional) of `top` are then inherited by classes like `person`, and `organizational-person`.

So, the mandatory attributes we are looking for actually lie in one or more of the parent classes. But who is the parent? Looking at the schema of the computer object again, find the value of the `subClassOf` attribute. This attribute points to the parent class; in the case of the `computer` class it happens to be the `user` class. I bet you weren't expecting that, were you? Here is the ancestry of the computer class:

```
computer -> user -> organizational-person -> person -> top
```

If you work your way through each of these classes, you will notice the mandatory attributes start appearing with the `top` class. The `person` class adds another, but the `organizational-person` and `user` classes don't add any. In addition, optional attributes are inherited from the parent classes. Eventually, we wind up with a fully formed computer class, completely defined and ready to use.

Now that you are getting the hang of inheritance, let's find out where something important is defined, like the account name. That property is stored as the `sAMAccountName`. But this time, let's do it the easy way by using the MMC and Active Directory Schema snap-in. Looking at the computer object, you will see a column labeled "Source Class," which points to the class that defines that attribute. The source class for `sAMAccountName` is `securityPrincipal`. But notice that the `securityPrincipal` class is not in our inheritance diagram. If we did not inherit from `securityPrincipal`, how did that attribute get there?

Auxiliary Classes

To answer that, we have to look at what *kind* of class we are talking about. Active Directory has four different types of classes. Some classes can be used to create objects and some classes cannot. Of the four types of classes, only structural classes can be instantiated.

When looking at the schema of a class, you can find out what type of class you are looking at by examining the `objectClassCategory` attribute. The `objectClassCategory` attribute contains a number that corresponds to what type of class it is. Table 17.2 lists the class types.

The `securityPrincipal` class is an auxiliary class; it provides additional attributes to the structural class. The `securityPrincipal` class is very important in that it allows the object created to be positively identified, which is the first step in providing security. Since it is an auxiliary class, it cannot be instantiated.

Understanding inheritance and the role of classes in the Active Directory schema will help you write scripts that return the properties of the objects that you are looking for. Even more important to someone potentially developing their own scripts is that inheritance makes your job a lot easier. If you know how one class implements an attribute, and that attribute is used in other classes because of inheritance, then you already know how to use that attribute in all those other classes.

TABLE 17.2:   Class Types

NAME	OBJECT CATEGORY	DESCRIPTION
88	0	These classes were defined before there was a specification to classify categories of classes. They behave like structural classes, but should be treated as abstract.
Structural	1	Active Directory objects are most often created from these classes. This includes users, computers, OUs, and so forth.
Abstract	2	These classes provide attributes that are inherited by child classes. Active Directory objects cannot be created from these classes.
Auxiliary	3	These classes provide additional attributes to a structural class. Active Directory objects cannot be created from these classes.

Common Active Directory Objects

We have talked about the schema, and how it defines the attributes that make up an object in Active Directory. Now it is time to start looking at the objects that we will be dealing with in more depth. We do not cover all the object classes here, or every single property and method, but we do talk about the more common ones that you will be working with as you develop your ADSI scripts.

As we look at the properties and methods, we mention some of the COM interfaces that implement those operations. ADSI implements both core interfaces for all Active Directory objects and specific interfaces for specific object types. We do not go into the interfaces themselves, but we do mention the functionality they provide. The property names provided in the tables in the following sections are the ldapDisplayNames that we use in our scripts.

Common Properties and Methods

The IADs interface is implemented by all ADSI objects. It describes the basic features of every object. It provides identification, parent container, and schema definition as well as providing the object with the ability to load its properties into the local property cache and commit any changes made to the directory service. Tables 17.3 and 17.4 describe the properties and methods, respectively, that are common to all Active Directory objects.

Container Properties and Methods

Container objects in Active Directory are designed to manage child objects, including their creation and removal. The IADsContainer interface is used to implement most of this functionality, and is used by containers and organizational units. Tables 17.5 and 17.6 describe the properties and methods of the Container object.

TABLE 17.3: Common ADSI Properties

PROPERTY	DESCRIPTION
ADsPath	Active Directory path to the object.
distinguishedName	Fully qualified name; specifies the complete path to the object.
objectGUID	Globally unique ID of the object.
name	Relative name (RN) of the object.
objectClass	Schema class of the object.
objectCategory	Category of the object. This is usually the same as the objectClass value, but not always.

TABLE 17.4: Common ADSI Methods

METHOD	DESCRIPTION
GetInfo	Loads all property values of the object into the local property cache.
SetInfo	Writes property values from the local property cache to the directory service.
Get	Gets a value by the property name.
Put	Sets a value by the property name.
GetEx	Gets property values from the local property cache.
PutEx	Sets property values into the local property cache.
GetInfoEx	Loads specific property values from the directory service.

TABLE 17.5: Container Properties

PROPERTY	DESCRIPTION
Cn	Common name of the container
Description	Description of the container
distinguishedName	Distinguished name of the container
Name	Name of the container

TABLE 17.6: Container Methods

METHOD	DESCRIPTION
GetObject	Retrieves an interface to the child object in the container
Create	Creates an instance of a child object in the container
Delete	Removes a child object from the container
CopyHere	Copies a child object into the container
MoveHere	Moves a child object into the container

Organizational Units

Organizational units (OUs) are used to manage other objects in the Active Directory hierarchy. They use the same properties and methods as the container. Note that organization units cannot be created inside a container object. This is a restriction of the Active Directory schema. The only way to change this behavior is through a modification to the organizationalUnit class to allow the container object to be a possible superior to an organizational unit. Tables 17.7 and 17.8 show the properties and methods of the Organizational Unit object.

TABLE 17.7: Organizational Unit Properties

PROPERTY	DESCRIPTION
cn	Common name of the organizational unit
description	Description of the organizational unit
distinguishedName	Distinguished name of the organizational unit
ou	Name of the organizational unit
managedBy	Distinguished name of the manager of the organizational unit
name	Name of the organizational unit

Organizational units also have properties similar to user objects, such as telephone and fax numbers. They are rarely used and difficult to access without a custom application.

TABLE 17.8: Organizational Unit Methods

METHOD	DESCRIPTION
GetObject	Retrieves an interface to the child object in the container
Create	Creates an instance of a child object in the container
Delete	Removes a child object from the container
CopyHere	Copies a child object into the container
MoveHere	Moves a child object into the container

User Properties and Methods

The IADsInterface is designed to manage user accounts in the directory. This interface inherits from the IADs interface, so it will also contain all the properties and methods described with that interface. The user object is one we will be spending quite a bit of time working with in our scripts, so it is a good idea to become familiar with its properties and methods.

Two more important reminders: not all the properties listed here will be available through the Active Directory Users and Computers console. The only way to access these properties is via ADSI or another utility application. Also, some properties will be set in accordance with the value set for other properties. For example, setting the country property (co) automatically sets the country abbreviation property (c). Table 17.9 shows the User object properties.

TABLE 17.9: User Properties

PROPERTY	DESCRIPTION
sAMAccountName	Account name for the user
givenName	First name of the user
middleName	Middle name of the user
sn	Last name of the user
initials	User's initials
physicalDeliveryOfficeName	Office location
streetAddress	Address
c	Country

TABLE 17.9: User Properties *(CONTINUED)*

PROPERTY	DESCRIPTION
streetAddress	Street address
postOfficeBox	Post office box
l	City
st	State
c	Country abbreviation
co	Country
postalCode	Zip code
telephoneNumber	Telephone number
facsimileTelephoneNumber	Fax number
mobile	Mobile telephone number
ipPhone	IP telephone number
info	Notes section on the telephone tab
homePhone	Home telephone number
pager	Pager number
profilePath	Path to the user's profile
scriptPath	Path to the user's logon script
homeDrive	Drive letter mapped to the user's home directory
homeDirectory	Path to the user's home directory
mail	Primary e-mail address
manager	Distinguished name of the user object who is the manager of this user
accountDisabled	A set of flags used to indicate if an account is disabled, locked out, password expiration disabled, etc.
accountExpirationDate	Date the account expires, if set
company	Company

TABLE 17.9:   User Properties *(CONTINUED)*

PROPERTY	DESCRIPTION
department	Department
departmentNumber	Department number
division	Division
employeeID	Employee ID
employeeNumber	Employee number
employeeType	Employee type
drink	Yes, there is a drink property. I kid you not.

Another property to be aware of is the memberOf property. This returns a collection of group objects to which the user directly belongs. This does not take into account any groups the user may belong to via group inheritance (groups that belong to other groups.) There is a way around that as well, which we see in action in the next chapter. Table 17.10 shows the methods of the User object.

TABLE 17.10:   User Methods

METHOD	DESCRIPTION
SetPassword	Set the user's password.
ChangePassword	Changes the password. The old password must be specified in addition to the new password.

Group Properties and Methods

The IADSGroup interface is used to manage group membership in Active Directory. This includes adding and removing users, as well as checking for group membership. Tables 17.11 and 17.12 show the properties and methods of the Group object.

TABLE 17.11:   Group Properties

PROPERTY	DESCRIPTION
cn	Common name of the organizational unit
description	Description of the organizational unit

TABLE 17.11: Group Properties *(CONTINUED)*

PROPERTY	DESCRIPTION
distinguishedName	Distinguished name of the organizational unit
groupType	Bitmap representing the type of group
ou	Name of the organizational unit
managedBy	Distinguished name of the manager of the organizational unit
mail	E-mail address for the group
name	Name of the organizational unit
sAMAccountName	Account name of the group

TABLE 17.12: Group Methods

METHOD	DESCRIPTION
Add	Add a new member to the group
Remove	Remove a member from the group
IsMember	Verifies an object is a member of the group

Computer Properties and Methods

The IADsComputer interface is used to manage computer objects in Active Directory. This includes servers and workstations on the network. It inherits from the IADs interface, so it will already have the properties and methods described in that interface. If you browse through the properties in more detail, you will notice it shares many properties with the user object as well. Table 17.13 shows the properties of the Computer object.

TABLE 17.13: Computer Properties

NAME	DESCRIPTION
cn	Common name for the computer
comment	Comment field
department	Department for the computer
description	Description of the computer

TABLE 17.13:   Computer Properties *(CONTINUED)*

NAME	DESCRIPTION
distinguishedName	Distinguished name of the computer
division	Division for the computer
dNSHostName	DNS host name of the computer
location	Location of the computer
name	Computer name
managedBy	Distinguished name of the manager of the computer
memberOf	Group memberships of the computer
operatingSystem	Operating system detected on the machine
operatingSystemServicePack	Service pack level of the operating system
operatingSystemVersion	Version number of the operating system
sAMAccountName	Account name of the computer
serialNumber	Serial number of the computer

The Basic ADSI Pattern

When you develop your script for Active Directory, from a programming standpoint you will notice that it follows a basic pattern. Patterns are a good thing for programmers. Using a pattern means you do not have to reinvent the wheel, or in the case of script writing, figure out how to write a script that manipulates your directory service. The pattern we'll be using in our ADSI scripts has three simple, basic steps. That pattern looks something like this:

1. Bind to an object in Active Directory. The object can be the top level of the domain, an OU in the domain, or an object in an OU, such as a user.

2. Read the data and work with the object. This includes (but is not limited to) querying the object, finding the child objects, changing the object's properties, creating a new object, or deleting the object.

3. Save changes to the object if you've made any changes to the object. Just like a word processor, if you don't save your work, no one can appreciate it or blame you for it later.

4. Rinse and repeat as needed.

Obviously this is not the complete list of steps you'll go through. In fact, things can get complicated in a hurry. You might have to query a database or write to a file along the way, but those steps can be inserted into the basic pattern. For now let's stick with the basics. Let's look at a simple example, adding a new user account:

```
Bind to the OU you want to create the user account in.
Create a user object.  Set the mandatory properties of the object.
Save the new user object.
```

Creating one object requires only one pass through the pattern. To see an example of the pattern being repeated, I will resort to a little pseudocode to give you the general idea. In this example, we want to modify the office location of 10 users, who we already have in a list:

```
While not at the end of the user list
        Bind to the user object.
        Modify the office attribute
        Save the user object
Return to the top of the loop and move to the next user
```

I want to give you one more example, but this one is a bit more complex (albeit more real-world in nature). We want to change the office location of a set of users again, but this time the users will belong to an OU in Active Directory.

```
Bind to the OU containing the users.
Query the OU for user objects
While not at the end of the user list
Bind to the user object
Modify the office attribute
Save the user object
Return to the top of the loop and move to the next user
```

In this example, I actually used the pattern inside another pattern. Notice that I also didn't save the OU object, but since no changes were made to it there was no need to. You could expand this pattern further to include a range of OUs.

You should be getting a feel for how most ADSI scripts are going to work, following this pattern. On your own, take a few minutes and think of how to use this pattern to accomplish some of these tasks:

◆ Adding an OU to the domain

◆ Adding an OU underneath an existing OU

◆ Deleting a user from the domain

◆ Resetting a user's password

Local Property Cache

Before we get into the scripting details of creating our ADSI scripts, it's important that you understand a little more about what ADSI is doing on your client machines as you go through the pattern we just explained.

When we bind to an object in ADSI, a region of memory on your client machine is set aside as a cache location for that object. This region is known as the *local property cache*. As you read property values from the object in Active Directory, they are stored locally in the cache. Placing a copy of the object in a local repository can speed up operations, as well as provide a layer of safety for our scripts. Figure 17.5 shows the local property cache and how it interacts with Active Directory.

Since all the changes made by a script are done to the object in the local cache, it means that those changes could be discarded or just plain lost. If, during the execution of your script, you want to undo all the changes that you have made, simply do not save the object. Likewise, if Fido comes along and decides your power cord would make an excellent chew toy, your work can be lost if you have not saved the object to Active Directory recently.

The key to the local property cache is finding the best time to save your work to an object. Each time the `SetInfo` method is called to write your object out to Active Directory, you will incur some network overhead. Some scriptwriters will set the mandatory properties of an object, save it to Active Directory, and then proceed to set the optional properties of the object and save again. Some will set all the properties and save the object at one time. As you write your scripts, you will develop a style that you are comfortable with and that works in your network environment.

Binding

You should have a pretty good grasp of the steps to take when writing an ADSI script. It is time to look at those steps in more details, starting with binding. At this point we are going to start talking more in terms of actual VBScript code.

Binding is basically assigning a variable name to an object in Active Directory. That explanation is oversimplified, but it works for now. During the execution of our script, whenever we want to read or change any attributes of that Active Directory object, we use that variable to refer to it. The actual name of the variable does not matter, but it should be something that is easy to associate with the object that we are manipulating.

BINDING SYNTAX

The first step in binding to an object in Active Directory is finding where that object is in Active Directory. Every object has to reside somewhere, either under the root of the domain itself or maybe buried in the depths of an OU structure seven levels deep. Finding some objects is like looking for that mysteriously missing watch in your house. If your house is like mine that usually means a search is required. For now let's assume that we know right where that object exists in Active Directory, and we can send the search party out to look for objects later.

FIGURE 17.5
The local property cache

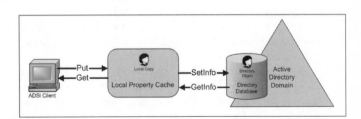

In VBScript, we can bind to an object in Active Directory with one statement. The statement itself has important parts: the Set keyword and the GetObject function. The Set keyword is used to bind a variable to an instance of an object, in our case the object resides in Active Directory. The GetObject function is used to return an instance of the requested object. The complete statement looks like this:

```
Set ADObject = GetObject("LDAP://CN=Scott,CN=Users,DC=zygort,DC=com")
```

There is one hitch to this method that you have to watch out for, and it is one of the most common problems when dealing with any directory services script. What if the object you are trying to bind to does not exist or the object does not exist where you think it exists?

First, before attempting to bind to any object in Active Directory, enable error trapping in your script. In VBScript, this is done with the On Error Resume Next statement. The error trap will let errors occur in the script without causing the script to end prematurely. An intrinsic object in VBScript called the Err object will hold the success or failure result of the last executing operation. You should check the value of the Number property of the Err object (Err.Number) immediately after you attempt to bind to the object. If the value is not zero, then something has gone wrong and you might want to consider terminating the script.

If you choose not to check the value of Err.Number, then at least check the object after you attempt to bind to see if it is Empty. If the object does not exist in Active Directory, it will not populate the variable with any information, hence leaving it as Empty. If the variable is Empty, then warn the user and possibly end the script gracefully. The following example will give you a better idea of how to handle binding and its potential for disaster:

```
On Error Resume Next
Set ADObject = GetObject("LDAP://CN=Scott,CN=Users,DC=zygort,DC=com")
If IsEmpty(ADObject) Then
        WScript.Echo "The object does not exist"
        WScript.Quit
End If
' Do your magic to the object
```

The path to the object you want to bind to is one of the most common places that errors can occur in your scripts. If you allow the user to enter the path to the object, this is going to increase the chances of a bad path. With a few additional lines of code, you can handle the situation more gracefully.

ADsPath

To bind to the Active Directory object, we have to know where it exists. Each object in Active Directory has a path that points to its current location known as the ADsPath, and this is the path we use to bind to that object. The ADsPath is basically the distinguished name of the object, preceded by the provider moniker. You can find the ADsPath attribute of any object by using the Active Directory Viewer, as shown in Figure 17.6.

To bind to the user object in VBScript, we use the Set keyword to associate the variable name to the object in Active Directory. In order for this work, we need to use a function called GetObject to point to the object in Active Directory. The GetObject function will connect to the directory service specified by the moniker, locate the object (if it exists where we say it is supposed to exist), and return the object's properties to a location known as the local property cache. The following example shows the code to bind to a variable to a user object, followed by using that variable to read the last name of the user:

```
Set User = GetObject("LDAP://CN=Scott,CN=Users,DC=zygort,DC=com")
Wscript.Echo User("sn")
```

An ADsPath is built with two parts: the protocol moniker for the directory service and the distinguished name of the object. You should already be familiar with distinguished names. We discussed the monikers for the directory service providers earlier in the chapter. For Active Directory, we use the LDAP:// provider.

```
<moniker>//<distinguished name>
```

There are also some variations to the distinguished name that offer a few more options when it comes to binding to an object. We will cover each of these variations in more detail in the following pages and discuss when you would want to use those variations.

FIGURE 17.6

Finding the ADsPath in the Active Directory Viewer

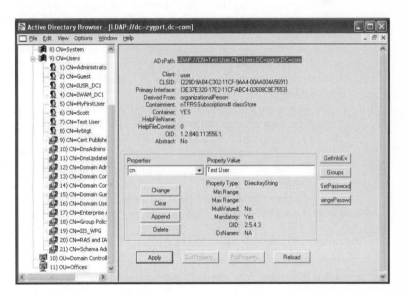

HARDCODED BINDING

Binding an object in a domain is fairly straightforward. Part of the ADsPath points to the domain to be contacted. These are the DC components of the distinguished name. For example, the domain name in the following ADsPath is zygort.com.

```
LDAP://CN=Scott,CN=Users,DC=zygort,DC=com
```

Instead of binding to a user object, let's bind to the default container that holds the user objects, the Users container:

```
LDAP://CN=Users,DC=zygort,DC=com
```

Let's take it a step further and imagine that this script will list every user object in the Users container. That might be a very useful report! Now let's take that script to another domain, such as the sybex.com domain. The script no longer works. Why?

Because the container it is trying to bind to, the Users container, is in the zygort.com domain. We've hardcoded the domain value in our script, and if the script cannot contact that domain then the script will not work. And if the script is able to contact the original domain, it will not give us the results from our new domain.

The solution is simple enough; just rename the ADsPath of the Users container from zygort.com to sybex.com. Oh, and make sure that if there are any other references throughout the *entire* script that you change those as well. And do not expect to make any changes to the script and take it back to the zygort.com domain, because it will not work again until you rename (again) the domain throughout the script. Sound like fun?

SERVERLESS BINDING

The above scenario certainly does not thrill me. I like my scripts to be as portable as possible. I want to be able to take a script from one domain to another and do as little rewriting as possible, preferably none!

To bind to an object, the ADsPath must have a domain component to it. There is just no way around it. So in order to make our scripts portable, we have to basically "teach" the script to fill in the domain components for itself. In Active Directory (and other LDAP services), the means to do just that is at our fingertips.

We can make use of a special object called RootDSE in our scripts. The RootDSE is a unique object created on each domain controller. Its job is to provide information about the capabilities of the domain controller and directory services available on that domain controller. By reading the attributes of the RootDSE object, our script can find out what domain our script is running in, what the path is to the schema container for the domain, what the current time is, and a host of other useful information.

We start by binding to the RootDSE object itself with the LDAP moniker. Because the RootDSE object is providing us with the domain information, there are no DC components in the ADsPath.

```
Set RootDSE = GetObject("LDAP://RootDSE")
```

After binding to the RootDSE object, we can reference its attributes to find out the information we need. Table 17.14 lists some of the more useful attributes of the RootDSE object. For a complete listing of the RootDSE attributes, pay a visit to the following URL:

```
http://msdn.microsoft.com/library/default.asp?url=library/en-us/wmisdk/wmi/
rootdse.asp
```

As you can see, you can retrieve the distinguished names of several important containers through the RootDSE object. In our case, we are looking for the distinguished name of the current domain. To find that, we can read the defaultNamingContext attribute of the RootDSE object. The following code shows the whole process in action:

```
Set RootDSE = GetObject("LDAP://RootDSE")
Wscript.Echo RootDSE("defaultNamingContext")
' On my domain, this returns DC=zygort,DC=com
Set UserCN = GetObject("LDAP://CN=Users, " & _ RootDSE("defaultNamingContext"))
```

TABLE 17.14: RootDSE attributes

ATTRIBUTE	DESCRIPTION
configurationNamingContext	Returns the distinguished name of the configuration container in the domain
currentTime	Returns the current time on the domain controller
defaultNamingContext	Returns the distinguished name of the domain that the domain controller is a member of
dnsHostName	Returns the DNS name of the domain controller
schemaNamingContext	Returns the distinguished name of the schema container

The process is simple: Start by binding a variable to the RootDSE object. With that variable, we read the contents of the defaultNamingContext property, which will return the domain components of the current domain. Since our imaginary script was binding to the Users container of the domain, I have prepended the LDAP moniker and container name to the value returned from the RootDSE object and submitted it the GetObject function. The end result should be the UserCN object bound to the Users container (which still has a chance of failing, so always use the error trap discussed earlier!).

Binding to the RootDSE object is a standard practice in most ADSI scripts. Besides giving you lots of useful information about the domain itself, getting and keeping an object bound to the RootDSE object can also give you a performance boost. Later in this chapter we talk about how this works.

USING AN ALTERNATE DOMAIN CONTROLLER

So far all the binding statements we have looked at have one thing in common; we have never specified a domain controller to use. Each ADsPath simply lists the domain components, but never a server name. To bind to an object and retrieve its information, we have to contact a domain controller for that given domain. So which domain controller are we talking to?

Remember that domain controllers are peers in Active Directory, so each should contain roughly the same information (keep in mind there is always some latency involved in replicated data between domain controllers). If your binding statement does not specify a specific domain controller, you should be talking to the same domain controller that authenticated your account when you logged on. If you want to see which domain controller authenticated you, take a look at the value of the %logonserver% environment variable.

Now, what happens if that domain controller is unavailable? DNS will be queried for other available domain controller services on the local site. You should have one available, or you might (unintentionally) find your work being done at another site and discover that WAN lines do little to improve performance. If you have no domain controllers available at your site, you might want to put this book down and find out why.

The recommended practice for writing ADSI scripts is not to specify a certain domain controller when binding to Active Directory objects. This lets Active Directory and DNS do their respective jobs, providing a list of services available and which service providers are preferred based on your network location. A good domain administrator should have setup sites and services to be readily available to his or her users (and to their scripts.).

However, if you are really picky about where your Active Directory work gets done, then ADSI does let you specify which domain controller you want to communicate with. By changing the ADsPath used to a different format, we can specify a domain controller and, optionally, the port to be used if the directory service is running on a port other than the default (port 398). To support this, the ADsPath can take on one of the following alternate formats:

```
LDAP://<domain controller>,<distinguished name>
LDAP://<domain controller>:<port>,<distinguished name>
```

Let me give you a couple of examples. The first two are typical examples of an ADsPath, and the rest are variations that specify to use the BranchOffice domain controller:

```
LDAP://DC=zygort,DC=com
LDAP://CN=Scott,CN=Users,DC=zygort,DC=com
LDAP://BranchOfficeDC
LDAP://BranchOfficeDC:5151
LDAP://BranchOfficeDC,CN=Scott,CN=Users,DC=zygort,DC=com
LDAP://BranchOfficeDC:5151,OU=Offices,DC=zygrot,DC=com
```

This is not the recommended practice. Specifying a domain controller to use will essentially tie the successful execution of your script to the status of the specified domain controller. You have also severely limited the portability of your script to other domains. Using the RootDSE object to obtain the current domain components will still work, but unless that domain has a domain controller with the same name as you've just specified in the ADsPath, then you will still be out of luck.

Having said all that, this technique does have some situations that weigh in its favor. Let's say you have a domain controller that is busy (perhaps performing double duty as a print server) and one that is idly waiting for authentication requests; which would you rather use? Trust me when I say that a heavy Active Directory script can bring a print server running on the domain controller to its virtual knees (this was when I learned to check which domain controller I was authenticating against).

Let's say you need to make a change for a specific site. You could make the change to your local domain controller and let replication propagate to the rest of the domain controllers. Or, you can target a domain controller at that site. The change will be made immediately at that site and be available to the local users. Eventually the change will replicate through the rest of the domain according to the replication schedule.

Binding to global catalog Servers

While binding to a single domain directory tree is good for most scripts, there are situations where you may need to get information from a broader authority. For example, if your current domain is just one of a larger domain forest, you may need to bind to a global catalog server to find the data you need, which may be spread across the forest.

To summarize the global catalog server's functions, think of it as a domain controller that replicates a subset of domain information from each domain in a forest. Directory attributes that are defined as part of the *partial attribute set* will be replicated to all domain controllers that have been configured as global catalog servers. Binding to the global catalog server and using it as the source of your queries can yield information for each domain in the forest.

Global catalog servers separate directory queries from global catalog queries by using separate TCP/IP ports (the global catalog server uses port 3268 by default). ADSI already knows the default port for binding to the global catalog server, so it's not necessary to specify the port unless it has been changed by an administrator. Instead, we only have to change the provider that we wish to use. To use the global catalog server, use GC:// instead of LDAP://, like so:

```
Set GC = GetObject("GC://RootDSE")
```

Notice that we can still use the RootDSE object when querying a global catalog server. In the next chapter, I will give you some scripts to work with the global catalog server and go over them in more detail.

GUID BINDING

To refresh your memory, a GUID is a 128-bit value that is guaranteed to be unique in the span of the networked world (but I've never heard it called a money-back guarantee, I wonder why?). Active Directory uses not only distinguished names to identify objects, but it also generates a GUID for each new object that is created. Although a distinguished name may change over time (and its location in Active Directory), the same GUID remains with the object throughout its lifetime.

Knowing this, it is possible to bind to an object using its GUID instead of its distinguished name. This assumes that you know the GUID of the object beforehand, of course. The beauty in this method is that you can always bind to *that* object, no matter where in the Active Directory tree it happens to be. When you see the code to do this, you'll see the ugly side of binding to a GUID instead of a distinguished name:

```
Set MyObject = GetObject("LDAP://<GUID=AC54…91BF74,DC=zygort,DC=com>")
```

First, notice that I have enclosed the GUID piece of the ADsPath between a set of less-than (<) and greater-than (>) symbols. GUIDs are represented in hexadecimal notation, and typing out the entire GUID would have run well beyond the edge of the page or taken up several lines of text. Not to mention, it would not have corresponded to any object in anyone else's Active Directory tree but my own (hopefully!). To view the GUID of an object, you can use Active Directory Viewer or reference the GUID property of an object that you have bound to, as shown here:

```
Set MyObject = GetObject("LDAP://CN=Scott,CN=Users,DC=zygort,DC=COM")
WScript.Echo MyObject.Get("objectGUID")
' or
WScript.Echo MyObject.GUID
```

WELL-KNOWN GUIDS

Getting past the ugliness of GUIDs for everyday objects such as user and computers objects, there are some containers where knowing the GUID is critical to finding it. Several standard containers in Active Directory that are used on an everyday basis can be renamed, thus changing their distinguished name and potentially breaking our scripts. Microsoft knew this was possible, and assigned each of these containers a consistent GUID (which defeats the purpose of a GUID, don't you think?) so that they could always be bound to regardless what their current name happened to be. These are called Well-Known GUIDS, and are shown in Table 17.15.

TABLE 17.15:   Well-Known GUID Values

CONTAINER	WELL-KNOWN GUID
Users	A9D1CA15768811D1ADED00C04fD8D5CD
Computers	AA312825768811D1ADED00C04FD8D5CD
System	AB1D30F3768811D1ADED00C04FD8D5CD
DomainControllers	A361B2FFFFD211D1AA4B00C04FD7D83A
Infrastructure	2FBAC1870ADE11D297C400C04FD8D5CD
DeletedObjects	18E2EA80684F11D2B9AA00C04F79F805
LostAndFound	AB8153B7768811D1ADED00C04FD8D5CD

To use a Well-Known GUID, we have to vary our binding syntax a bit (I know, you were just getting used the last set of variations). In the next example, we'll bind to the Users container of the zygort.com domain. For the sake of brevity, I'll use the constant from the earlier file.

```
Set UsersCN = GetObject("LDAP://<WKGUID=" & WKGUID_USERS & _ ",DC=zygort,DC=com>"
```

Again, notice that I am enclosing the GUID between a set of less-than (<) and greater-than (>) symbols. Using the keyword WKGUID= tells the query engine that we are going reference a well-known GUID. You should also notice that the domain components are also included *inside* the symbols. These GUID values are consistent across all Active Directory domains, but we still need to specify which domain we are targeting. However, we can still retrieve the domain components from the RootDSE object rather than hardcoding them.

INTERFACES

Now that you have a handle on binding with GUIDs, you should not use them in place of binding with distinguished names. Don't you just hate it when people show you something cool and then tell you that you can't have it? Well, not to worry, I would never do that to you.

Instead, you should use them in *conjunction* with distinguished names. Why? Because when binding with the GUID syntax, certain attributes and methods that worked when binding with distinguished name suddenly stop working. What's happening behind the scenes is that a different interface is being used when you bind to the object using a GUID.

An interface is simply a contract between the client and object. The interface states that "I support attributes A, B, and C." If the client tries to use attribute D, E, or F, then an error occurs. You know by now that different classes in Active Directory (user, computer, etc.) sometimes have different attributes and methods to them. These are enabled by implementing class-specific interfaces on those objects. Depending on the object you bind to, you will wind up using an interface specific for that class—at least, until you try to bind using a GUID.

When binding using a GUID, ADSI does not use the interface for the class of the object you are binding to. GUID binding was not designed to support all the functionality of the object class, but rather was intended as a fast method of connecting to an object. Since the class-specific interface is not used, this also results in low overhead. In fact, the GUID itself is an indexed attribute in Active Directory, which improves query performance, as well as being part of the partial replica set that is replicated to every global catalog server.

So how do we regain our lost functionality? The answer is actually simple; bind with the GUID first, retrieve the distinguished name, then bind to the object using the distinguished name. This will allow you bind to the correct object, no matter what it is currently named, as well as give you access to all the attributes and methods of the object. The following is an example, from start to finish, of binding to the Users container from a domain:

```
Set RootDSE = GetObject("LDAP://RootDSE")
UsersGUID = "<WKGUID=" & WKGUID_USERS & "," & _
        RootDSE.Get("defaultNamingContext") & ">"
Set UsersGUIDCN = GetObject("LDAP:// " & UsersGUID)
Set UsersCN = GetObject("LDAP:// " & _ UsersGUIDCN.Get("distinguishedName"))
```

This code first binds to the RootDSE object. It then creates a string, which combines the well-known GUID from the constant value with the default naming context from the RootDSE object. This string is then used to bind to the Users container. The distinguished name property of the Users container is retrieved, and we bind to the container again using the distinguished name of the container. We now have all the attributes and methods of the object that we would normally be used to dealing with.

OpenDSObject

Permissions in Active Directory can be very selective, right down to the attribute level. Normal users do not typically have the permissions necessary to create or delete objects. A network administrator might grant one everyone access to view the user's location attribute, while granting only a managers group access to view their homeTelephone attribute.

Up until now, we've been using the credentials of the logged-on user for authorization to access Active Directory. Active Directory naturally has a set of security permissions in place by default to keep unauthorized users from creating, modifying or (even worse) deleting objects. Depending on the task at hand, we need to run our scripts in the context of security account with the rights to perform the tasks we have written the script to do.

When a script executes, it runs in the security context of the currently logged-on user. By using the RunAs command, the security context of running instance of the script can be changed, as long as a valid username and password are supplied. Since the GetObject function does not accept a username and password as arguments, it must attempt to bind to an object using whatever security context the script is running in.

If we want to bind to an object using a different set of security credentials, and we do not want to use the RunAs command, we can use a function called OpenDSObject. This function takes four arguments in the following order: the object to bind, a username, a password, and the type of authentication mechanism to use. Using OpenDSObject in our script would look similar to this (hopefully with a stronger password!):

```
Set MyObject = _ OpenDSObject("LDAP://CN=Scott,CN=Users,DC=zygort,DC=com", _
    "ZYGORT\ScriptingAdmin", "P@ssw0rd", ADS_SECURE_AUTHENICATION)
```

Before continuing, it is necessary to point out the obvious danger at hand. Using this function puts a password in clear text for anyone with access to the script to see. I should not have to say this, but I will anyway: Do not use any account with domain administrator rights in this function! Create a special, very restricted account with just enough rights to perform the task at hand, and give it a strong password. (Hint: Make sure the password does not expire or your script will suddenly stop working one day.)

You should also download the Script Encoder from Microsoft and apply it to any scripts that put a password in clear text. The Script Encoder will essentially hide the code from prying eyes conducting a surface-level search. A known cipher is applied to the code, rendering the code unreadable. When the code is executed, the encoded script is read into the scripting engine and decoded for execution. It is not encrypted, though, and the cipher is well known by this point. Cracking tools are freely available on the Web to reverse your encoded script into a readable form.

There is one more catch to using `OpenDSObject`; you must already have a reference to an ADSI object before you can use it. Any object will do, not necessarily the object you want to work with at the moment. The trick is to bind to an object that does not require authentication, such as the LDAP object itself. So, prior to calling `OpenDSObject`, we would execute the following line of code:

```
Set NonSecureObject = GetObject("LDAP:")
```

With those important warnings out of the way, let's look at the method in more detail. The `ADsPath` is nothing new to us by now. The password is simply a string value. The username is a string value as well, but it can take a number of formats:

Username: `ScriptingAdmin`

User principal name: `ScriptingAdmin@zygort.com`

Domain\username: `ZYGORT\ScriptingAdmin`

Distinguished name: `cn=ScriptingAdmin,cn=Users,dc=zygort,dc=com`

I should point out that while the `OpenDSObject` has arguments for username and password, nothing says that you *have* to use them! To use the current security context of the script, simply put the VBScript keyword `Nothing` in the `username` and `password` arguments. As you look at some of the authentication types below, you will notice some have less to do with security and more to do with performance, which we can take advantage of.

The authentication type specified is one of several constants defined elsewhere (see `\includes\ADSI_CONSTANTS.vbs`). These constants are hexadecimal values that set security flags on or off, depending on the security behavior desired. These flags form a bit mask, so they can be combined to produce the desired result by using the `OR` keyword to form the final bit mask. I should also point out that none of these options are supported by the NDS or NWCompat providers. The constants include the following authentication flags. (The value of each flag, in hexadecimal, is shown in parentheses.)

ADS_SECURE_AUTHENICATION (0x1) Uses secure authentication. When connecting to Active Directory, Kerberos will be used if it is available; otherwise it uses NTLM. If the username and password are set to NULL, the binding takes place using the security context of the running script.

ADS_USE_ENCRYPTION (0x2) Requests that ADSI use encryption for data exchanges over the network. This option is not supported by the WinNT provider.

ADS_USE_SSL (0x2)   Attempts to encrypt the communications channel use SSL. This requires that a certificate server be installed on the domain to support SSL. This option is not supported by the WinNT provider.

ADS_READONLY_SERVER (0x4)   Indicates that a writable server is not required for serverless binding. On a Windows NT network, this allows ADSI to connect to either a Primary Domain Controller (PDC) or a Backup Domain Controller (BDC), since BDCs are read-only. On a Windows 2000 or 2003 network, this flag has no effect since all domain controllers are writable.

ADS_PROMPT_CREDENTIALS (0x8)   Is no longer used.

ADS_NO_AUTHENICATION (0x10)   Explicitly requires no authentication. Active Directory will attempt to establish a connection between the client script and the object, but it will not perform authentication. This flag requests an anonymous binding, which is equivalent to binding using the Everyone group credentials. This option is not supported by the WinNT provider.

ADS_FAST_BIND (0x20)   Causes ADSI to expose only the base interfaces supported by all ADSI objects. This flag is not so much a security directive as a performance directive. Setting this flag will allow the LDAP provider to skip several steps, improving performance.

ADS_USE_SIGNING (0x40)   Verifies sent and received data. This should be set in conjunction with the **ADS_SECURE_AUTHENICATION** flag. This option is not supported by the WinNT provider.

ADS_USE_SEALING (0x80)   Uses Kerberos to encrypt data. This should be set in conjunction with the **ADS_SECURE_AUTHENICATION** flag. This option is not supported by the WinNT provider.

ADS_USE_DELEGATION (0x100)   Allows ADSI to delegate the user security context. To move objects between domains, this must be used.

ADS_SERVER_BIND (0x200)   Indicates the **ADsPath** includes a server name. Do not use this flag with serverless binding or if the binding syntax includes domain components. Using a server name without setting this flag can result in extra network traffic.

To define these flags as constants in your VBScript, you should change the 0x notation to the VBScript &H notation. For example, the ADS_USE_ENCRYPTION value of 0x2 would become &H2 in your VBScript.

PERFORMANCE CONSIDERATIONS

As I mentioned before, ADSI handles the mechanics of connecting to objects in the directory service for you, basically shielding you from the dirty work. This can be a good thing, but it can also be a bad thing because it makes it difficult to troubleshoot an ADSI script that is performing poorly.

Each time you bind to an object in Active Directory, some overhead is incurred. DNS records may have to be accessed to find a domain controller. The schema may have to be referenced. Certainly the object itself will have to be located and its attributes read into the local property cache. There are some steps you can take in your script to reduce the total amount of overhead generated when binding, especially when your script binds to many Active Directory objects in succession.

One of the simplest ways to improve performance is by taking advantage of connection caching. When you bind to an object in Active Directory, your script must first authenticate itself to the domain controller servicing the request. This authentication takes time, and repeating the authentication takes additional time. Connection caching simply keeps one connection that has successfully authenticated to a domain controller open and uses the same server for all subsequent object requests. When the script is ready to end, the connection is finally dropped by setting the object to Nothing (which will also happen automatically when the script terminates). This is why opening a connection to the RootDSE object at the beginning of a script and leaving it open can be a simple and easy performance enhancement.

Other performance gains can be made by taking advantage of some of the flags available through the OpenDSObject function. These flags basically tell ADSI to skip some steps that would normally be taken during the process of binding to an object. While eliminating steps will obviously increase performance (less work takes less time to perform, right?), there will always be a trade-off in exactly what steps were skipped.

The first flag to consider is the ADS_FAST_BIND flag. This flag will allow the LDAP provider to skip the steps of verifying that the object exists and getting the object's class. If the object does not exist and you attempt to access one of its attributes or methods, an error will be raised. Since the object's class is not known, ADSI will not be able to use the class-specific interface for the object, meaning that you will also lose the specific functionality of the object's class.

To successfully use this flag, you should always be certain that the object(s) you are going to work with exist, and run your code in an error trap just in case. You should know what attributes and methods will be available on the object. Only the base interface of the object will be used, which exposes the ADsPath, Class, GUID, Name, and Parent attributes and the Get, GetEx, GetInfo, GetInfoEx, Put, PutEx, and SetInfo methods.

The other flag to consider is the ADS_SERVER_BIND flag. This flag eliminates the steps of locating a domain controller on your behalf, which means you must take the initiative to provide a suitable server name in your ADsPath!

Reading Data

After binding to an object, most scripts read the attributes of that object at some point. Remember that ADSI will always set up a cached copy of our Active Directory objects in a region of memory called the local property cache. Even though we have a cache location, we have no data in that cache yet. Binding to the object doesn't download any of its attributes into the local property cache; that task is left to us. ADSI provides three methods for populating the local property cache; the GetInfo method, the Get method, and the GetInfoEx method.

Before I tell you the differences between them, I have to point out the issue of latency involved in ADSI scripting. Simply put, someone can change the value of an attribute in Active Directory after we've read it into the cache. By the same token, our script could change the value of an attribute immediately after someone else has submitted a change for the same attribute. In either case, someone's going to be confused about why their change didn't appear to take place. There are no provisions for "locking" the values of an object while we manipulate them. Essentially, the last change submitted to Active Directory wins.

GETINFO METHOD

The GetInfo method is used to initialize the local property cache or to refresh the values that are stored in it. All the supported attributes of the object will be loaded into the cache. This method will also overwrite all the existing values in the cache with the current values from Active Directory. If you haven't saved your work before you call GetInfo, all your changes are lost. The method takes no arguments, so the code looks like this:

```
User.GetInfo
```

GET AND *GETEX* METHODS

The Get method retrieves object attribute values from the local property cache and is called with one attribute at a time. If the cache is already loaded with the object's attributes (via GetInfo, perhaps), then you are ready to go. However, if the cache hasn't retrieved the attributes from Active Directory yet, then the first call to the Get method will implicitly invoke the GetInfo method to populate the local property cache.

The method takes one argument: the LDAP display name of the attribute to retrieve. It will retrieve the value (assuming there is one) and return it to a variable. The code to use the Get method looks like this:

```
UserFirstname = User.Get("givenName")
```

The Get method is also "implied" when you refer to the property name directly from the object. For example, here are two equivalent lines of code:

```
WScript.Echo User.Get("givenName")
WScript.Echo User.givenName
```

That seems simple enough, which usually means it's not. There are some attributes that return other objects. If this is the case, you have to use the Set keyword in front of the variable, like this:

```
Set Security = User.Get("ntSecurityDescriptor")
```

We're not out of the woods yet! Some attributes in Active Directory contain more than one value as well (appropriately called multivalued attributes). These values will return an array of values to the variable. Since an array is not considered an object, we can skip the Set keyword. The trick comes when reading the values of that attribute. Luckily, reading values from an array is simple:

```
PhoneNumbers = User.Get("otherHomePhone")
For each PhoneNumber in PhoneNumbers
    Wscript.Echo PhoneNumber
Next
```

As if that's not enough fun, ADSI will return a different type of structure if that multivalued attribute has only one value in it. Using the home PhoneNumber attribute, if the attribute only contains one value, ADSI will return it as a string type. If it has several values, it will return them in an array.

This is where the GetEx method comes into play, as well as your newly acquired knowledge of the Active Directory schema. If you know that an attribute is multivalued but you don't know how many values it contains, using the GetEx method will always return the attribute value(s) in an array. This saves you from having to look at the value returned, figuring out if it is a string or an array, and then displaying the value(s) appropriately. Since the GetEx method will always give you an array, we can modify the previous code ever so slightly to accommodate the GetEx method:

```
PhoneNumbers = User.GetEx("otherHomePhone")
For each PhoneNumber in PhoneNumbers
    Wscript.Echo PhoneNumber
Next
```

There is one more catch to all of this reading and displaying data. This catch has to deal with the type of data returned by the attribute. Some attributes contain numbers; some contain characters or strings. Some contain data that is more complex, such as 64-bit unsigned integers. We'll talk about the details soon in the section "Active Directory Data Types."

GETINFOEX METHOD

This method is the middle ground between GetInfo and Get. First, it reads the value of an attribute from Active Directory, not the local property cache. It then stores that value in the cache, overwriting the current value if one exists. It can be used to refresh the value of selected attributes, rather than refreshing the entire set of attributes that belong to an object. Even better, it can retrieve several specific attributes with one line of code, as you will see in a moment.

The method looks like it takes two arguments, but in its current version it really only takes one. The first argument is an array of attributes to retrieve. The second argument is reserved for some later use, so for now we always set it to 0.

```
AttributeArray(0) = "AdsPath"
AttributeArray(1) = "givenName"
AttributeArray(2) = "sn"
User.GetInfoEx AttributeArray,0
Wscript.Echo User.Get("AdsPath")     ' from the Local Property Cache
```

This piece of code puts three values in an array named AttributeArray. It passes that array into the GetInfoEx method, which populates the local property cache with those three attributes. If you do not like populating an array one element at a time, the alternative is to use the Array function, like this:

```
User.GetInfo Array("AdsPath","givenName","sn"), 0
Wscript.Echo User.Get("Adspath")
```

The Array function takes a list of comma-separated values and returns them in an array. You can return that list directly into the first argument of the GetInfoEx method.

Saving Data

I know, in our ADSI pattern, saving your work is the last step. So why am I mentioning it now? Well, a couple of reasons come to mind. First, it's a very important step. If you do not save your work, then why run the script? Second, it is a short step, and it is easy to forget about. And it is a step that neither your script nor the scripting engine will complain about when you forget it. Your only clue (assuming the rest of your script functions properly) will be the lack of changes when you check Active Directory. Finally, we refer to it in upcoming sections, so it's good that you know what it does ahead of time.

As I said, it is a short step. All you need to do is call the SetInfo method of the object that you have been modifying. This will write out the current values of that object in the local property cache to the directory service itself. The method has no arguments, so the code to use it will look like this:

```
User.SetInfo
```

You can call `SetInfo` any time you like, but think about the lack of arguments in the method. That means you cannot save only certain attributes from the local property cache; it is an all-or-nothing deal. You can minimize the amount of network traffic by batching your changes to an object together and saving them at one time. A common practice when creating objects is to populate the mandatory attributes for the new object, save the object, populate whatever optional attributes you choose, and save again. Definitely do not call `SetInfo` after every attribute change you make!

After writing the object to the Active Directory, it will then query the object for its values. As you will see in the next section, even if we do not explicitly set an attribute, Active Directory will fill in certain attributes for us. At a minimum, when an object is first created, Active Directory will make sure that the mandatory attributes for that class have a value.

Modifying Data

We have seen how to bind to objects, how to read the values of their attributes, and how to save changes to those attributes. Now we can dive into the depths of actually modifying data in Active Directory. As one last-minute reminder, always check that the object you've bound a variable to actually exists—that is to say, it does not have a value of `Nothing`. If you have missed the target, it is a lot easier to stop and adjust your aim than to keep firing errant shots into the hillside.

In this section, we talk about creating objects, modifying objects, and deleting objects. We will also talk in more depth about the different data types that Active Directory uses, and how to work with them.

By this point, you should know that the first step is always binding to an object. We will talk about which object you should bind to, but we won't go into depth about the binding process anymore. We also will not go into depth about creating specific classes of objects, which we cover in the next chapter.

A word of warning: We are officially about to start playing with your Active Directory hierarchy for real. I highly recommend working with the scripting examples in the book and the downloadable material on a test domain. A virtual environment is ideal for these types of learning exercises.

CREATING OBJECTS

Creating an object in Active Directory requires two decisions to be made; first, what object do you want to create, and second, where do you want to create that object in the hierarchy? Thinking back to our Active Directory schema, remember there are a number of structural classes that Active Directory is capable of creating an object from. For the majority of directory structures, you will use a standard set of classes; the user, the group, the organization unit, and the container.

Once you have decided the what and where, you can get down to work. When we perform the binding step of our pattern, we want to bind to the container object that is going to hold our new object (either an OU or an actual container). For example, if I want to create a new user in an organization unit called "Sybex", I would bind to the Sybex OU.

One mistake I have seen a few times by new ADSI scriptwriters is forgetting to bind to the container itself. Instead, they bind to the root of the domain and create their new object. Then they cannot find the object. At first, they will think that their new user has been created in the default container for that object, such as the `Users` container for new users, but that is not the case. ADSI is going to do exactly what you tell it to do, and create that new object in the root of your Active Directory hierarchy. So be specific!

```
Set Parent = GetObject("LDAP://CN=Users,DC=zygort,DC=com")
```

To create the new object, we use the `Create` method of the parent container. It returns an object, so we have to use the `Set` keyword. The `Create` method is available on any object that is capable of holding Active Directory objects. The method requires two arguments: the type of class to create and the Common Name (CN) value of the object.

```
Set NewUser = Parent.Create("user","CN=MyFirstUser")
```

The first argument (`"user"`) tells ADSI to refer to the `user` class to create the object. This is the LDAP display name for the class. The second argument (`"CN=MyFirstUser"`) gives ADSI a value to assign the Common Name of the object. It must be unique in the container. It is a good practice to create new objects within an error trap, just in case the situation arises.

At this point, you have a variable pointing to your new object. Now is the perfect time to start assigning values to the mandatory attributes of the object. One of the mandatory attributes of the `user` object is the `sAMAccountName` (we'll go more into the `Put` method in a moment).

```
NewUser.Put "sAMAccountName", "MyFirstUser"
```

Now, believe it or not, mandatory attributes are not mandatory in the sense that you have to fill them in yourself. Mandatory attributes like the `objectSid` (which is a GUID and you would not want to create it yourself anyway!) are generated by the system in the event you leave them empty when you save your object. Just for fun, I left the `sAMAccountName` attribute blank on my `NewUser`, and the value I found in Active Directory was $L21000-QV9063NT6GK3. Definitely a secure name, but not one I would like to type in on a daily basis!

When you have finished assigning values to the attributes of your newly created object, do not forget to call the `SetInfo` method of the object:

```
NewUser.SetInfo
```

DELETING OBJECTS

You have a few options for deleting objects in Active Directory. The first is the most straightforward method: simply bind to the object and call the `DeleteObject` method. The `DeleteObject` method takes one argument, which is reserved, so for now we simply use 0 as the argument value. This code shows you how to delete a user:

```
Set UserToDelete = GetObject("CN=Scott,DC=zygort,DC=com")
UserToDelete.DeleteObject(0)
```

The second method of deleting an object in Active Directory is similar to the process of creating a user. We will bind to the parent container, call the `Delete` method, and specify the object class and name of the object to be removed. The code to remove a user would look like this:

```
Parent.Delete "user", "CN=Scott"
```

Using this method, if you had a variable bound to the object that you just removed, you will want to set the variable to `Nothing`. In the local property cache, the object still exists. If you were to call the `SetInfo` method, your script would return an error. Basically, the local property cache would be trying to save changes to an object that no longer existed! Even worse, it would not be readily obvious why your script was failing; the error would occur on the `SetInfo` line of code. Here is some code to show the whole process in action:

```
Set User = GetObject("LDAP://CN=Scott,CN=Users,DC=zygort,DC=com")
' Make and save changes to the user object here…
Set Parent = GetObject("LDAP://CN=Users,DC=zygort,DC=com")
Parent.Delete "user", User.Name
Parent.SetInfo
Set User = Nothing
```

How do you know which method to use? Think about the job your script is going to do. If you are deleting one object, use the `Delete` method. One binding followed by one deletion and you are done. If you are examining many objects that exist in a container, use the `DeleteObject` method. You only bind to the parent object as opposed to each individual leaf object to delete. Binding is an operation that causes overhead, so reducing that overhead will help your scripts perform better.

You will also want to consider what type of objects you are deleting. You can technically use either method of deletion for container objects. The difference will be that the `Delete` method will generate an error if the container contains child objects below it, while the `DeleteObject` method will delete the container and everything below it in one fell swoop. While efficient, using the `DeleteObject` method on containers is also dangerous.

How do you know if the container has any child objects? One sure way is to try to delete the container! If it has child objects, it will return an error stating that "The directory service can perform the requested operation only on a leaf object."

Before deleting objects en masse, consider the repercussions of your action. As with databases, there is no undo button if you wipe out the wrong object. If your script is the interactive sort, displaying an "OK to delete?" prompt might prevent the user from making a big mistake. In an automated script, you will have to use your best judgment about when it is truly safe to delete an object.

PUT AND PUTEX METHODS

The `Put` and `PutEx` methods are used for modifying a property of an existing Active Directory object. The property may or may not have a current value, but if a value does exist in the property then it will be overwritten. Remember that this only changes the values in the local property cache, not the directory service. To set your changes in the Active Directory, execute the `SetInfo` method.

When modifying the properties of an Active Directory object, you must first bind to it (of course!). Executing the `GetInfo` method will populate the local data cache with the object's properties. You can then examine the current property values to determine which (if any) values need to be modified, or you can begin making your changes immediately.

To make changes to the property, you must first know what kind of property you are dealing with in terms of the data type that it holds and if the property holds a single value or multiple values. Active Directory data types are discussed in the next section, but most of the values modified in scripts are simple string, date, or numeric values.

Properties that hold a single value use the `Put` method to assign a new value to the property. The `ldapDisplayName` is specified when assigning the new value.

```
User.Put("givenName") = "Scott"
```

Assigning values to a property that holds multiple values is a bit trickier. The first step is deciding if you want to overwrite all the values currently stored in the property or simply append a new value to the existing values.

The PutEx method accepts three arguments: a numeric value that represents the operation to perform, the ldapDisplayName of the property to modify, and the values to use in the operation.

The numeric value representing the operation specifies what type of operation is going to take place on the property values. You may clear the current property values, update the current values, append a new value, or delete a property value. Their values are usually assigned to a set of constants in the script.

```
Const ADS_PROPERTY_CLEAR = 1
Const ADS_PROPERTY_UPDATE = 2
Const ADS_PROPERTY_APPEND = 3
Const ADS_PROPERTY_DELETE = 4
```

The value arguments are almost always going to be an array of values. The only exception to this rule is when you are clearing the current values from a property. The easiest way to create an array of new values to pass into the PutEx method is to use the built-in function Array(). The Array() function is passed a comma-separated list of values, which are then returned in an array structure. We will see this in action in the following sets of example code.

To clear the existing property values, we would use the following code:

```
User.PutEx ADS_PROPERTY_CLEAR, "middleName", 0
```

Again, the only time an array is not passed to the PutEx method is when clearing the property values. However, the method is expecting an argument so we simply pass it the number 0.

When updating a property, the array in the third argument has two elements. The first element is the current value to be replaced, and the second element is the new value.

```
User.PutEx ADS_PROPERTY_UPDATE, "otherTelephoneNumber", _
    Array(" (971) 555-1234", " (971) 555-1122")
```

To append additional values to a property, create an array of the new values to append and pass to the PutEx method. If a duplicate value is passed to the property, it will be ignored.

```
User.PutEx ADS_PROPERTY_APPEND, "otherTelephoneNumber", _
    Array(" (971) 555-1111"," (971) 555-2222")
```

When removing a value from a value from a property, the third argument contains an array of the current values of the property to remove. If one of the current values is not found, it is ignored.

```
User.PutEx ADS_PROPERTY_DELETE, "otherTelephoneNumber", _
    Array("(971) 555-1122")
```

Active Directory Data Types

Active Directory holds several types of data in its attributes. To write a script that successfully displays and manipulates the properties of an Active Directory object, you have to understand how the information in those properties is stored. Some properties store their data in simple strings or numeric values. Other properties will return whole objects that you will have to work with. In this section, we take a brief look at the some of the different data types you will be dealing with in Active Directory and show you how to work with them in your scripts.

DN (DISTINGUISHED NAME)

Not to be confused with the distinguishedName attribute, the DN data type is used to link one Active Directory object to another. For example, the manager attribute links one user object to another. Most servers will return an error if the DN value does not point to a valid existing Active Directory object. The DN property is treated as a string for reading and writing.

OCTETSTRING

An attribute of this data type is returned as an array of bytes. This is used to represent a string of binary data. Normally these are used to store security IDs and are returned as byte arrays. Byte arrays are not a common thing to work with in VBScript and are typically set by the system. If you would like to see the value stored in an octet string, we can accommodate that with the following code (thanks to MVP Richard Mueller for reminding me how this works):

```
Set User = GetObject("LDAP://CN=Scott,CN=Users,DC=zygort,DC=com")
UserSID = User.Get("objectSID")
SIDString = ""
For X = 1 To LenB(UserSID)
SIDString = SIDString & " 0x" & _
Right("0" & Hex(AscB(MidB(UserSID, X, 1))), 2)
Next
WScript.Echo SIDString
```

DNWITHBINARY

This is also known as a Distinguished Name with an octet string.

CASEEXACTSTRING AND CASEIGNORESTRING

Attributes of these data types represent case-sensitive and case-insensitive strings, respectively. These strings may or may not contain Unicode strings. ADSI will accept and return either. Many of the attributes in Active Directory will use these two data types.

DIRECTORYSTRING

A DirectoryString attribute is a Unicode string, which is treated as a CaseIgnoreString.

IA5STRING

An IA5String is treated as a CaseIgnoreString.

NUMERICSTRING

Attributes of this data type contain string values. All space characters are ignored when comparisons are made. ADSI does not perform verification to ensure that the value is actually numeric or contains spaces.

PRINTABLESTRING

Attributes of this data type contain string values. These strings are considered case-sensitive when comparisons are made. ADSI will accept any values without verifying that the value is actually printable.

BOOLEAN

This attribute is stored as a 32-bit value. Zero is considered false, and all other values are considered true.

UTCTIME

This attribute is used to store date and time information. Attributes of this data type are stored as an ASCII string. The date and time is represented in either the YYMMDDHHMM or YYMMDDHHMMSS format. Appended to this is either the character "Z" to indicate Greenwich Mean Time or the +/-HHMM format to indicate the offset from Greenwich Mean Time. In other words, adding the local time to the time offset should equal Greenwich Mean Time (local + offset = GMT).

ADSI will accept any string values without verifying the value is a valid time string. Ordering is done by treating the value as an ASCII string, not a date/time value.

GENERALIZEDTIME

This data type is used to store date and time information. Attributes of this data type are stored as an ASCII string. The date and time are represented in the same way as for the UTCTime data type, except that four characters are used to represent the year value instead of only two. When extending the schema with a new date or time attribute, this is the preferred data type to use.

INTEGER

This attribute is a 32-bit signed numeric value.

INTEGER8

This attribute is a 64-bit unsigned numeric value. Attributes of the Integer8 data type can represent one of three different types of values: they can be a date/time field, an interval field, or a counter field.

The Integer8 data type is also known as a Large Integer. VBScript does not know how to work with 64-bit values; it is limited to 32-bit values. Therefore, these attributes are returned as COM objects implementing the IADSLargeInteger interface, which makes them a bit easier to deal with. This interface defines two properties—HighPart and LowPart—which divides the 64-bit integer into two 32-bit integers.

When storing a time value, it is used to represent time in intervals of 100 nanoseconds. Since one nanosecond is 1 billionth (.000000001) of a second, we are dealing with intervals of .0000001 of a second. One second is made of up 10 million of these intervals.

When storing a date/time value, it is used to represent the number of these intervals since midnight on January 1, 1601. Even with the IADSLargeInteger interface, we have going to have to perform some math.

For `Interval` values, such as the maximum password age, the following code should give us the value in minutes, hours, and days:

```
Const Int8Minutes = 600000000        '60 seconds * 10000000
Set Domain = GetObject("LDAP://DC=zygort,DC=com")
Set MaxPwdAgeLI = Domain.Get("maxPwdAge")
HighPart = MaxPwdAgeLI.HighPart
LowPart = MaxPwdAgeLI.LowPart
If LowPart < 0 Then HighPart = HighPart + 1
MaxPwdAge = Abs(HighPart * (2^32) + LowPart) / Int8Minutes
WScript.Echo "Maximum Password Age is " & MaxPwdAge & " minutes. "
WScript.Echo "Maximum Password Age is " & MaxPwdAge/60 & " hours. "
WScript.Echo "Maximum Password Age is " & MaxPwdAge/60/24 & " days. "
```

The math is not fun, but I will try to explain it. First we get the two 32-bit values from `HighPart` and `LowPart`. If `LowPart` is negative, we have to add 1 to `HighPart`; otherwise the calculation will be off by a little over 7 minutes. This is just a "gotcha" of unsigned arithmetic (which VBScript is also not fond of dealing with), so we work around it with one line of code.

Next, we shift the `HighPart` by 32 bits and add the value of `LowPart`. We want the absolute value of this calculation, so it is enclosed in the `Abs` function. At this point, we have the number of 100-nanosecond intervals that makes up the value. Since we want the value in minutes, we divide the number of intervals by the number of intervals in a minute (60 seconds * 10,000,000 intervals in 1 second = 60,000,000 intervals). Is this giving you a headache yet?

I took the more illustrative route to display the value in hours and days by doing the division in the Echo statement. You could easily have computed it right off the bat by changing the value of the constant to the proper number of intervals for an hour and day.

For date/time values, such as the date the password was last set for a user object, the following code should give us the correct date and time value:

```
Set User = GetObject("LDAP://CN=Scott,CN=Users,DC=zygort,DC=com")
Set PwdLastSetLI = User.Get("PwdLastSet")
HighPart = PwdLastSetLI.HighPart
LowPart = PwdLastSetLI.LowPart
If LowPart < 0 Then HighPart = HighPart + 1
PwdLastSet = #1/1/1601# + _
(Abs((HighPart * (2^32)) + LowPart) /Int8Minutes) /  MinutesInDay
WScript.echo CDate(PwdLastSet)
```

The date from this code will be in UTC, or Universal Coordinated Time. It should be adjusted by the appropriate time zone bias, which we can get from Windows Management Instrumentation (WMI) and add into our code. The bias is reported in number of minutes; for example, the Central Time Zone is 6 hours behind, or –360 minutes.

```
Set WMIService = GetObject("winmgmts:\\.\root\cimv2")
Set Items = WMIService.ExecQuery("Select * from Win32_TimeZone",,48)
For Each Item in Items
    Bias = Item.Bias
    DaylightSavings = Item.DaylightBias
Next
TimeBias = Bias - DayLightSavings
```

Notice that I have also checked for any daylight savings adjustments that need to be made and added them to the time zone value. Finally, add the time zone adjustment to the `Int8Minutes` value in the statement that computes the date.

```
PwdLastSet = #1/1/1601# + _
    (Abs((HighPart * (2^32)) + LowPart) / Int8Minutes + TimeBias) / _ MinutesInDay
```

Notice the use of parentheses in this statement. This is important, because if you remember the order of precedence from math class, you'll know that multiplication and division operations take place before addition and subtraction operations. This will screw up the calculation unless we use parentheses to add the `Int8Minutes` value to the time bias before dividing by the number of minutes in a day and raise an error.

For `Counter` values, we do not have to do any conversions at all.

Unfortunately, there is no specific naming convention that you can reference to find out what type the field represents. Which of the three types the attribute represents will affect how you compute its value.

SECURITY DESCRIPTORS

Security descriptors contain the access control lists for Active Directory objects. When accessing one of these properties, ADSI will return an object with the `IADSSecurityDescriptor` interface. Access control lists (ACLs) contain a list of access control entries (ACEs), each of which represents a user or group that their rights to an object. This list is exposed through the `DiscretionaryACL` property, which returns an object containing the individual entries. Creating a new ACE is beyond the scope of this book, but we can look at the entries with the following code (this will be expanded for more detail in the next chapter).

```
Set User = GetObject("LDAP://CN=Scott,CN=Users,DC=zygort,DC=com")
Set UserSec = User.Get("ntSecurityDescriptor")
WScript.Echo "Owner -> " & UserSec.Owner
WScript.Echo "Group -> " & UserSec.Group
Set DACL = UserSec.DiscretionaryACL
WScript.Echo "List Count -> " & DACL.AceCount
For Each Entry In DACL
    WScript.Echo "Trustee ---->" & Entry.Trustee
    WScript.Echo "AccessMask -> " & Entry.AccessMask
    WScript.Echo "Ace Type ---> " & Entry.AceType
Next
```

Searching for Data

Since Active Directory is a directory service, it only makes sense that we are going to search it from time to time. One way to do this is by binding to each container and recursively searching through every child container, one object at a time. While this will surely get the job done, the performance penalty will be enough to make you never want to do it again.

The more efficient option is to use the built-in search provider from ADSI, the `ADSDSoObject` provider. This provider is used with the ActiveX Data Objects (ADO) library to provide a simple and powerful method to query Active Directory and process the results.

THE QUERY PATTERN

Let's start by defining a pattern to query Active Directory, similar to the pattern we described earlier for working with Active Directory objects. It consists of six steps: specifying a search root, defining the filter, selecting the properties, defining the scope, executing the search, and looping through the results. Here are those steps in more detail:

Select the search root.   In the case of Active Directory, we select what container object we want to query. This can be the root of the domain or any child container below it. To this container, we bind a variable and use it as the base for our search.

Define a filter.   The filter defines what criteria that the object must meet to be returned. This is usually based on certain object properties, such as `objectClass` or `objectCategory`. The filter syntax can get very complicated, and we cover it in more detail soon.

Define the properties to retrieve.   These are the attributes you want to read from the objects in the result set. Leaving this portion empty will return all the object properties, but for most queries this is overkill.

Specify the scope.   The scope is the depth to which the search should go below the search root. The search can be limited to the search root itself, the search root, and the immediate child containers, or every container below the search root.

Execute the search.   This step passes the query to Active Directory for processing, and then passes the results into an object we can process later.

Process the results.   In this step we go through the results one record at a time and display the returned property values or use them for further processing.

To execute our queries against Active Directory, let's use a set of objects designed for querying all kinds of data sources. The ActiveX Data Object type library, or ADO, has three objects we can take advantage of: the `Connection` object, the `Command` object, and the `Recordset` object.

The `Connection` object is used to point to the data source, Active Directory in our case. The `Command` object is used to actually execute the query and return the result set in a `Recordset` object.

When we create instances of ADO objects, remember that these are not Active Directory objects, so we need to use the `CreateObject` function instead of the `GetObject` function. The object classes reside in the ADODB type library, so we have to reference the type library with the `ProgID` when we create the objects, as you will see in the code samples that follow.

SPECIFY THE SEARCH ROOT

The search root defines where in the Active Directory tree we want our search to begin. While the search root should probably always be a container object, you can technically use any object you want.

Rather than using the distinguished name of the container object, the search root is specified as an `ADsPath`. The search root can be a domain object, a global catalog server, or a member of one of the well-known container objects such as the `Configuration` container for querying the Active Directory schema.

The final step to constructing a search root is enclosing the `ADsPath` of the container object in angle brackets. Here are a few examples of search roots:

```
<LDAP://DC=zygort,DC=com>
<LDAP://CN=Users,DC=zygort,DC=com>
<GC://DC=zygort,DC=com>
```

The search root value will eventually find a home in the `CommandText` property of the `Command` object. You can use the properties of the `RootDSE` object to find the values of the `defaultNamingContext` or `rootDomainNamingContext` to build the search root value on the fly rather than hardcoding it in your script.

DEFINING THE SEARCH FILTER

Undoubtedly the most difficult portion of the query process is constructing the search filter. Even for experienced query writers, writing a query typically starts simple and become more complex as the result set gets smaller and more focused until finally only the desired data is returned. The search filter is the Active Directory equivalent of a SQL WHERE clause, but many would say less readable. We will take the syntax one step at a time and you'll have it under control in no time.

The basic filter syntax looks something like this:

```
( attribute = value )
```

With the code enclosed in parentheses, we compare a property to a value. We can check for equality (=), less than or equal to (<=), greater than or equal to (>=). There is also an approximately equal-to operator (~=), but this is ignored by Active Directory and treated as an equality comparison. Note that the less-than and greater-than operators are not supported, but there are a few ways to achieve the same result with the operators we do have. If you would like your filter to return all objects where a property value is less than 50, then you can create your filter to check that the property value is less than or equal to 49.

The search filter allow for either exact matches or wildcard searches using the asterisk character. Most people are familiar with using the asterisk in wildcard searches, but its behavior in ADSI takes on two personalities. When used by itself, it becomes a present operator and tests for the presence of a value in the attribute. When used with other characters, it tests for any number (including zero) characters in the wildcard location. Wildcards can be used multiple times in the statement. Here are a few examples to give you an idea:

```
(attribute=*)        ' Present operator.  Matches objects that contain
                     ' a value in the attribute field
(attribute=*son)     ' Matches values ending in "son"
(attribute=A*)       ' Matches values beginning with the letter A
(attribute=*ste*)    ' Matches values with "ste" anywhere in the value
```

The use of a wildcard does not guarantee that a value will contain anything in the wildcard location. The last example, `*ste*`, will match words like Stephen, Austen, or Paste. Wildcards will nearly always return a larger result set, so be prepared for a longer query and more processing time on the result set.

Another useful operator we can use in the value comparison is the Not operator, represented by an exclamation mark (!). The Not operator reverses the result of a comparison; in other words, if a statement was true, it becomes false. It is used in front of the attribute value rather than with the equals sign.

```
(!givenName=Scott)   ' Returns all objects except those with a
                     ' givenName attribute of Scott
```

Now, remember those missing less-than or greater-than operators? By using the Not operator, we can achieve the same result of those missing operators. Consider the following example:

```
(!attribute>=50)
```

This filter states that if an attribute value is greater than or equal to 50, then do *not* return it (by way of the Not operator). This is the same as saying that any value less than 50 should be returned. While the code does its job, it's a bad practice to get into, and it can hurt performance of your queries.

Consider this: You are examining 1,000 records. The server takes X number of steps to perform a comparison. This gives us X*1000 operations to get the final result set. It takes an additional step per record to reverse the result of the comparison. Now we are looking at (X+1) * 1000 operations to get the final result set. Each additional operation step takes more time to return the final result set. To optimize your queries, you should avoid the use of the Not operator whenever possible.

Finally, let's talk about handling those Active Directory attributes that implement bitmaps. We can still use bitmap attributes in our comparisons, but we have to use a set of comparisons defined by LDAP known as the matching rule object identifiers, or OIDs. Those two rules are shown in Table 17.16.

TABLE 17.16: Match Rule OIDs

MATCH RULE OID	DESCRIPTION
1.2.840.113556.1.4.803	Matches only if all bits from the attribute match the value. Equivalent to a bitwise AND operator.
1.2.840.113556.1.4.804	Matches if any bits from the attribute match the value. Equivalent to a bitwise OR operator.

To use the bitwise comparison rules, we have to specify the OID of the rule with the attribute, separated by colons on either side of the OID value. It makes the filter a little convoluted to read, so let's use an example to explain it:

```
(groupType:1.2.840.113556.1.4.803:=2147483648)
```

Here, we are looking at the groupType attribute. The comparison is performed using the bitwise AND rule. When we look at the groupType documentation, we see that the bitmask that defines a group as a security group is the hexadecimal value 0x80000000, which translates to the numeric value 2147483648.

Let's finish looking at a single comparison filter by seeing some actual examples:

```
(objectClass=user)        ' Returns objects of the user class
(objectCategory=person)   ' Returns objects of the person category
(sn=Fenster*)             ' Returns objects with the surname property
                          ' beginning with the letters "Fenster"
```

We've seen almost every variation of a single comparison that we can use in a query. By itself, a single comparison isn't very powerful, though. By combining comparisons, we can either narrow down our result set or make it larger. At this point things start to get more complicated, so as you make changes to your filter statement you might want to consider keeping a copy of your last couple filter statements to revert back to in case you make a change in the wrong direction.

To combine single filters, we group them in a set of parentheses. In addition, we need to specify exactly how we want the combine the results. Do we want to combine the results together into one huge result set or do we want to specify that the result set has to satisfy each and every individual filter? The And operator (&) and the Or operator (|) are used to combine the individual results sets into the final result set. Here are a couple of examples to get you started:

```
(&(objectClass=user)(givenName=Scott))
(|(givenName=Scott)(givenName=Brad))
```

The first example uses the And operator. It says that if the object class is a user and the givenName attribute is Scott, then return the row in the final result set. The second example uses the Or operator. It says that if the givenName attribute is either Scott or Brad, then return the row in the final result set.

In the next chapter, we'll examine queries specific to each type of Active Directory object in more detail.

DEFINING THE SEARCH ATTRIBUTES

We can specify which attributes of the objects matching the filter criteria we would like to view. The attribute search list is simply a comma-separated list of the attribute's LDAP display names. If you would like to see all the attributes, you can use the wildcard character (*) in place of the list.

Returning all of the attributes is very wasteful of server and network resources. During the development of a script, if you are unsure which attributes you are going to need during the processing, you can rewrite the search attribute list each time to add or remove an attribute from the processing section. When you are ready to put your script into production, you should limit the attribute list to only those attributes used during processing.

One attribute that you should keep in mind is the ADsPath attribute of the object. If you need to modify any object attributes during processing, having the ADsPath will allow you to bind to the object to make your changes.

SPECIFY THE SEARCH SCOPE

The depth of the query is controlled by the search scope. This is the only optional portion of the Active Directory query, because a default value (subTree) is defined. Even though it is optional, it is still a good practice to go ahead and specify the search scope to keep your intentions clear. There are three search scopes to choose from, as shown in Table 17.17.

TABLE 17.17: Search Scope Options

SCOPE	DESCRIPTION
Base	Searches only the search root container.
OneLevel	Searches only the child objects of the search root container.
SubTree	The default search scope, this searches the search root container and all the child objects below, regardless of the depth of the child object.

PUTTING THE LDAP QUERY TOGETHER

At this point we have defined the search root, the filter, the attribute list, and the search scope. Now it is time to put them together and use them with the ADO objects and execute the query. We start with the `Connection` object, move on to the `Command` object, and use it to create a `Recordset` object. With the `Recordset` object full of data, we move on to process the results.

ADO *CONNECTION* OBJECT

The `Connection` object is used to point to the data source. It is responsible for loading the appropriate data source provider and validating the user credentials. To query Active Directory, we use the `ADsDSOObject` as the provider:

```
Set Conn = CreateObject("ADODB.Connection")
Conn.Provider = "ADsDSOObject"
```

By default, the credentials of the user running the script will be used for validation. We can specify an alternative set of credentials by setting the `User ID` and `Password` properties of the `Connection` object. We can also optionally encrypt the password for transmission across the network.

The last property, `ADSI Flag`, sets the authentication options for the connection. The authentication options are the same options we discussed back in the binding section. The default value is 0, which sets no authentication flags.

```
Conn.Properties("User ID") = "Scott"
Conn.Properties("Password") = "P@ssw0rd"
Conn.Properties("Encrypt Password") = True
Conn.Properties("ADSI Flag") = 0x1    ' Secure authenication
```

ADO *COMMAND* OBJECT

The Command object is used to execute queries and other commands against a data source using the `Connection` object as the pathway. The `ActiveConnection` property is set to the `Connection` object.

```
Set Cmd = CreateObject("ADODB.Command")
Set Cmd.ActiveConnection = Conn
Cmd.CommandText = ADQuery    ' To be revealed soon
```

The `CommandText` property will hold our Active Directory query we just built with the search root, filter, attribute list, and search scope. We will combine all four pieces into one statement for execution. When put together, the statement will look something like this:

```
<LDAP://DC=zygort,DC=com>;(&(objectClass=User)(objectCategory=person));
    ADsPath,givenName,sn;subtree
```

Notice how we have used semicolons to separate the individual parts of the query. We are going to use this statement as a string in the `CommandText` property of the `Command` object. The following example will give you an easy method to put the pieces together for the `CommandText` property:

```
SearchRoot = "<LDAP://DC=zygort,DC=com>"
Filter = " (&(objectClass=user)(objectCategory=person))
AttributeList = "ADsPath,givenName,sn"
```

```
Scope = "subTree"
Cmd.CommandText = SearchRoot & ";" & _
        Filter & ";" & _
        AttributeList & ";" & _
        Scope
```

By separating the Active Directory query into individual variable names, then concatenating the strings together, the code becomes a bit easier to read and change later. Again, notice the semicolons separating each piece of the query.

The Command object has additional properties can be useful as well. The Size Limit property limits the final result set size. By default there is no limit. The TimeOut property sets the maximum time, in seconds, for the client to wait for results from the server. The default is no timeout. Setting this property even for smaller searches can act as a safety net in case network or other problems prevent a script from blocking indefinitely.

The Page Size property specifies the maximum number of results to be returned in a result page. While the Command object itself sets no default page size, Active Directory limits result returns to the first 1,000 items. When there is a possibility that the result set to be returned will contain more than 1,000 items, using a page search will return all the results (one page at a time) until the end of the results are reached.

Setting the page size also improves performance by allowing the server to send the results one page at a time, rather than waiting for the entire result set to be compiled. Paged searches also allow the client to stop the operation before the entire result set is returned. In a search operation that does not use pages, the client is blocked from doing anything else until the result set is compiled.

The Cache Results property specifies if the results should be cached on the client. This property is set to true by default. For large search operations, you may improve performance by setting this property to false.

The Sort By property sorts the result set on the server prior to returning it to the client. The property supports a comma-separated list of attributes to sort by, but Active Directory only supports sorting on a single key. Since the sorting is done on the server and prior to the result set being returned to the client, this can severely impact the performance of your queries.

```
Cmd.Properties("TimeOut") = 30
Cmd.Properties("Page Size") = 500
Cmd.Properties("Cache Results") = True
```

After setting the Command object properties, we are ready to execute the command. To run the query, call the Execute method of the Command object. This method will return a Recordset object, so the code will look like this:

```
Set RS = Cmd.Execute
```

ADO *RECORDSET* OBJECT

The Recordset object holds the results of the Active Directory query. More accurately, it holds the results of the query whether there are any results or not. The ADO Recordset object has several properties that let you iterate through the query results and access the fields. Unlike binding to an object to access its properties, the Recordset is a read-only copy of data.

With a populated Recordset, the only task remaining is to process the results. Keep in mind that we are processing Active Directory data, and some data types will return objects or multivalued properties that will have to be handled differently than straightforward values like integers and strings.

PROCESS THE SEARCH RESULTS

When the Recordset is first returned, the current row marker will be at the beginning of the file, making the BOF property true. If the query did not return any results, then the current row marker will also be at the end of the file, making the EOF property true as well. By checking the values of the BOF and EOF properties before processing the result set, you will know if the result is empty or not.

```
If RS.BOF and RS.EOF Then
    WScript.Echo "No results were found!"
End If
```

If the Recordset does contain results, then it is a simple matter to iterate through the result set. The only trick, and for some reason one of the easiest lines of code to forget, is to move the current row marker to the next row in the result set. The method is called MoveNext. Each time we move to the next row in the Recordset, we need to check if that row is at the end of the file with the EOF property. When we reach the end of the file, it's time to stop processing the result set. Trying to move beyond the end of the result set will cause an error.

To iterate through the result set while checking for the end of file, we can use a Do-Until loop. To retrieve the attribute values from the result set, we can access the Fields property of the Recordset and supply the name of the attribute we want to retrieve. To refer to the Fields property of the Recordset object, we use the current row marker to retrieve the value of each attribute in the current row in the result set. The following code puts the pieces together:

```
Do Until RS.EOF
    WScript.Echo RS.Fields("ADsPath")
    RS.MoveNext
Loop
```

As you can see in this example, we have printed out the value of the ADsPath property for each result. The Fields property allows you to enter either the field name, which will match the ldapDisplayName specified in the query, or the position of the field in the result set. This is also known as the ordinal value. Fields start at the number 0. In the query we've been building so far, the attributes selected were ADsPath, givenName, and sn, respectively. The ADsPath field would be field 0, the givenName field would be field 1, and the sn field would be field 2. Accessing a field by ordinal value looks like this:

```
WScript.Echo RS.Fields(0)
```

When accessing a field by name, the Recordset object has to look up the field name and finds its ordinal position. Fields are stored in the Recordset in the same order they were defined in the query; therefore you should already know the position of the field you want to access. You can increase the performance of your scripts a bit by using the ordinal values rather than the field names.

Handling Errors

Rarely does a script get written perfectly the first time. When a script uses an outside resource, such as a database or a directory service, the chances that something could go wrong only increase. Now not only do you have to account for the usual scripting errors, but you also have to be prepared to handle errors that might occur on that resource.

There are three types of errors you can run into when developing a script:

♦ Syntax

♦ Runtime

♦ Logical

Syntax errors result when your script breaks the rules of the language. This is typically the result of misspelling something or improper use of parentheses when calling a subroutine. The interpreter will catch these for you, one line at a time, when you try to execute your script. It will even tell you what line number the error is on and what the error is. Using a good editor can help you avoid syntax mistakes by offering color coding for recognized keywords and IntelliSense to fill in the syntax for you. A good editor will also let you see the line numbers of your script, which makes it easier to go right to the offending line of code. Syntax errors are very common and easily fixed.

Runtime errors occur when your script attempts to do something and fails. Maybe it is trying to read a file that doesn't exist. It could be trying to divide a number by zero (always a classic!). The interpreter will tell you what line the error occurred on and what error was reported when you execute your script. The chance for runtime errors increases when your script uses an external resource.

Logical errors occur when your script executes without crashing but does not produce the correct results. For example, if you design a script to create a user in Active Directory but the new user never gets created, your script has a logical error in it. Logical errors require more detective work to find because as far as the interpreter is concerned, your script does not have a problem.

This is where debuggers come in. A debugger is a tool that lets you step through your code, execute one line at a time, and watch the results. A good debugger will let you view values in your script as they change, and allow you to change them yourself. It will also give you the ability to jump over pieces of code that you know work and do not want to waste your time with.

To execute a script in a debugger, you should add the //X option to the command line when you execute the script. For example:

```
CScript //X MyBuggyScript.vbs
```

As shown in Figure 17.7, if you have more than one debugger installed on your system, you should be prompted to select which debugger you should use (unless you have already specified a debugger as the default). Believe it or not, you might have a debugger installed already and don't know it. Now we have to answer the question of which debugger you should use. I will give you two possibilities, both from Microsoft, one of which is free and one of which you might already have.

MICROSOFT SCRIPT DEBUGGER

First, Microsoft provides its Script Debugger as a free download. It is far from the most powerful script editor available, but it will do in a pinch. Be sure to download the correct version for your operating system (for Windows XP, the file is scden10.exe). Microsoft's Script Debugger (see Figure 17.8) has the features shown in Table 17.18.

FIGURE 17.7

Choosing a debugger

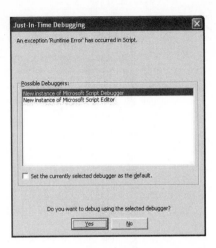

TABLE 17.18: Microsoft Script Debugger Features

FEATURE	DESCRIPTION
Breakpoints	Allows the user to specify a line of code to stop script execution and begin debugging
Bookmarks	Allows the user to jump to a bookmarked line of code
Command window	Displays or sets the value of a variable; executes subroutines or functions
Call stack	Displays the script call stack
Running documents	Displays the currently running scripts

When a debugging session begins, the first executable line of code is highlighted. At this point, the highlighted line of code has not been executed yet. You can execute the line by pressing the F8 key or by selecting Debug ➢ Step. On the Debug menu, you will also see two other stepping options: Step Over (Shift+F8) and Step Out (Shift+Ctrl+F8).

The Step Over option allows you to execute a procedure (either a subroutine or function) without actually stepping through the procedure itself. The procedure will execute as it normally would, and debugging would resume at the line of code following the procedure call. This saves you debugging time by not having to continually step through a procedure that you already know works.

You can also use the Step Over option on lines of code that do not call a procedure, and it will function like the Step Into option. This trick is useful to avoid falling into a procedure by accident. Debugging is can be a monotonous job, and you will find yourself pressing the F8 key absentmindedly. Without realizing it, you will find yourself stepping through lines of code in a procedure that you already know works. At that point you have to choose to step the rest of the way through the procedure or use the Step Out option. By using the Step Over keys, you can avoid the situation altogether.

FIGURE 17.8
Microsoft Script
Debugger

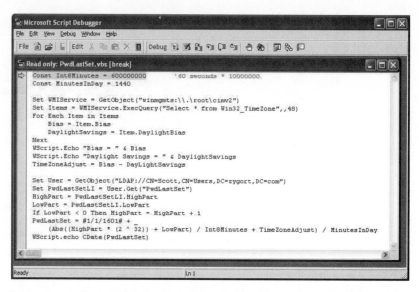

The Step Out option allows you to complete the execution of a procedure and resume debugging on the line of code following the procedure call. This is more useful than it sounds, especially when you find yourself stepping through a long procedure call that you know works.

While you are stepping through your script code, you will want to examine the values being stored in your variables. This is done in the Command window, which you can open by selecting View ➤ Command Window from the menu. You cannot have the Command window open and step through the code at the same time. To view the value of a variable, enter a question mark followed by a space and the name of the variable to view. Such a command would look like this:

```
? MyVariable
```

The Command window retains the commands that have been entered into it. This allows you to view the value of the variable at a later time; simply scroll up to the command that displayed it and press the Enter key. The new value will appear immediately below the command, moving the old value (and all other statements in the window) down one line.

The Command window also gives you the ability to change the current value of a variable. You can also set the value of a variable with a command such as this:

```
MyVariable = 100
```

Finally, the Command window allows you to execute a subroutine, procedure, or other line of valid VBScript code simply by entering it into the window and pressing Enter. Depending on the procedure being executed, this can be useful in testing and resetting values in your script.

While the Script Debugger works, it is not my tool of choice. The Microsoft Script Editor offers a better script debugger, and you might already have it. If you have Microsoft Visual Studio already installed, you will be doing yourself a favor by not even installing Script Debugger, as it will change some of your system debugging settings in its favor.

MICROSOFT SCRIPT EDITOR

The second option is Microsoft's Script Editor, which comes as part of the Microsoft Office installation. It is installed with Word if you have chosen the HTML editing option and with FrontPage. It offers a similar debugging experience that is much more powerful than Script Debugger. Many times I will choose the Script Editor as my script debugging tool, simply because I don't need the extra overhead of Visual Studio to debug a Visual Basic script.

Script Editor offers the same features as Script Debugger: breakpoints, bookmarks, an Immediate window in place of the Command window, call stack, and running documents. It also offers some additional features you might find useful, as shown in Table 17.19.

TABLE 17.19:   Additional Features

FEATURE	DESCRIPTION
DataTips	Pop-up windows that display the value of the variable currently under the mouse pointer
QuickWatch	A modal dialog window to quickly display a variable value or an expression
Watch window	Displays selected variable values and expressions
Autos window	Displays variable values used in the current and previous statement
Locals window	Displays variable values local to the current procedure
Object Browser	Displays object properties and methods and their arguments

In fact, if you are looking for a decent affordable script editor to build your scripts in, the Script Editor (see Figure 17.9) may be just to tool you need. To execute the Script Editor by itself, locate the MSE7.exe file on your system (assuming your system is using Office 2003). The file is usually located in the \Program Files\OfficeXX folder (where XX is the installed Office version number).

When you select Script Editor as your debugger, you will first be prompted to select the program types that you want to debug, and Script will be the only option. Click the OK button and the debugger will open up with an arrow pointing to the first line of executable code. Again, this line of code has not yet been executed. If you already have the Script Editor open, you can choose to debug the script in the existing instance of Script Debugger or open a new instance. Figure 17.10 shows the Step Into screen of the Microsoft Script Editor.

When you're debugging a script, you want to monitor the values of your variables and how they change throughout the execution of your script. The tools of Script Editor are wonderful at this. The DataTips pop-up windows allow you to place your mouse over a variable name and view its current value. By right-clicking on the variable, you are given the choice of adding a watch on the variable or viewing a QuickWatch of the variable.

FIGURE 17.9
Microsoft Script Editor

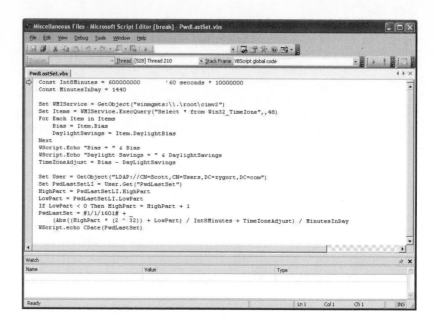

FIGURE 17.10
Microsoft Script Editor:
the Step Into window

The QuickWatch is a modal dialog window (see Figure 17.11); you cannot continue stepping through your code while it is open. It can display the value of the variable you selected, or you can type another variable in the Expression field to view its value. You can also type an expression, such as **25*25**, into the Expression field and it will evaluate it for you. A button on the right side allows you to create a Watch expression from the value.

A Watch expression also displays the value of a variable or the result of an expression, but it does it in a non-modal window. The window can be docked in the editor or allowed to float. This window remains open while you step through your code, allowing you to see changes to your variables as they occur. When the value of a variable changes, the color of the value changes to red to alert you that it has changed.

You can open the Watch window by selected Debug ➢ Windows ➢ Watch Window. When the Watch window is open, you can add any new watch expressions you like by simply typing the expression into the next available line. You can also select a line and delete a watch when you have finished with it. All watches will remain in the window until you remove them, even if the expression being watched is no longer valid.

When you are watching a variable type with multiple values, such as an object or an array, a tree view is available to view the various values of that variable. If a tree view is available, a plus sign will appear to the left side of the variable name. Clicking on the plus sign will expand the view, as shown in Figure 17.12.

The Autos window displays a set of Watch expressions. These Watch expressions are controlled by the debugger, automatically displaying the values of the variables in the current and previous lines of code. In practice, I have found the Locals window to be far more useful than the Autos window when debugging.

The Locals window also automatically displays a set of Watch expressions, but these expressions correspond to all the variables that are visible at the current location in your script. Think of it like a Watch window that automatically makes the changes for you. As you step into a procedure, any variables declared in that procedure are automatically added to the watch list. When you leave that procedure, they are removed. Open the Locals window (shown in Figure 17.13) by selecting Debug ➢ Windows ➢ Local Window.

All windows providing the ability to watch a variable also give you the ability to change the value of that variable. Simply edit the value directly in the window's Value column and the new value is immediately put in place. Keep in mind that this is only truly effective on variables that do not point to objects. The properties of an object can be modified, but not the object reference itself.

FIGURE 17.11

Microsoft Script Editor: the QuickWatch window

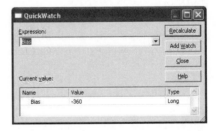

FIGURE 17.12

Microsoft Script Editor: the Watch window

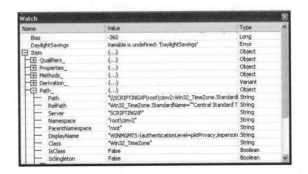

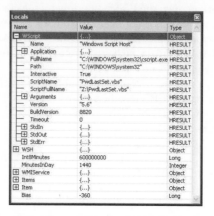

The Object Browser is not a debugging tool as much as it is an informational tool. It is primarily used to probe the properties and methods of objects, giving you information about what their function is and arguments required by the methods.

Stepping through code in the Script Editor is done with the F11 key. To use the Step Over option, press the F10 key. To Step Out of a procedure, press the Shift+F11 key combination.

You also have the option of changing the next line of code to be executed. By clicking and dragging the yellow arrow pointing to the next line of code, you effectively change the execution path of your script. You can either skip one or more lines of code entirely or reexecute a line of code.

BREAKING YOUR CODE ON PURPOSE

Believe it or not, the debugger is not only good for debugging. I already mentioned the Script Editor does indeed make a good script editor, but I am referring to using the debugger to actually break your script code. We would all like to think our scripts are bulletproof, but that can only be verified by actually firing bullets at it. It is time to start thinking about testing your scripts.

In the watch windows, you have the ability to change values. When you change values, try using a value that is out of the ordinary and see what your script does in response. Test a variety of data and note the outcome, especially every error code that is raised. By knowing the error codes ahead of time, you can build effective error traps into your code to handle them when they arise.

You can also try a less code-invasive approach to testing your code. Unplug your computer from the network to simulate losing connectivity. Log in as different user, preferably one with reduced privileges, and execute your scripts. Test your script across slow links, dial-up, VPN, any remote access system that might be in place. In a test domain, you might even have the opportunity to load-test a domain controller while running your script.

The idea behind all this mayhem is to create a more robust script. Few things are as frustrating as a script that crashes halfway through its execution. Not only will you have to clean up whatever it left behind, you will also have to find out why it crashed and fix the cause. Testing allows you to identify as many causes as possible ahead of time.

OPTION EXPLICIT

You do not need to use VBScript very long to have seen the statement `Option Explicit` at the beginning of a script. This setting causes the interpreter to stop script execution when it comes across a variable that you have not defined yet. It is possibly the easiest methods to avoiding the dreaded logic error. Consider this code:

```
OneLongTextString = "Why in the world would I use Option Explicit?"
MsgBox OneLongTextStrng
```

This code displays an empty message box, because it is trying to display a variable that didn't exist until that point. Without `Option Explicit` in effect, the interpreter would recognize that the variable didn't exist and happily create it for you with no value assigned to it. This is obviously just a typographical error, but if you type like I do this scenario could be all too common.

Take the same code but add `Option Explicit` to the beginning. This time the code will raise an error on the `MsgBox` line, stating that the variable was not declared. We would instantly know where the mistake is and zero in on the needed correction.

Always use `Option Explicit`. It should be in any templates that you create for scripts. It is very cheap insurance for avoiding logic errors.

ERROR TRAPS

In VBScript, we have the ability to enable and disable an error trap with the `On Error` statement, like this:

```
On Error Resume Next    ' enables the error trap
```

This statement tells the interpreter to continue executing the script if an error should occur, rather than abruptly ending the script. This is good in that your script does not crash halfway through a task. It is also bad that if the error has an effect on the rest of the script, the results could be chaotic.

You can place the error trap statement anywhere in your script. Placing the error trap statement at the beginning of a script ensures that it remains in effect throughout the entire script. If the error trap is placed inside a procedure, it will only be in effect until that procedure is finished. Error traps can be placed in multiple locations within the script.

The key to using an error trap is the `Err` object. The `Number` property of the `Err` object will report the error number of the last statement that was executing. If no error occurred, then `Err.Number` will equal 0. If `Err.Number` does not equal 0, then a problem has occurred that you will potentially have to deal with.

You do not have to check the value of `Err.Number` after every statement. However, the value of `Err.Number` should always be checked after "risky" statements. Risky statements are pieces of code that have a higher chance of raising an error than most. Message boxes, for example, seldom fail. Binding to an object in Active Directory, on the other hand, could fail for any number of reasons. Code that connects with a resource, such as Active Directory, should always be considered risky.

When developing a script, many times I will "hide" the error trap statement in a comment to disable it. This allows me to let the interpreter tell me where my errors are during the initial phases of testing, so I can zero in on syntax and runtime errors and fix them quickly. Using a comment serves as a reminder to me to enable the error trap before I put the script into production.

ADSI and COM Errors

The errors returned by ADSI code are well documented. There is also a strong possibility of errors coming from the COM system. In this section, we look at the more common errors your Active Directory script could run into. The error codes will be in hexadecimal format, and the descriptions will begin with the ADSI or COM constant name for the error code. ADSI errors are prefixed with LDAP_ and COM errors are prefixed with E_ADS_.

These constant names are not available directly in VBScript, which means that you will have to define your own constants to use them. In the next chapter, we see how to make this a painless process.

This is not the complete list of possible errors your scripts may run into. Along with ADSI and COM errors, there are several possible VBScript errors that your scripts might encounter as well. Along with the normal regimen of testing a script, perform a more invasive set of tests on your script in the debugger. This should only be done in a safe test environment such as a virtual machine or a test domain. Try to see what kind of errors will result when you break your own script, then build your error traps to handle those errors.

CONNECTION ERRORS

Connection errors typically occur for simple, easy-to-correct reasons. The LDAP server, especially if you have specified a particular server, might be unavailable. If you are using GetDSObject and have supplied an alternate set of credentials, those credentials may not be valid (hint: did the password on the account expire?).

A referral usually occurs when you are attempting to bind to a domain that is unavailable on your current network. This typically occurs when you hardcode the domain into the script rather than retrieving the domain information from the RootDSE object. Finally, the LDAP server might require a stronger form of connection. Table 17.20 shows a short list of possible error codes that ADSI might return when a connection fails.

TABLE 17.20:   ADSI Connection Error Codes

ADSI ERROR	DESCRIPTION
0x800704C9	LDAP_CONNECT_ERROR A connection could not be established.
0x8007052E	LDAP_INVALID_CREDENTIALS The credentials supplied are invalid.
0x8007200E	LDAP_SERVER_BUSY The LDAP server is too busy to service your request.
0x8007200F	LDAP_SERVER_UNAVAILABLE There is no LDAP server available.

TABLE 17.20: ADSI Connection Error Codes *(CONTINUED)*

ADSI ERROR	DESCRIPTION
0x80072027	LDAP_AUTH_METHOD_NOT_SUPPORTED The authentication method is not supported.
0x80072028	LDAP_STRONG_AUTH_REQUIRED The LDAP server requires strong authentication.
0x8007202A	LDAP_AUTH_UNKNOWN An unknown authentication error occurred.
0x8007202B	LDAP_REFERRAL A referral occurred; check your LDAP syntax.
0x8007203A	LDAP_SERVER_DOWN The LDAP server cannot be contacted.

SECURITY ERRORS

Security issues are also common in Active Directory scripts, particularly when those scripts are automated. Remember to configure your scripts to run in a security context with enough rights to perform the required actions. Always test your scripts using whatever security context will be used in production. Table 17.21 shows common security error codes which might be returned from ADSI.

TABLE 17.21: ADSI Security Error Codes

ADSI ERROR	DESCRIPTION
0x80070005	LDAP_INSUFFICIENT_RIGHTS The security context of the script has insufficient rights to perform its actions.
0x8007052E	LDAP_INVALID_CREDENTIALS The supplied credentials are invalid.
0x80072024	LDAP_ADMIN_LIMIT_EXCEEDED Administration limit is exceeded on the server.
0x80072029	LDAP_INAPPROPRIATE_AUTH The authentication is inappropriate.
0x8007202A	LDAP_AUTH_UNKNOWN An unknown authentication error has occurred.

OPERATION ERRORS

Operation errors compose the majority of problems experienced in ADSI scripts. Some errors have nothing to do with your script, but indicate that the server might be experiencing a problem. This will usually result in a timeout or server unavailable error.

If an error points to an unknown or invalid object, verify that the AdsPath to the object is valid. Table 17.22 shows a list of common operational error codes which might be returned by ADSI.

TABLE 17.22:   ADSI Operational Error Codes

ADSI ERROR	DESCRIPTION
0x0	LDAP_SUCCESS The operation succeeded.
0x80005000	E_ADS_BAD_PATHNAME An invalid ADSI pathname does not point to an existing object in Active Directory. Verify the domain path.
0x80005004	E_ADS_UNKNOWN_OBJECT An unknown object was requested. Verify the path to the object.
0x80005006	E_ADS_PROPERTY_NOT_SUPPORTED The requested property is not supported. Verify the property name for the object.
0x80005009	E_ADS_OBJECT_UNBOUND The ADSI object is not bound to a directory services object (call GetInfo).
0x8000500D	E_ADS_PROPERTY_NOT_FOUND The property is not in the local property cache. Call GetInfo and verify the property is set on the server.
0x8000500E	E_ADS_OBJECT_EXISTS The object already exists in Active Directory.
0x8000500F	E_ADS_SCHEMA_VIOLATION The operation attempted to perform an action that is not allowed by the schema.
0x80005014	E_ADS_INVALID_FILTER The filter syntax for the LDAP query is invalid.
0x8007001F	LDAP_OTHER An unknown error has occurred.
0x800705B4	LDAP_TIMEOUT The LDAP search timed out.
0x80071392	LDAP_ALREADY_EXISTS The object already exists in Active Directory.

TABLE 17.22: ADSI Operational Error Codes *(CONTINUED)*

ADSI ERROR	DESCRIPTION
0x8007200A	LDAP_NO_SUCH_ATTRIBUTE The attribute requested from an object does not exist.
0x8007200B	LDAP_INVALID_SYNTAX The syntax of your LDAP query is invalid.
0x80072015	LDAP_NOT_ALLOWED_ON_NONLEAF The attempted operation is not allowed on a non-leaf object, such as a container.
0x80072023	LDAP_SIZELIMIT_EXCEEDED The size limit on the query has been exceeded. Consider using the Page Size property.
0x80072030	LDAP_NO_SUCH_OBJECT The requested object does not exist. Verify the path.
0x80072032	LDAP_INVALID_DN_SYNTAX The distinguished name is invalid.
0x80072037	LDAP_NAMING_VIOLATION A naming violation has occurred.
0x8007203E	LDAP_FILTER_ERROR The search filter is invalid.
0x80072040	LDAP_NOT_SUPPORTED An attempt has been made to access a feature of LDAP that is not supported by the server.

Coming Up Next

In this chapter, you have seen many of the different factors involved in creating a successful ADSI script. From binding syntax to search filters, from class inheritance to error codes, we have covered a lot of programming ground. And this chapter has really only scratched the surface.

You should now have a better understanding of Active Directory from a programmer's point of view. While Active Directory does not truly hide information, the tools you have used as an administrator have also exposed it all to you. This wealth of data is available through ADSI to your scripts.

In the next two chapters, we build scripts to manage Active Directory and monitor Active Directory. Many of these scripts use a more modular approach than traditional VBScripts. We take advantage of the features of the Windows Scripting Files (WSF) format to make many of these tasks as simple as including a file and calling a function.

Chapter 18

Active Directory Scripts

In Chapter 17, we looked at the various pieces of VBScript code that are used to build an Active Directory script. This chapter focuses on putting those pieces together into usable scripts. We also devote some time to examining different techniques that you can incorporate into your scripts to customize them to suit your particular needs.

We begin with some of the most commonly run scripts, those that deal with users and groups. Later we work with scripts that submit queries to Active Directory. Finally we look at scripts that deal with organizational units (OUs) and containers.

All the script examples provided are available for download. Instead of reproducing the downloadable scripts line by line in this book, we instead work on building a set of tools that allow you to create your own scripts in the future.

We will be using a format of scripting files known as a Windows script file (WSF). This file format allows you to reference existing scripts and incorporate their functionality into your new script without copying and pasting lines of code. Using the WSF format, you can reference existing type libraries, which allows you to take advantage of the constant declarations present in that type library.

Our scripts also make use of classes and objects coded in VBScript. That's right—we define our own objects in VBScript. This gives us the ability to define a set of functionality in a class, such as a user or group, and reuse that functionality in every new script we create.

Fully documenting the use of Windows script files and VBScript classes is beyond the scope of this book, but to prepare you for the road ahead it is a good idea to cover the basics. The primary functionality of the Windows script files we introduce is the ability to integrate external source files into our scripts. This will have an effect similar to performing a copy-and-paste operation, but with only one line of code. Furthermore, if the external source file should ever be revised, every script that references that file will immediately use the updated code.

While I always encourage people to modify my sample code as they see fit, always maintain a backup of the original code to fall back on if their modifications don't work out as planned. Always test your scripts in a lab environment before unleashing them in your production environment. And above all, don't be afraid to ask for assistance in any of the online forums or newsgroups.

Windows Script File Basics

Windows script files are written in an XML format. For our purposes, they have two elements that must exist: `<job>` and `<script>`. A basic WSF file might look something like this:

```
<job>
<script language="VBScript">
WScript.Echo "This is a sample Windows script file."
</script>
</job>
```

XML files are used to represent data. The use of bracketed tags (`<tag>`) is similar to the tags used in HTML, but the rules governing the use of tags are much stricter. XML tags are case sensitive. All tags must be closed in the same order in which they were opened. HTML parsers will simply ignore any tags that are out of order, but the XML parser will throw a fit if proper nesting is not observed.

Element tags in XML can also make use of attributes to further define the usage of the data stored in the element. In the `<script>` tag earlier, the language of the script is specified as VBScript. The `<script>` tag can also use an attribute named `src` to reference an external script:

```
<job>
<script language="VBScript" src="Output.vbs" />
<script language="VBScript">
Display "This is a sample Windows script file."
</script>
</job>
```

The first `<script>` tag references a script named `output.vbs`. The lack of a path statement usually means that the file exists in the same folder as the referencing script. The tag also specifies the language of the external script as VBScript. External scripts are not confined to a single language; scripts written in any supported scripting language can be referenced. Be sure to specify the appropriate language in the attribute.

While the previous example only references a single external file, you could instead reference as many as you need. This gives you the ability to create a new script, using the functionality of the existing scripts, in a very short amount of time. It also gives you the ability to update (or fix) the functionality in an external file, and immediately use that new functionality in every script that references it. This can save potentially hundreds of hours of script updates.

VBScript Class Basics

Creating your own classes in VBScript is undoubtedly one of the more daunting tasks we will undertake as we create the scripting toolbox. It will also be one of the most useful, as you will be able to build your own new objects from scratch or extend existing objects without requiring a programming suite such as Visual Studio and without encountering the difficulties that can accompany the distribution of compiled objects and object libraries.

Recall from the previous chapter that classes are the blueprints for objects. We cannot use the code written in a class until we create an instance of the class. Since our VBScript classes will essentially become part of the main script when they are referenced in the Windows script file, we can use the following syntax in our main script:

```
Set MyObject = New ObjectClass
```

Designing a class requires a slightly different train of thought than you might be used to when it comes to writing scripts. When writing scripts, we tend to think in terms of getting input from the user and producing output for the user to read. As a general guideline, an object typically provides data, not output, for the main script. This separation of duties keeps our object relatively clean of extraneous code and focused on performing only the tasks it is designed to do. For example, we focus the user class on providing functionality specific to a User object in Active Directory, such as creating the user, getting and setting the user properties, and so forth. We leave the user input and output functions up to the main script.

A VBScript class is written as a structure. Inside the structure, we define properties and methods that give the class object its functionality. Do not let the terms *property* and *method* intimidate you. Creating a property is just like creating a variable, and creating a method is just like creating a subroutine or function. Let's create a simple class to use as an example:

```
Class MySampleClass
Public FirstName
Public LastName
Public BirthDate

Public Function GetAge
    GetAge = DateDiff("yyyy",BirthDate,Now)
End Function

Public Sub DisplayFullName
    WScript.Echo FirstName & " " & LastName
End Sub
End Class
```

The eagle-eyed readers out there will have undoubtedly noticed I just broke my guideline about classes displaying output. Since this is only an example script, I felt it was justifiable.

The class begins with the keyword `Class`, followed by the class name, and ends with the keywords `End Class`. These statements enclose our class structure. Within the structure, we have defined the properties `FirstName`, `LastName`, and `BirthDate` and the methods `GetAge` and `DisplayFullName`. To use this class in a script, we might use the following code:

```
<job>
<script language="VBScript" src="MySampleClass.vbs" />
<script language="VBScript">
Set MyObject = New MySampleClass
MyObject.FirstName = "Tom"
MyObject.LastName = "Sawyer"
MyObject.BirthDate = #10/31/1970#
MyObject.DisplayFullName
WScript.Echo "is " & MyObject.GetAge & " years old."
Set MyObject = Nothing
</script>
</job>
```

Notice the main script itself is in the WSF format with a `<script>` tag referencing the external script `MySampleClass.vbs`, which holds the class definition. The object syntax should look familiar after dealing with objects in Chapter 17. A new object named `MyObject` is created using the `Set` and `New` keywords. The object is then used to reference the properties and methods of the class. Finally, the object is cleaned up by setting it equal to the keyword `Nothing`.

Scope

In the class definition, all the statements were declared with the keyword Public. This is an operator used to define the scope or visibility of a property or method. Think of the class; to expose anything inside the box to the outside (such as our main script) we have to create an opening in the box. This is done programmatically by using the keyword Public. We can also create variables and procedures inside the box that can only be seen by other procedures inside the box. These are declared with the keyword Private.

This begs the questions, why would you create a private variable or procedure? There are actually many reasons to do create private variables and procedures, but the most common reason is that they are simply not needed outside the object itself. Their functionality is confined inside the object, typically to manipulate the object itself or to refine some aspect of the object's behavior. Allowing access to them from outside the object could create unpredictable results.

Property Procedures

This leads to another facet of object class design we must examine in the class variables themselves. In our example class, all the variables were defined as Public, which allowed the main code to manipulate their values directly. Now think about what would happen if this excerpt of code were run in the main script:

```
MyObject.BirthDate = "Today"
WScript.Echo MyObject.GetAge
```

This would result in an error because the DateDiff function cannot convert Today into a date. This is a pitfall of declaring a variable itself as Public. We can control the value in the variable through the use of property procedures. Property procedures look exactly like regular procedure calls, but they are treated as variables in the main code. Using property procedures allows you to programmatically control the values set in the main code. In the following example, I will fix the MySampleClass definition for the BirthDate variable using property procedures:

```
Class MySampleClass
Private m_BirthDate
Public Property Get BirthDate
    BirthDate = m_BirthDate
End Property

Public Property Let BirthDate(Value)
If IsDate(Value) Then
    m_BirthDate = Value
Else
    Err.Raise 100,"MySampleClass","Invalid Date"
End If
End Property
End Class
```

First, the originally Public variable was redefined as Private. It was also renamed by prefixing m_ to the beginning of the variable name. This is a common notation used to denote a variable as private to the module (m_, get it?). Next, two property procedures were added. The first property procedure has the keyword Get and the second has the keyword Let. The Get procedures are used to return a value to the calling code; in this case the value of the m_BirthDate variable is returned. The Let procedure is used when the main code attempts to set a value for the variable. The new value is passed into the variable Value. In this example, the new value is checked to see if it is a valid date. If it is a valid date, then the new value is assigned to the private variable. If it fails, an error is raised. The main code requires no changes, because the procedure name used matches the original property name.

Class Initialization and Termination

There are always at least two events in an object's life: It is initialized and it is destroyed or terminated. An object is initialized when an instance of the class is created. An object is destroyed when the object is set to Nothing (or the script ends and the object goes out of scope). Two optional pieces of code can be coupled to these events.

VBScript has two subroutines that tie to these two events. The names of these subroutines are reserved and must be used to properly link the event to the subroutine. When the object is created, the Class_Initialize subroutine is called. When the object is destroyed, the Class_Terminate subroutine is called. Omitting either or both of these procedures is acceptable; their absence is simply ignored by the interpreter.

Using these two subroutines allows the object to set itself up for business when it is created and close down shop when it is finished. In the Class_Initialize procedure, variables can be set up and given initial values. In the Class_Terminate procedure, any internal objects can be set to Nothing and any other work necessary to clean up after the object can be performed.

Script Locations

Like most files on a system, script files tend to have a habit of getting saved wherever is most convenient. This can is a very bad practice, especially when external script files are being referenced. The path in the src attribute is very important and will cause a script to fail if it cannot find the external script. Organizing your script files will save you many hours of hair-loss treatment.

There are typically two types of scripts: *user-invoked* scripts, typically for regular administrative duties such as creating new users, and *unattended* scripts, which are usually invoked by the Task Scheduler or in response to a defined server event. This can affect how and where you locate your scripts.

All scripts should be located on a file server share that is backed up regularly. Locating the script files on a share ensures that they will be accessible from any network computer, depending on share and NTFS security assigned to the folder.

Since all scripts are executed within a security context, permissions on the share and folders beneath are important to consider. For unattended script execution, a normal user account should be created with very limited permissions and a very strong password (depending on your network security restrictions, you might want to consider exempting the password from expiring). Unattended scripts can be located in a secured folder beneath the script share.

The location of any scripts referenced by another script must also be factored into the script layout. Most of these resource scripts rarely change. I typically setup a separate folder named includes to store my resource files. This allows me to have a consistent path to my external script files, no matter what location the main script is being executed from. Figure 18.1 gives you an example of a folder hierarchy that you might find useful.

FIGURE 18.1
Script folder hierarchy

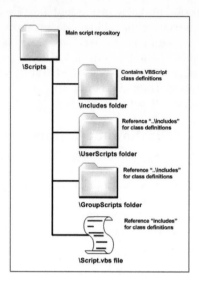

RootDSE Scripts

We will start by creating a fairly straightforward VBScript class to represent the RootDSE of an Active Directory domain and using it in some scripts. Creating an instance of this class will give us an object whose properties we can reference when we need information from the RootDSE object of AD.

RootDSE Class

The RootDSE object initializes by creating a reference object to the RootDSE of the Active Directory domain. This object is assigned to a private variable to the object. All of the RootDSE object properties are exposed through function calls.

```
Option Explicit
'==================================================================
Class RootDSEClass
'==================================================================
Private m_RootDSEObject
Private m_DomainObject
'==================================================================
Private Sub Class_Initialize
    Set m_RootDSEObject = GetObject("LDAP://RootDSE")
End Sub
'==================================================================
Private Sub Class_Terminate
    Set m_RootDSEObject = Nothing
End Sub
'==================================================================
```

```
Public Function ConfigurationNamingContext
    ConfigurationNamingContext = _
        m_RootDSEObject.Get("configurationNamingContext")
End Function
'=====================================================================
Public Function CurrentTime
    CurrentTime = m_RootDSEObject.Get("currentTime")
End Function
'=====================================================================
Public Function DefaultNamingContext
    DefaultNamingContext = m_RootDSEObject.Get("defaultNamingContext")
End Function
'=====================================================================
Public Function DnsHostName
    DnsHostName = m_RootDSEObject.Get("dnsHostName")
End Function
'=====================================================================
Public Function DsServiceName
    DsServiceName = m_RootDSEObject.Get("dsServiceName")
End Function
'=====================================================================
Public Function HighestCommittedUSN
    HighestCommittedUSN = m_RootDSEObject.Get("highestCommittedUSN")
End Function
'=====================================================================
Public Function LDAPServiceName
    LDAPServiceName = m_RootDSEObject.Get("LDAPServiceName")
End Function
'=====================================================================
Public Function NamingContexts
' Returns an array!
    NamingContexts = m_RootDSEObject.Get("namingContexts")
End Function
'=====================================================================
Public Function RootDomainNamingContext
    RootDomainNamingContext = _
        m_RootDSEObject.Get("rootDomainNamingContext")
End Function
'=====================================================================
Public Function SchemaNamingContext
    SchemaNamingContext = m_RootDSEObject.Get("schemaNamingContext")
End Function
'=====================================================================
Public Function ServerName
    ServerName = m_RootDSEObject.Get("serverName")
End Function
'=====================================================================
```

```
Public Function SubschemaSubentry
    SubschemaSubentry = m_RootDSEObject.Get("subschemaSubentry")
End Function
'==================================================================
Public Function SupportedCapabilities
' Returns an array!
    SupportedCapabilities = m_RootDSEObject.Get("supportedCapabilities")
End Function
'==================================================================
Public Function SupportedControls
' Returns an array!
    SupportedControls = m_RootDSEObject.Get("supportedControl")
End Function
'==================================================================
Public Function SupportedLDAPPolicies
' Returns an array!
    SupportedLDAPPolicies = m_RootDSEObject.Get("supportedLDAPPolicies")
End Function
'==================================================================
Public Function SupportedLDAPVersions
' Returns an array!
    SupportedLDAPVersions = m_RootDSEObject.Get("supportedLDAPVersion")
End Function
'==================================================================
Public Function SupportedSASLMechanisms
' Returns an array !
    SupportedSASLMechanisms = _
        m_RootDSEObject.Get("supportedSASLMechanisms")
End Function
'==================================================================
End Class
```

This object allows you to have a RootDSE object at your disposal in any script simply by adding a reference to the RootDSEObject.vbs script and creating an instance of the object. Now we can create some scripts to use this class and see it in action. All the scripts that follow use this same approach.

Viewing *RootDSE* Properties

This script uses the RootDSEClass class and simply calls each of the functions mapped to a RootDSE property. Keep in mind that some RootDSE properties contain an array of values, and that array is passed back to the main code. In the main code, a loop must be used to cycle through each item in the array.

```
<job>
<script langauge="VBScript" src="includes\RootDSEClass.vbs" />
<script>
Option Explicit
Dim RootDSE, Element
```

```
Set RootDSE = New RootDSEClass
WScript.Echo "Configuration Naming Context = " & _
    RootDSE.ConfigurationNamingContext
WScript.Echo "Current Time = " & RootDSE.CurrentTime
WScript.Echo "Default Naming Context = " & RootDSE.DefaultNamingContext
WScript.Echo "Dns Host Name = " & RootDSE.DnsHostName
WScript.Echo "DS Service Name = " & RootDSE.DsServiceName
WScript.Echo "Highest Committed USN = " & RootDSE.HighestCommittedUSN
WScript.Echo "LDAP Service Name = " & RootDSE.LDAPServiceName
WScript.Echo "Naming Contexts : "
' this for-next structure is the loop
' each element in the naming contexts is cycled through
For Each Element In RootDSE.NamingContexts
    WScript.Echo vbTab & Element
Next
WScript.Echo "Root Domain Naming Context = " & _
    RootDSE.RootDomainNamingContext
WScript.Echo "Schema Naming Context = " & RootDSE.SchemaNamingContext
WScript.Echo "Server Name = " & RootDSE.ServerName
WScript.Echo "Subschema Subentry = " & RootDSE.SubschemaSubentry
WScript.Echo "Supported Capabilities : "
For Each Element In RootDSE.SupportedCapabilities
    WScript.Echo vbTab & Element
Next
WScript.Echo "Supported Controls : "
For Each Element In RootDSE.SupportedControls
    WScript.Echo vbTab & Element
Next
WScript.Echo "Supported LDAP Policies : "
For Each Element In RootDSE.SupportedLDAPPolicies
    WScript.Echo vbTab & Element
Next
WScript.Echo "Supported LDAP Versions : "
For Each Element In RootDSE.SupportedLDAPVersions
    WScript.Echo vbTab & Element
Next
WScript.Echo "Supported SASL Mechanisms : "
For Each Element In RootDSE.SupportedSASLMechanisms
    WScript.Echo vbTab & Element
Next
</script>
</job>
```

The RootDSE object is really simple, probably too simple for an actual class implementation such as this. But in this case it served a purpose, to familiarize you with the use of a VBScript class. Now we can proceed to some more complicated VBScript classes and their implementations.

Domain Scripts

Information from the domain is used by a number of other objects stored in Active Directory. The best and most familiar example is information about the password expiration on the domain. By implementing the domain object as a class in our VBScript, we can also save ourselves some work by making some less-intuitive information, such as the values of the well-known GUIDS, available through the use of the class.

DomainClass

The domain object can be used for accessing the default domain and its properties. When the object initializes, it creates a temporary object referencing the RootDSE of the domain. After using the object to get the default naming context of the domain, it dereferences the object.

One of the most frustrating things about VBScript classes is their lack of support for constants as class members. In other words, a constant can't be declared and used throughout the class definition. To work around this, several private variables are declared and then given their values in the Class_ Initialize procedure.

Two functions are used to get information from the domain. The GetProperty function is passed the property name to retrieve. From the previous chapter, we learned that the values stored in properties can be either a normal string or number value, or they could return an object.

In most cases, the object returned will be a LargeInteger value, which we can assume is going to represent either a time value or a counter value. Regardless of the value represented, it is still a 64-bit integer that must be converted to view. To handle this possibility, the code in the GetProperty procedure looks to see if an object was returned. If so, then the object is converted into a 32-bit integer before returning to the calling code.

Password properties are stored as a bitmap in the pwdProperties property of the domain. To determine what properties are set, the constant name for the property is passed into the GetPasswordProperty function as a string. A logical And operation is performed on the property bitmap and the appropriate value to determine if the bit is set.

```
Option Explicit
'====================================================================
Class DomainClass
'====================================================================
' Private and public variables
Private m_DomainObject
Private m_DefaultNamingContext
'====================================================================
Private Sub Class_Initialize
Dim RootDSE
Set RootDSE = GetObject("LDAP://RootDSE")
m_DefaultNamingContext = RootDSE.Get("defaultNamingContext")
Set m_DomainObject = GetObject("LDAP://" & m_DefaultNamingContext)
Set RootDSE = Nothing
End Sub
'====================================================================
Private Sub Class_Terminate
Set m_DomainObject = Nothing
End Sub
'====================================================================
```

```
Public Function GetProperty(PropertyName)
On Error Resume Next
If IsObject(m_DomainObject.Get(PropertyName)) Then
   Dim PropertyObject, PropertyValue
   Set PropertyObject = m_DomainObject.Get(PropertyName)
   If PropertyObject.LowPart = 0 Then
      PropertyValue = 0
   Else
      PropertyValue = Int(Abs((PropertyObject.HighPart * 2^32) _
                     + PropertyObject.LowPart)/600000000)
   End If
   GetProperty = PropertyValue
Else
   GetProperty = m_DomainObject.Get(PropertyName)
End If
End Function
'=======================================================================
Public Function GetPasswordProperty(PropertyName)
Dim PasswordProperties
PasswordProperties = m_DomainObject.Get("pwdProperties")
Select Case LCase(PropertyName)
   Case "domain_password_complex"
      GetPasswordProperty = CBool(PasswordProperties And _
           DOMAIN_PASSWORD_COMPLEX)
   Case "domain_password_no_anon_change"
      GetPasswordProperty = CBool(PasswordProperties And _
           DOMAIN_PASSWORD_NO_ANON_CHANGE)
   Case "domain_password_no_clear_change"
      GetPasswordProperty = CBool(PasswordProperties And _
         DOMAIN_PASSWORD_NO_CLEAR_CHANGE)
   Case "domain_lockout_admins"
      GetPasswordProperty = CBool(PasswordProperties And _
         DOMAIN_LOCKOUT_ADMINS)
   Case "domain_password_store_cleartext"
      GetPasswordProperty = CBool(PasswordProperties And _
         DOMAIN_PASSWORD_STORE_CLEARTEXT)
   Case "domain_refuse_password_change"
      GetPasswordProperty = CBool(PasswordProperties And _
         DOMAIN_REFUSE_PASSWORD_CHANGE)
   Case Else
      GetPasswordProperty = "Unknown Property"
End Select
End Function
'=======================================================================
Public Function GetPathFromWKGuid(WKGuidName)
Dim WKGuid, GuidObject
Select Case LCase(WKGUIDName)
   Case "users" : WKGuid = _
          "a9d1ca15768811d1aded00c04fd8d5cd"
```

```
        Case "computers" : WKGuid = _
                "aa312825768811d1aded00c04fd8d5cd"
        Case "systems" : WKGuid = _
                "ab1d30f3768811d1aded00c04fd8d5cd"
        Case "domaincontrollers" : WKGuid = _
                "a361b2ffffd211d1aa4b00c04fd7d83a"
        Case "infrastructure" : WKGuid = _
                "2fbac1870ade11d297c400c04fd8d5cd"
        Case "deletedobjects" : WKGuid = _
                "18e2ea80684f11d2b9aa00c04f79f805"
        Case "lostandfound" : WKGuid = _
                "ab8153b7768811d1aded00c04fd8d5cd"
        Case Else
            Err.Raise 120,m_ErrSource, _
                    "Unknown well-known GUID specified."
            GetPathFromWKGuid = ""
            Exit Function
    End Select
    On Error Resume Next
    Set GuidObject = GetObject("LDAP://<WKGuid=" & WKGuid & _
    "," & m_DefaultNamingContext & ">")
    If Err.Number = 0 Then
        GetPathFromWKGuid = GuidObject.Get("distinguishedName")
    Else
        GetPathFromWKGuid = "Error binding to Well-Known GUID"
    End If
    Set GuidObject = Nothing
End Function
'=======================================================================
Public Function GetDomainControllers
' This returns a Dictionary Object!
Dim DCList, NTDSObject, Server
DCList = m_DomainObject.GetEx("masteredBy")
Set GetDomainControllers = WScript.CreateObject("Scripting.Dictionary")
For Each NTDSObject in DCList
    Set Server = _
            GetObject(GetObject("LDAP://" & NTDSObject).Parent) _
        GetDomainControllers.Add Server.Get("dNSHostName"), Nothing
Next
End Function
'=======================================================================
Public Property Get m_ErrSource
    m_ErrSource = "DomainObject"
End Property
Public Property Get DOMAIN_PASSWORD_COMPLEX
    DOMAIN_PASSWORD_COMPLEX = &H1
```

```
    End Property
    Public Property Get DOMAIN_PASSWORD_NO_ANON_CHANGE
        DOMAIN_PASSWORD_NO_ANON_CHANGE = &H2
    End Property
    Public Property Get DOMAIN_PASSWORD_NO_CLEAR_CHANGE
        DOMAIN_PASSWORD_NO_CLEAR_CHANGE = &H4
    End Property
    Public Property Get DOMAIN_LOCKOUT_ADMINS
        DOMAIN_LOCKOUT_ADMINS = &H8
    End Property
    Public Property Get DOMAIN_PASSWORD_STORE_CLEARTEXT
        DOMAIN_PASSWORD_STORE_CLEARTEXT = &H16
    End Property
    Public Property Get DOMAIN_REFUSE_PASSWORD_CHANGE
        DOMAIN_REFUSE_PASSWORD_CHANGE = &H32
    End Property
    '========================================================================
End Class
```

WHY ARE THE DOMAIN OBJECT CONSTANTS DEFINED IN PROPERTY PROCEDURES?

Well, the answer is simple, and a bit complex. The simple answer is that we need those constants defined somewhere. The alternative is to hard-code the constant value into every line of code that requires it, and trust me when I say that is *not* a road you want to go down. The problem is that VBScript classes don't support class-level constants—for example, in our sample class the variable m_DomainObject at the top of the class definition. Notice that it is also not defined within the body of any procedure. This gives it a class-level scope, which basically means that the variable is "visible" from any location in the class (since it is defined as Private, it is not visible outside of the class).

Normally, we would use the keyword Const to define a constant. This reserves memory for the variable, assigns it a value, and prevents the code from changing it during the course of the script execution. Unfortunately, VBScript classes do not support the Const keyword at the class level. So we have to work around it somehow.

One option is to simply define the constants as variables. This would work perfectly well, except that you could inadvertently change the value and never be the wiser (that is, until you have to debug your script for the unexpected results). I don't want to deal with that possibility.

My solution is to define the constants as properties of the class, but only define the Get procedure, which returns the value of the constant. By not defining a Let procedure for the property, we have effectively made the property read-only, which fits the definition of a constant.

You might notice that the properties are defined with the Public scope as well. That will allow us to access those constant values from our new scripts as well! You'll see this design at work in most of the remaining class definitions as well.

View Domain Account Policies

This script uses the DomainClass class to find the default domain password policies. The password age properties return a value in minutes, which is then converted into a value representing days.

```
<job>
<script language="VBScript" src="includes/DomainClass.vbs" />
<script>
Option Explicit
Dim Domain
Set Domain = New DomainClass
WScript.Echo "Lockout Duration  = " & _
    Domain.GetProperty("lockoutDuration") & " minutes."
WScript.Echo "Lockout Threshold = " & _
    Domain.GetProperty("lockoutThreshold") & " attempts."
WScript.Echo "Lockout Observation Window = " & _
    Domain.GetProperty("lockoutObservationWindow") & " minutes."
WScript.Echo "Maximum Password Age = " & _
    Domain.GetProperty("maxPwdAge") / 60 / 24 & " days."
WScript.Echo "Minimum Password Age = " & _
    Domain.GetProperty("minPwdAge") / 60 / 24 & " days."
WScript.Echo "Minimum Password Length = " & _
    Domain.GetProperty("minPwdLength") & " characters."
WScript.Echo "Password History Length = " & _
    Domain.GetProperty("pwdHistoryLength") & " passwords remembered."
</script>
</job>
```

View Domain Password Policies

This script uses the DomainClass class to view the current settings for the domain's password policy. The string value passed into GetPasswordProperty is the same as the constant defined for the property bitmask.

```
<job>
<script language="VBScript" src="includes\DomainObject.vbs" />
<script>
Option Explicit
Dim Domain
Set Domain = New DomainObject
WScript.Echo "Complex Passwords Enabled  = " & _
Domain.GetPasswordProperty("domain_password_complex")
WScript.Echo "No Anonymous Changes  = " & _
    Domain.GetPasswordProperty("domain_password_no_anon_change")
WScript.Echo "No Clear Change  = " & _
    Domain.GetPasswordProperty("domain_password_no_clear_change")
WScript.Echo "Lockout Admins  = " & _
    Domain.GetPasswordProperty("domain_lockout_admins")
WScript.Echo "Store Password in Clear Text  = " & _
    Domain.GetPasswordProperty("domain_password_store_cleartext")
```

```
WScript.Echo "Refuse Password Changes  = " & _
    Domain.GetPasswordProperty("domain_refuse_password_change")
</script>
</job>
```

Active Directory Query Scripts

Before we get into creating and using classes to represent some of the various objects in Active Directory (such as users and computers), let's take a moment to look at the ability to query AD. Building and executing queries in Active Directory is often used as the basis for additional operations on other objects. For example, to change the value of a certain property for users on the domain, you first have to collect a list of users on the domain! That is best done with a query, so creating a class to help us quickly build AD queries makes a lot of sense.

QueryClass

The QueryClass class is designed to simplify creating and executing queries against Active Directory. Several steps must be performed to create an AD query; the search root must be selected, the filter must be created, the attributes must be selected, and the search scope must be defined.

The script typically uses several ActiveX Data Objects (ADOs) to define and execute the query. A Connection object is used to define a connection to an Active Directory source. A Command object is used to define, control, and execute the query itself. The results are returned in a Recordset object. With the QueryClass class, the creation and control of the ADO objects is done within the object itself.

The main script first creates an instance of the QueryClass class. Then the search root, filter, attributes, and search scope are defined by setting their respective properties in the QueryClass. Finally the query is executed by calling the ExecuteQuery function of the object. The results are returned in a Recordset; the main script iterates through the Recordset and processes the results.

In the previous chapter, we discussed the effect that the properties of the Command object have on the query result set and performance. Those properties are defined in a Dictionary object, which stores the property name as the key. The properties are loaded into the Dictionary object in the Class_Initialize procedure. You may modify these defaults to suit your environment as necessary. The properties can be changed, prior to executing the query, by calling the SetProperty procedure and passing in the property name and new value.

Two private utility functions appear at the bottom of the script. These functions examine the value entered for the SearchRoot property. The function FormatAdsPath attempts to correctly format the LDAP path entered. The function ADObjectExists checks Active Directory for the existence of the specified search root. These utility functions will also appear in other object classes.

```
Option Explicit
'=================================================================
Class QueryClass
'=================================================================
Private m_cn, m_cmd
Private m_SearchRoot
Private m_FilterText
Private m_Attributes
Private m_SearchScope
Private m_CmdProperties
'=================================================================
```

```
Private Sub Class_Initialize
Set m_cn = WScript.CreateObject("ADODB.Connection")
m_cn.Provider = "ADsDSOObject"
Set m_cmd = WScript.CreateObject("ADODB.Command")
Set m_CmdProperties = WScript.CreateObject("Scripting.Dictionary")
m_CmdProperties.Add "Asynchronous", False
m_CmdProperties.Add "Cache results", True
m_CmdProperties.Add "Chase referrals",ADS_CHASE_REFERRALS_EXTERNAL
m_CmdProperties.Add "Column Names Only", False
m_CmdProperties.Add "Deref Aliases", False
m_CmdProperties.Add "Page size", 1000
m_CmdProperties.Add "SearchScope", ADS_SCOPE_SUBTREE
m_CmdProperties.Add "Size Limit", 0' No limit
m_CmdProperties.Add "Sort On", ""' No sort
m_CmdProperties.Add "Time Limit", 600      ' 600 seconds = 10 Minutes
m_CmdProperties.Add "Timeout", 600
m_SearchScope = "subtree"                  ' Set a default scope
End Sub
'=====================================================================
Private Sub Class_Terminate
m_cn.Close
Set m_cn = Nothing
Set m_cmd = Nothing
Set m_CmdProperties = Nothing
End Sub
'=====================================================================
Public Property Get FilterText
   FilterText = m_FilterText
End Property

Public Property Let FilterText(FilterValue)
   m_FilterText = FilterValue
End Property
'=====================================================================
Public Property Get Attributes
   Attributes = m_Attributes
End Property

Public Property Let Attributes(AttributeList)
   m_Attributes = AttributeList
End Property
'=====================================================================
Public Property Get Scope
   Scope = m_SearchScope
End Property

Public Property Let Scope(ScopeText)
   Select Case UCase(ScopeText)
      Case "BASE" : m_SearchScope = "base"
```

```
         Case "ONELEVEL" : m_SearchScope = "onelevel"
         Case "SUBTREE" : m_SearchScope = "subtree"
         Case Else
             Err.Raise 100, m_ErrSource, "Invalid Scope"
             m_SearchScope = "subtree"' Set a default scope
      End Select
End Property
'========================================================================
Public Property Get SearchRoot
      SearchRoot = m_SearchRoot
End Property

Public Property Let SearchRoot(AdsPath)
      If ADObjectExists(AdsPath) Then
         m_SearchRoot = "<" & FormatAdsPath(AdsPath) & ">"
      Else
         Err.Raise 101, m_ErrSource, "Invalid AdsPath"
      End If
End Property
'========================================================================
Public Sub SetProperty(PropertyName,PropertyValue)
If m_CmdProperties.Exists(PropertyName) Then
      m_CmdProperties(PropertyName) = PropertyValue
Else
      Err.raise 105, m_ErrSource, "Unknown command property"
End If
End Sub
'========================================================================
Public Function ExecuteQuery
Dim CmdProperty
If IsEmpty(m_SearchRoot) Then
      Err.Raise 102, m_ErrSource, "No search root defined"
      Exit Function
End If
If IsEmpty(m_Attributes) Then
      Err.Raise 103, m_ErrSource, "No attributes defined"
End If
m_cn.Open
m_cmd.ActiveConnection = m_cn
For Each CmdProperty In m_CmdProperties.Keys
      m_cmd.Properties(CmdProperty) = m_CmdProperties(CmdProperty)
Next
m_cmd.CommandText = m_SearchRoot & ";" & _
                    m_FilterText & ";" & _
                    m_Attributes & ";" & _
                    m_SearchScope
Set ExecuteQuery = m_cmd.Execute
End Function
'========================================================================
```

```
Private Function ADObjectExists(ADsPath)
Dim ADObject, LDAPObject
ADSPath = FormatAdsPath(AdsPath)
On Error Resume Next
Set LDAPObject = GetObject("LDAP:")
Set ADObject = _
     LDAPObject.OpenDSObject(ADsPath,vbNullString,vbNullString, _
                            ADS_FAST_BIND)
If Err.Number = 0 Then
   ADObjectExists = True
Else
   ADObjectExists = False
End If
Set ADObject = Nothing
Set LDAPObject = Nothing
End Function
'=====================================================================
Private Function FormatAdsPath(ADsPath)
If Not CBool(Instr(ADsPath,"LDAP://")) Then
   FormatAdsPath = "LDAP://" & ADsPath
Else
   FormatAdsPath = AdsPath
End If
End Function
'=====================================================================
Public Property Get m_ErrSource
m_ErrSource = "QueryClass"
End Property
Public Property Get ADS_CHASE_REFERRALS_NEVER
   ADS_CHASE_REFERRALS_NEVER = &H00
End Property
  Public Property Get ADS_CHASE_REFERRALS_SUBORDINATE
   ADS_CHASE_REFERRALS_SUBORDINATE = &H20
End Property
Public Property Get ADS_CHASE_REFERRALS_EXTERNAL
   ADS_CHASE_REFERRALS_EXTERNAL = &H40' Default
End Property
Public Property Get ADS_CHASE_REFERRALS_ALWAYS
   ADS_CHASE_REFERRALS_ALWAYS = &H60
End Property
Public Property Get ADS_SCOPE_BASE
   ADS_SCOPE_BASE = 0
End Property
Public Property Get ADS_SCOPE_ONELEVEL
   ADS_SCOPE_ONELEVEL = 1
End Property
Public Property Get ADS_SCOPE_SUBTREE
   ADS_SCOPE_SUBTREE = 2
End Property
```

```
Public Property Get ADS_FAST_BIND
    ADS_FAST_BIND = &H20
End Property
' ============================================================================
End Class
```

Using the *QueryClass*

This class only requires you to set four properties: the `SearchRoot`, the `Attributes` to be returned, the `Scope` of the search, and the `FilterText`. After setting those four properties, you can call the `ExecuteQuery` method, and assign the result to an object. The resulting object will be an ADO `Recordset`.

`Recordsets` must be looped through until the `EOF` property of the `Recordset` is `True`. Do not forget to execute the `MoveNext` method of the `Recordset` in the loop!

They `QueryClass` object is the third VBScript class we have examined. As you look at the code for the class itself, and then the code for the script that uses the class, take a moment to notice the difference in their sizes. While the class code is large (and they are going to get larger yet!), the script that uses the class is relatively small. When you consider the timesavings in both writing code and then debugging code, using classes in your scripts should prove to be more cost- and time-effective than writing several stand-alone scripts.

Search for User Accounts

This script uses the `QueryClass` class to return a list of the `User` objects in the specified Active Directory domain. The domain is specified by using the `RootDSEClass`, which we examined earlier, and retrieving the default naming convention property.

```
<job>
<script language="VBScript" src="includes\RootDSEClass.vbs" />
<script language="VBScript" src="includes\QueryClass.vbs" />
<script>
Dim RootDSE
Set RootDSE = New RootDSEClass
Dim Query
Set Query = New QueryClass
Query.SearchRoot = RootDSE.DefaultNamingContext
Query.Attributes = "cn,AdsPath"
Query.Scope = "subtree"
Query.FilterText = "(&(objectClass=user)(objectCategory=person))"
Dim Results
Set Results = Query.ExecuteQuery
Do Until Results.eof
    WScript.Echo Results.Fields(0) & "," & Results.Fields(1)
    Results.MoveNext
Loop
Set QueryObject = Nothing
Set RootDSE = Nothing
</script>
</job>
```

Search for Computer Accounts

This script uses the QueryClass class to return a list of the Computer objects in the specified Active Directory domain:

```
<job>
<script language="VBScript" src="includes\RootDSEClass.vbs" />
<script language="VBScript" src="includes\QueryClass.vbs" />
<script>
Dim RootDSE
Set RootDSE = New RootDSEClass
Dim Query
Set Query = New QueryClass
Query.SearchRoot = RootDSE.DefaultNamingContext
Query.Attributes = "cn,AdsPath"
Query.Scope = "subtree"
Query.FilterText = "(&(objectClass=computer)(objectCategory=computer))"
Dim Results
Set Results = Query.ExecuteQuery
Do Until Results.eof
    WScript.Echo Results.Fields(0) & "," & Results.Fields(1)
    Results.MoveNext
Loop
Set QueryObject = Nothing
Set RootDSE = Nothing
</script>
</job>
```

Search for Groups

This script uses the QueryClass class to return a list of the Group objects in the specified Active Directory domain:

```
<job>
<script language="VBScript" src="includes\RootDSEClass.vbs" />
<script language="VBScript" src="includes\QueryClass.vbs" />
<script>
Dim RootDSE
Set RootDSE = New RootDSEClass
Dim Query
Set Query = New QueryClass
Query.SearchRoot = RootDSE.DefaultNamingContext
Query.Attributes = "cn,AdsPath"
Query.Scope = "subtree"
Query.FilterText = "(&(objectClass=group)(objectCategory=group))"
Dim Results
Set Results = Query.ExecuteQuery
```

```
Do Until Results.eof
    WScript.Echo Results.Fields(0) & "," & Results.Fields(1)
    Results.MoveNext
Loop
Set QueryObject = Nothing
Set RootDSE = Nothing
</script>
</job>
```

Search for Organizational Units

This script uses the QueryClass class to return a list of the OUs in the specified Active Directory domain:

```
<job>
<script language="VBScript" src="includes\RootDSEClass.vbs" />
<script language="VBScript" src="includes\QueryClass.vbs" />
<script>
Dim RootDSE
Set RootDSE = New RootDSEClass
Dim Query
Set Query = New QueryClass
Query.SearchRoot = RootDSE.DefaultNamingContext
Query.Attributes = "name,AdsPath"
Query.Scope = "subtree"
Query.FilterText = "(objectClass=organizationalUnit)"
Dim Results
Set Results = Query.ExecuteQuery
Do Until Results.eof
    WScript.Echo Results.Fields(0) & "," & Results.Fields(1)
    Results.MoveNext
Loop
Set QueryObject = Nothing
Set RootDSE = Nothing
</script>
</job>
```

User Scripts

Finally, we start getting into building classes that will represent real Active Directory objects, starting with the User object. The User object is possibly the most-used object in AD; it is constantly being created, deleted, and modified in one way or another. Again, our goal here is to reduce some of the complexity of the ADSI object model by use of a class.

UserClass

The UserClass class obviously represents a User in Active Directory. To use this object, it must be instantiated like the other classes and then either bound to an existing User object in AD or used to create a new user. User properties can then be modified, the password reset, or the account unlocked. The group membership of the user can be returned, a group can be joined, or the group membership can be copied from another user. Finally, the object can be saved to AD.

Creating a new user is done with the Create method. This method takes three arguments: the ADsPath to the container that will hold the User object, the Common Name (CN) of the new object, and the SAM account name of the new object. The object will be created and saved to Active Directory, and a reference to the new User object will be returned.

Binding to an existing user is done with the BindToUser method. This method only takes the ADsPath to the object as an argument. A reference is returned to the object. When a reference is returned, it may be ignored if you don't need it, as you will see in the example scripts that follow the class definition.

```
Option Explicit
'=======================================================================
Class UserClass
'=======================================================================
Private Sub Class_Initialize
End Sub
'=======================================================================
Private Sub Class_Terminate
End Sub
'=======================================================================
' Private and public variables
Private m_UserObject
'=======================================================================
Public Function BindToUser(UserPath)
If ADObjectExists(UserPath) Then
    Set m_UserObject = GetObject(FormatAdsPath(UserPath))
    m_UserObject.GetInfo
    Set BindToUser = m_UserObject
Else
    Err.Raise 102,m_ErrSource,"Object does not exist"
End If
End Function
'=======================================================================
Public Function Create(ContainerPath,CN,AccountName)
If CN = "" Or ContainerPath = "" Or AccountName = "" Then
    Err.Raise 101,m_ErrSource,"Missing arguments"
    Exit Function
End If
Dim Container
If ADObjectExists(ContainerPath) Then
    Set Container = GetObject(FormatAdsPath(ContainerPath))
    Set m_UserObject = Container.Create("user",FormatCN(CN))
```

```
      m_UserObject.Put "sAMAccountName", AccountName
      m_UserObject.SetInfo
      m_UserObject.GetInfo
      Set Create = m_UserObject
   Else
      WScript.Echo "Error connecting to container!"
      WScript.Quit(1)
   End If
End Function
'=========================================================================
Public Function Copy(Destination,CN,AccountName)
If CN = "" Or AccountName = "" Then
   Err.Raise 101,m_ErrSource,"Missing arguments"
   Exit Function
End If
If ADObjectExists(Destination) Then
   Dim PropertiesToCopy
   PropertiesToCopy = _
      Array("company","co","c","l","st","zipcode","scriptPath")
   Dim Container, ObjectCopy
   Set Container = GetObject(FormatAdsPath(Destination))
   Set ObjectCopy = Container.Create("user","CN=" & FormatCN(CN))
   ObjectCopy.Put "sAMAccountName", AccountName
   ObjectCopy.SetInfo
   ObjectCopy.GetInfo
   Dim PropertyName
   On Error Resume Next
   For Each PropertyName In PropertiesToCopy
      ObjectCopy.Put PropertyName,m_UserObject.Get(PropertyName)
   Next
   ObjectCopy.SetInfo
   Set Copy = ObjectCopy
Else
   Err.Raise 109,m_ErrSource,"Destination does not exist"
End If
End Function
'=========================================================================
Public Property Get AccountEnabled
   AccountEnabled = Not(m_UserObject.AccountDisabled)
End Property
'=========================================================================
Public Property Let AccountEnabled(EnableValue)
If CBool(EnableValue) Then
   m_UserObject.AccountDisabled = False
Else
   m_UserObject.AccountDisabled = True
End If
End Property
'=========================================================================
```

```
Public Property Let Password(NewPassword)
    m_UserObject.SetPassword(CStr(NewPassword))
End Property
'========================================================================
Public Property Get PasswordDoesntExpire
PasswordDoesntExpire = _
CBool(m_UserObject.Get("userAccountControl") And _
    ADS_UF_DONT_EXPIRE_PASSWD)
End Property
'========================================================================
Public Property Let PasswordDoesntExpire(ExpireValue)
Dim NewValue
If CBool(ExpireValue) Then
    NewValue = CalculateBitMask _
        (m_UserObject.Get("userAccountControl"), _
         ADS_UF_DONT_EXPIRE_PASSWD,True)
Else
    NewValue = CalculateBitMask _
        (m_UserObject.Get("userAccountControl"), _
         ADS_UF_DONT_EXPIRE_PASSWD,False)
End If
m_UserObject.Put "userAccountControl", NewValue
End Property
'========================================================================
Public Property Get LockedOut
    LockedOut = m_UserObject.IsAccountLocked
End Property
'========================================================================
Public Sub UnlockAccount
If CBool(m_UserObject.IsAccountLocked) Then
    m_UserObject.IsAccountLocked = False
End If
End Sub
'========================================================================
Public Property Get PasswordExpired
PasswordExpired = CBool(m_UserObject.Get("userAccountControl") _
                And ADS_UF_PASSWORD_EXPIRED)
End Property
'========================================================================
Public Function Move(Destination)
If ADObjectExists(Destination) Then
    m_UserObject.MoveHere FormatAdsPath(Destination), _
        m_UserObject.Get("distinguishedName")
Else
    Err.Raise 109,m_ErrSource,"Invalid object or destination"
End If
End Function
'========================================================================
```

```
Public Property Get Groups
' Returns a Dictionary object!
Dim GroupList, Group
Set GroupList = WScript.CreateObject("Scripting.Dictionary")
For Each Group In m_UserObject.GetEx("memberOf")
   GroupList.Add Group,0
Next
Set Groups = GroupList
End Property
'======================================================================
Public Property Get AllGroups
' Returns a Dictionary object!
Dim GroupList
Set GroupList = WScript.CreateObject("Scripting.Dictionary")
GetMembership m_UserObject.Get("distinguishedName"),GroupList
Set AllGroups = GroupList
End Property
'======================================================================
Private Function GetMembership(ObjectAdsPath,List)
Dim tmpObject, Group
Set tmpObject = GetObject(FormatAdsPath(ObjectAdsPath))
On Error Resume Next
For Each Group In tmpObject.GetEx("memberOf")
   If Err.Number = 0 Then
      If Not(List.Exists(Group)) Then
         List.Add Group,0
         GetMembership Group,List
      End If
   End If
   Err.Clear
Next
End Function
'======================================================================
Public Sub CopyGroupsFromUser(UserPath)
If ADObjectExists(UserPath) Then
   Dim GroupsToCopy
   Dim CopyObject
   Set CopyObject = GetObject(FormatAdsPath(UserPath))
   On Error Resume Next
   GroupsToCopy = CopyObject.GetEx("memberOf")
   If Err.Number <> 0 Then
      Dim Group, GroupObject
      For Each Group In GroupsToCopy
         Set GroupObject = GetObject(FormatAdsPath(Group))
         GroupObject.PutEx ADS_PROPERTY_APPEND, _
            "member", Array(UserPath)
         GroupObject.SetInfo
```

```
         Next
      End If
   Else
      WScript.Echo "User " & UserPath & " does not exist."
      WScript.Quit(1)
   End If
End Sub
'========================================================================
Public Sub JoinGroup(GroupPath)
If ADObjectExists(GroupPath) Then
   Dim GroupObject
   Set GroupObject = GetObject(FormatAdsPath(GroupPath))
   GroupObject.PutEx ADS_PROPERTY_APPEND, _
      "member", Array(m_UserObject.Get("distinguishedName"))
   GroupObject.SetInfo
Else
   WScript.Echo "Group " & GroupPath & " does not exist."
   WScript.Quit(1)
End If
End Sub
'========================================================================
Public Sub Save
m_UserObject.SetInfo
m_UserObject.GetInfo
End Sub
'========================================================================
Public Property Get PropertyList
' Returns a Dictionary object!
Dim Properties
Set Properties = WScript.CreateObject("Scripting.Dictionary")
Dim PropertyIndex, PropertyValue
For PropertyIndex = 0 To (m_UserObject.PropertyCount - 1)
   For Each PropertyValue In m_UserObject.Item(PropertyIndex).Values
      If Not (Properties.Exists( _
         m_UserObject.Item(PropertyIndex).Name)) Then
            Properties.Add _
               m_UserObject.Item(PropertyIndex).Name, _
               GetADsTypeValue(CInt( _
                  PropertyValue.AdsType),PropertyValue)
      End If
   Next
Next
Set PropertyList = Properties
End Property
'========================================================================
Public Sub SetProperty(PropName,PropValue)
On Error Resume Next
m_UserObject.Put PropName,PropValue
```

```
   If Err.Number <> 0 Then
      WScript.Echo "Error setting property " & PropName
   End If
   End Sub
   '================================================================
   Public Sub MultiPropertyClear(PropertyName)
      m_UserObject.PutEx ADS_PROPERTY_CLEAR,PropertyName,0
   End Sub
   '================================================================
   Public Sub MultiPropertyUpdate(PropertyName, PropertyArray)
      m_UserObject.PutEx ADS_PROPERTY_UPDATE,PropertyName,PropertyArray
   End Sub
   '================================================================
   Public Sub MultiPropertyAppend(PropertyName, PropertyArray)
      m_UserObject.PutEx ADS_PROPERTY_APPEND,PropertyName,PropertyArray
   End Sub
   '================================================================
   Public Sub MultiPropertyDelete(PropertyName, PropertyArray)
      m_UserObject.PutEx ADS_PROPERTY_DELETE,PropertyName,PropertyArray
   End Sub
   '================================================================
   Private Function ADObjectExists(ADsPath)
   Dim ADObject, LDAPObject
   ADSPath = FormatAdsPath(AdsPath)
   On Error Resume Next
   Set LDAPObject = GetObject("LDAP:")
   Set ADObject = LDAPObject.OpenDSObject( _
      ADsPath,vbNullString,vbNullString,ADS_FAST_BIND)
   If Err.Number = 0 Then
      ADObjectExists = True
   Else
      ADObjectExists = False
   End If
   Set ADObject = Nothing
   Set LDAPObject = Nothing
   End Function
   '================================================================
   Private Function GetADsTypeValue(AdsType,AdsValue)
   Select Case CInt(adsType)
      Case 1 : GetADsTypeValue = AdsValue.DNString
      Case 2 : GetADsTypeValue =  AdsValue.CaseExactString
      Case 3 : GetADsTypeValue =  AdsValue.CaseIgnoreString
      Case 4 : GetADsTypeValue =  AdsValue.PrintableString
      Case 5 : GetADsTypeValue =  AdsValue.NumericString
      Case 6 : GetADsTypeValue =  CStr(AdsValue.Boolean)
      Case 7 : GetADsTypeValue =  AdsValue.Integer
      Case 8 : GetADsTypeValue =  "Octet String"
      Case 9 : GetADsTypeValue =  AdsValue.UTCTime
```

```
    Case 10
            Dim PropertyLargeInteger, LargeIntegerValue
            Dim LargeIntegerDate, DateHigh, DateLow
            Set PropertyLargeInteger = AdsValue.LargeInteger
            DateHigh = PropertyLargeInteger.HighPart
            DateLow = PropertyLargeInteger.LowPart
            If DateLow < 0 Then
               DateHigh = DateHigh + 1
            End If
            If (DateHigh = 0) And (DateLow = 0 ) Then
               LargeIntegerDate = #1/1/1601#
            Else
               LargeIntegerDate = #1/1/1601# + (((DateHigh * _
                         (2 ^ 32)) + DateLow)/600000000)/1440
            End If
            If IsDate(LargeIntegerDate) And _
                  LargeIntegerDate > #1/1/1970# Then
               GetADsTypeValue = LargeIntegerDate
            Else
               GetADsTypeValue = _
                  PropertyLargeInteger.HighPart * 2^32 + _
                  PropertyLargeInteger.LowPart
            End If
    Case 11 : GetADsTypeValue = "Provider Specific"
    Case 12 : GetADsTypeValue = "Object Class"
    Case 13 : GetADsTypeValue = "Case Ignore List"
    Case 14 : GetADsTypeValue = "Octet List"
    Case 15 : GetADsTypeValue = "Path"
    Case 16 : GetADsTypeValue = "Postal Address"
    Case 17 : GetADsTypeValue = "TimeStamp"
    Case 18 : GetADsTypeValue = "BackLink"
    Case 19 : GetADsTypeValue = "Typed Name"
    Case 20 : GetADsTypeValue = "Hold"
    Case 21 : GetADsTypeValue = "Net Address"
    Case 22 : GetADsTypeValue = "Replica Pointer"
    Case 23 : GetADsTypeValue = "Fax Number"
    Case 24 : GetADsTypeValue = "Email"
    Case 25 : GetADsTypeValue = "NT Security Descriptor"
    Case 26 : GetADsTypeValue = "Unknown"
    Case Else : GetADsTypeValue = "Unknown - " & _
                  AdsValue.adsType
    End Select
End Function
'========================================================================
Private Function FormatCN(CNValue)
FormatCN = Replace(CNValue,"LDAP://","")
```

```
If Left(FormatCN,3) <> "CN=" Then
   FormatCN = "CN=" & FormatCN
End If
End Function
'=====================================================================
Private Function FormatAdsPath(ADsPath)
If CBool(Instr(ADsPath,"LDAP://")) Then
   FormatAdsPath = AdsPath
Else
   FormatAdsPath = "LDAP://" & ADsPath
End If
End Function
'=====================================================================
Private Function CalculateBitMask(CurrentMask,NewMask,EnableFlag)
If CBool(EnableFlag) Then
   CalculateBitMask = CurrentMask Or NewMask
Else
   If CurrentMask And NewMask Then
      CalculateBitMask = CurrentMask Xor NewMask
   Else
      CalculateBitMask = CurrentMask
   End If
End If
End Function
'=====================================================================
Public Property Get m_ErrSource
   m_ErrSource = "UserClass"
End Property
' ADS Constants defined as readonly properties of the class
Public Property Get ADS_UF_ACCOUNTDISABLE
' The user account Is disabled
  ADS_UF_ACCOUNTDISABLE =  &H2
End Property
Public Property Get ADS_UF_HOMEDIR_REQUIRED
' The home directory Is required
  ADS_UF_HOMEDIR_REQUIRED = &H8
End Property
Public Property Get ADS_UF_LOCKOUT
'The account Is currently locked out
  ADS_UF_LOCKOUT = &H10
End Property
Public Property Get ADS_UF_PASSWD_NOTREQD
' No password is required
  ADS_UF_PASSWD_NOTREQD = &H20
End Property
Public Property Get ADS_UF_PASSWD_CANT_CHANGE
' The user cannot change the password. This flag can be read,
```

```
' but not set directly.
   ADS_UF_PASSWD_CANT_CHANGE = &H40
End Property
Public Property Get ADS_UF_ENCRYPTED_TEXT_PASSWORD_ALLOWED
' The user can send an encrypted password
   ADS_UF_ENCRYPTED_TEXT_PASSWORD_ALLOWED = &H80
End Property
Public Property Get ADS_UF_TEMP_DUPLICATE_ACCOUNT
' This is an account for users whose primary account is in
' another domain.
' This account provides user access to this domain,
' but not to any domain that trusts this domain.
   ADS_UF_TEMP_DUPLICATE_ACCOUNT = &H100
End Property
Public Property Get ADS_UF_NORMAL_ACCOUNT
' This is a default account type that represents a typical user
   ADS_UF_NORMAL_ACCOUNT = &H200
End Property
Public Property Get ADS_UF_INTERDOMAIN_TRUST_ACCOUNT
' This is a permit to trust account for a system domain that
' trusts other domains
   ADS_UF_INTERDOMAIN_TRUST_ACCOUNT = &H800
End Property
Public Property Get ADS_UF_DONT_EXPIRE_PASSWD
' When Set, the password will Not expire on this account
   ADS_UF_DONT_EXPIRE_PASSWD = &H10000
End Property
Public Property Get ADS_UF_SMARTCARD_REQUIRED
' When set, this flag will force the user to log on using a smart card
   ADS_UF_SMARTCARD_REQUIRED = &H40000
End Property
Public Property Get ADS_UF_TRUSTED_FOR_DELEGATION
' When Set, the service account is trusted for Kerberos delegation.
   ADS_UF_TRUSTED_FOR_DELEGATION = &H80000
End Property
Public Property Get ADS_UF_NOT_DELEGATED
' When set, the security context of the user will not be delegated
' to a service even if the service account is set as trusted for
' Kerberos delegation.
   ADS_UF_NOT_DELEGATED = &H100000
End Property
Public Property Get ADS_UF_PASSWORD_EXPIRED
' The user password has expired. It is read-only and cannot be set.
   ADS_UF_PASSWORD_EXPIRED = &H800000
End Property
'=======================================================================
' OpenDSObject Constants
Public Property Get ADS_SECURE_AUTHENTICATION
```

```
        ADS_SECURE_AUTHENTICATION = &H1
    End Property
    Public Property Get ADS_USE_ENCRYPTION
        ADS_USE_ENCRYPTION = &H2
    End Property
    Public Property Get ADS_USE_SSL
        ADS_USE_SSL = &H2
    End Property
    Public Property Get ADS_READONLY_SERVER
        ADS_READONLY_SERVER = &H4
    End Property
    Public Property Get ADS_PROMPT_CREDENTIALS
        ADS_PROMPT_CREDENTIALS = &H8
    End Property
    Public Property Get ADS_NO_AUTHENTICATION
        ADS_NO_AUTHENTICATION = &H10
    End Property
    Public Property Get ADS_FAST_BIND
        ADS_FAST_BIND = &H20
    End Property
    Public Property Get ADS_USE_SIGNING
        ADS_USE_SIGNING = &H40
    End Property
    Public Property Get ADS_USE_SEALING
        ADS_USE_SEALING = &H80
    End Property
    Public Property Get ADS_USE_DELEGATION
        ADS_USE_DELEGATION = &H100
    End Property
    Public Property Get ADS_SERVER_BIND
        ADS_SERVER_BIND = &H200
    End Property
    '=====================================================================
    Public Property Get ADS_PROPERTY_CLEAR
        ADS_PROPERTY_CLEAR = 1
    End Property
    Public Property Get ADS_PROPERTY_UPDATE
        ADS_PROPERTY_UPDATE = 2
    End Property
    Public Property Get ADS_PROPERTY_APPEND
        ADS_PROPERTY_APPEND = 3
    End Property
    Public Property Get ADS_PROPERTY_DELETE
        ADS_PROPERTY_DELETE = 4
    End Property
    '=====================================================================
End Class
```

> ### BUT *CLASS_INITIALIZE* AND *CLASS_TERMINATE* ARE EMPTY!
>
> Think of these empty procedures as placeholders. The idea is simple: If later in the cycle of script management, we realize that it would be to our advantage to put some code in those procedures, they are already there and ready to be filled in. It also comes in handy if you decide that you would like to use these classes as templates for your own classes, and your new classes will make use of the Initialize and Terminate procedures.

Create a New User

This script uses the UserClass to create a new user. The ADsPath to the container, the Common Name (CN) and the SAM account name for the new object are passed to the Create method of the class. After successfully executing the Create method, the new User object has been created, but is essentially blank.

A few additional properties are then set for the new user account. The first name (givenName property) and last name (sn property) are set, followed by setting a new password.

When setting properties for the new User object using the class, it is important to note that the properties are not saved to the User object automatically. Rather, only after setting all the new properties must the object be saved. This is a design decision to prevent multiple trips to the domain controller as each and every property is set. The design of the class could easily be modified to enable this behavior if desired.

```
<job>
<script language="VBScript" src="includes\UserClass.vbs" />
<script>
Option Explicit
Dim UserObject
Set UserObject = New UserClass
UserObject.Create _
    "LDAP://OU=Users,DC=zygort,DC=com","ScriptUser","ScriptTest"
UserObject.AccountEnabled = True
UserObject.SetProperty "givenName", "Script"
UserObject.SetProperty "sn", "User"
UserObject.Password = "P@ssw0rd"
UserObject.Save
</script>
</job>
```

List User Properties

When not creating a new User object, all operations on User objects begin by binding to the User object in Active Directory with the BindToUser method. The method only takes the ADsPath to the User object as an argument.

A Dictionary object is returned by the PropertyList method of the class. The key value holds the property name and the value (obviously) holds that property's value. A simple For-Next loop iterates through the property list. Note that the list will only contain the properties for which values have been set on the User object.

```
<job>
<script language="VBScript" src="includes\UserClass.vbs" />
<script>
Option Explicit
Dim UserObject
Set UserObject = New UserClass
UserObject.BindToUser "CN=ScriptUser,OU=Users,DC=zygort,DC=com"
Dim PropertyList, Prop
Set PropertyList = UserObject.PropertyList
For Each Prop In PropertyList.Keys
    WScript.Echo Prop & "=" & PropertyList(Prop)
Next
</script>
</job>
```

Set User Properties

Setting user properties is one of the most common operations on User objects. Begin by binding to the User object, the set the property using the SetProperty method. The method takes the property name (the LDAP display name) and the new value as arguments.

After setting new property values on the User object, be sure to call the Save method. This method essentially executes a SetInfo method on the User object itself and writes the information back to Active Directory. This saves network traffic to the domain controller, as well as allows your script to be able to back-track out of an operation should the need arise.

The last property that is set does not use the SetProperty method, but rather sets a property of the UserClass called PasswordDoesntExpire. This one requires a little more explanation. The actual property that controls the password expiration on the user object is stored as a bitmap in the userAccountControl property. Rather than force the scriptwriter to memorize or build the new bitmap for the intended result, certain "bits" of the bitmap have been exposed through properties in the class, which will manipulate the bitmap for you. As a bit of homework, look at the code for the property Let PasswordDoesntExpire procedure and figure out how it works.

```
<job>
<script language="VBScript" src="includes\UserClass.vbs" />
<script>
Option Explicit
Dim UserObject
Set UserObject = New UserClass
UserObject.BindToUser "CN=ScriptUser,OU=Users,DC=zygort,DC=com"
UserObject.SetProperty "givenName", "FirstName"
UserObject.SetProperty "sn", "LastName"
UserObject.SetProperty "", ""
UserObject.PasswordDoesntExpire = True
UserObject.Save
</script>
</job>
```

Set User Password

This script lets you bind to a User object and reset the user's password. Don't forget to save the object when you have finished. In this example, a simple string value is used. This script could (and probably should) be updated with your own code to generate a pseudo-random and stronger password.

```
<job>
<script language="VBScript" src="includes\UserClass.vbs" />
<script>
Option Explicit
Dim UserObject
Set UserObject = New UserClass
UserObject.BindToUser "CN=ScriptUser,OU=Users,DC=zygort,DC=com"
UserObject.Password = "P@ssw0rd"
UserObject.Save
</script>
</job>
```

Set Password Not to Expire

This script allows you to bind to a User object and change settings so that the password does not expire. Changing the assignment value to False will re-enable password expiration.

```
<job>
<script language="VBScript" src="includes\UserClass.vbs" />
<script>
Option Explicit
Dim UserObject
Set UserObject = New UserClass
UserObject.BindToUser "CN=ScriptUser,OU=Users,DC=zygort,DC=com"
UserObject.PasswordDoesntExpire = True
UserObject.Save
</script>
</job>
```

Unlock a User Account

This script binds to a user account and, if the account is locked out, it will be unlocked. This script could be modified to run on the result set of a query that scanned Active Directory for locked User objects.

```
<job>
<script language="VBScript" src="includes\UserClass.vbs" />
<script>
Option Explicit
Dim UserObject
Set UserObject = New UserClass
UserObject.BindToUser "CN=ScriptUser,OU=Users,DC=zygort,DC=com"
If UserObject.LockedOut Then
    UserObject.UnlockAccount
```

```
End If
UserObject.Save
</script>
</job>
```

Enable and Disable a User Account

By default, a new user account is disabled. This script demonstrates how to enable and disable a user account with the UserClass object. Setting the AccountEnabled property for on the object to True enables the account, while False disables it.

```
<job>
<script language="VBScript" src="includes\UserClass.vbs" />
<script>
Option Explicit
Dim UserObject
Set UserObject = New UserClass
UserObject.BindToUser "CN=ScriptUser,OU=Users,DC=zygort,DC=com"
If UserObject.AccountEnabled Then
    UserObject.AccountEnabled = False
Else
    UserObject.AccountEnabled = True
End If
UserObject.Save
</script>
</job>
```

List Group Membership of a User

This script lists the immediate group membership of a user. By immediate group membership, I am referring to the group membership that you can see in the Members Of tab of the User object. Remember that while a user can belong to a group, that group could be a member of another group. This script will not list those groups.

```
<job>
<script language="VBScript" src="includes\UserClass.vbs" />
<script>
Option Explicit
Dim UserObject
Set UserObject = New UserClass
UserObject.BindToUser "CN=ScriptUser,OU=Users,DC=zygort,DC=com"
Dim GroupList, Group
Set GroupList = UserObject.Groups
For Each Group In GroupList.Keys
    WScript.Echo Group
Next
</script>
</job>
```

List All Group Membership of a User

This script lists the immediate group membership of a user plus group memberships of the user groups. Nested group membership can be a cause of different security problems, simply because the group membership hierarchy is difficult to see in Active Directory Users and Computers. This script reads the value of the AllGroups property of the UserClass object, while the earlier script (which only reads the immediate group membership) reads the value of the Groups property.

```
<job>
<script language="VBScript" src="includes\UserClass.vbs" />
<script>
Option Explicit
Dim UserObject
Set UserObject = New UserClass
UserObject.BindToUser "CN=ScriptUser,OU=Users,DC=zygort,DC=com"
Dim GroupList, Group
Set GroupList = UserObject.AllGroups
For Each Group In GroupList.Keys
    WScript.Echo Group
Next
</script>
</job>
```

Join the User to a Group

There are actually two different ways for a user to join a group via scripting. One is to bind to the group and add a new member (this will be demonstrated when we examine the GroupClass class). The other, demonstrated in the script that follows, binds to the user and joins that user to the group by calling the JoinGroup method of the UserClass object and passing the ADsPath of the group to join.

```
<job>
<script language="VBScript" src="includes\UserClass.vbs" />
<script>
Option Explicit
Dim UserObject
Set UserObject = New UserClass
UserObject.BindToUser "CN=ScriptUser,OU=Users,DC=zygort,DC=com"
UserObject.JoinGroup "LDAP:\\CN=ScriptGroup,OU=Users,dc=zygort,dc=com"
UserObject.Save
</script>
</job>
```

Copy a User Object

The process of creating new user accounts can be made simpler (and less susceptible to errors) by using a template user account as the basis for creating a new user account. Calling the Copy method of the UserClass object and passing the container, the Common Name (CN), and the SAM account name of the new user account can do this task for you. You will also want to set an initial password on the new account.

```
<job>
<script language="VBScript" src="includes\UserClass.vbs" />
<script>
Option Explicit
Dim UserObject, NewUserObject
Set UserObject = New UserClass
UserObject.BindToUser "CN=TemplateUser,OU=Users,DC=zygort,DC=com"
Set NewUserObject = UserObject.Copy _
    "LDAP://OU=Users,DC=zygort,DC=com","CopiedUser","CopiedUser"
NewUserObject.Password = "P@ssw0rd"
NewUserObject.Save
</script>
</job>
```

Copy Group Membership to Another User

Group membership is one of the main sources of aggravation for user administrators. A common practice is to create a template user account, which you then copy as new users are added. This script demonstrates how to take advantage of the existing group membership of a template user account (specifically, in light of the two group membership scripts shown earlier, immediate group membership) by reading the group membership of the template object and joining the bound User object to those groups.

```
<job>
<script language="VBScript" src="includes\UserClass.vbs" />
<script>
Option Explicit
Dim UserObject
Set UserObject = New UserClass
UserObject.BindToUser "CN=ScriptUser,OU=Users,DC=zygort,DC=com"
UserObject.CopyGroupsFromUser _
    "LDAP:\\CN=TemplateUser,OU=Users,dc=zygort,dc=com"
UserObject.Save
</script>
</job>
```

Move a User Object

Since a good Active Directory hierarchy uses containers (and/or organizational units) to organize objects, eventually you will have to deal with user accounts moving from one container object to another. Calling the Move method and passing the ADsPath of the destination container will move the bound User object to its new home.

```
<job>
<script language="VBScript" src="includes\UserClass.vbs" />
```

```
<script>
Option Explicit
Dim UserObject, NewUserObject
Set UserObject = New UserClass
UserObject.BindToUser "CN=ScriptUser,OU=Users,DC=zygort,DC=com"
UserObject.Move "LDAP://OU=Test,DC=zygort,DC=com"
UserObject.Save
</script>
</job>
```

Group Scripts

We've looked at groups in the User class, and now it is time to start working with Group objects all on their own. To do this, we are going to build a GroupClass class, which we can use in later scripts to easily build and manipulate real Active Directory Group objects.

GroupClass

Many of the functions of the GroupClass class mirror those found in UserClass. Using a common design helps when you are using the class to develop scripts by not requiring you to learn an entirely new set of properties and functions for every class utilized by your scripts.

A few additional aspects must be noted when dealing with groups. Groups can be one of two types: security or distribution. They can also have one of three different scopes: universal, global or domain local. Each of these must be specified when creating a new group. VBScript uses constant values to internally denote the type and scope of a group. At the bottom of the GroupClass code, you will see I have made these available through public properties to make life easier. (I have also given them friendlier names than you would find in the Microsoft documentation.)

```
Option Explicit
'================================================================
Class GroupClass
'================================================================
Private Sub Class_Initialize
End Sub
'================================================================
Private Sub Class_Terminate
End Sub
'================================================================
' Private and public variables
Private m_GroupObject
'================================================================
Public Function BindToGroup(GroupPath)
If ADObjectExists(GroupPath) Then
    Set m_GroupObject = GetObject(FormatAdsPath(GroupPath))
    m_GroupObject.GetInfo
    Set BindToGroup = m_GroupObject
Else
    Err.Raise 102,m_ErrSource,"Object does not exist"
```

```
End If
End Function
'=======================================================================
Public Function Create _
   (ContainerPath,CN,AccountName,GroupType,GroupScope)
If CN = "" Or ContainerPath = "" Or GroupType = "" Then
   Err.Raise 101,m_ErrSource,"Missing arguments"
   Exit Function
End If
Dim Container
If ADObjectExists(ContainerPath) Then
   Set Container = GetObject(FormatAdsPath(ContainerPath))
   Set m_GroupObject = Container.Create("group",FormatCN(CN))
   m_GroupObject.Put "groupType", GroupType Or GroupScope
   m_GroupObject.Put "sAMAccountName", AccountName
   m_GroupObject.SetInfo
   m_GroupObject.GetInfo
   Set Create = m_GroupObject
Else
   WScript.Echo "Container does not exist!"
   WScript.Quit(1)
End If
End Function
'=======================================================================
Public Property Get GroupType
If CBool(m_GroupObject.Get("groupType") And SECURITY_GROUP) Then
   GroupScope = "Global"
Else
   GroupScope = "Distribution"
End If
End Property
'=======================================================================
Public Property Let GroupType(TypeValue)
Select Case LCase(TypeValue)
   Case "distribution" : m_GroupType = DISTRIBUTION_GROUP
   Case "security" : m_GroupType = SECURITY_GROUP
End Select
End Property
'=======================================================================
Public Property Get GroupScope
CheckForBoundObject
If CBool(m_GroupObject.Get("groupType") And GLOBAL_GROUP) Then
   GroupScope = "Global"
Else
   If CBool(m_GroupObject.Get("groupType") And _
   DOMAIN_LOCAL_GROUP) Then
      GroupScope = "Domain Local"
   Else
```

```
            GroupScope = "Universal"
        End If
    End If
End Property
'=======================================================================
Public Property Let GroupScope(TypeValue)
Select Case lcase(TypeValue)
    Case "global" : m_GroupScope = GLOBAL_GROUP
    Case "domain local" : m_GroupScope = DOMAIN_LOCAL_GROUP
    Case "universal" : m_GroupType = UNIVERSAL_GROUP
End Select
End Property
'=======================================================================
Public Sub AddMember(Member)
If ADObjectExists(Member) Then
    On Error Resume Next
    m_GroupObject.Add FormatAdsPath(Member)
Else
    WScript.Echo "Member " & Member & " does not exist."
End If
End Sub
'=======================================================================
Public Sub RemoveMember(Member)
    m_GroupObject.Remove FormatAdsPath(Member)
End Sub
'=======================================================================
Public Property Get Members
' returns a Dictionary object!
Dim MemberList
Set MemberList = WScript.CreateObject("Scripting.Dictionary")
For each Member in m_GroupObject.Members
    MemberList.Add Member.Name,0
Next
Set Members = MemberList
End Property
'=======================================================================
Public Property Get AllMembers
' Returns a Dictionary object!
Dim MemberList
Set MemberList = WScript.CreateObject("Scripting.Dictionary")
GetMembership m_GroupObject.AdsPath,MemberList
Set AllMembers = MemberList
End Property
'=======================================================================
Private Function GetMembership(ObjectAdsPath,List)
Dim tmpObject, Member
Set tmpObject = GetObject(FormatAdsPath(ObjectAdsPath))
On Error Resume Next
```

```
    For Each Member In tmpObject.Members
        If Err.Number = 0 Then
            If Not(List.Exists(Member.Name)) Then
                List.Add Member.Name,0
                If Member.Class = "group" Then
                    GetMembership Member.AdsPath,List
                End If
            End If
        End If
        Err.Clear
    Next
End Function
'=====================================================================
Public Property Get MemberOf
' Returns a Dictionary object!
Dim MemberList, Member
Set MemberList = WScript.CreateObject("Scripting.Dictionary")
On Error Resume Next
For Each Member In m_GroupObject.GetEx("memberOf")
    MemberList.Add Member,0
Next
Set MemberOf = MemberList
End Property
'=====================================================================
Public Property Get Manager
    Manager = m_GroupObject.Get("managedBy")
End Property
'=====================================================================
Public Property Let Manager(ManagerPath)
If ADObjectExists(ManagerPath) Then
    m_GroupObject.Put "managedBy", FormatCN(ManagerPath)
End If
End Property
'=====================================================================
Public Sub SetProperty(PropName,PropValue)
On Error Resume Next
m_GroupObjectObject.Put PropName,PropValue
If Err.Number <> 0 Then
    WScript.Echo "Error setting property " & PropName
End If
End Sub
'=====================================================================
Public Sub DisplayProperties
Dim Element
For Each Element In m_PropertyList.Keys
    WScript.Echo Element & " = " & m_PropertyList(Element)
Next
End Sub
'=====================================================================
```

```
Public Sub Save
m_GroupObject.SetInfo
m_GroupObject.GetInfo
End Sub
'=====================================================================
Private Function GetADsTypeValue(AdsType,AdsValue)
Select Case CInt(adsType)
   Case 1 : GetADsTypeValue = AdsValue.DNString
   Case 2 : GetADsTypeValue =  AdsValue.CaseExactString
   Case 3 : GetADsTypeValue =  AdsValue.CaseIgnoreString
   Case 4 : GetADsTypeValue =  AdsValue.PrintableString
   Case 5 : GetADsTypeValue =  AdsValue.NumericString
   Case 6 : GetADsTypeValue =  CStr(AdsValue.Boolean)
   Case 7 : GetADsTypeValue =  AdsValue.Integer
   Case 8 : GetADsTypeValue =  "Octet String"
   Case 9 : GetADsTypeValue =  AdsValue.UTCTime
   Case 10
      Dim PropertyLargeInteger, LargeIntegerValue
      Dim LargeIntegerDate, DateHigh, DateLow
      Set PropertyLargeInteger = AdsValue.LargeInteger
      DateHigh = PropertyLargeInteger.HighPart
      DateLow = PropertyLargeInteger.LowPart
      If DateLow < 0 Then
         DateHigh = DateHigh + 1
      End If
      If (DateHigh = 0) And (DateLow = 0 ) Then
         LargeIntegerDate = #1/1/1601#
      Else
         LargeIntegerDate = #1/1/1601# + (((DateHigh * _
                   (2 ^ 32)) + DateLow)/600000000)/1440
      End If
      If IsDate(LargeIntegerDate) And _
      LargeIntegerDate > #1/1/1970# Then
         GetADsTypeValue = LargeIntegerDate
      Else
         GetADsTypeValue = _
            PropertyLargeInteger.HighPart * 2^32 + _
            PropertyLargeInteger.LowPart
      End If
   Case 11 : GetADsTypeValue = "Provider Specific"
   Case 12 : GetADsTypeValue = "Object Class"
   Case 13 : GetADsTypeValue = "Case Ignore List"
   Case 14 : GetADsTypeValue = "Octet List"
   Case 15 : GetADsTypeValue = "Path"
   Case 16 : GetADsTypeValue = "Postal Address"
   Case 17 : GetADsTypeValue = "TimeStamp"
   Case 18 : GetADsTypeValue = "BackLink"
   Case 19 : GetADsTypeValue = "Typed Name"
```

```
    Case 20 : GetADsTypeValue = "Hold"
    Case 21 : GetADsTypeValue = "Net Address"
    Case 22 : GetADsTypeValue = "Replica Pointer"
    Case 23 : GetADsTypeValue = "Fax Number"
    Case 24 : GetADsTypeValue = "Email"
    Case 25 : GetADsTypeValue = "NT Security Descriptor"
    Case 26 : GetADsTypeValue = "Unknown"
    Case Else : GetADsTypeValue = "Unknown - " & AdsValue.adsType
End Select
End Function
'=======================================================================
Private Function ADObjectExists(ADsPath)
Dim ADObject, LDAPObject
ADSPath = FormatAdsPath(AdsPath)
On Error Resume Next
Set LDAPObject = GetObject("LDAP:")
Set ADObject = _
    LDAPObject.OpenDSObject(ADsPath,vbNullString,vbNullString, _
ADS_FAST_BIND)
If Err.Number = 0 Then
    ADObjectExists = True
Else
    ADObjectExists = False
End If
Set ADObject = Nothing
Set LDAPObject = Nothing
End Function
'=======================================================================
Private Function FormatAdsPath(ADsPath)
If CBool(Instr(ADsPath,"LDAP://")) Then
    FormatAdsPath = AdsPath
Else
    FormatAdsPath = "LDAP://" & ADsPath
End If
End Function
'=======================================================================
Private Function FormatCN(CNValue)
FormatCN = Replace(CNValue,"LDAP://","")
If Left(FormatCN,3) <> "CN=" Then
    FormatCN = "CN=" & FormatCN
End If
End Function
'=======================================================================
Public Property Get m_ErrSource
    m_ErrSource = "GroupClass"
End Property
Public Property Get ADS_PROPERTY_CLEAR
    ADS_PROPERTY_CLEAR = 1
```

```
End Property
Public Property Get ADS_PROPERTY_UPDATE
   ADS_PROPERTY_UPDATE = 2
End Property
Public Property Get ADS_PROPERTY_APPEND
   ADS_PROPERTY_APPEND = 3
End Property
Public Property Get ADS_PROPERTY_DELETE
   ADS_PROPERTY_DELETE = 4
End Property
Public Property Get ADS_FAST_BIND
   ADS_FAST_BIND = &H20
End Property
'========================================================================
' I'm taking a little liberty in renaming these constants to something
' more friendly than ADS_GROUP_TYPE_DOMAIN_LOCAL_GROUP
Public Property Get DISTRIBUTION_GROUP
   DISTRIBUTION_GROUP = &h0
End Property
Public Property Get GLOBAL_GROUP
   GLOBAL_GROUP = &h2
End Property
Public Property Get DOMAIN_LOCAL_GROUP
   DOMAIN_LOCAL_GROUP = &h4
End Property
Public Property Get UNIVERSAL_GROUP
   UNIVERSAL_GROUP = &h8
End Property
Public Property Get SECURITY_GROUP
   SECURITY_GROUP = &h80000000
End Property
'========================================================================
End Class
```

Creating a New Group

To create a new group, start by creating an instance of the GroupClass class. Next, call the Create method and pass it the ADsPath of the parent container, the Common Name (CN) of the group, the SAM account name of the group, and finally the group type (security or distribution) and group scope (domain_local, global, or universal).

In the GroupClass class, the constants used to define the group are exposed as read-only properties. After you have created an instance of the class, you can read these property values from the instantiated object. In this example, the last argument uses the Security_Group and Domain_Local_ Group properties to define the group type and scope:

```
<job>
<script language="VBScript" src="includes\GroupClass.vbs" />
<script>
```

```
Option Explicit
Dim GroupObject
Set GroupObject = New GroupClass
GroupObject.Create _
    "OU=Users,DC=zygort,DC=com","ScriptGroup","ScriptGroup", _
GroupObject.Security_Group,GroupObject.Domain_Local_Group
</script>
</job>
```

To define the group type, the properties `Security_Group` and `Distribution_Group` are used. The properties `Domain_Local_Group`, `Global_Group`, and `Universal_Group` are used to define the group scope. Purists will probably notice that these are not the actual ADSI constant names. In the interest of readability, I have taken the liberty of exposing the properties by names that are much more friendly to read than ADS_GROUP_TYPE_DOMAIN_LOCAL_GROUP.

List Group Members

This script lists the immediate members of a group. Start by binding to the group, followed by setting a variable equal to the `Members` property. This property will return a `Dictionary` object containing a list of group members in the Key field. The value field will simply contain 0.

```
<job>
<script language="VBScript" src="includes\GroupClass.vbs" />
<script>
Option Explicit
Dim GroupObject, GroupMembers, Member
Set GroupObject = New GroupClass
GroupObject.BindToGroup "CN=ScriptGroup,OU=Users,DC=zygort,DC=com"
Set GroupMembers = GroupObject.Members
For Each Member In GroupMembers.Keys
    WScript.Echo Member
Next
</script>
</job>
```

List All Group Members

This script lists the immediate members of a group, as well as the group membership of any subordinate groups. After binding to the group with the `GroupClass` class, set a variable equal to the `AllMembers` property of the object. This property will return a `Dictionary` object with a list of group members in the Key field. The value field will contain 0.

Please note that the `Members` and `AllMembers` properties will (usually) return different result sets. Be sure to use the property that will return the set of members that you are looking for.

```
<job>
<script language="VBScript" src="includes\GroupClass.vbs" />
<script>
Option Explicit
Dim GroupObject, GroupMembers, Member
```

```
Set GroupObject = New GroupClass
GroupObject.BindToGroup "CN=ScriptGroup,OU=Users,DC=zygort,DC=com"
Set GroupMembers = GroupObject.AllMembers
For Each Member In GroupMembers.Keys
    WScript.Echo Member
Next
</script>
</job>
```

List Group Membership of a Group

This script lists the groups that the bound group is a member of (for example, the `ScriptTest` group might belong to the `DomainScripters` group). Begin by binding to the group. Next, set a variable equal to the `MemberOf` property of the group. This property will return a `Dictionary` object. We can then use a `For-Next` loop to iterate through the items in the `Dictionary` object.

```
<job>
<script language="VBScript" src="includes\GroupClass.vbs" />
<script>
Option Explicit
Dim GroupObject, GroupMember, Member
Set GroupObject = New GroupClass
GroupObject.BindToGroup "CN=ScriptGroup,OU=Users,DC=zygort,DC=com"
Set GroupMember = GroupObject.MemberOf
For Each Member In GroupMember
    WScript.Echo Member
Next
</script>
</job>
```

Add a New Group Member

One of the primary scripting tasks of a group is the addition (and later, removal) of members to the group. Start by binding the `GroupClass` to the group. Call the `AddMember` method and pass it the `ADsPath` of an existing `User` object in Active Directory.

```
<job>
<script language="VBScript" src="includes\GroupClass.vbs" />
<script>
Option Explicit
Dim GroupObject
Set GroupObject = New GroupClass
GroupObject.BindToGroup "CN=ScriptGroup,OU=Users,DC=zygort,DC=com"
GroupObject.AddMember "LDAP://CN=Scott,DC=zygort,DC=com"
</script>
</job>
```

Remove a Group Member

We can't have a script to add members to a group without a script to remove members from the group. Bind to the group, call the RemoveMember method, and specify the ADsPath of the group member to remove.

```
<job>
<script language="VBScript" src="includes\GroupClass.vbs" />
<script>
Option Explicit
Dim GroupObject
Set GroupObject = New GroupClass
GroupObject.BindToGroup "CN=ScriptGroup,OU=Users,DC=zygort,DC=com"
GroupObject.RemoveMember "LDAP://CN=Scott,OU=Users,DC=zygort,DC=com"
</script>
</job>
```

Change the Group Manager

This script allows you to change the manager of a group. The manager is exposed through the Manager property and should be passed the ADsPath to an existing User object in Active Directory.

```
<job>
<script language="VBScript" src="includes\GroupClass.vbs" />
<script>
Option Explicit
Dim GroupObject
Set GroupObject = New GroupClass
GroupObject.BindToGroup "CN=ScriptGroup,OU=Users,DC=zygort,DC=com"
GroupObject.Manager = "CN=Scott,OU=Users,DC=zygort,DC=com"
GroupObject.Save
</script>
</job>
```

Computer Scripts

Several management tasks involve the Computer objects in Active Directory. In order to simply deal with these tasks via VBScript, we create a class to do the grunt work for us just as we have done with the UserClass and GroupClass classes.

ComputerClass

Many of the functions of the ComputerClass class mirror those found in UserClass and GroupClass. Again, this allows you to use the same method calls and property names that you have used with the other VBScript classes presented in this module, rather than relearn a new set for every class.

```
Option Explicit
'======================================================================
Class ComputerClass
'======================================================================
```

```vbscript
' Private and public variables
Private m_ComputerObject
'================================================================
Private Sub Class_Initialize
End Sub
'================================================================
Private Sub Class_Terminate
End Sub
'================================================================
Public Sub BindToComputer(ComputerPath)
If ADObjectExists(ComputerPath) Then
   Set m_ComputerObject = GetObject(FormatAdsPath(ComputerPath))
   m_ComputerObject.GetInfo
   Set BindToUser = m_ComputerObject
Else
   Err.Raise 102,m_ErrSource,"Object does not exist"
End If
End Sub
'================================================================
Public Function Create(ContainerPath,CN,AccountName)
If CN = "" Or ContainerPath = "" Or AccountName = "" Then
   Err.Raise 101,m_ErrSource,"Missing arguments"
   Exit Function
End If
Dim Container
If ADObjectExists(ContainerPath) Then
   Set Container = GetObject(FormatAdsPath(ContainerPath))
   Set m_ComputerObject = Container.Create("computer",FormatCN(CN))
   m_ComputerObject.Put "sAMAccountName", AccountName & "$"
   m_ComputerObject.Put "userAccountControl", _
                     ADS_UF_WORKSTATION_TRUST_ACCOUNT
   m_ComputerObject.SetInfo
   m_ComputerObject.GetInfo
   Set Create = m_ComputerObject
Else
   WScript.Echo "Error connecting to container!"
   WScript.Quit(1)
End If
End Function
'================================================================
Public Sub Move(Destination)
If ADObjectExists(Destination) Then
   Dim NewContainer
   Set NewContainer = GetObject(FormatAdsPath(Destination))
   NewContainer.MoveHere m_ComputerObject.AdsPath, _
                     m_ComputerObject.Name
End If
End Sub
'================================================================
```

```
Public Sub SetProperty(PropName,PropValue)
On Error Resume Next
m_ComputerObject.Put PropName,PropValue
If Err.Number <> 0 Then
   WScript.Echo "Error setting property " & PropName
End If
End Sub
'=====================================================================
Public Sub MultiPropertyClear(PropertyName)
   m_ComputerObject.PutEx ADS_PROPERTY_CLEAR,PropertyName,0
End Sub
'=====================================================================
Public Sub MultiPropertyUpdate(PropertyName, PropertyArray)
m_ComputerObject.PutEx _
   ADS_PROPERTY_UPDATE,PropertyName,PropertyArray
End Sub
'=====================================================================
Public Sub MultiPropertyAppend(PropertyName, PropertyArray)
m_ComputerObject.PutEx _
   ADS_PROPERTY_APPEND,PropertyName,PropertyArray
End Sub
'=====================================================================
Public Sub MultiPropertyDelete(PropertyName, PropertyArray)
m_ComputerObject.PutEx _
   ADS_PROPERTY_DELETE,PropertyName,PropertyArray
End Sub
'=====================================================================
Public Sub Reset
On Error Resume Next
m_ComputerObject.SetPassword m_ComputerObject.Name
If Err.Number = 0 Then
   WScript.Echo "Computer " & m_ComputerObject.Name & " was reset."
   WScript.Echo "      It must now rejoin the domain!"
Else
   WScript.Echo "Error resetting computer account " & _
              m_ComputerObject.Name
End If
End Sub
'=====================================================================
Public Sub Save
m_ComputerObject.SetInfo
m_ComputerObject.GetInfo
End Sub
'=====================================================================
Private Function ADObjectExists(ADsPath)
Dim ADObject, LDAPObject
ADSPath = FormatAdsPath(AdsPath)
On Error Resume Next
```

```
    Set LDAPObject = GetObject("LDAP:")
    Set ADObject = _
      LDAPObject.OpenDSObject(ADsPath,vbNullString,vbNullString, _
                              ADS_FAST_BIND)
    If Err.Number = 0 Then
      ADObjectExists = True
    Else
      ADObjectExists = False
    End If
    Set ADObject = Nothing
    Set LDAPObject = Nothing
    End Function
    '========================================================================
    Private Function FormatAdsPath(ADsPath)
    If CBool(Instr(ADsPath,"LDAP://")) Then
      FormatAdsPath = AdsPath
    Else
      FormatAdsPath = "LDAP://" & ADsPath
    End If
    End Function
    '========================================================================
    Private Function FormatCN(CNValue)
    FormatCN = Replace(CNValue,"LDAP://","")
    If Left(FormatCN,3) <> "CN=" Then
      FormatCN = "CN=" & FormatCN
    End If
    End Function
    '========================================================================
    Public Property Get ADS_FAST_BIND
      ADS_FAST_BIND = &H20
    End Property
    Public Property Get m_ErrSource
      m_ErrSource = "ComputerClass"
    End Property
    Public Property Get ADS_UF_WORKSTATION_TRUST_ACCOUNT
      ADS_UF_WORKSTATION_TRUST_ACCOUNT = &H1000
    End Property
    '========================================================================
    End Class
```

Create a Computer Account

Creating a computer account is a common administrative function. After creating a new instance of the ComputerClass class, call the Create method. The Create method takes three arguments: the ADsPath of the computer account's container, and the Common Name (CN) and SAM account name of the new computer account.

After creating the new computer account, you can continue to set any additional properties necessary with the SetProperty method. The SetProperty method takes two arguments: the property

name and the new value. After setting the property values, be sure to call the Save method to write
the new property values back to Active Directory.

```
<job>
<script language="VBScript" src="includes\ComputerClass.vbs" />
<script>
Option Explicit
Dim ComputerObject
Set ComputerObject = New ComputerClass
ComputerObject.Create _
    "LDAP://OU=Test,DC=zygort,DC=com","ScriptComputer","ScriptComputer"
ComputerObject.SetProperty "description", "Scripting Test Computer"
ComputerObject.Save
</script>
</job>
```

Move a Computer Account

Computer accounts sometimes need to be moved between containers in order for the proper set of
Group Policy Objects (GPOs) to be applied to it. After binding to the Computer object in Active Directory, call the Move method and pass the ADsPath of the new container as the argument.

```
<job>
<script language="VBScript" src="includes\ComputerClass.vbs" />
<script>
Option Explicit
Dim ComputerObject
Set ComputerObject = New ComputerClass
ComputerObject.BindToComputer _
    "LDAP://CN=ScriptComputer,OU=Computers,DC=zygort,DC=com", _
        "ScriptComputer","ScriptComputer"
ComputerObject.Move "LDAP://OU=Test,DC=zygort,DC=com"
</script>
</job>
```

Reset a Computer Account

Just like user accounts, computer accounts have passwords as well. Occasionally, these passwords
might need to be reset just like a user's password. The Reset method of the ComputerClass object is
used to perform this task. This is actually a function call in the class, which will return True if the reset
operation was successful. In the script that follows, the result of the Reset method is used to display
a message to the user about the outcome of the operation.

```
<job>
<script language="VBScript" src="includes\ComputerClass.vbs" />
<script>
Option Explicit
Dim ComputerObject
Set ComputerObject = New ComputerClass
```

```
ComputerObject.BindToComputer _
   "LDAP://CN=ScriptComputer,OU=Test,DC=zygort,DC=com"
If ComputerObject.Reset Then
   WScript.Echo "Computer account was successfully reset."
   WScript.Echo "Please rejoin the computer to the domain!"
Else
   WScript.Echo "An error occurred resetting the computer account."
End If
</script>
</job>
```

Organizational Unit Scripts

Organizational units tend to be fairly static structures in an Active Directory hierarchy. In fact, the structure of a well-thought-out hierarchy almost never changes, except in response to changes within the organization itself, such as reorganizations or acquiring new businesses.

OUClass

While I'm personally not a fan of scripting organizational units (some things I just prefer to "see"), we should nonetheless build a class to represent the OU object and its capabilities. I should take this opportunity to warn you that not all the functionality you have for an OU in the graphical administration tools is available to you as a programmer. One of the most requested features I've seen in the newsgroups—the ability to create Group Policy Objects (GPOs)—is not available to programmers yet. However, the ability to link GPOs to organizational units is within our grasp.

```
Option Explicit
Class OUClass
'========================================================================
' Private and public variables
Private m_OUObject
'========================================================================
Private Sub Class_Initialize
End Sub
'========================================================================
Private Sub Class_Terminate
End Sub
'========================================================================
Public Function BindToOU(OUPath)
If ADObjectExists(OUPath) Then
   Set m_OUObject = GetObject(FormatAdsPath(OUPath))
   m_OUObject.GetInfo
   Set BindToOU = m_OUObject
Else
   Err.Raise 102,m_ErrSource,"Object does not exist"
End If
End Function
'========================================================================
```

```
Public Sub Create(ContainerPath,CN)
If CN = "" Or ContainerPath = "" Then
    Err.Raise 101,m_ErrSource,"Missing arguments"
    Exit Sub
End If
Dim Container
If ADObjectExists(ContainerPath) Then
    Set Container = GetObject(FormatAdsPath(ContainerPath))
    Set m_OUObject = Container.Create("organizationalUnit",FormatCN(CN))
    m_OUObject.SetInfo
    m_OUObject.GetInfo
    Set Create = m_OUObject
Else
    WScript.Echo "Error connecting to container!"
    WScript.Quit(1)
End If
End Sub
'=====================================================================
Public Sub Delete
    m_OUObject.DeleteObject(0)
End Sub
'=====================================================================
Public Sub Move(Destination)
Dim NewContainer
Set NewContainer = GetObject(FormatAdsPath(Destination))
NewContainer.MoveHere m_OUObject.AdsPath, m_OUObject.Name
m_OUObject.MoveHere FormatAdsPath(Destination),FormatCN(Destination)
End Sub
'=====================================================================
Public Property Get ChildCount
' Note: msDS-Approx-Immed-Subordinates is new to Windows 2003
m_OUObject.GetInfoEx Array("msDS-Approx-Immed-Subordinates"),0
ChildCount = m_OUObject.Get("msDS-Approx-Immed-Subordinates")
End Property
'=====================================================================
Public Property Get ChildObjects
' This returns a Dictionary object!
Dim Child
Set ChildObjects = WScript.CreateObject("Scripting.Dictionary")
For Each Child in m_OUObject
    ChildObjects.Add Child.Name, Child.Class
Next
End Property
'=====================================================================
Public Sub LinkGPO(GPOName)
Dim SearchRoot,FilterText,Attributes,SearchScope,GPOPath
Dim RootDSE
Set RootDSE = "LDAP://RootDSE"
```

```
    SearchRoot = "<LDAP://cn=policies,cn=system," & _
       RootDSE.Get("defaultNamingContext") & ">;"
    Set RootDSE = Nothing
    FilterText = _
       "(&(objectcategory=grouppolicycontainer)" & _
       "(objectclass=grouppolicycontainer)" & _
       "(displayname=" & GPOName & "));"
    Attributes = "AdsPath"
    SearchScope = "OneLevel"
    Dim Cn, Cmd, Results
    Set Cn = CreateObject("ADODB.Connection")
    Set Cmd = CreateObject("ADODB.Command")
    Cmd.ActiveConnection = Cn
    Cmd.CommandText = SearchRoot & ";" & FilterText & ";" & _
    Attributes & ";" & SearchScope
    Set Results = Cmd.Execute
    Select Case Results.RecordCount
       Case 0
          WScript.Echo "No GPO found named " & GPOName
          WScript.Quit(1)
       Case 1
          GPOPath = Results.Fields(0)
       Case Else
          WScript.Echo "More than 1 matching GPO found!"
          WScript.Quit(1)
    End Select
    Set Results = Nothing
    Set Cmd = Nothing
    Set Cn = Nothing
    On Error Resume Next
    Dim CurrentGPOLinks
    CurrentGPOLinks = m_OUObject.Get("gpLink")
    If Err.Number > 0 Then
       WScript.Echo "Error retrieving current GPO Links"
    End If
    On Error GoTo 0
    m_OUobject.Put "gpLink",CurrentGPOLinks & "[" & GPOPath & ";0]"
    End Sub
    '=====================================================================
    Private Function ADObjectExists(ADsPath)
    Dim ADObject, LDAPObject
    ADSPath = FormatAdsPath(AdsPath)
    On Error Resume Next
    Set LDAPObject = GetObject("LDAP:")
    Set ADObject = _
       LDAPObject.OpenDSObject(ADsPath,vbNullString,vbNullString, _
                              ADS_FAST_BIND)
```

```
If Err.Number = 0 Then
     ADObjectExists = True
Else
ADObjectExists = False
End If
Set ADObject = Nothing
Set LDAPObject = Nothing
End Function
'=======================================================================
Private Function FormatAdsPath(ADsPath)
If CBool(Instr(ADsPath,"LDAP://")) Then
   FormatAdsPath = AdsPath
Else
   FormatAdsPath = "LDAP://" & ADsPath
End If
End Function
'=======================================================================
Public Property Get m_ErrSource
   m_ErrSource = "OUClass"
End Property
Public Property Get ADS_FAST_BIND
   ADS_FAST_BIND = &H20
End Property
'=======================================================================
End Class
```

Create a New Organizational Unit

Creating a new organizational unit is similar to creating all the other objects we have looked at so far. Start by creating an instance of the OUclass class. Call the Create method and supply the ADsPath of the parent container and name of the new OU.

```
<job>
<script language="VBScript" src="includes\OUClass.vbs" />
<script>
Option Explicit
Dim OUObject
Set OUObject = New OUClass
OUObject.Create "LDAP://OU=Test,DC=zygort,DC=com","ScriptOU"
OUObject.SetProperty "description", "Scripting OU"
OUObject.Save
</script>
</job>
```

Delete an Organizational Unit

To delete an organizational unit, first bind to the OU and call the Delete method of the OUClass object. A check is performed first against the ChildCount property of the object to guard against deleting an OU that contains child objects.

```
<job>
<script language="VBScript" src="includes\OUClass.vbs" />
<script>
Option Explicit
Dim OUObject
Set OUObject = New OUClass
OUObject.BindToOU "LDAP://OU=Test,DC=zygort,DC=com"
If OUObject.ChildCount = 0 Then
OUObject.Delete
Else
    WScript.Echo "This OU contains child objects, aborting delete."
End If
</script>
</job>
```

List Child Objects in Organizational Unit

When reorganizing the hierarchy of organizational units in Active Directory, you may find it useful to get a list of child objects in an existing OU. If you bind to the OU, the ChildObjects property returns a Dictionary object with a list of the child objects of the organizational unit, which you can then iterate through and perform additional operations on.

```
<job>
<script language="VBScript" src="includes\OUClass.vbs" />
<script>
Option Explicit
Dim OUObject, ChildObjects, ChildObj
Set OUObject = New OUClass
OUObject.BindToOU "LDAP://OU=Test,DC=zygort,DC=com"
If OUObject.ChildCount > 0 Then
    Set ChildObjects = OUObject.ChildObjects
    For Each ChildObj In ChildObjects.Keys
        WScript.Echo ChildObj & ", " & ChildObjects(ChildObj)
    Next
Else
    WScript.Echo "OU contains no child objects"
End If
</script>
</job>
```

Excel Scripts

Beyond administration, scripting is used to gather information from Active Directory. Results from queries (see our discussion of `QueryClass` earlier in this chapter) can be displayed as command-line output, which can be redirected to a text file. The text file can then be loaded into Excel. If the information was formatted correctly in the output file (for example, by commas to separate different fields of information), then the information can be imported into separate columns, which might then need to be formatted, and column headers added, and all those other fun tasks that turns data into information.

The other option is to access Excel directly from VBScript. If Excel is loaded on the computer that is running the script, then an instance of the `Excel.Application` object can be created. You must then learn to use the object model that encompasses Excel in order to properly send your data to an Excel spreadsheet. Believe me when I say that the Excel object is not a trivial set of properties and methods.

To see what object model that makes up Excel, fire up Excel, open the Visual Basic editor (Tools ➢ Macros ➢ Visual Basic Editor), and press the F2 key. This will open the Object Browser window, which you might want to maximize. It will start by showing the objects in all the loaded modules, so click the drop-down box in the upper-left corner (which should say <All Libraries>) and select Excel. Now you will see only the objects, properties, methods, and enumerations that deal with Microsoft Excel.

Although there is no possible way to cover everything you see before you, let's go through a simple example. Find the `Application` object in the left window and select it. The right window will now show the properties and methods of the `Application` object. Select the `ActiveCell` property (see Figure 18.2). The definition of the property will be displayed in the bottom window. Notice that the property is going to return a `Range` object. Click on the underlined word *Range* in the bottom window; this selects the `Range` object. Unfortunately, it doesn't tell you much about the object, does it? Figure 18.2 shows the object browser in action.

Scripting Excel can be a complex task, but we hope that the `ExcelClass` definition that follows will make things easier for you. Rather than navigating the Excel object model, the functionality that moves from cell to cell and formats the data is provided through the class. This is not a full-featured class for handling Excel scripting, but it is plenty to get you started—and of course you can expand it as you see fit.

FIGURE 18.2

The Object Browser

ExcelClass

The ExcelClass class is definitely more complicated than the other class definitions that we have seen so far. Since we have not discussed anything about Excel up to this point, we need to take a few minutes to discuss the methodology used by the ExcelClass class before we can jump into using it. It is important to remember that this class is designed to act as a "middleman" between your script and the Excel application.

Most result sets are processed from left to right, top to bottom. In Excel, columns and rows are used. While columns are labeled with alphabetic letters, they are really represented by numbers.

In an instantiated ExcelClass object, there is always one (and only one) active cell. This cell is going to have a value assigned to or read from it. To get or set the value of the active cell, use the CellValue property of the object. Two methods are also available to read or set the values of any cells in the worksheet. The GetAbsoluteCellValue method takes two arguments: the row and column of the cell to read. The SetAbsoluteCellValue method takes three arguments: the row and column of the cell and the value to set in that cell. These methods can be very useful in making comparisons between cells in a workbook.

The active cell is also capable of having certain properties set through the class. The foreground, or text, color is set through the CellForeColor property. The background color can be set with the CellBackColor property. These are not the actual property names exposed by the Excel object model, but these names are more intuitive than referencing the Cell.Interior.Color property.

The cell font characteristics can be manipulated as well. The CellFont property can set or read the font name. The CellFontSize can set or read the size of the font. The CellBold property can be set to True or False to make the font bold or normal styled, respectively.

Setting the same font characteristics for every cell can be wasteful, so there are also a handful of methods in the ExcelClass class to manipulate them on a larger scale. To set the background or foreground color on an entire column, you can use the SetColumnBackColor and SetColumnForeColor methods, respectively. The method names for doing the same on a row basis are SetRowBackColor and SetRowForeColor. All of these methods (notice they are not properties!) take two arguments: the column or row number and the color value to set. At the present time, the methods cannot handle ranges of columns or rows.

The row height and column width can also be changed by your script. The CurrentRowHeight and CurrentColumnWidth properties will access the current column and row properties of the active cell. To change a specific row or column, you may use the SetRowHeight and SetRowWidth methods and pass the row or column number and height or width as arguments.

Navigating, or moving, the active cell is going to be a common task, and there are several methods available for doing so. Since the act of reading or populated a spreadsheet is done one cell at a time, from right to left and top to bottom, it made sense to use navigation methods that reflected this. Those methods are NextColumn and NextRow. The NextColumn method moves the active cell one column to the right, and the NextRow method moves it one row down.

Note that the NextRow method does not move the active cell to the first column! Moving the active cell to the first column on the next row is done by calling the StartNewRow method. Do not confuse these two methods.

To find the location of the current active cell, you may reference the Row and Column properties of the object. These will return the numeric value of the row and column. To translate the numeric value of the column into the standard alphabetic representation, you may pass the column number to the GetColumnLetters method of the object. You may also set the value for the current row and column if you wish. Because several other methods are available for moving the active cell, I would avoid directly setting the row and column values.

Other navigational methods are also provided. The MoveAbsoluteCell method takes two arguments—the row and column number—and moves the active cell to that specific cell. When looking at a spreadsheet in Excel, remember that the columns are represented by letters, and while you could mentally translate those alphabetic values into their numeric equivalents, I have provided a method to do it for you. Call the GetColumnNumber method and pass the string value of the column (case is ignored) to the method, and it will return the column number.

You can also move a number of cells relative to the active cell. The MoveRelativeCell method takes two arguments: the number of rows (positive or negative) to move and the number of columns (positive or negative) to move from the active cell.

You might find the need to populate two or more worksheets with information. The method NewWorksheet will create a new worksheet in the current workbook and make it the active worksheet. The active cell will be set to A1, and you can immediately begin entering data.

To save a workbook, use the SaveWorkbook method, passing it the filename you wish to use. If you attempt to exit the script without saving the workbook, you will be prompted by Excel to save your work (undoubtedly you've run into this behavior before with at least one other application, right?). If you truly wish to exit without saving your work, you should set the QuitWithoutSaving property of the object to true before the script ends.

To open an existing workbook, create an instance of the ExcelClass class and call the OpenWorkbook method, passing it the filename of the spreadsheet to open. The active cell will be on the first worksheet, cell A1.

By default, the spreadsheet is not visible while you are working with it (though you can tell Excel is running if you examine the running processes under Task Manager). If you wish to see what is going on, you may execute the Show method. To hide the spreadsheet, execute the Hide method.

```
Option Explicit
'==================================================================
Class ExcelClass
'==================================================================
' Private and public variables
Private m_ExcelObject
Private m_ActiveWorkbook, m_ActiveSheet
Private m_CurrentRow, m_CurrentColumn
Private m_QuitWithoutExiting
Private m_ErrSource
'==================================================================
Private Sub Class_Initialize
Set m_ExcelObject = WScript.CreateObject("Excel.Application")
m_ErrSource = "ExcelObject"
m_QuitWithoutExiting = False
End Sub
'==================================================================
Private Sub Class_Terminate
If m_QuitWithoutExiting Then
    m_ExcelObject.Visible = True
Else
    m_ActiveWorkbook.Close
    m_ExcelObject.Application.Quit
End If
```

```
        Set m_ActiveSheet = Nothing
        Set m_ActiveWorkbook = Nothing
        Set m_ExcelObject = Nothing
        End Sub
        '=================================================================
        Public Property Get Row
            Row = m_CurrentRow
        End Property

        Public Property Let Row(RowValue)
        If IsNumeric(RowValue) Then
            m_CurrentRow = RowValue
        Else
            Err.Raise 101,m_ErrSource,"Row must be a number"
        End If
        End Property
        '=================================================================
        Public Property Get Column
            Column = m_CurrentColumn
        End Property

        Public Property Let Column(ColumnValue)
        If IsNumeric(ColumnValue) Then
            m_CurrentColumn = ColumnValue
            Else
            Err.Raise 102,m_ErrSource,"Column must be a number"
        End If
        End Property
        '=================================================================
        Public Property Get QuitWithoutExiting
            QuitWithoutExiting = m_QuitWithoutExiting
        End Property

        Public Property Let QuitWithoutExiting(ExitValue)
            m_QuitWithoutExiting = ExitValue
        End Property
        '=================================================================
        Public Sub SetColumnForeColor(Column,ColorValue)
            m_ActiveSheet.Columns(Column).Font.Color = ColorValue
        End Sub
        '=================================================================
        Public Sub SetColumnBackColor(Column,ColorValue)
            m_ActiveSheet.Columns(Column).Interior.Color = ColorValue
        End Sub
        '=================================================================
        Public Sub SetRowForeColor(Row,ColorValue)
            m_ActiveSheet.Rows(Row).Font.Color = ColorValue
        End Sub
        '=================================================================
```

```
Public Sub SetRowBackColor(Row,ColorValue)
    m_ActiveSheet.Rows(Row).Interior.Color = ColorValue
End Sub
'=====================================================================
Public Property Get CellValue
    CellValue = m_ActiveSheet.Cells(m_CurrentRow,m_CurrentColumn).Value
End Property

Public Property Let CellValue(NewValue)
    m_ActiveSheet.Cells(m_CurrentRow,m_CurrentColumn).Value = NewValue
End Property
'=====================================================================
Public Property Get CurrentColumnWidth
CurrentColumnHeight = _
    m_ActiveSheet.Columns(m_CurrentColumn).ColumnWidth
End Property

Public Property Let CurrentColumnWidth(WidthValue)
If IsNumeric(WidthValue) Then
    m_ActiveSheet.Columns(m_CurrentColumn).ColumnWidth = WidthValue
End If
End Property
'=====================================================================
Public Sub SetColumnWidth(Column,WidthValue)
If IsNumeric(Column) Then
    If IsNumeric(WidthValue) Then
        m_ActiveSheet.Columns(Column).ColumnWidth = WidthValue
    Else
        Err.Raise 104,m_ErrSource,"Width must be a number"
    End If
Else
    Err.Raise 103,m_ErrSource,"Column must be a number"
End If
End Sub
'=====================================================================
Public Property Get CurrentRowHeight
    CurrentRowHeight = m_ActiveSheet.Rows(m_CurrentRow).RowHeight
End Property

Public Property Let CurrentRowHeight(WidthValue)
If IsNumeric(WidthValue) Then
    m_ActiveSheet.Rows(m_CurrentRow).RowHeight = WidthValue
End If
End Property
'=====================================================================
```

```
Public Sub SetRowHeight(Row,WidthValue)
If IsNumeric(Row) Then
   If IsNumeric(WidthValue) Then
      m_ActiveSheet.Rows(Row).RowHeight = WidthValue
   Else
      Err.Raise 104,m_ErrSource,"Width must be a number"
   End If
Else
   Err.Raise 103,m_ErrSource,"Row must be a number"
End If
End Sub
'=====================================================================
Public Property Get CellForeColor
CellForeColor = _
   m_ActiveSheet.Cells(m_CurrentRow,m_CurrentColumn).Font.Color
End Property

Public Property Let CellForeColor(ColorValue)
m_ActiveSheet.Cells(m_CurrentRow,m_CurrentColumn).Font.Color = _
                                             ColorValue
End Property
'=====================================================================
Public Property Get CellBackColor
CellBackColor = _
   m_ActiveSheet.Cells(m_CurrentRow,m_CurrentColumn).Interior.Color
End Property

Public Property Let CellBackColor(ColorValue)
m_ActiveSheet.Cells(m_CurrentRow,m_CurrentColumn).Interior.Color = _
                                             ColorValue
End Property
'=====================================================================
Public Property Get CellFont
CellFont = _
   m_ActiveSheet.Cells(m_CurrentRow,m_CurrentColumn).Font.Name
End Property

Public Property Let CellFont(FontValue)
m_ActiveSheet.Cells(m_CurrentRow,m_CurrentColumn).Font.Name = _
                                             FontValue
End Property
'=====================================================================
Public Property Get CellBold
CellBold = _
   m_ActiveSheet.Cells(m_CurrentRow,m_CurrentColumn).Font.Bold
End Property

Public Property Let CellBold(BoldValue)
```

```
If BoldValue Then
   m_ActiveSheet.Cells(m_CurrentRow,m_CurrentColumn).Font.Bold = _
                                                       True
Else
   m_ActiveSheet.Cells(m_CurrentRow,m_CurrentColumn).Font.Bold = _
                                                       False
End If
End Property
'====================================================================
Public Property Get CellFontSize
CellFontSize = _
   m_ActiveSheet.Cells(m_CurrentRow,m_CurrentColumn).Font.Size
End Property

Public Property Let CellFontSize(SizeValue)
If IsNumeric(SizeValue) And SizeValue >= 8 Then
   m_ActiveSheet.Cells(m_CurrentRow,m_CurrentColumn).Font.Size = _
                                               SizeValue
Else
   Err.Raise 106,m_ErrSource,"Invalid font size"
End If
End Property
'====================================================================
Public Sub NewWorkBook
Set m_ActiveWorkbook = m_ExcelObject.Workbooks.Add
Set m_ActiveSheet = m_ActiveWorkbook.Worksheets(1)
m_CurrentRow = 1
m_CurrentColumn = 1
End Sub
'====================================================================
Public Sub NewWorksheet
Set m_ActiveSheet = m_Worksheets.Add
m_CurrentRow = 1
m_CurrentColumn = 1
End Sub
'====================================================================
Public Property Get Worksheet
Worksheet = m_ActiveSheet.Name
End Property

Public Property Let Worksheet(WorksheetValue)
If IsNumeric(WorkSheetValue) Then
   If WorksheetValue <= m_ExcelObject.Worksheets.Count Then
      Set m_ActiveSheet = m_ExcelObject.Worksheets(WorksheetValue)
      m_CurrentRow = 1
      m_CurrentColumn = 1
   Else
      Err.Raise 111,m_ErrSource,"Invalid worksheet"
```

```vb
            End If
      Else
         Dim WSCount
         For WS = 1 To m_ExcelObject.Worksheets.Count
            If m_ExcelObject.Worksheets(WS).Name = WorkSheetValue Then
               Set m_ActiveSheet = m_ExcelObject.Worksheets(WS)
               Exit For
            End If
         Next
      End If
End Property
'=====================================================================
Public Sub MoveAbsoluteCell(Row,Column)
If IsNumeric(Row) Then
   m_CurrentRow = Row
Else
   Err.Raise 101,m_ErrSource,"Row must be a number"
End If
If IsNumeric(Column) Then
   m_CurrentColumn = Column
Else
   Err.Raise 102,m_ErrSource,"Column must be a number"
End If
End Sub
'=====================================================================
Public Sub MoveRelativeCell(Row,Column)
If IsNumeric(Row) Then
   m_CurrentRow = m_CurrentRow + Row
Else
   Err.Raise 101,m_ErrSource,"Row must be a number"
End If
If IsNumeric(Column) Then
   m_CurrentColumn = m_CurrentColumn + Column
Else
   Err.Raise 102,m_ErrSource,"Column must be a number"
End If
End Sub
'=====================================================================
Public Function GetColumnNumber(Column)
Select Case Len(Column)
Case 1
   GetColumnNumber = Asc(UCase(Column)) - 64
Case 2
   GetColumnNumber = (Asc(UCase(Left(Column,1))) -64) * 26 + _
                     Asc(UCase(Right(Column,1))) - 64
End Select
End Function
'=====================================================================
```

```vb
Public Function GetColumnLetters(Column)
If Column \ 26 > 0 Then
   Dim FirstLetter, SecondLetter
   FirstLetter = Chr((Column \ 26) + 64)
   SecondLetter = Chr((Column Mod 26) + 64)
   GetColumnLetters = FirstLetter & SecondLetter
Else
   GetColumnLetters = Chr(Column + 64)
End If
End Function
'===================================================================
Public Sub NextRow
   m_CurrentRow = m_CurrentRow + 1
End Sub
'===================================================================
Public Sub PreviousRow
If (m_CurrentRow - 1) > 0 Then
   m_CurrentRow = m_CurrentRow - 1
End If
End Sub
'===================================================================
Public Sub NextColumn
   m_CurrentColumn = m_CurrentColumn + 1
End Sub
'===================================================================
Public Sub PreviousColumn
If (m_CurrentColumn - 1) > 0 Then
   m_CurrentColumn = m_CurrentColumn - 1
End If
End Sub
'===================================================================
Public Sub StartNewRow
m_CurrentRow = m_CurrentRow + 1
m_CurrentColumn = 1
End Sub
'===================================================================
Public Sub OpenWorkBook(Filename)
On Error Resume Next
m_ExcelObject.Workbooks.Open FileName
If Err.Number <> 0 Then
   Err.Raise Err.Number,m_ErrSource,Err.Description
End If
Set m_ActiveWorkbook = m_ExcelObject.Workbooks(1)
Set m_ActiveSheet = m_ActiveWorkbook.Worksheets(1)
m_CurrentRow = 1
m_CurrentColumn = 1
End Sub
'===================================================================
```

```
Public Sub SaveWorkBook(FileName)
    m_ActiveWorkbook.SaveAs FileName
End Sub
'==================================================================
Public Property Get ActiveSheetName
    ActiveSheetName = m_ActiveSheet.Name
End Property

Public Property Let ActiveSheetName(NameValue)
    m_ActiveSheet.Name = NameValue
End Property
'==================================================================
Public Function GetAbsoluteCellValue(Row,Column)
If IsNumeric(Row) Then
    If IsNumeric(Column) Then
        GetAbsoluteCellValue = _
            m_ActiveSheet.Cells(Row,Column).Value
    Else
        Err.Raise 102,m_ErrSource,"Column must be a number"
    End If
Else
    Err.Raise 101,m_ErrSource,"Row must be a number"
End If
End Function
'==================================================================
Public Sub SetAbsoluteCellValue(Row,Column,CellValue)
If IsNumeric(Row) Then
    If IsNumeric(Column) Then
        m_ActiveSheet.Cells(Row,Column).Value = CellValue
    Else
        Err.Raise 102,m_ErrSource,"Column must be a number"
    End If
Else
    Err.Raise 101,m_ErrSource,"Row must be a number"
End If
End Sub
'==================================================================
Public Sub Hide
    m_ExcelObject.Visible = True
End Sub
'==================================================================
Public Sub Show
    m_ExcelObject.Visible = True
End Sub
'==================================================================
End Class
```

Export Users to Excel

This script demonstrates how to create an Excel spreadsheet with a list of User objects and their ADsPaths. It uses the QueryClass class to find the User object, and then uses the ExcelClass class to write the results to an Excel spreadsheet.

The QueryClass object is instantiated as we have seen before, and the values for the searchroot, attributes, scope, and filtertext are supplied. The resulting record set, Results, is then iterated through.

Before we start processing the results, the ExcelClass object is instantiated. This creates an instance of the Excel application in memory, but since we have not set the Visible property of the object to True, it will not be displayed. A new workbook is created with the NewWorkbook method. The active cell is the first cell in the workbook, A1 by default, which is given the value from the first field of the Recordset. The foreground color is changed to red and the background color is changed to blue for demonstration purposes. The NextColumn method moves the active cell to the next column in the workbook, B1, and the value is assigned. The cell's font is changed to Arial Narrow for demonstration. The StartNewRow method moves the active cell to the first column in the next row, much like sending a CRLF (carriage return-line feed) to a text file. The Recordset point is then moved to the next record and the process repeats.

The last section of the code demonstrates how to set the foreground color for an entire column and how to set the height for a row. This is a simple example to get you started. The main purpose is to get you used to the idea of navigating the Excel spreadsheet using the ExcelClass object.

```
<job>
<script language="VBScript" src="includes\RootDSEClass.vbs" />
<script language="VBScript" src="includes\QueryClass.vbs" />
<script language="VBScript" src="includes\ExcelClass.vbs" />
<script>
Dim RootDSE
Set RootDSE = New RootDSEClass
Dim Query
Set Query = New QueryClass
Query.SearchRoot = "OU=Users,DC=zygort,DC=org"
Query.Attributes = "cn,AdsPath"
Query.Scope = "subtree"
Query.FilterText = "(&(objectClass=user)(objectCategory=person))"
Dim Results
Set Results = Query.ExecuteQuery
Set Excel = New ExcelClass
Excel.NewWorkbook
Do Until Results.eof
    Excel.CellValue = Results.Fields(0)
    Excel.CellForeColor = vbRed
    Excel.CellBackColor = vbBlue
    Excel.NextColumn
    Excel.CellValue = Results.Fields(1)
    Excel.CellFont = "Arial Narrow"
    Excel.StartNewRow
    Results.MoveNext
```

```
Loop
Excel.SetColumnForeColor 1,vbRed
Excel.SetRowHeight 2,20
Excel.QuitWithoutExiting = True
Set Query = Nothing
Set RootDSE = Nothing
</script>
</job>
```

Import Users from Excel

This script will use the `ExcelClass` and the `UserClass` classes to read a list of settings from an Excel spreadsheet and to populate Active Directory with the users and their information. This can be a bit tricky, especially if you want to maintain flexibility in your script, so let me explain what I was trying to do here.

First, I do not like locking anyone into a given format. That means that I want users to be able to modify the spreadsheet as they see fit, and the script should adapt to it. However, to meet the requirements for adding users (specifically through the `Create` method of the `UserClass` object), three elements are required: the parent container, the Common Name, and the `SAMAccountName`. Other that that, anything should go.

To accomplish this, the first row is reserved for the `ldapDisplayName` of the property you wish to set. The only three required columns are "Container", "CN", and "SAMAccountName", which I have placed as the first three columns in the spreadsheet. After those columns, enter the `ldapDisplayName` for any other properties you wish to set on the first row. Then fill in the properties for the individual users that correspond to those properties on the subsequent lines.

The script begins by opening the spreadsheet and skipping the first row of property names. Each subsequent row of properties is read and stored in either a variable (for the required properties) or in a `Dictionary` object (for the optional properties). If all the required properties are included, the `UserClass` object is instantiated. The new `User` object is created, and the optional properties are set. This procedure repeats for each row in the spreadsheet.

```
<job>
<script language="VBScript" src="includes\ExcelClass.vbs" />
<script language="VBScript" src="includes\UserClass.vbs" />
<script>
Dim EndOfRow, EndOfFile
EndOfRow = False
EndOfFile = False
Set Excel = New ExcelClass
Excel.OpenWorkbook "NewUsers.xls"
' First row is the ldapDisplayName, skip it
Excel.NextRow
Dim User
Do Until EndOfFile
    If Excel.CellValue = "" Then
        EndOfFile = True
    Else
```

```
      Dim Container, CN, SAMAccountName, OtherProperties
      Set OtherProperties = _
         WScript.CreateObject("Scripting.Dictionary")
         Do Until EndOfRow
            If Excel.GetAbsoluteCellValue(1,Excel.Column) = "" Then
               EndOfRow = True
            Else
               Select Case _
                  LCase(Excel.GetAbsoluteCellValue(1,Excel.Column))
               Case "container"
                  Container = Excel.CellValue
               Case "cn"
                  CN = Excel.CellValue
               Case "samaccountname"
                  SAMAccountName = Excel.CellValue
               Case Else
                  If Not(Excel.CellValue = "") Then
                     OtherProperties.Add _
                        Excel.GetAbsoluteCellValue(1,Excel.Column), _
                        Excel.CellValue
                  End If
               End Select
               WScript.Echo _
                  Excel.GetAbsoluteCellValue(1,Excel.Column) & _
                     "=" & Excel.CellValue
               Excel.NextColumn
            End If
      Loop
      If Not(Container = "" And CN = "" And SAMAccountName = "") Then
         Dim UserObject
         UserObject = New UserClass
         UserObject.Create Container,CN,SAMAccountName
         Dim PropName
         For Each PropName In OtherProperties.Keys
            UserObject.SetProperty PropName, _
                                 OtherProperties(PropName)
         Next
         UserObject.Save
      Else
         WScript.Echo "Missing required values in row " & Excel.Row
      End If
      Excel.StartNewRow
      EndOfRow = False
   End If
Loop
</script>
</job>
```

Coming Up Next

In this chapter, you have seen an approach to building scripts by putting together reusable VBScript classes into a Windows script file. This approach is designed to make your scripts less error-prone and easier to construct, and to make better use of a system administrator's most valuable commodity—time.

In the next chapter, we build additional scripts aimed at monitoring Active Directory. Microsoft Operations Manager (MOM) already has an excellent feature pack designed exclusively for monitoring AD, but sadly this server product is beyond the budget of many IT departments. However, many of the monitoring functions of MOM can be duplicated by a combination of scripts and the Task Scheduler.

Chapter 19

Monitoring Active Directory

In this chapter, we will create scripts for monitoring your Active Directory installation. Microsoft already has an excellent server product, Microsoft Operations Manager (MOM), which supports a feature pack designed to manage Active Directory. This server product is unfortunately priced beyond the budget of many IT departments.

The functionality of the Active Directory Management Pack (ADMP) is documented on the Microsoft Operations Manager website. From that documentation, we learn what each individual monitoring task is designed to do, and how often each task executes. We can use this information to build a VBScript to replicate the original task, and use the Task Scheduler to execute the script on a regular schedule.

Following the same modular approach to script writing as we have seen in the previous chapter, we will use the Windows script file (WSF) format for our scripts. Along the way, a few additional VBScript classes will be built for use (and reuse) in our scripts. Of course, all these scripts will be available for download.

In this module, you will also be introduced to Windows Management Interface (WMI). WMI provides a standard interface we can take advantage of to monitor not only Active Directory functions, but most functions and settings on a local or remote computer as well.

OutputClass

In terms of output, monitoring scripts are a different animal compared with other scripts. What kind of information do we expect a monitoring script to provide? Most of the time, we do not want any information from the script unless it finds something wrong, in which case we want to know about the problem right away.

The OutputClass class object acts as a smart equivalent to the Wscript.Echo method. Rather than calling the Wscript.Echo method directly, you would instead instantiate an instance of the OutputClass, and call the Display method of the object. The object then decides, based on its own information, whether or not to actually display the output.

Why would we want to avoid displaying output from a script? Consider that when a script is executed with the WScript engine, output is presented in the form of a dialog box to the user. The execution of our script is blocked until the user answers the dialog box. This will irritate the user quickly considering how often these monitoring scripts are designed to execute. Therefore, by using this class as a sort of "middle-man" in displaying output, we give the script a built-in method to avoid the blocking behavior of dialog boxes.

Of course, executing a script with the CScript engine does not suffer this blocking because output is sent to a command prompt window. Normally, when scripts are scheduled by means of the Task Scheduler, CScript.exe is specified as the script engine. This will lead to a command prompt box popping up each time a script executes and then disappearing when the script has completed. This can be equally irritating to the user.

The question becomes, which behavior are we looking for? As we go over the code for the monitoring scripts, you will notice that we have designed them to serve a dual purpose; in addition to raising an alert to potential problems, they can also be used to present the monitored data to the user. This allows us to use one script for both alerts and to diagnose potential problems with Active Directory, depending on which engine we use to run the script.

Therefore, when scheduling our scripts with the Task Scheduler, we want to specify the WScript .exe scripting engine. If you wish to view the output from the script, use the CScript.exe engine.

The class itself is very simple. It starts by determining which scripting engine is being used to execute the script. If the scripting engine is WScript.exe, then the default behavior is to suppress the output. Otherwise, the script output is displayed as normal. You can also use a property named SuppressOutput to manually control the script output. Setting the property to True suppresses the script output, while setting it to False allows the output to be displayed.

The last method of the class is the ModalAlert method. This displays a system modal dialog box with the message passed to the method. This is simply a quick and easy way of interrupting the user with an important message, such as an alert to an impending problem with Active Directory.

This is, of course, only scratching the surface of what you can accomplish with a class like this. If your scripts use the same dialog boxes settings continuously, you could add a method similar to ModalAlert to reliably re-create the same dialog box time and time again.

```
'=================================================================
Class OutputClass
'=================================================================
' Private and public variables
Private m_SuppressOutput
'=================================================================
Private Sub Class_Initialize
    If Instr(LCase(WScript.FullName),"wscript.exe") > 0 Then
        SuppressOutput = True
    Else
        SuppressOutput = False
    End If
End Sub
'=================================================================
Private Sub Class_Terminate
End Sub
'=================================================================
Public Property Get SuppressOutput
    SuppressOutput = m_SuppressOutput
End Property

Public Property Let SuppressOutput(SuppressValue)
    m_SuppressOutput = CBool(SuppressValue)
End Property
'=================================================================
```

```
Public Function Display(Message)
If Not(m_SuppressOutput) Then
    WScript.Echo Message
End If
End Function
'=======================================================================
Public Sub ModalAlert(Message)
    MsgBox Message,vbExclamation+vbOKOnly+vbSystemModal,"ALERT!"
End Sub
'=======================================================================
End Class
```

Windows Management Instrumentation (WMI)

Windows Management Instrumentation (WMI) is a cornerstone technology when it comes to monitoring systems, whether client or server. You might also hear it referred to as Web-Based Enterprise Management (WBEM). WMI is Microsoft's implementation of an industry initiative to standardize management of systems in and enterprise environment.

WMI is ready to use in Windows 2003, XP, and Windows 2000 operating systems. In Windows NT 4.0 SP4 and Windows 98 or (gasp!) 95, WMI is available as a downloadable component.

WMI uses a Common Information Model (CIM) to represent systems, the applications on that system, networks, devices on that network, and a variety of other managed components. The goal of CIM is to present a view of the logical and physical elements of a system. It is also object-oriented and extensible.

One of the biggest strengths of WMI is its ability to pull or set configuration data from remote computers as well as the local system. The name of the system to connect to is passed in a connection string, and if the system name can be resolved, then an attempt to access the WMI repository on that system is attempted. On the surface, it seems simple enough. Remember, though, that we are remotely accessing and potentially modifying a system. This practice in general is one that network administrators tend to keep a close eye on and restrict where appropriate.

One of those restrictions is in the Windows Firewall. When enabled (which, by default, it should be), WMI requests are denied. This will usually result in an error message such as "RPC Server Unavailable". WMI must be allowed to establish a DCOM connection to the remote computer. Figure 19.1 shows how DCOM communication must get through the firewall on both the local and remote client.

FIGURE 19.1
WMI and DCOM
communication

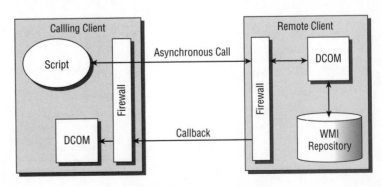

A full discussion of WMI programming is well beyond the scope of this module, but we can still cover the basics to help you understand how the `WMIClass` (discussed in the next section) works.

The process begins by establishing a connection to the WMI repository on the remote computer. There are actually several different methods available for connecting to the remote computer, but for the purposes of our reusable VBScript object we opted to use a more flexible approach. Specifically, the `WMIClass` uses an object called the `SWBemLocator`.

The `SWBemLocator` object is used to obtain an object that represents the connection to the WMI repository. The connection is created by calling the `ConnectServer` method of the object. The method takes four arguments: the name of the system to connect to, the WMI namespace to connect to, and the username and password to use to establish the connection. You should be familiar with three of those arguments, but the WMI namespace might require a little more explanation.

A WMI namespace is a method of grouping similar WMI classes together. During installation, a WMI provider will first register its namespace with the system and then register all the classes that will reside within that namespace. For example, all Win32 WMI classes can be found in the `root\cimv2` namespace.

To give you an idea of the query possibilities available with WMI, Table 19.1 lists some of the more useful Win32 WMI classes and their properties. This is far from a comprehensive list, so for more information visit Microsoft's website.

To get a better idea of what is available in WMI, let's look at a few tools. The first is a built-in utility named `WbemTest.exe`. This tool will allow you to browse the wealth of WMI information on a system. It is installed with Windows 2000, Windows 2003, and Windows XP, as well as available as a download for other systems. To start `WbemTest`, simply click Start▷ Run and enter **WbemTest**.

The first step in working with WMI is connecting to the system you wish to examine. The first dialog box will be presented with about 13 disabled buttons, which might give you the impression that you have already got a problem. You don't—you just haven't connected yet. Figure 19.2 shows the `WbemTest` dialog box in an unconnected state.

In the upper-right corner is a button labeled Connect. Click it and you will be presented with the Connect dialog box, shown in Figure 19.3. This dialog box allows you to specify any necessary connection information. The Namespace field allows you to specify a system and namespace to connect to. If your current security credentials are not enough to connect to the WMI repository, you can supply an alternate set of security information in the User, Password, and Authority fields.

FIGURE 19.2
WbemTest dialog box
(not connected)

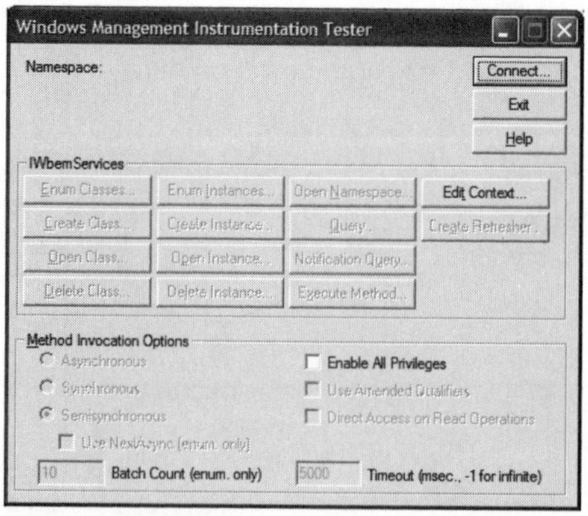

TABLE 19.1:   Commonly Used Win32 WMI Classes and Their Properties

CLASS	DESCRIPTION AND PROPERTIES
Win32_ComputerSystem	Represents the computer operating system. Useful properties include Name, Domain, DomainRole, PartOfDomain, Roles, and UserName.
Win32_DiskDrive	Represents the physical disk drives in the system. Useful properties include Name, Model, Size, and Status.
Win32_LogicalDisk	Represents both physical and mapped drives. Useful properties include Name, DriveType, FileSystem, and Size.
Win32_Network AdapterConfiguration	Represents the network adapters in a system. Useful properties include Caption, DHCPEnabled, DNSDomain, IPAddress, IPSubnet, DefaultIPGateway, and MACAddress.
Win32_OperatingSystem	Represents the operating system. Useful properties include Caption, BootDevice, CurrentTimeZone, CSName, FreePhysicalMemory, FreeVirtualMemory, SystemDrive, ServicePackMajorVersion, and Version.
Win32_Process	Represents the processes running on a system. Useful properties include CommandLine, ExecutablePath, ProcessID, and ParentProcessID.
Win32_Processor	Represents the system processor(s). Useful properties include Name, Availability, CPUStatus, MaxClockSpeed, CurrentClockSpeed, and Status.
Win32_Service	Represents the running services on a system. Useful properties include Caption, Name, PathName, Started, StartMode, StartName, and State.
Win32_Share	Represents the shared resources on a system. Useful properties include Name, Path, Type and Status.

By default, the Namespace field says "root\default" (on Windows XP, the field is sometimes not labeled). Let's change that "root\cimv2" and click the Connect button. This will return us to the WbemTest dialog box, and now all the buttons should be enabled. You'll also see the namespace we entered in the Connect dialog box listed under the Namespace label. We can now start to explore WMI.

Start by clicking the Enum Classes button. You'll be presented with a Superclass Info dialog box, shown in Figure 19.4. Since we are not going to narrow down our search, we can leave it blank and click the OK button.

This returns the Query Result dialog box shown in Figure 19.5. This box lists the results of our query for all the base-level classes. As you scroll through the list, you'll notice a few common prefixes to the classes, such as CIM_, Win32_, and MSFT_. You are also given two buttons to add or delete top-level classes to the WMI repository. We'll avoid that for now and go on to actually writing a few WMI queries, so click the Close button to return to the WbemTest dialog box.

FIGURE 19.3

Connect dialog box

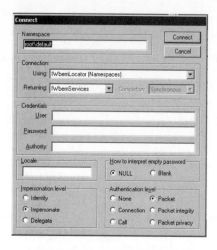

FIGURE 19.4

Superclass Info
dialog box

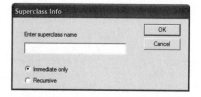

FIGURE 19.5

Query Result
dialog box

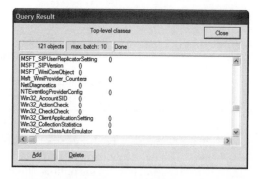

Writing queries in WMI is done with a language called the WMI Query Language (WQL). If you are familiar with Structured Query Language (SQL) used by most database packages, this will seem very familiar to you. For the rest, we'll cover the elements of a query along the way.

A query has two essential clauses: the Select clause, which is a list of attributes to return, and the From clause, which lists the data source containing the information. In the Select clause, we can submit a comma-separated list of individual attributes to return or we can use the asterisk (*) as a wildcard, which means "give me all the attributes." When developing queries, start by using the wildcard. You will get more information than you need at first, but you can whittle it down as you refine the query.

To write and submit a query, click the Query button. This brings up the Query dialog box, shown in Figure 19.6, which has a large text field for us to enter our query. We'll start with a very simple query to list the attributes of the local computer system. The text of that query will be simply `Select * From Win32_ComputerSystem`. Enter the query in the Enter Query field and click the Apply button.

This should return only one result, shown in Figure 19.7, namely your local computer. It doesn't seem like much information at first, but double-click on the single result.

You are now in the Object Editor dialog box, shown in Figure 19.8. This will allow you to browse the attributes for the instance of the `Win32_ComputerSystem` class that was returned from our query. The information in this dialog box, particularly the attribute names, is useful to note when developing your own WMI queries. When finished perusing the results, click the Close button in the Object Editor dialog box and then click the Close button in the Query Results dialog box to return to the `WbemTest` dialog box.

We've seen a simple two-part WMI query, using only the `Select` and `From` clauses, which returned only a single result. Let's submit another query that will give us more to work with. Click the Query button and enter the following WMI Query: `Select * from Win32_LogicalDisk`. Your results will look different from ours (which are displayed in Figure 19.9), but will list the physical and mapped disks.

By looking at the results, you can probably guess which drives are local and which are mapped. If we want to write a WMI query that will return only the local or only the mapped drives, we have to find something that differentiates the two. In your own result set, examine the value of the `DriveType` attribute for a local and a mapped drive. According to Microsoft's documentation, the `DriveType` of a local disk is 3, a network drive is 4, and a CD-ROM is 5. Therefore, to write a WMI query that targets only mapped drives, we need to add a clause to limit the result set to instances where the `DriveType` attribute is 4.

FIGURE 19.6
Query dialog box

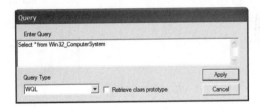

FIGURE 19.7
Query Result dialog box

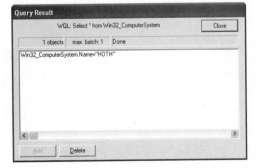

A `Where` clause is used to limit the result set of a query. The `Where` clause is added after the `From` clause in a query. Close the current Query Results dialog box and execute the following new query: `Select * from Win32_LogicalDisk Where DriveType='4'` (in this case, the single quotes around the 4 are optional, but we've found that it is a good habit to get into when specifying `Where` clause values). Our results are shown in Figure 19.10.

FIGURE 19.8
Object Editor
dialog box

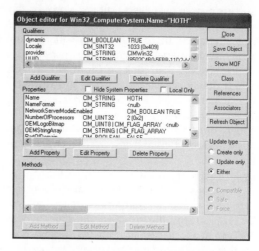

FIGURE 19.9
`Win32_LogicalDisk`
query results

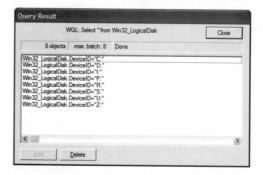

FIGURE 19.10
Network drive
query results

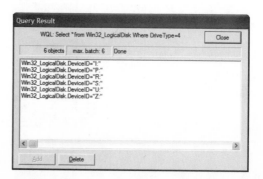

Finally, to query for the local drives, we can modify the `Where` clause to look for both local disks and CD-ROM drives. The `Where` clause supports logical operators just like the VBScript `If-Then` statement. Close the current Query Results dialog box and execute the following query: `Select * from Win32_LogicalDisk Where DriveType='3' or DriveType='5'`.

`WbemTest` is an excellent tool that lets you practice and hone your WMI queries before committing them to a script. You can continue to write and experiment with WMI queries without fear of causing irreparable harm to your system. The worst outcome is that `WbemTest` might lock up and you'll have to restart it, so feel free to explore.

If you would like some additional help in the form of prewritten WMI queries, we have another tool for your consideration. It is called Scriptomatic 2.0, and it is a free download from Microsoft (the URL is long and complicated, so do a Google search on the keywords "Scriptomatic 2 download" and you'll find a link right to it). Download the compressed executable file from Microsoft, extract the files, and double-click on the `ScriptomaticV2.hta` file to execute. Figure 19.11 shows the Scriptomatic tool after initializing. After using it a few times, I'm sure you will find it to be one of the most invaluable tools at your disposal.

The Scriptomatic tool is a hypertext application (HTA), which means it is essentially a local web application. You can open up the `ScriptomaticV2.hta` file in a text editor to see how it does its magic. Scriptomatic begins by loading all the namespaces available on the local computer. The default namespace used is `root\CIMv2`, but you can choose any other namespace with the WMI Namespace drop-down box. After selecting the appropriate namespace, use the WMI Class drop-down box to select the class you wish to query.

As you can see in Figure 19.11, we have selected the `Win32_LogicalDisk` class. The Scriptomatic tool has created a VBScript for us that will query the class and display all the attributes for the class. If you would like to see the script in another programming language, select that language from the Language frame on the right side.

FIGURE 19.11
Scriptomatic V2 tool

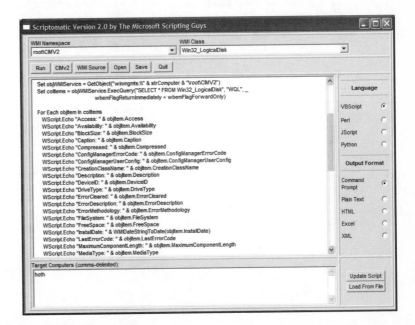

You can run the script by clicking the Run button near the top of the window. A list of output choices is available on the right side; by default the output will be sent to a command prompt window. When the Plain Text output option is selected, a file named Output.txt is created, filled, and opened in Notepad. The HTML output option creates an Output.htm file and opens it in Internet Explorer, as shown in Figure 19.12. We'll leave it as an exercise for you to discover the results of the remaining output options.

You can save the script created by Scriptomatic by clicking the Save button and supplying a path. The script can also be copied and pasted into your script editor and modified to suit your needs. Again, the best way to discover the true potential of the Scriptomatic tool is to experiment with it. A read_me.doc file comes along with the ScriptomaticV2.hta file that describes more of the functionality of the tool, along with a dose of humor from its creators, The Scripting Guys.

The Scriptomatic tool produces code with a few common traits. The code is designed to use an array of computer names, allowing you to run the same WMI query on multiple computers. It uses the same method of executing the WMI query. It also uses a For Each loop to cycle through each instance of the class in the query result set. You might question if this is necessary for all WMI classes, but it really is.

The CIM itself defines many base classes, which are inherited by other classes in the repository. These classes are used to represent the hardware and software in a system. All WMI classes are designed to support multiple instances of any given class. This makes WMI flexible enough to represent any computer configuration imaginable.

Multiple class instances can also complicate the task of processing WMI data. Let's look at a simple computer system. We typically have a motherboard, at least one processor, and at least one hard drive (we didn't say it was a complete system). These would be represented by one instance of the Win32_MotherboardDevice class, one instance of the Win32_Processor class for each processor, and one instance of the Win32_DiskDrive class for each hard drive.

To get information about the processor, we would execute a WMI query such as **Select * from Win32_Processor**. If you are familiar with SQL queries, this will make perfect sense to you. If not, the query simply says "Get all properties of the all instances of the Win32_Processor class". If you want the query to be more efficient, you could specify only the properties in which you are interested.

FIGURE 19.12
Scriptomatic
HTML output

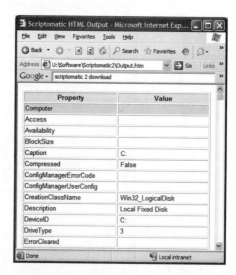

After executing the query, you process each instance of the Win32_Processor class that was returned. Depending on the computer system, this makes perfect sense. Servers tend to have more than one processor, while desktop clients tend to have a single processor. We cannot guarantee that every computer we contact has only one processor; therefore it makes sense to treat each query result set as if it contains more than one instance of the WMI class. The following example code will show you how to execute a WMI query and process the result set:

```
WMIQuery = "Select * From Win32_Processor"
Set ResultSet = WMILocator.ExecQuery(WMIQuery)
For Each Result in ResultSet
    WScript.Echo "Current Speed=" & Result.CurrentClockSpeed
    WScript.Echo "Max Speed=" & Result.MaxClockSpeed
Next
```

However, most common computer systems only have one motherboard, correct? While it might not make sense to treat the query result set as if there is only one instance of the Win32_MotherboardDevice class, this is still how it should be treated. In fact, all query results should be treated as if they might have multiple instances of the WMI class. The WMI query is always going to return a collection of instances, even if there is only one instance in that collection.

That said, there is a shortcut you can take if you are either absolutely sure there is only one instance of a class, or if you only want to process the first instance in the collection. By executing an Exit For command after processing the properties of the first instance, you can bypass the rest of the loop. The following code example shows how to do this with the Win32_MotherboardDevice class:

```
WMIQuery = "Select * From Win32_MotherboardDevice"
Set ResultSet = WMILocator.ExecQuery(WMIQuery)
For Each Result in ResultSet
    WScript.Echo "Caption=v & Result.Caption
    WScript.Echo "Description=" & Result.Description
    Exit For    ' Displays only the first motherboard's data
Next
```

Now that you have seen some of the basic concepts of WMI, it is time to start using it. As with other useful pieces of code, we have created a WMIClass VBScript class for you.

WMIClass

The WMIClass class is designed for two purposes. First, it has a set of methods designed for monitoring Active Directory. The WMI queries are contained in the appropriate method, and the output is typically packaged in a dictionary object to pass back to the calling script. The second purpose is that it gives you a template of sorts to follow for creating your own WMI queries. Looking closely, you will see that the methods tend to follow a predictable and repeatable pattern.

Creating the WMI class was not an easy task, mentally. There were several different approaches we could have used, from a generic and open-ended framework to a specific case-by-case methodology. For the purposes of the book format, we opted for a more specific approach. This allowed us to package the query results in a specific manner for consumption by the calling script. The generic approach would have required more "programming gymnastics" than we wanted to subject you to.

While the methods used to submit a WMI query to a target system are fairly straightforward, actually connecting to the target system is not. A few different methods are available. The main reason for this is security. Generally speaking, the code submitted in this book is intended for use by system administrators. As such, most of the code should run just fine with the security credentials of the user. However, since this might not always be true, we decided to use a WMI connection object that would easily allow a different set of security credentials to be passed to the target system.

The SWBemLocator object is used to create and open a connection to the WMI namespace on the target computer. A method named ConnectServer is used to connect to the system. This method allows us to pass in a username and password if the current user does not have adequate security rights to connect. Other connection methods either don't have this provision or require a few more hoops to be jumped through. By default, the username and password (set by the m_Username and m_Password variables, respectively) are set to a blank string. By leaving these fields blank, we ensure that the ConnectServer method uses the current security context when making the connection to the target server.

As we mentioned earlier, the methods in this VBScript class follow a pattern. You can reuse this pattern to create your own WMI query functions. When the class is instantiated by a calling script, an instance of the SWBemLocator is created for use in the method calls of the class. In the course of each method, this object is used to connect to and return a reference object to the WMI namespace on the target system. This reference object is used to submit the WMI query.

Each method starts by building the WMI query itself. The target server is then connected to, and the WMI query is submitted. The results are then processed and packaged in the appropriate manner and sent back to the calling script. The results are packaged differently in each method, but most of the methods shown here use a dictionary object to return the results to the client:

```
Option Explicit
'================================================================
Class WMIClass
'================================================================
Private m_UserName
Private m_Password
Private m_ADLogFile
Private WMILocator, WMIService, WMIQuery
Private Results, Result
'================================================================
Private Sub Class_Initialize
m_UserName = ""
m_Password = ""
Set WMILocator = CreateObject("WbemScripting.SWBemlocator")
End Sub
'================================================================
Private Sub Class_Terminate
End Sub
'================================================================
Public Property Get UserName
UserName = m_UserName
End Property

Public Property Let UserName(NameValue)
m_UserName = Trim(NameValue)
End Property
'================================================================
```

```
Public Property Get Password
Password = m_Password
End Property

Public Property Let Password(PasswordValue)
m_Password = Trim(PasswordValue)
End Property
'=================================================================
Public Function GetProcessorTimeForProcess(Server,Process)
' Returns a Dictionary Object
WMIQuery = "Select Name, PercentProcessorTime " & _
   "From Win32_PerfFormattedData_PerfProc_Process"
If IsArray(Process) Then
   Dim ServiceCount, X, WhereClause
   WhereClause = " Where "
   ServiceCount = UBound(Service)
   For X = 0 To UBound(Service)
      WhereClause = WhereClause & "name='" & Service(X) & "' or "
   Next
   WhereClause = Left(WhereClause,Len(WhereClause) - 4)
   WMIQuery = WMIQuery & WhereClause
Else
   WMIQuery = WMIQuery & " Where name='" & Process & "'"
End If
Set WMIService = WMILocator.ConnectServer _
   (Server,"\root\CIMV2",m_Username,m_Password)
Set Results = WMIService.ExecQuery(WMIQuery,,48)
Set GetProcessorTimeForProcess = _
   WScript.CreateObject("Scripting.Dictionary")
For Each Result in Results
   GetProcessorTimeForProcess.Add Result.Name, _
      CInt(Result.PercentProcessorTime)
Next
End Function
'=================================================================
Private Function TweakDate(TimeWritten)
' TimeWritten comes back in this format: 20050330085208.000000-360
' It needs a bit of tweaking to display properly
Dim Year,Month,Day,Hour,Minute
Year = Left(TimeWritten,4)
Month = Mid(TimeWritten,5,2)
Day = Mid(TimeWritten,7,2)
Hour = Mid(TimeWritten,9,2)
Minute = Mid(TimeWritten,11,2)
TweakDate = Month & "/" & Day & "/" & Year & " " & Hour & ":" & Minute
End Function
'=================================================================
Public Function GetServiceState(Server,Service)
' Returns a Dictionary Object
WMIQuery = "Select Name, State From Win32_Service"
```

```
If IsArray(Service) Then
    Dim ServiceCount, X, WhereClause
    WhereClause = " Where "
    ServiceCount = UBound(Service)
    For X = 0 To UBound(Service)
        WhereClause = WhereClause & "name='" & Service(X) & "' or "
    Next
    WhereClause = Left(WhereClause,Len(WhereClause) - 4)
    WMIQuery = WMIQuery & WhereClause
Else
    WMIQuery = WMIQuery & " Where name='" & Service & "'"
End If
Set WMIService = WMILocator.ConnectServer _
    (Server,"\root\CIMV2",m_Username,m_Password)
Set Results = WMIService.ExecQuery(WMIQuery,,48)
Set GetServiceState = WScript.CreateObject("Scripting.Dictionary")
For Each Result In Results
    GetServiceState.Add Result.Name, Result.State
Next
End Function
'=====================================================================
Public Function GetAvailableSpace(Server,DriveLetter)
' This value is returned in BYTES, not Megabytes or Gigabytes
WMIQuery = "Select FreeSpace From Win32_LogicalDisk " & _
            "Where DeviceID='" & DriveLetter & "'"
Set WMIService = WMILocator.ConnectServer _
    (Server,"\root\CIMV2",UserName,Password)
Set Results = WMIService.ExecQuery(WMIQuery,,48)
For Each Result In Results
    GetAvailableSpace = Result.FreeSpace
Next
End Function
'=====================================================================
Public Function GetTrustInfo(Server)
' This function returns a Dictionary Object!
WMIQuery = "Select * from Microsoft_DomainTrustStatus"
Set WMIService = WMILocator.ConnectServer _
    (Server,"\root\MicrosoftActiveDirectory",UserName,Password)
Set Results = WMIService.ExecQuery(WMIQuery,,48)
Set GetTrustInfo = WScript.CreateObject("Scripting.Dictionary")
Dim ResultString
For Each Result In Results
' The value contains a comma-delimited list.
' 0 = Trusted Domain, 1 = Trust Direction, 2 = Trust Type
' 3 = Trust attributes
' 4 = Trust Status
    ResultString = Result.TrustedDomain
```

```
    Select Case Result.TrustDirection
        Case 1 : ResultString = ResultString & ",Inbound"
        Case 2 : ResultString = ResultString & ",Outbound"
        Case 3 : ResultString = ResultString & ",Bidirectional"
    End Select
    Select Case Result.TrustType
        Case 1 : ResultString = ResultString & ",Downlevel"
        Case 2 : ResultString = ResultString & ",Uplevel"
        Case 3 : ResultString = ResultString & ",Kerberos Realm"
        Case 4 : ResultString = ResultString & ",DCE"
    End Select
    Select Case Result.TrustAttributes
        Case &h1 : ResultString = ResultString & ",Non-transitive"
        Case &h2 : ResultString = ResultString & ",Uplevel Clients Only"
        Case &h40000 : ResultString = ResultString & ",Tree Parent"
        Case &h80000 : ResultString = ResultString & ",Tree Root"
        Case Else
            ResultString = ResultString & "," & Result.TrustAttributes
    End Select
    ResultString = ResultString & "," & Result.TrustIsOk
    GetTrustInfo.Add Result.FlatName, ResultString
  Next
End Function
'=====================================================================
End Class
```

CPU Overload

This script is designed to monitor the LSASS CPU utilization on each domain controller and alert the user when the percentage of CPU use by the process exceeds a designated threshold.

The script starts by getting a list of all domain controllers from the DomainClass object. It then cycles through each domain controller and uses the WMIClass object to retrieve the percentage of processor time used by the LSASS process. The percentage at which an alarm is raised is set by the ThresholdAlarm constant, so feel free to modify this to suit your needs and schedule.

At first, raising an alarm when the CPU utilization was above the threshold value seemed simple enough. However, we all know that every process has spikes. For example, when you start Task Manager and click the Performance tab, you usually see a small spike right away. That spike occurs when you start the Task Manager itself and does not indicate a system problem. The same is true of the LSASS process. It may experience a series of spikes lasting a few seconds or a few minutes. These spikes tend to occur as groups of users are logging onto the system and probably are not a cause for alarm.

Therefore, the process of raising an alarm takes some additional steps. If the process is above the designated threshold, then we start another loop to watch that particular domain controller for a bit longer. The script is going to check to domain controller every 2 seconds for five cycles (which means the domain controller is monitored for an additional 10 seconds). The average CPU usage of the LSASS process is computed, and if that average is still above the threshold value, then an alarm is raised. You can adjust these settings by changing the values of the AlarmCycleCount and the TimeBetweenAlarmSamples constants.

```
<job>
<script language="VBScript" src="..\includes\OutputClass.vbs" />
<script language="VBScript" src="..\includes\WMIClass.vbs" />
<script language="VBScript" src="..\includes\DomainClass.vbs" />
<script>
Option Explicit
Dim Output
Set Output = New OutputClass
Dim WMI
Set WMI = New WMIClass
Dim Domain
Set Domain = New DomainClass
Dim Servers, Server
Set Servers = Domain.GetDomainControllers
' Threshold percentage to trigger some concern
Const ThresholdAlarm = 80
' Number of cycles above threshhold to raise alarm
Const AlarmCycleCount = 5
' Time between 'alarm mode' samples
' The time value is in milliseconds
Const TimeBetweenAlarmSamples = 2000
Output.Display "Getting LSASS process CPU Usage"
For Each Server In Servers.Keys
    Dim ProcessorTime
    Set ProcessorTime = WMI.GetProcessorTimeForProcess(Server,"lsass")
    Dim PTime
    PTime = CInt(ProcessorTime("lsass"))
    Output.Display Server & " - " & PTime & "%"
    If PTime >= ThresholdAlarm Then
        Output.Display "Watching " & Server & " for alarm."
        Dim AlarmCycles
        ' Start at 2 because we already have the first sample.
        For AlarmCycles = 2 To AlarmCycleCount
            Set ProcessorTime = _
                WMI.GetProcessorTimeForProcess(Server,"lsass")
            PTime = PTime + ProcessorTime("lsass")
            WScript.Sleep(TimeBetweenAlarmSamples)
        Next
        If (PTime / AlarmCycleCount) >= ThresholdAlarm Then
            Output.ModalAlert Server & _
                " is above the lsass threshold."
        End If
    End If
Next
</script>
</job>
```

RegistryClass

Every so often, you'll need to access the Registry from a script. Like other scripting tasks, there are usually a few ways to accomplish it. For example, one of the easiest methods is to use the shell object with the RegRead, RegWrite, and RegDelete methods. Unfortunately, these don't address the needs of remote registry management.

However, WMI comes to the rescue by supplying a provider to handle Registry queries and updates. This provider gives us the ability to enumerate both keys and values residing under a key, retrieve values, create keys and values, delete keys and values, and check the access privileges of the current user on a key. It can perform all of these functions either on a local or remote computer. The implementation is a little cumbersome, so we have enclosed it in a VBScript class and added a few functions to make it a bit easier to use. The result is the RegistryClass class.

The class begins by assuming the local computer is the target of our Registry functions. In the Class_Initialize method, you'll see that the variable m_Server is set to a period, which represents the local machine. To target a remote server, set the Server property to the name of the remote server.

Before any operations can be performed on the Registry, the client must connect to the target server. This is done by invoking the Connect method of the RegistryClass object. After successfully connecting to the Registry provider, you can work with any Registry keys to which you have rights.

One of the more cumbersome aspects of using the WMI Registry provider is the requirement to supply the tree and key path as separate arguments. The tree value must also be supplied as a specific unsigned integer that corresponds to the desired tree. For example, the HKEY_LOCAL_MACHINE tree is defined by the hexadecimal number 80000002. The enumerations are supplied as public read-only properties in the class. Since almost every Registry path is viewed as a single line of text, with the tree as at the beginning of the path, we have designed the methods of this class to accept the Registry path in the same manner. The code in the method will parse the tree from the key path and use the appropriate tree value for calling the WMI methods. For example, to view the keys underneath a particular key, you can use the GetKeys method and pass the key path as a single string, like this:

```
Set Registry = New RegistryClass
Set KeyList = Registry.GetKeys("HKLM\Software\Microsoft")
```

The GetKeys method returns a dictionary object populated with a list of keys underneath the submitted key path. The GetKeyValues method returns a dictionary object populated with the value names and their current value underneath the submitted key path.

The GetValue function returns a single value. It requires the key path, the name of the value, and the type of the value passed as arguments. The type of value should be one of the publicly exposed value type properties in the class, such as REG_SZ, REG DWORD, etc. The following code demonstrates its use:

```
Set Registry = New RegistryClass
MyValue = Registry.GetValue _
    ("HKLM\Software\Microsoft","MyValue",Registry.REG_SZ)
```

The DeleteKey and DeleteValue methods are used to delete keys and values, respectively. Both require the key path as the first argument, and the DeleteValue method also requires the value name.

The CreateKey and CreateValue methods are used to create keys and values, respectively. Both require the key path as the first argument. The CreateValue method also requires a value name, the new value, and the value type as arguments. The value type is also passed as one of the public value type properties, as this code demonstrates:

```
Set Registry = New RegistryClass
Registry.CreateValue_
    ("HKLM\Software\Microsoft","MyValue",0,Registry.REG_SZ)
```

WARNING   Before turning you loose with this Registry class, we must reiterate the standard Registry warning that you have heard many times before. Changes to the Registry take effect immediately and can have a disastrous effect on your system. Make changes to the Registry at your own risk. Always be sure to test your Registry changes on a system that you can afford to wipe out in case of an accident. Testing in an environment such as Virtual PC or VMWare is ideal as you can easily undo your changes in the event of a mishap.

```
Option Explicit
'==============================================================
Class RegistryClass
'==============================================================
' Private and public variables
Private m_Registry
Private m_Server
'==============================================================
Private Sub Class_Initialize
    m_Server = "."
End Sub
'==============================================================
Private Sub Class_Terminate
    Set m_Registry = Nothing
End Sub
'==============================================================
Public Property Get Server
    Server = m_Server
End Property

Public Property Let Server(ServerName)
    m_Server = Trim(ServerName)
End Property
'==============================================================
Public Sub Connect
Set m_Registry = _
    GetObject("winmgmts:{impersonationLevel=impersonate}!\\" & _
        m_Server & "\root\default:StdRegProv")
End Sub
'==============================================================
Public Function GetKeys(Key)
' Returns a Dictionary Object!
```

```
Set GetKeys = WScript.CreateObject("Scripting.Dictionary")
Dim Keys(), KeyCount
m_Registry.EnumKey GetTree(Key),GetSubKey(Key), Keys
For KeyCount = 0 to UBound(Keys)
   GetKeys.Add Keys(KeyCount), Nothing
Next
End Function
'=========================================================================
Public Function GetKeyValues(Key)
' Returns a Dictionary object!
Dim Values(), ValueType()
m_Registry.EnumValues GetTree(Key), GetSubKey(Key), Values, ValueType
Set GetKeyValues = WScript.CreateObject("Scripting.Dictionary")
If Not IsNull(Values) Then
Dim ValueCount, Value
   For ValueCount = 0 To UBound(Values)
      Select Case ValueType(ValueCount)
         Case REG_SZ
            m_Registry.GetStringValue _
               GetTree(Key), GetSubKey(Key), Values(ValueCount), Value
            GetKeyValues.Add _
               CheckValueName(Values(ValueCount)), CheckValue(Value)
         Case REG_EXPAND_SZ
            m_Registry.GetExpandedStringValue _
               GetTree(Key), GetSubKey(Key), Values(ValueCount), Value
            GetKeyValues.Add _
               CheckValueName(Values(ValueCount)), CheckValue(Value)
         Case REG_BINARY
            m_Registry.GetBinaryValue _
               GetTree(Key), GetSubKey(Key), Values(ValueCount), Value
            GetKeyValues.Add _
               CheckValueName(Values(ValueCount)), Join(Value,"")
         Case REG_DWORD
            m_Registry.GetDWORDValue _
               GetTree(Key), GetSubKey(Key), Values(ValueCount), Value
            GetKeyValues.Add _
               CheckValueName(Values(ValueCount)), CheckValue(Value)
         Case REG_MULTI_SZ
            m_Registry.GetMultiStringValue _
               GetTree(Key), GetSubKey(Key), Values(ValueCount), Value
            GetKeyValues.Add _
               CheckValueName(Values(ValueCount)), Join(Value,",")
      End Select
   Next
End If
End Function
'=========================================================================
```

```
Public Function GetValue(Key,ValueName,KeyType)
Dim KeyValue
Select Case KeyType
  Case REG_SZ
    m_Registry.GetStringValue _
      GetTree(Key), GetSubKey(Key), ValueName, GetValue
  Case REG_EXPAND_SZ
    m_Registry.GetExpandedStringValue _
      GetTree(Key), GetSubKey(Key), ValueName, GetValue
  Case REG_BINARY
    m_Registry.GetBinaryValue _
      GetTree(Key), GetSubKey(Key), ValueName, KeyValue
    GetValue = Join(KeyValue,"")
  Case REG_DWORD
    m_Registry.GetDWORDValue _
      GetTree(Key), GetSubKey(Key), ValueName, GetValue
  Case REG_MULTI_SZ
    m_Registry.GetMultiStringValue _
      GetTree(Key), GetSubKey(Key), ValueName, KeyValue
    GetValue = Join(KeyValue,",")
End Select
End Function
'==================================================================
Private Function CheckValueName(ValueName)
If ValueName = "" Then
  CheckValueName = "(Default)"
Else
  CheckValueName = ValueName
End If
End Function
'==================================================================
Private Function CheckValue(Value)
If Value = "" Then
  CheckValue = "(value not set)"
Else
  CheckValue = Value
End If
End Function
'==================================================================
Public Function CreateKey(Key)
  CreateKey = m_Registry.CreateKey(GetTree(Key),GetSubKey(Key))
End Function
'==================================================================
Public Function CheckAccess(Key,AccessLevel)
m_Registry.CheckAccess _
  GetTree(Key),GetSubKey(Key),AccessLevel,CheckAccess
End Function
'==================================================================
```

```
Public Function DeleteKey(Key)
   DeleteKey = m_Registry.DeleteKey(GetTree(Key),GetSubKey(Key))
End Function
'=================================================================
Public Function DeleteValue(Key, ValueName)
DeleteValue = _
   m_Registry.DeleteValue(GetTree(Key),GetSubKey(Key),ValueName)
End Function
'=================================================================
Public Function CreateValue(Key,ValueName,KeyValue,KeyType)
Select Case KeyType
   Case REG_SZ
      CreateValue = m_Registry.SetStringValue _
         (GetTree(Key),GetSubKey(Key),ValueName,KeyValue)
   Case REG_EXPAND_SZ
      CreateValue = m_Registry.SetExpandedStringValue _
         (GetTree(Key),GetSubKey(Key),ValueName,KeyValue)
   Case REG_BINARY
      CreateValue = m_Registry.SetBinaryValue _
         (GetTree(Key),GetSubKey(Key),ValueName,KeyValue)
   Case REG_DWORD
      CreateValue = m_Registry.SetDWORDValue _
         (GetTree(Key),GetSubKey(Key),ValueName,KeyValue)
   Case REG_MULTI_SZ
      CreateValue = m_Registry.SetMultiStringValue _
         (GetTree(Key),GetSubKey(Key),ValueName,KeyValue)
End Select
End Function
'=================================================================
Private Function GetTree(KeyValue)
Dim TreeName
Select Case Left(KeyValue,InStr(KeyValue,"\")-1)
   Case "HKCR" : GetTree = HKCR
   Case "HKCU" : GetTree = HKCU
   Case "HKLM" : GetTree = HKLM
   Case "HKU"  : GetTree = HKU
   Case "HKCC" : GetTree = HKCC
   Case Else
      GetTree = Nothing
End Select
End Function
'=================================================================
Private Function GetSubKey(KeyValue)
   GetSubKey = Right(KeyValue,Len(KeyValue)-InStr(KeyValue,"\"))
End Function
'=================================================================
' Tree enumerations
Public Property Get HKCR
```

```
        HKCR = &H80000000
    End Property
    Public Property Get HKCU
        HKCU = &H80000001
    End Property
    Public Property Get HKLM
        HKLM = &H80000002
    End Property
    Public Property Get HKU
        HKU = &H80000003
    End Property
    Public Property Get HKCC
        HKCC = &H80000005
    End Property
    '=====================================================================
    ' Key Value Type enumerations
    Public Property Get REG_SZ
        REG_SZ = 1
    End Property
    Public Property Get REG_EXPAND_SZ
        REG_EXPAND_SZ = 2
    End Property
    Public Property Get REG_BINARY
        REG_BINARY = 3
    End Property
    Public Property Get REG_DWORD
        REG_DWORD = 4
    End Property
    Public Property Get REG_MULTI_SZ
        REG_MULTI_SZ = 7
    End Property
    '=====================================================================
    ' Key Access Rights enumerations
    Public Property Get KEY_QUERY_VALUE
        KEY_QUERY_VALUE = &H1
    End Property
    Public Property Get KEY_SET_VALUE
        KEY_SET_VALUE = &H2
    End Property
    Public Property Get KEY_CREATE_SUB_KEY
        KEY_CREATE_SUB_KEY = &H4
    End Property
    Public Property Get KEY_ENUMERATE_SUB_KEYS
        KEY_ENUMERATE_SUB_KEYS = &H8
    End Property
    Public Property Get KEY_NOTIFY
        KEY_NOTIFY = &H10
    End Property
```

```
Public Property Get KEY_CREATE_LINK
   KEY_CREATE_LINK = &H20
End Property
Public Property Get DELETE
   DELETE = &H10000
End Property
Public Property Get READ_CONTROL
   READ_CONTROL = &H20000
End Property
Public Property Get WRITE_DAC
   WRITE_DAC = &H40000
End Property
Public Property Get WRITE_OWNER
   WRITE_OWNER = &H80000
End Property
' =====================================================================
End Class
```

AD Database and Log File Free Space

Every Active Directory database needs free disk space in order to grow. The log files of AD transactions also need free space. This script is designed to monitor the amount of available disk space on the drives holding the AD database file and log files and to raise an alert if the amount of available disk space drops below a minimum amount.

The script begins by retrieving a list of domain controllers from a `DomainClass` object. The location of the AD database and log files may be different on each domain controller. The Microsoft Operations Manager has an advantage over us in this case, as it installs a COM helper object, known as the OOMADs, which can be used to make several system calls that are not available through regular VBScript objects.

In order for our script to find the location of these files, we must read some values from the registry of the domain controller. We can do this by using an instance of the `RegistryClass` class described in the previous section. The location of the AD database and log files can be found in the following Registry key:

```
HKLM\System\CurrentControlSet\Services\NTDS\Parameters
```

The database location is stored in the value `DSA Database file` and the log file location is stored in the value `Database log files path`. The script is interested in only the drive letter rather than the full path. The `GetAvailableSpace` method of the `WMIClass` object is called, and the server and drive letter are passed as arguments. This method executes a WMI query on the server and returns the amount of available space in bytes. Since most people have become accustomed to reading drive space values in gigabytes rather than bytes, the number is converted into a gigabyte format.

The minimum amount of free drive space is set by the `DBThreshold` constant for the AD database and the `LogThreshold` constant for the log files. It is important to note here that the value used for each of these constants is going to depend on how we have chosen to display the value of available space. The script current displays the value in gigabytes, so the DBThreshold value of 1 means 1GB. If we decided to lower the threshold to 500MB, we must change two items in the code. The first is the value in the DBThreshold constant itself. The second item to change is the following line of code:

```
DBFreeSpace = FormatNumber _
    (WMI.GetAvailableSpace(Server,DBDrive) / GB)
```

The constant GB refers to the number of bytes in a single gigabyte. Constants have also been defined in the script for megabytes (MB) and kilobytes (KB). We simply need to substitute MB for GB in the script.

To change the threshold for the log files, a similar procedure is followed. The value of LogThreshold constant would be changed, and the line of code setting the LogFreeSpace variable would be changed as described earlier.

```
<job>
<comment>
Microsoft Operations Manager runs a script similiar to this
every 15 minutes in response to an event rule.
Schedule to your own liking.
</comment>
<script language="VBScript" src="..\includes\RegistryClass.vbs" />
<script language="VBScript" src="..\includes\DomainClass.vbs" />
<script language="VBScript" src="..\includes\WMIClass.vbs" />
<script language="VBScript" src="..\includes\OutputClass.vbs" />
<script>
Option Explicit
' Adjust thresholds to your minimum DB and Log free space.
' It currently uses Gigabytes as the unit of measure.
Const DBThreshold = 1
Const LogThreshold = 1
' Registry keys pointing to the AD Database and log file locations.
Const ADKey = "HKLM\System\CurrentControlSet\Services\NTDS\Parameters"
Const DBValue = "DSA Database file"
Const LogValue = "Database log files path"
' Number of bytes in a kilobyte, megabyte, and gigabyte.
Const KB = 1024
Const MB = 1048576
Const GB = 1073741824
Dim Registry
Set Registry = New RegistryClass
Dim Domain
Set Domain = New DomainClass
Dim Output
Set Output = New OutputClass
Dim WMI
Set WMI = New WMIClass
Dim Servers, Server
Set Servers = Domain.GetDomainControllers
For Each Server In Servers
```

```
      Dim DBDrive, LogDrive
      Dim DBFreeSpace, LogFreeSpace
      Registry.Server = Server
      Registry.Connect
      DBDrive = Left _
          (Registry.GetValue(ADKey,DBValue,Registry.REG_SZ),2)
      LogDrive = Left _
          (Registry.GetValue(ADKey,LogValue,Registry.REG_SZ),2)
      DBFreeSpace = FormatNumber _
          (WMI.GetAvailableSpace(Server,DBDrive) / GB)
      If DBDrive = LogDrive Then
          LogFreeSpace = DBFreeSpace
      Else
          LogFreeSpace = FormatNumber _
              (WMI.GetAvailableSpace(Server,LogDrive) / GB)
      End If
      Output.Display Server
      Output.Display "DBDrive = " & DBFreeSpace
      Output.Display "LogDrive = " & LogFreeSpace
      If DBFreeSpace < DBThreshold Then
          Output.ModalAlert _
              Server & " is low on DB space (" & DBFreeSpace & ")"
      End If
      If LogFreeSpace < LogThreshold Then
          Output.ModalAlert _
              Server & " is low on log space (" & LogFreeSpace & ")"
      End If
   Next
</script>
</job>
```

Active Directory Essential Services

Active Directory requires several services to be operational in order to function correctly. Those services include the File Replication Service (FRS), the Intersite Messaging Service (IsmServ), the Kerberos Key Distribution Center (KDC), the NetLogon service (Netlogon), and the Windows Time (W32Time) service. These services should be running on each domain controller. This script is designed to alert the user when one or more of these services are not running.

The script begins by retrieving a list of domain controllers from a `DomainClass` object. The `Get ServiceState` method of a `WMIClass` object is called, which submits a query to each server to check the current state of each service. The method returns the state of each service in a dictionary object. If any service is not currently in the running state, a modal alert dialog box is raised to alert the user.

```
<job>
<comment>
Microsoft Operations Manager runs a script similiar to this
every 11 minutes. Schedule to your own liking.
```

```
</comment>
<script language="VBScript" src="..\includes\OutputClass.vbs" />
<script language="VBScript" src="..\includes\WMIClass.vbs" />
<script language="VBScript" src="..\includes\DomainClass.vbs" />
<script>
Option Explicit
Dim Output
Set Output = New OutputClass
Dim WMI
Set WMI = New WMIClass
Dim Domain
Set Domain = New DomainClass
Dim Servers, Server
Set Servers = Domain.GetDomainControllers
Dim StateList, State
For Each Server In Servers.Keys
    Output.Display "Checking Active Directory Services on " & Server
    Set StateList = _
        WMI.GetServiceState(Server, _
                    Array("ntfrs","ismserv","kdc","Netlogon","w32time"))
    For Each State In StateList.Keys
        Output.Display State & " " & StateList(State)
            If Not(StateList(State) = "Running") Then
                Output.ModalAlert Server & " - " & State & _
                                " is not running!"
            End If
    Next
Next
</script>
</job>
```

Active Directory Response Time

Since Active Directory is only as fast as the servers supporting it, checking the responsiveness of your domain controllers makes good sense. This script is designed to do just that.

The script begins by retrieving a list of domain controllers by using a DomainClass object. The script then attempts to bind to the RootDSE of each domain controller. The response time for the bind operation is measured, and if the response time exceeds our maximum (set by the MaxResponseTime constant), then the script pays a little more attention to the server. The bind operation is attempted a few more times (set by the AlarmCycleCount constant) and the response time is measured. It is possible that the domain controller server is busy servicing other requests, and we do not want to raise a false alarm. If the average of the response time still exceeds our maximum, then a modal alert dialog box is raised to alert the user.

```
<job>
<comment>
Microsoft Operations Manager runs a script similiar to this
```

every 5 minutes in response to an event rule.
Schedule to your own liking.

```
</comment>
<script language="VBScript" src="..\includes\DomainClass.vbs" />
<script language="VBScript" src="..\includes\OutputClass.vbs" />
<script>
Option Explicit
Dim Domain
Set Domain = New DomainClass
Dim Output
Set Output = New OutputClass
Dim Servers, Server
Set Servers = Domain.GetDomainControllers
' Number of cycles to sample response
Const AlarmCycleCount = 5
' Time between 'alarm mode' samples
Const TimeBetweenAlarmSamples = 2000
' Maximum number of failures
Const MaxFailures = 2
' Maximum response time in seconds
Const MaxResponseTime = 2
Dim LDAPString
Dim TimeStart, TimeStop, ResponseTime
On Error Resume Next
For Each Server In Servers.Keys
    Dim TestServer
    LDAPString = "LDAP://" & Server & "/RootDSE"
    TimeStart = Timer
    Set TestServer = GetObject(LDAPString)
    TimeStop = Timer
    If Err.Number = 0 Then
        ResponseTime = TimeStop - TimeStart
        Output.Display Server & " responded in " & _
                    ResponseTime & " seconds."
        If ResponseTime > MaxResponseTime Then
            For AlarmCycles = 2 To AlarmCycleCount
                TimeStart = Timer
                Set TestServer = GetObject(LDAPString)
                TimeStop = Timer
                WScript.Sleep(TimeBetweenAlarmCycles)
                ResponseTime = ResponseTime + (TimeStop - TimeStart)
            Next
            ResponseTime = ResponseTime / AlarmCycleCount
            If ResponseTime >= MaxResponseTime Then
                Output.ModalAlert Server & " is averaging " & _
                            ResponseTime & " to respond."
            End If
        End If
    End If
```

```
        Else
            ' Server failed to respond.
            Err.Clear
            Dim AlarmCycles, FailureCounter
            FailureCounter = 1 ' It's failed once already
            For AlarmCycles = 2 To AlarmCycleCount
                Set TestServer = GetObject(LDAPString)
                If Err.Number <> 0 Then
                    FailureCounter = FailureCounter + 1
                End If
                WScript.Sleep(TimeBetweenAlarmCycles)
            Next
            If FailureCounter >= MaxFailures Then
                Output.ModalAlert Server & " has failed to respond " & _
                                FailureCounter & " times!"
            End If
        End If
    Next
</script>
</job>
```

Global Catalog Server Response

The response time of a global catalog server is important to many domain and forest operations. The Microsoft Operations Manager has a script that is run in response to an event that measures the response time of the global catalog server. Since we are not dealing with events in our scripts, we have simulated that script functionality and you may schedule it or run it manually.

The script begins by gathering a list of all the global catalog servers serving the domain. This is done in the function GetGlobalCatalogServers, which will return a dictionary object. Global catalog information is stored in the configuration naming context of the domain, and can be found by using the ADSI query:

```
(&(objectcategory=ntdsdsa)(options=1))
```

With the list of global catalog servers in hand, the script proceeds to test the servers for responsiveness. A query is submitted to each global catalog server and the response is timed. The query submitted to the server has to be both successful on a consistent basis and not cause a significant performance hit to the server. The documentation on the Active Directory Management Pack for Microsoft Operations Manager lists the following query as one that meets those criteria:

```
(objectCategory=DMD)
```

If the response time exceeds our maximum (set by the MaxResponseTime constant), then pay more attention to the server. The query is submitted a few more times (set by the AlarmCycleCount constant) and the response time is measured. It is possible that the global catalog server is simply experiencing a period of heavy activity, and we do not want to raise a false alarm. If the average of the response time still exceeds our maximum, then a modal alert dialog box is raised to alert the user.

```
<job>
<comment>
Microsoft Operations Manager runs a script similiar to this
every 5 minutes in response to an event rule.
Schedule to your own liking.
</comment>
<script language="VBScript" src="..\includes\RootDSEClass.vbs" />
<script language="VBScript" src="..\includes\QueryClass.vbs" />
<script language="VBScript" src="..\includes\OutputClass.vbs" />
<script>
Option Explicit
Dim RootDSE
Set RootDSE = New RootDSEClass
Dim Output
Set Output = New OutputClass
Dim GCServers, GCServer
Set GCServers = GetGlobalCatalogServers
' Number of cycles to sample response
Const AlarmCycleCount = 3
' Time between 'alarm mode' samples
Const TimeBetweenAlarmSamples = 2000
' Maximum response time in seconds
Const MaxResponseTime = 2
Dim GCQuery
Set GCQuery = New QueryClass
GCQuery.FilterText = "(objectCategory=DMD)"
GCQuery.Attributes = "distinguishedName"
GCQuery.Scope = "SubTree"
Dim TimeStart, TimeStop, ResponseTime
For Each GCServer In GCServers.Keys
    Output.Display "Querying " & GCServer
    GCQuery.RawSearchRoot = "GC://" & GCServer
    Dim Results
    TimeStart = Timer
    Set Results = GCQuery.ExecuteQuery
    TimeStop = Timer
    If Results Is Nothing Then
        Output.ModalAlert GCServer & " returned nothing!"
    Else
        Output.Display GCServer & " returned " & _
                    Results.RecordCount & " records."
        If Results.RecordCount = 0 Then
            Output.ModalAlert GCServer & _
                            " returned no results from query attempt!"
```

```
            End If
            ResponseTime = TimeStop - TimeStart
            Output.Display GCServer & " responded in " & _
                           ResponseTime & " seconds."
            If ResponseTime > MaxResponseTime Then
                For AlarmCycles = 2 To AlarmCycleCount
                    TimeStart = Timer
                    Set Results = GCQuery.ExecuteQuery
                    TimeStop = Timer
                    WScript.Sleep(TimeBetweenAlarmCycles)
                    ResponseTime = ResponseTime + (TimeStop - TimeStart)
                Next
                ResponseTime = ResponseTime / AlarmCycleCount
                If ResponseTime >= MaxResponseTime Then
                    Output.ModalAlert GCServer & " is averaging " & _
                                      ResponseTime & " to respond."
                End If
            End If
        End If
        GCQuery.Close
Next
'========================================================================
Function GetGlobalCatalogServers
' Find the Global Catalog Servers in this forest
' Returns a Dictionary Object!
Dim Query
Set Query = New QueryClass
Query.Searchroot = RootDSE.ConfigurationNamingContext
Query.FilterText = "(&(objectcategory=ntdsdsa)(options=1))"
Query.Attributes = "distinguishedName"
Query.Scope = "SubTree"
Dim Results
Set GetGlobalCatalogServers
WScript.CreateObject("Scripting.Dictionary")
Set Results = Query.ExecuteQuery
Do Until Results.EOF
    Dim Server
    Set Server = GetObject(GetObject("LDAP://" & _
        Results.Fields(0)).Parent)
    GetGlobalCatalogServers.Add Server.Get("dNSHostName"), Nothing
    Results.MoveNext
Loop
Set Query = Nothing
End Function
</script>
</job>
```

Lost and Found Object Count

Active Directory contains a Lost and Found container for orphaned objects. When objects start showing up in this container, the administrator should examine them to determine whether they should be deleted or moved into another container. Of course, this requires actually remembering to check the Lost and Found container on a regular basis. This script is designed to check the container for you and raise an alert when objects appear in it.

```
<job>
<comment>
Microsoft Operations Manager runs a script similiar to this
every 120 minutes. Schedule to your own liking.
</comment>
<script language="VBScript" src="..\includes\DomainClass.vbs" />
<script language="VBScript" src="..\includes\OutputClass.vbs" />
<script>
Option Explicit
' Microsoft Operations Manager runs a script similiar to this
' every 120 minutes. Schedule to your own liking.
' Change the Threshold value to your desired threshold
Const Threshold = 10
Dim Domain
Set Domain = New DomainClass
Dim Output
Set Output = New OutputClass
Dim LostAndFound, ObjectCount
LostAndFound = Domain.GetPathFromWKGuid("LostAndFound")
WScript.Echo "Lost and Found container path is " & LostAndFound
Set LostAndFound = GetObject("LDAP://" & _
    Domain.GetPathFromWKGuid("LostAndFound"))
LostAndFound.GetInfoEx Array("msDS-Approx-Immed-Subordinates"),0
ObjectCount = LostAndFound.Get("msDS-Approx-Immed-Subordinates")
Output.Display "Lost and Found container holds " & ObjectCount & _
                " objects."
If ObjectCount > Threshold Then
    Output.ModalAlert "Lost and Found object count (" & _
                    ObjectCount & ")" & _
                    " is greater than the threshold value (" & _
                    Threshold & ")"
End If
</script>
</job>
```

PingClass

If you ask any administrator what their first course of action would be to diagnose an unresponsive system, we're betting 9 out of 10 would say "Ping it." However, in VBScript, there is no native method available to perform the simple act of pinging a network system. This is not to say it can't be done, however.

One alternative is to purchase a custom library of objects, such as those from ActiveXperts (www.activexperts.com). Another option is to create a Shell object, execute the ping.exe command, capture the output stream, and then parse the results from that stream of text. Trust us, it's not fun.

Our alternative is to use WMI. The Win32_PingStatus class provides all the values returned by the ping command. By enclosing its functionality into a VBScript class, we can easily reuse it in any script we wish. Most of the properties of the Win32_PingStatus class are read-only, so we have no need to expose them in our class as writeable properties.

The main method of the PingClass class is the PingHost method. The address of the server to ping is passed to the method as its only argument. The address can be passed either as a DNS name, NetBIOS name, or IP address. When passing the address as a name, be sure you have the proper services available to resolve that name to its IP address (DNS, WINS, or a local HOSTS or LMHOSTS file).

The PingHost method will execute a WMI query to ping the system. If the ping is successful, the method returns True to the calling script. If it fails, False is returned. The values from the ping command, such as response time, protocol address, and status code, are set as read-only properties of the PingClass object.

```
Option Explicit
'=====================================================================
Class PingClass
'=====================================================================
' Private and public variables
Private m_PingWMIService
Private m_PrimaryAddressResolutionStatus
Private m_ProtocolAddress
Private m_ResponseTime
Private m_StatusCode
Private m_StatusCodeMessage
'=====================================================================
Private Sub Class_Initialize
Set m_PingWMIService = _
   GetObject _
      ("winmgmts:{impersonationLevel=impersonate}//./root/cimv2")
End Sub
'=====================================================================
Private Sub Class_Terminate
Set m_PingWMIService = Nothing
End Sub
'=====================================================================
Public Function PingHost(Host)
Dim PingQuery
PingQuery = "SELECT * FROM Win32_PingStatus WHERE Address = '" & _
Host & "'"
```

```
Dim WMIPingResults, Result
Set WMIPingResults = m_PingWMIService.ExecQuery(PingQuery)
For Each Result In WMIPingResults
    m_PrimaryAddressResolutionStatus = Result.PrimaryAddressResolutionStatus
    m_ProtocolAddress = Result.ProtocolAddress
    m_ResponseTime = Result.ResponseTime
    m_StatusCode = Result.StatusCode
    If Result.StatusCode = 0 Then
        PingHost = True
    Else
        PingStatus = False
    End If
Next
End Function
'=================================================================
Public Property Get PrimaryAddressResolutionStatus
    PrimaryAddressResolutionStatus = m_PrimaryAddressResolutionStatus
End Property
'=================================================================
Public Property Get ProtocolAddress
    ProtocolAddress = m_ProtocolAddress
End Property
'=================================================================
Public Property Get ResponseTime
    ResponseTime= m_ResponseTime
End Property
'=================================================================
Public Property Get StatusCode
    StatusCode = m_StatusCode
End Property
'=================================================================
Public Property Get StatusCodeMessage
    StatusCodeMessage = GetStatusMessage(m_StatusCode)
End Property
'=================================================================
Private Function GetStatusMessage(Code)
Select Case Code
    Case 0 : StatusCodeMessage = "Success"
    Case 11001 : StatusCodeMessage = "Buffer Too Small"
    Case 11002 : StatusCodeMessage = "Destination Net Unreachable"
    Case 11003 : StatusCodeMessage = "Destination Host Unreachable"
    Case 11004 : StatusCodeMessage = "Destination Protocol Unreachable"
    Case 11005 : StatusCodeMessage = "Destination Port Unreachable"
    Case 11006 : StatusCodeMessage = "No Resources"
    Case 11007 : StatusCodeMessage = "Bad Option"
    Case 11008 : StatusCodeMessage = "Hardware Error"
    Case 11009 : StatusCodeMessage = "Packet Too Big"
    Case 11010 : StatusCodeMessage = "Request Timed Out"
```

```
      Case 11011 : StatusCodeMessage = "Bad Request"
      Case 11012 : StatusCodeMessage = "Bad Route"
      Case 11013 : StatusCodeMessage = "TimeToLive Expired Transit"
      Case 11014 : StatusCodeMessage = "TimeToLive Expired Reassembly"
      Case 11015 : StatusCodeMessage = "Parameter Problem"
      Case 11016 : StatusCodeMessage = "Source Quench"
      Case 11017 : StatusCodeMessage = "Option Too Big"
      Case 11018 : StatusCodeMessage = "Bad Destination"
      Case 11032 : StatusCodeMessage = "Negotiating IPSEC"
      Case 11050 : StatusCodeMessage = "General Failure"
      Case Else : StatusCodeMessage = "Unknown Status Code"
    End Select
    End Function
    '=====================================================================
    End Class
```

Operation Master Response

This script checks the Active Directory operations masters for responsiveness. The Flexible Single Master Operations (FSMO) roles include the PDC emulator, the RID master, the Infrastructure Operations Master, the Domain Naming Operations Master, and the Schema Operations Master. The health and availability of the servers holding these operation master roles is crucial.

The script starts by finding the server that owns each FSMO role. This entails finding the object in Active Directory linked to each role, followed by binding to that object to discover its DNS name. Each distinct server is added to a dictionary object with a comma-separated list of the roles held by that server.

The dictionary object allows the script to be more efficient. It is not uncommon in an AD installation to have one server hold multiple FSMO roles. In that case, the dictionary object allows us to check the responsiveness of each server once regardless of the number of roles it owns.

This script makes use of the PingClass described in the previous section. We start by sending a ping to check that the server is alive and responding to network traffic.

If the ping is successful, then an attempt is made to bind to the RootDSE of the server. If the ping is not successful, or takes longer to respond than we consider to be acceptable (configured with the MaxResponseTime constant), then the server is pinged a few additional times to verify that it really is being unresponsive. If the server is still unresponsive, a modal alert is raised.

```
    <job>
    <comment>
    Microsoft Operations Manager runs a script similiar to this
    every 5 minutes. Schedule to your own liking.
    </comment>
    <script language="VBScript" src="..\includes\RootDSEClass.vbs" />
    <script language="VBScript" src="..\includes\OutputClass.vbs" />
    <script language="VBScript" src="..\includes\PingClass.vbs" />
    <script>
    Option Explicit
    ' Number of cycles to sample response
```

```
Const AlarmCycleCount = 5
' Time between 'alarm mode' samples
Const TimeBetweenAlarmSamples = 2000
' Maximum number of failures
Const MaxFailures = 2
' Maximum response time in seconds
Const MaxResponseTime = 2
' Delay between ping attempts
Const TimeBetweenAlarmPings = 2000
Dim RootDSE
Set RootDSE = New RootDSEClass
Dim Output
Set Output = New OutputClass
Dim RoleOwners
Set RoleOwners = WScript.CreateObject("Scripting.Dictionary")
Dim FSMORoleOwner,RoleOwner,Host
Dim PDC,RID,SM,IM,DNM
' Find the PDC Emulator
Set PDC = GetObject("LDAP://" & RootDSE.DefaultNamingContext)
Set FSMORoleOwner = GetObject("LDAP://" & PDC.fsmoRoleOwner)
Set RoleOwner = GetObject(FSMORoleOwner.Parent)
Host = RoleOwner.Get("dNSHostName")
Output.Display "PDC Emulator = " & Host
RoleOwners.Add Host, "PDC Emulator"
' Find the RID Master
Set RID = GetObject("LDAP://cn=RID Manager$,cn=system," & _
    RootDSE.DefaultNamingContext)
Set FSMORoleOwner = GetObject("LDAP://" & RID.fsmoRoleOwner)
Set RoleOwner = GetObject(FSMORoleOwner.Parent)
Host = RoleOwner.Get("dnsHostName")
Output.Display "RID Master = " & Host
If RoleOwners.Exists(Host) Then
    RoleOwners(Host) = RoleOwners(Host) & ",RID Master"
Else
    RoleOwners.Add Host,"RID Master"
End If
' Find the Schema Master
Set SM =  GetObject("LDAP://" & RootDSE.SchemaNamingContext)
Set FSMORoleOwner = GetObject("LDAP://" & SM.fsmoRoleOwner)
Set RoleOwner = GetObject(FSMORoleOwner.Parent)
Host = RoleOwner.Get("dnsHostName")
Output.Display "Schema Master = " & Host
If RoleOwners.Exists(Host) Then
    RoleOwners(Host) = RoleOwners(Host) & ",Schema Master"
Else
    RoleOwners.Add Host,"Schema Master"
End If
' Find the Infrastructure Master
```

```
Set IM = GetObject("LDAP://cn=Infrastructure," & _
   RootDSE.DefaultNamingContext)
Set FSMORoleOwner = GetObject("LDAP://" & IM.fsmoRoleOwner)
Set RoleOwner = GetObject(FSMORoleOwner.Parent)
Host = RoleOwner.Get("dnsHostName")
Output.Display "Infrastructure Master = " & Host
If RoleOwners.Exists(Host) Then
   RoleOwners(Host) = RoleOwners(Host) & ",Infrastructure Master"
Else
   RoleOwners.Add Host,"Infrastructure Master"
End If
' Domain Naming Master
Set DNM = GetObject("LDAP://cn=Partitions," & _
   RootDSE.ConfigurationNamingContext)
Set FSMORoleOwner = GetObject("LDAP://" & DNM.fsmoRoleOwner)
Set RoleOwner = GetObject(FSMORoleOwner.Parent)
Host = RoleOwner.Get("dnsHostName")
Output.Display "Domain Naming Master = " & Host
If RoleOwners.Exists(Host) Then
   RoleOwners(Host) = RoleOwners(Host) & ",Domain Naming Master"
Else
   RoleOwners.Add Host,"Domain Naming Master"
End If
Dim Ping
Set Ping = New PingClass
Dim Owner, ResponseTime, OwnerRootDSE
For Each Owner In RoleOwners.Keys
   Output.Display "Pinging " & Owner
   If Ping.PingHost(Owner) Then
      ResponseTime = Ping.ResponseTime
      Output.Display Owner & " is responding at " & _
                     ResponseTime & "ms."
      If ResponseTime > MaxResponseTime Then
         For AlarmCycles = 2 To AlarmCycleCount
            WScript.Sleep(TimeBetweenAlarmCycles)
            Ping.PingHost(Owner)
            ResponseTime = ResponseTime + Ping.ResponseTime
            WScript.Sleep(TimeBetweenAlarmPings)
         Next
         ResponseTime = ResponseTime / AlarmCycleCount
         If ResponseTime >= MaxResponseTime Then
            Output.ModalAlert Server & " is averaging " & _
                              ResponseTime & " to respond."
         End If
      End If
      On Error Resume Next
      Set OwnerRootDSE = GetObject("LDAP://" & Owner & "/RootDSE")
      If Err.Number = 0 Then
```

```
        Output.Display Owner & " connected via RootDSE."
      Else
        Err.Clear
        Output.ModalAlert Owner & " failed to bind to RootDSE!"
      End If
    Else
      Output.ModalAlert Owner & " is not responding."
    End If
  Next
</script>
</job>
```

Monitor Trust Relationships

Our last script is a simple one. It starts by obtaining a list of trusts and their current properties from the WMI provider \root\MicrosoftActiveDirectory, which is returned from the WMIClass object by calling the GetTrustInfo method and passing it the name of a domain controller to contact. In this case, there should be no need to contact every domain controller for this information, so we have selected one local domain controller to query.

The GetTrustInfo method returns a dictionary object. The key is the trust name and the value is a comma-separated list of the trust properties. The property names are listed as comments in the code below. The main property that we are interested in is the TrustIsOK property. If the trust is OK, then this will return True. If this value is False, then an alert is raised.

```
<job>
<comment>
Microsoft Operations Manager runs a script similiar to this
every 17 minutes. Schedule to your own liking.
</comment>
<script language="VBScript" src="..\includes\WMIClass.vbs" />
<script language="VBScript" src="..\includes\OutputClass.vbs" />
<script language="VBScript">
Option Explicit
Dim WMI
Set WMI = New WMIClass
Dim DC, TrustList, Trust
' Set DC to the domain server to contact
DC = "DC1.zygort.com"
Set TrustList = WMI.GetTrustInfo(DC)
Dim Output
Set Output = New OutputClass
Dim TrustProperties
For Each Trust In TrustList.Keys
  TrustProperties = Split(TrustList(Trust),",")
  ' 0 = Trusted Domain, 1 = Trust Direction, 2 = Trust Type
  ' 3 = Trust attributes
  ' 4 = TrustIsOK (aka Trust Status)
```

```
      Output.Display "Trust : " & Trust
      Output.Display "Trusted Domain: " & TrustProperties(0)
      Output.Display "Trust Direction: " & TrustProperties(1)
      Output.Display "Trust Type: " & TrustProperties(2)
      Output.Display "Attributes: " & TrustProperties(3)
      Output.Display "Status: " & TrustProperties(4)
      Output.Display "--------------------"
      If Not(TrustProperties(4)) Then
        Output.ModalAlert "Trust " & Trust & _
          " has a failure code (" & TrustProperties(4) & ")"
      End If
    Next
</script>
</job>
```

Index

Note to the reader: Throughout this index **boldfaced** page numbers indicate primary discussions of a topic. *Italicized* page numbers indicate illustrations.